Contemporary Issues in Sociology of Sport

Andrew Yiannakis, PhD
University of Connecticut

Merrill J. Melnick, PhD
State University of New York
College at Brockport

Editors

Human Kinetics

Library of Congress Cataloging-in-Publication Data

Contemporary issues in sociology of sport / [edited by] Andrew Yiannakis, Merrill J.
Melnick.-- Rev. ed.
    p. cm.
  Rev. ed. of: Sport sociology. 4th ed. c1993.
  Includes bibliographical references and index.
  ISBN 0-7360-3710-1
    1. Sports--United States--Sociological aspects. 2. Sports--United States. I. Yiannakis,
Andrew. II. Melnick, Merrill J. III. Sport sociology.

GV706.5 .C647 2001
306.4'83'0973--dc21   00-053860

ISBN: 0-7360-3710-1

This book is a revised edition of *Sport Sociology: Contemporary Themes, Fourth Edition,* published in 1993 by Kendall/Hunt Publishing Company.

Acquisitions Editor: Linda Anne Bump; **Managing Editor:** Amy Stahl; **Assistant Editor:** Derek Campbell; **Copyeditor:** Bob Replinger; **Proofreaders:** Jim Burns, Sue Fetters, Julie Marx, Amy Stahl; **Indexer:** Sharon Duffy; **Permission Managers:** Courtney Astle, Dalene Reeder; **Graphic Designer:** Robert Reuther; **Graphic Artists:** Dody Bullerman, Sandra Meier; **Cover Designer:** Jack W. Davis; **Art Manager:** Craig Newsom; **Illustrator:** Tom Roberts; **Printer:** Versa Press

Printed in the United States of America

10 9 8 7 6 5 4 3 2 1

Human Kinetics
Web site: **www.humankinetics.com**

United States: Human Kinetics
P.O. Box 5076, Champaign, IL 61825-5076
800-747-4457
e-mail: humank@hkusa.com

Canada: Human Kinetics
475 Devonshire Road Unit 100, Windsor, ON N8Y 2L5
800-465-7301 (in Canada only)
e-mail: hkcan@mnsi.net

Europe: Human Kinetics
P.O. Box IW14, Leeds LS16 6TR, United Kingdom
+44 (0) 113 278 1708
e-mail: humank@hkeurope.com

Australia: Human Kinetics
57A Price Avenue, Lower Mitcham, South Australia 5062
08 8277 1555
e-mail: liahka@senet.com.au

New Zealand: Human Kinetics
P.O. Box 105-231, Auckland Central
09-523-3462
e-mail: hkp@ihug.co.nz

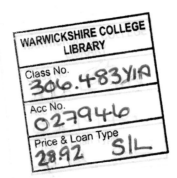

Contents

Preface

Contemporary Issues in Sociology of Sport, formerly published in four editions as *Sport Sociology: Contemporary Themes*, strikes a balance between theoretical and empirical works; includes a variety of data sources, authors, and topics; and most important, encompasses the major contemporary issues presently being discussed, debated, and researched by sport sociologists. Although the book is intended for both beginning and intermediate-level students in sociology of sport, some exposure to course work in the social sciences (e.g., sociology, social psychology, psychology, anthropology) is helpful. Some articles will inevitably prove more intellectually challenging than others. But because this book contains a broad variety of selections, instructors should have no difficulty identifying articles that suit the needs, interests, and backgrounds of their students.

To enhance the teaching and learning process, we have written informative introductions to each of the 12 units of the anthology. We recommend that students read the introduction to each unit before the selections because they highlight important concepts, offer cogent summaries, and pose challenging questions.

To assist the reader further, we offer both general and specific discussion questions about each article. The questions are intended to help the reader know "what to look for" in each of the selections. The answers to these questions should also provide the student with a helpful summary of each article, which, in turn, should prove useful in small-group discussion, in writing papers, or in studying for examinations. We recommend that students peruse the questions before reading a particular article because they help draw attention to major points, ideas, and concepts.

The book includes 34 articles organized into 12 thematic units. Twenty-eight articles (82 percent) are new to this edition. Many are unique in the sense that they explore concepts, topics, or themes that have received only scant attention in other readers and anthologies in sociology of sport. In particular, the units titled Sport, Power, and Ideology; Big-Time Sports and the College Experience; The Body in Culture and Sport; Sport and the Mediated Image; Sport and Deviance: The Darker Side of Sportsworld; and Sport and Globalization include some of the best scholarship available in the field. These units will provide especially interesting reading.

We have deliberately included works representing diverse theoretical orientations, such as conflict theory, structural functionalism, critical feminist theory, and cultural studies. Moreover, this text offers a careful balance among various research paradigms and perspectives and includes works of both a quantitative and qualitative nature. In choosing the selections, we were able to draw upon the outstanding corpus of female-authored scholarship that has emerged since publication of the last edition.

The main focus of the book remains the identification and critical examination of contemporary sport themes. All 12 units of the anthology reflect, as far as possible, the most exciting theoretical perspectives, research findings, and thinking in the field, and represent, in our judgment, "where the action is" in sociology of sport today.

An anthology is the work of many individuals. In particular, we wish to thank the authors and copyright holders who graciously permitted their work to appear in *Contemporary Issues in Sociology of Sport*.

Andrew Yiannakis (University of Connecticut)
Merrill J. Melnick (SUNY Brockport)

Credits

Article 1 Reprinted, by permission, from George H. Sage, 1997, "Physical Education, sociology, and sociology of sport: Points of intersection," *Sociology of Sport Journal,* **14**(4): 317-339.

Article 2 Reprinted, by permission, from Douglas E. Foley, 1990, "The great American football ritual: Reproducing, race, class and gender inequality," *Sociology of Sport Journal* 7(2): 111-135.

Article 3 Reprinted, by permission, from J. Harry, 1995, "Sports ideology, attitudes toward women and anti-homosexual attitudes," *Sex Roles,* **32**(1-2): 109-116.

Table 3.1 Reprinted, by permission, from J. Harry, 1995, "Sports ideology, attitudes toward women, and anti-homosexual attitudes," *Sex Roles,* **32**(1-2): 113.

Table 3.2 Reprinted, by permission, from J. Harry, 1995, "Sports ideology, attitudes toward women and anti-homosexual attitudes," *Sex Roles* **32**(1-2): 114.

Article 4 Reprinted, by permission, from Becky Beal, 1995, "Disqualifying the official: An exploration of social resistance through the subculture of skateboarding," *Sociology of Sport Journal* 12: 252-267.

Article 5 Reprinted, by permission, from E.C. Devereux, 1971, "Backyard versus little league baseball: Some observations on the impoverishment of children's games in contemporary America." Presented at Conference on Sport and Social Deviancy, SUNY, Brockport, 12/11/71.

Article 6 Reprinted, by permission, from M.A. Landers and G.A. Fine, 1996, "Learning life's lessons in tee ball: The reinforcement of gender and status in kindergarten sport," *Sociology of Sport Journal* 13(1): 87-93.

Article 7 Reprinted, by permission, from B.C. Green, 1997, "Action research in youth soccer: Assessing the acceptability of an alternative program," *Journal of Sport Management* 11: 29-44.

Table 7.1 Reprinted, by permission, from B.C. Green, 1997, "Action research in youth soccer: Assessing the acceptability of an alternative program," *Journal of Sport Management* 11: 34.

Table 7.2 Reprinted, by permission, from B.C. Green, 1997, "Action research in youth soccer: Assessing the acceptability of an alternative program," *Journal of Sport Management* 11: 35.

Table 7.3 Reprinted, by permission, from B.C. Green, 1997, "Action research in youth soccer: Assessing the acceptability of an alternative program," *Journal of Sport Management* 11: 38.

Table 7.4 Reprinted, by permission, from B.C. Green, 1997, "Action research in youth soccer: Assessing the acceptability of an alternative program," *Journal of Sport Management* 11: 40.

Article 8 Reprinted, by permission, from N. Fejgin, 1994, "Participation in high school competitive sports: A subversion of school mission or contribution to academic goals?" *Sociology of Sport Journal* **11**: 211-230.

Table 8.1 Reprinted, by permission, from N. Fejgin, 1994, "Participation in high school competitive sports: A subversion of school mission or contribution to academic goals?" *Sociology of Sport Journal* **11**: 217.

Table 8.2 Reprinted, by permission, from N. Fejgin, 1994, "Participation in high school competitive sports: A subversion of school mission or contribution to academic goals?" *Sociology of Sport Journal* **11**: 219.

Table 8.3 Reprinted, by permission, from N. Fejgin, 1994, "Participation in high school competitive sports: A subversion of school mission or contribution to academic goals?" *Sociology of Sport Journal* **11**: 221.

Table 8.4 Reprinted, by permission, from N. Fejgin, 1994, "Participation in high school competitive sports: A subversion of school mission or contribution to academic goals?" *Sociology of Sport Journal* 11: 222.

Article 9 Reprinted, by permission, from K.E. Miller, D.F. Sabo, M.P. Farrell, G.M. Barnes and M.J. Melnick, 1998, "Athletic participation and sexual behavior in adolescents: The different worlds of boys and girls," *Journal of Health and Social Behavior (June 1998).*

Table 9.1 Reprinted, by permission, from K.E. Miller, D.F. Sabo, M.P. Farrell, G.M. Barnes and M.J. Melnick, 1998, "Athletic participation and sexual behavior in adolescents: The different worlds of boys and girls," *Journal of Health and Social Behavior (June 1998):* 115.

Table 9.2 Reprinted, by permission, from K.E. Miller, D.F. Sabo, M.P. Farrell, G.M. Barnes and M.J. Melnick, 1998, "Athletic participation and sexual behavior in adolescents: The different worlds of boys and girls," *Journal of Health and Social Behavior (June 1998):* 116.

Table 9.3 Reprinted, by permission, from K.E. Miller, D.F. Sabo, M.P. Farrell, G.M. Barnes and M.J. Melnick, 1998, "Athletic participation and sexual behavior in adolescents: The different worlds of boys and girls," *Journal of Health and Social Behavior (June 1998):* 117.

Figure 9.1 Reprinted, by permission, from K.E. Miller, D.F. Sabo, M.P. Farrell, G.M. Barnes and M.J. Melnick, 1998, "Athletic participation and sexual behavior in adolescents: The different worlds of boys and girls," *Journal of Health and Social Behavior (June 1998):* 118.

Figure 9.2 Reprinted, by permission, from K.E. Miller, D.F. Sabo, M.P. Farrell, G.M. Barnes and M.J. Melnick, 1998, "Athletic participation and sexual behavior in adolescents: The different worlds of boys and girls," *Journal of Health and Social Behavior (June 1998):* 120.

Article 10 J.S. Eccles and B.L. Barber, 1999, "Student council, volunteering, basketball, or marching band: What kind of extracurricular involvement matters?" *Journal of Adolescent Research* **14**(1): 10-43. Reprinted by permission of Sage Publications.

Tables 10.1–10.16 J.S. Eccles and B.L. Barber, 1999, "Student council, volunteering, basketball, or marching band: What kind of extracurricular involvement matters?" *Journal of Adolescent Research* **14**(1): 16-38. Reprinted by permission of Sage Publications.

Figure 10.1 J.S. Eccles and B.L. Barber, 1999, "Student council, volunteering, basketball, or marching band: What kind of extracurricular involvement matters?" *Journal of Adolescent Research* **14**(1): 16-38. Reprinted by permission of Sage Publications.

Article 11 From: "The Athletic Department vs. the University," from COLLEGE SPORTS INC., © 1990 by Murray Sperber. From *Phi Delta Kappan,* **72**(2), 1-10, 1990. Excerpted by arrangement with Henry Holt and Company, LLC. Reprinted by permission of Henry Holt and Company, LLC.

Article 12 E.M. Blinde, D.E. Taub, and L. Han, "Sport participation and women's personal empowerment: Experiences of the college athlete," *Journal of Sport & Social Issues* **17**(1): 47-60. © 1993 by Sage Publications, Inc. Reprinted by permission of Sage Publications Inc.

Article 13 Reprinted, by permission from R. Sellers, G. Kuperminc, and A. Damas, 1997, "The college life experiences of afro-american women athletes," *American Journal of Community Psychology,* **24**(5): 699-720.

Emergence and Development of Sociology of Sport

Objectives

The article provides historical background to the development of the sociology of sport and addresses several critical issues about the relationships between sociology, physical education, and sport sociology.

Sport sociologist and Alliance Scholar George Sage launches our book with a discussion of the relationships among physical education, sociology, and the sociology of sport. He begins by outlining the early connections between physical education and sociology. Sage then addresses the rift that ensued from a shift in emphasis in sociology, the change from a "reform perspective" model to a "science of society" model.

The author further discusses the growth of the New Physical Education and its link to "the social development principle" and outlines some of the early influences that helped shape educational theory in the United States. Sage then traces the forces that gave rise to the academic study of sport and exercise and helps explain the emergence and growth of the sociology of sport.

In recent years the relationship between sport sociology and physical education has experienced tension and strain. Sage describes the causes of this strain and proposes some possible new directions. One promising link, according to the author, is with the emerging field of sport pedagogy. The field is engaging in greater critical scrutiny and debate of the practices and assumptions employed in the training of teachers of physical education. Much attention is directed toward the study of "oppression, inequity and social injustices perpetuated by teachers in the schools." In these endeavors, Sage points out, critical sport pedagogy and sport sociology have similar intellectual orientations, especially in the critical study of class, ethnicity, gender, and race. The author rightly concludes that "with respect to both theory and practice, there is a number of relevant mutual intersections for these two subdisciplines."

Sport sociology received a considerable boost in 1978 with the formation of the North American Society for the Sociology of Sport. In 1980 the society held its first conference, and the event has been held annually ever since. The field has grown considerably since 1980. Today, many universities and colleges around the world offer sport sociology. Books and journals abound, and conferences and symposia are held on a regular basis.

In closing, the author suggests that future growth in the sociology of sport is likely to be "situated" within a broader framework, under the umbrella terms of sport and cultural studies. The link with sociology may be further strained. A major paradigm shift that appears to be in progress (Greendorfer, 1994) suggests that future scholarship in the area may adopt a more inclusive perspective that incorporates a wider array of "physical activity phenomena" than merely sport.

Finally, Sage suggests that we may also begin to see developments along applied lines as the relevance of the knowledge that sport sociologists produce is more effectively demonstrated to "various public and professional groups."

Reference

Greendorfer, S. (1994). Sociocultural aspects. In Ziegler (Ed.), *Physical education and kinesiology in North America: Professional and scholarly foundations* (pp. 99-123). Champaign, IL: Stipes.

Discussion Questions

George Sage

1. Describe and explain the early connections and links between sociology and physical education.
2. By the beginning of the 20th century sociology had rejected the reform perspective and adopted a "science of society" model. What were the implications of such a shift for sociology and its relationship with physical education?
3. Discuss and explain the growth of the New Physical Education and its links to the "social development principle."
4. Discuss and explain the three major influences that shaped early educational theory in the United States.
5. Discuss and explain the forces that gave rise to the academic study of sport and exercise, and to sport sociology in particular.
6. Discuss and explain the issues that in recent years have strained the relationship between physical education and sport sociology.
7. Speculate and comment on the possible future theoretical and applied directions of sport sociology.

Physical Education, Sociology, and Sociology of Sport: Points of Intersection

George H. Sage

This paper examines the linkages between physical education, sociology, and sociology of sport in North America. Physical education and sociology in North America have had numerous mutual ties since the beginnings of both fields. In the first section of the paper, I describe the rise of sociology and physical education in North America, emphasizing the linkages that initially existed between physical education and sociology, and then the separation that transpired between the disciplines. The second section examines the connections between social theory and physical education before the sociology of sport was formally developed. The final section details the rise of sociology of sport, with the main focus on the role of physical educators (a.k.a. sociocultural kinesiologists, sport studies scholars, human kinetics scholars) in the development of sociology of sport. This section concludes with a discussion of the linkages of social theory, critical pedagogy in physical education, and sport sociology in physical education.

In this paper I examine the linkages between physical education, sociology, and sociology of sport in North America. A deliberate attempt has been made in this paper not to duplicate content, themes, and topics covered by Ingham and Donnelly (1997) in this issue. Furthermore, several previous efforts to chronicle the evolvement of the sociology of sport have been made by scholars who were instrumental in the founding and development of the sociology of sport in North America (Frey & Eitzen, 1991; Greendorfer, 1981, 1994; Loy, Kenyon, & McPherson, 1980; Loy, McPherson, & Kenyon, 1978a; Luschen, 1980; McPherson, 1975; Snyder & Spreitzer, 1979). Although those writings were valuable sources in the preparation of this paper, this paper differs from the others in that the focus here is on the social organization of physical education in relation to its historical intersections with sociology and sport sociology.

Physical education and sociology in North America have had numerous mutual ties since the beginnings of both fields. Both emerged as distinct fields of study in North America at about the same time—the mid-19th century. During the first half century of both, a number of common interests and concerns helped bind physical educators and sociologists together in their professional endeavors. The ties between the two fields loosened in the first half of the 20th century, except that a central component of "The New Physical Education" was grounded in a recognition of social structure and social processes—both central concerns in sociology.

Throughout the 20th century, social theory has been present in pedagogy and curriculum theories and practices in physical education because physical education has drawn extensively from education curriculum theories which, in turn, have borrowed from social theories. With the emergence of the sociology of sport as a distinct academic specialty in the 1960s, physical education and sociology have been drawn closer together because scholars in both fields have been involved in teaching and research in sociology of sport.

Reprinted from Sage, 1997.

In the first section of the paper, I describe the rise of sociology and physical education in North America, emphasizing the linkages that initially existed between physical education and sociology, and then the separation that transpired between the disciplines. The second section examines the connections between social theory and physical education before the sociology of sport was formally developed. The final section details the rise of sociology of sport, with the main focus on the role of physical educators (a.k.a. sociocultural kinesiologists, sport studies scholars, human kinetics scholars) in the development of sociology of sport. This section concludes with a discussion of the linkages of social theory, critical pedagogy in physical education, and sport sociology in physical education.

Because of the close associations among scholars and professionals in the United States and Canada during the evolution of physical education, sociology, and the sociology of sport, relevant events in both countries are addressed.

The Rise of Sociology and Physical Education in North America

Both sociology and physical education in North America emerged in the latter 19th century as culminating products of historical forces. The antecedents of sociology are found in several political, social, and intellectual movements. The most significant were the scientific revolution, which began in the 15th century; it, in turn, was a major spur for the industrial revolution, which had its first major impact in England in the 18th century. Also in the 18th century, political and social revolutions in America and France and the social philosophical movement, the Enlightenment, helped create the social and intellectual context for the rise of sociology. It was Auguste Comte who gave this field of study the name "sociology" in the early 19th century (Marvin, 1965); the first two books in America bearing the concept "sociology" in their titles were both published in 1854: *Sociology of the South* (Fitzhugh, 1854) and *Treatise on Sociology, Theoretical and Practical* (Hughes, [1854] 1968).

In the formative years, American sociologists focused their attention on the forces that hold society together and on the foes that fragment it. Many believed that the direct application of sociological knowledge to the world about them would enable them to solve many problems endemic to indus-

trial society. So a number of first generation North American sociologists strongly emphasized ameliorating social problems, taking the purpose of sociology as supplying guidance for needed social reforms. House (1970) noted that early sociology in the United States was "strongly influenced and shaped by the humanitarian, philanthropic, and social reform movements that were actively under way in the country during the 19th century" (p. 220; see also Camic & Xie, 1994). The records and reports of the American Social Science Association (ASSA) are characterized by the dominant theme of "the science of reform, or reform as science" (Silver, 1983, p. 115). Charles Sanborn, a founder of the ASSA, viewed the role of the social scientist as improving conditions of life and eliminating misery (Manicas, 1987).

Antecedents to the field of physical education in North America are to be found in the social conditions of the rapidly growing industrial revolution of the early 19th century. Even though efforts to provide education for children and youth began early in the American colonial period, formal programs of physical education were not part of these efforts. As industrialization took off in the Antebellum Period, some of the most acute problems centered on growing urbanization, the large numbers of industrial workers living under marginal economic conditions, unemployment, poverty, high city crime rates, juvenile delinquency, the intermingling of different racial and ethnic groups, and articulations between local, state (or province), and national levels of government. The transformation in personal and social conditions were of such scope and intensity that traditional practices and customs were simply incapable of coping with these new forces (Licht, 1995; Monkkonen, 1988; Stelter & Artibise, 1986).

Physicians, educators, and social reformers were in general agreement that many of the social conditions described above were contributing to poor public health, so they sought ways to improve public health, especially for children and youth. Increasingly, their attention converged on the need for physical activities as a means for improving health, and the first physical education programs were undertaken for schoolchildren, college students, and adults. The underlying theoretical foundation on which the field of physical education emerged was that physical activity was related to personal health status, and a systematic program of vigorous physical activity could enhance personal health, thus alleviating some of the effects of industrial-age living.

Proponents of the theory that vigorous physical activity could improve health advanced various kinds of physical education regimes (e.g., German gymnastics, Swedish gymnastics, the Sargent system) as the best means for achieving improved health. In 1889, Edward M. Hartwell (1889), at the Boston Conference in the Interest of Physical Training, suggested that the aim of physical education was to promote health. Ten years later, at the annual convention of the American Association for the Advancement of Physical Education, one of the speakers declared: "Physical education justifies itself by its relation to the new" promotion of health (Report, 1899, p. 217).

As physical educators advanced the cause of physical activity for the promotion of public health during the latter 19th and early 20th century, sociologists championed the cause of physically active leisure time and recreational facilities as a means for alleviating some of the social problems of industrial society. In cooperation with civic-minded citizens, clergy, and physicians, leaders in both physical education and sociology joined forces for the promotion of playgrounds and public parks in the major cities of the East and Midwest before 1910.

The successful establishment of city playgrounds and public parks in the latter 19th century were brought about by the joint efforts of many physical educators and sociologists who labored tirelessly on committees, commissions, and various community groups on behalf of play for children and outdoor leisure facilities and activities for adults. Professionals in both fields published papers advancing the cause of parks, playgrounds, physical activity, and increased leisure time to ameliorate social conditions of an increasingly industrialized society (Goodman, 1979; Hardy, 1981; Hofstadter, 1955; Martindale, 1976; Riess, 1989).

Sociology Opts for Science

By the first decade of the 20th century, a new emphasis in sociology began to distinguish between a scientific and a reform orientation to the study of society. This new approach rejected the reform model for sociology, holding that the purpose of sociology was to develop a science of society, regardless of whether that science contributed to the solution of social problems. According to this perspective, sociology, like the natural sciences, should pursue knowledge for its own sake (Coser, 1976; House, 1970; Martindale, 1976).

The "science" model had become well-entrenched in sociology by the latter 1920s. In 1929,

William F. Ogburn, president of the American Sociological Society (predecessor to the American Sociological Association), articulated this point of view in his presidential address to members:

> Sociology as a science is not interested in making the world a better place in which to live, in encouraging beliefs, or in spreading information, in dispensing news, in setting forth impressions of life, in leading multitudes, or in guiding the ship of state. Science is interested in one thing only, to wit, discovery of new knowledge. (Quoted from Becker, 1971, p. 28)

Sociology departments became oriented to systematic empirical research employing quantitative methodology. With the rise of academic/empirical sociology, sociology and physical education grew apart from each other, as sociologists evidenced little interest in play, games, sport, or leisure and recreation in general (Camic & Xie, 1994; Manicas, 1987).

The New Physical Education and Social Development

Meantime, as sociology withdrew from social reformism, physical education became increasingly dissatisfied with the various gymnastic systems and increasingly supportive of the educational developmentalism that was sweeping the nation. During the first two decades of the 20th century, Thomas Wood at Columbia University and Clark Hetherington at the University of Missouri (and later at Wisconsin, New York University, and Stanford) adapted the theoretical orientation of educational developmentalism to physical education, formulating what became known as "The New Physical Education" (Hetherington, 1910; Wood, 1910).

Hetherington (1910) articulated the meaning of this new approach, suggesting it

> be called the new physical education, with the emphasis on education, and the understanding that it is "physical" only in the sense that the activity of the whole organism is the educational agent and not the mind alone.... The general idea [is] that education is neither for body nor for mind alone, but for all human powers that depend on educational activities for development. (p. 350)

In the new physical education formulated by Wood and Hetherington, "social development" had a privileged position. It was firmly based on a belief that games and sport experiences develop qualities essential to social living, such as cooperation, self-sacrifice, self-discipline, teamwork, and others, that it promoted habits and attitudes conducive to good citizenship in a democracy, and that it gave rise to ideals and practices of good sportsmanship and ethical conduct (Wood & Cassidy, 1927; Williams, 1927). With the popularity of the new physical education, games and sports gradually became the major component of the physical education curriculum because physical educators viewed sport as a means for the socialization of American youth and the assimilation of American culture.

Now, while the new physical education was not "sociological" in any strict sense, it was grounded in a recognition and understanding of the importance of social structures, social processes, and cultural practices, all fundamental considerations in sociology. Thus, it is clear that sociological concepts and ideas were linked to the new physical education curriculum (I have more to say about social theory in physical education in the next section).

Jesse Feiring Williams succeeded Wood and Hetherington and, under his leadership, the theories of the new physical education dominated the profession from the 1920s through the 1950s. Williams' (1930) well-known statement that "the modern spirit in physical education seeks . . . Education . . . through physical activities as one aspect of the social effort for human enlightenment. . . . education through the physical is based on the . . . unity of mind and body" (p. 279) became the guiding principle in physical education. According to Williams, (1927) "physical education should aim to provide skilled leadership and adequate faculties that will afford an opportunity for the individual or group to act in situations which are physically wholesome, mentally stimulating and satisfying, and socially sound" (p. 284). Thus, a socially grounded component was prominent in his aim of physical education.

Williams' book, *Principles of Physical Education*, went through six editions and was a basic textbook for physical education students for more than 30 years. Beginning with the third edition, Williams devoted a separate chapter to "The Nature of Man: His Sociological Foundations." In it, he states, "There are sociological aspects of contemporary American culture that bear upon physical education" (Williams, 1938, p. 121). On another page, he says, "American sport reflects American life. Sport with other social forces over a long period of time may modify American life" (Williams, 1938, p. 155).

The social development principle in physical education flourished with the continued popularity of athletic sport and the prodigious growth of public school programs in physical education. Clearly, connections between physical education and the subject matter of sociology were prevalent in the new physical education that dominated American physical education up to 1960.

Neither Wood, Hetherington, Williams, nor any of their disciples attempted to ground their ideas about social development with a program of empirical research, using social theories and social research methodology. There were, however, some exceptions to this picture. Charles Cowell (1935, 1958) at Purdue University published a few empirical studies between 1935 and 1960. In 1960, Cowell published an article in the *Research Quarterly*, reviewing the empirical research literature on the contributions of physical activity to social development. Although 114 references were listed by Cowell, he admitted that selecting the articles was very arbitrary and that the instruments used to collect data in most of the studies were used without enough attention to what the scores and ratings actually meant. He also complained that most of the studies were merely descriptive.

Most physical educators were content to evangelize about the "social development" objective of games and sports. They did not seek interdisciplinary connections between sociology and physical education, nor did they attempt to develop a body of knowledge in the sociology of sport.

Social Theory and Physical Education

For the past 75 years, there have been articulations between physical education and sociology that went beyond the "social development" objective of the new physical education that was discussed previously. Since physical education became a distinct academic field of study, theories and practices employed in physical education have drawn assumptions and insights from social theories generated in sociology.

Dominant Social and Educational Theories Adopted by Physical Education

As physical education struggled for identity and legitimacy in the latter 19th century, some of its early leaders wished to position it with other scientific disciplines that existed, or were in the process of becoming disciplines (e.g., psychology, sociology). Luther Gulick, one of the most respected physical educators in the latter 19th and early 20th centuries, declared that physical education was not only a "new profession" but also a "scientific field" that offered opportunities for the study of problems of great value for the human species (Gulick, 1890). In spite of the aspirations of Gulick and other physical educators, many of whom were medical doctors, few made any effort to advance physical education as a science by engaging in theoretical endeavors or developing research programs of high scientific standards (Park, 1987).

By the early years of the 20th century, teacher education had become the dominant concern of departments of physical education in higher education. Physical educators in higher education were increasingly called on to prepare teachers for the expanding public school system and faculty for the proliferating departments of physical education in colleges and universities. Teacher preparation in physical education closely followed the trends and fashions in the broad field of education, since many college physical education departments were component parts of colleges of education. As educational theories and practice changed, physical education largely followed along.

As the public school system grew in the decades between 1900 and 1950, pedagogical theories and practices were largely forged in relation to three influences: (a) the reports of various committees and commissions; (b) the educational philosophy of John Dewey; and (c) the systems paradigm of other scientific disciplines.

Throughout the first half of the 20th century, a series of national committees, task forces, and commissions (e.g., The Seven Cardinal Principles of Education, 1918; Educational Policies Commission, 1938; General Education in a Free Society, 1945) were called on to establish the aims for American education. The message of these groups made clear that public schools were expected to prepare students with the personal-social dispositions and technical skills required to successfully carry out their adult roles in a democratic capitalist society, and that students were to learn to adjust to the norms, values, and expectations of the dominant social order. Thus, curriculum derived from these reports largely involved reinforcing and reproducing the dominant social and cultural practices and traditions (Apple, 1982, 1990; Cremin, 1964).

John Dewey was the eminent American educational philosopher of the first half of the 20th century, and a dominating influence on American education. The pedagogy derived from his social philosophy infused a vitality to the themes of voluntarism, optimism, individualism, and accommodation, all of which were part of the progressive reformism of that period (Cremin, 1964; Spring, 1985). But his was not a pedagogy of empowerment or emancipatory social transformation; instead, it was a liberal reformist pedagogy congruent with the social liberalism of the progressive movement. Education, Dewey argued, should contribute to industrial democracy by developing moral enlightenment and social harmony (Dewey, 1916; Giroux, 1981, 1989; Popkewitz, 1991).[1]

A third, and more subtle, influence impinging on the field of education emanated from the other scientific disciplines of the academy. During the first half of the 20th century, a systems paradigm dominated the physical, biological, and social scientific disciplines. In this approach, emphasis was on the contributions (or functions) of component parts to the maintenance of the larger system. Functions of physical, biological, or social phenomena were examined in relation to the larger system of which they are a part. When applied to society, the social theory was called structural-functionalism, and it emphasized the contributions of various social institutions and processes to the maintenance and stability of society (Barnes, 1995; Parsons, 1937, 1951).

The fledgling professional field of education was almost entirely shaped by the prevalent physical, biological, and social science systems models. Structural-functional theory was incorporated into educational pedagogy, not in any deliberate or direct way, but subtly though the professional discourse and belief system that pervaded all of the scientific disciplines and most educated enclaves during the first half of the 20th century. From a functionalist standpoint, the special function of the formal system of education in the U.S., as a component of the larger social system, was to promote the maintenance of American society by teaching youth of the nation attitudes, values, and beliefs congruent with its traditions, while developing in youth necessary occupational skills. Thus, schools were seen as adapting and integrating students in the culturally prescribed ways, thus preserving American culture (Morrow & Torres, 1995).

Based on the influences just described, and with only a few exceptions (e.g., Counts, 1932; Rugg, 1931) before World War II, the professional field of education viewed the aim of schools as one of integrating students into the imperatives of American culture, with social adjustment as the main outcome goal. Schooling was seen as a place where students learned the norms, values, and customs of American culture as preparation for adult life in American society.

From the progressive era in the early 20th century to the present, physical education has largely followed the structural-functional perspective of mainstream professional education, emphasizing integration and social adjustment of the individual to the social order, portraying the political order as unproblematic, and promoting unquestioning allegiance to Americanism. Professional practice in physical education has been devoted to the reinforcement and reproduction of current practices, beliefs, and values (Booth & Loy, in press; Kozman, 1951; Siedentop, Mand, & Taggart, 1986). Research in physical education has been firmly ensconced in positivistic, empirical-analytical traditions popularized by the natural sciences. Recent trends representing an alternative to this pattern are discussed in the last section of this paper.

Toward a Sociology of Sport by Physical Educators in Higher Education

Prior to the mid-1960s, physical education in higher education was largely focused on the preparation of teachers for the public schools and faculty for college physical education departments. But physical education, as well as other departments with an applied professional emphasis, came under increasing pressure to demonstrate a basic academic body of knowledge. In some universities there were threats that unless this could be demonstrated, departments would be eliminated (Kerr, 1991; Sage, 1984).

Physical educators in higher education had to respond to these challenges or face an uncertain future at some colleges and universities. As a result, the physical education literature throughout the 1960s was filled with programmatic essays purporting to show that physical education was indeed an academic discipline and articulating the conceptual and theoretical foundations of that discipline (Abernathy & Waltz, 1964; Brown, 1967; Nixon, 1967; Rarick, 1967; Steinhaus, 1967). Arguably the most persuasive voice was that of Franklin Henry, a University of California physical educator. In a now-classic article titled, "Physical Education: An

Academic Discipline," Henry (1964) asserted that "there is indeed a scholarly field of knowledge basic to physical education. It is constituted of certain portions of such diverse fields as anatomy, physics and physiology, cultural anthropology, history and sociology, as well as psychology" (p. 32).

Responses, such as Henry's, to the pressures in higher education for physical education to demonstrate a basic disciplinary foundation, set in motion a paradigm shift in physical education during the latter 1960s and 1970s (Newell, 1990). Departments of physical education adapted their curricula from solely the preparation of physical education teachers to the preparation of young scholars whose training was linked to an established academic discipline and to the study of exercise and sport. New specialized subdisciplines and graduate majors in those subdisciplines arose, such as physiology of exercise, biomechanics, motor learning, sport psychology, sociology of sport, and so forth.

Graduates of such programs took as their model the scientific disciplines, not the professional schools, so their focus on the analysis of exercise and sport turned to disciplinary concepts and theories and methods of empirical research, rather than the preparation of physical education teachers. As many of the younger scholars studying in physical education distanced themselves from teacher preparation, a major shift in intellectual perspective in physical education was created (Sage, 1991).

In addition to the trends in higher education, organized sports of all kinds—youth, high school, intercollegiate, professional, Olympic—were becoming a more prominent feature of North American culture in the 1960s. Sport was receiving greater mass media attention, and televised sports were beginning to play a dominant role in TV programming. At the same time, serious scholarly studies about sports were being undertaken. Renowned sociologist James S. Coleman's (1961) *The Adolescent Society* clearly demonstrated that high school athletics is more important as a value among high school students than intellectual achievements. *Sport: Mirror of American Life* by Robert Boyle, senior editor for *Sports Illustrated*, examined the impact of sport on American life. Collectively, these and other trends and events made it evident that sports had become a very important cultural practice and thus an appropriate subject for sociological analyses.

It may be seen, then, that several events in higher education, and in the broader social culture in the 1960s, coalesced to set the stage for the beginnings of sociology of sport as a distinct subdiscipline in physical education. But the most notable catalyst for actually launching sociology of sport as a field of study in North America came when Gerald Kenyon and John Loy (1965), both with terminal degrees in physical education, authored the first programmatic statement of a need for a sociology of sport. Their article entitled, "Toward a Sociology of Sport," was published in the May 1965 issue of the *Journal of Health, Physical Education, and Recreation*. Kenyon followed with other position papers and calls for a sociology of sport, such as his essay, "A Sociology of Sport: On Becoming a Subdiscipline" (Kenyon, 1969a).

These writings served to stimulate and/or support more formalized efforts that subsequently took place, such as conferences and meetings, publications, scholarly societies, and university courses in sport sociology. Before describing these, I want to emphasize quite emphatically that the development of the sociology of sport has been a joint venture for physical educators and sociologists. For example, in some universities the sociology of sport courses required by departments of physical education have been taught in sociology departments. Physical education graduate students taking a major emphasis in sport sociology have typically taken course work in sociology departments as part of their program, and sociologists have often served on thesis and dissertation committees. In a few cases, physical education faculty with sport sociology expertise have held joint appointments in departments of sociology. Sociologists have sat on editorial boards of sociology of sport journals and held offices in sociology of sport societies. Thus sociologists have actually played an important and continuing role in the evolution of sport sociology.[2] However, the main focus of this paper is on physical education and its linkages to sociology and sociology of sport, so the role of sociologists working in sociology departments is not pursued to any extent.

Intellectual Boundaries: Relationship Between Sociology of Sport and Physical Education

In the sociology of sport, much of the work of early leaders involved establishing the intellectual boundaries of the specialty and making initial research probes. An inevitable part of establishing a new specialty's boundaries is that someone, acknowledged as its leader, sets the theoretical and methodological agenda and others join in support for it. For the sociology of sport, Gerald Kenyon in the Department of Physical Education at the University of Wisconsin quickly emerged as the spokesperson, largely through his programmatic speeches at various national conventions, hosting a Big Ten symposium on the sociology of sport, joint editorship of the first anthology on the sociology of sport, and through his sponsorship of a group of graduate students at Wisconsin who were destined to become the vanguard in the first generation of scholars specifically trained as sport sociologists.

Kenyon was a key figure in defining the scope and task of the emerging field of sport sociology. He helped clarify definitions and concepts, as well as mapping out theoretical and methodological frameworks and suggesting favorable areas of future research in the sociology of sport. In a series of publications between 1965 and 1969, Kenyon emphatically situated the sociology of sport firmly within the positivistic perspective of science. Sociology was defined as the "study of social order" (Kenyon & Loy, 1965, p. 24) and "sport sociology . . . is a value-free social science" (p. 25); the function of the sport sociologist "is not to shape attitudes and values but rather to describe and explain them" (p. 25; see also Kenyon, 1969a). It is clear that Kenyon was asserting that the scientific legitimacy of sport sociology was tied to what he thought was the appropriate model of sociology, namely the positivist, empirical-analytical paradigm of the established sciences.[3] Some of the consequences of this position are discussed in the last section of this paper.

Conferences and Symposia

Whenever a topic of intellectual curiosity attracts a group of interested persons, they typically organize meetings to get acquainted with each other, establish social ties (network), and share their ideas and research. Conferences and symposia were especially helpful in the early development of sport sociology because scholars interested in this field were scattered across several disciplines: physical education, sociology, anthropology, political science, social psychology. It was through opportunities to meet and discuss mutual interests, theoretical ideas, and report their research that social linkages developed between sport sociologists working in physical education and sport sociologists working in sociology. These linkages, in turn, helped form a cohesive group committed to advancing this subdiscipline.

The first program on the sociology of sport sponsored by the American Association for Health, Physical Education, and Recreation (AAHPER) (the name was changed to the American Alliance for

Health, Physical Education, Recreation, and Dance [AAHPERD] in 1979) took place in 1966. Gerald Kenyon, John Loy, and Cyril White were the keynote speakers. During the next few years, the annual meetings of AAHPER usually included a session devoted to the sociology of sport.

In the mid-1970s, AAHPER underwent a major restructuring, one outcome of which was the creation of what were called "academies." A major function of the academies was to organize sessions related to particular areas of scholarly inquiry and professional concerns at the annual meetings of AAHPERD. In 1976, a Sociology of Sport Academy was founded by AAHPER to coordinate and promote the study of sport sociology. The Sociology of Sport Academy organizes three or four sessions at the annual AAHPERD conference, thus providing sport sociologists an opportunity to hear and report research but also providing an opportunity for nonsport sociologists attending the conference to attend sport sociology sessions and learn about the ideas and research findings in this subdiscipline.

In 1968, at the annual convention of the American Sociological Association (ASA), a luncheon roundtable discussion on the sociology of sport was held, led by Charles Page of the University of Massachusetts, a strong supporter for the advancement of the sociology of sport. For the past 30 years, the ASA and its regional affiliates have regularly sponsored sessions on the sociology of sport at their annual meetings.

In 1970, the Canadian Association for Health, Physical Education, and Recreation (CAHPER) sponsored a seminar on sociology of sport at McMaster University. At that seminar, a committee was established to prepare a special issue for the *CAHPER* journal devoted to sport sociology. That special issue was published in February 1971. CAHPER also sponsored the publication of a set of monographs titled "CAHPER Sociology of Sport Monograph Series," composed of more than a dozen topics relevant to sport sociology. The series was initiated by the Sociology of Sport Committee of CAHPER in response to a need expressed by physical educators who were teaching courses in the sociology of sport in Canadian universities.

As the sociology of sport inched its way into higher education in the United States in the late 1960s and '70s, the greatest support for this field of study was shown by faculty and graduate students in graduate departments of physical education at Big Ten universities. In November 1968, a symposium on the sociology of sport was held at the University of Wisconsin under the auspices of the Committee for Institutional Cooperation (CIC), composed of one member from each of the Big Ten universities and the University of Chicago. More than 50 participants were in attendance. The conference proceedings were edited by Kenyon and published under the title of *Aspects of Contemporary Sociology of Sport* (Kenyon, 1969b). A second CIC symposium on the sociology of sport was held 10 years later at the University of Minnesota in April 1978; the proceedings were published under the title of *The Dimensions of Sport Sociology* (Krotee, 1979).

Several other notable conferences were organized or jointly organized by departments of physical education and sociology during the late 1960s and early 1970s that focused on issues relevant to sport sociology. In 1967, the University of Illinois hosted an international workshop on the "Cross-Cultural Analysis of Sport and Games" sponsored by the UNESCO Committee on the Sociology of Sport (Luschen, 1970). At the State University College of New York at Brockport in 1971, a conference titled "Symposium on Sport and Social Deviancy" dealt with cheating, gambling, political activism, and racism (Landers, 1976). In 1972, three prominent conferences were held. A symposium on problems associated with "Athletics in America" took place at Oregon State University (Flath, 1972). "Sport in a Changing World" was the title of a symposium held at the University of Wisconsin, Madison. A "Conference on Women and Sport" was held at Pennsylvania State University (Harris, 1972).

All of these conferences helped link physical educators and sociologists through a central topic that was of mutual interest to both. More than that, they were actually multidisciplinary because speakers and participants included philosophers, psychologists, historians, and so forth, in addition to sport sociologists.

Throughout the past 30 years, many international conferences and symposia on the sociology of sport have been held. But because the focus of this paper is North America, international meetings are not identified, except to note that the International Committee for Sport Sociology (ICSS) has held annual symposia since 1966, and North American sport sociologists have always had a prominent presence in ICSS (the name was changed to the International Sport Sociology Association in 1994).

Sport Sociology in Physical Education Publications

As interest and scholarship grows in any field of study, publications are created to allow scholars to discuss mutual concerns, issues, and problems, as well as share theoretical ideas and research findings.

Periodicals

Two physical education publications have had a sustaining record of publishing articles on sport sociology. *Quest*, a publication of National Association for Physical Education in Higher Education, has been a popular publishing outlet for sport sociologists over the years, and the *Research Quarterly for Exercise and Sport*, the AAHPERD research journal, has regularly published empirical research in sport sociology.

During the late 1970s and early 80s, the Sport Studies Research Group in the School of Physical and Health Education at Queen's University in Canada published some excellent critical and theoretically oriented work in a series titled "Working Papers in the Sociological Study of Sports and Leisure."

Although not under the sponsorship of physical education, I would be remiss not to identify the *Sociology of Sport Journal* and the *International Review for the Sociology of Sport* (IRSS) at this point. The first is the major publication outlet for North American sport sociologists, and the second is the major international outlet for sport sociologists. Although the founders of the North American Society for the Sociology of Sport (NASSS) (to be described later) aspired from their first organizational meeting in 1978 to sponsor a journal, it was not until 1984 that their aspirations reached fruition with the first issue of the *Sociology of Sport Journal*, with Human Kinetics Publishers as the publisher and sociologist Jay Coakley of the University of Colorado, Colorado Springs as editor. Peter Donnelly from the School of Physical Education at McMaster University followed Coakley as editor; the present editor, Cynthia Hasbrook, is with the Department of Human Kinetics at the University of Wisconsin, Milwaukee. Thus, two of the three editors of *Sociology of Sport Journal* have been from the field of physical education.

The International Committee for Sport Sociology began publication of the *International Review of Sport Sociology* (currently titled the *International Review for the Sociology of Sport*) in 1966. It was published in Poland under the editorship of Andrzej Wohl until 1984. From 1984 to 1988, Kurt Weis was the editor and from 1988 to 1996, Klaus Heinemann was editor; both are from Germany. It is presently edited by James McKay of Queensland University, Brisbane, Australia and is published by Sage Publications.[4]

Anthologies and Textbooks on Sport Sociology

As any new academic field of inquiry begins to grow and courses are offered on that subject, anthologies are published to bring the literature together because the written materials that do exist on that subject are typically scattered through many diverse publications. Such was the case for sport sociology. Those working in physical education were the first in publishing anthologies. Beginning in 1969 with John Loy and Gerald Kenyon's (1969) *Sport, Culture, and Society* and George Sage's (1970) *Sport and American Society* one year later, a half-dozen books of readings appeared in the next few years edited or coedited by scholars working in physical education departments (Ball & Loy, 1975; Hart, 1972; Yiannakis, McIntyre, Melnick, & Hart, 1976).

There were no textbooks devoted exclusively to sport sociology prior to the mid-1970s. However three books authored by physical educators, Cozens and Stumpf's (1953) *Sports in American Life*, Bryant J. Cratty's (1967) *Social Dimensions of Physical Activity*, and Celeste Ulrich's (1968) *The Social Matrix of Physical Education* were all pioneering efforts to focus on the social aspects of physical activity. In doing this, they contributed to the promotion of a sociology of sport.

The first books written specifically as textbooks for sport sociology classes and authored or coauthored by physical educators appeared in the late 1970s (Ibrahim, 1975; Eitzen & Sage, 1978; Loy, McPherson, & Kenyon, 1978b). Sport sociology textbooks authored by sociologists appeared at about the same time (Coakley, 1978; Edwards, 1973; Nixon, 1976; Snyder & Spreitzer, 1978). A half-dozen additional textbooks have been published in the past 20 years. All of these texts have been used in sport sociology courses offered in physical education departments as well as in sociology departments. Thus, the intellectual endeavors of sport sociologists from physical education and from sociology were being read by students in both academic fields.

Data Base for Sport Sociology Literature

A major contribution to the preservation of and access to the literature in sport sociology was made by Gerald Kenyon. In the late 1960s, he created a basic data retrieval system, which he took with him to the University of Waterloo in 1970 when he became Dean of the Faculty of Human Kinetics and Leisure Studies at that university. At Waterloo, Kenyon established the unique and valuable computerized information retrieval system for the Sociology of Leisure and Sport (SIRLS). When the University of Waterloo sold the SIRLS collection to the Sport Information Resource Centre (SIRC) in Gloucester, ON, Canada in the early 1990s, SIRLS contained more than 17,000 references in the sociology and social psychology of sport and leisure.

Emergence of the North American Society for the Sociology of Sport

Individuals with common interests tend to organize together into clubs, societies, associations, and so forth. This is especially true in the academic world. Every academic discipline has at least one society or professional association, and many have several. In sport sociology, the conferences and symposia, the growing literature, the collaborations among scholars during the 1970s all set the stage for the founding of a scholarly organization for this subdiscipline.

It was at the 1978 CIC symposium at the University of Minnesota that the participants—mostly physical educators and sociologists—assembled in the foyer of Mayo Memorial Auditorium just before the symposium ended and discussed the need for founding a scholarly society for sport sociology in North America. During the discussion, a consensus emerged that such an organization was needed and a name was agreed on: the North American Society for the Sociology of Sport (NASSS). A steering committee was established and entrusted with the tasks of developing a newsletter, beginning a membership drive, planning a conference, publishing the proceedings, and considering the feasibility of founding a journal.

Andrew Yiannakis, a physical educator at the University of Connecticut, planned the first NASSS conference held in Denver in 1980. He was assisted by Susan Greendorfer, a physical educator from the University of Illinois, who also served as treasurer for seven years; James Bryant, a physical educator from Metropolitan State College, Denver, CO, who helped with site arrangements; and James Frey, a sociologist from UNLV, who assisted with publicity. NASSS conferences have been held annually ever since.

From its beginnings until the present, the majority of NASSS members have been employed in departments of physical education (a.k.a. kinesiology, human movement, exercise science, and sport studies, etc.), but numerous sociologists have held membership as well. Leadership in NASSS has always been shared by scholars from both physical education and sociology. Between 1980 and 1998, of the 16 presidents of NASSS, nine have been employed in departments of physical education (or one

of the other titles used) and seven in departments of sociology.

Sociology of Sport in Physical Education: Status and Intersections With Other Subdisciplines

The status of sociology of sport in departments of physical education (or similar titles) has been strained for the past 30 years, which is rather ironic because the most articulate initial thrusts for a sociology of sport came from persons trained in physical education, and the primary location for most persons who are teaching and doing research in sport sociology has been in departments of physical education. There are two main reasons for the uneasy pattern of relations between those who teach and research in sport sociology and other faculty in physical education. First, as I noted in a previous section, Gerald Kenyon went to great lengths in his early programmatic essays to differentiate sport sociology from physical education. Several additional statements of his may be used to illustrate this. He said,

> I cannot conceive of sport sociology and physical education as one and the same things. . . . Just as sociology is not social work, neither is sport sociology motor therapy. . . . Sport sociology . . . does not endeavor to . . . find support for the so-called "social development" objective of physical education . . . the sport sociologist is neither a spreader of gospel, nor an evangelist for exercise. (Kenyon, 1969a, pp. 166, 172)

While Kenyon (1969a) was willing to grant that some of the findings of sport sociology "might well be useful to the physical educator" (p. 178) and that the sport sociologist might "benefit from an exposure to a wide array of physical activities and sport" (pp. 178-179), he cautioned that there was potential for such "exposure" to cause the sport sociologist to become "a devoted apologist for exercise" and "there is a danger of contaminating one's objectivity" (p. 179). One can readily imagine the tensions that such statements might create between sport sociologists and other faculty working in departments of physical education.

The second issue that has tended to trouble relations between sport sociology and physical education centers around the fact that sport sociologists are often critical of sport organizations and practices as they are presently constituted, whereas other physical education faculty tend to be advocates for these same sport organizations and practices. Hollands (1984) described the problem in this way: "The very structure of sport study in North America ironically pairs the social critic [sport sociologist] with those very individuals in sport science whose professional ideology reinforces ahistorical and functionalist approaches to the subject" (p. 73).

It is easy to see, then, that the role of sport sociologists in departments of physical education can become paradoxical. On the one hand, physical education departments (or similar names) are an ideal location for studying play, games, and sport phenomena because these human movement activities are significant cultural practices in North American society. On the other hand, critical analyses, especially when they problematize current sporting practices, are often discounted as unscientific by colleagues whose orientation is the positivist science model; worse, some colleagues, as well as students taking courses in sport sociology, perceive social critiques of sports as being antisport, even unpatriotic, and thus having no legitimate place in the physical education course offerings.

A third issue that has been a problem for sport sociology in physical education departments is that faculty and students tend to see direct career linkages to the content in courses of most of the subdisciplines (e.g., exercise physiology) and perceive their bases of knowledge as relevant to careers in teaching, athletic training, coaching, sports medicine, etc. Sport sociology, on the other hand, doesn't provide a foundational knowledge base for any specific career outlet in the physical activity professions.

Notwithstanding the problems and tensions that sport sociology has encountered in departments of physical education, it must be emphasized that departments of physical education have provided the primary support for the development of sport sociology through offering (even requiring) sport sociology courses and by employing sport sociologists to teach courses and develop graduate programs in sport sociology. Indeed, it has been departments of physical education that sponsored most graduate degree specialization in sport sociology. Without the support of physical education departments, the field of sport sociology would have had far greater difficulty gaining a foothold in higher education.

There is no doubt many different reasons for this support, but the apparent overarching reason appears to be that physical education faculty believe that sport sociology does have an important and relevant body of knowledge for students in the teacher education curriculum, as well as for students in other programs under the auspices of physical education, such as coaching, athletic administration, sport management, and the various kinesiological sciences and sport studies. An important intellectual affinity that seems to be recognized between sport sociology and the other areas in physical education is that they are all "embodied," and the literature in the sociology of sport seems to provide a bridge between the various physical activity sciences and professions.

Critical Social Pedagogy in Physical Education

One subdiscipline within physical education where promising linkages with sport sociology are emerging is sport pedagogy.[5] Some scholars in both sport sociology and sport pedagogy employ critical[6] social theory in their teaching and research. Only the outlines of this mutual interest in critical social theory can be sketched in this paper.

In a previous section, I argued that physical education has largely followed a structural-functional orientation. But the hegemony of structure-functionalism in social theory, like hegemony in any social entity, has never been complete. Beginning in the late 1960s, the assumptions and tenets of structural-functionalist thought were contested in a variety of ways. This was a period of social and political upheaval in the U.S. and several social movements coalesced—university campus protests against the war in Vietnam, the women's liberation movement, the Civil Rights Movement—to challenge traditional oppression and injustices found in American social institutions and culture.

This critical scrutiny and debate spilled over into the academic and scientific community where a diverse group of neo-Marxist social theories challenged the hegemony of positive science and structural-functionalism as a way to understand late capitalist society. Positive conceptions of science and functionalism as a social model were attacked for their perceived tendency to exaggerate consensus, stability, and integration to the point of essentially disregarding conflict, change, and disorder (Bernard, 1983; Giddens, 1977, 1987; Sewart, 1978;

Stockman, 1983). Critical social thought, which included important work grounded in feminist and race theories, began to make significant inroads into American cultural attitudes and values (Gouldner, 1970; Jay, 1984; Leonard, 1990; Turner, 1990).

In parallel with critical social trends in the social sciences, scholarship in educational pedagogy and curriculum theory began to employ critical analyses during the late 1970s and early 1980s. Michael Apple (1979, 1982) and Henry Giroux (1981, 1983) emerged as two of the earliest educational theorists to advocate a critical pedagogy.[7]

In sport pedagogy, critical social work began to appear in the literature in the mid-1980s. During the past decade there has been an expanding literature of socially critical work in physical education. Much of this work has been a critique of positivistic approaches to research and technocratic views of teaching and curriculum in physical education (Fernández-Balboa, 1993, 1995, 1997; Schempp, 1987). Other work has analyzed and proposed alternatives to the hidden curriculum and physical education curricula for students who are considered "at risk" (Bain, 1975, 1985, 1990; Fernández-Balboa, 1993; Hellison, 1985, 1988).

Most of the socially critical literature in sport pedagogy has been directed at sensitizing those aspiring to work in physical education and those who are currently professionals in physical education to the effects of their taken-for-granted assumptions and practices (Bain, 1989; Dewar, 1987, 1991; Griffin, 1985, 1991). These analyses and critiques have highlighted the oppression, inequity, and social injustices perpetuated by teachers in the schools. They have emphasized and critiqued the dominant values that underlie school structure, teaching and administrative practices, approaches to learning, curricular approaches, and particular conceptions of subject matter. Rovegno and Kirk (1995) argue that critical social physical education has attempted to "locate physical education within the constellations of other practices that constitute society, and to begin to suggest how physical education might contribute to, and be shaped by, social, cultural, political, and economic forces" (p. 452). Most importantly, the socially critical research has raised persuasive arguments in support of empowerment and emancipation as important goals for physical education.

In these endeavors, critical pedagogy in physical education shares intellectual affinities with sport sociology in physical education about social constructions, body culture, physicality and sexuality, personal health versus public policy, and especially the embodiment of class, ethnicity, gender, and race. In short, with respect to both theory and practice, there is a number of relevant mutual intersections for these two subdisciplines.

Future Directions for Physical Education, Sociology, and Sport Sociology

It is abundantly clear that physical education and sociology have had close connections since the beginnings of both in the latter 19th century, and those linkages continue today, primarily through the subdiscipline of sport sociology. Over the past 30 years, the sociology of sport has emerged as a distinct academic specialty, and its roots are firmly embedded in departments of physical education (and the other names being used). Departments of physical education have given support to sport sociology by creating undergraduate and graduate courses, as well as graduate programs, in sport sociology.

The academic status of sport sociology in physical education appears to have a stable foundation, especially through the growing intersections with other physical activity subdisciplines. On the other hand, the marginalization of sociology of sport in sociology seems destined to continue. There has been no notable growth in the number of sociologists who claim sport as a specialty in the past 20 years.

Current trends suggest that a paradigm shift is already underway in the study of the sociocultural aspects of sports, and that the designation "sociology of sport" may become outdated. Early definitions and boundary mappings tended to constrain sociology of sport to the domain of sociology proper, which tended to limit interdisciplinary analysis. However, much of the diverse and critical theoretical and methodological knowledge production that has been gaining momentum over the past decade situates sport sociology within a broader framework of what many call "sport studies" (Harris, 1989). Greendorfer (1994) noted that sport sociology "seems to be shifting from one whose attention was solely devoted to the study of sport to one more inclusive of a broad range of physical activity phenomena" (p. 113).

Some consider the broader orientation of sport sociology coalescing with the cultural studies tradition (Harris, 1989; Hollands, 1984). Scholars on the forefront of the sport/cultural studies movement have emphasized that its fusion of perspectives carries the promise of developing a comprehensive model to analyze relations of dominance and subordination simultaneously contoured along class, race, and gender lines (Birrell, 1989). These are promising signs that the sociocultural aspects of sport will continue to grow as a fertile field of study.

Along applied lines, more and more sport sociologists are being consulted by various public and professional groups and asked to share their research and insights. *Applied Sociology of Sport*, edited by Andrew Yiannakis and Susan Greendorfer (1992), was a recent effort "to articulate a theoretical framework for the conceptual development of an applied sociology of sport" (p. vii). The growth of physical activities of all kinds in the popular culture of North America seems assured, and it is likely that new applied opportunities will become available for sport sociologists, or whatever scholars working in this field will be called in the future.

References

Abernathy, R., & Waltz, M. (1964, April). Toward a discipline: First steps first. *Quest, 2,* 1-7.

American Sociological Association. (1990). *Biographical directory of members*. Washington, DC: American Sociological Association.

Apple, M.W. (1979). *Ideology and curriculum*. Boston: Routledge & Kegan Paul.

Apple, M.W. (1982). *Education and power*. Boston: Routledge & Kegan Paul.

Apple, M.W. (1990). *Ideology and curriculum* (2nd ed.) New York: Routledge.

Bain, L.L. (1975). The hidden curriculum in physical education. *Quest, 24,* 92-101.

Bain, L.L. (1985). The hidden curriculum reexamined. *Quest, 37,* 145-153.

Bain, L.L. (1989). Implicit values in physical education. In T.J. Templin & P.G. Schempp (Eds.), *Socialization into physical education: Learning to teach* (pp. 289-314). Columbus, OH: Merrill.

Bain, L.L. (1990). A critical analysis of the hidden curriculum in physical education. In D. Kirk & R. Tinning (Eds.), *Physical education, curriculum, and culture: Critical issues in the contemporary crisis* (pp. 23-42). New York: Falmer Press.

Bain, L.L. (1997). Sport pedagogy. In J.D. Massengale & R.A. Swanson (Eds.), *The history of exercise and sport science* (pp. 15-37). Champaign, IL: Human Kinetics.

Ball, D.W., & Loy, J.W. (Eds.) (1975). *Sport and social order*. Reading, MA: Addison-Wesley.

Barnes, B. (1995). *The elements of social theory*. Princeton, NJ: Princeton University Press.

Becker, E. (1971). *The lost science of man*. New York: Braziller.

Bernard, T.J. (1983). *The consensus-conflict debate: Form and content in social theories*. New York: Columbia University Press.

Birrell, S. (1989). Racial relations theories and sport: Suggestions for a more critical analysis. *Sociology of Sport Journal, 6,* 212-227.

Booth, D., & Loy, J.W. (in press). Functionalism, sport, and society. In J.J. Coakley & E. Dunning (Eds.), *Handbook of sport and society*. Thousand Oaks, CA: Sage Publications.

Boyle, R.H. (1963). *Sport: Mirror of American life*. Boston: Little, Brown.

Brown, C. (1967). The structure of knowledge of physical education. *Quest, 9,* 53-67.

Camic, C., & Xie, Y. (1994). The statistical turn in American social science: Columbia University, 1890 to 1915. *American Sociological Review, 59,* 773-805.

Coakley, J.J. (1978). *Sport in society: Issues and controversies*. St. Louis: C.V. Mosby.

Coleman, J.S. (1961). *The adolescent society*. Glencoe, IL: Free Press.

Coser, L.A. (1976). Sociological theory from the Chicago dominance to 1965. In *Annual Review of Sociology, Vol. 2* (pp. 145-160). Palo Alto, CA: Annual Reviews, Inc.

Counts, G.S. (1932). *Dare the school build a new social order*. New York: John Day Co.

Cowell, C.C. (1935). An abstract of a study of differentials in junior high school boys based on the observation of physical education activity. *Research Quarterly, 6,* 129-136.

Cowell, C.C. (1958). Validating an index of social adjustment for high school use. *Research Quarterly, 29,* 7-18.

Cowell, C.C. (1960). The contributions of physical activity to social development, No. 2, Part II. *Research Quarterly, 31,* 286-306.

Cozens, F., & Stumpf, F. (1953). *Sports in American life*. Chicago: University of Chicago Press.

Cratty, B.J. (1967). *Social dimensions of physical activity*. Englewood Cliffs, NJ: Prentice-Hall.

Cremin, L.A. (1964). *The transformation of the school: Progressivism in American education, 1876-1925*. New York: Vintage.

Dewar, A.M. (1987). The social construction of gender in physical education. *Women's Studies International Forum, 10,* 453-465.

Dewar, A.M. (1991). Feminist pedagogy in physical education: Promises, possibilities, and pitfalls.

Journal of Physical Education, Health, and Recreation, **62**(6), 8-21.

Dewey, J. (1916). *Democracy and education.* New York: Macmillan.

Edwards, H. (1973). *Sociology of sport.* Homewood, IL: Dorsey Press.

Eitzen, D.S., & Sage, G.H. (1978). *Sociology of American sport.* Dubuque, IA: W.C. Brown.

Fernández-Balboa, J.-M. (1993). Sociocultural characteristics of the hidden curriculum in physical education. *Quest, 45,* 230-254.

Fernández-Balboa, J.-M. (1995). Reclaiming physical education in higher education through critical pedagogy. *Quest, 47,* 91-114.

Fernández-Balboa, J.-M. (1997). Knowledge base in physical education teacher education: A proposal for a new era. *Quest, 49,* 161-181.

Fitzhugh, G. (1854). *Sociology of the South.* Richmond, VA: A. Morris.

Flath, A. (Ed.) (1972). *Athletics in America.* Corvallis, OR: Oregon State University Press.

Freire, P. (1970). *Pedagogy of the oppressed.* New York: Herder and Herder.

Frey, J.H., & Eitzen, D.S. (1991). Sport and society. In W.R. Scott & J. Blake (Eds.), *Annual Review of Sociology, Vol. 17* (pp. 503-522). Palo Alto, CA: Annual Reviews, Inc.

Giddens, A. (1977). *Studies in social and political theory.* New York: Basic Books.

Giddens, A. (1987). *Social theory and modern sociology.* Stanford, CA: Stanford University Press.

Giroux, H.A. (1981). *Ideology, culture, and the process of schooling.* Philadelphia: Temple University Press.

Giroux, H.A. (1983). *Theory and resistance in education.* South Hadley, MA: Bergin & Garvey.

Giroux, H.A. (Ed.) (1989). *Critical pedagogy, the state, and cultural struggle.* Albany, NY: SUNY Press.

Gonzalez, G.B. (1982). *Progressive education: A Marxist interpretation.* Minneapolis: Marxist Educational Press, University of Minnesota.

Goodman, C. (1979). *Choosing sides: Playground and street life on the Lower East Side.* New York: Schocken.

Gouldner, A.W. (1970). *The coming crisis of Western sociology.* New York: Basic Books.

Greendorfer, S.L. (1981). Emergence of and future prospects for sociology of sport. In G.A. Brooks (Ed.), *Perspectives on the academic discipline of physical education* (pp. 379-398). Champaign, IL: Human Kinetics.

Greendorfer, S.L. (1994). Sociocultural aspects. In E.F. Zeigler (Ed.), *Physical education and kinesiology in North America: Professional and scholarly foundations* (pp. 99-123). Champaign, IL: Stipes.

Griffin, P.S. (1985). Teachers' perceptions of and responses to sex equity problems in a middle school physical education program. *Research Quarterly for Exercise and Sport,* **56,** 103-110.

Griffin, P.S. (1991, August). The challenge to live up to our ideals: Appreciating social diversity and achieving social justice in schools. *Journal of Physical Education and Recreation,* **62,** 58-61.

Gulick, L.H. (1890). Physical education: A new profession. *Proceedings of the 5th annual meeting of the American Association for the Advancement of Physical Education* (pp. 9-66). Ithaca, NY: Andrus & Church.

Hardy, S. (1981). The city and the rise of American sport: 1820-1920. In D.I. Miller (Ed.), *Exercise and Sport Sciences Reviews, Vol. 9* (pp. 183-219). Philadelphia: Franklin Institute.

Harris, D. (Ed.) (1972). *Women and sport: A national research conference.* University Park, PA: College of Health, Physical Education, and Recreation, Pennsylvania State University.

Harris, J.C. (1989). Suited up and stripped down: Perspectives for sociocultural sport studies. *Sociology of Sport Journal,* **6,** 335-347.

Hart, M. (Ed.) (1972). *Sport in the sociocultural process.* Dubuque, IA: W.C. Brown.

Hartwell, E.M. (1889). The nature of physical training and the best means of securing its ends. In I. Barrows (Ed.), *Physical training: A full report of the papers and discussions of the conference held in Boston in November 1889* (pp. 5-22). Boston: George H. Ellis.

Hellison, D.R. (1985). *Goals and strategies for teaching physical education.* Champaign, IL: Human Kinetics.

Hellison, D.R. (1988). Our constructed reality: Some contributions to an alternative perspective to physical education. *Quest,* **40,** 80-90.

Henry, F.M. (1964, September). Physical education: An academic discipline. *Journal of Health, Physical Education, and Recreation,* **35**(7), 32-33, 69.

Hetherington, C. (1910). Fundamental education. *Journal of Proceedings and Addresses of the National Education Association,* **48,** 350.

Hofstadter, R. (1955). *The age of reform: From Bryan to FDR.* New York: Knopf.

Hollands, R.G. (1984). The role of cultural studies and social criticism in the sociological study of sports. *Quest,* **36,** 66-79.

House, F.N. (1970). *The development of sociology.* Westport, CT: Greenwood Press.

Hughes, H. (1968). *Treatise on sociology, theoretical and practical.* New York: Negro Universities Press. (Original work published in 1854).

Ibrahim, H. (1975). *Sport and society: An introduction to sociology of sport*. Long Beach, CA: Hwong Publishing Co.

Ingham, A.G., & Donnelly, P. (1997). A sociology of North American sociology of sport. *Sociology of Sport Journal*, **14**, 362-418.

Jay, M. (1984). *Marxism and totality: The adventures of a concept from Lukacs to Habermas*. Berkeley, CA: University of California Press.

Kenyon, G.S. (1969a). A sociology of sport: On becoming a subdiscipline. In R.C. Brown & B.J. Cratty (Eds.), *New perspectives of man in action* (pp. 163-180). Englewood Cliffs, NJ: Prentice-Hall.

Kenyon, G.S. (1969b). *Aspects of contemporary sport sociology*. Chicago: The Athletic Institute.

Kenyon, G.S., & Loy, J.W. (1965, May). Toward a sociology of sport. *Journal of Health, Physical Education, and Recreation*, **36**, 24-25, 68-69.

Kerr, C. (1991). *The great transformation in higher education, 1960-1980*. Albany, NY: SUNY Press.

Kozman, H.C. (Ed.) (1951). *Developing democratic human relations through health, physical education, and recreation* (First Yearbook). Washington, DC: American Association for Health, Physical Education, and Recreation.

Krotee, M. (Ed.) (1979). *The dimensions of sport sociology*. West Point, NY: Leisure Press.

Landers, D.M. (Ed.) (1976). *Social problems in athletics*. Urbana, IL: University of Illinois Press.

Leonard, S.T. (1990). *Critical theory in political practice*. Princeton, NJ: Princeton University Press.

Licht, W. (1995). *Industrializing America: The nineteenth century*. Baltimore: Johns Hopkins University Press.

Loy, J.W., & Kenyon, G.S. (Eds.) (1969). *Sport, culture, and society: A reader on the sociology of sport*. New York: Macmillan.

Loy, J.W., Kenyon, G.S., & McPherson, B.D. (1980). The emergence and development of the sociology of sport as an academic specialty. *Research Quarterly for Exercise and Sport*, **51**, 91-109.

Loy, J.W., McPherson, B.D., & Kenyon, G.S. (1978a). *The sociology of sport as an academic specialty: An episodic essay on the development and emergence of an hybrid subfield in North America*. Ottawa, ON: CAHPER.

Loy, J.W., McPherson, B.D., & Kenyon, G.S. (1978b). *Sport and social systems*. Reading, MA: Addison-Wesley.

Luschen, G. (Ed.) (1970). *The cross-cultural analysis of sport and games*. Champaign, IL: Stipes Publishing.

Luschen, G. (1980). Sociology of sport: Development, present state, and prospects. In A. Inkeles, N.J. Smelser, & R.H. Turner (Eds.), *Annual review of sociology, Vol. 6* (pp. 315-347). Palo Alto, CA: Annual Reviews, Inc.

Manicas, P. (1987). *A history and philosophy of the social sciences*. New York: Blackwell.

Martindale, D. (1976). American sociology before World War II. In A. Inkeles, J. Coleman, & N. Smelser (Eds.), *Annual review of sociology, Vol. 2* (pp. 121-143). Palo Alto, CA: Annual Reviews, Inc.

Marvin, F.S. (1965). *Comte, the founder of sociology*. New York: Russell & Russell.

McPherson, B.D. (1975). Past, present, and future perspectives for research in sport sociology. *International Review of Sport Sociology*, **10**, 55-72.

Monkkonen, E.H. (1988). *America becomes urban: The development of U.S. cities and towns, 1780-1980*. Berkeley, CA: University of California Press.

Morrow, R.A., & Torres, C.A. (1995). *Social theory and education*. Albany, NY: SUNY Press.

Newell, K.M. (1990). Physical education in higher education: Chaos out of order. *Quest*, **42**, 227-242.

Nixon, II, H.L. (1976). *Sport and social organization*. Indianapolis: Bobbs-Merrill.

Nixon, J.E. (1967). The criteria of a discipline. *Quest*, **9**, 42-48.

Park, R. (1987, April). *Formation of paradigms: Some considerations*. Paper presented at the National Association for Sport & Physical Education Symposium on Science, Inquiry, and Progress: The Future of Physical Education, Las Vegas, NV.

Parsons, T. (1937). *The structure of social action*. New York: McGraw-Hill.

Parsons, T. (1951). *The social system*. Glencoe, IL: Free Press.

Popkewitz, T.S. (1991). *A political sociology of educational reform*. New York: Teachers College Press.

Rarick, G.L. (1967). The domain of physical education as a discipline. *Quest*, **9**, 49-52.

Report of the first national convention of the AAAPE, April 4, 5, 6, 1899, held at the girls' Latin school, Boston. (1899). *American Physical Education Review*, **4**, 139-244.

Riess, S.A. (1989). *City games: The evolution of American urban society and the rise of sports*. Urbana, IL: University of Illinois Press.

Rovegno, I., & Kirk, D. (1995). Articulations and silences in socially critical work on physical education: Toward a broader agenda. *Quest*, **47**, 447-474.

Rugg, H. (1931). *Culture and education in America*. New York: Harcourt Brace.

Sage, G.H. (1970). *Sport and American society*. Reading, MA: Addison-Wesley.

Sage, G.H. (1984). The quest for identity in college physical education. *Quest*, **36**, 115-121.

Sage, G.H. (1991). Paradigms, paradoxes, and progress: Reflections and prophecy. In R.J. Park & H.M. Eckert (Eds.), New possibilities, new paradigms? (pp. 154-161). *American Academy Papers*, **24,** Champaign, IL: Human Kinetics.

Schempp, P. (1987). Research on teaching in physical education: Beyond the limits of natural science. *Journal of Teaching in Physical Education*, **6,** 111-121.

Sewart, J.J. (1978). Critical theory and the critique of conservative method. *American Sociologist*, **13,** 15-22.

Siedentop, D., Mand, C., & Taggart, A. (1986). *Physical education: Teaching and curriculum strategies from grades 5-12*. Palo Alto, CA: Mayfield.

Silver, H. (1983). *Education as history: Interpreting 19th and 20th century education*. New York: Methuen.

Snyder, E.E., & Spreitzer, E. (1978). *Social aspects of sport*. Englewood Cliffs, NJ: Prentice-Hall.

Snyder, E.E., & Spreitzer, E. (1979, Winter). Sport sociology and the discipline of sociology: Present status and speculations about the future. *Review of Sport and Leisure*, **4,** 10-29.

Spring, J. (1985). *American education: An introduction to social and political aspects*. New York: Longman.

Steinhaus, A. (1967). The disciplines underlying a profession. *Quest*, **9,** 68-72.

Stelter, G.A., & Artibise, A.F. (Eds.) (1986). *Power and place: Canadian urban development in the North American context*. Vancouver, BC: University of British Columbia Press.

Stockman, N. (1983). *Antipositivist theories of the sciences*. Boston: D. Reidel.

Turner, J.H. (1990). The past, present, and future of theory in American sociology. In G. Ritzer (Ed.), *Frontiers of social theory: The new syntheses* (pp. 371-391). New York: Columbia University Press.

Ulrich, C. (1968). *The social matrix of physical education*. Englewood Cliffs, NJ: Prentice-Hall.

Williams, J.F. (1927). *Principles of physical education*. Philadelphia: W.B. Saunders.

Williams, J.F. (1930, May). Education through the physical. *Journal of Higher Education*, **1,** 279-282.

Williams, J.F. (1938). *Principles of physical education* (3rd ed.) Philadelphia: W.B. Saunders.

Wood, T.D. (1910). The new physical education. *The ninth yearbook of the National Society for the Study of Education* (pp. 75-104). Chicago: University of Chicago Press.

Wood, T.D., & Cassidy, R.F. (1927). *The new physical education*. New York: Macmillan.

Yiannakis, A., & Greendorfer, S.L. (1992). *Applied sociology of sport*. Champaign, IL: Human Kinetics.

Yiannakis, A., McIntyre, T.D., Melnick, M.J., & Hart, D.P. (1976). *Sport sociology: Contemporary themes*. Dubuque, IA: Kendall/Hunt.

Notes

1. One neo-Marxist interpretation claims that Dewey "was at all times proposing an educational enterprise whose ideological content was consonant with the determining economic structure and the social and political relationship inherent in that structure" (Gonzalez, 1982, p. 104).

2. Despite the important contributions that a few sociologists have made to the development of sociology of sport, the overall interest in sport by members of the American Sociological Association (ASA) has been extremely limited. In the biographical questionnaire sent to ASA members for its 1990 Membership Directory (American Sociological Association, 1990), each member received a list of 54 specialty areas within sociology and was asked to specify up to four "areas of interest." Of the 13,265 members who responded, *less than 2%* of the members marked the category "Leisure/Sport/Recreation."

3. Over the years there has been some criticism about Kenyon's positivist bias. My comments about Kenyon's theoretical orientation are not meant to be judgmental but rather descriptive.

4. The *Journal of Sport and Social Issues* is another journal that is a frequent outlet for sport sociology research. The current editor is Toby Miller of New York University, and it is published by Sage Publications.

5. During the 1970s, physical educators developed a distinct area of scholarly inquiry and research and began referring to this specialization as sports pedagogy (Bain, 1997).

6. I have opted to use the word "critical," even though I recognize that there are differences in meanings for this term, but this is the term adopted and used by those with a commitment to the traditions of Marxist and neo-Marxist scholarship.

7. Both Apple and Giroux drew inspiration from Brazilian social philosopher Paulo Freire (1970).

UNIT II

Sport, Power, and Ideology

Objectives

The unit illustrates the functions, power, and influence of sport on values, attitudes, behaviors, and cultural practices, and their manifestation in interpersonal and gender relations, especially in the reproduction of class, gender, and racial inequality. Further, it demonstrates how, under given conditions, certain sport environments serve as arenas for social resistance to oppressive ideologies and practices.

Although some would argue that sport is a frivolous activity removed from the business of everyday life (and some argue that it may not even be worthy of scholarly investigation!), the pervasiveness of sport in practically every sector of American life—social, political, and economic—renders such a position terribly suspect.

Since the publication of Robert Boyle's classic treatise *Sport: Mirror of American Life* (1963), novelists, journalists, and researchers have devoted much thought to the relationship between sport and American life. An analysis of the literature suggests that sport is inextricably linked to religion, the military, the polity, the economy, education, cultural heroes and heroines, and everyday language. Furthermore, it can be argued that sport transmits cultural values, maintains the status quo, and serves as a focal point for rallying and unifying loosely knit social groups and communities. And, as with other institutions, it is suggested that sport is employed as a tool for transmitting the ideology of rul-

ing elites, an ideology that helps ensure the maintenance of their legitimacy, domination, and control over the sources of wealth, power, and influence in society. This influence often manifests itself in practices, values, and attitudes that sow the seeds of divisiveness by empowering some ethnic groups over others and by contributing to social and political rifts in gender relations and attitudes toward homosexuals. Such practices appear to occur in many "mainstream" institutionalized sports. But humans have a curious habit of resisting oppressive practices and attempts at cultural indoctrination. We see evidence of this in emerging and nontraditional sports that lie outside the mainstream, sports that have not yet come under the complete influence and control of the sport institution. These encompass such sports as skateboarding, windsurfing, dog sledding, and a category known as extreme sports.

It appears, therefore, that under certain conditions sport also can serve as an arena for social resistance to dominant values and oppressive ideologies and practices. The substance of those conditions has been the subject of considerable speculation, but we do know that the sports that offer a venue for social resistance are newer, nonmainstream sports with low market demand. They generally attract nontraditional groups who tend to stress the experience for its own sake and who generally avoid imbuing their sport with a high degree of competitiveness. Play, or the process, is the primary focus rather than display for mass-entertainment purposes. At least, this is how many such sports start. As they evolve, however, they go through varying degrees of institutionalization and begin to attract participants whose motivation and goals tend to differ from the original group of "pioneers." As more mainstream types join the activity, they tend to drive out the original founders. The sport gradually comes under the influence and hegemonic practices of the sport institution. Yet pockets of resistance remain. Participants continue to negotiate for their survival by employing strategies that set them apart from the mainstream. They tend to remain small in number, they often maintain a low profile, they avoid elite-level competitive practices that draw the attention of spectators or potential sponsors, and they continue to emphasize the process, the intrinsic satisfactions associated with the experience itself rather than the outcomes associated with superior performance. Many martial-arts groups, besides the sports alluded to in this unit, fall in this category. Ultimately such sports develop subcultures that serve as safe havens for their members. While engaging in their chosen activities, such individuals can escape, for a short time, the oppressive practices and pressures to conform to dominant ideologies. They reaffirm, in the safety of the boundaries of their group, their shared values, beliefs, and practices. Clearly, such practices serve as forms of resistance and stand out as examples of the ways that sport empowers groups with shared values and beliefs to combat hegemonic practices and oppressive institutional ideologies.

In the three selections that follow, the authors discuss how sport is employed as a tool for social resistance and how sport can be used to transmit ideologies and cultural practices that help reproduce class and gender inequalities and antihomosexual attitudes.

In the first selection, Foley, a cultural anthropologist, reports on his observations from an ethnographic study of a football season in a small town in Texas. In particular, the author documents the extent to which community sport, in this case football, is "implicated" in the reproduction of class, gender, and racial inequality despite moments of "resistance" by those involved in the activity. The author concludes his analysis by stating that "when seen from a historical community perspective, sport may be less a site for progressive, counterhegemonic practices than critical sport theorists hope."

Clearly, Foley's analysis holds little hope for resistance in sports such as football that are so intimately tied to community life and commercial and business interests. Nonetheless, the author's analysis helps identify the structure and cultural practices associated with fully co-opted sports and provides the reader with markers that help identify the conditions under which oppressive ideologies and practices, including the reproduction of class, gender, and racial inequalities, are most likely to occur. These conditions include the use of sport as a form of display and entertainment, association with business and commercial interests, existence of a large and committed school and community fan base, management of such activities by adult groups such as coaches and other vested interests (a process that disempowers the athletes because they have no say in decision making), and, of course, media participation. Play, as Gregory Stone noted over 40 years ago, is turned into display for the entertainment of the masses! Effective resistance by athletes under such conditions is often futile. Individuals who speak out, who dare to challenge "the system," are easily squashed and silenced. Yet even in such oppressive environments various forms of resistance are possible, and the literature, especially at the collegiate level, is replete with such examples.

Harry demonstrates, in the second selection, how males who most embrace the ideology of sport and the competitive sport ethos hold the strongest antihomosexual and antigay attitudes. Among females, sexist attitudes are associated with negative beliefs about gays and lesbians. Further, among men the socialization process into sports, and its accompanying sports ideology, appears to serve as a form of training in sexism and homophobia. The socialization process for females, however, does not appear to entail the learning of similar attitudes and prejudices. The author concludes that sport has different meanings for men and women. For men, "sports may help to define and validate prejudices against women, gays and lesbians. For women, sports ideology seems largely devoid of implications for gender roles" (Harry, 1995, p. 115).

Beal discusses, in the third selection, how participants in one sport, the emerging subculture of skateboarding, attempt to resist the dominant competitive ethos by opting for a more participatory, egalitarian, and less commercialized form of play. Despite the fact that the social impact of skateboarding is not "transformative" for most people, it is noteworthy that the participants in this study were empowered to act in their best interests. The author sees this as positive and suggests that "other activities can be created" that will enable participants to reclaim varying degrees of power.

Beal concludes that although such forms of resistance in sport have the power to change dominant social relations, such resistance is often accompanied by a variety of compromises, accommodations, and contradictions. The skateboarders' sexist behavior is one example of such a contradiction.

References

Beal, B. (1995). Disqualifying the official: An exploration of social resistance through the subculture of skateboarding. *Sociology of Sport Journal,* **12**: 252–267.

Boyle, R. (1963). *Sport: Mirror of American life.* Boston: Little, Brown & Co.

Foley, D. (1990). The great American football ritual. *Sociology of Sport Journal,* **7**(2): 111–135.

Harry, J. (1995). Sports ideology, attitudes toward women and anti-homosexual attitudes. *Sex Roles,* **32**(1-2): 109–116.

Discussion Questions

Douglas Foley

1. Describe and explain how this study was conducted.
2. What is meant by the term "multiple systems of dominance"? Explain.
3. Foley reports that football in this small community serves to reproduce class, gender, and racial inequalities. What evidence does the author provide to warrant this conclusion? Identify and discuss.
4. According to the author, in what ways do football rituals help reproduce various forms of social inequality? Identify some of these rituals and explain their function.
5. What forms of resistance did Foley observe? To what extent were these attempts successful? Discuss and explain.
6. Do you believe that, in general, sport settings are effective sites of resistance and counterhegemonic practices? Debate and take a position on the issue.

Joseph Harry

1. The author suggests that individuals high in support of the sport ideology would also be antihomosexual. Discuss and explain the logic underlying this viewpoint.
2. The author reports that different scales were employed to measure antigay and antilesbian attitudes. Explain the reasoning of this approach.
3. Discuss and explain why the sport ideology appears to be linked to traditional sexist views and prejudices against lesbians and gays only among men.
4. Discuss and explain why the sport ideology appears to be unrelated to the attitudes held by women toward gays and lesbians.
5. The author suggests that the meanings of sport differ for men and women. What does he mean and what explanations does he offer?

Becky Beal

1. In what ways is skateboarding used to resist dominant values and norms? Discuss and explain.
2. Explain the meaning of hegemony.
3. How do the values of skateboarders differ from those of mainstream society?
4. Discuss and explain the two most common forms of resistance, challenge, and accommodation.
5. What is meant by the term "infrapolitics"?
6. What values of mainstream society do skateboarders challenge or resist?
7. Discuss and speculate about the possible effects of resistance within the skateboarding subculture on mainstream society.

The Great American Football Ritual: Reproducing Race, Class, and Gender Inequality

Douglas E. Foley

An ethnographic study of one football season in a small South Texas town is presented to explore the extent that community sport is, as various critical theorists have suggested, a potential site for counterhegemonic cultural practices. Football is conceptualized as a major community ritual that socializes future generations of youth. This broad, holistic description of socialization also notes various moments of ethnic resistance engendered by the Chicano civil rights movement. Other moments of class and gender resistance to the football ritual are also noted. Finally, the way players generally resisted attempts to thoroughly rationalize their sport is also described. In spite of these moments of resistance, this study ultimately shows how deeply implicated community sport—in this case high school football—is in the reproduction of class, gender, and racial inequality. The white ruling class and the town's patriarchal system of gender relations are preserved in spite of concessions to the new ethnic challenges. When seen from a historical community perspective, sport may be less a site for progressive, counterhegemonic practices than critical sport theorists hope.

This analysis of a football season is part of a larger study of the popular culture practices of youth in one South Texas town (Foley, 1990). Theoretically, it has a great affinity with a Gramscian perspective (Critcher, 1986; Deem, 1988; Gruneau, 1983; Har-

greaves, 1986; McKay, 1986; Whitson, 1984) of sport as a site of contested popular cultural practices. Although there are significant differences between these authors, the Gramscian perspective advocated by the Birmingham Centre for Contemporary Cultural Studies (CCCS) generally informs many new critical studies of sports. The cultural studies perspective has been employed to study a wide array of popular or leisure practices (Bennett, Mercer, & Wollacott, 1986; Chambers, 1986; Fiske, 1989a, 1989b). Increasingly, sport sociologists are arguing that sports must also be studied as an autonomous cultural activity with the potential to challenge the commercialization and rationalization of sports activities.

This study seeks to ground recent critical perspectives of sports in the everyday cultural practices of one small, historical community. It explores the way high school sport reproduces social inequalities with the kind of detailed ethnographic data used in other microstudies of sport subcultures (Donnelly & Young, 1988; Fine, 1987). Like those microethnographic studies, this one is concerned with describing sports as a socialization process. Unlike other socialization studies, however, a historical[1] community with a social structure, not a group of people practicing a particular sport, is the focus. In addition, the reproduction and resistance perspective of popular culture theory is used rather than a functionalist or symbolic interactionist perspective (Donnelly & Young, 1988; Loy & Ingham, 1973).

The anthropological concept of a dramatic community ritual (Turner, 1974) is also used to give a

Reprinted from Foley, 1990.

holistic portrait of how major popular or leisure cultural practices (in this case, football) socialize people into community structures of inequality. The following description of the ritual complex surrounding high school football games concentrates on the rites, ceremonies, and events that socialize youth in the community and that symbolically stage class, gender, and racial inequality. Two basic premises not generally used in anthropological studies of ritual, but commonly shared by critical theorists of sport, guided this study. First, capitalist societies and their sport scenes are marked by multiple systems of dominance (Birrell, 1984, 1989; Deem, 1988; Hall, 1984, 1985; Messner, 1988). Consequently, a multiple-system-of-dominance perspective was used to explore the intersections of class, gender, and racial practices and relations and the way in which they are dialectically related in local community sport rituals. Second, any ideological hegemony constructed by a capitalist class is never secure and is often contested through various popular culture practices. Consequently, this study also explores the extent to which community sport scenes are sites of resistance and counterhegemonic popular or leisure cultural practices.

The setting of this field study was "North Town," a small (8,000 population) South Texas farming/ranching community with limited industry, considerable local poverty, and a population that was 80% Mexican-American. North Town was one of three towns in this winter-vegetable-producing area where a Chicano third party emerged to challenge the segregated racial order. The third party, the Partido Raza Unida, has since disbanded, but their impact was felt in all walks of life and sport was no exception. "North Town High" had an enrollment of 600 students and its sports teams played at the Triple-A level in a five-level state ranking system.

During the football season described here, I attended a number of practices, rode on the players' bus, and hung out with the coaches at the fieldhouse and with players during extensive classroom and lunchtime observations. I also participated in basketball and tennis practices and interviewed students extensively about student status groups, friendship, dating, and race relations. The participant observation and interviewing in the sports scene involved hundreds of hours of fieldwork over a 12-month period. The larger community study[2] also included three full-time research assistants, and the fieldwork took place over a 2-year period. The traditional anthropological field methods used in this study are reported in great detail in Foley, Mota, Post, and Lozano (1988) and Foley (1990).

The Ritual Complex

The Weekly Pep Rally

Shortly after arriving in North Town I attended my first pep rally. Students, whether they liked football or not, looked forward to Friday afternoons. Regular 7th-period classes were let out early to hold a mass pep rally to support the team. Most students attended these events but a few used it to slip away from school early. During the day of this pep rally I overheard a number of students planning their trip to the game. Those in the school marching band (80) and in the pep club (50) were the most enthusiastic. Students were plotting secret rendezvous with boyfriends and girlfriends or were fantasizing about fateful meetings with their secret loves. Fewer students and townspeople than usual would follow the team on this first long road trip.

Nevertheless, as on most Fridays, teachers and students were talking about The Game. Some teachers engaged the players in lively banter during classes about "whipping" Larson City. In senior English class a long analysis of last year's bad calls, missed kicks, and fumbles ensued. The history of this event had already been reconstructed, and those students interested in it shared that moment with the players. Players and nonplayers collectively plotted and reveled in mythical feats of revenge. There was much brave talk about "kicking their asses this year."

Some high school students considered the idea of young males in padded armor crashing into each other as dumb and boring. Some adults also thought that the sport was silly or too rough or a waste of time. Generally, however, most North Town students, like the adults, looked forward to football season and the Friday night games. The games enlivened the community's social life. Adults, especially the local chamber of commerce types, articulated this view even more than the students. Community sports was the patriotic, neighborly thing to do. Many students felt deep loyalties to support their team, but others used these community events to express their disgust for the game and the players, hence for "respectable" mainstream society.

This Friday afternoon the pep rally started like most school pep rallies. As the last bell rang, the halls were crammed with students rushing to put books away and to find their friends. Various students claimed their rightful territory on the bleachers facing the microphones. Months later, when I knew them better, I could see the pattern to this mad scramble for seats: It was age-graded. The older, most prominent students took the center seats, thus signaling their status and loyalty. Younger first- and second-year students sat next to the leaders of the school activities if they were protégés of those leaders.

In sharp contrast, knots and clusters of the more socially marginal students, the "druggers," and the "punks and greasers," usually claimed the seats nearest the exits, thus signaling their indifference to all the rah-rah speeches they had to endure. The "nobodies" or "nerds," those dutiful, conforming students who were followers, tended to sit in the back of the center regions. Irrespective of the general territory, students usually sat with friends from their age group. Teachers strategically placed themselves at the margins and down in front to assist in crowd control.

The pep rally itself was dominated by the coaches and players, who were introduced to the audience to reflect on the coming contest. In this particular pep rally the team captains led the team onto the stage. All the Anglo players entered first, followed by all the Mexicano players. Coach Trujillo started out with the classic pep talk that introduced the team captains, who in turn stepped forward and spoke in an awkward and self-effacing manner, thus enacting the ideal of a sportsman—a man of deeds, not words. They all stuttered through several "uhs" and "ers," then quickly said, "I hope y'all come support us. Thanks." Generally students expected their jocks to be inarticulate and, as the cliché goes, strong but silent types. Coach Trujillo then elaborated on how hard work, loyalty, and dedication would bring the school victory. He also brought up last year's defeat at the hands of Larson City to jibe the present seniors that this would be their "last chance to beat the Raiders."

Between the brief comments made by players and coaches, the cheerleaders and pep squad tried to involve the student body through cheers. A small contingent of the 80-piece marching band tooted and banged out the proper drum rolls for the speakers and cheerleaders. Other band members dispersed among the crowd and helped the pep squad lead cheers. Being a part of the band was also an important way of establishing one's loyalty to school and community. Later, during the game, the marching band would entertain the crowd at halftime while the players rested. Halftime performance also showcased the youth of North Town.

The Marching Band and Band Fags

The quality of the marching band was as carefully scrutinized as the football team by some community members. The band director, Dante Aguila, was keenly aware of maintaining an excellent winning band. Like sport teams, marching bands competed in local, district, and statewide contests and won rankings. The ultimate goal was winning a top rating at the state level. In addition, each band sent its best players of various instruments to district contests to compete for individual rankings. Individual band members could also achieve top rankings at the state level.

A certain segment of the student body began training for the high school marching band during their grade-school years. Band members had a much more positive view of their participation in band than the players did. The band was filled with students who tended to have better grades and came from the more affluent families. The more marginal, deviant students perceived band members as "goodie goodies," "richies," and "brains." This characterization was not entirely true because the band boosters club did make an effort to raise money to help low-income students join the band. Not all band students were top students, but many were in the advanced or academic tracks. Band members were generally the students with school spirit who were proud to promote loyalty to the school and community. The marching band was also a major symbolic expression of the community's unity and its future generation of good citizens and leaders.

The view that band members were the cream of the crop was not widely shared by the football players. Many female band members were socially prominent and "cool," but some were also studious homebodies. On the other hand, "real men" supposedly did not sign up for the North Town band. According to the football players, the physically weaker, more effeminate males tended to be in the band. Males in the band were called "band fags." The only exceptions were "cool guys" who did drugs, or had their own rock and roll band, or came from musical families and planned to become professional musicians. The males considered to be fags were sometimes derided and picked on as "sissies." Occasional gender jokes were made about their not having the "balls" to date the cute female band members.

The main masculinity test for band fags was to punch their biceps as hard as possible. If the victim returned this aggression with a defiant smile or smirk, he was a real man; if he winced and whined, he was a wimp or a fag. The other variations on punching the biceps were pinching the forearm and rapping the knuckles. North Town boys generally punched and pinched each other, but this kind of male play toward those considered fags was a daily ritual degradation. These were moments when physically dominant males picked on allegedly more effeminate males and reaffirmed their place in the male pecking order. Ironically, however, the players themselves rarely picked on those they called band fags. Males who emulated jocks and hoped to hang out with them were usually the hit men. The jocks signaled their real power and prestige by showing restraint toward obviously weaker males.

Cheerleaders and Pep Squads

As in most pep rallies, on the Friday I am describing, the cheerleaders were in front of the crowd on the gym floor doing dance and jumping routines in unison and shouting patriotic cheers to whip up enthusiasm for the team. The cheerleaders were acknowledged as some of the prettiest young women in the school and they aroused the envy of nobodies and nerds. Male students incessantly gossiped and fantasized about these young women and their reputations.

One frequently told story was about a pep rally when students started throwing pennies at Trini, a cheerleader. Initially this curious story made no sense to me. Trini struck me as the perfect all-American girl next door. She was widely acknowledged as cute and perky, got above average grades, and was on her way to college, a good career, and marriage. She also dated an Anglo from another town. That fact, and the relentless gossip about her being a "slut" and "gringo-loving whore," had hurt her; but being strong willed, she would not quietly accept these putdowns. She lashed back by criticizing people for being small-townish and small-minded.

The rest of the girls, four Mexicanas and two Anglos, were more or less alike both physically and socially. One Anglo girl was particularly athletic, which often prompted Anglos to make negative remarks about a Mexicana who was popular but considered a bit plump. Students invariably had their favorites to adore and/or ridicule. Yet they told contradictory stories about the cheerleaders. When privately reflecting on their physical attributes and social status, males saw going with a cheerleader as guaranteeing their coolness and masculinity. Particularly the less attractive males plotted the seduction of these young women and reveled in the idea of having them as girlfriends. When expressing their views of these young women to other males, however, they often accused the cheerleaders of being stuck-up or sluts.

This sharp contradiction in males' discourse about cheerleaders makes perfect sense, however, when seen as males talking about females as objects to possess and dominate and through which to gain status. Conversations among males about cheerleaders were rhetorical performances that bonded males together and established their rank in this patriarchal order. In public conversations, males often expressed bravado about conquest of these "easy lays." In private conversations with intimate friends, they expressed their unabashed longing for, hence vulnerable emotional need for, these fantasized sexual objects. Hence, cheerleaders as highly prized females were dangerous, status-confirming creatures who were easier to relate to in rhetorical performances than in real life. Only those males with very high social status could actually risk relating to and being rejected by a cheerleader. The rest of the stories the young men told were simply male talk and fantasy.

Many young women were not athletic or attractive enough to be cheerleaders, nevertheless they wanted to be cheerleaders. Such young women often joined the pep squad as an alternative, and a strong esprit de corps developed among the pep squad members. They were a group of 50 young women in costume who came to the games and helped the cheerleaders arouse crowd enthusiasm. The pep squad also helped publicize and decorate the school and town with catchy team-spirit slogans such as "Smash the Seahawks" and "Spear the Javelinos." In addition, they helped organize after-the-game school dances. Their uniforms expressed loyalty to the team, and pep squad members were given a number of small status privileges in the school. They were sometimes released early for pep rallies and away games.

Teachers were often solicitous to pep squad members and labeled them good students. Pep squad members were usually students who conformed to the school rules and goals, thus were good citizens, but being in the pep squad also afforded them an opportunity to break home rules. Students and some teachers joked with pep squad members about "getting out of the house" to go to the games for romantic reasons. On road trips these young women momentarily escaped parental supervision and had opportunities to publicly attract and flirt with young men from other towns. This helped establish their gender status among other students as more "hip," even though being in the pep squad was a "straight" activity.

Homecoming:
A Rite of Community Solidarity and Status

Ideally, North Town graduates would return to the homecoming bonfire and dance to reaffirm their support and commitment to the school and team. They would come back to be honored and to honor the new generation presently upholding the name and tradition of the community. In reality, however, few ex-graduates actually attended the pregame bonfire rally or postgame school dance. Typically, the game itself drew a larger crowd and the local paper played up the homecoming game more. College-bound youth were noticeably present at the informal beer party after the game. Some townspeople were also at the pregame bonfire rally, something that rarely happened during an ordinary school pep rally.

That afternoon, bands of Anglo males riding in pickup trucks began foraging for firewood. Other students not involved in hauling the wood gathered in the school parking lot. They wanted to watch what was brought for burning and meanwhile shared stories about stolen outdoor wooden outhouses, sheds, posts, and packing crates. It was important to the onlookers just which community members donated burnable objects, how cleverly objects were procured, and what outrageous objects were to be burnt this year. This was obviously a traditional event that entertained and bestowed status on both the procurers and donors of burnable objects.

Three groups of boys with pickup trucks eventually created a huge pile of scrap wood and burnable objects that had been donated. The cheerleaders, band, and pep squad members then conducted the bonfire ceremonies. Several hundred persons, approximately an equal number of Anglo and Mexicano students, showed up at the rally along with a fair sprinkling of older people and others who were not in high school. Nearly all of the leaders were Anglos and they were complaining that not enough students supported the school or them. The cheerleaders led cheers and sang the school fight song after brief inspirational speeches from the coaches and players. Unlike the school pep rally, the police arrived to survey the fire. Rumors circulated that the police were there to harass people because some crates might have been stolen from a local packing shed. It was also rumored that some of the football players were planning to get drunk after the bonfire died down.

The huge blazing fire in the school parking lot made this pep rally special. The fire added to the festive mood, which seemed partly adolescent high jinks and partly serious communion with the town's traditions. The collective energy of the youth had broken a property law or two to stage this event. Adults laughed about the "borrowed" packing crates and were pleased that others "donated" things from their stores and houses to feed the fire. The adults expressed no elaborate rationale for having a homecoming bonfire, which they considered nice, hot, and a good way to fire up the team.[3] Gathering around the bonfire reunited all North Towners, past and present, for the special homecoming reunion and gridiron battle. Whatever the deeper symbolic meaning, those attending seemed to enjoy the pep rally. Several of the organizers and friends remained behind to watch the fire burn down. They gossiped about friends and acquaintances and told sport stories.

After the homecoming game, a school dance was held featuring a homecoming court complete with king and queen. The queen and her court and the king and his attendants, typically the most popular and attractive students, were elected by the student body. Ideally they represented the most attractive, popular, and successful youth. They were considered the best of a future generation of North Towners. Following tradition, the queen was crowned during halftime at midfield as the band played and the crowd cheered. According to tradition, the lovely queen and her court, dressed in formal gowns, were ceremoniously transported to the crowning in convertibles. The king and his attendants, who were often football players and dirty and sweaty at that, then came running from their halftime break to escort the young women from the convertibles and to their crowning. The king and his court lingered rather uneasily until the ceremony was over and then quickly returned to their team to rest and prepare for the second half.

This particular homecoming halftime ceremony took place as it always did, but with one major difference. The customary convertibles for the queen and her court were missing; consequently, the queen and her court, on this occasion all Mexicanas, had to walk to their crowning. This evoked numerous criticisms among Mexicano students and parents in attendance. Many felt it was a "gringo plot" to rob them of their chance to be leaders in the community. The *Chicano Times*, a radical San Antonio newspaper, screamed out headlines that accused the school officials of blatant discrimination. The administrators and teachers in charge of organizing the event denied these charges but were left embarrassed and without any acceptable defense.

In this particular instance, this rite of solidarity became instead a source of divisiveness in North Town. A number of Better Government League (BGL) Anglos perceived the Mexicanos as politicizing the event and causing trouble. Another way of interpreting their criticism, however, was as an attempt to preserve the pomp and splendor of the ceremony that marked the social status of the town's future leaders. Those Mexicanos seeking to become integrated into and leaders of the community were not willing to be treated differently. They demanded that football and its homecoming ceremony serve its traditional purpose of creating continuity and unity. Mexicanos were trying to preserve a cultural tradition that would finally serve their children the way it had those of Anglos.

The Powder-Puff Football Game: Another Rite of Gender Reproduction

A powder-puff football game was traditionally held in North Town on a Friday afternoon before the seniors' final game. A number of the senior football players dressed up as girls and acted as cheerleaders for the game. A number of the senior girls dressed up as football players and formed a touch football team that played the junior girls. The male football players served as coaches and referees and comprised much of the audience as well. Perhaps a quarter of the student body, mainly the active, popular, successful students, drifted in and out to have a laugh over this event. More boys than girls, both Anglo and Mexicano, attended the game.

The striking thing about this ritual was the gender difference in expressive manner. Males took the opportunity to act in silly and outrageous ways. They pranced around in high heels, smeared their faces with lipstick, and flaunted their padded breasts and posteriors in a sexually provocative manner. Everything, including the cheers they led, was done in a very playful, exaggerated, and burlesque manner.

In sharp contrast, the females donned the football jerseys and helmets of the players, sometimes those of their boyfriends, and proceeded to huff and puff soberly up and down the field under the watchful eyes of the boys. They played their part in the game as seriously as possible, blocking and shoving with considerable gusto. This farce went on for several scores, until one team was the clear winner and until the females were physically exhausted and the males were satiated with acting in a ridiculous manner.

When asked why they had powder-puff football games, most male students could not articulate a very deep meaning for the event. Most said things like, "It's good for a laugh," "It's fun," "It's a good break from school; school's boring." Others hinted at something more than recreation and teenage fun:

> I don't know, I guess it gives guys a chance to have a little fun with the girls. . . . It makes the girls see how rough it is to play football. . . . The guys get to let off a little steam, tease their girlfriends a little, maybe show them who's the boss.

Some girls earnestly suggested the following meanings for the event:

> It gives us a chance to show the guys that we can compete too. We aren't sissies. We can take getting hit too. . . . We can show them that football isn't just for guys. . . . Girls are athletic, too. We can run and throw the ball pretty good, too. . . . God, I don't know, just to have a break from sixth period. . . . The guys get to have all the fun, why shouldn't we?

Teachers tended to look on the game as a silly, harmless event that helped build school spirit. One boldly suggested that maybe these big jocks were putting on bras because they secretly wanted to be girls. That tongue-in-cheek interpretation of football players has already been seriously proposed by one prominent folklorist (Dundes, 1978). Alan Dundes understands the butt-slapping and talk about "hitting holes" and "penetrating the other team's endzone" as a form of male combat that masks latent homosexuality. Such an interpretation would undoubtedly shock North Towners, who generally regarded this sort of thing as simply fun and silliness.

This interpretation also completely misses the cultural significance of such an event. Anthropologists have come to call such curious practices "rituals of inversion" (Babcock, 1978), specially marked moments when people radically reverse everyday cultural roles and practices. During these events people break, or humorously play with, their own cultural rules. Such reversals are possible without suffering any sanctions or loss of face. These moments are clearly marked so that no one familiar with the culture will misread such reversals as anything more than a momentary break in daily life.

Males of North Town High used this moment of symbolic inversion to parody females in a burlesque and ridiculous manner. They took great liberties with the female role through this humorous form of expression. The power of these young males to appropriate and play with female symbols of sexuality was a statement about males' social and physical dominance. Conversely, the females took few liberties with their expression of the male role. They tried to play a serious game of football. The females tried earnestly to prove they were equal. Their lack of playfulness was a poignant testimony to their subordinate status in this small town.

This moment of gender role reversal was a reflection of sexual politics, not of sexual preference. A psychological interpretation overlooks the historical pattern of patriarchy in the entire football ritual. The powder-puff football game, although seemingly a minor event, was an important part of the total football ritual. This ritual generally socialized both sexes to assume their proper, traditional gender roles. On the other hand, one could argue that the assertive, serious way they played the game may also be teaching these young women some new lessons in competing with males. Perhaps the girls were also trying to invert this inversion ritual, thus turning boys into real rather than symbolic buffoons. Generally, however, the women seemed to participate unwittingly in staging this expression of male dominance and privilege.

The Coach:
A Mexicano Coach on the Firing Line

The North Town adult primarily responsible for making high school football an important, well-attended ritual was the head coach. Unfortunately, a good deal of local politics made it difficult for Coach Roberto Trujillo, North Town's first Mexicano head coach, to do his job. Coach Trujillo's father ran a dance hall that alternately hosted Anglo country and western as well as Mexicano "conjunto" (country, polka, and Caribbean) music. More important, his father had been a charter member in the new BGL political organization, which opposed North Town's new Chicano civil rights organization, Partido Raza Unida (PRU). The Trujillos' alliance with the Anglo BGL made both father and son "vendidos" (sellouts) in the eyes of most Raza Unida members. Coach Trujillo, in reality not a politically involved person, had a reputation as "a nice man but a little weak." He was the perfect compromise candidate for the BGL liberals who controlled the school board. He was a native son, college educated, polite, respectful, and generally mild mannered. His coaching record, though not exceptional, was considered acceptable. Most important, he was from a successful middle-class Mexicano family who renounced the extreme views of the PRU. Coach

Trujillo was the BGL liberals' model of an accommodating, reasonable Mexican.

A number of other BGL Anglos were outraged, however, at his appointment over an Anglo coach, Jim Ryan, also a native son and one who had the distinction of leading North Town to their only regional finals. He was a likeable "good ole' boy" who was very approachable and had deep South Texas roots. Liberal BGLers viewed him as a poorly educated redneck who lacked the new ethnic tolerance they sought to project as school board leaders. Coach Ryan was a staunch conservative who constantly railed against what he termed communists, welfare loafers, and PRU radicals. Many Mexicano players actually considered him a good disciplinarian and coach, but a number of them also felt that he was indeed partial toward Anglo players.

Coach Trujillo, on the other hand, was considered too friendly and soft on the players. Stories circulated about his easy practices and indecisive play calling. What many of the critics wanted was a military-style coach, a stern disciplinarian. They constantly criticized the star North Town players as being lazy and too soft. Trujillo was in the proverbial coach's hot seat for all the classic reasons, and for uniquely racial ones as well. He had the double jeopardy of being neither manly enough nor white or brown enough to lead North Town youth into battle. He was constantly challenged to prove himself both to the Mexicano activists and to the more redneck Anglos.

Coaches As Storytellers:
Reproducing and Resisting Inequality

The first out-of-town trip proved to be revealing on the subject of race relations. The players took their seats as if some crusading liberal had written the script. All the Mexicano players quietly seated themselves at the back of the bus. Then all the Anglo players brashly seated themselves in the front of the bus with the coaching staff. At first I was taken aback by this event, which seemed an unmistakable sign of Anglo racial dominance. Yet I wondered how such a seating arrangement could possibly signify subservience in a town full of politically assertive Mexicano adults. Before we reached Larson City, at least 10 racial jokes were hurled between the front and the back of the bus. One giant Anglo tackle, the high school principal's son, cracked perhaps the best joke. He bellowed out, "Shewt, if we lose this game, *we* are going to ride home in the back of the bus." This brought a nervous reply from Coach Trujillo that he might have to join them (the Anglos) there too. Having just heard the story of his compromised political position with Mexicanos, I thought the comment was his way of downplaying the controversy over him. Or perhaps he was as subservient to Anglos as the Raza Unida leaders claimed.

As we neared Larson City, to my great surprise Trujillo cracked the following joke with the Anglo players: "We are going to have to take some of you boys to Boystown to show you how the *other* half lives." Anyone familiar with Texas border culture knows that the whorehouse sections of Mexican border towns are called Boystown. The classic rite of passage for South and West Texas males[4] is to lose their virginity in one of these Boystowns. This embattled Mexicano coach was joking about Anglo mates using Mexicana prostitutes. He was suggesting to the Anglo players that they were about to become men and friends with his race, if they would let him make men out of them. The coach was evoking a common male bonding ritual and using humor to displace the racial tensions. He was also saying that they were all heading for "the border" of race relations in search of a new understanding.

During the fieldwork, I spent a great deal of time watching for examples of coaches serving as mediators of racial conflict, and at least one other coach and Coach Trujillo did indeed take it upon themselves to mediate racial attitudes and images. They directly intervened as peacemakers in at least two incidents of conflict between players and students. More important, they often tried to redefine the reality of North Town race relations by telling a story or homily to their players. An excellent example of their role in redefining racial/ethnic relations was a story I overheard Coach Trujillo tell several Anglo players after practice one day. He had just finished putting the boys through a brutal 2-1/2 hour full-pads scrimmage. This occurred during the dog days of late September and the temperature on the playing field was at least 100°F. The boys were exhausted and began joking and complaining about what a dictator the coach was. One quipped, "Man, I thought Hitler was a German."

Coach Trujillo read this ethnic reference as an invitation to launch into a racial treatise on the sense of equality and character of the Mexicano people, and himself in particular. Trujillo had been the first Mexicano player with a scholarship to play for a "lily-white" West Texas college. He then recounted his own version of the brutal two-a-day summer practice story that all football players tell. Usually this tale is told to illustrate one's pain threshold and ability to survive hot, sweaty practices. Often such practices do seem like the nightmarish inventions of a sadistic coach. Only "real men" survive these hot summer practices, and the worse the practices, the better the telling of the tale. Young players usually recount these practices to older relatives and former players who hang out in local gas stations and restaurants.

Coach Trujillo created an interesting variant of this tale that also had a racial lesson. After the exhausted players returned to the locker room, one of the Anglo players had the gall to toss the coach's equipment away from the coach's locker, thus invading his hard-earned resting space. The coach confronted the offending lockermate and reminded him that they were all in it together. They were all survivors of the football wars; consequently he was deserving of equal respect and space. With a twinkle in his eye, the coach explained, "I was telling this guy in a nice way, 'Hey, redneck, that's my space.'" According to Coach Trujillo, this bold, honest confrontation with the Anglo, and by extension American society, brought instant respect from the other players sitting nearby. They could see that he was ready to fight for his rights, which he had earned the hard way. Seeing this hulking white monster of a lineman being cowed by this little brown bulldog was a new experience for the Anglo players. They purportedly responded with warmth and admiration, and this was the beginning of the coach's acceptance among the Anglo players.

In a way, Coach Trujillo's story was much like the miraculous conversion tales born-again Christians often tell. In a trying and difficult moment, he acted with courage and humility to be accepted as an equal. He risked everything and stood up for the ideal that the races should live together in harmony rather than discord. According to his tale, from that day forward a new era of race relations began for his college and their football team. He relived his past to model what he wanted for his own players. He was no Hitler, nor were his people any different from Anglos. Moreover, he and his people were ready to fight for their rights. The coach told several homilies like this one. It is not clear how effective such moral lessons were, but this was how he dealt with the race problem.

But in the end, Coach Trujillo said he "threw in the towel." Despite a good season, second in the conference, and a 7-4 record, he resigned and left his hometown feeling, in his own words, "sick of the strife and the pressure on my family." The coach claimed that he had "lost a lotta friends" and had gotten an ulcer. He compared the South Texas racial situation unfavorably to other places he had been, such as Colorado and Michigan, and feared that North Town might never change. Being a political centrist, he had very little good to say about either political group:

> My daddy wants out of the BGL. He can see that the Anglos just won't change. They just want to use him, and one or two Anglo board members still think I am just a Meskin'. They'll never change. They always overreact to a Mexicano getting ahead. Look at the school elections. They handled the whole thing very poorly. Some kids were left off the ballot by mistake, and they should get rid of the rule that disqualified some of our best kids. They are just trying to protect their kids and hold us back. And the Anglos should not have quit the band trying to pressure the new Mexican-American band director. I'm sick of the Raza Unida too. They use these pressure tactics and call people "vendidos" and shoot off their mouths. The indictments of voters is real bad, and the Anglos are pressuring to control the school board votes, but Raza Unida has gone too far. I believe they did try to steal the city election, and they did shoot a gun at the mayor's house.

When Coach Trujillo reflected on his past, he came across as a man trapped in a painful process of cultural change. Unlike the new generation of students, he was not part of the civil rights movement and remained unsure how much to assert himself. The movement left him filled with a longing for change but a certain fear about breaking the cultural rules he hated. In the end, Coach Trujillo decided the situation was impossible to change or live with, so he moved on, but not without a great deal of sadness. He was unable to develop the type of relationship with North Town community leaders that would solidify his place in the local power structure.

Prominent Citizens and Their Booster Club: Reproducing Class Privileges

North Town was the type of community in which male teachers who had athletic or coaching backgrounds were more respected than other teachers. For their part, the other teachers often told "dumb coach" jokes and expressed resentment toward the school board's view of coaches. North Town school board members, many of them farmers and ranchers—rugged men of action—generally pre-

ferred that their school leaders be ex-coaches. Consequently a disproportionate number of ex-coaches became school principals and superintendents. The superintendent, himself an ex-coach, sported a 1950s-style flattop and loved to hunt. The junior high principal, also a former coach, owned and operated a steak house. The high school principal was an ex-coach but he lacked the capital to start a business. Three of the present coaching staff had farms or small businesses. School board members invariably emphasized an ex-coach's ability to deal with the public and to discipline the youth.

Once gridiron warriors, coaches in small towns are ultimately forced to become organization men, budget administrators, and public relations experts. These administrative Minotaurs are half-man, half-bureaucrat who are paid a small sum of money for hundreds of hours of extra work. Ultimately they must appease local factions, school boards, administrators, booster clubs, angry parents, and rebellious teenagers. The successful North Town coaches invariably become excellent public relations men who live a "down home" rural lifestyle; they like to hunt and fish and join local coffee klatches or Saturday morning quarterback groups. They must be real men who like fraternizing with the entrepreneurs, politicians, and good ole' boys who actually run the town. This role as a local male leader creates a web of alliances and obligations that put most coaches in the debt of the prominent citizens and their booster club.

North Town's booster club, composed mainly of local merchants, farmers, and ranchers, had the all-important function of raising supplementary funds for improving the sports program and for holding a postseason awards banquet. The club was the most direct and formal link that coaches had with the principal North Town civic leaders. Some prominent merchants and ranchers were absent from these activities, however, because they disliked sports or because they left it to those with more time and enthusiasm. North Town had a long history of booster club and school board interference in coaching the team. One coach characterized North Town as follows: "One of the toughest towns around to keep a job. Folks here take their football seriously. They are used to winning, not everything, not the state, but conference and maybe bidistrict, and someday even regional. They put a lot of pressure on you to win here."

The booster club that coach Trujillo had to deal with was run by a small clique of Anglos whom the BGL liberals considered "good ole' boys and redneck types." They became outspoken early in the season against their "weak Mexican coach." They fanned the fires of criticism in the coffee-drinking sessions over which of the two freshman quarterbacks should start, the "strongarmed Mexican boy" or the "all-around, smart Anglo boy." The Anglo boy was the son of a prominent car dealer and BGL and booster club activist. The Mexican boy was the son of a migrant worker and small grocery store manager. The freshman coach, Jim Ryan, chose the Anglo boy, and the PRU accused him of racial prejudice. In a similar vein, conflict also surfaced over the selection of the varsity quarterback. Coach Trujillo chose the son of an Anglo businessman, an underclassman, over a senior, the son of a less prominent Anglo. The less educated Anglo faction lambasted the coach for this decision, claiming he showed his preference for the children of the more socially and politically prominent BGL types.

One of Coach Trujillo's former players, who was a coach and community political leader, eloquently recounted to me "what physical education courses never teach you" about coaching:

I will never forget Coach Bowman. He was a hard-core sergeant-type who didn't give a damn about pleasing the booster club. During a real rough practice the Smith kid got beat up pretty bad by a Hispanic kid and Coach stopped starting him. His mother came into the office one day to chew out Coach Bowman, and she caught him sitting there in his shorts with his legs up on the desk puffing away on this stogie. He told her that her son was a "goddamn sissy and didn't deserve to start." From then on his days were numbered, and the booster club got him fired. . . . And it works both ways. Hispanics do the same thing. When we had the big school board change and Coach Fuentes was brought in, he gave me a list of three kids, a quarterback, linebacker, and running back, who he wanted me to play on the freshman team. They were all the kids of school board members or buddies of the politicos. It was bad, man. I threatened to walk off the field and let him coach, so he finally gave in.

The former player went on to explain how local pressures and influences on coaches get played out. He advised me to watch who got invited to the parties after the games and who got invited to hunt on certain ranches:

I'll tell you where you really see all this stuff, Doc. You never got invited to the parties, so you didn't see this. Every Friday night after the games, the prominent people in this town throw a barbecue and invite us coaches. The whole staff has gotta go and behave right if you wanna keep your job. That is where a coach can make or break himself. . . . No there wasn't but one or two Mexicanos at these parties. It was all Anglos, until the Mexicano school board came in. Then everything changed. Nobody invited Coach Fuentes and his staff to these parties. They started going to parties on the other side held by the Mexicano politicos. Most Anglos also dropped out of the booster club at that time too. . . . Really, there is no way that this town can have a good football program without a good mix of kids and the Anglo parents ramrodding the booster club. It is sad to say, but the Mexicanos will probably always be too divided to run the thing right. The booster club was in bad shape when they ran it. . . . The other important thing is getting invited by the people who have got money to hunt bird or deer on their land. It is kind of an honor for you to do this, and for them to have you. And if you've got good connections with star players and name coaches from the university or the pro ranks, then you bring them in to speak to the booster club. Local people like going hunting with a real sports celebrity even better. It's all part of the way it is down here, Doc. To survive, you gotta get along with certain people.

The pattern of community pressures observed in North Town was not particularly exceptional. A good deal of the public criticism and grumbling about choices of players had racial overtones. The debate over which Anglo varsity quarterback to play also reflected community class differences among Anglos. North Town students and adults often expressed their fears and suspicion that racial and class prejudices were operating. It would be an exaggeration, however, to portray the North Town football team as rife with racial conflict and disunity. Nor was it filled with class prejudice. On a day-to-day basis there was considerable harmony and unity. Mexicanos and Anglos played side by side with few incidents. A number of working-class Mexicano youths and a few low-income Anglos were also members of the football program. At least in a general way, a surface harmony and equality seemed to prevail.

The only rupture of such public accommodations came when Coach Trujillo and Coach Ryan exchanged sharp words and nearly got into a fistfight during practice. This led to Trujillo making what many Mexicano political activists considered a humiliating public apology to Ryan. The two coaches were also severely reprimanded by the principal and superintendent. Ultimately everyone, especially the two feuding coaches, tried to downplay the conflict for the good of the team. Powerful social pressures controlled any public expression of racial disunity and class conflict on the team.

Local sports enthusiasts are fond of arguing that coaches select players objectively, without class or racial prejudices, because their personal interest, and that of the team, is served by winning. Unfortunately, this free-market view glosses over how sport actually functions in local communities. Small-town coaches are generally subjected to enormous pressures to play everyone's child, regardless of social class and race. Success in sport is an important symbolic representation of familial social position. Men can reaffirm their claim to leadership and prominence through the success of their offspring. A son's athletic exploits relive and display the past physical and present social dominance of the father. In displaying past and present familial prominence, the son lays claim to his future potential. Every North Town coach lived and died by his ability to win games *and* his social competence to handle the competing status claims of the parents and their children.

Socially prominent families, who want to maintain their social position, promote their interests through booster clubs. The fathers of future community leaders spend much time talking about and criticizing coaches in local coffee shops. These fathers are more likely to talk to the coaches privately. Coaches who have ambitions to be socially prominent are more likely to "network" with these sportsminded community leaders. A symbiotic relationship develops between coaches, especially native ones, and the traditional community leaders. Preferential treatment of the sons of prominent community leaders flows from this web of friendships, hunting privileges, Saturday morning joking, and other such exchanges.

Moreover, considerable pressure to favor the sons of prominent citizens comes from within the school as well. The school and its classrooms are also a primary social stage on which students enact their social privilege. These youths establish themselves as leaders in academic, political, and social affairs, and teachers grant them a variety of privileges. This reinforces the influence of their parents in the PTA, the sports and band booster clubs, and the school board. Both generations, in their own way, advance the interests of the family on many fronts.

The Spectators: Male Socialization Through Ex-Players

Another major aspect of the football ritual is how the spectators, the men in the community, socialize each new generation of players. In North Town, groups of middle-aged males with families and businesses were influential in socializing the new generation of males. These men congregated in various restaurants for their morning coffee and conversation about business, politics, the weather, and sports. Those leading citizens particularly interested in sports could be heard praising and criticizing "the boys" in almost a fatherly way. Some hired the players for part-time or summer jobs and were inclined to give them special privileges. Athletes were more likely to get well-paying jobs as road-gang workers, machine operators, and crew leaders. Most players denied that they got any favors, but they clearly had more prestige than other high school students who worked. Nonplayers complained that jocks got the good jobs. On the job site the men regaled players with stories of male conquests in spoils, romance, and business.

Many players reported these conversations, and I observed several during Saturday morning quarterback sessions in a local restaurant and gas station. One Saturday morning after the all-important Harris game, two starters and their good buddies came into the Cactus Bowl Café. One local rancher-businessman shouted, "Hey, Chuck, Jimmie, get over here! I want to talk to you boys about that Harris game!" He then launched into a litany of mistakes each boy and the team had made. Others in the group chimed in and hurled jokes at the boys about "wearing skirts" and being "wimps." Meanwhile the players stood slope-shouldered and "uh-huhed" their tormentors. One thing they had learned was never to argue back too vociferously. The players ridiculed such confrontations with "old-timers" privately, but the proper response from a good kid was tongue-biting deference.

This sort of pressure on players began early in the week with various goodnatured jests and comments. The most critical groups were the cliques of ex-players who had recently graduated. Those who went off to college usually came back only a few weekends to watch games. If they continued to play, they returned as celebrities and tended to say very little. Being college players, they tended to be above any carping criticism of high school players. Usually, the more relentlessly critical groups were those ex-players who had never left town.

Some ex-players led the romanticized life of tough, brawling, womanizing young bachelors. These young men seemed suspended in a state of adolescence while avoiding becoming responsible family men. They could openly do things that the players had to control or hide because of training rules. Many of these ex-players were also able to physically dominate the younger high school players. But ex-players no longer had a stage on which to perform heroics for the town. Consequently they often reminded current players of their past exploits and the superiority of players and teams in their era. Current players had to "learn" from these tormentors and take their place in local sports history.

Players Talking About Their Sport: The Meaning of Football

The preceding portrayal of the community sports scene has already suggested several major reasons why young males play football. Many of them are willing to endure considerable physical pain and sacrifice to achieve social prominence in their community. Only a very small percentage are skilled enough to play college football, and only one North Towner has ever made a living playing professional football. The social rewards from playing football are therefore mainly local and cultural.

However, there are other more immediate psychological rewards for playing football. When asked why they play football and why they like it, young North Town males gave a variety of answers. A few openly admitted that football was a way for them to achieve some social status and prominence, to "become somebody in this town." Many said football was fun, or "makes a man out of you," or "helps you get a cute chick." Others parroted a chamber of commerce view that it built character and trained them to have discipline, thus helping them be successful in life. Finally, many evoked patriotic motives—to beat rival towns and to "show others that South Texas plays as good a football as East Texas."

These explicit statements do not reveal the deeper psychological lessons learned in sports combat, however. In casual conversations, players used phrases that were particularly revealing.

What they talked most about was "hitting" or "sticking" or "popping" someone. These were all things that coaches exhorted the players to do in practice. After a hard game, the supreme compliment was having a particular "lick" or "hit" singled out. Folkloric immortality, endless stories about that one great hit in the big game, was what players secretly strove for. For most coaches and players, really "laying a lick on" or "knocking somebody's can off" or "taking a real lick" was that quintessential football moment. Somebody who could "take it" was someone who could bounce up off the ground as if he had hardly been hit. The supreme compliment, however, was to be called a hitter or headhunter. A hitter made bone-crushing tackles that knocked out or hurt his opponent.

Players who consistently inflicted outstanding hits were called animals, studs, bulls, horses, or gorillas. A stud was a superior physical specimen who fearlessly dished out and took hits, who liked the physical contact, who could dominate other players physically. Other players idolized a "real stud," because he seemed fearless and indomitable on the field. Off the field a stud was also cool, or at least imagined to be cool, with girls. Most players expected and wanted strong coaches and some studs to lead them into battle. They talked endlessly about who was a real stud and whether the coach "really kicks butt."

The point of being a hitter and stud is proving that you have enough courage to inflict and take physical pain. Pain is a badge of honor. Playing with pain proves you are a man. In conventional society, pain is a warning to protect your body, but the opposite ethic rules in football. In North Town bandages and stitches and casts became medals worn proudly into battle. Players constantly told stories about overcoming injuries and "playing hurt." A truly brave man was one who could fight on; his pain and wounds were simply greater obstacles to overcome. Scars were permanent traces of past battles won, or at the very least fought well. They became stories told to girlfriends and relatives.

The other, gentler, more social side of football was the emphasis on camaraderie, loyalty, friendship between players, and pulling together. Players also often mentioned how much fun it was to hang out with the guys. Some of them admitted to being locker room and "gym rats," guys who were always hanging around the fieldhouse and gym. They told stories of their miraculous goal line stands, of last-minute comebacks against all odds, and of tearful, gutwrenching losses on cold muddy fields. Most of the players talked about the value of teamwork and how satisfying it was to achieve something together with other guys. Difficult, negative experiences were also shared. Long grueling practices without water and shade, and painful injuries—these were part of being teammates. Only other football buddies who had been in the football wars could appreciate the sacrifice and physical courage demanded in practices and games.

There were also shining tales of good sportsmanship. Players told stories about being helped up and helped off the field by opponents. They also prided themselves in learning how to lose gracefully and be good sports. At the high school level, winning was still the most important thing, and most coaches drilled that into their players. But if you could not win, the very least you could do was try as hard as possible, give all of yourself to the cause. The one cliché that North Town players constantly parroted back to me was "Winners never quit, and quitters never win." Most North Town players prided themselves on giving their best effort. If they did not, the townspeople would lose respect for them and grumble, as they did during two conference losses. As the chamber of commerce claimed, North Town youth acquire their aggressive, competitive spirit on the town's athletic fields.

Another positive, pleasurable part of the game that most players mentioned was the emotional thrill of performing before large crowds. Many stories were told about "butterflies" and "getting the adrenaline pumping." Players coming back to the bench during the game were quite aware of the crowd. They threw down their helmets in exaggerated anger and disgust. They shouted at each other, slapped high-fives, and smashed each others' shoulder pads. Meanwhile they cast furtive glances at girls in the pep squad or at older brothers prowling the sidelines. They had to constantly express their spirit and commitment to the game, even during sideline breaks. Others limped and ice-packed their injuries and grimaced broadly for all to see.

Many players, particularly the skilled ones, described what might be called their aesthetic moments as the most rewarding thing about football. Players sitting around reviewing a game always talked about themselves or others as "making a good cut" and "running a good route," or "trapping" and "blindsiding" someone. All these specific acts involved executing a particular type of body control and skill with perfection and excellence. Running backs made quick turns or cuts that left would-be tacklers grasping for thin air. Ends "ran routes" or a clever change of direction that freed them to leap into the air and catch a pass. Guards lay in wait for big opposing linemen or aggressive linebackers to enter their territory recklessly, only to be trapped or blindsided by them. Each position had a variety of assignments or moments when players used their strength and intelligence to defeat their opponents. The way this was done was beautiful to a player who had spent years perfecting the body control and timing to execute the play. Players talked about "feeling" the game and the ball and the pressure from an opponent.

Team sports, and especially American football, generally socialize males to be warriors. The young men of North Town were being socialized to measure themselves by their animal instincts and aggressiveness. Physicality, searching for pain, enduring pain, inflicting pain, and knowing one's pain threshold emphasizes the biological, animal side of human beings. These are the instincts needed to work together and survive in military combat and, in capitalist ideology, in corporate, academic, and industrial combat. The language used—headhunter, stick 'em, and various aggressive animal symbols—conjures up visions of Wall Street stockbrokers and real estate sharks chewing up their competition.

Other Males:
Brains, Farm Kids, and Nobodies

What of those males who do not play high school football? Does this pervasive community ritual require the participation of all young males? Do all nonathletes end up in the category of effeminate "band fags"? To the contrary, several types of male students did not lose gender status for being unathletic. There were a small number of "brains" who were obviously not physically capable of being gridiron warriors. Some of them played other sports with less physical contact such as basketball, tennis, track, or baseball. In this way they still upheld the ideal of being involved in some form of sport. Others, who were slight of physique, wore thick glasses, lacked hand-eye coordination, or ran and threw poorly, sometimes ended up hanging around jocks or helping them with their schoolwork. Others were loners who were labeled nerds and weirdos.

In addition, there were many farm kids or poor kids who did not participate in sports. They were generally homebodies who did not participate in many extracurricular activities. Some of them had to work to help support their families. Others had no transportation to attend practices. In the student peer groups they were often part of the great silent majority called "the nobodies."

Resistance to the Football Ritual: The Working-Class Chicano Rebels

There were also a number of Mexicano males who formed anti-school oriented peer groups. They were into a "hip" drug-oriented lifestyle. These males, often called "vatos" (cool dudes), made it a point to be anti-sports, an activity they considered straight. Although some were quite physically capable of playing, they rarely tried out for any type of team sports. They made excuses for not playing such as needing a job to support their car or van or pickup. They considered sports "kids' stuff," and their hip lifestyle as more adult, cool, and fun.

Even for the vatos, however, sports events were important moments when they could publicly display their lifestyle and establish their reputation. A number of vatos always came to the games and even followed the team to other towns. They went to games to be tough guys and "enforcers" and to establish "reps" as fighters. The vatos also went to games to "hit on chicks from other towns." During one road game, after smoking several joints, they swaggered in with cocky smiles plastered on their faces. The idea was to attract attention from young women and hopefully provoke a fight while stealing another town's women. Unlike stealing watermelons or apples from a neighbor, stealing women was done openly and was a test of courage. A man faced this danger in front of his buddies and under the eyes of the enemy.

Ultimately, only one minor scuffle actually occurred at the Larson City game. Some days after the game the vatos told many tales about their foray into enemy territory. With great bravado they recounted every unanswered slight and insult they hurled at those "geeks." They also gloried in their mythical conquests of local young women. For the vatos, fighting, smoking pot, and chasing females were far better sport than huffing and puffing around for "some fucking coach." As the players battled on the field, the vatos battled on the sidelines. They were another kind of warrior that established North Town's community identity and territoriality through the sport of fighting over and chasing young women.

The Contradiction of Being "In Training"

In other ways, even the straight young men who played football also resisted certain aspects of the game. Young athletes were thrust into a real dilemma when their coaches sought to rationalize training techniques and forbade various pleasures of the flesh. Being in training meant no drugs, alcohol, or tobacco. It also meant eating well-balanced meals, getting at least 8 hours of sleep, and not wasting one's emotional and physical energy chasing women. These dictates were extremely difficult to follow in a culture where drugs are used regularly and where sexual conquest and/or romantic love are popular cultural ideals. Add a combination of male adolescence and the overwhelming use of sex and women's bodies to sell commodities, and you have an environment not particularly conducive to making sacrifices for the coach and the team. North Town athletes envied the young bachelors who drank, smoked pot, and chased women late into the night. If they wanted to be males, American culture dictated that they break the rigid, unnatural training rules set for them.

Contrary to the vatos' caricature of jocks as straight and conformist, many North Town football players actually broke their training rules. They often drank and smoked pot at private teen parties. Unlike the rebellious vatos, who publicly flaunted their drinking and drugs, jocks avoided drinking in public. By acting like all-American boys, jocks won praise from adults for their conformity. Many of them publicly pretended to be sacrificing and denying themselves pleasure. They told the old-timers stories about their "rough practices" and "commitment to conditioning." Consequently, if jocks got caught breaking training, the men tended to overlook these infractions as slips or temptations. In short, cool jocks knew how to manage their public image as conformists and hide their private nonconformity.

One incident, when two of the players were caught drinking at a school livestock show, illustrates how many of the adults preferred to handle this cultural contradiction. The sons of two ranchers, Roddy, a senior tackle, and Bob, a senior linebacker, were suspended from school for this incident. Since football season was over, this only jeopardized their graduation, not the winning of a conference championship. The main line of argument made on their behalf was that "boys will be boys," and "these are good kids."[5]

Fathers who had experienced this training contradiction themselves made the boys-will-be-boys argument on behalf of their sons. They gave their sons and other players stern lectures about keeping in shape, *but* they were the first to chuckle at the heroic stories of playing with a hangover. They told these same stories about teammates or about themselves over a cup of coffee or a beer. As a result, unless their youth were outrageously indiscreet—for example passing out drunk on the main street or in class, getting a "trashy girl" pregnant—a "little drinking and screwing around" was overlooked. They simply wanted the school board to stop being hypocritical and acknowledge that drinking was all part of growing up to be a prominent male.

In the small sports world of North Town, a real jock actually enhances his public image of being in shape by occasionally being a "boozer" or "doper." Indeed, one of the most common genres of stories that jocks told was the "I played while drunk/stoned," or the "I got drunk/stoned the night before the game" tale. Olmo, a big bruising guard who is now a hard-living, hard-drinking bachelor, told me a classic version of this tale before the homecoming game:

> Last night we really went out and hung one on. Me and Jaime and Arturo drank a six-pack apiece in a couple of hours. We were cruising around Daly City checking out the action. It was real dead. We didn't see nobody we knew except Arturo's cousin. We stopped at his place and drank some more and listened to some music. We stayed there till his old lady [mom] told us to go home. We got home pretty late, but before the sun come up, 'cause we're in training, ha ha.

Olmo told this story with a twinkle in his eye, especially the part about being in training. I asked him how it was possible to play well if he had "hung one on" the night before. This launched him into the story that he wanted to tell about drinking before and even during games. This story had become part of local sports lore because other players also told it to me. Stories of players' sexual exploits were recounted in the same vein that drinking stories were. A real man could be "in shape" because his extraordinary will could overcome these allegedly debilitating vices. A real man could have it all and become complete through drugs, sex, violence, and glory.

Most players secretly admired such rule-breaking behaviors. Olmo was a model of ideal male behavior and, to a degree, other players who were cool emulated him. Homebodies, the farm kids, and goodie-goodies rarely broke training, but the pressures on them to do so were enormous. Drinking parties, like North Town's post-homecoming bash, made celebrities out of the players. Kids clustered around the bonfire and around various pickups and shared beer and pot with their warriors who had beaten the enemy.

Conclusions:
Some Theoretical Considerations

A number of critical sports theorists have begun to ask whether the legitimation of the ruling elites of both capitalist and communist states through mass sports rituals actually does create an ideological hegemony. Moreover, they ask, if sport is some dehumanizing form of ideological dominance, why do so many people enjoy and increasingly participate in organized popular sports? This raises the issue of whether sport scenes also become the site for resistance to ideological hegemony.

The answer that sports theorists (Critcher, 1986; Gruneau, 1983; Hargreaves, 1986) give, following a Gramscian perspective of popular culture studies, is that ruling-class cultural hegemony is never secure. These theorists generally argue that popular and leisure cultural practices such as sports always have the potential for autonomy and resistance to ruling-class hegemony. This is so, not because sport is inherently ludic but because the politicization and commercialization of local sports practices provoke some form of class consciousness and class resistance. In other words, the elite are never quite successful at appropriating popular cultural practices such as sport and recreation and turning them into mindnumbing, nationalistic forms of political conformity.

Other social theorists sympathetic to this perspective of class dominance (Birrell, 1984, 1989; Hall, 1984, 1985; McKay, 1986; Messner, 1988) suggest even more emphatically than the previously cited critical theorists that the ground of resistance to mass sport must be situated in multiple forms of dominance. In this view, the cultural practices of gender and racial dominance must *also* be included with a class theory perspective of sports. A multiple-dominance view of sports suggests that the commercializing and rationalizing tendencies in sports can at least be mediated and somewhat democratized through the more active participation of previously marginalized groups. Some feminists also argue that since women are more nurturing and humanistic, a massive new presence of women in organized sports will at least have a humanizing effect.

Finally, other popular culture theorists (Fiske 1989a, 1989b) suggest an additional ground for resistance and autonomy that is more general than class, gender, or racial consciousness. Fiske argues that all popular cultural forms have the potential to be pleasurable because they are profane, expressive cultural acts. Sport, like dance, music, or visual art, is a form of personal expression within a set of conventions or rules for self-expression. Within certain limits, these cultural performances manipulate the conventional symbols and expressive practices in new, self-gratifying ways. Students of popular cultural practices outside sport have shown a variety of creative resistance in the expressions of street graffiti, low-rider cars, pop art, informal clothes such as jeans, pop music, youth culture styles, and other unconventional popular expressive forms. This perspective generally suggests that the ultimate ground for resistance to the rationalization and commercialization of various expressive popular culture practices is the human preference to control and produce self-expression. Mass-produced overly standardized forms of self-expression such as commercialized art or sport will invariably run into some resistance because human beings are symbol-producing animals who invariably prefer to innovate with and invent expressive forms to represent themselves and create a social identity. Gruneau proposes some caution here that we "seem to have discovered resistance virtually everywhere in capitalist consumer cultures" (1988, p. 25).

This general question of how autonomous a cultural domain-organized sport is must be addressed, as Gruneau (1983) forcefully suggests, through historical studies of sport practices. Bourdieu (1988) also outlines a complementary programmatic statement for the sociology of sport that calls for intensive studies of the "habitus" of sport practices. I would add to these programmatic statements the addendum that a critical sociology of sport needs to conceptualize local studies of sports as historical community studies. Whatever resistance exists against sport rituals of socialization, it must be understood within the context of the local traditions of structural dominance.

In this particular study there were definitely signs of working-class resistance to the way the football ritual socializes youths to enact various forms of social inequality. The most dramatic example was the way the rebellious vatos used the games to parody football as a ritual of class and racial privilege. According to them, football was not the only way to prove one was a real man and warrior. Moreover, even the most straight, conformist youths who played football, especially those who knew they would never play beyond the community level, did not simply go along with the increasing rationalization of their sport. They were far less likely to follow modern scientific training practices than coaches and the booster club hoped. As Fiske (1989a, 1989b) suggests, leisure culture practices such as football have pleasurable expressive and aesthetic moments. The real joy of playing hometown football is still some kind of ludic or expressive moment that may survive more on the local level than in big-time college and professional sports.

In addition, in a town experiencing the Chicano civil rights movement, there were many signs of an ethnic resistance to the reproductive character of local sports. Many Mexicanos protested strongly when the Anglos enacted the homecoming ceremony in a way that marginalized them. The same could be said for the Mexicano players who defiantly sat in the back of the bus and who made it difficult for Anglo coaches to unquestioningly put Anglo players in the high status positions. Moreover, Coach Trujillo clearly played a mediating role in resisting racial dominance until he was forced out. Finally, even the Mexicana cheerleader, Trini, was making her own statement about the reproductive character of the football ritual.

Yet, all of the previously mentioned signs of resistance notwithstanding, the football ritual remains a powerful metaphor of American capitalist culture. In North Town, football is still a popular cultural practice deeply implicated in the reproduction of the local ruling class of white males, hence class, patriarchal, and racial forms of dominance. The larger ethnographic study (Foley, 1990) details how the football ritual was also tied to student status groups, dating, friendship, and social mobility patterns. Local sports, especially football, are still central to the socialization of each new generation of youth and to the maintenance of the adolescent society's status system. In addition, this ritual is also central to the preservation of the community's adult status hierarchy. The local politics of the booster club, adult male peer groups, and Saturday morning coffee klatches ensnare coaches and turn a son's participation in the football ritual into an important symbolic reenactment of the father's social class and gender prominence.

Despite continuous claims about the autonomous and liberating effects of organized sports, this study appears to indicate that organized sports, as presently practiced at the community level, is still a rather archaic, conservative force in our society. This is not to claim that sport is an inherently conservative popular culture practice in the sense that Critcher (1986) seems to suggest. Following Gruneau (1983) and Bourdieu (1988), I would argue that sport, like all cultural practices, is never intrinsically reactionary or progressive. Each cultural context or habitus of practices has a history and set of traditions that can either endure or change, depending on what the people living out that tradition choose to do. These data suggest the emergence of some forms of human agency and autonomy. There were Mexicano, female, and working-class challenges to the maintaining of traditional forms of dominance through local sports practices.

Nevertheless, it is clear that such challenges have done little to transform the everyday culture that this major community ritual enacts. The football ritual continues to stage North Town's contemporary system of class dominance and its archaic system of patriarchal dominance. The transformation of sports at the community level will require a deeper cultural change in this community socialization process that re-creates each new generation. Without political movements that are stronger than the Chicano civil rights movement, local sport scenes like North Town's will not easily become sites of progressive, counterhegemonic forces.

References

Babcock, B. (Ed.) (1978). *The reversible world: Symbolic inversion in art and society.* Ithaca, NY: Cornell University Press.

Bennett, T.C., Mercer, C., & Wollacott, J. (1986). *Popular culture and social relations.* Milton Keynes, England: Open University Press.

Birrell, S. (1984). Studying gender in sport: Issues, insights, and struggle. In N. Theberge & P. Donnelly (Eds.), *Sport and the sociological imagination* (pp. 125-135). Fort Worth, TX: Texas Christian University Press.

Birrell, S. (1989). Race relations theories and sport: Suggestions for a more critical analysis. *Sociology of Sport Journal,* **6,** 212-227.

Bourdieu, P. (1988). Program for a sociology of sport. *Sociology of Sport Journal,* **5,** 153-161.

Chambers, I. (1986). *Popular culture: The metropolitan experience.* London: Methuen.

Critcher, C. (1986). Radical theorists of sport: The state of play. *Sociology of Sport Journal,* **3,** 333-343.

Deem, R. (1988). "Together we stand, divided we fall"; Social criticism and the sociology of sport and leisure. *Sociology of Sport Journal,* **5,** 341-354.

Donnelly, P., & Young, K. (1988). The construction and confirmation of identity in sport subcultures. *Sociology of Sport Journal,* **5,** 223-240.

Dundes, A. (1978). Into the endzone for a touchdown: A psychoanalytic consideration of American football. *Western Folklore,* **37,** 75-88.

Fine, G.A. (1987). *With the boys: Little League baseball and preadolescent culture.* Chicago: University of Chicago Press.

Fiske, J. (1989a). *Understanding popular culture.* Boston: Unwin Hyman.

Fiske, J. (1989b). *Reading the popular.* Boston: Unwin Hyman.

Foley, D. (1990). *Learning capitalist culture: Deep in the heart of Tejas.* Philadelphia: University of Pennsylvania Press.

Foley, D., with Mota, C., Post, D., & Lozano, I. (1988). *From peones to politicos: Class and ethnicity in a south Texas town, 1900-1987.* Austin, TX: University of Texas Press.

Gruneau, R. (1983). *Class, sports, and social development.* Amherst: The University of Massachusetts Press.

Gruneau, R. (1988). Introduction: Notes on popular culture and political practice. In R. Gruneau (Ed.), *Popular cultures and political practices* (pp. 11-32). Toronto: Garamond Press.

Hall, M.A. (1984). Toward a feminist analysis of gender inequality it sport. In N. Theberge & P. Donnelly (Eds.), *Sport and the sociological imagination* (pp. 82-103). Fort Worth: Texas Christian University Press.

Hall, M.A. (1985). Knowledge and gender: Epistemological questions in the social analysis of sport. *Sociology of Sport Journal,* **2,** 25-42.

Hargreaves, J. (1986). *Sport, power and culture: A Social and historical analysis of popular sports in Britain.* London: St. Martins Press.

Loy, J.W., & Ingham, A.G. (1973). Play, games, and sport in the psychosocial development of children and youth. In G.L. Rarick (Ed.), *Physical activity—Human growth and development* (pp. 257-302). New York: Academic Press.

McKay, J. (1986). Marxism as a way of seeing: Beyond the limits of current critical approaches to sport. *Sociology of Sport Journal, 3,* 261-272.

Messner, M. (1988). Sports and male domination: The female athlete as contested ideological terrain. *Sociology of Sport Journal, 5,* 197-211.

Turner, V. (1974). *Dramas, fields, and metaphors: Symbolic action in human societies.* Ithaca, NY: Cornell University Press.

Whitson, D. (1984). Sport and hegemony: On the construction of the dominant culture. *Sociology of Sport Journal, 1,* 64-78.

Notes

1. The distinction here is between a community and a subculture or lifestyle group. A historical community is a geopolitical territory that has its own political, economic, and cultural systems—a collective of people who share a set of memories and traditions about past political, economic, and cultural practices. A subculture of sports enthusiasts such as surfers or skiers do not live in and share a community mode of production and its traditional social structure of class, gender, and racial dominance.

2. The community study includes a historical analysis of how the county's political economy evolved into a fully capitalist mode of agricultural production and a major recomposition of social classes. This economic transformation engenders ethnic politics and the gradual dismantling of this capitalist racial order. The community study also analyzes how these broader transformations affect the local youth scene and race relations in the high school.

3. The firing-up-the-team pun was actually a fairly good explanation of the bonfire. It was a kind of tribal fire around which the community war dance was held. The event was preparing these young warriors for battle, and the cheerleaders and band replaced painted dancers and tom tom drums. In addition, the fire was a kind of community hearth. At least some people were literally returning to the "home fires" of their village and tribe.

4. This South Texas rite of passage was beautifully portrayed in Peter Bogdanovich's *The Last Picture Show,* which is based on a novel by Larry McMurtry.

5. This is of course the classic defense often used to condone the drinking and vandalism of privileged college fraternity kids.

Sports Ideology, Attitudes Toward Women, and Antihomosexual Attitudes

Joseph Harry

The present work tests the associations of sports ideology with sexist and antihomosexual attitudes in a sample of 304 college students. It was found that sports ideology is positively associated with sexist and antihomosexual attitudes, but only among males. Among females only sexist attitudes were associated with negative attitudes toward gays and lesbians. Among males, the link of sports ideology to antihomosexual attitudes was independent of sexist beliefs. Reciprocal causal influences between sexist attitudes and sports ideology are discussed.

A common view is that the institution of sports is one of our most gender-traditional social arrangements which fosters sexism and support for patriarchy (Kidd, 1990; Messner, 1988). It attempts to define and celebrate arenas in which men are superior to women, especially in strength, assertiveness, and competitiveness. It represents "athletics as a masculine drama, involving the display of power, aggression, and violence" (Pronger, 1990, p. 187). However, women have increasingly entered the fields of sports and thereby challenged the view of athletics as an exclusive domain of and for men (Bryson, 1990). The entry of women into sports has been repeatedly challenged and resisted either by claiming that sports participation is unfeminine or by marginalizing that participation (Lenskyj, 1986).

The present work empirically tests the association between sports ideology and attitudes toward women in a population of college students. Athletic ideology consists of a set of moral beliefs that sports confers important benefits on both society and the individual, e.g., its "character-building" qualities. We are not here interested in the narrower topic of sports participation. While there have been numerous studies of the characteristics and attitudes of athletes, research on attitudes toward the institution of sport, among both participants and nonparticipants is limited (Spreitzer and Snyder, 1975). If sports, as hypothesized, generates or supports sexist ideologies, the effects most likely operate through the ideology of sports rather than through simple participation.

A second focus of the present work is whether sports ideology is also associated with negative attitudes toward gays and lesbians. Sports ideology and imagery serve to define heterosexual manliness. As Lehne (1976) has argued, gays are the heterosexual image of male failure. He argues that the image of gays serves a useful purpose in the world of gender politics by providing an object to be criticized and contrasted with the ideal of athletic manliness. Hence, the frequent antigay comments made in athletic situations (Messner, 1992, pp. 34-37). Pronger (1990, pp. 76-77) extends Lehne's argument by observing that a key component of masculinity as expressed in heterosexuality is gender differences in power. Within male gender myths heterosexuality is a symbolic reaffirmation of those power differences. Thus, homosexuality is a loss of masculine power over women. Hence, "the heart of homophobia—the fear of the loss of power" (p. 77). This fear of loss of power may simply be a fear of

Reprinted from Harry, 1995.

loss of power over women or it may also include a fear of being subject to the power of other men through homosexual involvement. We therefore hypothesize that those high in support for sports ideology would also be quite antihomosexual.

Although it is anticipated that sports ideology is associated with both sexism and negative attitudes toward gays and lesbians, these associations may differ by gender. The relationships of the institutions of sports with women, both physical and symbolic, have often been subject to tensions. Women have been "welcomed unconditionally as spectators and cheerleaders for men's games" (Lenskyj, 1986, p. 101). In this capacity as audience to men's performances women have been invited to subscribe to a highly traditional interpretation of sports and of gender roles. Women's participation in sports has been another matter. It has often been resisted, considered unfeminine, and been a basis of questioning the sexual orientation of those women who took sports too seriously, e.g., the stereotype of the female physical education teacher (Lenskyj, 1986, pp. 102-107).

In more recent years women have come to see a place for themselves in sports. This may mean that they have also come to subscribe more to the sports ideology, i.e., sports is good for you. If so, it seems dubious that they would also subscribe to an associated ideology of sexism and male dominance. Whether sports ideology is also associated with antihomosexual attitudes among women is arguable since that association might also require a sexist interpretation of sports. We expect little association between sports ideology and sexism among women.

The association of negative attitudes toward gays and lesbians with sports ideology may also depend on the sex of the homosexual. The image of being a lesbian or "tomboy" has usually been less negative in our culture than that of being a gay male or "sissy." As reported by Duncan and Duncan (1978, p. 272) from national survey data, "It was more important to these fathers that a 'boy act like a boy' should than that a 'girl act like a girl' should." The stereotype of a lesbian seems little inconsistent with that of athlete while that of a gay male is highly inconsistent. Hence, the association of sports ideology with antihomosexual attitudes may depend on both the sex of the respondent and the sex of the hypothetical homosexual. For this reason we have used separate scales measuring antigay attitudes and antilesbian attitudes.

Research Methods

The subjects for the present research consist of a systematic sample from the undergraduate students at a large residential Midwestern university. There were 327 respondents to a mailback questionnaire sent to 677 students. There was one follow-up employed consisting of a new copy of the questionnaire. The response rate was 48.3 percent. Using listwise deletion of cases with missing data in the analysis below reduces the effective N to 304. Comparing the demographics of the respondents with institutional data, the median age of the sample is 20.0 years compared to 20.1 for the university as a whole. There is some underrepresentation of freshmen and sophomores in the sample: 19.6 percent freshmen compared to 24.4 percent for the population. Mean ACT score for the sample is 23.3 and 22.0 for the population. Females are overrepresented in the sample: 63 percent versus 54 percent. These differences between the sample and the population suggest that the sample underrepresents poorly performing students who others have found to be somewhat more antigay. Kurdek (1988) reported a negative .34 correlation of grades with antigay attitudes among male college students and a −.24 one among female students—both significant. The racial distribution for the sample is 6 percent African American, 86 percent Caucasian, 4 percent Asian, with the rest being "Other." The class backgrounds for the sample are very largely upper working-class and middle class. Median maternal education is 13.0 years with nine percent of the mothers having less than a high school education and 26 percent possessing 16 years or more. The students come primarily from the Chicago suburbs and secondarily from Chicago.

Two scales were employed measuring attachment to sports. Sports ideology was measured through the Psychosocial Functions of Sport Scale which consists of seven items measuring belief in the moral qualities of sports, e.g., "Sports are valuable because they help youngsters become good citizens" (Martin and Dodder, 1993; Spreitzer and Snyder, 1975). In the present data the alpha-reliability of this scale is .80. A second five-item scale measuring personal satisfaction from sports, e.g., "Sports are a good way for me to relax," has an alpha-reliability of 0.85 (Martin and Dodder, 1993).

To measure support for sexism/patriarchy the widely used Attitudes Toward Women Scale (AWS) of Spence and Helmreich (1978, pp. 237-239) was employed. This 14 item scale measures the extent to which men should be the leaders in various sectors of society, e.g., "The intellectual leadership of a community should be largely in the hands of men." Its alpha-reliability here is .84. Conceptually the AWS measures support for traditional gender roles or, perhaps, sexism. However, given that a number of its items reflect restricting women's participation in the "public sphere" and leadership roles, it may also measure the conceptually overlapping concept of patriarchy.

Separate scales were employed to measure attitudes toward lesbians and attitudes toward gays. Ten items referring to lesbians and 10 items referring to gays were taken from Herek's (1984) 38 item Condemnation-Tolerance Factor on homosexuality, e.g., "Lesbians are sick," "Male homosexuality is a perversion." The antilesbian scale has an alpha-reliability of 0.93, as does the antigay scale.

Results

Table 3.1 presents the means, standard deviations, and correlations among the above described scales separately for each gender. We begin by comparing gender differences in the means. No significant difference was found in the sports ideology scale, apparently indicating that men and women subscribe equally to this ideology. However, men were found to report significantly more satisfaction from involvement in sports. This is consistent with findings that adult males participate in sports considerably more (Fishwick and Hays, 1989). As others have found (Spence and Helmreich, 1978, p. 39), the men in this sample were also significantly more

sexist on the AWS. While men and women did not differ in their views on lesbians, male subjects were significantly more antigay than female subjects. This gender difference is consistent with other findings that males, and especially young males, are more antigay than females. However, the literature is not completely consistent on this point (Kite, 1984).

Turning to comparisons of the correlation among the males and females, we find that sports ideology is significantly and positively related to patriarchal beliefs, antilesbian views, and antigay views among men but not among women. Significance tests for interactions were performed by regressing each of the latter three scales on sports ideology, gender, and their product term. The predictors were entered hierarchically with the product term entered last. In all three cases the interactions proved significant at at least the .05 level. It thus seems that sports ideology is linked to traditional sexist views and prejudices against lesbians and gays but only among men. These data also imply that the meanings of sports may differ among men and women since support for sports does not also entail a broader set of traditional prejudices among women.

The data of table 3.1 also reveal that sexist scores on the AWS are positively and significantly associated with antilesbian and antigay views. The strength of these associations is about equal among both men and women. These data are consistent with the findings of others that college students who are more traditional in gender roles are also more antigay (Kurdek, 1988; Whitley, 1987). Traditional gender roles appear to provide cultural support for antigay and antilesbian prejudice and encourage views of homosexuals as gender deviants.

Table 3.1   Correlations Among Scales by Sex[a]

	Ideology	Satisfaction	AWS	Antilesbian	Antigay	Mean[b]	SD
Ideology	X	.39**	.03	.10	.08	23.24	4.34
Satisfaction	.59**	X	−.01	.02	−.01	19.76**	3.96
AWS	.31**	.07	X	.46**	.49**	25.17**	6.24
Antilesbian	.37**	.23*	.52**	X	.93**	26.25	8.59
Antigay	.33**	.17	.53**	.79**	X	24.82*	8.78
Mean[b]	23.68	21.22**	32.23**	27.95	31.18**	X	
SD	4.66	3.43	7.85	8.89	9.67		X

[a]Females above the diagonal (N = 193); males below (N = 111). The asterisks attached to the correlation coefficients indicate the correlations are significantly different from zero; unlike the asterisks for the means, they do not indicate significant gender differences.

[b]T-tests for independent groups with separate variance estimates; two-tailed tests.

*$p < .05$.

**$p < .01$.

Reprinted from Harry, 1995.

In table 3.2 we sort out the separate effects of sports ideology and sexist beliefs by regressing antigay and antilesbian attitudes on those two scales separately by gender. The sports satisfaction scale has been dropped from these analyses because its significance uniformly vanishes with the introduction of the sports ideology measure. The data indicate that among females only support for traditional gender roles is a significant predictor of antilesbian attitudes or of antigay attitudes while sports ideology has no significant effects. Among men both sports ideology and sexist beliefs are significant predictors of both antilesbian and antigay attitudes. Comparing the two betas predicting antigay attitudes among men, it was found that traditional attitudes toward women was a significantly stronger predictor than sports ideology (t = 2.20, $p < .05$; Cohen and Cohen, 1983, pp. 479-480). However, predicting antilesbian attitudes among men, the two corresponding betas were not significantly different (t = 1.66, p = ns), although both differed significantly from zero. Among men only, sports ideology thus seems to have an independent link to antihomosexual beliefs, both directly and indirectly through its link with support for traditional gender roles.

Discussion

Given that the above data are all attitudinal, it would be hazardous to make commitments about certain attitudes being causally prior to others. However, the data seem to indicate that sports and its associated ideology have different cultural significance for men and women. This difference is expressed in the different structurings of these attitudes rather than in a mean sex difference in sports ideology which did not appear in the present data. For men sports seems to be a part of the large set of cultural attitudes associated with and expressive of gender. For women, sports is less expressive of gender differences. In factor analytic terms, sports is part of the patriarchal gender factor for men but not for women. For men sports may help to define and validate prejudices against women, gays, and lesbians. For women sports ideology seems largely devoid of implications for gender roles. While many women believe that sports is good for one, that belief does not carry with it a traditional view of female subordination.

In the above analysis sports ideology has been taken as a predictor of gender attitudes. However, in the course of childhood socialization the causal directions may be reversed or reciprocal. Boys are offered sports and its ideology as a means of validating their manhood. Indeed, given the immense amount of time many boys spend in competitive sports, one could argue that sports *is* the normative gender role for boys while a boy who is not interested in sports is considered a likely gender deviant (Lever, 1976, 1978). Boys interested in proving that manhood or showing that they are better than

Table 3.2   Predicting Antilesbian and Antigay Scales from AWS and Sports Ideology by Sex

Predictors	B	SE B	Beta	t	Sign.	df	Mult. R
Females							
Dependent variable: antilesbian							
Ideology	.18	.13	.09	1.40	ns		
						2,190	.47
AWS	.63	.09	.46	7.19	.01		
Dependent variable: antigay							
Ideology	.12	.13	.06	.96	ns		
						2,190	.50
AWS	.69	.09	.49	7.81	.01		
Males							
Dependent variable: antilesbian							
Ideology	.45	.16	.24	2.84	.01		
						2,108	.57
AWS	.51	.09	.45	5.41	.01		
Dependent variable: antigay							
Ideology	.38	.17	.18	2.17	.05		
						2,112	.57
AWS	.58	.10	.47	5.58	.01		

Reprinted from Harry, 1995.

girls may then adopt sports ideology and activities. In this scenario sports becomes a largely symbolic and even ritual activity through which traditional gender roles and gender prejudices are validated for boys. Such a strong link between competitive sports activities and gender roles for children might imply that sports ideology is simply derivative of rather than contributory to traditional gender ideology. However, the above shown direct link of sports ideology to antigay and antilesbian attitudes among men suggests that that ideology makes some separate contribution to traditional gender-related prejudices.

Conclusions

The above data have shown that sports ideology is associated with sexist attitudes and with prejudices against both gays and lesbians among male college students. Among female college students sports ideology revealed no such associations. Among the women respondents, only high scores on the AWS were associated with antilesbian and antigay attitudes. These data suggest that the meanings of sports differ for men and women. For men sports seem to be a means of validating male ideals and superiority to women. For women, sports ideology is not supportive of traditional gender attitudes, even among those women who subscribe to the ideology of sports.

These data also suggest that among men socialization into sports and its associated ideology constitutes training in sexism and homophobia. Such "character-building" seems to be unanticipated consequences of a seemingly innocuous and wholesome pastime, although for some participants such consequences may be fully intentional. However, sports socialization for women does not appear to entail the learning of these prejudices.

References

Bryson, L. (1990). Challenges to male hegemony in sport. In M. Messner & D. Sabo (Eds.), *Sport, men, and the gender order*. Champaign, IL: Human Kinetics Books.

Cohen, J., & Cohen, P. (1983). *Applied multiple regression/correlation analysis for the behavioral sciences* (2nd ed.). Hillsdale, NJ: Erlbaum Associates.

Fishwick, L., & Hays, D. (1989). Sport for whom: Differential participation patterns of recreational athletes in leisure time physical activities. *Sociology of Sport Journal, 6*, 269-277.

Herek, G. (1984). Attitudes toward lesbians and gay men: A factor-analytic study. *Journal of Homosexuality, 10*, 39-51.

Kidd, B. (1990). The men's cultural centre: Sports and the dynamic of women's oppression/men's repression. In M. Messner & D. Sabo (Eds.), *Sport, men, and the gender order*. Champaign, IL: Human Kinetics Books.

Kite, M. (1984). Sex differences in attitudes toward homosexuals: A meta-analytic review. *Journal of Homosexuality, 10*, 69-81.

Kurdek, L. (1988). Correlates of negative attitudes toward homosexuals in heterosexual college students. *Sex Roles, 18*, 727-738.

Lehne, G. (1976). Homophobia among men. In D. David & R. Brannon (Eds.), *The forty-nine percent majority*. Reading, MA: Addison-Wesley.

Lenskyj, H. (1986). *Out of bounds: Women, sport, and sexuality*. Toronto: Women's Press.

Lever, J. (1976). Sex differences in the games children play. *Social Problems, 23*, 479-487.

Lever, J. (1978). Sex differences in the complexity of children's play and games. *American Sociological Review, 43*, 471-483.

Martin, D., & Dodder, R. (1993). A reassessment of the psychosocial functions of sport scale. *Sociology of Sport Journal, 10*, 197-204.

Messner, M. (1988). Sports and male domination: The female athlete as contested ideological terrain. *Sociology of Sport Journal, 5*, 197-211.

Messner, M. (1992). *Power at play*. Boston: Beacon Press.

Pronger, B. (1990). *The arena of masculinity: Sports, homosexuality, and the meaning of sex*. New York: St. Martin's Press.

Spence, J., & Helmreich, R. (1978). *Masculinity and femininity: Their psychological dimensions, correlates, and antecedents*. Austin, TX: University of Texas Press.

Spreitzer, E., & Snyder, E. (1975). The psychosocial functions of sport as perceived by the general population. *International Review of Sport Sociology, 10*, 87-93.

Whitley, B. (1987). The relationship of sex-role orientation to heterosexual attitudes toward homosexuals. *Sex Roles, 17*, 103-113.

Disqualifying the Official:
An Exploration of Social Resistance
Through the Subculture of Skateboarding

Becky Beal

This paper describes some of the ways in which popular culture may be a site of social resistance. The subculture of skateboarding is described as one form of popular culture that resists capitalist social relations, and the skateboarders' particularly overt resistance to an amateur contest provides a framework for characterizing their daily and more covert behaviors of resistance. Although social resistance has the potential to change dominant social relations, it is often limited by contradictions and accommodations. In this case, the skateboarders' sexist behavior is one of their significant contradictions. Finally, some implications of social resistance are addressed.

Popular cultural activities, including sport, have typically been analyzed as a means of reproducing dominant cultural norms and values. From a critical perspective, sport has been viewed as maintaining the dominant group's position by reaffirming and reproducing inequitable social relations associated with capitalism, patriarchy, and racism (e.g., Bray, 1988; Messner, 1992; Sage, 1990). More recently, sport has also been analyzed as a place where dominant values and norms are challenged and where alternative norms and values are created (e.g., Birrell & Richter, 1987; Klein, 1991; Stevenson, 1991; Young, 1983). This study considers the way in which one form of popular culture, skateboarding, has been used to resist dominant norms and values.

Reprinted from Beal, 1995.

Hegemony Theory

Gramsci's (1971) concept of hegemony, his insight and analysis of power and social change, necessitates a serious investigation of culture. Hegemony is not simply the notion that dominant group ideas are transferred to the minds of subordinate groups through superstructural means. It implies the active consent of the subordinate group in creating and maintaining its subordinate status. This active consent is encouraged by the dominant group's ability to create limits on the range of what is perceived to be acceptable or even possible. In this way, subordinate groups actively choose from the dominant group's agenda, maintaining a semblance of freedom while reinforcing the dominant group's interests.

Active consent occurs not simply by consciously acknowledging certain ideas but by arranging one's behaviors by those ideas. In other words, active consent occurs by embracing and living out dominant values and norms, and this occurs in the ordinary experiences of people. Hegemony is the process by which ideologies become materialized through the everyday experiences of people: how ideologies are internalized, struggled over, negotiated, opposed, and lived out. Hebdige (1979) described this relationship of ideology and everyday practices: "Since ideology saturates everyday discourse in the form of common sense, it can not be bracketed off from everyday life as a self-contained set of 'political opinions' or 'biased views'" (p. 12). Williams described this relationship as a "decisive" component of hegemony: "What is decisive is not only the conscious system of ideas and beliefs, but the whole lived process as practically organized by specific dominant meanings and values" (1977, p. 109).

Resistance to hegemonic forms of everyday life represents a significant foundation for social change. This change may be reformist or revolutionary, but in any case, social change is created by social actors and not by a predetermined system of evolutionary economics. Notably, the challenge to hegemony occurs in the civil society, in the everyday experiences of people, and this includes popular practices such as sport.

Hegemony, as a theoretical framework, brings light to how the issues of ideology and everyday life are not distinct entities but are interactive: how the dominant ideology affects subordinate subcultures and how those subcultures, in turn, respond to the effects of the dominant ideology. In this way, popular culture is more complex than just a breeding ground of false consciousness or simply a separate social space in which subordinate groups can express their interests. Instead, it is indicative of a dynamic culture, one that is continually being shaped by both hegemonic and counterhegemonic interests.

Capitalist Ideology and Sport Practices

Many researchers have described a dominant sport culture as one in which competition, extrinsic rewards, elitism based on skill, and specialization are central components (e.g., Donnelly, 1993; Stevenson, 1991). In addition, mainstream sport in North America has been associated with bureaucratic social relations (Berlage, 1982; O'Hanlon, 1980; Whitson, 1984). It has been argued that these structures of sport in North America are connected with capitalist ideology and therefore reinforce the lived practices and experiences of capitalist relations (Bray, 1988; Foley, 1990; O'Hanlon, 1980; Whitson, 1984). For example, Whitson (1984) argues that mainstream sports have been framed in the value structures of advanced capitalism: discipline, control, accountability, and bureaucratic rationalization that has created a managerial level of "experts." Whitson claims that this reaffirmation of capitalistic values outside of the work force confirmed those

values as natural or as "common sense." Similarly, Foley notes, "The great ideological struggle in advanced capitalist societies is not only over explicit political ideologies but also over one's mode of identity expression" (1990, p. 186), and, "Youths practice, learn, and anticipate their different class identities and roles through the way they play football, display peer status, and horse around in the classrooms" (p. 192).

In summary, the structure and relations of corporate bureaucracies are prevalent in mainstream North American sport. When popular cultural activities are structured by corporate bureaucratic social relations, they reproduce the dominant group's position by promoting and legitimizing the values and norms that underlie capitalism. This also decreases the validity of alternative relations. As Donnelly (1988) notes, "Such standardization of cultural forms has carried with it a powerful tendency to naturalize the dominant values and social relations of capitalist consumer culture. With this naturalization comes a loss of choice and a loss of awareness of choices which may be available" (p. 73).

Challenges to Capitalist Ideologies and Practices in Sport

As stated previously, hegemony is never secured, and within most practices of popular culture there are elements of hegemony and counterhegemony. Alternative practices, or resistances, are continually challenging the hegemony of the dominant group, but this struggle is full of apparent contradictions because it is encased in a hegemonic while simultaneously trying to break it down. Therefore, many resistant subcultures are not singularly transformative, but they do include forms of challenge as well as forms of accommodation.

Numerous individual and daily resistances occur in mainstream sport, but this study investigates a subcultural form of resistance which entails ritualistic patterns that go beyond individuals testing the limits of organized sport practices. In the subculture of skateboarding, the most blatant form of resistance revealed in this study was the opposition to the corporate bureaucratic forms of sport (and, as a consequence, corporate bureaucratic social relations). This subculture of skateboarding resisted by creating alternative norms and relations that emphasized participant control of the physical activity and open participation rather than elite competition.

Methods

Observation, participant-observation, and semi-structured in-depth interviews were used to investigate the subculture of skateboarding in northeastern Colorado. In June 1989, I began observing skateboarders in Jamestown and Welton, Colorado, at popular skateboard spots (e.g., parking lots, university pedestrian walkways), skateboard shops, and a locally sponsored skateboard exhibition.[1] The first subjects were friends' children and employees at skateboard shops. I introduced myself to others while they were skateboarding on the streets and asked if I could talk with them. They call themselves "skaters," and the act of skateboarding they call "skating." I met one of the female skaters (a rarity) through mutual membership in a local feminist group. I used snowball sampling, so these initial contacts led to many others. Over a 2-year period (1990-1992), I talked with 41 skaters, 2 skateboard shop owners, and several parents and siblings.

Of the 41 skateboarders, 24 were interviewed more than once, and 6 of those became my best informants since we formed a closer relationship that fostered more trust. This relationship consisted of continual feedback by which they checked the reliability of the information I was gathering and I, in turn, could continually refine and ask more pertinent questions. In addition, I spent over 100 hours observing skateboarders, many of whom I did not interview (they were observed in public spaces). Only 4 of the 41 participants were female. In addition, all were Anglo except for two Hispanic males. The average age of those participating was 16, but ages ranged from 10 to 25 years. The participants had skateboarded for an average of 4 years, but the range of their participation was from 1 to 15 years. My most consistent contacts were from two friendship groups of skaters. The group from Jamestown was younger (ages 10–16 years) and included two Hispanic males; the second group was from Welton, was older (ages 15–25 years), and included a female.

Once the study was complete, the analysis of their subculture was presented to approximately one third of the participants. Their comments served to reaffirm and fine-tune my conclusions. They especially wanted me to note their heterogeneity: Although they shared many norms and values, they did not share all values, and, therefore, just because they were all skateboarders did not mean that they were all good friends or were as homogenous as they are often portrayed in the media.

It is necessary to elaborate on the above comment because there was not a ubiquitous skateboard subculture. In fact, a variety of subgroups skateboarded. The skateboarders demonstrated a continuum of hegemonic to counterhegemonic behavior ranging from those who embraced the corporate bureaucratic form of the activity to those who resisted it. This study focused on those who resisted, but even within that group resistance was demonstrated through a variety of styles.

Skaters described those involved in corporate bureaucratic skating as "rats," individuals who bought the commercially produced paraphernalia and plastered all their belongings with corporate logos. But, more distinctively, they were defined as kids who aspired to skate professionally. These skaters frequently sought sponsorship, which was pursued, for example, by creating videotapes of their skating and sending them to different corporations. In addition, these skaters entered competitions with the intent of seeking the needed recognition for sponsorship.

Another group of skaters resisted the professionalization of their physical activity. They defined skateboarding as a way of living and rejected any notions that the activity should be used as a way of making a living. As a consequence, their relationship with commercially produced products was carefully negotiated. For example, they bought commercially produced skateboards (many tried to make their own but claimed they were not as good) but decorated their boards with their own symbols, which, in a few cases, included poetry. They no longer bought the "right" clothes or commercially produced stickers; instead they were more innovative with their clothing and often created their own stickers, leaving samples displayed where they skated. The styles of expression varied greatly, and the skaters classified each by an association with a type of music or style of skating. Some of these included "hippies," "punks," "skinheads," "frat boys," "metalers" (i.e., those who listened to heavy metal music), "rappers," and "old timers" (e.g., those who did slalom skating as opposed to "trick" skating).

Although the skaters recognized and labeled their internal differences, they also acknowledged their own subcultural status. The following letter to a newspaper editor from a teenage skater illustrates this self-definition:

Skaters have a completely different culture from the norms of the world's society. We dress differently, we have our own language, use our own slang, and live by our own rules. People feel threatened by foreign attitudes.

Everyone has his own views on different types of society and their own stereotypes. . . . Please stop viewing us as a totally negative race of people. The few people who have come up and watched us skate and spoken to us know that we are nice, educated, and intelligent. (Maeda, 1991, p. 17)

This study concentrates on those who opposed the professionalization of their activity.

Skateboarding As a Cultural Site of Social Resistance

As with other popular cultural activities, skateboarding is not inherently counterhegemonic or hegemonic; instead, it may carry both sets of meanings, sometimes simultaneously. As Bennett (1986) stated,

The field of popular culture is structured by the attempt of the ruling class to win hegemony and by the forms of opposition to this endeavor. As such, it consists not simply of an imposed mass culture that is coincident with dominant ideology, nor simply of spontaneously oppositional cultures, but is rather an area of negotiation between the two within which . . . dominant, subordinate and oppositional cultural and ideological values and elements are "mixed" in different permutations. (pp. xv-xvi)

Since the early 1960s, skateboarding in the United States has gone through periods of popularity. At times of high popularity, various commercial interests have tried to capitalize on the activity by promoting it as part of the dominant sport culture, that is, as a legitimate sport, one which promotes competition, win-at-all-costs attitude, and extrinsic rewards. This trend toward commercialization and legitimization appears to be common with many nontraditional sports, such as rock climbing (Donnelly, 1993) and mountain biking (Gray, 1992). The following outlines how this process has occurred in skateboarding.

Corporate Bureaucracy of Skateboarding

The governing body for skateboarding is the National Skateboard Association (NSA). It was founded in 1981 by Frank Hawk, the father of a tal-

ented skater, Tony Hawk, and was initially associated with the Boy Scouts of America. In 1986, the NSA received nonprofit corporation status from the State of California. Since then, the board of directors have included the chief executive officers of the major corporations who market to skateboarders (e.g., Vision, Powell/Peralta, Santa Cruz, and *Transworld Skateboard* and *Thrasher* magazines; NSA, 1990). At this time, the NSA is the main agency for the industry to encourage the commercial growth of the sport. In order to promote the sport, the NSA sponsors amateur and professional events throughout the country. Recently, state affiliates have been created (e.g., the Colorado Skateboard Association, or CSA).

The aim of the NSA is clearly to create an organized, competitive, and commercialized sport of skateboarding. The NSA states its purposes as follows:

1. To maintain the NSA as a nonprofit corporation for the international betterment of skateboarding and recognition of skateboarding as a sport.
2. To establish an office to be the headquarters for the association in order to communicate with the world on skateboard matters and keep records. (NSA, 1990)

The current president of the NSA, Don Bostick, reiterated this commitment to a corporate form of sport by describing the NSA's goal as making skateboarding "more professional and more accepted, . . . similar to Little League" (personal communication, November 25, 1991).

Subculture of Skateboarding

Members of the subculture whom I observed used the materials created by the skateboard industry, but they did so in a manner that did not fully support the industry's goal of mainstreaming ("Little Leaguing") skateboarding. Resistance to such bureaucratization was also demonstrated in the structure and values of the subculture. There were no exclusive positions, no championships, no elite standards, no end goal to achieve, and nothing to win. Doug, a 25-year-old skater from Welton, described how skating was different from organized sports: "I don't hear skaters whining about, you know, other people being better than them or striving to be, or bumming out because they're not mastering something, whereas in other athletics they do, they're really, ya, there's a pressure to succeed where there isn't in skateboarding because there's not huge goals to attain." In this environment there was little need to compete, as Sam, a young teen from Jamestown, stated: "You don't need to be all that good to have fun . . . [you] don't have to compete to have fun." In fact, competitive attitudes were discouraged, as reflected in the following statement by Jeff, a 17-year-old from Welton: "Nobody really seemed to like competitive natures. For instance, me, Philip, and a couple of our friends all found that to be a really turn off. This guy would pull a really good trick and rub it in their faces. And then there's Hugh who can do stuff and he doesn't go, 'oh wow, bet you can't.' But he's fun to be with . . . and he encourages you, so that's pretty cool."

Within this flexible and informal structure, the skateboarders controlled the physical activity, and they were the experts. This popular practice of skateboarding had no rules, no coaches, and no referees. As Craig, a 21-year-old from Welton, suggested, "It's not as military minded [as other sports] there are no manuals or no coaches . . . [you're] not part of a machine, [you] go at your own pace, to each his own." The participants created their own tricks and games and they determined which tricks they practiced and how long. In the process of controlling their own physical activity, the participants also controlled their own bodies. Such values and behaviors oppose those associated with corporate bureaucratic relations, and in the grassroots practice of skateboarding resistance is evident in the creation of a participant-controlled activity that deemphasizes competition. There is also tension between the grassroots practice of skateboarding and the bureaucratized form of the activity. The following example of overt and explicit resistance is reprised in the more covert and subtle everyday acts of resistance described subsequently.

Amateur Contest
As an Overt Example of Resistance

In the summer of 1991 the Colorado Skateboard Association (CSA) sponsored a series of eight amateur contests along the eastern flank of the Rocky Mountains including the cities of Colorado Springs, Denver, and Jamestown. I attended three of these events. Although the CSA was the major sponsor, most of the work was done at the local level. In each of the cities a local skateboard shop created the contest course and coordinated staff and officials including the CSA volunteers, the judges, and commentators. The CSA volunteers were adult women who handled the finances, registration, and record keeping. The judges were the local skateboarding leaders who were older and also employees at the local skateboard shop. Another local skater would comment in disc jockey style between the music that was blasted over a public address system. Those who officially participated paid an initial $40 fee and $10 more for each competition in which they participated.

Most of those attending the contests were not actually competing but rather participating in the peripheral activities of watching, fraternizing, and skating apart from the contest. These skaters used the contests to meet new people, learn new tricks, and skate on new and challenging courses which they rushed to during the warm-up periods. In addition, many of the contestants were skaters who closely associated with the grassroots form of skateboarding but who defined and used the contest as an opportunity to meet personal needs as opposed to fully adopting the values of the CSA. As Doug stated, "Skaters, even in contests, it's more an attitude of having your best run, making all your tricks as opposed to beating somebody. It's not 'I got to beat this guy, this is the guy I'm going to beat.'" This negotiation between a corporate form of skateboarding and the interests of the skaters is reflected in the registration process. Contestants placed themselves into an appropriate category based on age and experience. Each contestant then had a corresponding registration number and color to denote the category pinned on his shirt (there were no females in the competition). Many of the skaters pinned their numbers so they were difficult to read (e.g., upside down, or at the very bottom of the shirt). This intentional rejection of conformity demonstrates that these skaters were not fully dedicated to values of mainstream sport.

The contests generally followed a set pattern. The order of participation was from the youngest and least experienced to the oldest and most experienced. Between each category there were warm-up periods in which only those who were about to compete were supposed to skate. For the competition, the participants in each category were to perform two rounds of a 2-minute routine on a skateboard course that consisted of a variety of obstacles such as ramps and parking blocks (none of the courses was standardized).

At one of the competitions, the CSA volunteers became concerned about the use of the warm-up periods because several skaters who were not officially entered were using the facilities, and even some who had officially entered were warming up out of sequence. This breach of CSA rules led to an announcement that only those who were about to compete could skate during the warm-up periods, and that included those who had paid an entrance fee but were skating out of turn. The CSA volunteers backed the announcement by adding that anyone who broke these rules would be disqualified. Neither the contestants nor the other skaters paid any heed to this and continued to skate on the equipment during the warm-up periods. The CSA representatives went out on the course and started to police the event. They ejected those who did not have a registration number pinned to their clothes and wrote down the numbers of those who were skating out of turn. Next, they announced over the public address system the numbers of those who had been disqualified.

The loose but smoothly running competition halted as skaters went to the judges' stand to protest. The judges referred the protests to the CSA volunteers. Three skaters argued that the purpose of the event was to encourage skateboarding and that the organizers were not accomplishing that goal by limiting the use of the course. As the argument took place, most of the other skaters observed it, and the announcer started rapping, "You have all been D.Q.'ed . . . D.Q., you went to the Dairy Queen . . . D.Q., dumb queer, the dumb queer went to the Dairy Queen." Finally, a resolution was reached and it was announced that no one was disqualified, but instead the skaters were asked to allow the contestants to use their warm-up period without interference. In other words, the contest returned to a "free-skate" event. At the next competition, which was held 2 weeks later, the commentator sarcastically reminded people, while nonregistered skaters were on the course, that if anyone broke the rules they could be disqualified. No disqualifications occurred. The ability of the skaters to resist and negotiate with the CSA representatives demonstrated that they successfully challenged the official agenda.

The skateboarders' resistance to the CSA-sponsored competition is an overt example of the struggle between the values of corporate bureaucratic interests (e.g., control by authority, elite competition) and the grassroots interests (e.g., control by participants, open participation). This overt opposition was indicative of the more subtle resistance that also occurred at these competitions.

De-Emphasizing Elite Competition

The most frequently observed form of resistance during these amateur contests was opposition to the competetive environment. This was displayed through a variety of behaviors. First, the lack of anxiety about competing was pervasive. The skaters had 2 minutes to impress the judges, but it was quite apparent that very few of the skaters had practiced a routine and there were few attempts to maximize the number of tricks. The majority of the skaters took their time skating a few tricks, taking a breather, and then continuing. This lack of concern for the outcome was particularly striking for one who had been heavily engaged in competitive athletics—the atmosphere was quite different. Not only did the skaters not have a planned routine or try to maximize their number of tricks, but they actually made fun of themselves while performing. For example, at one event the participants passed a curly brown wig through the crowd. Several skaters of various skill levels wore this during their 2 minutes. In addition, skaters who fell or made obvious errors in their tricks commonly stopped and bowed or laughed at themselves and then continued with their 2-minute run (as opposed to, for example, throwing a board or yelling obscenities in disgust).

The second behavior that contradicted the competitive environment that the CSA was trying to create was the extraordinary amount of support, both physical and emotional, the skaters gave each other. For example, most skaters do not own protective gear such as helmets and knee pads, yet the CSA required them to wear such equipment during contests. During these events, the skaters who owned protective gear commonly shared it among the participants. Skaters also demonstrated support when participants lost control and possession of their skateboards during the 2-minute run. In these cases, either the skateboards were quickly recovered by other participants, or other participants rolled their own skateboards out to the skater who had lost his. In addition, when participants made exceptional tricks or good runs, the skaters would show their support by clapping, screaming, and whistling.

I saw no overt signs of competitive attitude, no "in your face, I'm better than you are" gestures such as finger pointing at other participants. No one boasted after a good run, and there were no "end zone" dances of celebration. When skaters were satisfied they expressed it as a personal accomplishment, such as, "Wow, that's the first time I ever pulled off that trick." They did not openly express these as a means of demonstrating superior qualities or of socially bettering themselves.

The competitive environment was often mocked through the explicit lack of concern with regard to time. In all the competitions, the precision and accuracy of timing were disregarded. The commentator had the job of starting and stopping the participant through verbal cues. Often, the commentator would purposefully miscue the participant. For example, the commentator would start the run and then say "time over" 20 seconds later, followed by "just kidding." In addition, the participants often felt no obligation to the clock because several skaters ended their run after they felt it was completed, and not when the official time had expired.

Daily Practices of Resistance

Scott (1990) argues that most resistances occur on a subtle and daily basis, what he refers to as "hidden transcripts." These hidden resistances occur in a language that only the subculture can understand, and it is within subordinate subcultures that a logic of resistance is created. This subtle, covert and daily resistance is what Scott calls "infrapolitics," because it is the grounding on which overt political movements stand. As Scott states, "Each of the forms of disguised resistance, of infrapolitics, is the silent partner of a loud form of public resistance. Thus, piecemeal squatting is the infrapolitical equivalent of an open land invasion: both are aimed at resisting the appropriation of land" (1990, p. 199). The overt resistance to the CSA-sponsored contest exemplifies the skaters' behaviors and the values of their typical daily interactions; it illuminates the infrapolitics of the subculture of skateboarding. One parallel that can be drawn between the amateur contest and the skateboarders' daily practices is the opposition to elite competition.

De-Emphasizing Elite Competition

Especially significant for the subculture of skateboarders was creating a physical activity in which most people could participate, and to encourage participation they de-emphasized the role of competition. In fact, the skaters were very outspoken against competition when used as a means to an elite and exclusive status. All the skaters were asked to describe the characteristics of a skater, and I phrased the question as, "What makes a skater cool or uncool?" Overwhelmingly, they responded that an uncool skater was competitive and exclusive, while a cool skater was supportive and did not show off. Charles blatantly stated, "Skaters who are assholes are people who brag or skate to compete." Within the subculture there were status differences,

but they were not established through competition with others. There were two criteria for high status: One must be highly skilled and creative, and one must not use those skills to belittle others. Although there was skill differentiation, it was not used to promote exclusivity from others because status is gained primarily by promoting cooperation and inclusion. Brian, a young teenager from Welton, commented on this attitude:

> Well, we don't, we're not like competitive, like saying, "I can ollie [a specific skater stunt] higher than you so get away from me," and stuff like that. We're like, we just want to do a few things people are doing, and skaters help out skaters . . . and if I were to ask a good skater like some people I skate with, like Brad Jones, he's the best skater I know in Welton. If I asked him, he would like give me tips and stuff, you know, on how to do it, and that's just how we do it, we want to show other people how to skate.

My 2 years of observing skaters' interactions confirms these statements. Skaters were very supportive of each other. It was common to see skaters who on their first meeting encouraged each other, gave tips, and laughed at their own mistakes. When I frequented the various privately owned skateboard parks, I often saw the more skilled skaters help the newcomers, especially in the skill of dropping into a half-pipe ramp. A half-pipe is a ramp that literally looks like piping cut in half lengthwise. The basic technique is to roll back and forth in the half-pipe. The next step is to "drop in" to the half-pipe. To drop in is to start skating from the top edge of the ramp. The skater situates the board so that only the two back wheels are touching the edge of the ramp while most of the board is extended in the air and toward the middle of the ramp. The skater places most of his or her weight on the back wheels, and then to drop in, the skater rolls the back wheels over the edge and drops the nose of the board into the ramp, which starts the rolling motion down the side of the ramp. Dropping in is nerve-racking, and, therefore, emotional support along with technical tips is very helpful.

The support given by skaters is in marked contrast to what is common in more traditional sports being played by young people. For example, one day I passed a public tennis court where two preadolescent boys were playing tennis. They were yelling at each other about how good they were and announcing how they were going to "kick" the other one's "ass." Unlike the skaters, they did not show each other tips on playing, support the good shots of the other, or laugh at each other. The significant aspect of this observation was the response I received when describing this incident to a group of skaters in Welton. One of the skaters, Doug, commented, "That's because we don't skate against somebody, we skate with them."

The implications of competition for friendships and self-esteem were concerns addressed by many skaters. They felt that the lack of competition enhanced opportunities for friendship and self-esteem, while sport that emphasized competition was a difficult place to make friendships and foster self-esteem. For example, Eric stated, "In skating you're only responsible for you. If you mess up, you won't mess up the whole team, [you're] not going to lose friends over messing up in skating. . . . If you're the worst one on the baseball team others give you shit [and that] makes you feel bad. In skating if you are bad, no one makes you feel bad about that."

The vast majority of skaters explicitly differentiated skateboarding from mainstream competitive sport. Pamela, a 19-year-old skater, made this comparison:

Soccer is a lot of pressure . . . you have to be as good if not better than everybody else, you have to be, otherwise you don't get to play at all. Skating you can't do that. You just have to push yourself harder and harder. Swimming is just sort of there, you get timed, now for me you go against the clock. Now when you skate you don't go against anything, you just skate. That's what it is.

In addition, skaters often mocked the mainstream emphasis on competition and winning. For example, Jeff and Philip shared with me an inside joke about dancing that they used to ridicule the pervasiveness of competition and the win-at-all-costs attitude. Philip, Jeff's younger brother, plays in a local rock-and-roll band, and the type of music they play usually involves a "pit," which is a dance space where dancing is rough and there is plenty of physical contact. Philip: "And this guy walks by and he's wearing a Yankees hat and a Jordan T-shirt, a typical jock looking guy, and he walks by and he leans over to his friend and he goes, 'Man, is there going to be a pit here, if there is, dude, I'm going to win.'" Both Philip and Jeff laughed, and Jeff commented, "The object is not to win." The general de-emphasis on competition indicates that the meaning of skating is based on other standards, and for skaters

I talked with, these were values that promoted the participants' control of the activity.

Participant Control

Another parallel that can be drawn between the skateboarders' behavior at the amateur contest and their daily practices was the resistance to an elite or authoritarian-controlled sport, because in both situations the participants controlled their activity. The popular practice of skateboarding does not use rules, referees, coaches, or organized contests. As Paul claimed, "[You] don't need uniforms, and no coach to tell you what to do and how to do it." Kathleen, an 18-year-old skater, added, "No referees, no penalties, no set plays. You can do it anywhere and there is not a lot of training." This lack of formal structure led to a very flexible environment where the participants not only controlled their own activity but engaged in creative endeavors. Often, the skaters created and named their own games and tricks. The two brothers, Jeff and Philip, discussed this flexible and creative emphasis. Philip: "Skateboarding is young and there are so many new tricks people are doing, it's not like baseball where all the rules have been set down." Jeff: "Well, there are no rules to skating." Philip: "When was the last time someone invented something in baseball?"

Most of the skating I observed was not bound by rules; rather, it tested the physical limits and imagination of the participants. Generally, a skating session involved practicing certain techniques, finding fun places to skate, and trying to do new tricks on the new obstacles found. When skaters created more organized forms of games, they were the ones who made the rules. Different groups of skaters created different games, but all incorporated some form of risk-taking challenges. Variations of follow-the-leader were common. Generally, a skater led a line of others through various tricks and obstacles; when the leader made a mistake (couldn't "land" a trick), then he or she went to the back of the line and the next person was the new leader.

The lack of elite control was reflected in the lack of elite standards; as Craig commented, "There is no such thing as a perfect '10' for a trick." Skaters challenged themselves at whatever level of skill they had. Effort and participation were essential to skating, not achieving some elite defined objective. These values and the ability to control their physical activity often led to feelings of empowerment. Many skaters expressed this simply by stating that they loved to learn new tricks and enjoyed seeing themselves improve. Grace, a 21-year-old skater, drew the connection more explicitly by discussing how she did not want skating to become a sport because she did not want practices, coaches, and specific tricks to learn: "For who's to say what trick is better? I like to do stuff that feels cool, that gives me butterflies in my stomach."

The participants' desire to control their activity was reflected in their statements about having more flexibility to be creative or to be expressive through skateboarding. For example, James, a college freshman, wrote this in an English paper: "Skating to me is all about having a good time. This is easy to do while skating since to me skating is relaxing. Skating is all based on being creative with the mind. This starts with the mind, then goes to the tricks I do." Doug claimed,

> A lot of them [skaters] are really involved with artistic endeavors, are very artistic. You can see the parallel; it's kind of a freedom of expression that skating is. How do you express yourself playing football, playing basketball? When you're skating it's, basically skating reflects your mood at the time and how you're skating, what you are doing, you know, it's definitely, you know, a way to express yourself.

Although it can be argued that one can express oneself through organized sport, what Doug argued for was the degree of flexibility in that expression. In a separate interview, Mark explicitly addressed this by claiming that different styles of skating are accepted, whereas he felt one would be kicked off the football team for having a different style. Grace's statement about her frustration over skating epitomizes these concerns: "[Skateboarding] is a symbol of freedom that can't be cut up and processed and sold, [one] can't do that with freedom."

The opposition of skateboarders to the CSA-sponsored contest is an overt and explicit example of the daily and more subtle resistance to the values and norms associated with corporate bureaucracies and corporate bureaucratic sport. Skateboarders resisted the values and norms of elite competition, and authority as expert, by encouraging cooperation and creating a participant-controlled activity.

Resistance and Social Change

Popular culture is a site in which both hegemonic and counterhegemonic interests are expressed and lived simultaneously, and although resistance behaviors have the potential to transform dominant social relations into more equitable social relations, resistance does not automatically lead to wide-scale social change. Many resistance theorists note that the behavior they study may ostensibly oppose or challenge dominant social relations, but that does not guarantee that social change will take place (Aggelton, 1987; King, 1982; Lesko, 1988; Scott, 1990; Stevenson, 1991; Willis, 1977; Young, 1983). In fact, oppositional behavior is often full of contradictions that can lead to the reproduction of dominant social relations. Those who study resistance place the outcome of that behavior on a continuum of social change, from behavior that leads to social change to behavior that actually reproduces the dominant norms and values (e.g., Willis, 1977).

The two most common categories of resistance behavior are challenges and accommodations. Challenges are the behaviors that effectively change dominant relations, whereas accommodations are behaviors full of contradiction that do not effectively change dominant relations and, therefore, may sometimes reproduce them. For example, Stevenson (1991) described some of the contradictions he found in elite Christian athletes that limited the potential for social change. Although their Christian behavior challenged some common forms of cheating, their behavior did not effectively challenge or change the dominant structure of elite sport. Similarly, Young (1983) found that the rugby players in his study resisted some dominant relations but simultaneously reinforced others. The rugby players resisted the mainstream values that emphasize winning and the work ethic but reproduced sexist values through their behavior at social occasions, most notably in the ritual drinking songs.

The most common contradiction evident in the skateboarders was their sexist behavior. The female skater is a notable exception: Only 4 of the 41 skaters I interviewed were females. Females who were associated with skateboarding were commonly placed in the marginal roles of girlfriend or supporter and were often referred to as "Skate Betties." The females I interviewed were quite aware of these attitudes that discouraged their participation, yet they continued to skateboard because they enjoyed it for many of the same reasons as males. For many females, the males' behavior discouraged them from participating or marginalized them by labeling them as Skate Betties. Therefore, the transformative benefits of resistance were limited primarily to males. In addition, a small faction of the skateboarders were self-proclaimed racists, calling themselves "skinheads." The comments about the disqualifications during the contest, such as "the dumb queer went to the Dairy Queen," may also indicate homophobia. Although the subculture of skateboarders resists many of the social relations associated with capitalism, in an apparent contradiction to what might be expected it generally does not resist those associated with sexism, racism, and homophobia.

Also, the vast majority of the skaters did not intend their behavior to have widespread social ramifications; their intention was much more individual or small-group oriented, local rather than global. The contradictions that arise in oppositional subcultures limit the potential and scale of change. Notwithstanding, some change did occur because of the alternative nature of the subculture. Essentially, the skaters wanted and created an alternative sport, one that fit their needs of participation and control. This type of resistance is more closely associated with Scott's (1990) notion of "infrapolitics" because its emphasis is on creating and maintaining a self-governing activity in which alternative relations can be lived, rather than advancing these relations to alter other social institutions. However, given the recent admonitions to "act locally and think globally," the potential for more widespread social change exists in such local "alternatives."

Implications of Social Resistance

The implications of social resistance are based on the assumption that human behavior is not determined solely by a dominant ideology or economic relations, but rather that humans are able to respond creatively to their social and economic conditions through various daily and cultural practices. As McLaren (1985) stated, "At the level of human agency, hegemony is both sustained and contested through our 'style' of engaging in the world and the ways in which we ritualize our daily lives: our general embodiments, our rhythmical practices, and our lived forms of resistance" (p. 92). The implication is that humans can challenge dominant practices, create alternative practices, and potentially create social change through cultural practices.

One of the main criticisms of resistance theorists is that they have a tendency to romanticize the revolutionary aspects of oppositional behavior, but many resistance theorists explicitly note that such behavior does not automatically produce social change. They argue that both challenges and accommodations occur in oppositional behaviors, and that contradictory behavior does not undermine their significance for human agency in social change:

> Certainly many "resistances" fall short of challenging basic social structures—but to ask for their success is to ask for an epochal shift every Sunday afternoon! We've been exploring the possibility of a middle course which avoids saying just because resistances do not overthrow a dominant system, then they are related only to its support. Resistance may be deeply implicated in accommodation, but not in a way which is inevitable, planned and wholly programmed as a pre-existing function of dominant institutions and ideology.... Here is a scope for change, for politics, for becoming,—not for utopianism or despair. (Willis, 1983, pp. 136-137)

Even though the social impact of skateboarding is not transformative for most people, the significance lies in the fact that these participants were empowered to act in their best interests; they created and experienced alternative types of relations that met their needs. The ability of skaters to use a physical activity in this manner suggests that other activities can be created to reclaim power. The knowledge of creating alternatives can serve as a blueprint for future interaction or social actions and cultural products, and it can also inspire and give credence to the idea that there are social choices and that groups of people have the ability to create alternatives.

References

Aggelton, P. (1987). *Rebels without a cause? Middle class youth and the transition from school to work.* London: The Falmer Press.

Bennett, T. (1986). Introduction: Popular culture and "the turn to Gramsci." In T. Bennett, C. Mercer, & J. Woollacott (Eds.), *Popular culture and social relations* (pp. xi-xix). Milton Keynes, England: Open University Press.

Berlage, G.I. (1982, May). Are children's competitive team sports teaching corporate values? *ARENA Review,* **6**(1), 15-21.

Birrell, S., & Richter, D. (1987). Is a diamond forever? Feminist transformations of sport. *Women's Studies International Forum,* **10**, 395-409.

Bray, C. (1988). Sport and social change: Socialist feminist theory. *Journal of Physical Education, Recreation and Dance, 59,* 50-53.

Donnelly, P. (1988). Sport as a site for popular resistance. In R. Gruneau (Ed.), *Popular cultures and political practices* (pp. 69-82). Toronto, ON: Garamond Press.

Donnelly, P. (1993). Subcultures in sport: Resilience and transformation. In A. Ingham & J. Loy (Eds.), Sport in social development: Traditions, transitions, and transformations (pp. 119-145). Champaign, IL: Human Kinetics.

Foley, D. (1990). *Learning capitalist culture: Deep in the heart of Tejas.* Philadelphia: University of Pennsylvania Press.

Gray, J. (1992, November). *Mountain biking as counterculture.* Paper presented at the North American Society for the Sociology of Sport Conference, Toledo, OH.

Gramsci, A. (1971). *Selections from prison notebooks of Antonio Gramsci.* New York: International Publishers.

Hebdige, D. (1979). *Subcultures: The meaning of style.* London: Metheun.

King, N. (1982). Children's play as a form of resistance in the classroom. *Journal of Education, 164,* 320-329.

Klein, A. (1991). *Sugarball: The American game, the Dominican dream.* New Haven, CT: Yale University Press.

Lesko, N. (1988). The curriculum of the body: Lessons from a Catholic high school. In L. Roman & L. Christian-Smith (Eds.), *Becoming feminine: The politics of popular culture* (pp. 123-142). London: The Falmer Press.

Maeda, K. (1991, October). Rights for skateboarders [Letter to the editor]. *Windsor Beacon,* p. 17.

McLaren, P. (1985). The ritual dimensions of resistance: Clowning and symbolic inversion. *Journal of Education, 167,* 84-97.

Messner, M. (1992). *Power at play: Sports and the problem of masculinity.* Boston: Beacon Press.

National Skateboard Association. (1990). Packet for new members.

O'Hanlon, T. (1980). Interscholastic athletics, 1900-1940: Shaping citizens for unequal roles in the modern industrial state. *Educational Theory, 30,* 89-103.

Sage, G. (1990). Power and ideology in American sport: A critical perspective. Champaign, IL: Human Kinetics.

Scott, J. (1990). *Domination and the arts of resistance: Hidden transcripts.* New Haven, CT: Yale University Press.

Stevenson, C. (1991, November). *Christianity as a hegemonic and counter-hegemonic device in elite sport.* Paper presented at the annual conference for the North American Society for the Sociology of Sport, Milwaukee, WI.

Whitson, D. (1984). Sport and hegemony: On the construction of the dominant culture. *Sociology of Sport Journal, 1,* 64-78.

Williams, R. (1977). *Marxism and literature.* Oxford, UK: Oxford University Press.

Willis, P. (1977). *Learning to labour: How working class kids get working class jobs.* New York: Columbia University Press.

Willis, P. (1983). Cultural production and theories of reproduction. In L. Barton & S. Walker (Eds.), *Race, class, and education* (pp. 107-138). London: Croom Helm.

Young, K. (1983). *The subculture of rugby players: A form of resistance and incorporation.* Unpublished master's thesis, McMaster University, Hamilton, ON.

Note

1. The names of cities and participants have been changed to help ensure the anonymity of the participants.

Acknowledgments

I would like to thank George Sage and Peter Donnelly for their insightful suggestions. I would also like to acknowledge James Beal and the anonymous reviewers for their helpful comments. I appreciate the support of the Department of Physical Education at Northern Illinois University during the writing of this manuscript.

Author Note

At the time of publication, the National Skateboard Association was defunct.

UNIT III

Children in Sport

Objectives

The unit examines how organized competitive sports for children measure up to the characteristics of what Moore and Anderson, and Devereux, have called "the essential features of a really good learning environment." Further, the unit examines the structure and impacts of highly organized sports programs on children.

Since the founding of Little League Baseball at Williamsport, Pennsylvania, in 1939, adult-controlled sports programs for children have grown dramatically. Current estimates are that more than 30 million children now participate in over 40 sports in these highly popular programs. The expansion of such sports programs initially generated little interest among social scientists, and the sociopsychological impacts on the participants were little understood. In fact, scholarly investigation of youth sports programs suffered, until the early 1970s, from what we can only describe as benign neglect. More recently, several researchers have attempted to answer the question, "How good are organized sports programs for children?"

The current literature suggests that high-performance children's sports are quasi-professionalized environments that place inordinate demands, both physically and psychologically, on young children. As a society, we assume that parents, coaches, and program administrators have the children's best interests at heart and protect them from abuses and excesses. Yet the available evidence suggests otherwise. The three selections that follow suggest that basic changes may be needed, including the way these programs are organized and managed.

In the initial reading, Devereux focuses on what participation in highly competitive, adult-organized athletic programs does *not* do for young children. He argues that "Little Leaguism" is threatening to wipe out the spontaneous culture of free play and games among American children, thereby robbing them of "childish fun" and valuable learning experiences.

Noteworthy in this article is Devereux's discussion of the characteristics of what Moore and Anderson (1969) suggest are the "essential features" of a good learning environment. That is, a good learning environment should

- permit free and safe exploration by the child,
- be self-pacing,
- be "agent responsive" in the sense that the environment should provide the child with immediate and relevant feedback,
- permit the discovery and learning of underlying principles and rules,
- be autotelic (self-rewarding), and
- be responsive to a child's activities in a way that permits and encourages the enactment of the roles of "agent" (initiator, such as leader) and "patient" (recipient, such as follower).

What do children learn in environments possessing such characteristics? The literature suggests the following:

- They learn to take a reflexive view of themselves and develop insight and self-understanding.
- They learn about competition and winning and losing in relatively nonthreatening contexts and can experiment with different success styles.
- Such play environments provide "buffered learning experiences" for dangerous or anxiety-

59

producing psychological problems in the context of play.

- Children learn in mock combat that they can safely express aggression without hurting others.
- Children learn to master dangerous emotions in situations in which they do not face "reality consequences" (as with real life) until they are mature and able to deal with them effectively.
- In the context of play, children learn the underlying principles of rules, their underlying logic, and the notion of fair play.
- Children also learn about social relationships and the informal rules that govern group conduct.
- Finally, through exploration and discovery in the context of play, they learn how to formulate general moral principles that help them make independent decisions.

Devereux, drawing on the works of early psychologists such as Piaget and Kohlberg, among others, suggests that the authoritarian control of sports by adults hinders children's growth and development and stifles the development of mature moral judgment.

If indeed the traditional model of sport as employed in children's Little League, Pop Warner Football, and other similar programs stifles important learning in children, it behooves us to examine such activities and evaluate them using the criteria provided by Devereux.

We believe that Devereux develops a strong case that the culture of children's games in America is sadly impoverished. Less structure and a return to spontaneity is perhaps the most defensible direction for the future if we care about what our children learn in sport. The reader is encouraged to review the "essential features of a good learning environment" and evaluate just how well, or poorly, adult-controlled programs for children measure up.

In the second selection, Landers and Fine describe how status, competitiveness, and gender roles are reinforced by participation in organized tee ball. This process appears to be encouraged both by the structure of the activity, that is, the reward system for superior skill and performance, and by the expectations of the coaches, who clearly stressed and rewarded winning above all else. In particular, coaches perceived the girls as less skilled and less serious, and consequently assigned them to noncentral positions—positions that required less ball handling. The resulting skill-prestige hierarchies in favor of the boys, and the differential treatment they received, created a setting that further reinforced gender differences

in athletic skill. The girls were made to feel inferior. Consequently, the girls did not feel welcome, and their interest in tee ball waned during the season.

In the third selection, Green, a sport-management expert, studied the effects of an alternative sports program on several measures of satisfaction, sport involvement, and attitude. The program was designed as a child-centered alternative to more traditional programs. The findings were supportive, although some modifications appeared necessary to infuse the program with some "real soccer." The author also found that parents who preferred the modified program differed from parents with children in traditional programs in several significant ways. In particular, they were more concerned about adult intrusion in children's sports and held less professionalized attitudes toward play than parents of children in traditional programs.

References

Devereux, E. (1971). Backyard vs. Little League baseball. Paper presented at conference on sport and deviance, Brockport, NY (by permission of author).

Green, B. (1997). Action research in youth soccer: Assessing the acceptability of an alternative program. *Journal of Sport Management*, **11**: 29-44.

Landers, M.A., & Fine, G.A. (1996). Learning life's lessons in tee ball. The reinforcement of gender and status in kindergarten sport. *Sociology of Sport Journal*, **13**: 87-93.

Moore, O.K., & Anderson, A.R. (1969). Some principles for the design of clarifying educational environments. In D. Goslin (Ed.), *Handbook of socialization theory and research* (pp. 571-613). New York: Rand McNally.

Discussion Questions

Edward Devereux

1. According to the author, what has happened to children's games in America, and why? Discuss and explain.
2. List some of the functions of informal children's play activities.
3. What are the essential features of a "good" learning environment? Identify and discuss.
4. Do you agree with Devereux's contention that children have more fun in unstructured play and game settings (in which they run the show)

than in structured, adult-controlled activities? Discuss and explain.

5. Describe and evaluate the research findings on competition the author refers to in this article.

6. Compare backyard versus Little League baseball as learning settings and evaluate their possible impacts on children.

7. Observe young children in your community in both formal and informal play settings and relate your observations to the points raised in Devereux's article.

Melissa Landers and Gary Alan Fine

1. Briefly explain the purpose of the study.

2. Explain the various ways low-status players were made to feel that they did not really count.

3. (a) In what ways did the coaches and the peer group reinforce athletic skill? (b) What are the possible impacts of this process on young children? Discuss and explain.

4. (a) In what ways did the program help decrease the girls' interest in tee ball? (b) What role did the coach play in this process? Discuss and explain.

5. (a) What were the coaches' views about girls in tee ball? (b) How did they express these views? Discuss and explain.

6. (a) Describe and explain the differences in the duties of the male and female coaches. (b) Speculate about the messages that such differences send to young children in sport.

7. What do children, females in particular, learn about gender, athletic ability, and status inequality in sport? Discuss and debate.

Christine Green

1. Identify and explain the factors that influenced the development of this modified soccer league.

2. Identify and discuss the structure and goals of the modified soccer league. How do these differ from conventional soccer leagues?

3. Discuss and explain the purpose of the project.

4. Summarize and comment on the findings of the project.

5. Discuss and speculate on the implications of the findings with respect to children in sport.

6. Parents who preferred a more traditional model of sport differed from parents who espoused the alternate sports program. (a) Discuss and speculate on the possible differences among the two groups of parents. (b) In class, develop profiles of the two groups of parents based on the information provided in the article and your own knowledge and experience.

Backyard Versus Little League Baseball: Some Observations on the Impoverishment of Children's Games in Contemporary America

Edward C. Devereux

In this presentation, I plan to focus on a few more general issues. Most generally, my critique of Little League Baseball, and other such major sports programs for children, will be based not so much on what participation in such activities does for the child-participants as on what it does not do for them. I will argue that "Little Leaguism" is threatening to wipe out the spontaneous culture of free play and games among American children, and thus that it is robbing our children not just of their childish fun but also of some of their most valuable learning experiences.

On the Impoverishment of Children's Games in America

One way to gain insight about what is happening in contemporary America is to look at ourselves in cross-cultural and historical perspective. Earlier this year, I spent two months in Japan, carrying out a survey among Japanese school children. While there, I spent as much time as I could observing children in informal play settings such as parks, neighborhood playgrounds, school yards, apartment court yards and city streets. What struck me most forcefully was the observation that Japanese children seem to spend very little time just "hang-ing around"; whenever two or more children found themselves together, they seemed to move very quickly into some kind of self-organized but rule-oriented play. Though I made no formal inventory, I was impressed with the great variety and richness of the games I observed. Although the Japanese also have Little League Baseball, most of the games I observed were carried out wholly without adult instigation or supervision.

On one occasion my wife and I observed a group of some dozen kindergarten children playing ring games in a public park. I have no doubt that these children were brought to the park by some teacher or adult supervisor, and I kept waiting for some adult to appear to structure the next game for them. But during the 45 minutes we remained in the vicinity no adult ever approached or spoke to the children. Evidently the game repertory, the motivation to play, and the ability to organize and pace their own activities were well rooted in the children's own heads.

Later in the year, I went to Israel on another research project, and again I spent as much time as I could observing the informal play activities of the Israeli children. Here also I was impressed with the enormous variety of spontaneous games and play activities I observed. On this, we also have some impressive research documentation in the work of the Israeli psychologist Rivka Eifermann (1971a). In her study, a team of some 150 observers recorded

Reprinted from Devereux, 1971.

the play activities of some 14,000 Israeli school children in Kibbutzim, Moshavim and cities, in school yards, playgrounds, and streets over a two-year period. One result of this research was the compilation of an encyclopedia of over 2,000 games the children were observed to be playing, including many bewildering variants on such well-known games as soccer, tag, and hop-scotch, as well as hundreds of less well-known games, also in endless variations (Eifermann, 1971b). Most of these games, moreover, were being played wholly without adult instigation or supervision.

All this challenges us to raise the question: What has happened to the culture of children's games in America? Looking back to my own childhood, some 50 years ago, I can recall literally dozens of games we played regularly and with enthusiasm—puss in the corner, red rover, capture the flag, one-o-cat, statues, stealing sticks, blind man's buff, croquet, leap frog, duck on the rock, prisoner's base, and many, many more. No doubt some of these are still around, in vestigial form; but my impression is that I rarely see these, or other games like them, being played spontaneously by children. Those which are played seem to be adult-instigated and supervised in schools, camps or other organized play settings, or in party settings in homes. And even here, our game culture has become sadly impoverished. Ask any group of children what they did at a birthday party and nine out of ten will say they pinned the tail on the donkey. Halloween? Bob for apples and tricks or treats! What ever happened to the tricks, incidentally? We have institutionalized and sterilized Halloween, and thereby killed most of its creativity and fun. Most generally, it appears that our game culture has become sadly impoverished from lack of use and from an excess of adult supervision and control. "Come on, children, we're all going to play a game now!" "Do we *have* to?" You can almost hear the groans.

On these trends, there is also some research evidence in a fascinating study by Sutton-Smith and Rosenberg (1971). In their monograph, these authors compare game preferences of American children as documented in four different research studies spanning a 60-year period from the late 1890s to the late 1950s. Even though these four studies are not strictly comparable, nevertheless certain general trends are impressively clear. The great variety of once-popular indoor and backyard skill games, such as croquet and quoits, have all declined in interest, to be replaced by the ubiquitous ping-pong. Leader games, such as Simon Says, statues, and follow the leader, are now of little interest for boys. Chasing games, like tag, are now acceptable only to very little children. Central person parlor games, such as hide the thimble, forfeits, and twenty questions, have mostly disappeared, as have the endless varieties of ring games, such as drop the handkerchief and London Bridge, and the team guessing and acting games, like charades. Individual games of skill—remember mumble-de-peg?—are withering away. Virtually all of the undifferentiated team games, such as hare and hound, prisoner's base, etc., have either disappeared or declined in interest, as boys have devoted more of their attention to a few major sports. And even here, the authors conclude, the range of choice has narrowed significantly: ". . . trends would indicate that boys are spending more and more time on fewer sports. Bowling, basketball, and football improve in rank positions, but all other sports decline . . . This would appear to be further evidence of the increasing circumscription of the boy's play role" (p. 47).

How can we account for this apparently very real constriction in the game culture of American children? How do American children really spend their spare time? In the presence of this audience, I am tempted to say that they are all out there on the baseball and football fields, or on the hockey rinks, participating according to season in the sports programs organized for them by schools and other adult sponsoring agencies. In fact, as we all know, several hundred thousand of them are doing just that, for example, as members of the now more than 40,000 Little League Baseball teams. For these children, there can be no doubt that such team activities capture a very large share of their time and attention. In one study reported by Skubic (1956), for example, 81 out of 96 Little League players in the Santa Maria area "reported that half to most of their leisure time during the whole year is spent on baseball" (p. 102).

But even conceding that a very large absolute number of children are now involved in such organized sports, the fact remains that the vast majority of children in the 8 to 12 age range are not. What do they do instead? A great deal of unstructured, non-rule-oriented play: bike riding, for example, still ranks very high with both boys and girls. In American homes, toys, hobby kits, and various proprietary games such as Monopoly still find wide acceptance among children. Just hanging around and talking, or very informal horseplay with friends, now occupies a very large share of the typical preadolescent's time. Finally, and by far the most important, there is television watching, to which this age group now devotes some 20 hours per week.

On this, I would speculate that the availability of a mass television audience has had a lot to do with the extraordinary ascendancy of Big Leaguism in America, and perhaps indirectly, of Little Leaguism as well. By focusing the attention of millions of viewers on a handful of major sports, and on the heroic teams and individual stars within them, we have converted ourselves to a nation of spectators. For most of us, sports are something to be watched, not played—or at least not by amateurs.

Personally, I doubt that very many children in the 8-12 range are television sports addicts, though some undoubtedly are. But children surely perceive where their father's interests are focused, and by 10 or 12 are well aware of the extraordinary pay-off value of success in major sports in America. They see how the star athletes are rewarded in college and high school sports, and how pleased their fathers are at any athletic achievements of their own. I suspect that Little Leaguism for elementary school children is fostered more by the parents than by the children themselves, though for some it falls on well-cultivated ground. Here is a chance to "play" at something really important that parents and adults generally seem to take very seriously.

But even for the children who have no special interest or competence in any major sport, probably a majority of all children, or who are actually alienated by the whole subculture of organized, competitive sports, the model is still there and highly salient. Against the heroic, if perhaps somewhat myopic, standards of Big League or Little League sports who would dare propose a simple game of puss in the corner, capture the flag, or red rover? Kid stuff, unworthy of the time and attention of any redblooded American boy past the age of seven or eight!

On the Educational Functions of Play and Games

Why should we care about what has been happening to the recreational and spare time activities of our children? In approaching an answer to this question, I would like to say just a bit about the functions of games and informal play activities in childhood and comment specifically about the kinds of learning which may occur in spontaneous, self-organized children's games. I will then go on to assess how organized, adult sponsored competitive sports stack up against this model.

It has long been recognized that children's games and play activities represent miniature and playful models of a wide variety of cultural and social activities and concerns. To take a familiar example, the activities of little girls revolving about dolls and playing house undoubtedly serve some function in the process of anticipatory socialization to future roles as mothers and housekeepers. Similarly, in the games of boys, such elemental social themes as leading and following, of capturing and rescuing, of attacking and defending, of concealing and searching, are endlessly recombined in games of varying complexity in what Sutton-Smith (1971) has called a syntax of play. For example, the chase and elude themes of tag are combined with the capture and rescue elements of release in the more complex game of prisoner's base. When the chase and elude themes of tag are combined with the attack and defend themes of dodge ball, we have the more complex game type represented in football.

As Roberts and Sutton-Smith (1962) have pointed out, games of different types represent microcosmic social structures in which various different styles of competing, and of winning or losing, are subtly encoded. Through their participation in a wide variety of *different* game types, in which the various elements of skill, chance, and strategy are variously recombined in gradually increasing complexity, children find an opportunity to experiment with *different* success styles, and gain experience in a variety of cognitive and emotional processes which cannot yet be learned in full scale cultural participation.

I would stress in particular, at this point, that for game experiences to serve their socialization functions effectively, it is essential that children engage in a wide variety of different types of games, and at varying levels of complexity appropriate to their stage of development. If the American game culture is becoming overly constricted, will our coping styles and success strategies as adults also become constricted? Could it be, as journalists have speculated, that America's inability to cope with the realities of world politics stems in part from the fact that our president, a football addict, is committed to a narrow-gage game plan and success style which is grossly inadequate to deal with those of opponents who are skilled in such sophisticated games as chess and go?

There is another feature of spontaneous games which renders them especially effective in serving as "buffered learning experiences" for our children: The fact that the models they embody are miniaturized and rendered relatively safe by the "having fun" context in which they typically occur. As Lewin (1944) noted, games tend to occur on a "plane of unreality," a fact which renders them especially well suited as contexts in which to "toy" with potentially dangerous psychological and emotional problems. Thus Phillips (1960) has observed that many children's games provide a miniature and relatively safe context in which children may gain useful experience in the mastery of anxiety. Consider in this connection the titillating joys of peek-a-boo, the universally popular game in which infants toy with the anxieties associated with mother-absence, and the happy resolution achieved in the discovery that one can bring her back by uncovering one's eyes. In playful games, older children deliberately project themselves into situations involving risk, uncertainty and insecurity, and the tensions generated by the conflicting valences of hope and fear. Particularly where some element of chance is involved, as it is in many children's games, failure is less invidious and hence more easily bearable. Similarly, in games involving mock combat, aggression may be safely expressed because, as Menninger (1942, p. 175) pointed out, "one can hurt people without really hurting them"; and of course without too much danger of being really hurt yourself.

I must stress in particular the point that children's games are effective as expressive models for gaining experience in the mastery of dangerous emotions very largely because of their miniature scale and their playful context. They are rendered safe by remaining on a plane of unreality, in which "reality consequences" do not have to be faced.

I would like to go on to argue that "child's play," far from being a frivolous waste of time as it is so often pictured in our task-oriented, Puritan culture, may in fact represent an optimum setting for children's learning.

To gain some perspective on this matter, consider what psychologists are saying about the kinds of conditions in which optimum learning may occur. In designing their famous computer-typewriter-teaching-machine, or "automatic reflexive environment," O.K. Moore and A.R. Anderson (1969) were careful to take into account what they believe to be the essential features of a really good learning environment: That it should permit free and safe exploration; that it should be self-pacing; that it should be "agent-responsive"; that it should provide immediate and directly relevant feedback; that it should be "productive," that is to say, so structured that a wide variety of ramifying principles and interconnections can be learned; that it should be "autotelic" or self-rewarding, that is to say, related directly to the child's own spontaneous interests and motivations; and finally, that it should be responsive to the child's own initiatives in a way which will permit him to take a "reflexive view of himself." Otherwise put, the environment should be such that the child may alternate in the roles of "active agent" and "patient," and at times may step back and view the whole setting from the viewpoint of an "umpire."

If we take these principles seriously, as I believe we must, it is easy to see why many children do not learn very much in traditionally structured school settings. For in such traditional schools, the pupils are "patients" and the teacher is the active agent. The "principles" to be learned are explained, perhaps even demonstrated by the teacher, rather than being discovered by the children themselves. Learning is defined as "work," with all the implications that the children, left to follow their own motivations and interests freely, would rather be doing something else. The pacing of activities is rigidly controlled by the teacher, or by the school schedules, or by the tyranny of the lesson plan. And the evaluative feedback, coming from the teacher rather than from the materials themselves, is often delayed, irrelevant, and peculiarly invidious.

I will try to show you that these principles, so widely violated in the regular educational settings in which children are supposed to be learning, are all admirably incorporated in a spontaneous, self-organized, and self-paced game of backyard baseball, and in many other children's games and play activities. And I will argue that Little League Baseball—and other adult-organized and supervised sports—do a pretty good job of bankrupting most of the features of this, and other, learning models.

But first I would call your attention to the observations of another eminent child psychologist about the functions of spontaneous, self-organized children's games. In his classic study of the moral development of children, Jean Piaget (1932) noted that social rules, for the young child, originally appear as part of the external situation, defined and enforced by powerful adults. At an early stage of "moral realism," the child conforms because he must to avoid punishment and to maintain the needed goodwill of his parents. But he feels no internalized moral commitment to these rules, because he had no share in defining them, because they often seem arbitrary or unnecessary, and because they are often imposed in an arbitrary and punitive fashion. Piaget argued that the experiences children have in informal games and play activities with their own age mates play an essential role in moving them beyond this stage of moral realism. In an informal game of marbles, for example, where there is no rule book and no adult rule-imposer or enforcer, and where the children know "the rules" only vaguely or have differences of opinion about what they really are, the children must finally face up to the realization that some kinds of rules really are necessary; they must decide for themselves what kinds of rules are "fair," to keep the game going, and interesting, and fun for all; they must participate in establishing the rules and must learn how to enforce them on themselves and others. Experiences like this, Piaget theorized, play a vital role in helping the child grow to a more mature stage of moral development based on the principles of cooperation and consent.

Along somewhat similar lines, Parsons and Bales (1955) have argued that the enormous power differentials between adults and children present serious obstacles to certain kinds of essential learning. For example, adult authority usually appears to young children to be heavily ascriptive in character; authority flows from the fact that one is a parent, a teacher, a coach, or simply an "adult," possessed of awesome powers to punish or reward. But the relevance of this power is not always obvious. Within the peer group, however, where differences in power are on a much smaller scale, leadership is much more likely to be based on relevant, universalistic criteria. A child leader is accepted and followed only to the extent that he effectively expresses the children's own values and helps them to work or play together in self-satisfying ways. It is largely within the framework of informally organized peer groups, these authors reason, that the child learns to conceive of social relationships as being patterned on relevant, universalistic principles in which people must get along in common subjection to general rules.

Kohlberg (1962) has pointed to yet another feature of unstructured children's play for the processes of moral development. If the "rules" are rigidly fixed once and for all by parents, teachers, coaches, or rule books, the child may learn them and perhaps accept them. But he will not gain much experience in the development of mature moral judgment. According to Kohlberg, it is only with some real experience with dissonance, as when the rules are ambiguous or when there is some cross-pressure or opinion difference about which rules should apply, that children learn to understand how certain more general moral principles must be formulated to help them decide for themselves what they should do. Much of my own recent research

has tended to support the notion that informal peer group experiences and their accompanying dissonance contribute to the development of moral autonomy in children (Devereux, 1970) and that authoritarian control by adults has precisely the opposite effect (Devereux, 1972).

Backyard Versus Little League Baseball, Viewed As Learning Settings

In the light of what has been said thus far, I would now like to comment on what I see as some crucial differences between an informal and spontaneous version of backyard baseball and the organized and adult-controlled Little League version of the same game. Let me grant at once that the latter form of the game is obviously much better equipped, better coached and probably also a good deal safer. No doubt Little League children really do get better training in the official rules and strategies of our national sport and better experience in the complex physical skills of ball handling, fielding, and so on. If the purpose of the game is to serve as an anticipatory socialization setting for developing future high school, college and professional ball players, the Little League sport is clearly the winner.

But if we look at the matter in a more general educational perspective, it appears that those aims are not achieved without serious cost. In educational terms, the crucial question must always be not what the child is doing to the ball, but what the ball is doing to the child. My most general point must be that in Little League baseball this is often not the case. Almost inevitably, in a highly organized, competitive sport, the focus is on winning and the eye is on the ball. How often does the well-intentioned volunteer coach from the phys-ed department really think about what kind of total experience his boys are having, including those who have warmed the bench all afternoon, or who were not selected for League competition?

Of that, more shortly. But first let me describe a typical variant of backyard baseball, as played in my own neighborhood some 50 years ago. We called it One-o-Cat. There were no teams. With a minimum of five kids you could start up a game, though it was better with seven or eight; once the game got started, usually a few more kids would wander over to join in, often kids of the wrong age or sex. But no matter: It was more fun with more kids, and the child population was a bit sparse back then. One base—usually a tree, or somebody's sweater or cap.

Home plate usually a flat stone. Two batters, a catcher, a pitcher, and a first baseman. If other kids were available, you had some fielders, too. If someone had a catcher's mitt, we'd use a hard ball; otherwise a softball, or tennis ball or anything else. If someone had a face mask, the catcher would play right behind the batter; otherwise way back. There was no umpire to call balls and strikes, so the pitcher was disciplined mostly by shouts of "put it over!" Fouls were balls that went to the right of the tree marking first base or to the left of a shrub on the other side; in other yards or fields, other foul markers would have to be agreed on.

The "rules" of the game, as we vaguely understood or invented them, were fairly simple. Pitched balls not swung at didn't count either as balls or strikes. Three swings without a hit and you were out. In principle you could go on hitting fouls indefinitely, but after a while the other kids would complain and make you go shag a wild one. A caught fly put you out. A good hit could get you to the tree and back for a home run; a lesser hit could leave you stranded at first, to be hit in, maybe, by the other batter. Or you could be put out either at first base or at the home plate in the usual fashion. Since there were no fixed base lines, when a runner was caught between the first baseman and the catcher, a wild chase all over the yard frequently ensued. When you went out, you retired to right field and everybody moved up one notch, catcher to batter, pitcher to catcher, first baseman to pitcher, left fielder to first, etc. There were no teams and nobody really bothered to keep score, since the personnel of the game usually changed during the session anyway, as some kids had to go do their chores or as others joined in. The object seemed to be to stay at bat as long as you could: but during the afternoon every kid would have plenty of opportunities to play in every position, and no one was ever on the bench. If a few more kids showed up, the game was magically transformed to Two-o-Cat, now with three rotating batters and a second base somewhere over there where third would have been; the runners now had to make the full triangular circuit before completing their run.

Maybe we didn't learn to be expert baseball players, but we did have a lot of fun; moreover, in an indirect and incidental way, we learned a lot of other kinds of things which are probably more important for children in the 8 to 12 age range to learn. Precisely because there was no official rule book and no adult or even other child designated as rule enforcer, we somehow had to improvise the whole thing all by ourselves—endless hassles about whether a ball was fair or foul, whether a runner was

safe or out, or more generally, simply about what was fair. On the anvil of experience we gradually learned to control our affect and to understand the invisible boundary conditions of our relationships to each other. Don't be a poor sport or the other kids won't want you to play with them. Don't push your point so hard that the kid with the only catcher's mitt will quit the game. Pitch a bit more gently to the littler kids so they can have some fun too; and besides, you realize it's important to keep them in the game because numbers are important. How to get a game started and somehow keep it going, so long as the fun lasted. How to pace it. When to quit for a while to get a round of cokes or just to sit under a tree for a bit. How to recognize the subtle boundaries indicating that the game was really over—not an easy thing, since there were no innings, no winners or losers—and slide over into some other activity. "Let's play tag"— "Not it!" Perhaps after supper, a game of catch with your father, who might try to give you a few very non-professional pointers. Perhaps for a few, excited accounts to the family of your success at bat that day and momentary dreams of later glory in the big leagues. But mostly on to the endless variety of other games, pastimes and interests which could so engage a young boy on a summer afternoon or evening.

In terms of the learning models proposed by Roberts, Sutton-Smith, Moore, Piaget, Parsons, Kohlberg, and many others, it was all there. It was fun; the scale was small, and the risks were minimal; we felt free and relatively safe (at least psychologically); it was spontaneous, autotelic, and agent responsive; it was self-pacing and the feedback was continuous and relevant; and the game was so structured that it required us to use our utmost ingenuity to discover and understand the hidden rules behind the rules—the general principles which make games fair, fun and interesting, and which had to govern our complex relationships with each other; the recognition of the subtle differences in skills, including social skills, which gave added respect and informal authority to some; the ability to handle poor sports, incompetents, cry-babies, little kids and girls, when the easy out of excluding them from the game entirely was somehow impractical. How to handle it when your own anger or frustrations welled up dangerously close to the point of tears. Most generally, although the formal structure of the game was based on a model of competition and physical skill, many of its most important lessons were in the social-emotional sector—how to keep the group sufficiently cohesive to get on with the play, and how to handle the tensions which arose within us and between us.

All these are things which were happening to the boys when left to themselves in this informal game situation. And it seems to me that they are far more important than what was happening to the ball. By now the ball is lost, anyway, somewhere in the bushes over by left field. Perhaps someone will find it tomorrow. And besides, it's too hot for baseball now, and the kids have all gone skinny-dipping in the little pond down the road a bit.

How does Little League Baseball stack up against this model? Rather badly, in my opinion. The scale is no longer miniature and safe, what with scoreboards, coaches, umpires, parents, and a grandstand full of spectators all looking at you and evaluating your every move with a single, myopic criterion: Perform! Win! The risks of failure are large and wounding. And in the pyramidal structure of league competition only a few can be winners and everybody else must be some kind of loser.

In Little League ball, the spontaneity is largely killed by schedules, rules, and adult supervision—a fixed time and place for each game, a set number of innings, a commitment to a whole season's schedule, at the expense of all alternative activities. Self-pacing? Obviously not. Fun? Yes, in a hard sort of way; but please, no fooling around or goofing off out there in right field; keep your eyes on the ball. Instant feedback? Yes, loud and clear from all sides, if you make a mistake; but mostly from adults in terms of their criteria of proper baseball performance.

But the major problem with Little League Baseball, as I see it, is that the whole structure of the game is rigidly fixed once and for all. It's all there in the rule books and in the organization of the League and of the game itself. It is all handed to the children, ready-made, on a silver platter, together with the diamonds, the bats and the uniforms. It is all so carefully supervised by adults, who are the teachers, coaches, rule enforcers, decision makers, and principal rewarders and punishers, that there's almost nothing left for the children to do but "play" the game. Almost all of the opportunities for incidental learning which occur in spontaneous self-organized and self-governed children's games have somehow been sacrificed on the altar of safety (physical only) and competence (in baseball only).

Competition and Little Leaguism in Contemporary America

No doubt there are some who will argue that ours is a tough, competitive society and that somehow, during the educational process, children must be hardened up and readied for the rigorous competition of real life they will face later on. It is certainly true that competition has indeed played a central role in American society, and for generations there were many, like Theodore Roosevelt, who thought of it as the backbone of American character and achievement. But at what cost to other values? More than 30 years ago the great psychoanalyst, Karen Horney, in her classic analysis of *The Neurotic Personality of Our Time* (1937) saw fit to devote an entire chapter to "neurotic competitiveness." But while Horney saw the problem clearly enough, most psychologists and educators of that generation did not. It is interesting to note that among the 23 experimental studies of competition reported by Murphy, Murphy and Newcomb (1937), the focus is almost invariably on the effects of competition on the performance of some task; not a single one of these studies dealt with any measures of the effects of competition on the subjects themselves!

But effects there undoubtedly are, among them the apparent inability of American children, reared in a competitive style, to know when *not* to compete. This point was neatly demonstrated in an experiment by Madsen and Shapira (1970) in which an apparatus was so arranged that no child could get any reward at all without cooperating with the others. Mexican children, and in another study by Shapira and Madsen (1969), Israeli Kibbutz children, were quick to fall into a cooperative plan to everybody's mutual advantage, but the American children continued to compete even after it became quite obvious that no one could "win" anything at all.

The time has surely come to reassess the heavy stress we have placed on competition in our educational system, and in our culture generally. In this connection it is interesting to note that recent movements toward educational reform call for a drastic reduction in the role of competition. More generally, the new "counter culture" flourishing on our college campuses is strongly anticompetitive in basic orientation. Somehow a whole generation of fathers, still deeply involved in major sports and other facets of the old American dream, has managed to rear a generation of sons among which a very substantial segment will have no part of it.

What can we say, more specifically, of the effects of Little League competition for children? I shall not take space here to consider such measured physiological side effects as the famous Little League elbow, or the evidences of measured Galvanic Skin Responses of young boys before and after competition (Skubic, 1955), or the reported losses of sleep and appetite before or following competition (Skubic, 1956). I have no reason to doubt that first rate child athletes, like the adult athletes studied by Ogilvie and Tutko (1971), are better built physically, better coordinated and have fairly well integrated, if somewhat aggressive personalities, in comparison with less athletic peers.

But the crucial question must be whether participation in Little League sports helps make them that way, or whether the reported differences are a result of the selection processes involved. In the adult study cited above, the authors believe that most of observed differences result from the selection processes rather than from the character-molding experiences of athletic competition. Hale's (1956) finding that the Little League players who made it to the Williamsport national competition had more, darker and curlier pubic hair than non-playing age mates almost certainly reflects a selective factor rather than a consequence of ball playing.

Similarly, in Seymour's (1956) study, it is clear that all the major reported differences between the Little Leaguers and their classmates, all documenting the "superiority" of the League players, existed *before* the season began. On all the self-rating scales used in this study, moreover, the nonparticipants actually *improved more* than the participants, ending ahead of the participants in their post-season self-ratings of their feelings about "me and my school" and "me and my home." In this study, the nonparticipants also gained somewhat more than the participants in the teacher ratings on "social consciousness," "emotional adjustment," and "responsibility." On the sociometric ratings, as expected, the boy athletes were the sociometric stars in their classrooms both before and after the season. The author does note, however, that on the post-season sociometric test, the Little League boys were somewhat *less* accepting of their peers, as measured by ratings they extended to others, than they had been before the season started. Could these results represent a gentle forecast of the Ogilvie-Tutko description of adult athletes: "Most athletes indicate low interest in receiving support and concern from others, low need to take care of others and low need for affiliation. Such a personality seems necessary to achieve victory over others" (pp. 61-62).

If some processes of selection are at work in sifting out the children who get to play in League or interscholastic competition, as they quite obviously are, and if both the adult and peer culture shower these children with special attention and kudos, as they surely do, then responsible educators must have some concern about all the other children, who are losers or nonparticipants in this one-dimensional competition. How sure are we that the values and character traits selected and carefully reinforced in Little League sports are really the best for wholesome child development? In a culture as fanatically dedicated to excellence in competitive sports as we have become in modern America, are we needlessly and cruelly punishing the children who are physically smaller or less mature, or less well coordinated or aggressive, who can't compete successfully and perhaps don't even want to? Many will no doubt turn into fine and productive adults, but only following a childhood in which they were never able to live up to the myopic values of the peer culture or to the expectancies of their sport-addicted fathers.

Let me not be misunderstood. I am certainly not coming out against baseball as such, though for reasons indicated, I believe the informal, backyard variants have far more learning values for children than the formally organized, adult-supervised version. My most fundamental opposition to Little League Baseball, however, is based not so much to what it does by way of either harm or good to the player, as it is on what Little Leaguism is doing to the whole culture of childhood, to participants and nonparticipants alike, and to the schools, families, neighborhoods and communities where Little Leaguism has taken root.

Look first at what has happened to organized sports in high schools, and the picture is perhaps clearer. In a high school of two thousand students, only a relative handful get to participate even on the squads of any of the major sports teams. All the rest are consigned to the role of frenzied spectators at interscholastic meets, or still worse, in many sportminded communities, to nonparticipant-nonspectators, perceived by adults and peers alike as odd-balls pariahs, or queers. As Coleman (1961) showed, this group may in fact include some of the best students, but they get precious little reward for their academic efforts. And the kids who do go out in earnest for a high school sport find that, to compete at all effectively against our fanatic standards of excellence, they have to make it almost a full time job both in season and out, at the expense of virtually all other extracurricular and leisure time activities. In one way, you're damned if you don't participate; in another way, you're damned if you do . . .

In Little League and other variations of organized interscholastic sport we now see clear indications of the invasions of this sports culture into the much more precious and vulnerable world of little children. Like the bad currency in Gresham's famous law, it is an inferior product which ends by driving out the good. Because of its peculiar fascination, more for the parents than for the children themselves, it ends by nearly monopolizing the field and driving almost to bankruptcy the natural and spontaneous culture of play and games among American children.

References

Coleman, I., *The Adolescent Society*, Glencoe, Ill: Free Press, 1961.

Devereux, E.C., "Authority and moral development among American and West German children," *Journal of Comparative Family Studies*, Vol. III, Spring, 1972. In press.

———, "The role of peer-group experience in moral development," in J.P. Hill, ed., *Minnesota Symposia on Child Psychology*, Minneapolis: University of Minnesota Press. 1970. Vol. IV, pp. 94-140.

Eifermann, Rivka R, *Determinants of children's game styles*, Jerusalem: The Israel Academy of Sciences and Humanities, 1971b. In press.

———, "Social play in childhood," in R.E. Herron & Brian Sutton-Smith, eds., *Child's Play*, New York: John Wiley & Sons. 1971a. pp. 270-297.

Hale, C.J., "Physiological maturity of Little League baseball players," *Research Quarterly*, 1956, **27,** 276-282.

Herron, R.E., and Sutton-Smith, B., *Child's Play*, New York: Wiley & Son, 1971.

Horney, Karen, *The Neurotic Personality of Our Time*, New York: W.W. Norton & Co. 1937.

Kohlberg, L., "Development of moral character and moral ideology," in M.L Hoffman and L.W. Hoffman, eds., *Review of Child Development Research*, New York: Russell Sage Foundation, 1964, Vol. 1, pp. 383-431.

Lewin, Kurt, et al., "Level of Aspiration," in J.M. Hunt, ed., *Personality and Behavior Disorders*, New York: Ronald Press, 1944.

Madsen, M.C., and Shapira, A., "Cooperative and competitive behavior of urban Afro-American, Anglo-American, Mexican-American and Mexi-can village children," *Developmental Psychology*, 1970, **3**(l), 16-20.

Menninger, Karl, *Love Against Hate*, New York Harcourt, 1942.

Moore, Omar Khayyam & Anderson, A.R., "Some principals for the design of clarifying educational environments," in D. Goslin, ed., *Handbook of Socialization Theory and Research*, New York: Rand McNally, 1969, pp. 571-613.

Murphy, G., Murphy, L.B. & Newcomb, T.M., *Experimental Social Psychology*, New York: Harper Bros., rev. ed., 1937.

Ogilvie, B.C., and Tutko, T.A., "If you want to build character, try something else," *Psychology Today*, 1971, Vol. 5, pp. 60-63.

Parsons, T., and Bates, R.F., *Family, Socialization and Interaction Process*, Glencoe, Ill.: Free Press, 1955.

Phillips, R.H., "The nature and function of children's formal games," *Psychoanalytic Quarterly*, 1960, **29,** 200-207.

Piaget, J., *The Moral Judgment of the Child*, New York: Harcourt, 1932.

Roberts, J.M., & Sutton-Smith, B., "Child training and game involvement," *Ethnology*, 1962, **1,** 166-185.

Seymour, E.W., "Comparative study of certain behavior characteristics of participants and non-participants in Little League Baseball" *Research Quarterly*, 1956, **27,** 338-346.

Shapira, A., and Madsen, M.C., "Cooperative and competitive behavior of Kibbutz and urban children in Israel," *Child Development*, 1969, **40,** 609-617.

Skubic, E., "Emotional responses of boys to Little League and Middle League competitive baseball." *Research Quarterly*, 1955, **26,** 342-352.

———, "Studies of Little League and Middle League Baseball," *Research Quarterly*, 1956, **27,** 97-110.

Sutton-Smith, B., "A syntax for play and games," in R.E. Herron and B. Sutton-Smith, eds., *Child's Play*, New York: John Wiley & Sons, 1971, pp. 298-307.

Sutton-Smith, B., and Rosenberg, R.G., "Sixty years of historical change in the game preferences of American children," in R.E. Herron and B. Sutton-Smith, eds., *Child's Play*, New York: John Wiley & Sons, 1971, pp. 18-50.

Learning Life's Lessons in Tee Ball: The Reinforcement of Gender and Status in Kindergarten Sport

Melissa A. Landers
Gary Alan Fine

Sport serves as a crucible for the inculcation of traditional values regarding competence and gender. That this process is well-established in late childhood and adolescence has been widely documented (e.g., Fine, 1987; Kleiber, 1981; Smith, 1978; Vaz, 1982; Yablonsky & Brower, 1979). What is less clear is the depth of the roots of this sport socialization. Though socialization to gender and competence begin at birth within the family, the school, day care, and sport team represent the earliest public organizations that attempt to channel children's behavior according to where they stand relative to others. Within most communities, organized sport starts at about age 5 or 6; a younger child is not seen as capable of socially coordinated action (see Mead, 1934).

Our goal is to describe how status and gender roles can become reinforced at the earliest stage of organized sport. Both coaches and peers convey traditional attitudes that girls do not fully belong in certain—traditionally male—sports (Eder & Parker, 1987; Lenskyj, 1991) and that competitiveness plays an important role in sporting activity. These attitudes lead to rewards and training for those who enter as competent, and to relatively higher behavioral expectations for those, notably girls, who are not seen as equally proficient or enthusiastic.

Reprinted from Landers and Fine, 1996.

The World of Tee Ball

The entry point for a child's baseball "career" is tee ball. In this version of America's pastime, children bat in turn, hitting a ball placed on a sturdy, rigid rubber hose, which is called the tee. When they hit the ball, they run bases. The other team fields: following the adult baseball model, they are expected to catch the hit ball and/or throw the runner out. Typically at this stage the batters (and runners) are more successful than the fielders. To ensure that the game does not last too long, there is a limit of six innings per game. In the league that we observed, approximately 12 children played on each team. All 12 batted, and all played in the field simultaneously.

The first author observed a tee ball group, organized by the YMCA in a small southeastern U.S. city during the spring 1993 baseball season. The primary method of data collection consisted of field notes taken during participant observation. Approximately 22 hours were spent in observation. Informal interaction and conversation with the children supplemented the data and were incorporated into field notes. A formal, taped interview was also conducted with each of the two head coaches near the end of the season.

The tee ball group met two afternoons a week for practices and one afternoon a week for formal games. Some 24 five- and six-year-old kindergarten children participated, including 13 Caucasian boys, 6 Caucasian girls, 4 African-American boys, and 1 Asian-American boy. Most of the children were from working-class or middle-class backgrounds.

The children were divided into two teams: the Braves, directed by Coach Carol, and the Flames, directed by Coach Bobby. Wayne was the assistant coach for both teams. The two teams generally practiced together, although they separated before scrimmages to perform batting or catching drills. During games they played each other or a third YMCA team composed of kindergarten children who attended a local private school. For all these children, tee ball was an introduction to organized athletics. The socialization function of tee ball was illustrated after the first game as the children were lined up and taught how to walk in a line past the opposing team, hands extended, for a congratulatory "good-game" high five. Tee ball has an important effect on children's perceptions of the rules of athletic participation.

All-male athletic teams have long been recognized as traditional sites for male bonding and learning about masculinity (Fine, 1987; Kimmel & Messner, 1989; Sabo & Messner, 1993). Thus, the coed composition of tee ball might have been expected to lead to a softening of gender roles. As Thorne (1993) notes, many schools intentionally attempt to create mixed-gender activities to diminish traditional behavioral expectations of boys as active and formal game oriented and girls as more sedentary and informal play oriented (see Lever, 1976). Richer (1984) specifically advocates cross-gender play as a key to eliminating gender inequality. Our original expectation was that tee ball might provide girls with a nurturing environment in which to develop their athletic skills. This proved not to be the case.

The Aristocrats of Tee Ball

Hierarchies of skill are readily apparent in childhood, in schools and elsewhere. Those at the top and bottom of the skill hierarchy were readily visible among the tee ball players, to the coaches and other players and to the researcher. Those in the middle were more difficult to place in the hierarchy. However, the coaches envisioned a more precise skill hierarchy and made it more tangible by favoring those they perceived as their most skilled players in terms of both their placement on the field

(better players were allowed more ball contact) and special attention and instruction during games and practices.

This hierarchy had behavioral effects in that it was coupled with a strong competitive urge. Coaches, even those with 5-year-old charges, desire to win. Although the YMCA as an organization emphasized teamwork and the development of physical skills over competition, the coaches accepted the hierarchical "culture of competition" (Goldman & McDermott, 1987). The teams' win/loss records, though unofficial, were kept diligently and discussed daily by the coaches. Coach Carol in particular made frequent reference to her team's successful record.

Among the 24 kindergartners, two boys were regarded by adults as exhibiting great athletic prowess. One played first base for the Flames; the other was the pitcher for the Braves. Below these two were six boys who played infield positions. The others were assigned to the remaining positions according to the coaches' perceptions of their skill, including the low-status outfield slots. Playing outfield in tee ball is even less educational than in baseball, as batters rarely hit the ball outside the infield. The outfielders are sufficiently distant from the coach that they receive little instruction. In terms of the amount of time handling the ball and receiving instruction during practice and games, the infielders we observed, already more skilled, were at a tremendous advantage.

Skilled players also received special coaching. During one practice, Coach Carol ordered her outfielders to run to the bleachers and back, then to take a water break. While they were doing this, she taught the infielders how to execute a double play.

Even when low-status players have the opportunity to play important roles, it is made clear that they do not really count. For example, before a game in which her regular first baseman was missing, Coach Carol instructed the pitcher to run the ball to first base instead of throwing it to the substitute first baseman, avoiding the possibility of error. As a result, it was apparent to the substitute that he did not have the requisite skills for the position and, of course, was unable to improve. Likewise, Coach Bobby altered the normal fielding pattern during a game when facing a weak batter. He told his shortstop to move forward to compensate for the short hit that was likely. Hearing this, other fielders moved forward in unison, embarrassing and disconcerting the batter.

The coaches clearly emphasized winning rather than the equal participation of all players. Such coaching values at this young age enable those who enter tee ball relatively skilled to become even more skilled and those who enter with few or undeveloped skills to remain unskilled. If the object was to educate children, while emphasizing teamwork, the coaches might have attempted to undermine the skill hierarchy by ensuring that children play all positions for a relatively equal span of time.

Even by the age of 5, the importance placed on athletic skill is real. The children themselves were perfectly capable of discerning who among them possessed the greatest and least skill. Athletically skilled individuals occupied positions atop the skill hierarchy, which led to high social status, just as it does in preadolescence and early adolescence (Eder & Parker, 1987; Fine, 1987). For instance, during one pregame practice coaches asked children to select a partner for catch. Three boys chose Scott, the most talented boy on the team. All three boys surrounded Scott and began pulling on his arms. Scott's expression was first one of surprise, but gradually it turned into pleasure as he seemed to realize that his ability was bringing him popularity. From this point on, when the children were asked to choose a partner, all clamored for Scott.

Likewise, the association with skilled players occurred at one practice when Rex followed Danny and Chad, two of the best players on the Flames, in the lineup. Rex hit the ball well and upon returning to the bench asked Danny, "Didn't I have a good hit? On Friday, you're gonna have a good hit. Me, you, and Chad. Yeah, me, you, and Chad" (field notes). Rex claimed his position in the triumvirate with these better ballplayers. In contrast, at one practice Paul was in charge of teeing up balls for each batter. Regarding a learning-disabled child, he proclaimed, "Ted only gets two." Each other child was permitted three balls (field notes). How you play determines the respect you receive as a moral actor, even in kindergarten.

In this way, children played their part in reinforcing the importance of athletic skill within the peer group. They acted according to the competitive athletic culture established by coaches. In effect, they were "embellishing" (Corsaro, 1992) the athletic values passed down to them by their adult caretakers.

Gender Politics of Tee Ball

While for boys the program probably did little to decrease the interest level of relatively untalented players, for girls the program might actually have caused a decline in their level of interest.[1] Both head coaches perceived significant gender differences in the interest and skills of their players. During separate interviews they both indicated that they believed parents, through discriminatory practices, were more concerned with the athletic development of their sons. For instance, the coaches felt that parents were more inclined to throw the ball around with their sons than with their daughters. Indeed, most of the girls did not have baseball gloves, whereas the large majority of boys did, reinforcing the view that parents did not take their daughters' participation in tee ball seriously. Coach Carol: "None of the girls want to be there. Not one. If I put a coloring station in the corner, every girl would be there. . . . Dads take their sons outside to throw with. Girls stay inside and play dolls" (personal interview).

This interpretation gave Coach Carol little incentive to overcome the perceived barriers to female participation in tee ball. Rather than attempting to be a role model for these girls, the coach was content to reproduce the social order found in family and media representations of baseball. These expectations of girls' lack of interest affected the treatment of girls, exemplifying the "Pygmalion effect" (Rosenthal & Jacobson, 1968) and discouraging their potential involvement and motivation to excel in tee ball. Whether the girls' feelings about playing tee ball were a cause or effect of this treatment, the three girls questioned by the first author at the end of the season claimed not to enjoy playing tee ball. The coach failed to consider that the girls (or their parents) must have had sufficient interest in tee ball initially to sign up for the activity.

The coaches' views about girls in baseball prevented them from taking an active interest in the girls' athletic development and instead caused them to focus on the attention and behavior deficits that they perceived were displayed by the girls. Girls were reprimanded more frequently and more harshly than boys, often for the same behavior that was acceptable for boys:

Coach Carol gave each child a number. When she called their number, they were to come to bat. When she called out number eleven, two boys approached her claiming that number. She sent one of them back to his place by smiling and telling him that he was now number eleven and one-half. As she was doing this, Ellen approached her from the outfield, saying that she was number eleven. Coach Carol looked at her angrily and snapped, "You're now number twenty-one!" Ellen protested confusedly, saying, "But I know I was number eleven." Coach Carol looked at her in disgust and barked, "You're number twenty-one!" Ellen walked back to the outfield with her head down. (field notes)

Richard, a member of the Braves, ran out onto the field doing cartwheels. Not five minutes later, Helen ran out on the field also doing cartwheels. Suddenly, I heard Coach Carol yelling at Helen, "Get over here!" As Helen approached, Coach Carol added, "Do you know why you are sitting out?" Helen was looking down as she walked off the diamond toward Coach Carol. She shook her head, "No." Coach Carol said, "You were out there doing cartwheels and everything else! You don't even want to play!" Yet, Coach Carol had failed to reprimand or scold Richard for similar behavior. (field notes)

Ellen and Helen were placed together in the batting lineup. Both girls hit the ball solidly, but neither ran with confidence toward first or second base. Both were tagged out, despite Coach Carol's pleas to "run to second." Their outs ended the inning, but instead of switching to the field, Coach Carol made everybody remain on the field while Helen and Ellen ran around the bases twice, leading one boy to mutter, "Girls don't know where the bases are." Boys did not receive similar treatment for their baserunning errors. (field notes)

Even when the criticism was not directed at particular girls, the image of girls as incompetent was evident. When Coach Wayne accidentally dropped a ball he was trying to throw, he commented, "Look, I throw like a girl," achieving some role-distance from his error at the expense of girls. Before throwing it, he contorted his arms and awkwardly threw the ball toward Helen, who was standing in front of him. This behavior both illustrated and created the image of girls as inferior, bringing one female player into the scene as a prop for depicting her own incompetence. On another occasion after dropping a ball, Coach Wayne said to one of the girls, "I'm a little girl. I can't catch the ball."

On the few occasions when girls became upset at their treatment, the coaches conspired to smooth over the situation:

When it was Becky's turn to bat, Coach Bobby threw a ball at her teed up ball, knocking it off just before she swung. The ball rolled on the field fair. Scott picked it up and threw to first base. This was the third out, and the coaches yelled "Switch," as Becky was tagged out. The entire time, Becky was very upset. She crossed her arms, stuck her bottom lip out, and began to cry, demanding another try. When the coaches realized how upset she was, Coach Wayne told both teams to sit down. He went to the pitcher's position, and waited for Becky to hit. He captured her ball easily, and tagged her out, telling her, "OK, now switch." Thus, Becky was cooled out, while simultaneously receiving a dose of public humiliation. (field notes)

A consciousness of gender was also evident in the division of coaching duties. The male coaches usually performed activities that involved "active coaching," such as throwing and batting. Female coaches performed duties that involved organization and paperwork. Coach Bobby led the batting and catching drills for the Flames, and Coach Wayne typically led these drills for the Braves while Carol coached verbally from the sidelines. When it became necessary to collect money from the children for an end-of-the-season party, Coach Carol was given this assignment, working closely with the "tee ball mother." Coach Janie, the coach for the private school team, was assigned the job of ordering pizza. The two male coaches were not involved in planning the party.

Gender differences in athletic skill and interest are created and reinforced in a dynamic process of interaction with team members and coaches. Tee ball is yet another forum in which children are introduced to socially acceptable gender roles and forms of play, a forum in which girls are not made to feel welcome. Girls have been shown to be athletically influenced by coaches as role models. Negative treatment by coaches, lack of peer support, and observation of males in active coaching roles and females in more passive roles contributed to the waning interest of girls during the season.

Tee Ball Days

Our observation of a kindergarten tee ball group points to the placement of children into a skill hierarchy by coaches. This hierarchy was made real by giving the children semipermanent field positions, which encouraged the development of the most skilled players, who occupied central positions. In turn, these players received more positive attention and compliments from peers, coaches, and parents. This increased their athletic and social confidence as well as their likelihood of continued participation (Gras, 1974). In contrast, those positions involving the least ball handling were given to children perceived as less skilled or less interested. Most of the girls were included in this second group. Girls' behavior was singled out as less serious and involved; as a result, they were held by their coaches to a more stringent code of behavior. Those children—particularly boys—who enter organized athletics with a "head start" will move farther and farther ahead, confirming their early skills, even when this head start occurs as early as kindergarten. Children quickly picked up on the cultural importance placed on athletic skill. They found ways to embellish this theme and reinforce its importance in the peer group.

Every group has unique characteristics, and we do not claim that the findings from this setting, with these coaches and children, would necessarily generalize to other organized sport settings involving young children. However, it does suggest that skill hierarchies and gender divisions can occur at an early age, without participants, their parents, or those overseeing the program perceiving that anything is amiss. To change the gendered, competitive structure of athletics appears, from this research, to require consciousness of the power of expectations at a very early age.

References

Corsaro, W. (1992). Interpretive reproduction of children's peer cultures. *Social Psychology Quarterly*, **55**(2), 160-177.

Eder, D., & Parker, S. (1987). The cultural production and reproduction of gender: The effect of extracurricular activities on peer group culture. *Sociology of Education*, **60**, 200-213.

Fine, G.A. (1987). *With the boys: Little League baseball and preadolescent culture*. Chicago: University of Chicago Press.

Goldman, S.V., & McDermott, R. (1987). The culture of competition in American schools. In G. Spindler (Ed.), *Education and cultural process: Anthropological approaches* (2nd ed., pp. 282-299). Prospect Heights, IL: Waveland Press.

Gras, F. (1974). The shaping of the interest in the need for sport among children and adolescents as a condition for the development of a positive attitude to physical culture and sport. *International Review of Sport Sociology*, **9**, 75-80.

Kimmel, M.S., & Messner, M.A. (1989). *Men's lives*. New York: Macmillan.

Kleiber, D. (1981). Searching for enjoyment in children's sports. *The Physical Educator*, **38**, 77-84.

Lenskyj, H. (1991). *Women, sport, and physical activity research and bibliography*. Ottawa, ON: Minister of Supply and Services.

Lever, J. (1976). Sex differences in the games children play. *Social Problems*, **23**(4), 478-487.

Mead, G.H. (1934). *Mind, self, and society*. Chicago: University of Chicago Press.

Richer, S. (1984). Sexual inequality and children's play. *Canadian Review of Sociology and Anthropology*, **21**, 166-180.

Rosenthal, R., & Jacobson, L. (1968). *Pygmalion in the classroom*. New York: Holt, Rinehart and Winston.

Sabo, D., & Messner, M.A. (1993). Whose body is this? Women's sports and sexual politics. In G.L. Cohen (Ed.), *Women in Sport* (pp. 15-24). Newbury Park, CA: Sage.

Smith, M. (1978). Social learning of violence in minor league hockey. In F. Smoll & R.E. Smith (Eds.), *Psychological perspectives in youth sports* (pp. 91-106). Washington, DC: Hemisphere.

Thorne, B. (1993). *Gender play: Girls and boys in school*. New Brunswick, NJ: Rutgers University Press.

Vaz, E.W. (1982). *The professionalization of young hockey players*. Lincoln: University of Nebraska Press.

Yablonsky, L., & Brower, J. (1979). *The Little League game*. New York: Times Books.

Note

1. We would like to emphasize that this is a case study and that interpretations, while highly suggestive, do not necessarily generalize beyond the particular league that was observed.

Action Research in Youth Soccer: Assessing the Acceptability of an Alternative Program

B. Christine Green

Critics of youth sport have argued that competitive pressures engendered by adult supervision have robbed sport of its play and socialization values. Others contend that sport can be redesigned to enhance the benefits children obtain. This study describes an action research project designed to evaluate a soccer program that was devised as a child-centered alternative to traditional programs. On the basis of deliberations with the parent volunteers who created and implement the program, two surveys were designed: one for parents and one for children. Parents in the alternative program and in two traditional programs completed measures of satisfaction, sport involvement, purchase-decision involvement, and attitude. Children completed measures of satisfaction, enjoyment, and attitude. Analysis revealed that the alternative program is well-liked by parents and children, and that parents choosing the alternative program are psychographically distinct from parents who choose traditional programs. Necessary improvements in the alternative program were identified. Use of the study's findings and implications for sport programs and action research are discussed.

Recent exposés of the abuse of young athletes (e.g., Ryan, 1995) and the mismanagement of sport organizations (e.g., Prouty, 1988) have focused on programs designed for elite athletes. Those exposés have been concerned about the quality of judgment evidenced by coaches and administrators. They have sometimes questioned the pressures placed on athletes undergoing intensive daily training. They have not, however, questioned the fundamental design of our sport systems. It is not suggested, for example, that our sport programs need to be redesigned at their very roots. Perhaps that is because those exposés never question the value of formal sport competition per se.

However, there are two complementary discussions in the literature that do wonder about the value of formal competition and urge us to rethink the design of sport programs, particularly those for children. The first (and older) criticizes adult-supervised sport programs, arguing that competitive pressures have removed key elements of fun and peer socialization from sport (e.g., Devereux, 1976; Horn, 1977; Kohn, 1986; Martens, 1978). The second suggests that existing sport programs can become venues in which to imbed secondary training in social skills, self-regulation, and ethics (e.g., Hellison, 1995; Martens, 1988; Shields & Bredemeier, 1995; Voyle, 1989). What these discussions share is the contention that sport programs can and should be focused on the social and developmental needs of the children they purport to serve. The discussions suggest that the preoccupation with competition and win/loss records, which is characteristic of organized youth sport, deflects attention from the needs of children.

Reprinted from Green, 1997.

This study describes consultation with a community youth soccer program that was designed to provide a child-focused alternative. The program was devised with reference to the literatures that have been critical of youth-sport programming (e.g., Devereux, 1976; Horn, 1977; Martens, 1978), derivative work suggesting modifications to children's sports (e.g., Hutslar, 1985), and the associated research literature demonstrating that children's sport experience can be improved by modifying the games played (e.g., Chase, Ewing, Lirgg, & George, 1994; Martens, Rivkin, & Bump, 1984; Satern, Messier, & Keller-McNulty, 1989; Watson, 1986). The consultation was formulated as action research (Argyris, Putnam, & Smith, 1985; Whyte, 1991) aimed to answer the questions uppermost in the minds of the parents who had conceived and implemented the program.

In order to provide background, the program and its community are described. Research objectives of the program's staff of parent volunteers are noted. The resulting study is then reported. Research methods, results, and their use are reviewed. Implications for sport programming and for action research in sport contexts are then discussed.

The Modified Soccer Program

The modified soccer program was founded in a suburb of Washington, D.C., three years prior to commencement of the research project reported here. Its founder was an executive in the county health department who, as a volunteer, had administered a traditional youth soccer program. He was struck by the discrepancy between recommendations derived from youth-sport research and the practices that are common to youth-sport administration. He concluded that traditional programs are not sufficiently child-centered. He wrote:

> I started this alternative program . . . because the existing youth-sport programs . . . although well-intentioned, seemed to be organized with either disregard for or ignorance of the rich knowledge base in the pediatric sport science literature. . . . In a child-centered program, the games are dramatically modified to meet the developmental needs of children—all children. (Dutrow, 1994)

Like other soccer programs in its region, the modified program runs a 10-week fall season and an 8-week spring season. However, its similarity to other soccer programs ends there. Unlike traditional programs, games in the modified program do not emulate the professional version of soccer. There are no formal competitions, no league standings, no trophies, and no all-star games. Rather, each participant is assigned to a coeducational play group that is led by an adult play leader. Play group sessions do not rely on drills and scrimmages. Instead, play leaders organize (and often participate in) a variety of games using soccer balls and goals. The program philosophy, "let the game be the teacher," emphasizes a spirit of playfulness. Play leaders are trained in a repertoire of dozens of games (the number increasing throughout the season as new games are invented). All games are organized to include every member of the play group. The games are designed to emphasize one or more soccer skills, and to maximize the number of times each player gets to touch the ball. Games can be as small as 2 versus 2, and never become larger than 7 versus 7. Each game is tailored to the developmental level of players, and is structured so that it can be played with minimal (if any) adult intervention. Players can (and are encouraged to) design their own games. Play leaders are instructed that their purpose is to foster children's intrinsic satisfaction by helping them to develop friendships, self-esteem, physical skill, creativity, and independent decision making.

The focus on play and the consequent elimination of interteam competition combine to change the role of parents. In traditional youth-sport programs, parents who do not coach are relegated to cheering from the sidelines, often in ways that some participants find abusive (Devereux, 1976; Fine, 1987; Horn, 1977). In the modified program, parents who are not play leaders are invited to join the action by playing along with their children. In practice, most parents decline, choosing instead to sit on the sidelines and chat with other parents. There is no cheering of the kinds observed during games in traditional programs, although some parents do occasionally shout encouragement or praise—not only to their own children, but to others in the play group.

Implementation of the modified program was supported by a local, elite soccer program. The elite program sought to incorporate the modified program as a potential feeder system. It was hoped that the modified program would be attractive to families who were not adequately served by the city's existing traditional programs. However, the demand for spaces to play soccer exceeds the city's available supply, thus it was important to determine whether the modified program does serve a distinctive market. Further, because the modified program lacks any formal competitive structure, it obtains little media attention. Consequently, some administrators worried that parents and children might find the modified program less satisfying than a traditional program. Those who were active in implementing the modified program were further concerned about the degree to which the program was meeting its underlying objectives—namely to provide a positive social and psychological experience for its participants.

Method

Project Initiation and Planning

The research project was initiated when the program's founder approached a local university seeking research assistance to address the questions uppermost in the minds of the parents and volunteers responsible for implementing the modified program. Initially, the program personnel could only articulate general evaluative questions, such as, "Is what we are doing worthwhile?" "Do people like it?" "Do people see us differently than traditional programs?" These questions were explored through discussion with program administrators and play leaders throughout an entire fall and spring season. At the end of that period, 11 key questions were identified:

1. Are parents of children in the modified program satisfied with the modified program?
2. How does their satisfaction compare to the satisfaction of parents whose children are in traditional programs?
3. Are children in the modified program satisfied with it?
4. How does their satisfaction compare to that of children in traditional programs?
5. Do children in the modified program feel that they obtain friendships with others in the program?
6. How does their sense of friendship compare with that of children in traditional programs?
7. Do children in the modified program have a positive sense of their soccer skill, and do they enjoy soccer?
8. How does their sense of skill and enjoyment compare to that of children in traditional programs?
9. How does their attitude toward competition compare to that of children in traditional programs?

10. Do the parents who choose the modified program for their children have different levels of sport involvement or different attitudes than do parents who choose a traditional program for their children?
11. Is there any evidence that parents who choose a modified program for their children are actively seeking an alternative to traditional programs?

Sample and Procedure

Three groups were identified for analysis: parents and children in the modified program, parents and children in the city's traditional recreational soccer program, and parents and children in the city's other elite soccer program (i.e., not the one that had sponsored implementation of the modified program). The total population of parents and children in the modified program was solicited by questionnaires distributed and collected at play group during the fall season. A total of 87 athlete questionnaires and 73 parent questionnaires was returned (representing a response rate of 52% for the athletes and 62% for the parents).

Selection of the comparison samples followed a two-stage random sampling method recommended by Kalton (1983). The program directors for the traditional recreational program and the elite program were contacted during the fall season to obtain access to families in the program. Target participants were selected by first identifying teams whose players were similar to those in the modified program in terms of age and experience. Teams were then randomly selected from the identified clusters. Once teams had been selected, participants from those teams were chosen randomly. Once selected, both the player and his or her parent were surveyed. As with the modified program, questionnaires were distributed and collected at practice. Fifty parent/child pairs were surveyed in each program. In the recreational program, 34 athlete questionnaires and 33 parent questionnaires were returned (a response rate of 68% and 66%, respectively). In the elite program, 30 athlete questionnaires and 28 parent questionnaires were returned (a response rate of 60% and 56%, respectively).

Parents and children were instructed to complete their respective surveys independently and asked to return them in sealed envelopes. Instructions specified that the parent questionnaire be completed by "the parent most involved in your child's soccer experience." Because young children (typically younger than 8 years old) needed some assistance to complete the questionnaire, they were aided by a research assistant who was naive to the research questions underlying the measures. Research assistants were instructed to read questions to children, but to allow the children to formulate answers for themselves.

Parent respondents ranged in age from 25 to 49 years (M = 37.1 years). Sixty-two percent of parent respondents were mothers, and 38% were fathers. Eighty-one percent of the parents had completed a university degree. There were no statistically significant differences between the groups in the age, gender, or educational attainment of the parent who responded. Only four respondents identified themselves as African American, Hispanic, or Asian.

Athletes ranged in age from 5 to 13 years (M = 8.3 years). The athlete sample is 84% male, which reflects the dominance of males in all three programs.

Questionnaire Design

Following procedures recommended by Chalip (1989), two questionnaires were developed, one for athletes and one for parents. The literature was surveyed to identify measures appropriate to the questions identified during the two seasons of discussions with those implementing the modified program.

Parents' Questionnaire

Seven variables were measured in the parents' questionnaire: their satisfaction with program administration (ADMIN), their satisfaction with the coaching (P-COACH), their purchase-decision involvement (PDI), their level of primary sport involvement (PSI) and secondary sport involvement (SSI), their concerns about adult imposition in youth sport (ADIMP), and their professionalization of attitude toward play (WEBB). These variables and the items that comprise them are listed in table 7.1.

The four items measuring satisfaction with coaching are derived from Chelladurai's (1984) study of relations among leadership behaviors and participants' satisfaction in sport settings. The items are rated on a 6-point Likert scale ranging from strongly disagree to strongly agree. The 4-item coach-satisfaction scale is internally consistent (Cronbach's alpha = .77). The items are averaged to obtain an overall index of satisfaction with coaching.

The two items measuring satisfaction with administration were derived from Harrison (1994). They are measured on a 6-point Likert scale ranging from strongly disagree to strongly agree. The two items are correlated (r = .52, p < .001). They are

averaged to provide an overall index of satisfaction with program administration.

Mittal's (1989) purchase-decision involvement scale is used to measure the degree to which program design was an important factor in determining the respondent's choice. Mittal describes purchase-decision involvement as "the extent of interest and concern that a consumer brings to bear upon a purchase-decision task" (p. 150). He reports test-retest reliability of .79. Criterion validity was established by correlations with a measure of consumer information search (.50 < r < .67). The four items are each rated on 10-point bipolar scales, and then averaged to form an overall index of purchase-decision involvement.

The measures of primary and secondary sport involvement are taken from Orlick's (1974) family sports environment interview schedule. Orlick reports that the interview schedule successfully differentiates families of children involved and not involved in sport, an indicator of discriminant validity. Primary sport involvement refers to parents' current levels of participation in sport. Secondary sport involvement refers to parents' current levels of passive consumption of sport as spectators or as consumers of sport media. The three items in each subscale are measured on 5-point scales, with each of the five points anchored by a behavioral description. For each subscale, the three items are averaged to provide overall measures of primary and secondary sport involvement.

Gould and Martens (1979) identify adult imposition as a pivotal dimension of adults' concerns about youth sport. They report that the three items making up this scale load together unidimensionally in factor analysis. Each item is measured on a 10-point bipolar scale ranging from "thoroughly disagree" to "thoroughly agree." The three items are averaged to obtain a single measure of parents' concerns about adult imposition in youth sport.

Kidd and Woodman's (1975) modification of the original Webb (1969) scale was used to measure parents' professionalization of attitude toward their children's play. Respondents are asked to rank the importance of winning, skill development, and fun. Responses are scored from 1 (least professionalized attitude) to 6 (most professionalized attitude) according to the six possible permutations of ranking. The scale consistently obtains reliabilities in the .9 range.

Athletes' Questionnaire

Six variables were measured in the children's questionnaire: their satisfaction with the coach

Table 7.1 Parents' Items and Variables

ADMIN   *satisfaction with the program administration*

Includes: I am unhappy with the administration of this program.
I like the way the program is structured.

P-COACH   *satisfaction with the coach*

Includes: My child's coach makes it easy for children to learn soccer skills.
My child's coach is knowledgeable about soccer.
I would describe my child's coach as "good with children."
My child's soccer practices are well-organized and controlled by the coach.

PDI   *purchase-decision involvement*

Includes: In selecting from the many youth-sport opportunities in the area, would you say that:
I would not care a great deal as to which one I join.
I would care a great deal as to which one I join.
Do you think that the various soccer programs in the area are all very alike or are all very different?
How important would it be to you to choose the right soccer program?
In making your selection of this program, how concerned were you about the outcome of your choice?

PSI   *primary sport involvement*

Includes: Do you currently take part in any sports, games, or physical activities?
Were you or your spouse ever athletes or active in sports?
Do you belong to any sports clubs, YMCA, recreation centers, or fitness clubs?

SSI   *secondary sport involvement*

Includes: How often do you read about sports?
How often do you attend athletic events (e.g., pro, semi-pro, college) as a spectator?
How often do you watch sports on television?

ADIMP   *concern with adult imposition in youth sport*

Includes: Parents frequently interfere with running children's sport programs.
Coaches of children's sports typically provide poor leadership.
There is too much emphasis on winning in children's sport.

WEBB   *professionalization of attitude toward play*

In playing soccer, which of the following do you think is most important?
To defeat the other team
To play as well as you can
To have fun

Reprinted from Green, 1997.

(C-COACH), their satisfaction with the team (TEAM), their perception that they have friends on the soccer team (FRIENDS), feelings about playing soccer (DOSOC), perceived soccer skill (SKILL), and professionalization of attitude toward play (WEBB). These variables and the items that comprise them are listed in table 7.2.

The two items measuring children's satisfaction with their coach were derived from the work of Smith, Smoll, and Curtis (1978) and McCormack and Chalip (1988). The items were reviewed for face validity and readability by a sport psychologist, a sport sociologist, and a curriculum specialist. The items are scored on a 10-point scale ranging from "no, not at all" to "yes, very much." The two items are significantly correlated ($r = .49, p < .001$). The items are averaged to obtain an overall index of children's satisfaction with their coach.

The two items measuring children's satisfaction with the team were derived from the work of Wankel and his colleagues (Wankel & Kreisel, 1985; Wankel & Sefton, 1989). The items were reviewed for face validity and readability by a sport psychologist, a sport sociologist, and a curriculum specialist. The items are scored on a 10-point scale ranging from "no, not at all" to "yes, very much." The two

Table 7.2   Children's Items and Variables

C-COACH	*satisfaction with the coach*
	Includes: My coach knows a lot about soccer.
	My coach helps me learn new soccer skills.
TEAM	*satisfaction with the team*
	Includes: Soccer practice is exciting and fun.
	I really like to play soccer with my team.
FRIENDS	*perception of having friends on the team*
	Includes: I have a lot of friends on my soccer team.
DOSOC	*positive feelings about the soccer playing experience*
	Includes: How does it feel to do soccer skills like running, kicking, and dribbling?
	How do you feel when you are playing soccer?
SKILL	*perceived soccer skill*
	Includes: How good at soccer are you?
	How good at soccer would your parents say you are?
	How good at soccer would your coach say you are?
WEBB	*professionalization of attitude toward play*
	In playing soccer, which of the following do you think is most important?
	To defeat the other team
	To play as well as you can
	To have fun

Reprinted from Green, 1997.

items are significantly correlated ($r = .63$, $p < .001$). The items are averaged to obtain an overall index of children's satisfaction with the team.

Research into youth sport consistently finds that children's enjoyment of the experience is determined, in part, by their perception that they have friends on the team (e.g., Gill, Gross, & Huddleston, 1983; Gould & Petlichkoff, 1988; Scanlan, Stein, & Ravizza, 1989). This factor is measured by the single statement, "I have a lot of friends on my soccer team," which is scored on a 10-point scale ranging from "no, not at all" to "yes, lots."

Children's enjoyment while playing soccer was measured using two enjoyment items from Wankel and Kreisel's (1985) minor sport enjoyment inventory. Wankel and Kreisel report test-retest reliability of .73. The items are each scored on a 5-point Likert scale. They are averaged to form an overall index of children's enjoyment of playing soccer.

Perceived soccer ability was measured using three items developed from McElroy and Kirkendall's (1980) single-item measure. Whereas McElroy and Kirkendall used parents' perceptions only, the literature suggests the need to incorporate children's perceptions of their ability and their perception of the coach's opinion of their ability (Horn

& Hasbrook, 1986, 1987; Ommundsen & Vaglum, 1991). The three items are scored on a 5-point Likert scale ranging from "very good" to "poor" and averaged to provide an overall index of perceived soccer ability. Principle components analysis of data from this study showed the three items to share a single common factor: only one eigenvalue exceeded unity, and all three items had loadings above .7 on the first principle component.

Children's professionalization of attitude toward play was measured using the same scale as that given to parents (viz., Kidd & Woodman, 1975).

Results

Parents

The question uppermost in the minds of those who had designed and implemented the modified program asked whether the parents were satisfied with the modified program. The midpoint of each item in the two satisfaction scales (ADMIN and P-COACH) represents a point of indifference. To facilitate interpretation, the scores for each item were centered on their midpoint so that positive scores would represent satisfaction and negative scores would represent dissatisfaction. The resulting scores were then tested against zero (i.e., indifference) using one-sample t-tests. Both scores were positive and significantly different from zero (for ADMIN: $M = 1.55$, $SD = .75$, $t(72) = 17.62$, $p < .001$; for P-COACH: $M = 1.65$, $SD = .64$, $t(72) = 22.09$, $p < .001$). It is concluded that parents of children in the modified program reported significant levels of satisfaction with the program's coaching and administration.

The remaining research questions about parents are comparative; they ask whether parents who choose the modified program for their children differ from those who choose traditional programs. The responses of parents from each of the three programs (modified, traditional recreation, and elite) were tested using MANOVA. The seven variables (ADMIN, P-COACH, PDI, PSI, SSI, ADIMP, and WEBB) were entered as dependent variables, and the three programs were entered as the grouping (i.e., independent) variable. The MANOVA was significant; $F(14,250) = 6.34$; $p < .001$. It is concluded that parents in the three programs differ significantly.

In order to explore these differences among parents in the three programs, the seven dependent variables were tested via ANOVA using Helmert contrasts. Helmert contrasts provide a direct test of the key question of interest: whether parents of children in the modified program differ from parents of children in the traditional programs. They also test whether parents in the two traditional programs differ significantly. Thus, the two hypothesis degrees of freedom in the ANOVA are orthogonally decomposed into two precise tests. Means, standard deviations, and F-ratios are reported in table 7.3.

Inspection of table 7.3 shows that parents of children in the modified program were significantly more satisfied with their program's administration than were parents of children in the traditional programs. However, parents of children in the traditional programs did not differ significantly in their levels of satisfaction.

Parents in the three programs did not differ in their levels of satisfaction with coaching.

Parents of children in the modified program evidenced significantly higher levels of purchase-decision involvement than did parents in the traditional programs. Parents of children in the elite program evidenced significantly higher levels of purchase-decision involvement than did parents of children in the recreational program.

Parents of children in the three programs did not differ significantly in their levels of primary sport involvement, but they did differ significantly in their levels of secondary sport involvement. Parents of children in the modified program reported lower levels of passive sport consumption than did parents of children in the traditional programs. Parents of children in the elite programs reported significantly higher levels of passive sport consumption than did parents of children in the recreational program.

Parents of children in the modified program were significantly more concerned about adult impositions in youth sport than were parents of children in the traditional programs. Parents of children in the recreation and elite programs did not differ significantly in their concerns about adult imposition in youth sport.

Parents of children in the modified program had significantly less professionalized attitudes toward play than did parents of children in the traditional programs. Parents of children in the traditional programs did not differ significantly in their professionalization of attitude toward play.

Children

The staff of the modified program wanted to know whether the children liked the modified program. As with the parents' scales, the midpoint of each item in the two satisfaction scales (C-COACH and TEAM) represents a point of indifference. To facilitate interpretation, the scores for each item were centered on their midpoint so that positive scores would represent satisfaction and negative scores would represent dissatisfaction. The resulting scores were then tested against zero (i.e., indifference) using one-sample t-tests. Both scores were positive and significantly different from zero (for C-COACH: $M = 3.49$, $SD = 1.46$, $t(86) = 22.25$, $p < .001$; for TEAM: $M = 3.64$, $SD = 1.29$, $t(86) = 26.25$, $p < .001$). It is concluded that children in the modified program reported significant levels of satisfaction with the program's coaching and play group environment.

Staff of the modified program also wanted to know whether the children felt that they had friends in the program (FRIENDS), enjoyed playing soccer (DOSOC), and felt positively about their soccer skill (SKILL). The program had been designed with these objectives in mind. As with the satisfaction measures, the measures for each of these three variables are centered on a midpoint representing

Table 7.3   Helmert Contrasts: Parent Variables

Variable	Mean	SD	Modified vs traditional F(1, 131)	Recreational vs elite F(1, 131)
ADMIN				
Modified	1.55	.75	5.48*	.92
Recreational	1.12	.81		
Elite	1.32	.90		
C-COACH				
Modified	1.65	.64	.06	2.61
Recreational	1.55	.66		
Elite	1.80	.53		
PDI				
Modified	2.92	1.24	18.06***	7.62**
Recreational	1.50	1.62		
Elite	2.42	1.01		
PSI				
Modified	.03	.89	1.32	3.39
Recreational	−.34	.70		
Elite	.06	.88		
SSI				
Modified	−.08	1.05	15.29***	7.56**
Recreational	.25	1.07		
Elite	.97	.87		
ADIMP				
Modified	.71	1.79	7.67**	.37
Recreational	−.28	1.87		
Elite	.00	1.48		
WEBB				
Modified	1.25	.64	37.33***	.58
Recreational	2.10	1.11		
Elite	2.27	1.11		

*** $p < .001$; ** $p < .01$; * $p < .05$.

Reprinted from Green, 1997.

indifference. Positive scores, thus, represent a positive sense of friendships, enjoyment, and skill; negative scores represent a perception that friendships, enjoyment, or skill are lacking. Consequently, the observed scores for these three variables were tested against zero (i.e., indifference) using one-sample t-tests. All three scores were positive and significantly different from zero (for FRIENDS: $M = 1.92$, $SD = 2.92$, $t(86) = 6.35$, $p < .001$; for DOSOC: $M = 1.75$, $SD = .42$, $t(86) = 38.59$, $p < .001$; for SKILL: $M = 1.26$, $SD = .75$, $t(86) = 15.73$, $p < .001$). It is concluded that children in the modified program perceive they have friends in their play group, enjoy playing soccer, and have a positive sense of their soccer skills.

Remaining questions about the children are comparative; they ask whether children in the modified program differ from those in traditional programs. The responses of children from each of the three programs (modified, traditional recreation, and elite) were tested using MANOVA. The six variables (C-COACH, TEAM, FRIENDS, DOSOC, SKILL, and WEBB) were entered as dependent variables, and the three programs were entered as the grouping (i.e., independent) variable. The MANOVA was significant; $F(12,286) = 2.24$; $p = .01$. It is concluded that children in the three programs differ significantly.

In order to explore differences among children in the three programs, the six dependent variables were tested via ANOVA using Helmert contrasts. As with the examination of parent differences, the Helmert contrasts were structured to test whether children in the modified program differ from those in the traditional programs, and whether children in the two traditional programs differ significantly. Means, standard deviations, and F-ratios are reported in table 7.4.

Inspection of table 7.4 shows that children in the modified program and children in the traditional programs did not differ significantly in their satisfaction with the coaching. However, children in the elite program were significantly more satisfied with the coaching they received than were children in the recreational program. There were no differences among the three programs in children's level of satisfaction with their team.

Children in the modified program perceived a significantly lower level of team friendships than was reported by children in the traditional programs. Children in the elite program reported higher levels of perceived team friendships than were reported for children in the recreational program.

Children in the three programs did not differ in their levels of enjoyment when playing soccer nor in their professionalization of attitude toward play. However, children in the modified program reported a lower perception of their soccer skill than is reported by children in the traditional programs. Children in the two traditional programs did not differ in their perceived level of soccer skill.

Utilization of Results

Results were tabulated and provided in writing to the parents responsible for implementation of the modified program. The results and their interpretation were discussed in detail in six separate meetings. The sequential discussions were found to be important so that the meaning of results could be explored and policy implications could be derived.

The findings of high levels of parent and child satisfaction were encouraging. However, it was the comparative research that yielded the most substantial impacts. The most significant outcome resulted from the conclusion that the modified program was reaching a psychologically different market segment than was being reached by traditional programs. Several factors combined to persuade soccer administrators that this was the case. First, the significantly higher purchase-decision involvement of parents in the modified program suggested that these parents were actively seeking something different from the typical program. This conclusion was bolstered by their significantly higher concerns about adult imposition in youth sport, their markedly lower level of professionalized attitude toward play, and their

lower level of secondary sport involvement. Taken together, these findings persuaded administrators that the modified program appealed to parents who might otherwise be wary of organized sport for their children.

When combined with the high levels of reported satisfaction, this conclusion was important because it recommended the value of retaining the modified program. Given the high demand for time on soccer fields, there had been some concern that the modified program was merely a distraction from "real soccer." However, the fact that the program could generate high levels of satisfaction among clients who might not otherwise be so appropriately served was deemed advantageous for soccer's growth in the community.

Administrators also were encouraged by the finding that children in the modified program enjoyed playing soccer and felt positively about their skills and friendships. However, the fact that children in the modified program perceived their skills and friendships less favorably than did children in the traditional programs worried administrators. This difference led to a great deal of discussion and rethinking of the program.

After discussions with parents and children, it was concluded that the differences in perceived skill were due, in part, to the fact that children in the modified program do not have an opportunity to measure their skill in "real" games of soccer. Although the program had been designed to provide high volumes of play at soccer-like skills, the program's lack of soccer scrimmages or league games precluded children from obtaining the kinds of social comparison information that is obtained by children in traditional programs. Indeed, when queried, children reported that the games of the modified program "aren't real soccer." Their point of comparison is the kind of soccer they see being played on television or at the local high school, not their execution of specific ball skills (which is demonstrably high).

Consequently, two adjustments were made in the program. First, there is more effort to point out to children their specific skill improvements. Second, a "challenge program" has been introduced. This program provides children the option of playing standard games of seven-a-side soccer during the second half of some play group sessions. However, the play group is retained such that the team composition varies on each occasion, and there is no league structure. Two speculations were advanced to explain the differences in perceptions about friendships. First, it was noted that teams in the traditional programs are often formed around friends

Table 7.4 Helmert Contrasts: Child Variables

Variable	Mean	SD	Modified vs traditional $F(1, 131)$	Recreational vs elite $F(1, 131)$
C-COACH			.46	4.00*
Modified	3.49	1.46		
Recreational	3.27	2.17		
Elite	4.07	1.06		
TEAM			.51	.82
Modified	3.64	1.29		
Recreational	3.65	1.75		
Elite	3.95	.82		
FRIENDS			13.10***	5.06*
Modified	1.92	2.82		
Recreational	2.71	2.56		
Elite	4.11	.85		
DOSOC			3.42	.42
Modified	1.75	.42		
Recreational	1.84	.36		
Elite	1.90	.24		
SKILL			7.62**	.00
Modified	1.26	.75		
Recreational	1.57	.58		
Elite	1.57	.49		
WEBB			.38	.08
Modified	1.97	1.48		
Recreational	1.89	1.07		
Elite	1.79	1.13		

*** $p < .001$; ** $p < .01$; * $p < .05$.

Reprinted from Green, 1997.

who play together year after year. Second, it was noted that the competitive element in traditional programs provides teammates a superordinate goal that is lacking in the modified program: winning.

These conclusions led to two plans for improving the potentials for children to develop friendships in the modified program. First, wherever possible, play groups are formed from families in the same neighborhood to increase the likelihood that there will be some continuity between children's choice of playmates at home and in soccer. Second, the "challenge program" is used to provide children in the play group a consistent opportunity to share the goal of winning in a game of "real soccer."

Implications

At the time of this writing, the modified program has continued to grow in popularity, and the con-

cept is being expanded into other sports in the same community. The experiences of this program and the findings of this study suggest that modified sports activities for children can be well-received by parents and their children. Further, their inclusion in the array of sport offerings may expand the diversity of markets served by sport programs.

Nevertheless, the kinds of changes represented by the program studied here are not easily implemented. Although the literature is replete with recommendations for child-centered modifications (e.g., Chase, Ewing, Lirgg, & George, 1994; Hellison, 1995; Hutslar, 1985; Martens, Rivkin, & Bump, 1984; Satem, Messier, & Keller-McNulty, 1989; Shields & Bredemeier, 1995; Voylé, 1989; Watson, 1996), conventional versions of sport programming are more readily accepted by the volunteers who implement youth sport programs. In the case studied here, it took substantial entrepreneurial zeal to get the modified program started. Once it was going, there was considerable skepticism about its value, particularly among administrators who had extensive experience implementing traditional programs. The research reported here provided vital insight into the program's underlying value and dynamics, thus helping to sustain and advance it. This suggests the value of action research as a tool for nurturing alternative sport programs.

Several lessons for future projects emerge from this study. The most subtle but important is the demonstrated value of triangulation. In this study, no single finding was itself persuasive to administrators. However, when the data were considered as a whole, they were consistent in suggesting the unique nature of the market served by the modified program.

It was particularly enlightening to survey children and parents. Program administrators had been concerned primarily about parents' satisfaction because parents make the decision to enroll their children (cf. Howard & Madrigal, 1990). Administrators were surprised to learn from the comparisons with traditional programs that although parents and children were satisfied with the modified program, parents were relatively happier with it than were their children. This persuaded the administration to strengthen its efforts to meet the expressed needs of children.

Interpretation of the data was furthered by the interactions between the researcher and the program staff before and after study implementation (cf. Chalip, 1990). Prior to commencement of the study, it was necessary to spend substantial time clarifying questions and ascertaining the utility of operationalizations chosen. Once the data were collected and analyzed, it was helpful to spend time discussing meanings and implications. Discussion and observation as the study was being designed allowed it to be tailored to the needs and wants of stakeholders. Discussions following completion of the study helped to give the findings the necessary depth of meaning to make them useful to those responsible for maintaining program integrity while implementing necessary change.

Traditional recommendations for program evaluation (e.g., Rossi & Freeman, 1989) focus on examination of the program being evaluated. However, a program of the kind studied here has to establish itself in the midst of existing, traditional programs. In this study, data comparing the modified program to traditional programs provided essential insights into the nature of the market served. Perhaps one of the fundamental contributions of this kind of action research is its capacity to clarify the ways in which new programs and services contribute to the sport service mix.

References

Argyris, C., Putnam, R., & Smith, D.M. (1985). *Action science.* San Francisco: Jossey-Bass.

Chalip, L. (1989). The postseason assessment survey: A simple tool for sports organisation development. *New Zealand Journal of Sports Medicine.* **17**(2), 28-31.

Chalip, L. (1990). Rethinking the applied social sciences of sport: Observations on the emerging debate. *Sociology of Sport Journal,* **7,** 172-178.

Chase, M.A., Ewing, M.E., Lirgg, C.D., & George, T.R. (1994). The effects of equipment modification on children's self-efficacy and basketball shooting performance. *Research Quarterly for Exercise and Sport,* **65,** 109-116.

Chelladurai, P. (1984). Discrepancy between preferences and perceptions of leadership behavior and satisfaction of athletes in varying sports. *Journal of Sport Psychology,* **6,** 27-41.

Devereux, E. (1976). Backyard versus little league baseball: The impoverishment of children's games. In D. Landers (Ed.), *Social problems in athletics* (pp. 37-56). Urbana, IL: University of Illinois Press.

Dutrow, J. (1994, May 19). Writer cites benefits of alternative youth sports program. *The Bowie* (MD) *Blade-News,* p. A 15.

Fine, G.A. (1987). *With the boys: Little league baseball and preadolescent culture.* Chicago: University of Chicago Press.

Gill, D.L., Gross, J.B., & Huddleston, S. (1983). Participation motivation in youth sports. *International Journal of Sport Psychology,* **14,** 1-14.

Gould, D., & Martens, R. (1979). Attitudes of volunteer coaches toward significant youth sport issues. *Research Quarterly,* **50,** 369-380.

Gould, D., & Petlichkoff, L. (1988). Participation motivation and attrition in young athletes. In F. Smoll, R. Magill, & M. Ash (Eds.), *Children in sport* (3rd ed., pp. 161-178). Champaign, IL: Human Kinetics.

Harrison, M.I. (1994). *Diagnosing organizations: Methods, models, and processes* (2nd ed.) Newbury Park, CA: Sage Publications.

Hellison, D. (1995). *Teaching responsibility through physical activity.* Champaign, IL: Human Kinetics.

Horn, J.C. (1977). Parent egos take the fun out of little league. *Psychology Today,* **11**(9), 18, 22.

Horn, T.S., & Hasbrook, C.A. (1986). Informational components underlying children's perceptions of their physical competence. In M.R. Weiss & D. Gould (Eds.), *Sport for children and youths* (pp. 81-88). Champaign, IL: Human Kinetics.

Horn, T.S., & Hasbrook, C.A. (1987). Psychological characteristics and the criteria children use for self-evaluation. *Journal of Sport Psychology, 9,* 208-221.

Howard, D., & Madrigal, R. (1990). Who makes the decision: The parent or child? *Journal of Leisure Research, 22,* 244-258.

Hutslar, J. (1985). *Beyond Xs and Os.* Welcome, NC: Wooten.

Kalton, G. (1983). *Introduction to survey sampling.* Sage University Paper Series on Quantitative Applications in the Social Sciences (Series No. 07-035). Beverly Hills, CA & London: Sage.

Kidd, T., & Woodman, W. (1975). Sex and orientations toward winning in sport. *46,* 476-483.

Kohn, A. (1986). *No contest: The case against competition.* Boston: Houghton Mifflin.

Martens, R. (Ed.) (1978). *Joy and sadness in youth sport.* Champaign, IL: Human Kinetics.

Martens, R. (1988). Helping children become independent, responsible adults through sports. In E.W. Brown & C.F. Branta (Eds.), *Competitive sports for children and youth: An overview of research and issues* (pp. 297-307). Champaign, IL: Human Kinetics.

Martens, R., Rivkin, F., & Bump, L.A. (1984). A field study of traditional and nontraditional children's baseball. *Research Quarterly for Exercise and Sport, 55,* 351-355.

McCormack, J.B., & Chalip, L. (1988). Sport as socialization: A critique of methodological premises. *Social Science Journal, 25,* 83-92.

McElroy, M.A., & Kirkendall, D.R. (1980). Significant others and professionalized sport attitudes. *Research Quarterly for Exercise and Sport, 51,* 645-653.

Mittal, B. (1989). Measuring purchase-decision involvement. *Psychology & Marketing, 6,* 147-162.

Ommundsen, Y., & Vaglum, P. (1991). Soccer competition anxiety and enjoyment in young boy players: The influence of perceived competence and significant others' emotional involvement. *International Journal of Sport Psychology, 22,* 35-49.

Orlick, T.D. (1974). An interview schedule designed to assess family sports environment. *International Journal of Sport Psychology, 5,* 13-27.

Prouty, D.F. (1988). *In spite of us: My education in the big and little games of amateur sports in the U.S.* Brattleboro, VT: Velo-News.

Rossi, P.H., & Freeman, H.E. (1989). *Evaluation: A systematic approach.* Newbury Park, CA: Sage.

Ryan, J. (1995). *Little girls in pretty boxes: The making and breaking of elite gymnasts and figure skaters.* New York: Doubleday.

Satern, M.N., Messier, S.P., & Keller-McNulty, S. (1989). The effects of ball size and basket height on the mechanics of the basketball free throw. *Journal of Human Movement Studies, 16,* 123-137.

Scanlan, T.K., Stein, G.L., & Ravizza, K. (1989). An in-depth study of former elite figure skaters: II. Sources of enjoyment. *Journal of Sport and Exercise Psychology, 11,* 65-83.

Shields, D.L.L., & Bredemeier, B.J.L. (1995). *Character development and physical activity.* Champaign, IL: Human Kinetics.

Smith, R.E., Smoll, F.L., & Curtis, B. (1978). Coaching behaviors in little league baseball. In F.L. Smoll & R.E. Smith (Eds.), *Psychological perspectives in youth sports* (pp. 176- 201). New York: Wiley.

Voyle, J. (1989). Adolescent administration of a leisure centre: Lessons for sports organisations. *New Zealand Journal of Sports Medicine, 17,* 31-34.

Wankel, L.M., & Kreisel, P.S.J. (1985). Factors underlying enjoyment of youth sports: Sport and age group comparisons. *Journal of Sport Psychology, 7,* 51-64.

Wankel, L.M., & Sefton, J.M. (1989). A season-long investigation of fun in youth sports. *Journal of Sport and Exercise Psychology, 11,* 355-366.

Watson, G.G. (1986). A field experiment in sport socialization and boys' field hockey. *Journal of Human Movement Studies, 12,* 1-26.

Webb, H. (1969). Professionalization of attitudes toward play among adolescents. In G.S. Kenyon (Ed.), *Aspects of contemporary sport sociology* (pp. 161-178). Chicago: The Athletic Institute.

Impacts of High School Sports Participation

Objectives

The unit examines the impacts of high school sports and other extracurricular activities on the educational process and sexual behavior among adolescents.

According to the National Federation of State High School Associations (NFSHA), approximately 6.5 million boys and girls participated in some 33 sports during the 1998-1999 school year. No longer an exclusive arena for athletically inclined boys, high school sports now attract the participation of one girl in three.

Given the extraordinary popularity of high school sports today and the commanding presence they enjoy in most American high schools, both the general public and the academic community have seen fit to offer opinions about the pros and cons of this highly visible, resource-demanding extracurricular school activity. For the general public, the positives include the strong conviction that interscholastic sports teach prosocial values (e.g., "sport builds character") and contribute to school spirit and student-body morale. On the other hand, concern is voiced about how participation in such athletic programs diverts student attention from the classroom, contributes to high injury rates, and causes disruption of family activities.

For sport researchers, the most frequently addressed questions have focused on the educational and developmental experiences of the student-athlete. Simply stated, do interscholastic sport programs contribute to the academic goals of a school or do they interfere with its educational mission? Sociologist James S. Coleman, arguably the first social scientist to formally and systematically investigate the role interscholastic athletics play in American secondary education, noted almost half a century ago that male athletes enjoy high peer-group status within the adolescent subculture. Although Coleman was no fan of interscholastic sports, he was nevertheless compelled to conclude that male participation in high school sports was positively related to popularity, exemplar status, and membership in the leading crowd. Perhaps inspired by Coleman's seminal work, a legion of sport researchers over the past four decades has investigated a plethora of social (e.g., peer group status, dating behavior, delinquency), psychological (e.g., locus of control, self-concept, eating disorders), and educational (grades, school retention, educational aspirations) consequences thought to be associated with high school sports participation.

The findings from mostly cross-sectional studies suggest that students who participate in high school sports tend to earn better grades, are less likely to drop out of school, have higher educational expectations, are more popular with their peers, identify more strongly with their schools, have lower delinquency rates, and possess higher self-esteem. A number of sport sociologists, however, have pointed out that these research findings must be viewed with caution because conclusions are based primarily on correlational data, with little control exercised over self-selection factors. That is, high school athletes already possessing traits or characteristics known to be associated with academic success, social standing, and psychological well-being select themselves for, or are recruited by others (e.g., coaches) into, athletic teams. If this is the case, then attributing beneficial effects to athletic participation is suspect.

The validity and generalizability of sport participation research findings are further called into question by the fact that athletes are continually being filtered out of the athletic stream for a variety of reasons including loss of interest; injury; nonconformity to sport, school, and community standards; and failure to meet performance expectations (e.g., through the practice of "cutting" athletes from a team). Thus, the "typical" group of athletes included in many research studies of athlete versus nonathlete is often a highly filtered group. This circumstance makes it difficult for researchers to isolate the independent socialization effects of the sport experience.

Even when researchers have taken care to control for potentially confounding variables, it is difficult to attribute differences favoring athletic samples to the sport experience because participation in high school sports is just one of many possible influences in the lives of active, high-energy teenagers. As sport sociologist Jay Coakley (1998) has pointed out, kids do other things besides sports in their teen years. To suggest that sports participation is directly responsible for this or that developmental change is to run the risk of oversimplifying the complex maturational and developmental processes associated with early and late adolescence.

Coakley offers the following four general observations about the "state of the field" with respect to the socialization consequences of high school sports participation:

1. We need to show considerable caution before generalizing about the educational values of high school sports participation.
2. We need to do additional longitudinal, long-term studies that address not just the sport lives of teenagers but also their lives in general.
3. We need to do a better job in comparing the educational lives of athletes and nonathletes to see whether the favorable findings associated with the athlete group have more to do with preferential treatment from teachers, coaches, counselors, and school administrators.
4. We need to extend our research focus to examine how varsity sports fit within the larger high school student culture.

Sport sociologist George Sage (1998) predicts that the next decade will see researchers moving beyond statistical comparison studies of "athlete" versus "nonathlete" and using more sophisticated methods to investigate how high school sports programs, as cultural practices, serve as vehicles for inculcating the norms, values, and beliefs of dominant groups. As Sage has astutely observed, "Dominant groups use various institutional and cultural resources to legitimate and disseminate their ideologies and interests. Modern sport forms are cultural practices that are part of the terrain on which the dominant ideology is built and sustained" (pp. 262-263).

For researchers in general, and critical theorists in particular, identifying and mapping the ideological terrain of high school sports and the ways in which athletes incorporate, struggle with, and resist the ideological messages contained in their sport experiences will prove to be a challenging but exciting new research direction to pursue.

In the first selection, Fejgin uses longitudinal data from a nationally representative sample of American 10th graders to examine the relationship between participation in high school competitive sports and grades, self-concept, locus of control, discipline problems, and educational aspirations. In addition, student background factors (gender, social class) and school attributes (private versus public) are analyzed to determine their contribution to degree of athletic participation. On the basis of her findings, the author recommends that academic schoolwork be designed in ways similar to the ways sport is structured.

In the second selection, Miller, Sabo, Farrell, Barnes, and Melnick introduce cultural resource theory to explain why female athletes report significantly lower rates of sexual activity, including unwanted pregnancy, than female nonathletes. They theorize that athletic participation reinforces traditional gender scripts for boys but gives female participants more "bargaining chips" in the negotiating process associated with teen sexual activity. The implications of these findings for programs aimed at the prevention of adolescent pregnancy are worth serious consideration.

In the third selection, Eccles and Barber examine the potential benefits and risks of four kinds of extracurricular involvement among male and female adolescents (church and volunteer activities, team sports, school involvement, performing and academic clubs). Of interest to the reader will be the mixed findings for participation in team sports. Most important, the researchers identify two significant mediating variables, peer association and activity-based identity, that help explain the obtained extracurricular activity group differences.

References

Coakley, J.J. (1998). *Sport in society: Issues and controversies.* New York: McGraw-Hill.

Eccles, J., & Barber, B.L. (1999). Student council, volunteering, basketball, or marching band. What kind of extracurricular involvement matters? *Journal of Adolescent Research, 14*: 10-43.

Fejgin, N. (1994). Participation in high school competitive sports: A subversion of school mission or contribution to academic goals? *Sociology of Sport Journal, 11*: 211-230.

Miller, K., Sabo, D.F., Farrell, M.P., Barnes, G.M., & Melnick, M.J. (1998). Athletic participation and sexual behavior in adolescents: The different worlds of boys and girls. *Journal of Health and Social Behavior, 39*: 108-123.

Miracle, A.W., & Rees, C.R. (1994). *Lessons of the locker room: The myth of school sports.* Amherst, NY: Prometheus Books.

Sabo, D., Melnick, M.J., & Vanfossen, B.E. (1989). *The Women's Sports Foundation Report: Minorities in sport—the effect of varsity sports participation on the social, educational, and career mobility of minority students.* New York: Women's Sports Foundation.

Sage, G.H. (1998). *Power and ideology in American sport.* Champaign, IL: Human Kinetics.

Spreitzer, E. (1992, August). *Does participation in interscholastic athletics affect adult development: A longitudinal analysis of an 18-24 age cohort.* Paper presented at the annual conference of the American Sociological Association, Pittsburgh.

Discussion Questions

Naomi Fejgin

1. Discuss and compare the functionalist and conflict theory explanations for the hypothesized consequences of high school sports participation.
2. How did participation in high school athletics compare with participation in other extracurricular activities, including intramurals?
3. Do school type and school size encourage or discourage athletic participation? Explain.
4. Do these findings support the predictions of developmental or conflict theory? Explain.
5. Do high school sports play a role in nurturing individual achievement motivation? Explain.
6. Identify and discuss some policy recommendations based on the results of this study.

Kathleen Miller, Donald Sabo, Michael Farrell, Grace Barnes, and Merrill Melnick

1. How serious is the adolescent pregnancy problem in the United States?
2. Briefly describe how control, resource, and exchange theory processes might affect adolescent sexuality.
3. Identify and discuss some predictors of adolescent sexual activity.
4. What did the researchers discover about the impact of sports participation on male and female sexual behavior? Discuss and explain.
5. In terms of adolescent sexual activity, how did participants in athletics and "academic" extracurricular activities compare?
6. Which theory (control theory, exchange theory, cultural resources theory) did the best job of explaining the gender-specific effects that sport has on adolescent sexual behavior? Explain.

Jacquelynne Eccles and Bonnie Barber

1. Why does participation in organized extracurricular activities result in better use of an adolescent's free time? Discuss and explain.
2. Identify the five types of constructive leisure activity that adolescents typically favor.
3. Identify the concurrent and long-term correlates (i.e., benefits and risks) of participation in prosocial activities, team sports, performing arts, school-involvement activities, and academic clubs.
4. Identify the link between activity participation and peer-group characteristics. To what degree does the peer group mediate the association between activity-group membership and adolescent outcomes? Discuss and explain.
5. To what degree do activity-based identities explain the potential benefits and risks of extracurricular involvement? Discuss and explain.
6. Based on these findings, which type of extracurricular activity deserves the most school support? Discuss and explain your position.

Participation in High School Competitive Sports: A Subversion of School Mission or Contribution to Academic Goals?

Naomi Fejgin

Longitudinal data from a nationally representative sample of 10th graders (National Educational Longitudinal Study of 1988 First Follow-Up) were used to assess the net effect of athletic participation on student outcomes after controlling for student background and 8th-grade measures of the dependent variables. The analyses show positive effects of sport participation on grades, self-concept, locus of control, and educational aspirations, and a negative effect on discipline problems. Analysis also shows that athletic participation is unequally distributed across gender and socioeconomic groups: Males, students from higher socioeconomic levels, students attending private and smaller schools, and those with previous experience in school and private sport teams are more engaged in high school competitive sport.

The social significance of high school sport has been approached in social science research from a number of theoretical positions, four of which have received significant attention in the literature. Individual student outcomes have been considered by developmental theory, which emphasizes the "socializing" or "character-building" effects of athletic participation (Rees, Howell,& Miracle, 1990; Spady, 1970), and zero-sum theory, which is concerned with athletic participation diverting attention from academic work (Coleman, 1961).

Organizational and macrosocial positions are addressed by functional theory, which advocates the positive, integrational effects of high school sports (Waller, 1961), and conflict theory, which notes the unequal distribution of sports participation among different social groups and the reproductive effects of school sport on acceptance of existing social structure and stratification (Sage, 1990).

These contrasting pairs of theories are related in that, if the developmental approach is supported, and participation has positive student outcomes, attention is drawn to those who do not participate. Conversely, if the predictions of the zero-sum theory are supported, attention is drawn to those who waste energy on sports rather than use it for academic pursuits.[1] Thus, it is important to have accurate, up-to-date knowledge about the contribution of high school sports to student characteristics, especially the characteristics central to schoolwork, before considering the unequal distribution of sports activities.

Most studies testing the predictions of developmental versus zero-sum theories are inconclusive, leaving room for researchers who hold opposing views of school sports to draw different conclusions about their outcomes (Rees et al., 1990). The various studies addressing this issue either have serious methodological problems or use old data sets; these flaws leave room for a longitudinal analysis, employing a nationally representative sample of U.S. high school sophomores in the 1990s.

This study examines the relationship between participation in high school competitive sports and student outcomes such as grades, self-concept, locus of control, discipline problems, and educational

Reprinted from Fejgin, 1994.

aspirations. Then, assuming that participating in sports may have certain effects, this study also analyzes background factors that relate to participation, such as family and school attributes.

Effects:
Is School Sport a Character Builder?

Functional theorists have long viewed school sport as an integration mechanism for individual students, for school as an organization, and for society at large (Coleman, 1985). It has been argued (Evans & Davies, 1986; Frey, 1986) that team sports, especially interscholastic competitions, offer an opportunity for all students—active athletes, cheerleaders, and spectators—to congregate and fight for a common goal. These events are viewed as social rituals that socialize youth into some of the basic values of American life: competition, determination, fair play, and achievement.

At the individual level, in light of the developmental model, participation in school teams is viewed as affecting outcomes and building character. Character aspects and outcomes said to be affected include honesty, courage, cooperation, acceptance of authority, social prestige, and opportunities for educational and occupational advancement (Frey, 1986). Various studies have examined different psychological, attitudinal, and behavioral aspects of school and work performance in relation to sport participation. Several reviews of empirical studies of the effects of sport participation (Holland & Andre, 1987; Marsh, 1993; Otto, 1982; Stevenson, 1975) reported that the most commonly studied outcomes were academic achievement, educational and occupational aspirations, educational and occupational attainments, self-concept, and popularity. These outcomes tend to be positively related to participation in sport. For example, Otto and Alwin (1977) found that sport participation of male students in the senior year of high school was positively related to educational and occupational aspirations, after controlling for socioeconomic status (SES), IQ, and school grades. In a subsequent study Otto (1982) reported that sport participation in high school positively affected educational attainment, occupational status, and income 15 years later.

Howell, Miracle, and Rees (1989) found that sport participation in high school was related to educational attainment 5 years later, but not to income of those who did not attend college. Later, using the same sample, they reported that some forms of sport participation affected several measures of educa-

tional/occupational motivation, such as valuing of academic achievement, self-esteem, college plans, occupational plans, and positive attitudes toward the high school experience, but also some antisocial outcomes, such as irritability and reduced belief in "being honest" and in "social responsibilities" (Rees et al., 1990).

In more recent studies Melnick, Vanfossen, and Sabo (1988), using the nationally representative High School and Beyond data, found that girls' athletic participation was positively related to extracurricular involvement, educational aspirations, and perceived popularity. They also found differential effects of sport participation on perceived popularity, extracurricular involvement, school grades, standardized achievement scores, dropout rates, educational aspirations, college attendance, degree sought, and advancement in college—for Hispanic boys and girls from urban, suburban, and rural areas (Melnick, Sabo, & Vanfossen, 1992a). In a subsequent study (Sabo, Melnick, & Vanfossen, 1993) they reported other differential effects on educational and occupational attainment of black, white, and Hispanic boys and girls from different areas; sport participation positively affected mostly suburban white male students and, to a lesser degree, white female students and Hispanic females from rural areas.

Marsh (1993), using the same sample, found that sport participation during the last 2 years of high school favorably affected 14 of 22 outcomes, including social and academic self-concept, educational aspirations, course work selection, homework, reduced absenteeism, and college attendance.

Other studies have suggested a zero-sum model in which more time spent on nonacademic goals—for example, sports (Coleman, 1961) or part-time employment (Marsh, 1991)—diverts attention from school, leading to less time spent on homework and less investment in school. Greenberger and Steinberg (1986) found that student part-time employment was related to lower GPA, and Marsh (1991) found that total hours of work during high school "unfavorably affected going to college, high school attendance, academic track, parental involvement, educational aspirations, standardized test scores, staying out of trouble, . . . and academic self-concept" (p. 179). Coleman's argument about sport participation relied on his findings that athletic participation was the main determinant of social status of male high school students (1961). Therefore, he argued, students may prefer to invest time and energy in sport activities and neglect academic work that is not as valued by their peers. Later studies, however, found that athletic participation ranked only fifth among six status criteria for female high school students (Felz, 1978), and fourth for boys (Thirer & Wright, 1985). None of the studies actually found that sport participation negatively affected academic outcomes.

Most of the studies, however, especially those taking the developmental approach, had serious methodological problems. Nearly all of them used small, nonrepresentative samples (Hauser & Lueptow, 1978; Otto & Alwin, 1977; Snyder & Spreitzer, 1977; Spady, 1970). Many employed cross-sectional comparisons, without longitudinal perspectives (Braddock, 1981; Edwards, 1967; Hanks, 1979; Johnson, 1972; Malumphy, 1968; Pyecha, 1970; Snyder & Spreitzer, 1977). These cross-sectional studies may have found different attitudes and behaviors between athletes and nonathletes, but could not determine causality and direction of effect. They could not conclude, for example, whether sports participation builds self-discipline, or whether self-disciplined students choose to participate in sport teams and are able to endure the strenuous training regime.

Several studies employing longitudinal perspectives and using nationally representative samples (Hanks & Eckland, 1976; Howell et al., 1989; Rees et al., 1990) also used data from the 1960s and 1970s, and thus lack current relevance. The most recent studies employing a longitudinal perspective used data from the nationally representative sample of the High School and Beyond survey collected in the early to mid-1980s. Three of the four studies published by Melnick, Sabo, and Vanfossen examined subsamples of girls (Melnick et al., 1988), Hispanic students (Melnick et al., 1992a), or Hispanic and African-American youths (Melnick, Sabo, & Vanfossen, 1992b). One study considered educational and occupational mobility after high school, finding differential effects for various subgroups of students (Sabo et al., 1993).

Only one study examined some character-building effects (i.e., behaviors, attitudes, and concepts relevant to schoolwork), together with postsecondary achievement for the whole sample (Marsh, 1993). Marsh's conclusions, however, are different from those of Melnick et al. (1992a), although both agree that sport participation has no negative effects. While Melnick et al. concluded that "the 17 statistically or marginally significant, positive findings do not represent an overwhelming endorsement of the competitive high school sport experience" (p. 65), Marsh concluded that "participation in sport has many positive effects with no apparent negative effects and these positive effects are very robust," and "participation in sport leads to an increased commitment to, involvement with, or identification with school and school values" (p. 35). He also suggested that future studies take into account the type of sport the student is involved in and the degree of commitment to sport participation, variables not available in the High School and Beyond data set. The present study uses a more recent data set, which enables a more detailed measure of athletic participation.

Juxtaposing the predictions of the developmental and the zero-sum theories, this study addresses the effects of participation in school competitive sport on several student outcomes. Not all student outcomes examined in previous studies are analyzed in the present study, only those central to the predictions of these theories and to the key school missions. They are academic achievement and educational aspirations (for which the theories have opposing predictions). Also examined are self-concept, locus of control, and discipline problems, which have long been related in social-psychological theory to the first two outcomes. These behaviors and attitudes are seen here as important characteristics that contribute to individual advancement in school. Other characteristics such as moral or prosocial behaviors, which some scholars argue are positively affected by school sport (Arnold, 1984) (although others hold a contrary view; Eitzen, 1992), are not examined here.

The effect of athletic participation is also compared to that of participation in other extracurricular activities, such as academic clubs, music/drama, student government, and other hobby clubs. These activities have been positively related to several school-related behaviors (Finn, 1989; Spady, 1970), and to the total development of the individual (Holland & Andre, 1987).

Background Factors: School Sport and Conflict Theory

In contrast to those who espouse the functional arguments, conflict theorists argue that while participation in school teams may result in a variety of positive outcomes, school sport is often detrimental to those individuals who do not participate and to the school organization, since it has the potential of increasing tension and antagonism between groups within the school. Hendry (1978) found underinvolvement of lower class students in sports teams in Britain, which resulted in an antisport, antischool subculture. Other studies speculate on the harmful effects that unequal opportunity in sports and physical education may have for girls (Carrington & Leaman, 1986; Schafer, 1981; Scraton, 1986), enhancing their passivity, lack of competitiveness, and low self-esteem. Hargreaves (1986) put sport in a larger, macrosocial perspective, suggesting that it is used by more powerful groups in society for their benefit. Sage (1990) added that college and professional sport opportunities in America are unequally distributed across race, gender, and social class, and that the few cases of "rags to riches" athletes are made so visible in order to maintain belief in social mobility and equal opportunity, and to preserve the existing social structure. These beliefs trickle down to lower grades and encourage minority youth to invest in sport instead of academic work, believing it will offer them opportunities for social mobility.

Following these suggestions, this study addresses a second issue, whether sports in American high schools in the 1990s are unequally distributed across race, gender, and socioeconomic levels, and whether these variations are associated with certain school attributes.

Methodology

Sample

This study draws on data from the National Educational Longitudinal Study (NELS) of 1988 Base Year and First Follow-Up (Ingels, Scott, Lindmark, Frankel, & Myers, 1992). The base-year study (NELS 88) was carried out on a clustered, stratified national probability sample of 1,052 schools and 26,432 students (8th graders), while the first follow-up studied the same students in 10th grade (22,696) as well as a freshened sample to replace dropouts. The analyses in the present study use the panel sample of sophomores in 1990, who were in 8th grade in 1988, in order to present a longitudinal perspective. The sample was adjusted and weighted according to the formula suggested by the study's designers (Ingels et al., 1992, p. 58), to correct for sample design effects and ensure representativeness. The data for each student were collected by four questionnaires administered to students, parents, teachers, and schools. The present study uses mainly information available through the student questionnaire, some parent information, and school reports, together with standardized test scores from tests administered specifically for this study.

Measures

Most of the variables used for the examination of this study's questions are clearly defined in the NELS 88 data set—either as simple measures or as composites, compiled by the NCES (National Center for Education Statistics). Some are new measures composed for this study from the available data. The variables are described in detail in the appendix. Following are the variables, as used in the model. The main independent variable, athletic participation, is described in detail.

Independent Variables

The independent variable used in the main model, athletic participation (Athletic), is a continuous measure, composed of student self-reports on nine questionnaire items regarding participation in one or more sports, such as baseball/softball, basketball, football, soccer, swim team, other team sport, individual sport, cheerleading, or pom-pom. Participation in each sport was ranked on a scale of 0 to 3 (*did not participate* = 0, *participated in intramural sport* = 1, *participated on a junior varsity/freshmen team* = 2, *participated on a varsity team, or as a captain* = 3). Scores for each sport were summed so that the composite score (0 to 27) reflects athletic involvement as a combined measure of number of sports played, and the level of participation.

Also an alternative model considers the following independent variables: participation in music/drama (Music/Play), academic clubs (Academic Cl), student government (Student Cl), and other hobby clubs (Other Cl). In the model where athletic participation is the dependent variable, additional independent variables were introduced: school size, school affiliation (Private Scl), and 8th-grade participation in varsity sport (8th Varsity), intramural sport (8th Intramur), and private sport lessons after school (8th Private Sports AS).

Dependent Variables

Dependent variables were student 10th-grade measures of grades, self-concept (Self Cpt), locus of control (Locus), discipline problems (Discip), and educational aspirations (Ed Asp).

Background and Control Variables

These variables included gender (Female), race (Black, Asian, Hispanic), standardized composite test score (Std Ach), family income (Fam Inc), parent education (Par Ed), and 8th-grade measures of student grades (8th Grade), self-concept (8th Self), locus of control (8th Locus), discipline problems (8th Discip), and educational aspirations (8th Asp).

Statistical Analysis

Multiple regression analysis was used to examine the relationship between background, independent variables, and dependent variables. Multiple regression explains the extent to which variance in the dependent variable can be accounted for by the variance in a set of independent variables. Standardized beta coefficients indicate the weight of each variable in explaining the variance in the dependent variable (Norusis, 1993).

In order to estimate the effects of athletic participation on student grades, self-concept, locus of control, discipline problems, and educational aspirations, a set of independent multiple regressions were performed, where the background variables and athletic participation were regressed with each dependent variable separately. For each dependent variable, the 8th-grade measure was added to the equation in order to control for prior level and to show the net effect of athletic participation. Such a strategy allows interpretation of the relations between sport participation and outcome variables as effects of sport participation, since not only student background was controlled for but also prior measures of the outcome variables.

In order to examine relationships between background variables and sport participation, some cross-tabulations were presented first to demonstrate rates of participation of various groups in various sports. Then, another regression analysis examined in four steps the relative effect of each background variable on athletic participation, and the additional contribution of some school properties and prior athletic experience to the explained variance in 10th-grade athletic participation.

Findings

Effects of Athletic Participation

In table 8.1, after controlling for the background variables and for prior measures of each dependent variable, I show additional significant effects of athletic participation on grades ($\beta = .041$), self-concept ($\beta = .053$), locus of control ($\beta = .057$), educational aspirations ($\beta = .068$), and discipline problems ($\beta = -.057$).

Evidently, each dependent variable is mostly related to its measure in 8th grade (e.g., student grades in 10th grade are highly related to grades in 8th grade; student self-concept in 10th grade is

Table 8.1 Standardized Regression Coefficients From Regressions of Background Variables and Athletic on Dependent Variables

Independent variables	Dependent variables				
	Grades	Self Cpt	Locus	Ed Asp	Discip
Fam Inc	−.016	.006	.005	.037**	−.008
Par Ed	.031	−.021	.008	.112***	−.031
Std Ach	.218***	.106***	.165***	.239***	−.099***
Female	.024	−.052***	.039**	.071***	.057***
Black	.025	.113***	.037*	.086***	−.060***
Asian	.036*	−.008	.001	.035**	−.020
Hispanic	.000	.038**	.031	.042**	.035*
8th Grade	.287***				
8th Self		.454***			
8th Locus			.373***		
8th Asp				.387***	
8th Discip					.337***
Athletic	.041**	.053***	.057***	.068***	−.057***
R-square adjusted	.188	.267	.210	.384	.152

*$p < .05$. **$p < .01$. ***$p < .001$.

Reprinted from Fejgin, 1994.

highly related to self-concept in 8th grade, and so on). However, additional direct effects of athletic participation on each of these variables are observed, meaning that athletic participation appears to contribute to increased levels of grades, self-concept, locus of control, and educational aspirations, and to decreased levels of discipline problems. In fact, in each of these models except for educational aspirations, the effect of athletic participation is greater than that of family income, parent education, gender, and Asian or Hispanic origin.[2] These variables explain about 38% of the variance in educational aspirations, 27% of the variance in self-concept, 21% of the variance in locus of control, 19% of the variance in student grades, and 15% of the variance in discipline problems.

In order to look for differential effects of being involved with sports at higher levels of intensity and exposure, varsity team players and intramural players were entered into the model and computed against nonplayers (in place of the Athletic variable). In these models (table not shown), playing on intramural teams has diminishing or insignificant effects on the dependent variables, while playing on varsity teams has increasing effects ($\beta = .053$ for grades, $\beta = .063$ for self-concept, $\beta = .102$ for educational aspirations, and $\beta = -.064$ for discipline problems).

This analysis shows that students who are more involved in school sports have higher grades, higher self-concept, more internal locus of control, higher educational aspirations, and less discipline problems in school. The longitudinal approach, which enabled me to control for these behaviors prior to students' participation in high school sports teams, permits a cautious causal interpretation of the relationship between the intervening and the dependent variables. That is, regardless of whether students with higher grades, self-concept, locus of control, and educational aspirations and fewer discipline problems choose to participate in sport teams in high school, participation seems to affect in turn the same outcomes.

When participation in specific sports such as baseball/softball, basketball, football, and so on replaces athletic participation in these models, no significant effects are shown on any of the dependent variables (table not shown). This does not necessarily mean that different sports do not have distinct effects, but rather that these effects cannot be sorted out in the analysis, since all sports categories are not mutually exclusive and some students participate in more than one sport.

Other Extracurricular Activities

The contribution of participation in high school athletic competitions may also be assessed in comparison to other extracurricular activities. Each activity has a different nature and is expected to draw different students and to have distinct effects on development. Some activities are more competitive than others, some are more creative, and some demand high intellectual ability, specific physical skills, or social skills. It is logical to assume that participation in any extracurricular activity has some effects on student behavior. When such participation is entered into the model along with athletic participation, the relative effects may be compared.

In table 8.2 the partial regression coefficients for participation in athletic teams are compared to those of participation in other clubs, when all are regressed with each of the dependent variables separately. Participation in nonathletic clubs was grouped into four categories, according to the nature of the activities: academic clubs (math, science, debate), creative clubs (music, drama), student self-management clubs (student council, school paper), and other activities, usually labeled as hobbies. When the relative effects within each regression are compared, it appears that the effects of athletic participation resemble more the effects of participation in academic clubs than those of other clubs. The effect of athletic participation is similar to the effect of participation in academic clubs for educational aspirations ($\beta = .082$ and .080, respectively) and locus of control ($\beta = .043$ and .055); smaller than the effect of participation in academic clubs and similar to the effect of participation in music/drama ($\beta = -.045$ and $-.075$ and $-.050$) for discipline problems and for grades ($\beta = .032$ and .092); and larger than the effect of participation in academic clubs for self-concept ($\beta = .061$ and .034). All the other effects are insignificant.

The interesting point here is the consistency of effects of participation in these two types of extracurricular activities on all the dependent variables, while participation in other activities is mostly insignificant (except music/drama on educational aspirations and discipline, student clubs on educational aspirations, and other clubs on grades). While the effects of participation in academic clubs on these variables, especially on educational aspirations and grades, would be more readily anticipated, the effects of athletic participation are more surprising, since no clear link has been established between such physical and mental activities. Furthermore, partici-

Table 8.2   Standardized Regression Coefficients From Separate Regressions of Background Variables and Extracurricular Activities on the Dependent Variables

Independent variables	Dependent variables				
	Ed Asp	Grades	Self Cpt	Locus	Discip
Fam Inc	.035*	−.012	.008	.011	.010
Par Ed	.107***	.026	−.025	.007	−.027
Std Ach	.217***	.200***	.095***	.148***	−.078***
Female	.054***	.010	−.053***	.033*	.077***
Asian	.032*	.034*	.005	−.001	−.019
Hispanic	.041**	.000	.034*	.029	.031
Black	.082***	.024	.115***	.039*	−.057***
8th Asp	.369***				
8th Grades		.277***			
8th Concept			.449***		
8th Locus				.369***	
8th Discip					.333***
Academic Cl	.080***	.092***	.034*	.055***	−.075***
Music/Play	.035*	.006	−.018	−.004	−.050**
Student Cl	.046***	.020	.026	.023	.008
Other Cl	.025	.033*	−.003	−.014	−.028
Athletic	.082***	.032*	.061***	.043**	−.045**
R-square adjusted	.401	.198	.269	.211	.162

$*p < .05.$ $**p < .01.$ $***p < .001.$

Reprinted from Fejgin, 1994.

pation in school sport teams is sometimes considered an alternative activity and an energy release outlet for low-performing students, which may have positive effects on self-esteem and conformity to school rules but not on academic values. It seems, however, that contrary to the zero-sum theory assumptions, there is no negative academic price for the positive effects that athletic participation has on self-concept and locus of control.

Athletic Participation and Student Background

Since the apparent contribution of athletic involvement to the development of certain student qualities has been established, the question that follows is what factors determine the degree of participation. Available data do not permit control for physical ability, which is probably related to participation in school sport. However, it is important to examine whether such participation is equally distributed across certain social groups. Table 8.3 shows clearly that it is not. In that table, the percent of athletes (in any sport, on both intramural or varsity teams) is presented for each sex, SES quartile, school type,

urban status (within the public sector only), and school size. Cross-tabulations were subjected to chi-square tests, and significance levels are reported.

Table 8.3 shows total participation of 53.4% in high school sports and significant differences in rates of participation between all categories except race. Male students participate more than female; students from higher SES quartiles participate more than their counterparts in lower SES quartiles; students who attend private (non-Catholic) schools participate more than those who attend Catholic schools; and those attending Catholic schools participate more than students who attend public schools. In the public sector, students attending suburban schools participate more than urban students. And finally, athletic participation increases as school size decreases.

In order to examine the relative contribution of background variables and school attributes to athletic participation, a set of regressions were performed, where background variables were regressed with athletic participation first. School size, school type, and previous engagement in school or private sports teams were then entered as additional steps.

The first column of table 8.4 shows that participation is affected first by gender ($\beta = -.119$ for

Table 8.3   Participation in School Sports by Sex, Race/Ethnicity, SES Quartile, School Type, School Urban Status, and School Size (N = 3,783)

Variable	% Participation	Significance
Sex		.000
Male	59.7	
Female	47.5	
Total	53.4	
Race/ethnicity		.110
Asian	54.1	
Hispanic	47.4	
Black	54.6	
White	54.0	
SES quartile		.000
Low quartile	41.7	
Second quartile	50.3	
Third quartile	54.8	
High quartile	63.9	
School type		
Public	52.1	
Catholic	65.7	
Private	67.2	
School urban status (public)		.033
Urban	49.7	
Surburban	53.7	
School size		.000
Small[a]	60.8	
Medium[b]	51.7	
Large[c]	46.6	

[a]1–799 students. [b]800–1,599 students. [c]Over 1,666 students.

Reprinted from Fejgin, 1994.

females), and then by parent education ($\beta = .075$) and family income ($\beta = .050$). Standardized achievement score and race/ethnicity have no additional significant effects. It seems then, contrary to common myth, that youths from lower SES families do not engage in sports activities more than do those from higher SES families, at least when it comes to school-organized activities. Except for the traditional relationship of gender and sport, the single most powerful explanation for individual athletic involvement is parent education. When the model is estimated for males and females separately (table not shown), it shows an even more powerful influence of parent education on female sport participation. Gender differences are even more extreme when participation in varsity teams is considered. And when such participation is used as the dependent variable instead of Athletic, the effect of being female increases ($\beta = .133$; table not shown), but that of race/ethnicity stays insignificant.

School Attributes

Another explanation for student participation in school sport may be derived from the opportunity structure within the school. Some schools offer many different sports, while others offer only a few. Some schools focus mainly on interscholastic teams, which can involve only a small number of athletes, and only the best, while other schools offer more opportunities to participate via intramural teams.

Table 8.4   Standardized Regression Coefficients From Regressions of Background Variables and School Attributes on Athletic Participation

	Step 1	Step 2	Step 3	Step 4
Fam Inc	.050**	.047*	.054**	.020
Par Ed	.075***	.070***	.083***	.069***
Std Ach	.025	.023	.026	.017
Female	−.119***	−.119***	−.119***	−.069***
Asian	−.020	−.021	−.006	−.009
Hispanic	−.006	−.007	.027	−.003
Black	.013	.012	.030	.001
Private scl		.038*		
School Size			−.154***	
8th Varsity				.255***
8th Intramur				.071***
8th Private Sports AS				.127***
R-square adjusted	.027	.028	.049	.139

*p < .05. **p < .01. ***p < .001.

Reprinted from Fejgin, 1994.

Some schools offer various kinds of sports, but do not encourage students to participate, while others do everything to promote school sport involvement. The position of sport is an important aspect of the school's culture and probably depends on community norms and values as well as the relative power of the principal, coaches, and teachers, who strive to promote certain ideas (Coleman, 1985). The sport culture of a school undoubtedly affects student participation.

Available data in this set do not allow detailed analysis of actual sport opportunities in each school. Although the students were asked whether the school offered each sport, their answers did not reflect enough variance to enable any meaningful statistical analysis. Only about 1 to 5% of the students stated that their schools did not offer baseball/softball, football, basketball, cheerleading, or any individual sport, and 13 to 27% said that their schools did not offer pompom, soccer, or swimming. Still, in some schools there was a higher participation rate than in others. The question is whether rate of participation is related only to individual student inclination or to some school properties that may be indirect measures of an opportunity structure within the school. Therefore, four different proxies for such opportunity structure were entered into the model separately: school affiliation, size, region, and urban status, all of which are known to affect certain school outcomes. Region and urban status had insignificant effects on athletic participation, and therefore are not shown in table 8.4.

In the second column of table 8.4, a small additional effect of private school attendance ($\beta = .038$) is shown, and in the third column a larger effect of school size is reported ($\beta = -.154$). When both school type and school size are introduced into the same equation, school type loses significance, probably due to the high correlation between the two, and possibly to the small cell number, after controlling for all other variables. It seems, then, that school type and school size are related to some type of opportunity structure that encourages or discourages athletic participation. Note that these are net school effects, after individual socioeconomic measures have been controlled, so that school size is not another proxy for family income, or educational level, but a school property.

Since school attributes together with background variables explain a small percent of the variance in athletic participation (about 5% with school size), another group of variables were introduced to the equation in Step 4: previous involvement in sports in 8th grade. The coefficients here suggest that students who played on varsity teams in 8th grade are much more likely to play in high school ($\beta = .255$). So are students who played on intramural teams ($\beta = .071$) and those who played in private nonschool clubs ($\beta = .127$). One may argue that these effects conceal the contribution of natural physical skills to participation in high school sports. While this is probably partially true, it may also point to earlier effects of parent education and income, which are correlated with each of these variables.

Summary and Conclusions

The information from students in this nationally representative sample about their involvement in school-organized sports seems to support the predictions of developmental theory on the one hand and those of conflict theory on the other. The main goal of this study was to examine whether sport participation in high school was positively related to some school-related behaviors that enhance individual academic success, as several researchers maintain (Grove & Dodder, 1979; Marsh, 1993; Otto & Alwin, 1977), or whether the "sport builds character" belief is just a myth supported by conventional wisdom, as Rees et al. (1990) argued, and may even impede investment in academic work, as Coleman (1961) suggested.

As predicted by developmental theory, students who are more involved in high school competitive sports have higher grades, a higher self-concept, higher educational aspirations, a more internal locus of control, and fewer discipline problems. Although the effects are small, they are statistically significant and very consistent across all the analyses.

It appears that the repetitive experiences associated with competitive athletic activities may have some character-building qualities. The mechanisms through which these qualities are developed are not entirely clear. Possible explanations are offered here; some are supported by previous research while others are mere speculations.

First, I will consider the relationship between competitive sport activities and the development of locus of control. These activities offer experiences of both success and failure, which are highly visible to the individual and to the peer group. The clear and direct link between performance and achievement, as measured in a game score or a swimming time, may very well help to establish a more internal locus of control. The individual realizes that it is up to him or her to perform better or worse, and that it is difficult to blame other people or circumstances for failure.

Although sport competitions offer both success and failure experiences, being admitted to any sports team is a recognition of some kind of physical (and sometimes social) capability or skill. This recognition is associated with some social rewards, which probably help to develop a more positive self-concept. The higher social status of high school athletes (Coleman, 1961), together with physical skill itself, may very well feed the ego and enhance self-esteem (Snyder & Spreitzer, 1990).

Participation in sports teams requires adjustment to rigid rules, regulations, and practice times, as well as to the coach's authority (Whitson, 1986). Ongoing training of individuals to comply with these rules and to endure long hours of practice, while delaying the fulfillment of other physical and social needs, teaches the importance of and the rewards associated with such compliance, possibly making it easier to accept other school rules and formal authority. Furthermore, being on a school team means being recognized by the system as a "good citizen" who participates in community life beyond basic requirements. This may in turn create deeper commitment by the student, not only to the school's rules but also to its basic values and to the academic work that is its main mission. Thus, conforming to school rules and values may result in more disciplined behavior and higher grades. Higher grades could reflect either student self-discipline and willingness to put forth effort, learned partially through sport training, or teacher inclination to prefer these students and mark their work more favorably (Snyder & Spreitzer, 1990). Other studies have suggested that sport participation positively affects academic performance and acceptance of school rules through identification with the school (Finn, 1989; Marsh, 1993).

The effect of athletic participation on educational aspirations may be attributed to students' plans to use athletic prowess as "human capital" in gaining access to college, as Snyder and Spreitzer (1990) posited. Or, as Spady (1970) suggested, athletic participation may enhance educational aspirations through increased perceived social status. Or, it may be that athletic involvement affects educational aspirations not only directly, but also through self-concept, locus of control, discipline, and grades.[3] The positive effects of these variables on educational aspirations are well-known although not always clear-cut, as in the case of female students, who have lower self-concept but higher educational aspirations.

Whatever the explanations, it appears that participation in high school competitive sports provides some kinds of positive experiences that enhance student adjustment to school rules, schoolwork, and the basic values of an achievement-oriented society.

Lately several sport sociologists have embraced a more critical approach to school sports, pointing out the possible negative aspects of high school and college competitive sport. Eitzen (1992), for example, claimed that school sports as they are organized now are nondemocratic, opportunistic, and oppressive; they legitimate income inequalities between players, coaches, and managers; and they leave no room for freedom of choice, privacy, and individualism. Fernandez-Balboa (1993) argued that through the hidden curriculum in physical education and sport in school, students are socialized into "accepting particular modes of thinking and acting that support and legitimize power structures and social inequalities. These modes are characterized by apathy, indifference, apolitical attitudes, dependence on institutional control, compliance with authority, anxiety and powerlessness" (p. 248). Thus, he added, physical education lacks some fundamental human values, such as equity, freedom, cooperation, and self-actualization. Sage (1993) called on physical educators to rethink their roles and to challenge "the values that are unjust, insensitive, sexist, racist, and limiting" (p. 162), so that they would not automatically reproduce the power system that supports the interests of the dominant elites.

That critique is mostly theoretical, but one aspect central to the idea of social reproduction is reflected in the present findings. The statistical analysis supports the basic arguments of conflict theory and reaffirms the established knowledge that the school curriculum is unequally distributed across gender and socioeconomic groups. In this case, it is school extracurricular activities that are disproportionately used by different groups. As might be expected, gender is the strongest determinant of participation in school sport, and a great deal of work in the sociology and history of sport has been devoted to explaining such findings. Some advocates of equal rights for women, particularly those adopting a liberal feminist perspective, argue that since sports are an important aspect of modern American life, women should participate not just as spectators but as players. And, the exclusion of any social group from any form of social activity, whether by law, force, or negative socialization, is coercion used by the dominant group for its benefit. In fact, there is growing evidence that schools contribute to the observed disproportionality (Scraton, 1990; Wright, 1993). Accordingly, an appropriate part of the school mission could be to change this situation.

The other major bias in sports participation is that of social class. The model shows that once again, and against common myth, youths from lower socioeconomic groups have less opportunities to use this "social good" in order to better their educational and cultural adjustment. There are several theoretical explanations for this finding, and two clues are evident in the data presented here. First, the model shows that after gender, parents' educational level is the strongest determinant of athletic participation in school; thus, parental attitudes may be involved. Parents with more education may value the benefits of sport participation and possibly may encourage their children to participate. They also probably give them a head start in participation at a younger age, via private or community classes and summer camps. Second, the negative effects of public school affiliation and school size, which are related to student socioeconomic background, offer another explanation: Students from lower socioeconomic groups have fewer opportunities to participate in school sports because the schools they attend offer fewer such activities or do not encourage active participation. This finding is in line with other findings about unequal opportunities for students in public versus private and Catholic schools (Coleman, Hoffer, & Kilgore, 1982). One may argue, at least against the first explanation, that extracurricular sport activities are voluntary and that it is up to the student to use them. The same is true, however, regarding regular academic work. School is mandatory but studying is not. Still, we look for ways to reduce dropout rates and achievement gaps between social groups, and research in the sociology of education is primarily concerned with finding the factors that make a difference and suggesting ways of using them to increase all students' opportunities for better social adjustment.

Some policy implications of this study are that school sports have some positive effects, but their social distribution is unequal, and we should increase opportunities to participate. More teams for each type of sport would enable students to participate at different levels. Transportation home after practices and competitions would ease burdens of after-school participation. Incorporating sports in the schedule as elective classes, for credit, would facilitate during-school participation. Accommodating the needs of special populations may help make school sport less elitist and more humane. More research about methods that schools use to encour-

age sport participation, and about criteria that they use to allocate time and money and to select athletes, would assist policy makers in such decisions.

Another possible implication of this study is that educational research, and schools, should look into ways of organizing academic schoolwork following the sport pattern. It seems that school sport has some characteristics that may enhance student and coach self-worth and achievement orientation: It is voluntary, it is competitive, it is established on both intra- and interschool comparisons, and it rewards all participants—students (and indirectly their parents), coaches, principals, and schools as a whole. This structure has a built-in incentive system for each participant and for the group to put forth effort, as well as cooperation, in order to achieve a clear, measurable, externally established goal (Coleman, 1993).

In some ways school sports, normally perceived as leisure activities, are more like work (Fine, 1987) or like the business world, since performance is judged not only against one's colleagues but also against the competition—the team of another school, another district, or another state. From this point of view, school sport is the only activity that may help students to internalize the universalistic norms that Dreeben (1968) argued to be an important latent function of school, while carrying achievement orientation to its limits. In most schools, universalistic criteria are not employed regarding academic work, since different teachers and different schools set different criteria. Therefore, the "universe" against which the student is judged is very small—his or her specific class, or the wider age group in the school. Following Coleman's suggestions for output-driven schools (1993), if schools could reorganize academic work to operate more like sports teams, where universalistic criteria are employed and a reward system is built in, they could inject into the system what is missing in so many schools today—a real achievement orientation.

References

Arnold, P.J. (1984). Sport, moral education and the development of character. *Journal of Philosophy of Education*, **18**, 275-281.

Baird, L. (1969). Big schools, small schools: A critical examination of the hypothesis. *Journal of Educational Psychology*, **60**, 253-260.

Braddock, J.H. (1981). Race, athletics, and educational attainment. *Youth and Society*, **12**, 335-350.

Carrington, B., & Leaman, O. (1986). Equal opportunity and physical education. In J. Evans (Ed.), *Physical education, sport and schooling: Studies in the sociology of physical education* (pp. 215-227). London: The Falmer Press.

Coleman, J.S. (1961). *The adolescent society.* New York: Free Press of Glencoe.

Coleman, J.S. (1985). Sports in school. *Sport and Education, 1,* 6-10.

Coleman, J.S. (1993, March). *The design of organizations and the right to act.* Paper presented at the Eastern Sociological Society annual meeting.

Coleman, J.S., Hoffer, T., & Kilgore, S. (1982). *High school achievement: Public, Catholic, and private schools compared.* New York: Basic Books.

Dreeben, R. (1968). *On what is learned in school.* Reading, MA: Addison-Wesley.

Edwards, T.L. (1967). Scholarship and athletics. *Journal of Health, Physical Education and Recreation, 38,* 75.

Eitzen, D.S. (1992). Sports and ideological contradictions: Learning from the cultural framing of Soviet values. *Journal of Sport and Social Issues, 16,* 145-149.

Evans, J., & Davies, B. (1986). Sociology of schooling and physical education. In J. Evans (Ed.), *Physical education, sport and schooling: Studies in the sociology of physical education* (pp. 11-37). London: The Falmer Press.

Felz, D.L. (1978). Athletics in the status system of female adolescents. *Review of Sport & Leisure, 3,* 98-108.

Fernandez-Balboa, J.M. (1993). Sociocultural characteristics of the hidden curriculum in physical education. *Quest, 45,* 230-254.

Fine, G.A. (1987). *With the boys: Little League baseball and preadolescent culture.* Chicago: University of Chicago Press.

Finn, J.D. (1989). Withdrawing from school. *Review of Educational Research, 59,* 117-142.

Frey, J. (1986). College athletics: Problems of a functional analysis. In C.R. Rees & A.W. Miracle (Eds.), *Sport and social theory* (pp. 199-209). Champaign, IL: Human Kinetics.

Greenberger, E., & Steinberg, L. (1986). *When teenagers work: The psychological and social costs of adolescent employment.* New York: Basic Books.

Grove, S.J., & Dodder, R.A. (1979). A study of functions of sport: A subsequent test of Spreitzer and Snyder's research. *Journal of Sport Behavior, 2,* 83-91.

Hanks, M.P. (1979). Race, sexual status and athletics in the process of educational achievement. *Social Science Quarterly, 60,* 482-496.

Hanks, M.P., & Eckland, B.K. (1976). Athletic and social participation in the educational attainment process. *Sociology of Education, 49,* 271-274.

Hargreaves, J. (1986). *Sport, power and culture.* Cambridge, UK: Polity Press.

Hauser, W.J., & Lueptow, L.B. (1978). Participation in athletics and academic achievement: A replication and extension. *The Sociological Quarterly, 19,* 304-309.

Hendry, L.B. (1978). *School, sport and leisure.* London: A & C Black.

Holland, A., & Andre, T. (1987). Participation in extracurricular activities in secondary school: What is known, what needs to be known? *Review of Educational Research, 57,* 437-466.

Howell, F.M., Miracle, A.W., & Rees, C.R. (1989). Do high school athletics pay? The effects of varsity participation on socioeconomic attainments. *Sociology of Sport Journal, 1,* 15-25.

Ingels, S.J., Scott, L.A., Lindmark, J.T., Frankel, M.R., & Myers, S.L. (1992). *National education longitudinal study of 1988: First follow-up: Student component datafile. User's manual.* National Center for Education Statistics.

Johnson, P.A. (1972). A comparison of personality traits of superior skilled female athletes in basketball, bowling, field hockey and golf. *Research Quarterly, 43,* 409-415.

Malumphy, T.M. (1968). Personality of female athletes in intercollegiate competition. *Research Quarterly, 39,* 610-620.

Marsh, H.W. (1991). Employment during high school: Character building or a subversion of academic goals? *Sociology of Education, 64,* 172-189.

Marsh, H.W. (1993). The effects of participation in sport during the last two years of high school. *Sociology of Sport Journal, 10,* 28-43.

Melnick, M.J., Sabo, D.F., & Vanfossen, B.E. (1992a). Effects of interscholastic athletic participation on the social, educational, and career mobility of Hispanic girls and boys. *International Review for the Sociology of Sport, 27,* 57-75.

Melnick, M.J., Sabo, D.F., & Vanfossen, B.E. (1992b). Educational effects of interscholastic athletic participation on African-American and Hispanic Youth. *Adolescence, 27,* 295-308.

Melnick, M.J., Vanfossen, B.E., & Sabo, D.F. (1988). Developmental effects of athletic participation among high school girls. *Sociology of Sport Journal, 5,* 22-36.

Morgan, D.L., & Alwin, D.F. (1980). When less is more: School size and social participation. *Social Psychology Quarterly, 43,* 241-252.

Norusis, M.J. (1993). *SPSS for Windows. Base system user's guide, release 6.0.* Chicago: SPSS Inc.

Otto, L.B. (1982). Extracurricular activities. In H.J. Walberg (Ed.), *Improving educational standards and productivity* (pp. 217-233). Berkeley, CA: McCuthan.

Otto, L.B., & Alwin, D.F. (1977). Athletics, aspirations, and attainments. *Sociology of Education,* **42,** 102-113.

Pyecha, J. (1970). Comparative effects of judo and selected physical education activities on male university freshmen personality traits. *Research Quarterly,* **41,** 425-431.

Rees, C.R., Howell, F.M., & Miracle, A.W. (1990). Do high school sports build character? A quasi-experiment on a national sample. *The Social Science Journal,* **27,** 303-315.

Sabo, D.F., Melnick, M.J., & Vanfossen, B.E. (1993). High school athletic participation and post-secondary educational and occupational mobility: A focus on race and gender. *Sociology of Sport Journal,* **10,** 44-56.

Sage, G.H. (1990). *Power and ideology in American sport.* Champaign, IL: Human Kinetics.

Sage, G.H. (1993). Sport and physical education and the new world order: Dare we be agents of social change? *Quest,* **45,** 151-164.

Schafer, W.E. (1981). Sport and sex-role socialization. In J.W. Loy, C.S. Kenyon, & B.D. McPherson (Eds.), *Sport, culture and society* (pp. 211-215). Philadelphia: Lea & Febiger.

Scraton, S. (1986). Images of femininity and the teaching of girls physical education. In J. Evans (Ed.), *Physical education, sport and schooling: Studies in the sociology of physical education* (pp. 71-94). London: The Falmer Press.

Scraton, S. (1990). *Gender and physical education.* Geelong, Victoria, Australia: Deakin University Press.

Snyder, E.E., & Spreitzer, E. (1977). Participation in sport as related to educational expectations among high school girls. *Sociology of Education,* **50,** 47-55.

Snyder, E.E., & Spreitzer, E. (1990). High school athletic participation as related to college attendance among black, Hispanic and white males: A research note. *Youth and Society,* **21,** 390-398.

Spady, W.G. (1970). Lament for the letterman: Effects of peer status and extracurricular activities on goals and achievement. *American Journal of Sociology,* **75,** 680-702.

Stevenson, C.L. (1975). Socialization effects of participation in sport: A critical review of the research. *The Research Quarterly,* **45,** 287-300.

Thirer, J., & Wright, S.D. (1985). Sport and social status for adolescent male and females. *Sociology of Sport Journal,* **2,** 164-171.

Waller, W. (1961). *The sociology of teaching.* New York: Russell & Russell.

Whitson, D. (1986). Structure, agency and the sociology of sport debates. *Theory, Culture and Society,* **1,** 64-78.

Wright, J. (1993, April). *The construction of gendered subjectivity in physical education: A study of discourse and discourses.* Paper presented at the AERA annual meeting, Atlanta, GA.

Notes

1. It should be noted that these either/or positions only concern established views of high school sport as it is usually practiced in the United States; they do not represent the entire range of possible positions or practices concerning high school sport.

2. Note that the effects of the background variables are smaller than they would be if 8th-grade measures were not accounted for, since some of their effects on each variable are transmitted through these measures. For example, the effect of Female on 10th-grade self-concept, before controlling for 8th-grade self-concept, is $\beta = -.134$, and for 10th-grade educational aspirations $\beta = .091$.

3. When these variables are entered into the equation together with athletic participation and background variables and regressed with educational aspirations, they have additional effects.

Appendix

Background Variables

Gender is used as a dummy variable (Female = 1).

Race is used as a dummy variable (Asian = 1, Hispanic = 2, Black = 3).

Student standardized test score (Std Ach) is a continuous composite of standardized test scores in English and math, available in the data set.

Family income (Fam Inc) is a continuous measure, the logged yearly income of the family.

Parents' educational level (Par Ed) is measured as number of years beyond or below high school completed by the parent with the highest educational level.

Independent (Predictor) Variables

Athletic participation (Athletic) is a continuous measure, composed of student self-reports on nine questionnaire items regarding participation in any one or more sports, such as baseball/softball, basketball, football, soccer, swim team, other team sport, individual sport, cheerleading, or pom-pom. Participation in each sport was ranked on a scale of 0 (did not participate) to 3 (participates in varsity team). Thus, the composite score reflects athletic involvement as a combined measure of number of sports played and the intensity (level) of participation.

Varsity in 8th grade (8th Varsity) is a dummy variable for participation in any varsity team.

Intramural in 8th grade (8th Intramural) is a dummy variable for participation in any intramural team.

Private sports in 8th grade (Private Sports AS) is a dummy variable for participation in any private sport classes, or teams, after school.

Academic club (Academic Cl), *Music/drama* (Music/Play), *student self-management clubs* (Student Cl), and *other clubs* (Other Cl) are used as dummy variables.

School affiliation (Private Scl) is used as a dummy variable.

School size is a continuous measure, reflecting entire school enrollment.

Dependent Variables

Grades are student self-reports of English and math grades since the beginning of 9th grade, and *8th Grades* are these grades from the beginning of 7th grade, used to control for prior relative achievement. Grades, originally ranked on a descending scale from 1 (mostly A's) to 8 (mostly D's), were recoded to an ascending scale of 1 (low) to 4 (high).

Self-concept (Self Cpt) is a continuous composite measure available in the data set, and *8th Concept* is used to control for prior self-concept. This is a composite index summing responses to eight items such as "I feel good about myself," "I feel I am a person of worth, the equal of other people," "I feel useless at times," "I feel I do not have much to be proud of."

Locus of control (Locus) is a continuous composite measure available in the data set, where high grades reflect a more internal locus. *8th Locus* is used to control for student locus of control in 8th grade. This is a composite index summing responses to six items such as "I don't have enough control over the direction my life is taking," "In my life good luck is more important than hard work for success," "My plans hardly ever work out, so planning only makes me unhappy."

The *discipline problems* (Discip) variable is a continuous composite measure constructed out of three items, describing how many times in the current school year a student was late, skipped classes, or was absent from school. *8th Discip* is used as a control measure.

Educational aspirations (Ed Asp) are measured by years beyond or below high school the student declares he or she will complete, and *8th Asp* is used to control for prior level of educational aspirations.

Athletic Participation and Sexual Behavior in Adolescents: The Different Worlds of Boys and Girls

Kathleen E. Miller
Donald F. Sabo
Michael P. Farrell
Grace M. Barnes
Merrill J. Melnick

Using multivariate analysis of covariance to test hypotheses about the effects of sports and sexual behavior on a sample of 611 western New York adolescents, this study concludes that athletic participation and gender interact to influence adolescent sexual outcomes. Female athletes report significantly lower rates of sexual activity than female nonathletes; male athletes report slightly (though not significantly) higher rates than male nonathletes. The gender-specific effect of sports on sexual behavior remains, net of the impacts of race, age, socioeconomic status, quality of family relations, and participation in other extracurricular activities. This paper introduces cultural resource theory to explain how athletic participation influences both traditional cultural scripts and exchange resources, which, in turn, condition the sexual bargaining process and its outcomes for adolescents.

Over the past two decades, policymakers have expressed concern regarding adolescent sexuality and its consequences (e.g., National Campaign to Prevent Teen Pregnancy 1997). Much of the disquiet revolves around the perception that the age of onset of sexual behavior has fallen: 5 to 10 percent of 12-year-olds and 15 percent of 13-year-olds report having had intercourse (Alan Guttmacher Institute 1994). At least half of all American women and more than 75 percent of all American men report having had intercourse by age 18 (Abma et al. 1997; Alan Guttmacher Institute 1994). Adolescent girls in particular are growing more sexually active as double standards in both opportunity for sexual intercourse and attitudes against engaging in sexual behavior wane. In addition, early and frequent sexual relations among teenagers are associated with both unwanted pregnancies and sexually transmitted diseases (Harvey and Spigner 1995).

Intervention programs to reduce teen sexual activity and pregnancy risk now operate throughout the United States. However, with a few notable

Reprinted from Miller, Sabo, Farrell, Barnes, and Melnick, 1998.

exceptions—such as Teen Outreach (Allen et al. 1997) and New York City's "In Your Face" pregnancy prevention program (Tiezzi et al. 1997)—most programs have yielded results that are disappointing at best (Males 1993). While intervention programs commonly employ laudable strategies to raise self-esteem and to educate teens, particularly girls, regarding sexuality and its consequences, they overlook the possibility that certain structured activities in the youth culture may reduce sexual activity. While a number of peer activities such as drug and alcohol use are associated with increased sexual activity, few researchers have explored the potential deterrent effect of routine extracurricular activity.

One adolescent activity that may reduce sexual behavior among teens is playing sports, particularly for girls. In 1971, only one in 27 American girls engaged in high school sports; by 1994, the ratio had jumped to one in three. Females now comprise approximately 40 percent of all high school athletes (National Federation of State High Schools Association 1997) and 38 percent of college athletes (Acosta and Carpenter 1996). While not yet comparable to the participation levels of boys (about half of whom play sports in high school), girls' growing athletic participation has been viewed by many as an indicator of changing cultural attitudes regarding femininity and fitness (Messner and Sabo 1990).

Only three recent studies have addressed the impact of sports on adolescent sexual behavior. Dealing only with girls and not assessing the impact of sports participation per se, Brown et al. (1997) found that the greater the frequency of physical exercise, the older the adolescent girl at first intercourse. In addition, Zill, Nord, and Loomis (1995) concluded that female varsity athletes were about a third less likely than female nonathletes to report being a parent by the twelfth grade; male athletes, on the other hand, were a third more likely to become a teen parent than their nonathletic counterparts. And in a preliminary analysis, Sabo et al. (1997) found sports participation to be associated with less sexual activity and lower pregnancy risk among western New York high school girls.

Yet there are several problems with the extant research in this area. The above-mentioned studies of the relationship between sports participation and adolescent sexual behavior are largely descriptive and atheoretical. Furthermore, neither Brown et al. nor Sabo et al. distinguished between sports and other extracurricular activities, leaving open the possibility that athletic participation was merely a proxy for social participation in general, nor do any of these studies examine whether the association between sports and sexual behavior is spurious. If athletic participation and sexual activity are affected by the same factors—such as race, socioeconomic status, and quality of family interaction—then it may be that, once these factors are controlled, the relationship between sports participation and sexual behavior is diminished if not altogether eliminated. Finally, with the exception of Sabo et al.'s preliminary analysis, the differential effects of sports on boys' and girls' sexual behavior have not been adequately addressed.

In the present study, we examine survey data from a longitudinal study of a random sample of 699 adolescent females and males from western New York families to analyze the relationships among gender, athletic participation, and sexual behavior. We review three theoretical frameworks relevant to the question of whether sports participation has different effects on the sexual behavior of girls and boys, deriving from each a set of testable hypotheses. Taking into account the impact of race, age, socioeconomic status, quality of family interactions, and involvement in other extracurricular activities, we examine the impact of athletic participation on adolescent sexual activity, including (1) overall number of sex partners, (2) frequency of intercourse over one's lifetime, (3) frequency of intercourse during the past year, and (4) age of first intercourse.

Theorizing Athletic Participation, Gender, and Sexual Behavior

Below we employ three conceptual frameworks in order to ground hypotheses about adolescent sexuality and sports. To sort out the unique effects of sports, we pay particular attention to the question of whether the effects of athletic activity may differ from the effects of other extracurricular activities.

Control Processes

The old saying "idle hands are the devil's workshop" has implications for deviance in general and sexual behavior in particular. Some researchers (e.g., Benda and DiBlasio 1994; Lauritsen 1994) have employed control theory (Hirschi 1969) to explain adolescent sexual behavior, though none have chosen to incorporate athletic participation in their analyses. Adolescents with substantial amounts of unstructured, unsupervised time are more likely to engage in risky behavior than those who are constructively engaged (Zill et al. 1995). Part of the logic behind midnight basketball and youth centers is that adolescents are most likely to stay out of trouble if they are given something else to do, that is, if they are provided with acceptable alternative activities that keep them off the streets. The largest window of opportunity for delinquency, and presumably teen sexual experimentation as well, occurs in the afternoon after school closes and before parents return home from work (Sabo and Melnick 1996). Participation in school-sponsored sports programs commonly fills that time slot with regularly scheduled activities. Adolescents who participate in sports may very well have fewer opportunities to be delinquent because their time is more structured than that of other teens and because coaches act in loco parentis.

Control theory suggests that involvement (devotion of time and energy to conventionally acceptable activities) is only one part of the picture. Affective attachment to coaches and teammates may also help to suppress deviance. Furthermore, student athletes may have more incentive not to be delinquent, since they have access to highly valued reward structures through sports and thus much to lose by being delinquent. Athletes may avoid behaviors (such as sexual intercourse that puts them at risk for unintended pregnancy) that they see as potentially threatening to their continued participation, ability to compete, or long-range goals to earn an athletic scholarship and play in college. Athletes presumably also experience a stronger connection to a sports ethic that emphasizes fair play, rule conformity, and self-discipline.

Control theory yields several hypotheses germane to the present investigation. Since sports participation requires similar time commitments from both female and male athletes, no significant gender differences should exist in the direction or magnitude of athletic effects on sexual behavior. Athletic involvement should be associated with lower frequency of sexual intercourse, fewer sex partners, and later age at onset of sexual activity for both sexes. Furthermore, the "idle hands" thesis recognizes no special power of the playing field. Any structured extracurricular activity should have essentially the same impact; thus formal participation in arts-based and academic-based extracurricular activities are also expected to be associated with lower levels of sexual activity.

Cultural Processes

A variety of recent works have examined the connections among athletic participation, gender, and sexuality from the perspectives of critical sociology, culture, and gender theory. Sports are viewed as a cultural site for the construction of traditional or hegemonic masculinity (Messner and Sabo 1990), serving as an institutional training ground for manhood. In fact, building on the work of Caron, Carter, and Brightman (1985) and Houseworth, Peplow, and Thirer (1989) on male college students, Andre and Holland (1995) found that younger athletes of both genders score higher on self-reported "masculine" traits (BEM Sex Role Inventory) than do their nonathletic counterparts, and male athletes display more traditional attitudes toward women (Attitudes Towards Women Scale).

As adolescence progresses, sexual identity emerges as an extension of an already formed gender identity; thus sexual behavior becomes scripted in accordance with the wider cultural norms that pattern gender relations (Sabo and Messner 1993). Cultural expectations attached to "masculinity" may encourage boys to initiate sex, to be sexually aggressive with girls, and to regard sexual conquest as a validation for male adequacy (Zilbergeld 1993). Cultural expectations may also encourage male involvement with risky behaviors such as use of alcohol and other substances, delinquency, and sexual promiscuity (Pleck, Sonenstein, and Ku 1993; Skolnick 1993).

But research and theory concerning the sexual behavior of female athletes are scarce. We speculate that high school sports may influence girls' psychosexual development and sexual choices in ways different from boys. While sport amplifies traditional gender scripts for males, it de-emphasizes or even contradicts conventional scripts for females. Gender identity formation for girls who participate in high school athletics may therefore result in a less traditional feminine orientation to dating and sexual 0relations. Female athletes, conditioned to view themselves and their surroundings in a more proactive way, should be less passive, less subservient, and, most importantly, less emotionally dependent on boys for attention and the establishment of self-worth. Girls entering the sports arena now may even feel empowered by challenging male privilege and chauvinistic beliefs concerning athletic ability. In addition, female athletes often derive social support from being a member of a team which, in turn, may furnish girls with networking opportunities to discuss their dating relationships or the sexual reputations and motives of boys. The homosocial ambience and esprit d'corps of the girls' locker room provides opportunities for female bonding and sport talk, thus rendering other popular topics like boys, sex, and dating less salient. Consequently, the pursuit of heterosexual appeal and engagement in sexual activity may become less important for female athletes, and, thus, more a matter of deliberate choice than scripted normative expectations.

In short, whereas boys' gender identity formation vis-a-vis athletics has been largely consistent with hegemonic masculinity, it has been the female athlete's resistance to a traditional cultural script dictating passive femininity that has largely informed her gender identity development. Though male and female athletics share many structural properties, the cultural processes active for boys and girls differ profoundly, producing potentially differential patterns of gender identity formation and approaches to sexual behavior.

This cultural framework suggests that athletic participation should increase sexual activity for boys, but female athletes should actually experience lower rates than female nonathletes. Furthermore, owing to the uniqueness of the sport subculture, other extracurricular activities—which are not so deeply colored by cultural expectations regarding masculinity—should not show the same pattern of interaction effects.

Exchange Processes

Control theory and the cultural processes explanation both focus on the direct effects of sports on individual behavior. However, sexual behavior inherently depends upon interaction with at least one other person. As such, sport may affect adolescent sexual activity through its effects on the bargaining process that occurs in dating relationships. For example, Waller (1951) explicitly linked social status with dating behavior, suggesting that, following traditional scripts, females exchange beauty, affection, and sex for status gains associated with dating prestigious males.

Participation in sports has consistently proven to be one way for adolescent boys to gain status; male athletes may therefore trade their status for affection and sexual favors. There is some evidence to suggest that girls also gain status through participation in sports, possibly affecting the balance of exchange. Both Kane (1988) and Holland and Andre (1994) found that participation in "sex-appropriate" sports (e.g., tennis, as opposed to

basketball) increases status for high school girls. Though sports have remained primarily a male status enhancement vehicle, both female and especially male students are now more likely to identify sports as a way for girls to gain prestige as well (Suitor and Reavis 1995). Indeed, Sabo, Melnick, and Vanfossen (1989) found that a national probability sample of females and males derived significant popularity gains from athletic participation.

Within the conceptual framework of exchange theory, we speculate that the popularity gains that both females and males derive from high school athletic participation influence their sexual behavior. Where cultural factors affect adolescents' preferences regarding sexual activity, exchange considerations affect their power to act on these preferences within dyadic relationships. Because athletic participation increases boys' social position within the high school status hierarchy, it may be easier for them to request or even demand sex from girls. Athletic participation also augments the social status of girls, but in contrast to boys, the status enhancement provides them with the power to resist male pressures. Social status accrued in this manner gives girls an alternative to trading sex for popularity or self-esteem. Athletic participation enhances the value of the package of resources that both girls and boys bring to the sexual bargaining table.

We assume here that, as a general rule, girls and boys bargain with very different goals in mind. Where possible, boys pressure girls for sex whereas girls seek to resist this pressure. While exceptions no doubt abound, it is axiomatic in exchange theory that—all other things being equal—people try to act in their own best interests. While both genders have the capacity to enjoy sexual experimentation, girls experience two costs that boys do not: first, the centuries-old stigma against female promiscuity, and, second, the risk of pregnancy. Girls may also be more viscerally aware of the potential negative social and economic consequences of an unplanned pregnancy and thus assign such consequences greater priority in weighing the potential costs of sexual involvement.

This framework generates hypotheses similar to those associated with the cultural processes approach. Male athletes are expected to use their status to bargain for sex, and, thus, to have higher rates of sexual activity, more partners, and earlier onset of intercourse than male nonathletes. Female athletes, following the same logic, should display depressed rates of activity compared to their nonathletic counterparts. Other status-enhancing extracurricular activities should have substantially the same effect, increasing male sexual activity and decreasing female sexual activity. Adolescents presumably make use of all status resources available to them, including participation in athletics, music, clubs, and so on. The greater the prestige gains associated with a given activity, the more participation in that activity should mediate sexual outcomes. Thus, we would expect the same interactions between gender and other extracurricular activities as we expect for sports and gender.

Predictors of Adolescent Sexual Activity: Controls

Several factors have been documented as predictors of teen sexual behavior and should be taken into account in this research, particularly those factors that might correlate with both sexual activity and participation in sports. Not surprisingly, a strong relationship has been documented among age of first intercourse, number of partners, and frequency of sexual activity (Koyle et al. 1989; Thornton 1990).

Demographic Factors

As children move into the teen years, their interest in sex increases, and as they are granted more autonomy, opportunities for sexual experimentation simultaneously proliferate. Hence, age is associated with several measures of sexual behavior, including early first intercourse (Miller et al. 1997); ever having had sex (Harvey and Spigner 1995); and lifetime frequency of sexual intercourse (Benda and DiBlasio 1994). Whether measured by parental educational attainment (Harvey and Spigner 1995; Miller et al. 1997) or poverty status (Males 1993), lower socioeconomic status is related to increased adolescent sexual activity (Miller and Moore 1990). Race also correlates with frequency of sexual activity and age of first intercourse. Even after controlling for low socioeconomic status, black adolescents engage in intercourse earlier and more often than white adolescents (Furstenberg et al. 1987; Miller and Moore 1990).

Family Relationships

Findings regarding the effect of quality of family relations on sexual behavior are mixed (Miller and Moore 1990). Previous studies have focused on a

variety of types of familial interaction, including communication, control, and cohesion. Though open communication between parent and child is often viewed as a critical factor in delaying or reducing adolescent sexual activity, White and White (1991) found that such communication did not consistently have the expected effect. No consensus exists regarding the effect of parental discipline and control, either. Some scholars argue that the impact of control is curvilinear, with moderate levels of parental strictness yielding lower rates of adolescent sexual activity than high or low levels (Miller et al. 1986); however, these findings may reflect a failure to adequately specify type of parental control (Barnes and Farrell 1992; Voydanoff and Donnelly 1990). In addition, high levels of parental support and monitoring have been shown to be associated with lower rates of sexual activity (Barnes and Farrell 1992; Benda and DiBlasio 1994). Family support and cohesion, or the degree of bonding among family members, also influence the frequency of delinquent behavior among adolescents (Barnes and Farrell 1992; Farrell and Barnes 1993; Barnes, Farrell, and Dintcheff 1997). However, researchers have not isolated sexual behavior from aggregate measures of delinquency (Farrell and Barnes 1993; Farrell, Barnes, and Banerjee 1995). Weighing these findings, family cohesion seems to be our best indicator of family process factors that might influence sexual behavior.

Other Extracurricular Activities

While substantial effort has been devoted to exploring the antecedents of adolescent sexual activity, surprisingly little attention has been paid to the impact of extracurricular school activities. Control theory suggests that teens with too much time on their hands can end up in trouble, but the proposition has not been applied empirically to sexual/reproductive outcomes—with one notable exception. Zill et al. (1995) found that female students who reported spending time in nonathletic extracurricular activities (band, orchestra, chorus, school play, or musical) were at less risk for pregnancy than those who did not, though they found even stronger effects of athletic participation on childbearing.

Despite the paucity of research on the linkage between extracurricular activity and sexual behavior, there is good reason to pursue this association. In assessing the effect of sports participation on girls' and boys' sexual activity, it is important to establish whether sports really do have a unique impact. It may be that, as Marsh (1992) suggests, both sports and other kinds of extracurricular activity are part of a more general pattern of social participation, heightening involvement in and commitment to school and conventional behavior patterns. Thus, in addition to controlling for demographic and family interaction variables, we analyze the effects of both athletic and nonathletic extracurricular activity in this study.

Hypotheses

In this analysis, we test two sets of hypotheses. Control theory yields the following hypotheses:

- H_1: Female athletes have lower rates of sexual activity (including lower frequency of intercourse, fewer partners, and later coital onset) than female nonathletes.
- H_2: Male athletes have lower rates of sexual activity (including lower frequency of intercourse, fewer partners, and later coital onset) than male nonathletes.

Although the cultural processes and exchange frameworks are conceptually different they suggest the same adolescent sexual outcomes:

- H_3: Female athletes have lower rates of sexual activity (including lower frequency of intercourse, fewer partners, and later coital onset) than female nonathletes.
- H_4: Male athletes have higher rates of sexual activity (including higher frequency of intercourse, more partners, and earlier coital onset) than male nonathletes.

Methods

Random-digit-dial procedures were used on a computer-assisted telephone network to obtain a representative household sample of 699 adolescents and their families in a large northeastern metropolitan area. In order to be included in the sample at time one, households had to have at least one adolescent aged 13 to 16 and at least one biological or surrogate parent. Black families were oversampled (N = 211) in order to permit more detailed analysis. Characteristics of the overall sample closely matched the census distributions in the area. Each eligible family was offered $50 to participate. Strin-

gent follow-up procedures yielded a completion rate of 71 percent in the first year, and retention rates of over 90 percent in subsequent years (see Barnes et al. 1991; Barnes and Farrell 1992 for a more detailed description of the sampling procedures and sample characteristics). The present analysis used the third wave of data, containing data on sexuality; wave three included 611 adolescent subjects aged 15 to 18. A team of two trained interviewers conducted face-to-face interviews with the target adolescent and one or both parents. Questions about sensitive issues such as sexual behavior were reported through a self-administered portion of the interview.

Dependent Measures

Measures of adolescent sexual behavior included self-reports of overall number of sex partners, lifetime frequency of sexual intercourse, frequency of intercourse in the past 12 months, and age of first sexual intercourse. Respondents were asked how many different people they had had sexual intercourse with in their lives, with response categories of none, one, two or three, and four or more. For both lifetime sexual experience and experience within the past 12 months, reported frequency of intercourse was divided into six categories:

1. never
2. once
3. two or three times
4. four or five times
5. six to nine times
6. ten or more times

The respondent's age when she or he first had intercourse was categorized as early (age 10-14), late (age 15-18), or never (respondent had never had sexual relations).

Independent Measures

Four demographic variables were included in the present analysis:

1. race
2. gender
3. age
4. family income

Race was coded into two categories: black and white/other. Black respondents comprised 30 percent of the unweighted sample and 14 percent of the weighted sample. Respondents ranged in age from 14 to 19. Family income served as an indicator of socioeconomic status. Family income was reported by the adolescent's parents: where the father was unavailable, the mother provided an estimate of his income. Income categories (recoded to midpoint) ranged from under $7,000 to $100,000 or more, with an overall sample mean of approximately $41,000.

To measure family cohesion, we employed Olson, Portner, and Lavee's 1985 FACES III scale, for which response choices range on a 6-point Likert scale from "almost never" to "almost always." Respondents were asked to describe their families with respect to the following statements:

1. "Family members ask each other for help."
2. "We approve of each other's friends."
3. "We like to do things with just our immediate family."
4. "Family members feel closer to other family members than to people outside the family."
5. "Family members like to spend free time with each other."
6. "Family members feel very close to each other."
7. "When our family gets together for activities, everybody is present."
8. "We can easily think of things to do together as a family."
9. "Family members consult other family members on their decisions."
10. "Family togetherness is very important."

Alpha reliability of the cohesion scale was .82 for the sample as a whole.

Athletic participation was measured by the question, "Do you participate in sports at school?" For a small number of cases (N = 26) where the respondent was no longer in school, wave four responses (i.e., responses from the following year) to the question "How often did you actively participate in sports, athletics, or exercising (other than during school hours) in the last year?" were recoded dichotomously (yes or no) and substituted.

Respondents were asked to indicate whether they participated in seven extracurricular activities:

1. sports
2. music
3. drama
4. literary organizations
5. academic clubs
6. sororities/fraternities
7. "other activities"

Sorority/fraternity involvement was discarded due to the small number of participants (N = 21); "other activities" was likewise eliminated as theoretically meaningless. Factor analysis was used to establish whether the remaining activities could be grouped into meaningful subcultures. The analysis yielded three factors, which accounted for 32.9 percent of the variance. After varimax rotation, school participation in music and drama loaded on factor one, the "arts" factor (eigenvalue = 1.65), with loadings of .84 and .77 respectively. School participation in literary organizations (e.g., yearbook, school newspaper) and/or academic clubs comprised factor two, the "academic" factor (eigenvalue = 1.07), with loadings of .81 and .75 respectively. Athletic participation constituted factor three, the "sports" factor. Although the eigenvalue for this factor was only .90, we retained it because sports alone loaded .97 on the factor. Bivariate correlations among the three factors were low: .23 (arts/academic), .16 (academic/sports), and .03 (sports/arts).

Results

Sociodemographic characteristics of the weighted sample approximated those of the general population (Barnes et al. 1991; Barnes and Farrell 1992).[1] (See table 9.1 for sample descriptives.) Sport appeared to be the extracurricular activity of choice: while fewer than one in four respondents participated in the arts or academic extracurricular activities, over half (55 percent) reported athletic involvement. Nearly two thirds of the boys reported sports participation, while almost half of the girls engaged in sport activity of some kind.

In order to provide unbiased estimates of sexual behavior, the weighted descriptive statistics were used. While over a third of the adolescents reported having never had a sex partner, nearly two thirds had at least some sexual experience, and nearly a fifth (18.5 percent) reported having four or more partners. For both lifetime and recent sexual experience, responses were bimodal: while more than 40 percent had never had sex, over a third had had sex 10 or more times overall, and over a quarter reported this frequency within the past year alone. Nearly a quarter of respondents (well over a third of those who had at least some sexual experience) reported that their first sexual encounter had occurred before age 15.

Males were more likely to participate in sports than females (65 percent versus 47 percent). When comparisons were made across gender and

Table 9.1 Weighted Descriptive Statistics: Sociodemographics, Family Interaction, Extracurricular Activities, and Sexual Behavior Variables

	All (N = 611) %	Females Athletes (N = 153) %	Females Nonathletes (N = 183) %	Males Athletes (N = 181) %	Males Nonathletes (N = 94) %
Race (unweighted)[a]					
White/other	70.4	74.5	65.6	69.6	74.5
Black	29.6	25.5	34.4	30.4	25.5
Gender					
Female	54.8	NA	NA	NA	NA
Male	45.2				
Age					
15 or younger	21.6	24.1	19.3	22.8	19.8
16	27.1	25.5	24.7	34.3	20.1
17	26.4	33.8	23.1	24.3	24.6
18 or older	24.9	16.6	32.9	18.5	35.4
Mean	16.6	16.4	16.7	16.4	16.8
Mean family income, in thousands					
(3.5–100)	40.9	44.6	39.3	44.0	32.1
Mean family cohesion					
(10-50)	31.6	32.4	30.7	32.7	30.8
Arts (music, drama)					
No	73.0	59.6	70.0	79.9	86.8
Yes	27.0	40.4	30.0	20.1	13.2
Academic (clubs, literary organizations)					
No	70.9	51.2	75.3	75.7	84.2
Yes	29.1	48.8	24.7	24.3	15.8
Athletic participation					
Yes	55.0	NA	NA	NA	NA
No	45.0				
Partners[b]					
None	38.3	48.1	36.8	32.8	33.8
One	20.5	28.0	24.2	10.9	18.6
Two or three	22.7	14.7	25.9	26.9	22.8
Four or more	18.5	9.2	13.0	29.4	24.8
Frequency sex, life[b]					
Never	41.1	53.6	40.6	33.8	34.7
1–3 times	13.1	12.2	6.6	18.2	16.8
4–9 times	10.4	8.4	8.9	11.2	15.3
10+ times	35.3	25.8	43.8	36.7	33.2
Frequency sex, past year[b]					
Never	43.3	53.7	41.9	38.9	36.7
1–3 times	16.7	15.7	8.7	23.1	20.5
4–9 times	11.9	9.7	13.5	10.7	14.5
10+ times	28.1	20.9	35.8	27.3	28.2
Age at onset (ordinal)					
Early (10–14)	24.3	11.2	24.1	33.5	28.9
Late (15–18)	39.1	41.5	40.8	34.8	41.0
Never had sex	36.6	47.2	35.1	31.8	30.2

[a]Percentages provided here for race are based on the unweighted sample. After weighting to correct for oversampling of black families, 86% of the sample was white/other and 14% was black. Percentages provided for all other descriptive statistics are weighted. The unweighted sample was used for the multivariate analysis.

[b]Excludes some missing cases recoded to the mean value in later analysis.

Reprinted from Miller, Sabo, Farrell, Barnes, and Melnick, 1998.

athletic-involvement categories, several differences were noted. Compared to females, males reported greater sexual experience overall, more partners, and an earlier onset of sexual behavior. The relationships between sports and sexual behavior differed by gender: while athletic participation was associated with lower rates of sexual activity for females, the reverse was true for males.

An examination of the bivariate correlations yielded some initial insights into the relationships involved. Number of sex partners, lifetime and past-year frequency of intercourse, and age of first intercourse were all highly intercorrelated, ranging from .67 to .93. Table 9.2 shows the bivariate correlations among the extracurricular and sexual behavior variables. These relationships are of particular interest, since—unlike the demographic and interaction variables—the impact of participation in extracurricular school activities on sexual behavior has not been tested previously. No clear difference between sports and other group activities emerged for the sample as a whole. There was a weak negative association between each type of activity and sexual activity, an effect that was weakest for sports. However, when separated out by gender, it became clear that different processes were operating for boys and girls. Where all three types of activities were associated with lower sexual activity for females, for males, only arts involvement had this effect. In fact, male sports participation—while not a significant outcome—showed a modest positive correlation with sexual activity.

Because the dependent measures were highly correlated, we employed multivariate analysis of covariance to explore the gender-differentiated impacts of sports participation on adolescent sexual behavior (table 9.3). As predicted, sociodemographic factors played a significant role in predicting teen sexual activity. Respondents' race significantly affected the multivariate factor, as well as a majority of the univariate indicators of sexual activity: whites were less sexually active on the whole. Gender as a main effect was important in predicting number of sex partners and age at first coitus, though not frequency of intercourse. Females had fewer partners and initiated sex at a later age. Not surprisingly, older adolescents reported more partners and more frequent intercourse, though they were no more likely to have initiated sexual activity at an early age than were younger respondents. While family income had no significant effect on the dependent variables taken separately or as a factor, family cohesion was clearly a consideration in the sexual behavior of adolescents, significantly reducing frequency of intercourse and number of partners, and increasing age of first intercourse on both the multivariate and univariate lev-

Table 9.2   Bivariate Correlations of Dependent Variables and Extracurricular Activities, by Gender

	# of partners	Lifetime sex	Past year sex	Early onset
All				
Arts	−.18***	−.15***	−.15***	−.14***
Academic	−.16***	−.14***	−.12**	−.12**
Sports	−.01	−.08*	−.10*	−.05
Females				
Arts	−.11*	−.14*	−.13*	−.12*
Academic	−.21***	−.18***	−.16**	−.18**
Sports	−.14**	−.17**	−.17**	−.17**
Males				
Arts	−.19**	−.15*	−.17**	−.12*
Academic	−.03	−.06	−.06	−.01
Sports	.04	.01	−.02	.02

*p < .05; **p < .01; ***p < .001; (two-tailed tests).

Reprinted from Miller, Sabo, Farrell, Barnes, and Melnick, 1998.

els. In fact, only in the case of this variable can a genuine if cautious claim be made regarding causality, since family cohesion was measured several years prior to reported frequency of intercourse.

Yet the relationship between extracurricular activity and sexual behavior remains a tangled one. None of the three factors (arts, academic, sports) proved significant for the multivariate factor as a whole; in fact, neither sports nor academic participation had significant main effects for any of the univariate or multivariate analyses. However, the univariate impacts of arts participation on sexual behaviors were significant, indicating that adolescents who participated in activities such as music and drama were less likely to be sexually active than those who did not participate in these activities. The effect of arts involvement on number of sex partners differed by gender: though musical or dramatic extracurricular pursuits were associated with lower rates of sexual activity for both girls and boys, the effect for boys was significantly stronger. Other than this specific interaction, though, the relationships between nonathletic extracurricular activities and sexual behavior were not significantly affected by gender.

The interaction between athletic participation and gender constitutes the pivotal finding of this analysis. The interaction was significant for the univariate tests of each of the four dependent measures of sexual activity. Clearly, sports had a very different impact on boys' and girls' sexual behavior. Main effects for sports (all measures) and for gender (two measures) were absent due to the conflation of these categories:

Table 9.3   Multivariate Analysis of Covariance Predicting Adolescent Sexual Behavior (Sequential Method[a])

Independent variables	Multivariate F Four dependent variables taken together	Standardized beta coefficients			
		# of partners	Lifetime sex	Past year sex	Early onset
Demographic factors					
Race	8.96***	.45***	.40*	.32	.28***
White/other (= 0)					
Black (= 1)					
Gender	15.68***	−.51***	−.29	−.19	−.26**
Male (= 0)					
Female (= 1)					
Age	31.12***	.23***	.47***	.43***	.02
Income	NS	−.00	−.00	−.00	−.00+
Family interaction					
Family cohesion	5.66***	−.03***	−.03**	−.03**	−.02***
Extracurricular activity					
Arts (1 = yes)	NS	−.26*	−.45*	−.50*	−.16*
Academic (1 = yes)	NS	−.12	−.28	−.20	−.02
Sports (1 = yes)	NS	.07	−.03	−.10	−.05
2-way interactions					
Gender* Arts	NS	.48*	.48	.54	.18
Gender* Academic	NS	−.20	−.05	.02	−.07
Gender* Sports	1.95++	−.43*	−.87*	−.72*	−.35**
Cell comparisons for gender sports interaction: effects of athletic participation within genders*					
Males	NS	.28+	.21	.04	.15
Females	3.62**	−.32*	−.80***	−.77***	−.29**

[a]Contrasts are simple, reference category is first.

*p < .05; **p < .01; ***p < .001; +p < .10; ++p = .101.

Reprinted from Miller, Sabo, Farrell, Barnes, and Melnick, 1998.

as the cell comparison for the gender-sports interaction demonstrates, sports participation was associated with lower sexual activity levels for females only. The effect was particularly striking when athletic participation was contrasted with participation in other extracurricular activities, which manifestly did not interact with gender in the same way.

Comparing adjusted means for each of the four gender/sport categories confirms that girls who participated in sports reported evidence of less sexual activity on all measures. Female athletes had substantially fewer sex partners, engaged in less frequent intercourse on both temporal scales, and began having sex at a later age. Figure 9.1 shows the plotted adjusted means for lifetime frequency of sexual intercourse, which are typical of the dependent variables. The directions of the effects for each of these four behaviors were consistent: sports involvement for girls resulted in lower levels of sexual activity. For boys, however, the effects were decidedly weaker and reversed in direction. That is, to the extent that sports made a difference in boys' sexual behavior at all, male adolescent athletes actually reported more partners, more sexual experience overall, and earlier sexual onset than did their noninvolved peers.

Discussion

This work shows that sports have unique and gender-specific effects on adolescent sexual behavior. Our

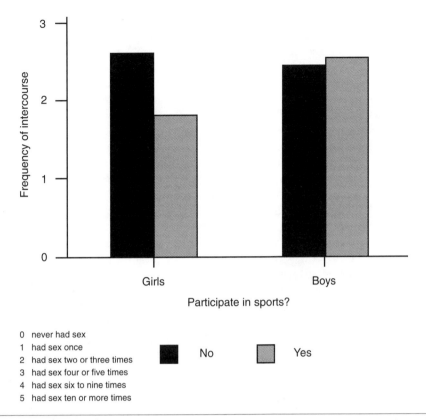

Figure 9.1   Adjusted means of dependent variables: lifetime frequency of intercourse, by gender and athletic participation.

Reprinted from Miller, Sabo, Farrell, Barnes, and Melnick, 1998.

findings indicate that, even after accounting for the effects of race, age, family income, family cohesion, and involvement in other extracurricular activities, athletic participation for girls was associated with: (1) lower frequency of sexual intercourse; (2) fewer sex partners; and (3) higher age at coital onset. For boys, these effects were very slight and in the opposite direction. What, then, are the implications of these results for the theories examined earlier?

The control or "idle hands" explanation received little support. Contrary to our findings, this theory predicts no significant gender differences in magnitude or direction of effects of sports on sexual behavior. Furthermore, control theory implies that sports should act to suppress sexual activity in more or less the same fashion as other extracurricular activities, a conclusion tentatively supported for girls but clearly not for boys. The interaction of gender and athletic participation raises doubts about the relevance of control theory for this analysis.

The cultural explanation fared better. After controlling for demographic and family relationship variables, the anticipated gender differences in the magnitude and direction of effects of sport on sexual behavior were borne out, as were clear differences between sports and other extracurricular activities. Whereas the effects of athletic participation on sexual activity were gender-specific, involvement in the arts (music or drama) had a depressive impact on the sexual activity of both genders. Academic extracurricular participation had little effect at all. These findings are consistent with the existence of diverse subcultures. Unlike sport, which for boys often enhances a sexually aggressive ethic of masculinity and, for girls, weakens their commitment to a sexually passive cultural script, arts involvement is less likely to promulgate a message of machismo.

Like the cultural explanation, the exchange framework suggests different sexual outcomes for female and male athletes. Girls who play sports do in fact report less frequent sexual intercourse, fewer partners, and later age at coital onset than those not involved in sports. These findings are consistent with the contention that social status gained through athletic participation is being used to resist sexual pressure. Though the difference is not statistically significant, male athletes report slightly more sexual activity than nonathletes, suggesting that they may employ sports-based resources to bargain for sex. Of course, the weakness of this tendency argues in favor of caution before accepting such an explanation. However, our descriptive analysis shows that boys in sports tend to polarize into two groups (those who are sexually inactive, and those who are very active), and this division may cloud somewhat the pattern of male athletic sexual behavior.

Furthermore, if the impact of sports on sexual behavior is largely mediated by a sexual bargaining process, the same dynamic presumably applies to other status-enhancing extracurricular activities. Any personal resources gained through involvement in academic or arts activities should have bargaining implications, with differences in the magnitude of the effect reflecting the status of the activity. Yet arts participation decreased sexual activity for boys as well as girls, an inconsistency that is difficult to explain using exchange theory alone unless participation in music or drama actually decreases social status.

Our findings do not negate control theory, which has proven highly effective in explaining other adolescent risky behaviors (Barnes and Farrell 1992), but suggest instead that there is something unique about the intersection of sports and sexual behavior which calls for an alternative theoretical approach. We suggest that athletic participation and sexual activity are distinct from the more general concepts of social participation and problem behavior. Unlike other extracurricular activities, the culture of sport is steeped in a tradition rooted in deeply cherished notions of discipline, manhood, and structured aggression. And unlike other risky behaviors, sexual activity involves negotiated patterns of interaction and resource exchange with others.

Cultural Resource Theory

We have developed an integrated framework called cultural resource theory to explain the apparent interface between the cultural and exchange processes at work here, wherein culture dictates the value of the resources brought to bear and resource availability influences adherence to cultural norms. Cultural resource theory explicitly recognizes the interaction of gender-specific cultural scripts and bargaining resources in the negotiation of sexual outcomes for adolescents. Sport provides both a set of cultural prescriptions and a set of bargaining resources that play key roles in determining an adolescent athlete's sexual behavior. Thus athletic status translates into bargaining power (to exploit or resist exploitation) for both

genders. Sport resources, along with a sport culture antithetical to normative expectations of passive femininity, allow girls to discard aspects of the traditional gender script that prioritize heterosexual appeal and vicarious status aggrandizement through social and/or sexual bonding with boys. The arts, conversely, provide girls with enhanced status which may be used in the bargaining process, but either confer little status on boys or, more likely, shake boys loose from a cultural script which equates masculine worth with sexual accomplishment.

Figure 9.2 provides a conceptual schematic of cultural resource theory. Athletic participation confirms traditional gender scripts for boys, while disconfirming traditional scripts for girls. Since these scripts promote (if not overtly) the exchange of female sexual favors for male prestige, athletic participation indirectly increases sexual activity for boys and decreases it for girls. Sports also enhance social status for both genders, giving male and female athletes greater power in negotiating sexual outcomes in their relationships.

Of course, care must be taken in attributing causality to any of the reported associations. As Frey and Eitzen (1991) point out, there is a powerful process of selection at work when children and adolescents enter the sports milieu. Spreitzer (1994) found that athletic participation is nonrandomly distributed: students who come from a higher socioeconomic family background, who have higher grades and score better on standardized tests, and who report higher levels of self-esteem are more likely to become athletes. Similarly, we found that athletes in the present analysis reported higher family incomes and higher levels of family cohesion. Still, selection and socialization are most likely mutually reinforcing processes. Selective recruitment into sports, then, does not mean that differences between athletes and nonathletes entirely predate their participation; it does, however, mandate the careful control of potential selector variables. We posit that the filtering processes involve both structural (e.g., race, age, socioeconomic status) and interactional (e.g., quality of family interaction) inputs. Even when these variables are controlled, however, a gender-differentiated effect of sports on adolescent sexual behavior remains.

Several additional caveats are in order. The foregoing discussion has focused exclusively on heterosexual adolescent sexual activity. Cultural resource theory emphasizes both the acquisition of resources that permit girls to diverge from traditional gender scripts if they so choose, and exposure to a nontraditional, androgynous gender script. While this

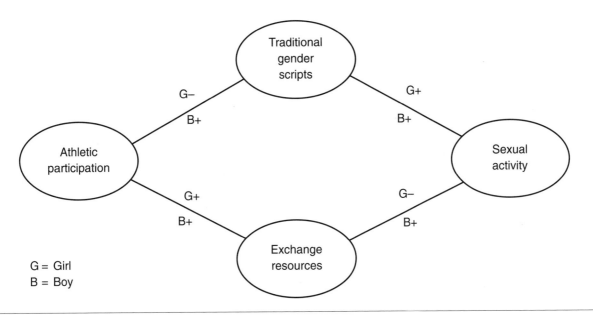

Figure 9.2   Cultural resource theory: conceptual model.

Reprinted from Miller, Sabo, Farrell, Barnes, and Melnick, 1998.

theory might lead one to predict same-sex sexual activity among female athletes, the data in this study did not permit empirical evaluation of this hypothesis. We have accordingly discussed only the heterosexual implications of the effects of athletic participation on adolescent sexual behavior.

In addition, parts of the preceding argument for cultural resource theory are based on deduction. Because we have little empirical evidence regarding the relative popularity associated with various extracurricular activities, we are unable to state unequivocally that popularity and sexual outcomes are related in a linear fashion. Nor can we entirely rule out a sociobiological explanation for these findings. For example, increased physical activity can delay menarche, deterring sexual interest and readiness among adolescent females (Freedson and Bunker 1997). It is also possible that females who reach sexual maturity at an early age tend to drop out of sports (Malina 1983), while boys who develop early are tracked into sports and enjoy greater athletic success because of their size and strength advantages.

Furthermore, within the rubric of cultural resource theory, we cannot assign greater or lesser importance to either the culture or exchange process in explicating the relationships among sports, gender, and sexual behavior. It may be, for example, that female athletes are less invested in the dating game altogether (culture), or just less likely to see sex as a necessary part of the game (exchange). They may be viewed by boys or perceive themselves as less desirable partners because of their divergence from conventional scripts; or, perhaps, they see themselves

or are viewed by boys as more desirable partners, and thus in a better position to dictate the terms of their relationships. High school sports may also be a cultural milieu in which platonic friendships between female and male athletes can be developed, bypassing the sexual bargaining process altogether. To some extent, these distinctions might be illuminated by comparing dating behavior and sexual outcomes. Ultimately, however, qualitative exploration of the gendered world of sport may be necessary in order to understand the meanings, and therefore the value, that adolescents assign their own activities.

The current study opens a window to an area of inquiry previously unexamined. Currently, intervention programs to combat adolescent behaviors leading to unwanted pregnancy operate in every state, and much research activity has been devoted to evaluating their efficacy. However, the results to date are varied, and many, if not most, of these programs appear to have no appreciable returns (Males 1993). None of these prevention programs, or the supportive research generated so far, address the contributions of athletic participation. While further research is needed to clarify the nature and nuances of the relationships found here, it is clear that involvement in sports affects girls and boys differently, and that for girls, athletic participation is associated with lower frequency of heterosexual intercourse, fewer partners, and later onset of intercourse. In light of the concern in contemporary America over adolescent sexuality, this promising connection would seem deserving of continued research attention.

Note

1. Because black families were disproportionately sampled in order to allow for more detailed race comparisons, the frequencies provided here have been weighted to correct for oversampling. However, since race is controlled for in the multivariate analysis, the unweighted sample is used in this procedure.

References

Abma, J. S., A. Chandra, W. D. Mosher, L. Peterson, and L. Piccinino. 1997. "Fertility, Family Planning, and Women's Health: New Data from the 1995 National Survey of Family Growth." National Center for Health Statistics. *Vital Health Statistics* 23:19.

Acosta, R. Vivian and Linda Jean Carpenter. 1996. *Women in Intercollegiate Sports: A Longitudinal Study—Nineteen Year Update, 1977–1996.* Brooklyn: Photocopied report.

Alan Guttmacher Institute. 1994. *Sex and America's Teenagers.* New York: Alan Guttmacher Institute.

Allen, Joseph P., Susan Philliber, Scott Heffling, and Gabriel P. Kuperminc. 1997. "Preventing Teen Pregnancy and Academic Failure: Experimental Evaluation of a Developmentally Based Approach." *Child Development* 64:729–742.

Andre, Thomas and Alyce Holland. 1995. "Relationship of Sport Participation to Sex Role Orientation and Attitudes Toward Women Among High School Males and Females." *Journal of Sport Behavior* 18 (4):24–36.

Barnes, Grace M. and Michael P. Farrell. 1992. "Parental Support and Control as Predictors of Adolescent Drinking, Delinquency, and Related Problem Behaviors." *Journal of Marriage and the Family* 54:763–776.

Barnes, Grace M., Michael P. Farrell, and Barbara A. Dintcheff. 1997. "Family Socialization Effects on Alcohol Abuse and Related Problem Behaviors Among Female and Male Adolescents." Pp. 156–175 in *Gender and Alcohol,* edited by S. and R. Wilsnack. Piscataway, NJ: Rutgers Center of Alcohol Studies.

Barnes, Grace M., Michael P. Farrell, Kevin W. Welch, Lois Uhteg, and Barbara A. Dintcheff. 1991. *Description and Analysis of Methods Used in the Family and Adolescent Study.* Buffalo: Research Institute on Alcoholism.

Benda, Brent B. and Frederick A. DiBlasio. 1994. "An Integration of Theory: Adolescent Sexual Contacts." *Journal of Youth and Adolescence* 23:403–420.

Brown, Janice T., Linda Ellis, Mary Lou Guerrina, Deborah M. Paxton, and Patricia Poleno. 1997. "The Relationship Between the Frequency of Exercise and the Age of Onset of Sexual Intercourse in Adolescent Females." *Nurse Practitioner* 22 (2):16–18+.

Caron, Sandra L., D. Bruce Carter, and Lloyd A. Brightman. 1985. "Sex-role Orientation and Attitudes Towards Women: Differences Among College Athletes and Nonathletes." *Perceptual and Motor Skills* 61:803–806.

Farrell, Michael P. and Grace M. Barnes. 1993. "Family Systems and Social Support: A Test of the Effects of Cohesion and Adaptability on the Functioning of Parents and Adolescents." *Journal of Marriage and the Family* 55:119–132.

Farrell, Michael P., Grace M. Barnes, and Sarbani Banerjee. 1995. "Family Cohesion as a Buffer Against the Effects of Problem-Drinking Fathers on Psychological Distress, Deviant Behavior, and Heavy Drinking in Adolescents." *Journal of Health and Social Behavior* 36:377–385.

Freedson, P. and L. Bunker. 1997. "Physiological Dimensions." Pp. 1–16 in *Physical Activity and Sport in the Lives of Girls.* Washington, DC: The President's Council on Physical Fitness and Sports.

Frey, James H. and D. Stanley Eitzen. 1991. "Sport and Society." *Annual Review of Sociology* 17: 503–522.

Furstenberg, Jr., Frank F., S. Philip Morgan, Kristin A. Moore, and James L. Peterson. 1987. "Race Differences in the Timing of Adolescent Intercourse." *American Sociological Review* 52: 511–518.

Harvey, S. Marie and Clarence Spigner. 1995. "Factors Associated With Sexual Behavior Among Adolescents: A Multivariate Analysis." *Adolescence* 30 (118):253–264.

Hirschi, Travis. 1969. *Causes of Delinquency.* Berkeley, CA: University of California Press.

Holland, Alyce and Thomas Andre. 1994. "Athletic Participation and the Social Status of Adolescent Males and Females." *Youth & Society* 25: 388–407.

Houseworth, Steve, Kenneth Peplow, and Joel Thirer. 1989. "Influence of Sport Participation Upon Sex Role Orientation of Caucasian Males and Their Attitudes Toward Women." *Sex Roles* 20:317–325.

Kane, Mary Jo. 1988. "The Female Athletic Role as a Status Determinant Within the Social Systems of High School Adolescents." *Adolescence* 23 (90):253–264.

Koyle, Priscilla Fay Carter, Larry Cyril Jensen, Joe Olsen, and Bert Cundick. 1989. "Comparison of Sexual Behaviors Among Adolescents Having an Early, Middle. and Late First Intercourse Experience." *Youth & Society* 20:461–476.

Lauritsen, Janet L. 1994. "Explaining Race and Gender Differences in Adolescent Sexual Behavior." *Social Forces* 72:859–84.

Males, Mike. 1993. "School-Age Pregnancy: Why Hasn't Prevention Worked?" *Journal of School Health* 63:429–432.

Malina, R. M. 1983. "Menarche in Athletes: A Synthesis and Hypothesis." *Annals of Human Biology* 10: 1–24.

Marsh, Herbert W. 1992. "Extracurricular Activities: Beneficial Extension of the Educational Curriculum or Subversion of Academic Goals?" *Journal of Educational Psychology* 84: 553–562.

Messner, Michael A. and Donald F. Sabo, ed. 1990. *Sport, Men and the Gender Order: Critical Feminist Perspectives.* Champaign, IL: Human Kinetics.

Miller, Brent C., J. K. McCoy, T. D. Olson, and C. M. Wallace. 1986. "Parental Discipline and Control Attempts in Relation to Adolescent Sexual Attitudes and Behavior." *Journal of Marriage and the Family* 48: 503–512.

Miller, Brent C. and K. A. Moore. 1990. "Adolescent Sexual Behavior, Pregnancy, and Parenting: Research Through the 1980s." *Journal of Marriage and the Family* 52: 1025–1044.

Miller, Brent C., Maria C. Norton, Thom Curtis, E. Jeffrey Hill, Paul Schvaneveldt, and Margaret H. Young. 1997. "The Timing of Sexual Intercourse Among Adolescents: Family, Peer, and Other Antecedents." *Youth & Society* 29:54–83.

National Campaign to Prevent Teen Pregnancy. 1997. *Whatever Happened to Childhood? The Problem of Teen Pregnancy in the United States.* Washington, DC: Author.

National Federation of State High Schools Association. 1997. *NFHS Handbook, 1997–98.* Kansas City, MO: NFSHSA.

Olson, D.H., J. Portner, and Y. Lavee. 1985. *FACES III.* St. Paul: University of Minnesota, Family Social Science.

Pleck, Joseph H., Freya L. Sonenstein, and Leighton C. Ku. 1993. "Masculinity Ideology: Its Impact on Adolescent Males' Heterosexual Relationships." *Journal of Social Issues* 49 (3):11–29.

Sabo, Donald F., Michael P. Farrell, Merrill J. Melnick, Grace M. Barnes, and Kathleen E. Miller. 1997. "High School Athletic Participation. Sexual Behavior and Adolescent Pregnancy: A Preliminary Analysis." Paper Presented at the 97th Annual Meeting of the American Sociological Association, August 9th, Toronto, Canada.

Sabo, Donald, Merrill Melnick, and Beth Vanfossen. 1989. *The Women's Sports Foundation Report: Minorities in Sport.* New York: The Women's Sports Foundation.

Sabo, Donald and Merrill Melnick. 1996. "Athletic Participation and Risk for Adolescent Pregnancy: Is There a Connection?" Paper Presented at the Population Council Family and Development Program Conference, June 4, New York City, NY.

Sabo, Donald and Michael Messner. 1993. "Whose Body Is This? Women's Sports and Sexual Politics." Pp. 37–51 in *Women in Sport: Issues and Controversies,* edited by Greta Cohen. Newbury Park, CA: Sage Publications.

Skolnick, Andrew A. 1993. "Studies Raise Doubts About Benefit of Athletics in Reducing Unhealthy Behavior Among Adolescents." *The Journal of the American Medical Association* 270:798–799.

Spreitzer, Elmer. 1994. "Does Participation in Interscholastic Athletics Affect Adult Development?" *Youth & Society* 25:368–387.

Suitor, J. Jill and Rebel Reavis. 1995. "Football, Fast Cars. and Cheerleading: Adolescent Gender Norms, 1978–1989." *Adolescence* 30 (118): 265–272.

Thornton, Arland D. 1990. "The Courtship Process and Adolescent Sexuality." *Journal of Family Issues* 11:239–273.

Tiezzi, Lorraine, Judy Lipshutz, Neysa Wrobleski, Roger D. Vaughan, and James F. McCarthy. 1997. "Pregnancy Prevention Among Urban Adolescents Younger Than 15: Results of the 'In Your Face' Program." *Family Planning Perspectives* 29 (4):173–176, 197.

Voydanoff, P. and B. W. Donnelly. 1990. *Adolescent Sexuality and Pregnancy.* Newbury Park, CA: Sage Publications.

Waller, Willard W. 1951. *The Family: A Dynamic Interpretation.* New York: Holt, Rinehart and Winston.

White, C. P. and M. B. White. 1991. "The Adolescent Family Life Act." *Journal of Clinical Child Development* 20 (1):50–70.

Zilbergeld, B. 1993. *The New Male Sexuality.* New York: Bantam Books.

Zill, Nicholas, C. Nord, and L. Loomis. 1995. *Adolescent Time Use, Risky Behavior, and Outcomes: An Analysis of National Data.* Rockville, MD: Westat, Inc.

Student Council, Volunteering, Basketball, or Marching Band: What Kind of Extracurricular Involvement Matters?

Jacquelynne S. Eccles
Bonnie L. Barber

We examined the potential benefits and risks associated with participation in five types of activities: prosocial (church and volunteer activities), team sports, school involvement, performing arts, and academic clubs. Our sample included 1,259 mostly European American adolescents (approximately equal numbers of males and females). First, we explore the link between involvement in these activities and our indicators of positive and negative development. Involvement in prosocial activities was linked to positive educational trajectories and low rates of involvement in risky behaviors. In contrast, participation in team sports was linked to positive educational trajectories and to high rates of involvement in one risky behavior, drinking alcohol. Then, we explore two possible mediators of these associations: peer associations and activity-based identity formation. The evidence supported our hypothesis that group differences in peer associations and activity-based identities help explain activity group differences.

The release of *A Matter of Time* by the Carnegie Corporation of New York (1992) put the spotlight on the role that productive use of time might play in successful adolescent development. It illustrated how much discretionary time adolescents have and how much of this time is spent on unstructured activities such as "hanging out" with friends, watching television, and listening to music. The authors argued that constructive, organized activities would be a better use of the adolescents' time for the following types of reasons: (a) idle time is the devil's playground—doing good things with one's time takes time away from opportunities to get involved in risky activities; (b) one can learn good things while engaged in constructive activities—for example, specific competencies and prosocial values and attitudes; and (c) involvement in organized activity settings increases the possibility of establishing positive social supports and networks. To date, however, there has been relatively little longitudinal, developmentally oriented research focused on either the benefits or costs of how adolescents spend their discretionary time. Most of the relevant research has been done in sociology and leisure

The research reported in this article was funded by grants from NICHD, NIMH, and NSF to the second author and by grants from NSF, the Spencer Foundation, and the W.T. Grant Foundation to both authors. We wish to thank the following people for their contributions over the years to this project: Carol Midgley, Allan Wigfield, David Reuman, Harriet Feldlaufer, Douglas Mac Iver, Janis Jacobs, Constance Flanagan, Andrew Fuligni, Deborah Josefowicz, Pam Frome, Lisa Colarossi, Amy Arbreton, Laurie Meschke, and Kristen Jacobson. Some of these data were presented by Eccles and Barber at the 1995 and 1997 Biennial Meetings of the Society for Research on Child Development.

Reprinted from Eccles and Barber, 1999.

studies, with some recent attention to the benefits of activity involvement growing out of concern with the potential importance of community-service activities for youth development. In this article, we investigate the longitudinal correlates of activity involvement during the high school years. Initially, we report on the patterns of involvement of high school sophomores to provide a richer picture of the social life of today's adolescents. Then, we report on both the short-term behavioral correlates and the long-term sequelae of engagement in different types of activities.

Most of the sociological research into the correlates of youth activity involvement has focused on extracurricular school activities. This research has documented a link between adolescents' extracurricular activities and adult educational attainment, occupation, and income, even after controlling for social class and ability (Landers & Landers, 1978; Otto, 1975, 1976; Otto & Alwin, 1977). Some of these studies also documented a protective association between extracurricular activity participation and involvement in delinquent and other risky behaviors (e.g., Landers & Landers, 1978).

Research within leisure studies has taken a slightly different path. In this area, there have been extensive discussions of the difference between relaxed leisure and constructive, organized activities. Relaxed leisure is characterized as enjoyable, but not demanding (watching TV). Constructive leisure requires effort and provides a forum in which to express one's identity or passion in sports, performing arts, and leadership activities (Agnew & Petersen, 1989; Csikszentmihalyi, 1990; Csikszentmihalyi & Kleiber, 1991; Fine, Mortimer, & Roberts, 1990; Grieves, 1989; Haggard & Williams, 1992; Kleiber, Larson, & Csikszentmihalyi, 1986; Larson & Kleiber, 1993; Larson & Richards, 1989). It is often assumed that there are more beneficial developmental outcomes for adolescents associated with constructive leisure than with relaxed leisure because constructive leisure provides the following opportunities: (a) to acquire and practice specific social, physical, and intellectual skills that may be useful in a wide variety of settings; (b) to contribute to the well-being of one's community and to develop a sense of agency as a member of one's community; (c) to belong to a socially recognized and valued group; (d) to establish supportive social networks of both peers and adults that can help one in both the present and the future; and (e) to experience and deal with challenges. We know little, however, about the instrumental role that relaxed and constructive leisure has on adolescent development.

Some recent research indicates positive consequences of participation in organized activities (e.g., Simmons & Blyth, 1987). For example, Mahoney and Cairns (1997) and McNeal (1995) found that extracurricular activities were related to a lower chance of school dropout, particularly during the early high school years and for high-risk youth. Mahoney (1997) has also shown a connection to reduced rates of criminal offending. In addition, adolescents involved in a broad range of adult-endorsed activities report lower rates of substance use than their noninvolved peers (Youniss, Yates, & Su, 1997). Sports, relative to other school-based activities such as student government and academic clubs, have been linked to lower likelihood of school dropout and higher rates of college attendance (Deeter, 1990; Elliott & Voss, 1974; Hanks & Eckland, 1978; Holland & Andre, 1987; Howell & McKenzie, 1987; Kirshnit, Ham, & Richards, 1989; McNeal, 1995); this is especially true for low-achieving and blue-collar male athletes (see Gould & Weiss, 1987; Holland & Andre, 1987; Melnick, Vanfossen, & Sabo, 1988).

Participation in extracurricular activities has also been linked to increases on indicators of positive development such as self-concept, high school grade point average (GPA), school engagement, and educational aspirations (Lamborn, Brown, Mounts, & Steinberg, 1992; Newmann, Wehlage, & Lamborn, 1992; Winne & Walsh, 1980). This is particularly true if one is involved in a leadership role. Similarly, involvement in high school extracurricular activities is predictive of several indicators of healthy adult development, including active participation in the political process and other types of volunteer activities, continued sport engagement, and better mental health (DeMartini, 1983; Glancy, Willits, & Farrell, 1986; Youniss, McLellan, Yang, & Yates, in press; Youniss, McLellan, & Yates, 1997; Youniss, Yates et al., 1997). In contrast, sports have also been linked to increased rates of school deviance (Lamborn et al., 1992).

A third line of research involves studies that focus on the question of causal direction and selection. For example, Larson (1994) used longitudinal analyses to study the association between sport participation and delinquency. His results suggest that the apparent protective relation of sports to low rates of delinquency actually reflects the negative impact of delinquency on sports participation: that is, adolescents engaged in delinquent behaviors drop out of school athletic participation over time. He found no evidence that participation in sports led to a decline in engagement in delinquent activities. In contrast, participation in other youth organizations did predict a decline in engagement in delinquent activities.

In this article, we examine both the potential benefits (psychological attachment to school, better GPA, lower rates of school absences, and higher rates of college attendance) and the potential risks (engagement in risky behavior, including substance use) associated with participation in various forms of constructive leisure. Five types of involvement are considered: prosocial (church and volunteer activities), team sports (any school team), school involvement (pep club, student council), performing arts (drama, marching band), and academic clubs (science club, foreign language club). These organized extracurricular activities were selected because they require effort and are settings in which adolescents can express their identities and passions (Csikszentmihalyi & Kleiber, 1991). In the first section of the article, we explore the link between involvement in these types of activities and our indicators of positive and negative developmental trajectories. To both control for selection factors and better understand the causal direction of the relation, we use longitudinal analyses. In the second half of the article, we explore possible reasons for these associations. In this section, we focus on two possible mediators: peer associations and activity-based identity formation.

Method

Study Design and Sample

The data come from the Michigan Study of Adolescent Life Transitions (MSALT). This is a longitudinal study that began (in 1983) with a cohort of sixth graders drawn from 10 school districts in southeastern Michigan. The vast majority of the sample is white and comes from working- and middle-class families living in small industrial cities around Detroit. We have followed approximately 1,800 of these youth through eight waves of data beginning in the sixth grade (1983-1984), and continuing into 1996-1997, when most were 25 to 26. The analyses presented here include 1,259 respondents who both completed the survey items about activity involvement and had outcome data from the waves of data collected in 1990-1991 (Wave 6— when most were 12th graders) and in 1992-1993 (Wave 7).

Measures

The adolescents were administered an extensive interview with items tapping a wide range of constructs. The specific constructs used for the first part of this article are summarized below.

Activity Involvement

In the 10th grade, we collected detailed information on the adolescents' involvement in a wide variety of activities in and out of school. Adolescents were provided with a list of 16 sports and 30 school and community clubs and organizations. They were asked to check off all activities in which they participated. We clustered the extracurricular activities into five categories: *prosocial activities*—attending church and/or participating in volunteer and community service-type activities; *performance activities*—participating in school band, drama, and/or dance; *team sports*—participating in one or more school teams; *school involvement*—participating in student government, pep club, and/or cheerleading; and *academic clubs*—participating in debate, foreign language, math or chess clubs, science fair, or tutoring in academic subjects. These categorizations focus on the actual content or domain of the activity.

Risk Behavior

In addition to information on involvement in positive extracurricular activities, we also collected detailed information on the adolescents' involvement in risky/problematic activities in 10th and 12th grades, such as drinking, getting drunk, skipping school, and using drugs. The risk behavior measures used the following categories to indicate frequency of engaging in the activity in the previous 6 months: $1 = none$, $2 = once$, $3 = 2$ to 3 times, $4 = 4$ to 6 times, $5 = 7$ to 10 times, $6 = 11$ to 20 times, and $7 = 21$ or more times. Drinking alcohol at Wave 6 had an extra category, with $7 = 21$ to 30 times and $8 = 31$ times or more.

Academic Outcomes

We also collected data on the students' attachment to school, using one 7-point item about how much they liked school in both 10th and 12th grades. In addition, information on academic performance and assessment test scores was obtained for every participant from their school files. For these analyses, we use school records of the participants' cumulative GPAs at the 11th and 12th grades, as well as verbal and numerical ability subscores on the

Differential Aptitude Test (The Psychological Corporation, 1981) administered in the ninth grade. Finally, in our 1992-1993 wave, we collected college attendance information.

Family Characteristics

We included mother's education as a measure of family social economic status to use as a control variable in the multiple regression analyses. This variable was assessed based on the mothers' questionnaire collected at the first wave, when the adolescents were in the sixth grade. Mothers indicated on a 9-point ordinal scale their highest level of education with 1 = *grade school*, 3 = *high school diploma*, 6 = *college degree*, and 9 = *Ph.D. or other advanced professional degree such as an MD*. The modal responses for this sample were 3 (high school degree, 37.8%) and 4 (some college or technical school, 34.1%). We then collapsed this scale into a 3-point ordinal scale with 1 = *no more than high school diploma* (46.2%), 2 = *some college* (38.3%), and 3 = *Bachelors' degree or more* (15.5%).

Procedure

The data were collected via self-administered questionnaires that were completed at school during regular school hours. For the 10th- and 12th-grade waves, the adolescents were released from their classrooms to fill out the questionnaire in a large common room—usually the lunchroom. In addition, complete school records from Grade 5 to Grade 12 were collected for all participants; these included grades, absences, courses taken, and any disciplinary measures taken by the schools. The young adult surveys were mailed to the participants' homes and returned via postage-paid envelopes. On completion of the survey, participants were sent $20.

Results

Descriptive Patterns

First, we describe the patterns of males and females in activity involvement in the 10th grade. These results are presented in tables 10.1 and 10.2. Table 10.1 summarizes the distribution of in-school and out-of-school activities by gender, with team sports aggregated into a single category. Table 10.2 breaks down the team sports into individual school-based competitive sports teams.

Next, we computed a total number of activities by summing all the in-school and out-of-school clubs and activities that were checked. On average, these adolescents participated in between one and two activities and/or clubs. Females participated at higher rates than males, $F(1, 1243) = 25.49$, $p < .001$; females' mean = 1.79 ($SD = 1.71$) and males' mean = 1.33 ($SD = 1.44$). However, 31% of the sample did not participate in any activities or clubs. Because sports were so common, we aggregated them separately by summing all of the different teams checked. Not surprisingly, males participated on more different teams than females. However, 45% of the sample had not competed on any school athletic team. Finally, we calculated the breadth of the adolescents' participation by summing the number of different types of activities for each adolescent (e.g., participation in several different sports, or several different types of clubs, only counted as one type of activity). Females also participated in a wider range of activities (mean = 1.54, $SD = 1.19$) than males (mean = 1.21, $SD = .90$; $F[1, 1243] = 28.21$, $p < .001$).

Next, we aggregated the adolescents' responses into five broad categories of activities: prosocial, sports teams, performing arts, school involvement, and academic clubs. Participants were given a yes score if they had checked off at least one activity/club within the broad category. A description of participation by gender is found in table 10.3. Consistent with results reported above, the males were more likely to engage in at least one sport activity than were females ($F[1, 1243] = 63.72$, $p < .001$). In contrast, the females were more likely to be involved in prosocial, performing arts, and school involvement activities ($F[1, 1243] = 23.71$, $p < .001$; $F[1, 1243] = 70.49$, $p < .001$; and $F[1, 1243] = 52.49$, $p < .001$, respectively).

We also assessed whether mother's education was related to participation in any of these five general categories. We divided mother's education into three categories and ran ANOVAs for each of the activity clusters. The only significant relation occurred for prosocial activity involvement ($F[2, 724] = 9.82$, $p < .01$): Adolescents with mothers having a college degree or higher were twice as likely (37%) to be involved in prosocial activities as adolescents with mothers having a high school degree or less education (18%); those with mothers having some college education fell in between (23%). Trends were evident for both team sports ($F[2, 724] = 2.82$, $p < .06$), and performing arts ($F[2, 724] = 2.60$, $p < .08$), with 53%, 63%, and 58% of adolescents in the three mother education categories participating in sports and 33%, 31%, and 42% of the adolescents in the three mother education categories participating in performing arts.

Table 10.1   Percentage of Females and Males Participating in Each Type of Activity

Activity	Females	Males
School team sports	45.6	66.7
Sports club	13.1	25.5
Dance classes	15.6	.7
Dance	14.4	5.2
Band/orchestra	19.1	14.3
Drama	13.0	6.1
Art	8.6	7.7
Student government	10.5	5.4
Pep club/cheerleading	12.4	3.1
Cheerleading as team sport	11.5	.2
Church	18.2	10.8
Service club	3.2	2.4
Tutoring/math, science, computers	2.3	2.3
Tutoring/other subjects	1.3	1.2
Science fair	1.0	.7
Math club	0.0	.5
Chess club	0.0	.7
Computer club	.6	2.3
Foreign language club	12.6	4.5
Debate club/forensics	1.2	1.4
Career-related clubs	2.9	2.4
Other school clubs	3.8	3.3
SADD	10.2	3.0
Peer counseling	3.5	1.2
ROTC	.4	3.3
Scouts/Girls' and Boys' Club	2.2	4.7
4H	3.5	1.9
Junior Achievement	.9	1.6

Reprinted from Eccles and Barber, 1999.

Table 10.2   Percentage of Females and Males Participating in Each Type of Competitive School Sports Team

Type of Sport	Females	Males
Baseball	3.2	26.3
Basketball	10.7	25.3
Football	2.9	31.9
Golf	.6	8.9
Ice hockey	1.3	9.1
Soccer	3.5	8.4
Wrestling	1.3	15.9
Field hockey	.6	1.6
Swimming/diving	11.8	12.7
Tennis	9.2	8.0
Track/cross-country	12.0	16.2
Gymnastics	4.7	1.4
Softball	16.5	3.0
Volleyball	17.1	5.2

Reprinted from Eccles and Barber, 1999.

Table 10.3   Participation Rates of Female and Male Students in Extracurricular Activities (in Percentages)

	Females		Males	
	No	Yes	No	Yes
Prosocial activities	498	187	481	91
	(73)	(27)	(84)	(16)
Sports teams	372	313	191	383
	(54)	(46)	(33)	(67)
Performing arts	389	297	450	122
	(57)	(43)	(79)	(21)
School involvement	526	157	519	46
	(77)	(23)	(92)	(8)
Academic clubs	572	113	509	63
	(83)	(17)	(89)	(11)

Reprinted from Eccles and Barber, 1999.

Concurrent and Long-Term Correlates

In this section, we report on the relation between 10th grade extracurricular activity involvement and other psychological and behavioral outcomes. We examine whether specific types of extracurricular activities are more beneficial or risky than others.

Prosocial Activity Involvement

Tables 10.4 and 10.5 illustrate the findings for involvement in prosocial activities. Adolescents involved in prosocial activities in 10th grade reported less involvement in problem behaviors; this difference is especially marked at Grade 12, 2 years after the activity data were collected. These results suggest that prosocial involvement is a protective factor with regard to the age-related increases in these risky behaviors. Prosocial involvement is also linked to better academic performance and greater likelihood of being enrolled full-time in college at age 21.

We tested this hypothesis more directly using longitudinal regression analysis. The results are shown in table 10.6. In each equation, we entered the 10th-grade level of the risky behavior to get an estimate of the extent to which each of the other predictors explained change in frequency of engaging in the particular risky behaviors. We also entered gender, mother's educational level, and two intellectual aptitude variables (performance on the Differential Aptitude Tests for verbal and mathematical abilities) as controls because these constructs have emerged in other studies as predictors of both academic achievement and involvement in risky behaviors. Finally, we entered 10th-grade prosocial activity involvement. The standardized betas for each of these predictors are included in table 10.6 to allow for comparisons of the magnitude of the

Table 10.4　Mean Levels (and Standard Deviations) of Risk Behaviors and Attachment to School in 10th Grade by Participation in Extracurricular Activities

	Prosocial activities		Sports teams		Performing arts		School involvement		Academic clubs	
	No	Yes	No	Yes	No	Yes	No	Yes	No	Yes
Drink alcohol	2.7	2.0**	2.5	2.6	2.6	2.4**	2.5	2.6	2.6	2.4
	(1.9)	(1.4)	(1.8)	(1.8)	(1.9)	(1.6)	(1.8)	(1.6)	(1.8)	(1.5)
Skip school	1.7	1.4**	1.7	1.6	1.7	1.5**	1.7	1.5+	1.7	1.5
	(1.0)	(.7)	(.9)	(.9)	(1.0)	(.7)	(1.0)	(.8)	(1.0)	(.9)
Use drugs	1.5	1.2**	1.5	1.4	1.5	1.4	1.5	1.4	1.5	1.3
	(1.4)	(1.0)	(1.3)	(1.2)	(1.3)	(1.2)	(1.3)	(1.2)	(1.3)	(1.1)
Like school	4.4	4.8**	4.3	4.7**	4.3	4.9**	4.4	5.0**	4.5	4.8**
	(1.7)	(1.6)	(1.8)	(1.6)	(1.7)	(1.6)	(1.7)	(1.6)	(1.7)	(1.5)

+$p < .10$. **$p < .01$.

Reprinted from Eccles and Barber, 1999.

Table 10.5　Mean Levels (and Standard Deviations) of Risk Behaviors and Academic Outcomes in 12th Grade and College Attendance in Young Adulthood by Participation in Extracurricular Activities

	Prosocial activities		Sports teams		Performing arts		School involvement		Academic clubs	
	No	Yes	No	Yes	No	Yes	No	Yes	No	Yes
Drink alcohol	4.5	2.8**	3.5	4.4**	4.3	3.6**	4.0	4.1	4.0	4.0
	(2.5)	(2.0)	(2.4)	(2.5)	(2.5)	(2.3)	(2.5)	(2.4)	(2.5)	(2.5)
Get drunk	3.9	2.4**	3.2	3.8**	3.7	3.2**	3.5	3.6	3.6	3.3
	(2.2)	(1.8)	(2.1)	(2.2)	(2.3)	(2.1)	(2.2)	(2.1)	(2.2)	(2.1)
Skip school	3.2	2.6**	3.1	3.0	3.0	3.1	3.0	3.1	3.1	2.8
	(1.6)	(1.5)	(1.7)	(1.5)	(1.5)	(1.7)	(1.6)	(1.5)	(1.6)	(1.6)
Use marijuana	2.0	1.3**	1.7	1.9	1.9	1.6+	1.8	1.6+	1.8	1.7
	(1.8)	(.9)	(1.5)	(1.6)	(1.7)	(1.4)	(1.7)	(1.1)	(1.6)	(1.5)
Use hard drugs	1.4	1.2*	1.3	1.4	1.4	1.3	1.4	1.1*	1.4	1.3
	(1.2)	(.8)	(1.0)	(1.2)	(1.2)	(1.0)	(1.2)	(.5)	(1.1)	(1.1)
Like school	4.6	4.8	4.5	4.8**	4.7	4.7	4.6	4.8	4.6	4.8
	(1.8)	(1.8)	(1.8)	(1.8)	(1.8)	(1.9)	(1.8)	(1.8)	(1.8)	(1.8)
High school grade point average	2.5	2.9**	2.6	2.6	2.5	2.8**	2.6	2.9**	2.5	3.0**
	(.7)	(.6)	(.7)	(.7)	(.7)	(.7)	(.7)	(.7)	(.7)	(.7)
Percentage in full-time college	.48	.65**	.47	.56*	.49	.58**	.49	.68**	.48	.72**
	(.50)	(.48)	(.50)	(.50)	(.50)	(.49)	(.50)	(.47)	(.50)	(.45)

+$p < .10$. *$p < .05$. **$p < .01$.

Reprinted from Eccles and Barber, 1999.

predictive relationship. As one would expect, the strongest predictor is the 10th-grade level of involvement in the risky behavior, suggesting considerable stability in the individual differences in these behaviors over the high school years. Nonetheless, involvement in prosocial activities is related to change in this engagement in a protective direction; that is, the students who are involved in activities such as attending church and doing volunteer work show less of an increase in these risky behaviors over the high school years than their noninvolved peers.

Involvement in prosocial activities at Grade 10 is also positively related to both liking school at that level and a higher GPA at the 12th-grade level. In addition, being involved in prosocial activities in the 10th grade is positively related to attending college full-time at age 21. Only the relation to 12th-grade GPA remained significant in the multiple regression analyses.

Team Sports

Tables 10.4, 10.5, and 10.7 show the relation of involvement in team sports to engagement in risky

Table 10.6   Standardized Regression Coefficients for Risk Behaviors and Academic Outcomes in 12th Grade and College Attendance in Young Adulthood Predicted From 10th-Grade Participation in Prosocial Activities

Predictor Variable	Drink alcohol	Get drunk	Skip school	Use marijuana	Use hard drugs	Like school	High school grade point average	Full-time college
10th-grade level of dependent variable	.48**	.46**	.22**	.45**	.27**	.31**		
Gender	.07	.10*	−.03	.06	−.03	.01	−.14**	.00
Maternal education	.00	.00	−.05	.04	−.03	−.04	.07*	.13**
Verbal ability	−.05	.03	.05	.03	−.04	.00	.16**	.16**
Math ability	.05	.02	−.19**	.05	−.05	−.10	.47**	.16**
Prosocial activities	−.20**	−.20**	−.10+	−.14*	−.11*	.02	.13**	.04
Adjusted R^2	.31**	.30**	.10**	.23**	.10*	.09**	.42**	.12**

$^+p < .10.$ $^*p < .05.$ $^{**}p < .01.$

Reprinted from Eccles and Barber, 1999.

Table 10.7   Standardized Regression Coefficients for Risk Behaviors and Academic Outcomes in 12th Grade and College Attendance in Young Adulthood Predicted From 10th-Grade Participation in Sports

Predictor Variable	Drink alcohol	Get drunk	Skip school	Use marijuana	Use hard drugs	Like school	High school grade point average	Full-time college
10th-grade level of dependent variable	.51**	.50**	.23**	.47**	.29**	.29**		
Gender	.07	.11*	−.02	.07	−.02	−.01	−.18**	−.03
Maternal education	−.03	−.04	−.06	.01	.02	−.04	.08*	.13**
Verbal ability	−.04	.04	.06	.04	−.04	.01	.17**	.17**
Math ability	.03	−.02	−.21	.04	−.07	−.10+	.49**	.16**
Sports participation	.15**	.09*	.01	.04	.02	.12*	.07*	.10*
Adjusted R^2	.30**	.27**	.09**	.21**	.09**	.10**	.41**	.13**

$^+p < .10.$ $^*p < .05.$ $^{**}p < .01.$

Reprinted from Eccles and Barber, 1999.

behaviors. Apparently, involvement in team sports at Grade 10 is a risk condition for engagement in one of these risky behaviors at Grade 12; namely, drinking alcohol. When one tests this hypothesis using the type of longitudinal regression analyses just described for prosocial activities, being involved with team sports does indeed contribute significantly to an increase in alcohol use and getting drunk over the high school years after controlling for mother's education, student gender, and intellectual aptitude (see table 10.7).

Involvement in team sports also serves as a protective condition for academic outcomes. Sports participants liked school better at both the 10th and 12th grades. They were also more likely to be attending college full-time at age 21 than nonparticipants. Finally, sports participation predicted an increase in liking school between the 10th and 12th grades, a higher than expected 12th-grade GPA, and a greater than expected likelihood of being enrolled full-time in college at age 21.

Performing Arts

Those adolescents who were involved in performing arts at Grade 10 were less frequently engaged in risky behaviors at both Grade 10 and 12 than those who were not. This is particularly true for alcohol-related behaviors (see tables 10.4 and 10.5). However, when one controls for prior levels of drinking in the longitudinal regression analyses (see table 10.8), we could find no evidence that 10th-grade involvement in performing arts affects the direction or magnitude of change in drinking behavior over the high school years.

Participation in performing arts was also related to greater liking of school at both the 10th and 12th grades (see tables 10.4 and 10.5) and to higher 12th-grade GPA and a greater likelihood of attending college full-time at age 21. The longitudinal regression analyses suggest that this protective role is only significant for 12th-grade GPA. The other two longitudinal relations become nonsignificant once

Table 10.8　Standardized Regression Coefficients for Risk Behaviors and Academic Outcomes in 12th Grade and College Attendance in Young Adulthood Predicted From 10th-Grade Participation in Performing Arts

Predictor Variable	Drink alcohol	Get drunk	Skip school	Use marijuana	Use hard drugs	Like school	High school grade point average	Full-time college
10th-grade level of dependent variable	.52**	.51**	.23**	.47**	.29**	.31**		
Gender	.08	.12*	.01	.08	−.01	.01	−.12*	.02
Maternal education	−.02	−.03	−.06	.01	.02	−.04	.09*	.13**
Verbal ability	−.04	.03	.05	.03	−.04	.00	.14**	.15**
Math ability	.03	−.01	−.21	.04	−.07	−.09	.49**	.17**
Performing arts	−.10+	−.05	.10*	.01	.02	−.01	.13**	.07
Adjusted R^2	.28**	.27**	.10**	.21**	.09**	.09**	.42**	.12**

$^+p < .10.$ $^*p < .05.$ $^{**}p < .01.$

Reprinted from Eccles and Barber, 1999.

Table 10.9　Standardized Regression Coefficients for Risk Behaviors and Academic Outcomes in 12th Grade and College Attendance in Young Adulthood Predicted From 10th-Grade Involvement in School Leadership or School Spirit Activities

Predictor Variable	Drink alcohol	Get drunk	Skip school	Use marijuana	Use hard drugs	Like school	High school grade point average	Full-time college
10th-grade level of dependent variable	.53**	.51**	.22**	.46**	.28**	.30**		
Gender·	.11*	.14**	.01	.07	−.02	.02	−.14**	.02
Maternal education	−.02	−.02	−.04	.01	.01	−.03	.10**	.14**
Verbal ability	−.05	.01	.03	.04	−.03	−.01	.15**	.14**
Math ability	.03	−.01	−.21**	.04	−.07	−.09	.48**	.16**
School involvement	.03	.06	.10+	−.03	−.07	.04	.10**	.10*
Adjusted R^2	.27**	.27**	.10**	.21**	.09**	.09**	.41**	.12**

$^+p < .10.$ $^*p < .05.$ $^{**}p < .01.$

Reprinted from Eccles and Barber, 1999.

the various control variables are included in the equation.

Finally, this was the only activity domain in which we found consistent evidence of a gender-by-activity involvement interaction: Males, but not females, engaged in performing arts were less likely than their peers to drink alcohol and skip school in Grade 10 and to drink alcohol in Grade 12 ($p <. 01$ in each case).

School-Involvement Activities

As can be seen in tables 10.4 and 10.5, participation in school-related clubs and nonathletic activities was not related consistently to engagement in risky behaviors. In contrast, it was positively related to liking school at Grade 10 and to both 12th-grade GPA and the likelihood of attending college full-time at age 21. By and large, these patterns were confirmed in the longitudinal regression analyses (see table

10.9). Participating in these kinds of school-related activities predicted better than expected 12th-grade GPA and greater than expected likelihood of attending college full-time at age 21.

Academic Clubs

Participation in academic clubs was primarily related to academic outcomes (see tables 10.4, 10.6, and 10.10). This was true at both the bivariate and longitudinal multivariate level. Adolescents who participated in academic clubs had higher than expected high school GPAs and were more likely to be enrolled in college at 21 than their noninvolved peers.

Discussion

Consistent with the majority of studies, we found clear evidence that participation in extracurricular

Table 10.10   Standardized Regression Coefficients for Risk Behaviors and Academic Outcomes in 12th Grade and College Attendance in Young Adulthood Predicted From 10th-Grade Involvement in Academic Clubs

Predictor Variable	Drink alcohol	Get drunk	Skip school	Use marijuana	Use hard drugs	Like school	High school grade point average	Full-time college
10th-grade level of dependent variable	.53**	.51**	.22**	.47**	.29**	.31**		
Gender	.11*	.13**	−.02	.08	−.01	.02	−.15**	.02
Maternal education	−.03	−.03	−.05	.01	.02	−.04	.07*	.12**
Verbal ability	−.05	.03	.06	.03	−.05	−.01	.14**	.14*
Math ability	.03	−.01	−.20**	.04	−.07	−.10	.49**	.16**
Academic clubs	.02	−.02	−.06	.02	.02	.03	.11**	.13**
Adjusted R^2	.27**	.27**	.09**	.21**	.09**	.09**	.41**	.13**

*$p < .05$. **$p < .01$.

Reprinted from Eccles and Barber, 1999.

activities during the high school years provides a protective context in terms of both academic performance and involvement in risky behaviors. Participation in all five types of extracurricular involvement predicted better than expected high school GPAs. Participation in sports, school-based leadership, school-spirit activities, and academic clubs predicted increased likelihood of being enrolled full-time in college at age 21. Involvement in sports also predicted increases in school attachment. Participation in prosocial activities was related to lower increases in alcohol and drug use, as well as to lower levels at both Grades 10 and 12, and participation in performing arts served this same function for males. Furthermore, each of these results holds true when social class, gender, and academic aptitude are controlled.

In contrast, participation in sports is also linked to increases in use of alcohol. Contrary to the results reported by Larson (1994), our results provide good evidence that participation in sports does lead to increases in some behaviors that might be considered problematic. In addition, our results clearly support the conclusion that participation in sports has positive academic consequences. It is likely that the difference in our outcome measures explains this discrepancy. Larson (1994) used a very global indicator of delinquency, in which alcohol and drug use was only a small component. His measure also included no indicators of academic success. In contrast, we used quite specific outcome measures, and our results indicate that participation in sports has both positive and potentially negative consequences.

What can we conclude? The evidence presented thus far is mostly consistent with the conclusion reached in the Carnegie Corporation (1992) report, *A Matter of Time.* However, the pattern is not as simple as one might expect. Both the magnitude and the direction of the relations depend on the outcome being considered and, to some extent, on the gender of the adolescent. For example, although participation in team sports is related to increased GPA and increased probability of attending college full-time, it is also related among males to such risky behaviors as drinking alcohol. Similarly, although being involved in school spirit and leadership clubs does not appear to reduce the frequency with which one does risky things such as use drugs, drink alcohol, and skip school, it is related in a positive direction to our indicators of academic success. Only involvement in prosocial activities (in this case, primarily church attendance) appears to be protective against increases in alcohol and drug use and increases in skipping school.

Several investigators have offered explanations for these effects. For example, in 1969, Rehberg suggested five possible mediators for the effects of sports participation: association with college-oriented peers, exposure to academic values, enhanced self-esteem, generalization of a high sense of personal efficacy, and superior career guidance and encouragement. In 1961, Coleman stressed the values and norms associated with the different peer clusters engaged in various types of extracurricular activities. Spady (1970) stressed the benefits in self-esteem one attains from the increases in peer status associated with successful participation in extracurricular activities. Otto and Alwin (1977) added skill and attitude acquisition (both interpersonal and personal) and increased membership in important social networks (more recently relabeled social capital by Coleman and Hoffer, 1987).

More recently, investigators have focused on the links between peer group formation, identity formation, and activity involvement. For example, Fine (1987) has explored the relation of participating in Little League to both peer group and identity formation. He has stressed how participation in something like Little League shapes both children's self-definition as a "jock" and their most salient peer group (see also Eccles, 1993; Hantover, 1978; Kirshnit et al., 1989; Kleiber & Kirshnit, 1990). In turn, these characteristics (one's identity and one's peer group) influence subsequent activity choices—creating a synergistic system that marks out a clear pathway into a particular kind of adolescence. Similarly, Eckert (1989) has explored the link between peer-group identity formation and activity involvement. As one moves into and through adolescence, individuals become identified with particular groups of friends or crowds (see also Brown, 1990). Being a member of one of these crowds helps structure both what one does with one's time and the kinds of values and norms one is exposed to. Once again, over time, the coalescence of one's personal identity, one's peer group, and the kinds of activities one participates in as a consequence of both one's identity and one's peer group can shape the nature of one's pathway through adolescence. Consistent with these perspectives, we are interested in how activity participation is linked to both peer group and identity formation. We assume that activity choices are a part of a larger system of psychological and social forces that influence development—forces linked to peer group affiliation and identity formation. Knowing what an adolescent is doing often tells us a lot about who the adolescent is with. Many of the activities we study take up considerable amounts of the adolescents' time and are done with other adolescents and adults. Thus, it is likely that participation in some of these activities directly affects adolescents' peer groups precisely because such participation structures a substantial amount of peer group interaction. One's coparticipants become one's peer crowd, and such peer crowds often develop an activity-based culture, providing adolescents with the opportunity to identify with a group having a shared sense of style. Similarly, leisure may help to clarify personal identity while maintaining relationships with peers. Involvement in a school organization or sport links an adolescent to a set of similar peers, provides shared experiences and goals, and can reinforce friendships between peers (see also Larson, 1994). Thus, extracurricular activities can facilitate adolescents' developmental need for social relatedness and can contribute to one's identity as an important and valued member of the school community.

Synergistic Forces With Peer Group Cultures and Identity Formation

The ideas outlined above are consistent with the work of Erikson (1968), and more recently, Adams and Marshall (1996) and Youniss, Yates, and Su (1997). These scholars suggest that adolescents seek out an identity that allows them to be actors in their social world and that allows them to feel effective, successful, and connected in their everyday activities (see also Williams & McGee, 1991). Extracurricular activities of the kinds we are studying provide youth with the opportunity to form just such identities. In addition, because participation also influences peer group formation, participation feeds into the type of synergistic system described above and depicted in figure 10.1.

We explore these ideas in this section. This work represents the beginning of our efforts to explore these issues. In this section, we focus first on the link between activity participation and peer group characteristics and then on the link between activity participation and peer-group and activity-based identities.

Method

Additional Measures

Friend Characteristics

Composition of the peer network was measured in 10th grade with a series of questions asking "what proportion of your friends are each of the following?" The items included in these analyses were "planning to go to college," "doing very well in school," "regularly drink alcohol," "irregularly use drugs," and "likely to skip class." The response scale ranged from 1 = *none* to 5 = *all*, with 3 = *half*.

Identity Group

At the 10th grade, we asked the participants to make a prototype judgment regarding their identity. Because the movie *The Breakfast Club* (Hughes, 1985) was quite popular at the time, we decided to use it as the basis of our measure of identity. There are five main characters in this movie—each one representing a stereotypic adolescent type. We asked the participants to indicate which of five characters (the princess, the jock, the brain, the basket case, and the criminal) was most like them. We told them to ignore the sex of the character and base their selection

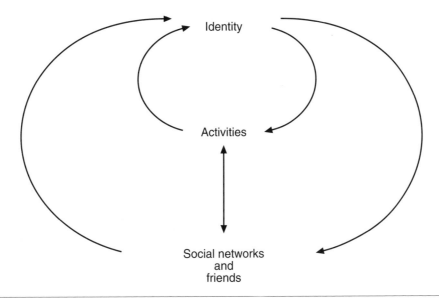

Figure 10.1   Synergistic influences among identity, friendship networks, and activity involvement.
Reprinted from Eccles and Barber, 1999.

on the type of person each character was. The adolescents had no difficulty with their selection—less than 5% left the question blank. About 9% selected the criminal, 11% selected the basket case, 12% selected the brain, 28% selected the jock, and 40% selected the princess. Although the gender distribution was sex-typed, there were substantial numbers of each sex in each of the given identity groups to allow for analyses.

Results and Discussion

Peer Groups

As noted above, activity settings provide a peer group as well as a set of tasks. To the extent that one spends a lot of time in these activity settings with the other participants, it is likely that one's friends will be drawn from among the other participants. It is also likely that the collective behaviors of this peer group will influence the behaviors of each member. To the extent that this is true, some of the behavioral differences associated with activity participation may be a consequence of the behavioral differences of the peer groups associated with these different activity clusters.

The relevant results are summarized in tables 10.11 and 10.12. At both 10th and 12th grades, the peer group characteristics were consistent with the outcomes reported in the first section of this article. This is particularly true at Grade 12. Consistent with the positive association of activity group membership with academic outcomes, the peer groups for participants are characterized by a higher proportion of friends who plan on attending college and are doing well in school (with the exception of the sports participants). Concordant with the protective association of prosocial participation with drug and alcohol use, adolescents involved in prosocial activities, compared to their peers, have fewer friends who use alcohol and drugs; they also have few friends who skip school. Finally, congruent with the association of sports participation with increased drinking, adolescents who participate in team sports have a higher proportion of friends who drink than their peers.

These results are compatible with the analysis outlined above. Consequently, it is certainly possible that peer group association is one of the mediators of the association between activity group membership and adolescent outcomes.

Identity Categories

Table 10.13 summarizes the distributions of identity types for each of our five activity groups. The significance levels for these one-way ANOVAs are indicated with stars after the activity group. The significant contrasts are summarized in the last column.

One of our activity groups is clearly related to the identity characters: sports. As one might expect, the jocks stand out in the team sports group. This is clearly an activity-based identity. The evidence for activity-based identities is less clear for the other

Table 10.11   Mean Levels (and Standard Deviations) of Friend Characteristics in 10th Grade by Participation in Extracurricular Activities

	Prosocial activities		Sports teams		Performing arts		School involvement		Academic clubs	
	No	Yes	No	Yes	No	Yes	No	Yes	No	Yes
College plans	3.7	4.0**	3.6	3.9**	3.7	3.9**	3.7	4.1	3.7	4.0**
	(1.1)	(.9)	(1.1)	(1.0)	(1.1)	(1.0)	(1.1)	(.9)	(1.1)	(1.0)
Do well in school	3.3	3.6**	3.3	3.5**	3.3	3.5**	3.4	3.6	3.4	3.6**
	(1.0)	(.9)	(1.0)	(.9)	(.9)	(1.0)	(1.0)	(.9)	(1.0)	(.9)
Drink regularly	2.8	2.4**	2.6	2.7	2.7	2.6*	2.7	2.8	2.7	2.6
	(1.3)	(1.1)	(1.2)	(1.3)	(1.2)	(1.2)	(1.3)	(1.2)	(1.2)	(1.2)
Use drugs	1.8	1.5**	1.9	1.7*	1.8	1.7**	1.8	1.6	1.8	1.6*
	(1.1)	(1.0)	(1.1)	(1.1)	(1.1)	(1.0)	(1.1)	(1.0)	(1.1)	(1.0)
Skip class	2.7	2.4**	2.8	2.6**	2.7	2.5**	2.7	2.6	2.7	2.5+
	(1.2)	(1.1)	(1.2)	(1.1)	(1.2)	(1.2)	(1.2)	(1.2)	(1.2)	(1.2)

$^+p < .10.$ $^*p < .05.$ $^{**}p < .01.$

Reprinted from Eccles and Barber, 1999.

Table 10.12   Mean Levels (and Standard Deviations) of Friend Characteristics in 12th Grade by Participation in Extracurricular Activities

	Prosocial activities		Sports teams		Performing arts		School involvement		Academic clubs	
	No	Yes	No	Yes	No	Yes	No	Yes	No	Yes
College plans	4.0	4.2**	3.9	4.1**	3.9	4.2**	4.0	4.4**	4.0	4.3**
	(1.0)	(.9)	(1.0)	(.9)	(1.0)	(.9)	(1.0)	(.7)	(1.0)	(.7)
Do well in school	3.4	3.6**	3.4	3.5	3.4	3.6**	3.4	3.7**	3.4	3.7**
	(.8)	(.8)	(.9)	(.8)	(.8)	(.8)	(.8)	(.8)	(.8)	(.8)
Drink regularly	3.2	2.6**	2.9	3.2**	3.2	2.9*	3.1	3.1	3.1	2.9
	(1.3)	(1.2)	(1.3)	(1.3)	(1.3)	(1.2)	(1.3)	(1.1)	(1.3)	(1.2)
Use drugs	2.0	1.6**	1.8	1.9	2.0	1.8*	1.9	1.8	1.9	1.8
	(1.1)	(.9)	(1.0)	(1.1)	(1.1)	(.9)	(1.1)	(.9)	(1.0)	(1.0)
Skip class	3.1	2.7**	3.0	3.0	3.0	3.0	3.0	3.1	3.1	2.9
	(1.2)	(1.2)	(1.3)	(1.2)	(1.2)	(1.3)	(1.2)	(1.3)	(1.2)	(1.2)

$^+p < .10.$ $^*p < .05.$ $^{**}p < .01.$

Reprinted from Eccles and Barber, 1999.

four identities, primarily due to the high proportion of adolescents in all identity groups who participated in at least one team sport during their 10th grade school year. Ignoring team sports, the princesses are overrepresented in both the performing arts and school-involved activity groups, and the brains are overrepresented in the prosocial activity group. The criminals are characterized by either very low or relatively low participation in all activity groups except team sports, and the basket cases are characterized by relatively low participation in all groups except the performing arts.

It is possible that some of the activity group differences on the outcomes identified in the first part of this article reflect behavioral differences associated with these different peer-group identity categories.

Tables 10.14 and 10.15 summarize the differences between these identity groups on both the risky behaviors and academic outcomes discussed earlier at both Grades 10 and 12. As one would expect, the criminal was highest on most of the risky behaviors, and the brain was the lowest at both grade levels. But consistent with the results reported earlier on the association of activity involvement with drinking behavior, the jocks reported relatively high levels of alcohol use at Grade 12. This finding is especially interesting given the stability of group differences across the 2-year gap between the self-identification as a criminal or jock and the rating of

Table 10.13   Mean Levels (and Standard Deviations) of Activity Participation in 10th Grade by *Breakfast Club* Identity

	Princess	Jock	Brain	Basket case	Criminal	Contrasts
Prosocial activities**	.26 (.44)	.16 (.37)	.35 (.48)	.26 (.44)	.12 (.32)	Br > P, J, C; Ba, P > J, C
Sports teams**	.45 (.50)	.87 (.34)	.49 (.50)	.28 (.45)	.47 (.50)	J > P, Br, Ba, C; P, Br, C > Ba
Performing arts**	.50 (.50)	.19 (.40)	.39 (.49)	.44 (.50)	.24 (.43)	P > J, Br, C; Br, Ba > J, C
School involvement**	.28 (.45)	.15 (.36)	.12 (.32)	.15 (.36)	.05 (.22)	P > J, Br, Ba, C; J > C
Academic clubs**	.19 (.39)	.08 (.27)	.21 (.41)	.18 (.39)	.12 (.32)	P, Br, Ba > J

**p < .01.

Reprinted from Eccles and Barber, 1999.

Table 10.14   Mean Levels (and Standard Deviations) of Risk Behavior in 10th Grade by *Breakfast Club* Identity

	Princess	Jock	Brain	Basket case	Criminal	Contrasts
Drink alcohol**	2.7 (1.8)	2.6 (1.8)	1.8 (1.1)	2.5 (1.7)	3.6 (2.4)	C > P, J, Br, Ba; P, J, Ba > Br
Skip school**	1.6 (.8)	1.6 (.9)	1.3 (.8)	1.7 (.9)	2.5 (1.5)	C > P, J, Br, Ba; P, J, Ba > Br
Use drugs**	1.4 (1.1)	1.3 (1.0)	1.1 (.5)	1.5 (1.4)	2.9 (2.5)	C > P, J, Br, Ba; P, Ba > Br
Like school**	4.8 (1.6)	4.8 (1.5)	4.8 (1.5)	4.0 (1.8)	3.6 (2.0)	P, J, Br > Ba, C

$^+p < .10.$ $^*p < .05.$ $^{**}p < .01.$

Reprinted from Eccles and Barber, 1999.

the risk behaviors. Interestingly, the princesses also report rather high levels of alcohol use in Grade 12.

Tables 10.14 and 10.15 also show the results for the positive academic outcomes. The expected pattern of results occurred for each of these measures as well: The brains had the highest rates of college attendance, followed closely, however, by the princesses and the jocks; the criminals had the lowest. Princesses, jocks, and brains also reported enjoying school the most at both grade levels. The results for college attendance are especially interesting, given that this outcome was measured 4 to 5 years after the self-categorization as a *Breakfast Club* stereotype.

These preliminary results suggest that there is a link between identity, patterns of activity involvement, and other indicators of successful and risky

adolescent development. This is most evident in the contrast between the jock and the criminal. These two groups are doing equally well in school in terms of their GPAs, and both are equally involved in alcohol consumption at Grade 12. What distinguishes them? The jock has a school-based activity identity whereas the criminal does not. It is not that the criminal is not involved in sports; although less likely to be involved in sports than the jocks, 47% of the criminals were participating in school-based team sports in the 10th grade. Unfortunately, this changed between 10th and 12th grades. Consistent with the findings of Larson (1994), 70% of these sports-participating criminals had dropped out of sports by Grade 12. This represents the largest dropout rate for all five identity types. Eckert (1989) suggested that one of the key distinguishing characteristics of the burnouts in her study (a group much like the groups who labeled themselves the criminal and the basket case in this study) was the lack of a school-based identity. Over time, this group became increasingly detached from school, leading in many cases to dropping out of high school prior to graduation. A similar process may be going on for our criminal group. They also appear to be disconnecting from school and school-based activities over their high school years and are least likely to graduate from high school and least likely to be attending college at age 21. Although not quite so

extreme, a similar process may also be going on in our basket case group.

As noted earlier, it is also likely that the nature of the peers one hangs out with as the result of one's identity and of one's activity patterns is a primary mediator of this link. Table 10.16 summarizes the identity group differences in peer network characteristics. Both the criminals and the brains had consistent profiles of friends. On one hand, the criminals stood out as having the fewest proportion of friends who were doing well academically and planning to attend college and the highest

Table 10.15   Mean Levels (and Standard Deviations) of Risk Behavior in 12th Grade by *Breakfast Club* Identity

	Princess	Jock	Brain	Basket case	Criminal	Contrasts
Drink alcohol**	4.4	4.8	2.9	3.5	5.2	P, J, C > Br, Ba
	(2.4)	(2.7)	(2.1)	(2.1)	(2.5)	
Get drunk**	3.8	4.1	2.6	3.3	4.5	J, C > Br, Ba
	(2.1)	(2.4)	(1.8)	(2.1)	(2.3)	P > Br
Skip school**	3.1	3.1	2.5	3.2	4.1	C > P, J, Br, Ba
	(1.5)	(1.5)	(1.7)	(1.7)	(1.6)	P, J, Ba > Br
Use marijuana**	1.6	2.0	1.4	1.9	3.2	C > P, J, Br, Ba
	(1.4)	(1.8)	(1.2)	(1.5)	(2.4)	J > Br
Use hard drugs**	1.3	1.4	1.2	1.4	2.0	C > P, J, Br, Ba
	(1.0)	(1.2)	(.9)	(.9)	(1.6)	
Like school	4.7	4.8	4.8	4.6	4.8	
	(1.8)	(1.8)	(1.7)	(1.8)	(1.9)	
High school GPA**	2.6	2.5	3.0	2.6	2.2	Br > P, J, Ba, C
	(.7)	(.7)	(.7)	(.7)	(.7)	P, J, Ba > C; P > J
Percentage in full-time college**	.55	.56	.62	.39	.31	P, J, Br > Ba, C
	(.50)	(.50)	(.49)	(.49)	(.46)	

$^+p < .10.$ $^*p < .05.$ $^{**}p < .01.$

Reprinted from Eccles and Barber, 1999.

Table 10.16   Mean Levels (and Standard Deviations) of Friend Characteristics in 10th Grade by *Breakfast Club* Identity

	Princess	Jock	Brain	Basket case	Criminal	Contrasts
College plans**	3.9	4.0	4.0	3.5	3.1	P, J, Br > Ba, C;
	(1.0)	(1.0)	(.9)	(1.2)	(1.2)	Ba > C
Do well in school**	3.5	3.5	3.6	3.2	2.9	P, J, Br > Ba, C;
	(.9)	(.8)	(.8)	(1.1)	(1.1)	Ba > C
Drink regularly**	2.7	2.8	2.2	2.6	3.4	C > P, J, Br, Ba;
	(1.2)	(1.2)	(1.1)	(1.1)	(1.2)	P, J, Ba > Br
Use drugs**	1.7	1.6	1.4	1.9	2.8	C > P, J, Br, Ba;
	(1.0)	(.9)	(.9)	(1.1)	(1.5)	Ba > P, J, Br; P > Br
Skip class**	2.8	2.6	2.1	2.8	3.5	C > P, J, Br, Ba;
	(1.2)	(1.1)	(1.0)	(1.1)	(1.2)	P, J, Ba > Br

$^+p < .10.$ $^*p < .05.$ $^{**}p < .01.$

Reprinted from Eccles and Barber, 1999.

proportion of friends engaged in risky behaviors. Consequently, it should not be surprising then that this group had the worst outcomes on both of these sets of outcomes despite the fact that they were actually doing all right in terms of their own GPAs.

On the other hand, the brains had the highest proportion of friends rated high on academic outcomes and low on risky behaviors. Consequently, it is not surprising that these youth themselves had the most consistent set of outcomes.

In contrast, the jocks and princesses had a more mixed pattern in terms of risks and protective factors. On one hand, the proportion of their friends with good academic outcomes was about the same as the brains' peer network. On the other hand, the proportion of their friends who drank and skipped school was also quite high. This pattern is consistent with the jocks' own behavior patterns.

Conclusions

The analyses reported in the second section represent the beginnings of our exploration of possible ways that participation in various types of activities might influence other indicators of adolescent development. In the first section, we documented a predictive link between activity participation and increases in both academic outcomes and engagement in risky behaviors. In the second part, we documented relations among activity participation, peer-group identity formation, and friendship networks. What can we conclude as we look across these three aspects of adolescents' lives? Adolescents who participated in prosocial activities had the most consistently positive outcomes—high academic achievement and low rates of involvement in risky behaviors. They were also the group most likely to identify themselves as brains and the group who had the most friends who were academic-oriented and the fewest friends engaged in risky behaviors. These identity and peer group patterns could help explain why it was only participation in prosocial activities that served as a protective influence for both sets of outcomes. It is among this group of adolescents that the three spheres of influence converge on both positive academic outcomes and low involvement in risky behaviors.

A different pattern of convergence characterized those youth involved in team sports. For this group, both identity group and peer group were associated with positive academic outcomes and relatively high levels of alcohol consumption. This pattern of convergence could help explain why being involved in team sports is associated with increases in both drinking and academic achievement.

A less extreme example of this type of convergence was also evident for those adolescents involved in school-related and school spirit-related clubs/organizations. This group also exhibited positive academic trajectories; in addition, however, they were just as likely to drink alcohol as their nonparticipating peers and showed a trend toward increasing rates of skipping school from the 10th to the 12th grade. They were also the group most likely to label themselves as princesses, who, in turn, were especially likely to have a high GPA, to be attending college at age 21, to drink alcohol and skip school on a fairly regular basis, and to have a substantial proportion of friends who evidenced the same profile.

Consequently, it should not be surprising that involvement in sports and school-based/school spirit-related activities was related to a different pattern of change over the high school years than participating in prosocial activities. The results for all three of these groups are consistent with the perspective on synergistic relations among these three domains of adolescent development outlined earlier and illustrated in figure 10.1. Activity choice is likely to both grow out of and reinforce emerging identities—particularly those aspects of identity linked to instrumental success and finding one's place in the social milieu. Activity choice also channels friendship networks due to propinquity and to shared interests. Friendship networks further reinforce the value of various types of activities and identities. Friendship networks also develop cultures of their own, which set the norms for a wide range of behaviors and long-term expectations and aspirations, thus influencing adolescents' behaviors across several domains (see Brown, 1990; Eckert, 1989; Sherif & Sherif, 1964). Consequently, the patterns of associations of activity participation with other indicators of adolescent development should depend on the nature of the peer culture and shared values associated with the groups of adolescents who dominate each activity setting.

Although our results are consistent with this analysis, the results reported here are basically correlational. In the future, we plan to do the detailed longitudinal causal modeling to verify the directional relations implied in this analysis. In addition, we will investigate the influences on activity participation. Given our interest in identity, we will pay particular attention to those characteristics of the self-system that are likely to influence activity choice, such as ability self-concept, expectations for success, subjective values, and perceived norms (see also Ajzen & Driver, 1991; Eccles, 1983; Fishbein & Ajzen, 1975). We also have data on the role of family, school, and elementary school participation patterns as influences on activity choices during adolescence.

We had a second goal in this article. Information regarding the patterns of involvement of adolescents in a variety of out-of-school and extracurricular activities provides us with a more complete picture of the social context of development during this period. What do adolescents do when they are not in formal educational or family settings? About 40% of adolescent waking hours are discretionary (no school, homework, employment, or chores), yet we know almost nothing about what teenagers do with their leisure time (for an exception, see Carnegie Corporation, 1992; Larson & Kleiber, 1993). We need to know more about a wider range of social settings, including athletics, school clubs and activities, and community service. Consequently, we also presented the patterns of activity involvement of this sample of adolescents as important descriptive information about the lives of today's youth.

The majority of the youth (69%) in this study were involved in some type of organized activity during their discretionary time. On average, most of the females were involved with more than one such activity, and most of the males were involved in less than two such activities. The range of activities was quite broad, with females exhibiting a more diverse pattern than males. For both males and females, the three most common activities were team sports, bands or orchestras, and church, with participation on sports teams being the most common by a substantial margin. Within sports, males and females exhibit sex role-stereotyped patterns. It is noteworthy, however, that the 10th-grade males and females in this sample were equally likely to be participating on swimming/diving teams and tennis teams, and females were more likely than males to be participating on softball and volleyball teams.

In conclusion, we have documented the types of activities U.S. adolescents were participating in during the early 1990s. We also documented the relation of activity participation to indicators of other positive and risky developmental outcomes. Involvement in prosocial activities was linked to positive educational trajectories and low rates of involvement in risky behaviors. In contrast, participation in team sports was linked to positive educational trajectories and to high rates of involvement in one type of risky behavior: drinking alcohol. The fact that this activity was associated with both good educational outcomes and drinking is consistent with other studies reporting that some involvement in risky activities such as drinking and cutting school is not necessarily problematic in terms of the consequences for long-term educational success (Schulenberg, Maggs, & Hurrelmann, 1997). One must take into account the meaning of the particular behavior in the broader context of the adolescent's life and development. If the risky behavior takes place in the context of a group of highly motivated and otherwise mentally healthy adolescents, it is unlikely that the risky behavior will, in and of itself, have extremely negative consequences (e.g., drinking among athletes and princesses). In contrast, if the risky behavior is part of a broader syndrome of behaviors and disaffection from socially accepted institutional settings such as schools, then the risky behavior is likely to be prognostic of poor subsequent developmental outcomes (Eckert, 1989; Jessor & Jessor, 1977).

References

Adams, G. R., & Marshall, S. K. (1996). A developmental social psychology of identity: Understanding the person-in-context. *Journal of Adolescence, 19*, 429-442.

Agnew, R., & Petersen, D. M. (1989). Leisure and delinquency. *Social Problems, 36*, 332-350.

Ajzen, I., & Driver, B. L. (1991). Prediction of leisure participation from behavioral, normative, and control beliefs: An application of the theory of planned behavior. *Leisure Sciences, 13*, 185-204.

Brown, B. B. (1990). Peer groups and peer cultures. In S. S. Feldman & G. R. Elliott (Eds.), *At the threshold: The developing adolescent.* Cambridge, MA: Harvard University Press.

Carnegie Corporation of New York. (1992). *A matter of time: Risk and opportunity in the non-school hours.* New York: Author.

Coleman, J. S. (1961). *The adolescent society.* New York: Free Press.

Coleman, J. S., & Hoffer, T. (1987). *Public and private high schools: The impact of communities.* New York: Basic Books.

Csikszentmihalyi, M. (1990). *Flow: The psychology of optimal experience.* New York: Harper & Row.

Csikszentmihalyi, M., & Kleiber, D. A. (1991). Leisure and self-actualization. In B. L. Driver, P. J. Brown, & G. L. Peterson (Eds.), *Benefits of leisure* (pp. 91-102). State College, PA: Venture.

Deeter, T. E. (1990). Remodeling expectancy and value in physical activity. *Journal of Sport and Exercise Psychology, 12*, 83-91.

DeMartini, J. (1983). Social movement participation: Political socialization, generational consciousness, and lasting effects. *Youth and Society, 15*, 195-223.

Eccles, J. S. (1983). Expectancies, values, and academic behaviors. In J. Spence (Ed.), *Achievement and achievement motivation* (pp. 75-146). San Francisco: W. H. Freeman.

Eccles, J. S. (1993). School and family effects on the ontogeny of children's interests, self-perceptions, and activity choice. In J. Jacobs (Ed.), *Nebraska symposium on motivation, 1992: Developmental perspectives on motivation* (pp. 145-208). Lincoln, NE: University of Nebraska Press.

Eckert, P. (1989). *Jocks and burnouts: Social categories and identity in the high school.* New York: Teacher College Press.

Elliott, D., & Voss, H. (1974). *Delinquency and dropout.* Lexington, MA: D. C. Heath.

Erikson, E. H. (1968). *Identity: Youth and crisis.* New York: Norton.

Fine, G. A. (1987). *With the boys: Little league baseball and preadolescent culture.* Chicago: University of Chicago Press.

Fine, G. A., Mortimer, J. T., & Roberts, D. F. (1990). Leisure, work, and the mass media. In S. S. Feldman & G. R. Elliott (Eds.), *At the threshold: The developing adolescent.* Cambridge, MA: Harvard University Press.

Fishbein, M., & Ajzen, I. (1975). *Belief, attitude, attention, and behavior: An introduction to theory and research.* Reading, MA: Addison-Wesley.

Glancy, M., Willits, F. K., & Farrell, P. (1986). Adolescent activities and adult success and happiness: Twenty-four years later. *Sociology and Social Research, 70*, 242-250.

Gould, D., & Weiss, M. R. (Eds.). (1987). *Advances in pediatric sport sciences, Vol. 2: Behavioral issues.* Champaign, IL: Human Kinetics.

Grieves, J. (1989). Acquiring a leisure identity: Juvenile jazz bands and the moral universe of "healthy" leisure time. *Leisure Studies, 8*, 1-9.

Haggard, L. M., & Williams, D. R. (1992). Identity affirmation through leisure activities: Leisure symbols of the self. *Journal of Leisure Research, 24*(1), 1-18.

Hanks, M., & Eckland, B. (1978). Adult voluntary associations and adolescent socialization. *The Sociological Quarterly, 19*, 481-490.

Hantover, J. P. (1978). The Boy Scouts and the validation of masculinity. *Journal of Social Issues, 34*, 184-195.

Holland, A., & Andre, T. (1987). Participation in extracurricular activities in secondary school: What is known, what needs to be known? *Review of Educational Research, 57*, 437-466.

Howell, F., & McKenzie, J. (1987). High school athletics and adult sport-leisure activity: Gender variations across the life cycle. *Sociology of Sport Journal, 4*, 329-346.

Hughes, J. (Director). (1985). *The Breakfast Club* [film]. Universal City, CA: Universal City Studios.

Jessor, R., & Jessor, S. L. (1977). *Problem behavior and psychological development: A longitudinal study of youth.* New York: Academic Press.

Kirshnit, C. E., Ham, M., & Richards, M. (1989). The sporting life. *Journal of Youth and Adolescence, 18*, 601-615.

Kleiber, D., & Kirshnit, E. E. (1990). Sport involvement and identity formation. In L. Diamant (Ed.), *Mindbody maturity: The psychology of sports, exercise, and fitness* (pp. 193-211). New York: Hemisphere.

Kleiber, D., Larson, R., & Csikszentmihalyi, M. (1986). The experience of leisure in adolescence. *Journal of Leisure Research, 18*, 165-176.

Lamborn, S. D., Brown, B. B., Mounts, N. S., & Steinberg, L. (1992). Putting school in perspective: The influence of family, peers, extracurricular participation, and part-time work on academic engagement. In F. M. Newmann (Ed.), *Student engagement and achievement in American secondary schools* (pp. 153-181). New York: Teachers College Press.

Landers, D., & Landers, D. (1978). Socialization via interscholastic athletics: Its effect on delinquency. *Sociology of Education, 51*, 299-301.

Larson, R. (1994). Youth organizations, hobbies, and sports as developmental contexts. In R. K. Silberiesen & E. Todt (Eds.), *Adolescence in context.* New York: Springer-Verlag.

Larson, R., & Kleiber, D. (1993). Free time activities as factors in adolescent adjustment. In P. Tolan & B. Cohler (Eds.), *Handbook of clinical research and practice with adolescents* (pp. 125-145). New York: John Wiley.

Larson, R., & Richards, M. (Eds.). (1989). The changing life space of early adolescence [Special issue]. *Journal of Youth and Adolescence, 18*, 501-626.

Mahoney, J. L. (1997, April). *From companions to convictions: Peer groups, school engagement, and the development of criminality.* Paper presented at the Biennial Meeting of the Society for Research on Child Development, Washington, DC.

Mahoney, J. L., & Cairns, R. B. (1997). Do extracurricular activities protect against early school dropout? *Developmental Psychology, 33*, 241-253.

McNeal, R. B. (1995). Extracurricular activities and high school dropouts. *Sociology of Education, 68*, 62-81.

Melnick, M. J., Vanfossen, B. E., & Sabo, D. F. (1988). Developmental effects of athletic participation among high school girls. *Sociology of Sport Journal,* **5**, 22-36.

Newmann, R.M., Wehlage, G.G., & Lamborn, S.D. (1992). The significance and sources of student engagement. In R M. Newmann (Ed.), *Student engagement and achievement in American secondary schools* (pp. 11-39). New York: Teachers College Press.

Otto, L. B. (1975). Extracurricular activities in the educational attainment process. *Rural Sociology,* **40**, 162-176.

Otto, L. B. (1976). Extracurricular activities and aspirations in the status attainment process. *Rural Sociology,* **41**, 217-233.

Otto, L. B., & Alwin, D. (1977). Athletics, aspirations, and attainments. *Sociology of Education,* **50**, 102-113.

The Psychological Corporation. (1981). *Differential Aptitude Test* (4th ed., Form VNW). San Antonio, TX: Harcourt Brace.

Rehberg, R. A. (1969). Behavioral and attitudinal consequences of high school interscholastic sports: A speculative consideration. *Adolescence,* **4**, 69-88.

Schulenberg, J., Maggs, J. L., & Hurrelmann, K. (1997). *Health risks and developmental transitions during adolescence.* Cambridge, UK: Cambridge University Press.

Sherif, M., & Sherif, C. (1964). *Reference groups: Exploration into conformity and deviation of adolescents.* Chicago: Henry Regnery.

Silbereisen, R. K., Naaco, P., & von Eye, A. (1999). Adolescents' development of romantic friendship and change in favorite leisure contexts. *Journal of Adolescent Research,* **7**(1), 80-93.

Simmons, R. G., & Blyth, D. A. (1987). *Moving into adolescence: The impact of pubertal change and school context.* New York: Aldine de Gruyter.

Spady, W. (1970). Lament for the letterman: Effect of peer status and extracurricular activities on goal and achievement. *American Journal of Sociology,* **75**, 680-702.

Williams, S., & McGee, R. (1991). Adolescent self-perceptions of their strengths. *Journal of Youth and Adolescence,* **21**, 325-337.

Winne, P. H., & Walsh, J. (1980). Self-concept and participation in school activities reanalyzed. *Journal of Educational Psychology,* **72**, 161-166.

Youniss, J., McLellan, J. A., Yang, S., & Yates, M. (in press). The role of community service in identity: Normative, unconventional, and deviant orientations. *Journal of Adolescent Research.*

Youniss, J., McLellan, J. A., & Yates, M., (1997). What we know about engendering civic identity. *American Behavioral Scientist,* **40**, 619-630.

Youniss, J., Yates, M., & Su, Y. (1997). Social integration: Community service and marijuana use in high school seniors. *Journal of Adolescent Research,* **12**, 245-262.

UNIT V

Big-Time Sports and the College Experience

Objectives

The unit examines the realities, demands, and opportunities created by commercialized, high-visibility college sports and their effect on athletes and the university.

Big-time college sports are multimillion dollar enterprises that employ students to conduct commercialized, high-visibility entertainment. Athletes are expected to be full-time students, are often required to put in over 40 hours a week at their sport, and are expected to perform at a level that helps fill stadiums and arenas. Essentially, athletes in the high-visibility, commercialized college sports are expected to work like athletes in the NBA or NFL while reaping few of the benefits. Their schedules are filled with practices, weightlifting, strategy sessions, obligatory attendance at banquets, media interviews, travel, and, of course, games. Such schedules strain the ability of young athletes to juggle the demands of school and athletics. They are often unable to have a meaningful social life, and their ability to pursue hobbies and other interests is impaired. This situation is especially pronounced for men in football and basketball, although the rise in women's sports is beginning to subject women athletes to similar pressures. Yet the literature suggests that women who participate in high-visibility sports may secure some benefits. Women athletes often report heightened levels of empowerment and

bodily competence, suffer less deterioration in their grades than the men do, achieve considerably higher graduation rates, and are able to develop a more proactive approach to life.

The three articles that follow provide glimpses to the various ways that participation in high-visibility sports affects the lives of both men and women athletes.

In the first selection, Sperber, author and professor of English and American Studies, laments the commercialization of college sports and their negative effect on the ideals of higher education. He identifies and discusses a number of "myths" that, he argues, help shield sports from scrutiny. Sperber demonstrates with several examples the often harsh realities of big-time college sports. Included among what he calls half-truths are the myth of amateurism and the myth that most big-time athletes are truly concerned with getting an education. He reminds the reader that universities often serve as minor-league farm teams for wealthy professional organizations, and he draws attention to the heavy time demands imposed on athletes in Division I programs. Sperber also attacks the myth that college sports are profitable enterprises. The reality, he argues, is that with the exception of a handful of schools, the majority of programs lose money. "Creative financing," according to Sperber, helps cover up mismanagement by athletic administrators and enables athletic departments to maintain the deception that they make money. The author concludes by making a number of recommendations for reforming College Sports, Inc. We are left to wonder, however, whether university faculties, students, presidents, and alumni are sufficiently concerned about the "creative accounting practices" and the corruption of academic ideals to demand meaningful change. Cynics would argue that so long as athletics provides exciting entertainment for the university community and the state and generates publicity and national exposure for the institution, calls for reform may be nothing more than wishful thinking!

In the second selection, Blinde, Taub, and Han studied 24 women athletes in Division I intercollegiate programs and found that participation was related to the enhancement of empowering attributes. These include, among others, a proactive approach to life and a more competent self. Because men often control women's sports, notions of competitiveness, a product orientation, and professionalized attitudes— attitudes associated with success and competence—dominate the activities. Because these attributes and teachings have traditionally been denied to women, participation in such environments provides women with opportunities to acquire such "success" skills and empowers them to gain greater control over their lives.

In the final selection, Sellers, Kuperminc, and Damas investigated the impact of athletic involvement on the lives of African American women. The authors focused on the athletes' academic performance, alienation and abuse, perceived social advantage resulting from athletic involvement, and life satisfaction. Among other findings, African American women athletes reported that it is somewhat "easier" for them to develop social skills and assertiveness because of participation in athletics. The authors note that academically these women perform "adequately," given the "time demands associated with athletics and their poorer academic preparation" in high school. Finally, the authors conclude that the life experiences of these women differ in significant ways from those of white women athletes, as well as those of African American male athletes.

Clearly, being a Division I athlete furnishes both benefits and drawbacks to the participants. Few would argue that participation in high-level intercollegiate athletics helps develop interpersonal skills, self-confidence, determination and perseverance, and a host of success skills that may well carry over into the business sector and life in general. And the friendships that one makes may last a lifetime. But a price tag is attached to those benefits, mostly tied to time demands that such programs place on athletes. When we take into account the athletic-related activities athletes are expected to engage in—weightlifting, media interviews, practice sessions, travel, and games—athletes often put in over 40 hours a week at their sports. In addition, we must factor in the psychic demands of the sport, all its pressures, and the fatigue resulting from intensive daily workouts and 6 A.M. lifting sessions. These activities take their toll on the athlete, with the result that little time remains for studying, pursuing personal hobbies and interests, or establishing meaningful and lasting relationships with the opposite sex. Moreover, the athletes who perform well academically in college probably "underperform." That is, they rarely manage to perform at their potential, and the quality and depth of their learning is often undermined. Athletes who come from poorer homes and who have received inadequate high school educational preparation for college are at considerable risk of failing out. Such athletes rarely achieve the dream of a college education. These students eventually "major in eligibility" and "struggle along," as Brede and Camp (1987) found in a study of NCAA Division I male athletes. Yet this is not how most athletes start college. Adler and Adler (1985), in an in-depth study of elite male basketball players, found that when athletes first arrive in college they often have high educational aspirations, want to get an education, and wish to graduate. But as the harsh realities and demands of high-level competition set in, they begin to change their perspectives and priorities. That is, they begin to make "pragmatic adjustments" in their academic attitudes and goals. About three-quarters of these athletes switch to what they perceive to be "easier" majors, and by their final year in college they abandon all concern with academic performance. As Adler and Adler note, "As a result of their experiences at the University, athletes grew increasingly cynical about and uninterested in academics. They accepted their marginal status and lowered their academic interest, effort, and goals" (p. 248).

The limited research available on women athletes is somewhat more positive, but until the last few years most women's Division I programs have not been subjecting their athletes to the same intense pressures as the men's high-visibility sports of football and basketball. Up to this point, research suggests that women athletes are often better prepared for college, outperform men athletes academically, and have higher graduation rates. As women's programs gradually become more professionalized, however, problems similar to those of the men may begin to surface. Only time will tell.

References

Adler, P., & Adler, P. (1985). From idealism to pragmatic detachment: The academic performance of college athletes. *Sociology of Education*, **58**, 241-250.

Blinde, E., Taub, D., & Han, L. (1993). Sport participation and women's personal empowerment: Experiences of the college athlete. *Journal of Sport and Social Issues*, **17**(1), 47-60.

Brede, R.M., & Camp, H.J. (1987). The education of college student athletes. *Sociology of Sport Journal*, **4**(3), 245-257.

Sellers, R.M., Kuperminc, G.P., & Damas, A. (1997). The college life experiences of Afro-American women athletes. *American Journal of Community Psychology*, **25**(5), 699-720.

Sperber, M. (1990). College sports inc. *Phi Delta Kappan*, **72**(2), 1-10.

Discussion Questions

Murray Sperber

1. Identify and discuss the myths identified by Sperber about college sports. In your opinion, what functions do such myths serve?
2. Sperber argues that universities provide free minor leagues for professional sports organizations. (a) What is the nature and extent of this "relationship" between universities and professional sports organizations? (b) Should professional sports organizations share some of the financial burden for training athletes presently incurred by universities? (c) What would the implications of such an arrangement be?
3. Sperber argues that athletic departments often employ "creative accounting" methods in the financial management of their programs. What does he mean? Discuss and explain.
4. Identify and discuss the pros and cons of having a big-time athletic program at your university. Develop a defensible position based on the available facts.
5. Class project: Each of the myths identified by Sperber is a potentially testable hypothesis.

Design and implement a research project to test one of these myths.

Elaine Blinde, Diane Taub, and Lingling Han

1. Discuss and explain the meaning of empowerment, especially in sport contexts.
2. Identify and react to each of the questions put to the athletes in this study.
3. How would you answer if these questions were put to you?
4. What did the investigators find regarding the issues of (a) bodily competence, (b) perception of a competent self, and (c) a proactive approach to life? Discuss and explain.
5. How does the nature of power as discussed by women athletes differ from definitions employed by male athletes? Discuss and explain.
6. According to the authors, linking "personal competence with the political realm" may be difficult for women to achieve. Do you agree or disagree? Discuss and explain.
7. In what ways can personal empowerment help women take more control over their lives? Discuss and explain.

Robert Sellers, Gabriel Kuperminc, and Alphonse Damas Jr.

1. Identify and discuss the major issues that prompted the authors to conduct this study.
2. Briefly summarize the findings of previous studies as reported in this article on (a) academic performance, (b) isolation and alienation, (c) perceptions of social advantage, and (d) satisfaction.
3. Identify and discuss the findings of this study with respect to the four areas listed in question 2.
4. Identify and discuss the authors' interpretation of the findings (found in Discussion section). Do you agree or disagree with them?
5. Identify and discuss the policy implications proposed by the authors. Do you agree or disagree with them?

College Sports Inc.:
The Athletic Department vs. the University

Murray Sperber

What was allowed to become a circus—college sports—threatens to become the means by which the public believes the entire enterprise [higher education] is a sideshow.*

—A. Bartlett Giamatti, former president of Yale University, former commissioner of Major League Baseball

A generation ago, when I was an undergraduate at Purdue, college sports were on the margin of university life. Today at Purdue and many other schools, athletic departments are much larger in size and scope, and they make greater demands on their institutions than ever before. Although I am a fan of college sports, I have long wondered whether and to what extent their increasing importance complements or corrupts the academic mission of their host universities.

After intensively researching these questions for a number of years, I came to one absolute conclusion: intercollegiate athletics, especially the big-time version, has become College Sports Inc., a huge commercial entertainment conglomerate, with operating methods and objectives totally separate from, and often opposed to, the educational aims of the schools that house its franchises. Moreover, because of its massive hypocrisy and fiscal irresponsibility, College Sports Inc. places many colleges and universities under the constant threat of scandal and other sports-induced maladies.

This situation is untenable for American higher education, and a basic redefinition of the role of intercollegiate athletics within the university is absolutely necessary. Therefore, throughout this Special Report and particularly in the conclusion, I suggest a number of radical ways to restructure college sports. Whether readers agree with my solutions or not, the research and arguments behind them will provide detailed and often surprising information about the nature of College Sports Inc. Moreover, this Special Report is designed to better prepare participants—everyone connected with and/or concerned about higher education—for the important public debate in the 1990s on the question, How can we cure the ills of American college sports?

When you go to college, you're not a student-athlete but an athlete-student. Your main purpose is not to be an Einstein but a ballplayer, to generate some money, put people in the stands. Eight or 10 hours of your day are filled with basketball, football. The rest of your time,

---

*Almost all the direct quotations and other cited material in this Special Report are referenced in my book, College Sports Inc.: The Athletic Department vs. the University. Those not cited in my book appear as footnotes at the end of this report.

Reprinted from Sperber, 1990.

you've got to motivate yourself to make sure you get something back.

—Isiah Thomas, former Indiana University basketball player, now a Detroit Pistons star

A great number of myths shield college sports from careful scrutiny and burden any discussion of the subject. The following refutations of the most common of these myths should introduce readers to the realities of College Sports Inc.

Myth: *College sports are part of the educational mission of American colleges and universities.*

Reality: The main purpose of college sports is commercial entertainment. Within most universities with big-time sports programs, the athletic department operates as separate business and has almost no connection to the academic departments and functions of the school—even the research into and teaching of sports is done by the physical education department.

The reason why elite athletes are in universities has nothing to do with the educational missions of their schools. Athletes are the only group of students recruited for commercial entertainment purposes—not for academic reasons—and they are the only students who go through school on grants based not on educational aptitude but on their talent and potential as commercial entertainers.

The system does not make sense. If colleges searched for and awarded scholarships to upcoming rock stars so that they could entertain the university community and earn money for their schools through concerts and tours, educational authorities and the public would call this "a perversion of academic values" and would not stand for it. Yet every year American institutions of higher education hand out more than 100,000 full or partial athletic scholarships, worth at least $500 million, for reasons similar to those that would justify grants to rock performers.

Myth: *College athletes are amateurs, and their athletic scholarships do not constitute professional payment for playing sports.*

Reality: A school gives an athlete a "full ride" grant worth up to $20,000 a year in exchange for the athlete's services in a commercial entertainment venture, that is playing on one of the school's sports teams. If the athlete fails to keep his or her part of the agreement and quits the team, the institution withdraws the financial package—even if the athlete stays in school as a regular student. Moreover, once the athlete uses up his or her playing eligibility, the school is under no obligation to continue to pay for the athlete's education—even though the athlete may be many semesters from graduation. Most schools stop the grants.

In its *NCAA Manual*, the National Collegiate Athletic Association lists the "benefits" of an athletic scholarship: free tuition and fees, room and board, and textbooks, as well as free tutoring, athletic medical insurance, rehabilitation expenses, on-campus career counseling, and advice from nonuniversity professionals. The athlete's freebies cost regular students thousands of dollars a year. Indeed, given escalating tuition and other school costs in the 1990s, the cost to a regular student for what an athlete receives in exchange for playing on a school's athletic team will soon reach $25,000 a year.

At one time in NCAA history, athletic scholarships were given for four years and, once awarded, could not be revoked. In 1973, under pressure from coaches who wanted greater control over their players and the ability to "fire" them for poor athletic performances, the NCAA instituted one-year scholarships, renewable annually at the athletic department's discretion.

Under their current terms, athletic scholarships appear indistinguishable from what the Internal Revenue Service (IRS) calls "barter payment for services rendered." According to IRS rules, "If you [the athlete] exchange your property and/or services [playing sports] for the property and/or services of another [a school's athletic scholarships], you have taxable income," and you are a professional.

Ironically, the NCAA itself endorses the concept of athletic scholarships as noncash payments when it forbids various "practices [that] constitute 'pay' for participation in intercollegiate athletics," among them, "complimentary admissions [to sports events] in excess of four per student-athlete per contest." Why does the fifth "admission" become "pay," whereas the first four are proof of a student-athlete's amateur standing? The IRS should consider athletic scholarship holders professionals and tax them accordingly.

Myth: *For college athletes, the opportunity of a university education is as important as playing intercollegiate sports.*

Reality: Formal and informal studies of why athletes choose colleges indicate that they make their selections primarily for athletic—not academic—reasons and that they consider universities as the pathway to professional sports. Specifically, top high school athletes want to play for a college coach with a winning record, on a team with a winning tradition, in the hope of receiving the best preparation for professional or Olympic careers. In addition, they want to "start" as freshmen and to receive maximum media exposure during their college careers. They believe that, if these ambitions are satisfied, they will be pro draft choices or Olympic team selections and acquire lucrative professional contracts. How coaches make use of these ambitions was explained by basketball's Larry Brown: "Every kid I recruited for college felt that he had an opportunity to play in the NBA, and I liked them to have those expectations. So they give themselves—their trust—to you from day one, hoping to reach that goal."

That very few college athletes ever fulfill their dream of playing professional sports is irrelevant to the dream's power over them and to its role in shaping their college careers, especially their willingness to devote as many as 60 hours a week to their sports and their frequent inability to sustain a serious course of studies. Jim Walden, head football coach at Iowa State University, says that in his sport "not more than 20% of the football players go to college for an education. And that may be a high figure."

But why blame the athletes? An anomaly of American history—that intercollegiate football and basketball began before the professional versions of those games and so precluded the formation of viable minor leagues in those sports—has created a situation that is unknown and unthinkable in other countries. In the U.S. outstanding high school football and men's basketball players, often with little interest in and preparation for higher education, are required to attend a university in order to gain an opportunity to play their sports at the pro level.

American higher education, however, has compounded the problem. Colleges now take on the training of many young athletes in sports for which there are excellent minor professional leagues and circuits, particularly baseball, hockey, golf, and tennis. In addition, colleges have undertaken the training of athletes for Olympic sports for which there is a strong club system. Almost 75% of current major league baseball players and a very high percentage of professional hockey, golf, and tennis players have passed through intercollegiate sports.

Thus American higher education provides free minor leagues for immensely wealthy pro sports organizations—the National Football League (NFL), the National Basketball Association (NBA), Major League Baseball, the National Hockey League (NHL), the Professional Golfers' Association (PGA), the Ladies Professional Golfers' Association (LPGA), professional tennis, and the United States Olympic Committee—and receives nothing in return. Moreover, most of these appropriately dubbed "nonrevenue" sports lose money for their schools. Hockey is a major money loser, but, in a typical instance, American college hockey supplied 12 players, many of them Canadian citizens, to the 1989-90 Boston Bruins, runners up in the Stanley Cup playoffs. Meanwhile, Canadian universities, because they do not give "full ride" athletic scholarships, had exactly one player in the entire NHL in 1989-90! As College Sports Inc. grows, increasing numbers of young athletes will enter American higher education primarily for athletic—not academic—training.

Myth: *What about those athletes like Bill Bradley and Tom McMillan who were outstanding in sports and in the classroom? Don't they prove that the system works?*

Reality: In any large sample of people in any endeavor, there are always a few at the high end of the bell-shaped curve. The renown of Bradley and McMillan as successes in sports and in academics suggests that intercollegiate athletics is a system that works for only a few. No one bothers to name all the outstanding Americans who were once top college students but not athletes; they are not unusual, and higher education is supposed to produce them.

Intercollegiate athletics should function for the majority of its participants. From their first day of college, however, athletes in big-time programs face a conundrum that few can solve: how to be a "student-athlete." Their only response is to erase one of the terms and to highlight the other: neglect a meaningful education and pursue sports full-time or, in a few cases, drop out of athletics and seriously go to school.

Harry Edwards, a sociologist at the University of California, Berkeley, has done extensive research on the time constraints on college athletes and concludes that NCAA Division I-A football players spend up to 60 hours a week during the season on their sport; basketball players spend 50 hours a week. Edwards succinctly explains the time dilemma that confronts most college athletes: "Education is activist. You have to be actively involved in your own education. When you're involved in sports 50 hours a week, maybe living in pain, you can't be actively involved [in your education]."

Edwards' comment also hints at the unrecorded hours that athletes spend on their sports: the time in recovery, the hours passed getting over headaches and other pains acquired in scrimmages, games, and so on. One former college basketball player described life under a coach who ran hard practices: "It was all you could do to drag yourself back to the dorm each day. By the time you ate and got back to your room, it was 8:30, and all you could think about was getting your weary bones in bed and getting some sleep. Who had time to study?" This player had placed second in his high school graduating class and had intended to prepare for medical school, but he had been channeled instead into physical education. He did not graduate from college.

If the coach demands that players spend 50 or more hours a week on a sport, an athlete cannot refuse—unless he or she wants to drop the sport and lose the athletic scholarship. And most athletes, because of their dream of making it to the pros or the Olympics, willingly participate in full-time sports regimens. Football and men's basketball programs are notorious for the time they require and the physical demands that they make on players, but many nonrevenue sports also require constant sacrifices from athletes. A recent NCAA survey noted that "women basketball players at major colleges spend as much time at their sport as their male counterparts." However, university authorities believe that a full-time student who is pursuing a meaningful degree should devote at least 40 to 50 hours a week to attending classes and studying—and that students who are ill-prepared for college, including large numbers of athletes, should spend significantly more time than that on their studies.

Even in an athlete's off-season, the time required for sports does not drop appreciably. A former athletic director at Southern Illinois University explained that, for off seasons, many coaches have "the mentality of 'more is better' . . . the longer the out-of-season practice period and the longer the weightlifting session, the better." In addition, the new high-tech machines, rather than cutting time from an athlete's training, have added to it. Coaches now demand longer hours on the Nautilus to increase strength and conditioning, and athletes are required to spend more time viewing videotapes of their own and their opponents' performance.

To put in perspective the amount of time that a college athlete spends on a sport, consider that the federal government allows a regular student receiving a work-study grant to spend a *maximum of 20 hours a week on his or her university job* (e.g., shelving books in the library). The government's rationale is that more than 20 hours a week cuts into the amount of time needed for a normal course of study by a full-time student. Nevertheless, according to Harry Edwards' figures, intercollegiate athletes regularly exceed this federal guideline by as much as 200%.

Most big-time athletic programs try to finesse the time constraints on athletes by parking them in special "hideaway curricula" and having them major in eligibility. (The NCAA has minimal rules for

"good academic standing" and playing eligibility.) But courses in a school's Division of Ridiculous Studies do not constitute a real college education. For the vast majority of athletic scholarship holders, the current system does not work.

Myth: *According to one of the NCAA's most basic rules, athletes may receive no more than "the same benefit generally available to the institution's [other] students."*

Reality: The NCAA invokes this rule to penalize a school for giving a T-shirt to a recruit, because regular students do not receive free T-shirts. But every big-time athletic program constantly breaks the "no extra benefit" rule by giving athletes special dormitories and dining facilities, special academic advisors and tutors, and a variety of other privileges unavailable and/or forbidden to the school's regular students. In fact, the blatant differences between the on-campus lives of jocks and those of regular students contribute to the cynicism with which many students and faculty members regard holders of athletic scholarships.

Compared to the usual small rooms, Spartan furnishings, and ordinary-to-awful food of the student dorms, jock housing tends toward the palatial. An individual unit for one or two athletes often consists of a nicely furnished suite—large living room, bedroom, and bathroom—with a stereo, color television, and VCR. The main dining room downstairs serves grade-A food in abundance. (The jock dorm at the University of Alabama is nicknamed "The Bryant Hilton," after its builder, former head football coach Paul "Bear" Bryant.) Moreover, even at those schools without jock dorms, special daily "training tables" are set up somewhere on campus for the athletes, and the free and plentiful food there is far superior to what their fellow dorm residents pay to eat. At the University of Nevada, Las Vegas, the "training table" is often off-campus. The men's basketball players can obtain a daily free meal at a number of Las Vegas casino restaurants.

Another standard jock privilege is access to free tutoring. To meet the minimal academic rules on playing eligibility, athletic departments hire large numbers of advisors and tutors. Wayne Yates, a former Division I basketball coach, said, "I believe academic counselors honestly want athletes to graduate, but I've heard an academic counselor say he could keep a cockroach eligible for two years. That's true."

NCAA Division I-A athletic departments now have an average of six full-time academic advisors, and some have a staffer for each sport. In addition, the full-time personnel hire large numbers of part-time assistants to do the bulk of the tutoring and "babysitting" (walking athletes to class, often taking notes for them, sometimes attending class for them). On occasion, these tutors write papers and take exams for their charges.

Pennsylvania State University prides itself on its academic advising program for athletes and spends $600,000 a year on advisors, tutors, study hall monitors, a career-development psychologist, and a sports psychologist. Penn State has 800 intercollegiate athletes; thus it spends an average of $750 per athlete for these NCAA-approved services. Penn State also has 35,000 other students, but if they need tutoring—and the limited university services are unavailable—they have to search the bulletin boards around campus for the names of professional tutors and pay the going rate of $10 to $15 an hour. (Penn State would not reveal how much it spends on free tutoring services for regular students, but, granting it a generous $1 million, the average would be about $27 per student.) Moreover, as at all Division I schools, athletes can use the universitywide services, but regular students are denied access to the athletic department's top-of-the-line program.

In spite of these special deals for athletes, many coaches and athletic directors are now demanding new NCAA legislation to allow athletes to receive "living expense" money—either direct payments of cash and/or an increase in their total grant package. Dick Schultz, executive director of the NCAA, argues, without a hint of irony, that this additional money will enable an athlete to "live like a normal college student."

Myth: *College sports provide an excellent opportunity for black youngsters to get out of the ghetto and to contribute to American society.*

Reality: Harry Edwards claims that many athletic programs treat black athletes as "gladiators," bringing them to campus only to play sports, not to obtain an education. And the low graduation rates of black college athletes support Edwards' thesis. From 1972-73 through 1985, Memphis State University, with men's basketball teams that were predominantly black, *did not graduate a single black player;* from the early to the mid-1980s, 4% of the black players on the men's basketball team at the University of Georgia graduated. Even Bob Knight of Indiana University, a supposedly pro-academics coach, has graduated just 12% of the black players whom he has recruited in the last 10 years.[1]

Most schools with major athletic programs, and many schools with smaller ones, recruit black athletes much more intensively and systematically than they do regular black students. In addition, some schools fund their "black gladiators" by diverting money from such scholarship sources as the Basic Education Opportunity Grants, earmarked for academically motivated minority students.

In late 1988 the NCAA reported on the University of Cincinnati's awarding of financial aid packages to six black freshman basketball players who were Proposition 48 nonqualifiers or partial qualifiers. The men's basketball coach at Cincinnati and the university's director of financial aid put together grants that included money from the University Honors Scholarship fund, the State Economic Opportunity Grant, and Student Financial Aid Discretionary Funds. The NCAA noted that, in this case and similar ones, "NCAA legislation actually permitted [Prop. 48] partial qualifiers to receive the aid that was awarded." According to Prop. 48 rules, these athletes had failed to achieve a combined score higher than 700 on the Scholastic Aptitude Test (SAT) and/or a 2.0 grade-point average on 11 core high school courses, but Cincinnati took money from its limited scholarship funds and gave it to them rather than to more academically qualified minority students. In 1990 the NCAA extended this financial aid benefit to Proposition 42 partial qualifiers—thus allowing institutions to continue to divert scarce funds in this way.

The final irony of the "black gladiator" situation is that many schools, instead of trying harder to locate and educate future black teachers, doctors, business leaders, and so on, spend large sums of money recruiting and then maintaining in college a group of black youths who are often the least prepared and the least interested in acquiring college educations.

> We've got the deal spotted. If they [athletic programs] don't get enough money, they steal it out of the education budget.
>
> —Don Tyson, chairman of Tyson Foods and a member of the Arkansas Higher Education Committee, commenting on the multimillion-dollar athletic department deficits in his state

Myth: *College sports are incredibly profitable, earning huge sums of money for American colleges and universities.*

Reality: One of the best-kept secrets about intercollegiate athletics—well-guarded because athletic departments are extremely reluctant to open their financial books—is that most college sports programs lose money. If profit is defined according to ordinary business practices, of the 802 members of the NCAA, the 493 members of the National Association for Intercollegiate Athletics (NAIA), and the more than 1,050 junior colleges, only 10 to 20 athletic programs make a consistent (albeit small) profit. In any given year, another 20 to 30 break even or do a little better. All the rest—more than 2,300 institutions—lose anywhere from a few dollars to millions of dollars annually on college sports.

Because athletic departments are allowed to engage in "creative accounting," covering many of their expenses with money from their schools' general operating funds and from other university resources, it is difficult to ascertain the full extent of their losses. One expert, Don Canham, longtime athletic director at the University of Michigan, estimated that "about 99% of the schools in this country don't balance their budgets in athletics." Canham balanced his, but the year after he retired (1988-89), Michigan's athletic program, with a consistently sold-out 101,701-seat stadium and victories in the Rose Bowl and in the NCAA men's basketball tournament (which earned more than $3.5 million), was $2.5 million in the red, and it projected a $5.3 million annual deficit by 1993.[2]

Even the NCAA acknowledges the poor financial health of college sports. Its most recent study on this topic, *The Revenues and Expenses of Intercollegiate Athletic Programs*, polled 795 athletic programs and reported that the vast majority lost money. Moreover, because only the big-time programs have a chance at college sports' pot of gold—lucrative bowl games and the NCAA men's basketball tournament—most NCAA members will continue to lose money indefinitely. (The NAIA schools and the junior colleges cannot even afford a lottery ticket.)

A few years ago, the regents of the Florida public universities investigated their state's athletic departments and found deficits at many institutions, including $1.1 million at the University of Central Florida in Orlando, $700,000 at Florida A & M, and $500,000 at the University of South Florida in Tampa. The chair of the Florida Board of Regents explained the core of the problem as "the general tendency of athletics administrators to overestimate the money that programs will bring in, then spend accordingly in advance. When faced with a shortfall, they have only two choices . . . ignore the bills, or pay with someone else's money."

These annual deficits prompt the creative accounting methods that athletic departments and their host universities employ. Among the most widespread practices are: placing the enormous maintenance costs on stadiums and other facilities (used exclusively by the athletic program and its elite athletes) in the "buildings and grounds" line in the universitywide budget; paying the multimillion-dollar debt servicing on these facilities by taxing regular students in the form of mandatory fees; moving coaches' salaries to regular faculty FTE lines; and funding athletic scholarships out of regular student financial aid.

If these bookkeeping tricks do not cover the deficit, schools take special subventions out of general operating funds, and, if they are public institutions, use taxpayers' money by diverting federal and state subsidies. Schools also siphon money from "unrestricted gift funds" (those donations not clearly marked for a specific use). Purdue University recently used $3 million of unrestricted gift funds to help pay for an indoor football practice facility, although many alumni (including this writer) thought that their contributions to their alma mater were used only for educational purposes. I now earmark my gifts to universities for specific academic programs.

A former NCAA Division I soccer coach succinctly summed up the finances of college sports: "Athletic administrators have one of the sweetest deals going. They have lots of the goodies of corporate America and few of the financial headaches. They can spend whatever they want, and every year Uncle University bails out the red ink. And the world hasn't caught on to their scam."

In truth, College Sports Inc. is an amazing hybrid of corporation and public agency. The men and women who run college sports consider themselves corporate officers managing large businesses, carefully amassing and guarding all revenue. They also reward themselves with the high salaries and perks of their corporate counterparts. On the other hand, the executives of College Sports Inc. do not wish to accept the financial responsibilities of every other businessperson in America—not even to paying the utility bills. Instead, they prefer the "no bottom line" mentality of some public agency bureaucrats, and they spend money far in excess of their revenues. Then, at the end of the fiscal year, they claim that their College Sports Inc. franchise is really an educational unit, like their school's math department and they appeal to the central administration for extra funds to balance their books.

University authorities, whether through collusion, fear of bad publicity, or confusion about the real issues, have long cooperated with athletic administrators and covered these losses. Rarely do school officials point out the fallacy in the appeal for supplementary funds: an athletic program is not an academic unit. If the math department has a budgetary shortfall one year because of underenrollment, the university absorbs the financial loss because the mission of an academic unit is education, not monetary profit, and because the value of teaching and research cannot be calculated in dollars and cents. However, the purpose of an athletic program is commercial entertainment, and, if its expenses exceed its revenues, then—like every other business in America—it should be held accountable.

The present financial situation in college sports continues for two main reasons: athletic departments refuse to reveal their true financial situations, and the majority of Americans—including college graduates, current students, and even faculty members—believe that College Sports Inc. is tremendously profitable and that the profits help higher education. In fact, to cover athletic program losses, most schools must divert dollars that could go to academic units, stuffing them down the college sports deficit hole.

Athletic department secrecy, combined with the myth of great profitability, allows university and athletic program administrators to perpetrate and perpetuate this money "scam." If the public understood how these financial losses hurt the schools involved, especially their academic programs, major reforms might come to college sports—and quickly.

Myth: *Schools receive millions of dollars when their teams play in football bowl games.*

Reality: The numbers reported are often for the "projected payout," whereas the actual payout can be much lower. Moreover, most participating schools must split their bowl revenues with other members of their conference. For example, when the headline announces that a Pac-10 team received $1 million for a bowl appearance, that school kept only $100,000 because of the conference's 10-way split.

Some schools even move money to the bowl sponsors by agreeing to take huge allotments of tickets. Although the University of Mississippi was rated 52nd nationally in *USA Today's Computer Rankings,* the Liberty Bowl invited Ole Miss to the 1989 game in part because the university guaranteed the sale of 20,000 tickets.

In addition, athletic departments like to turn bowl and tournament trips into all-expense-paid junkets for hundreds of people, including their employees and friends. These travel and hotel costs not only fritter away the bowl or tourney payout but often transform postseason play into a deficit item!

Myth: *Schools receive millions of dollars from the NCAA men's basketball tournament.*

Reality: The numbers given in newspaper articles are grossly inaccurate, because the NCAA bureaucracy keeps half of the revenue for itself. For example, of the millions received for the 1987 tourney, the association distributed only 44% to the schools involved.

The new contract giving Columbia Broadcasting System (CBS) the right to televise the NCAA tournament will increase tournament revenue. But, rather than share the pot of gold, the NCAA plans to exclude large numbers of schools from reaching into it at all. According to Tom Hansen, commissioner of the Pac-10, the NCAA may soon drop as many as 50 schools from Division I basketball. And, if past performance is any indication, the additional money will increase the lottery fever among the remaining 240 Division I basketball programs, with coaches engaging in "checkbook recruiting" and sparing no expenses to build winning teams.

In the 1990s NCAA "final four" squads will be the lottery winners. (Probably the perennial powers will dominate.) Schools whose teams are invited to the tournament will break even on their basketball program expenses, but the large number of also-rans will either pay huge sums of money to purchase losing tickets or be shut out entirely.

In addition, with the new NCAA/CBS contract have come increased demands to pay the players who make college sports extravaganzas possible. If athletic departments start paying cash to their athletes, the new television contract will not begin to cover the additional expenses.

Most important, the huge CBS contract points to the crucial problem in college sports: the network is not making a $1 billion contribution to American higher education; *it is buying a product*—the very best college basketball, played at the very highest level. *And it expects schools to deliver that product.* Amazingly, the president of CBS-TV, Neal Pilson, denies this commercial equation; he told those who attended a recent NCAA convention that television revenue "is money the schools can use for libraries, for scholarships, professors' salaries, research, and new classrooms, or for new football stadiums, recruiting athletes, or raising coaches' salaries. The choice is yours to make."

Pilson's comment is hypocritical for several reasons. As a television executive with extensive experience in college sports, he knows that athletic programs, because of the nature of their finances and their frequently incompetent management, need every penny of the television revenue that they can generate. He also understands the schools' true lack of choice. *If universities spend their television sports revenue on academic items, their athletic product will deteriorate.* And not having state-of-the-art facilities, not paying coaches their six-figure annual income packages, not recruiting the most talented athletes, and not requiring those athletes to train and play their sports full-time will definitely dilute the product. Then CBS-TV and the other telecasters *will pay less money to televise college sports events.*

Beneath this television executive's high minded rhetoric lies an attempt to distance the television industry from the very problems in college sports that it helped to create: the professional demands on student-athletes and the totally commercial atmosphere in which big-time athletic programs must exist in order to produce the highest-quality athletic product for television.

On the weekend after Pilson spoke, both the Harvard at Cornell and the Memphis State at Tulsa basketball games took place. The former game matched two schools that fulfill the criteria for much greater emphasis on academics than on athletic program items; the latter game featured two "jock factories" with the best facilities, players, and coaches that money can buy. CBS telecast Memphis State at Tulsa, as well as a game featuring the University of Nevada at Las Vegas.

Myth: *Alumni demand that their alma maters have large and successful college sports programs.*

Reality: Studies indicate that most alumni contribute to the academic units of their colleges and universities and that less than 2% of them donate to athletic programs. In fact, alumni often *withhold* contributions from their alma maters when the athletic teams are too successful or are involved in sports scandals; they are embarrassed by their schools' becoming "jock factories" and/or angered by the bad publicity. Moreover, they believe that their college degrees are being devalued.

Other research indicates that the major donors to athletic programs are boosters—people who never attended the school, who give money only to the athletic department and in proportion to its teams' success on the field or court, and who refuse to contribute to the institution's academic programs.

Even the alumni of the University of Notre Dame are less interested in sports than is generally believed. A major study of their attitudes concluded "When asked about their motivation for contributing to the alumni fund . . . [they] ranked the following as most important: alleviating the university's financial need, keeping private higher education viable, and recognizing Notre Dame's academic promise. At the bottom of the motivational scale . . . [was] endorsement of Notre Dame's athletic success."

Notre Dame, of course, is also famous for its boosters (known as the "subway alumni") and their generosity toward its athletic teams. Richard Conklin, a high official with the university for many years, offered this comment about them: "We at Notre Dame have had extensive experience trying to turn athletic interests of 'subway alumni' to academic development purposes and we have had no success. There is no evidence that the typical, nonalumnus fan of Notre Dame has much interest in its educational mission."

In fact, the nature of booster club appeals for money makes this situation inevitable. Club fund raisers tell boosters how much the athletic program is hurting financially and urge them to dig as deeply as possible to support it. After Booster Ed pays for his priority seats and also contributes to the "Save the Jocks Drive," he has little money—and even less inclination—to give to the physics department's scholarship fund.

Concomitant with the other myths concerning alumni support is the following one: schools that dare to drop or deemphasize a sports team will be hit by the wrath—emotional and financial—of their alumni. Only anecdotal evidence exists to refute this assertion, but it is important evidence nonetheless. According to the *Chronicle of Higher Education,* "Donations to Tulane University rose by $5 million in 1986, the year after the institution dropped basketball; annual giving at Wichita State University nearly doubled the year after officials suspended its debt-ridden football program."

Wichita State University presents a particularly interesting case because, as one official put it, there were warnings that enrollment would drop dramatically and that fund raising would fall off if the school discontinued football. In fact, "enrollment climbed, . . . and giving jumped to more than $25.5 million from just under $13.5 million" in the last football year. The president of the school, Warren Armstrong, who had been severely criticized by the local press and boosters when he made the decision to drop football, commented, "If a person's support is solely based on the athletic I think it's probably misplaced in the first place." Other Wichita State officials argued that "the lack of reaction to the university's decision indicates how soft the [boosters] support was to begin with."

Myth: *College sports programs generate great publicity and raise lots of money for their schools.*

Reality: A development officer at an East Coast university commented, "Schools with bigtime athletics get their names in the daily sports pages and on TV for free, but how does that help their academic missions or their fund raising? More probably, they're only convincing the public of their lack of educational seriousness."

In addition, when negative incidents occur in an athletic program, media attention intensifies, and the bad publicity tarnishes all parts of the institution. These days, such universities as Oklahoma, North Carolina State, and Kentucky are mainly known to the public for their sordid sports scandals, whereas their serious educational endeavors are ignored. Not surprisingly, schools in this situation often have difficulty raising money—not only for their athletic programs but also for their educational units.

The blade of negative publicity also swings back at a university when the attention generated by successful athletic teams overshadows academic programs and the institution gains a reputation as a "jock factory." This can permanently impair fundraising efforts.

Alumni give approximately $2 billion a year to their alma maters; however, the largest donations to colleges and universities come from private foundations and corporations. Last year these sources gave an estimated $3.45 billion to American higher education. According to the *Chronicle of Higher Education*, university fund raisers have long warned that a school with a big-time sports program risks being "known as a 'football factory' [rather] than as a first-rate university" and could have trouble obtaining grants, especially from the major foundations.

That private philanthropies take a dim view of "jock factories" and their attendant ills was underlined by an editorial in their newsletter, Foundation News, that urged "the foundations and corporations that give money to colleges and universities to make the integrity of a school's athletic program one of the conditions for providing grants." If these heavy hitters ever followed through on this threat, they could permanently change college sports.

Myth: *Big-time college sports programs boost student enrollment.*

Reality: This phenomenon is totally unproven; more important, even if it were true, is it desirable? Those students who apply to a school primarily because of the fame of its sports teams send strong signals about their lack of academic seriousness. Every school has its "beer and circus" contingent, but, if its membership reaches a critical mass, it changes the learning environment of the entire institution. Teaching or attending class on a Friday when a large number of students are absent because of a football or basketball weekend becomes a negative experience. Being in class on a Monday when students have not returned (or recovered) from their sports weekend also seems a waste of time. In such an atmosphere, even the serious minded students quickly become cynical and demoralized about the educational process.

Myth: *Big-time college sports programs build school spirit.*

Reality: All the evidence on this myth, pro and con, is anecdotal. When a school's team wins a championship, many members of the university community seem to feel good about it; however, for every champion, there are many more losing teams and disappointed fans.

I discovered a more important refutation of the school-spirit assertion while conducting research interviews. Throughout the country, at institutions with big-time programs, most administrators, faculty members, and students told private horror stories about coaches and athletes of their acquaintance who had received financial and/or academic privileges forbidden to all other members of the university community. ("Coach KickAss is allowed to skim money from his travel budget"; "Danny Dunk was in my Forensics 100 class, but one of the basketball managers took the exams for him.") These tales of corrupt practices emerged as regularly at schools known for abiding by NCAA rules as at those with a history of NCAA probations, and the stories were usually narrated in a spirit of resignation. ("This is the way that college sports works here, and there's nothing anyone can do about it.") The frequency of these negative anecdotes—as well as the scarcity of stories about the positive and unifying effects of college sports—suggests that big-time athletic programs mainly create distrust and opprobrium in their university communities. Thus College Sports Inc. does not seem to build school spirit; it breeds cynicism.

> Despite the pious half-time pronouncements we see on televised football and basketball games, in which the future of humankind is tied to the missions of universities with big-time athletic programs, these very programs contradict the fundamental aims of American higher education.
>
> —Richard Warch, president of Lawrence University, Appleton, Wisconsin

To solve the systemic problems in college sports, American higher education has to do the following: *Stop pretending that athletes can get decent college educations.* We can't expect intercollegiate athletes to work full-time in ambitious athletic programs and also to be full-time students in meaningful courses of study. Encourage those athletes who want preprofessional athletic training to enter the minor leagues in their sports, including the new foreign pro football and basketball leagues. Treat those athletes who want to attend the university the same as all regular students—admit them only if they achieve the minimum high school grade point average and SAT scores required of other incoming students. In other words, plug the "special admit" loophole that is now open to athletes with abysmal grades and test scores; abolish jock dorms and dining facilities and all other jock privileges; and give athletes only the same financial aid available to regular students, i.e., aid based on need and academic achievement.

If athletes were regular students, as responsible for their academic progress as every other fully enrolled student at the school, the need for hideaway curricula and other shams would no longer exist.

Stop pretending that athletic programs are financially self-supporting and that they never use public funds. Do not allow the franchises in College Sports Inc. to engage in creative accounting—moving as many of their expenses as possible to other parts of the university's financial books—and make athletic programs pay all their legitimate expenses. Schools should also inform state legislators, taxpayers, alumni, and other financial supporters when they cover athletic department expenses and deficits with general operating funds or with other money from university resources.

Stop pretending that athletic department deficits do not affect the academic programs of their schools. In an era when most colleges and universities operate under severe fiscal constraints, every dollar of university revenue is important. Schools must acknowledge that, when they siphon dollars from their budgets and other financial resources to cover athletic department deficits, they are using money that could go for academic programs, faculty and staff salaries, and the needs of regular students.

Many athletic directors like to proclaim that their departments' financial tubs "stand on their own bottoms." The time has come to make them live up to these proclamations or scale down their operations until these claims become true. Universities must insist that covering athletic program deficits with money that could go to education is an intolerable solution to the financial losses of College Sports Inc.

Stop pretending that coaches are college teachers, and stop tolerating their conflict-of-interest outside deals. Big-

time coaches are in the entertainment business. Few head coaches of Division I programs, especially in football and basketball, see the inside of a classroom on a regular basis; they devote their time and energies to administering their programs and promoting their careers. Their outside deals—including the endorsement of various products, television and radio shows, speaking engagements, sports clinics, private summer camps, and miscellaneous hustles—are often a major source of income. Schools should treat coaches just as they do all other university employees and demand that they devote a major portion of their time and energies to their full-time university jobs (or quit those positions).

Schools should also monitor coaches' outside-income deals for conflict-of-interest violations. They should not permit coaches to receive money from sporting goods companies in return for making their athletes wear (and thus advertise) particular brands of shoes and/or equipment. They should not allow coaches—on school property, wearing school colors and insignia—to endorse commercial products for their personal pin. They should not permit coaches free use of university athletic facilities and dorms to run private summer camps for personal profit. They should give coaches the same privileges that they grant to other university employees—but no more.

Stop pretending that all of the above and the hundreds of other abuses and disservices visited upon American higher education by College Sports Inc. have any reason to continue. Whatever set of circumstances transforms intercollegiate athletics, massive change will soon come to college sports. The present situation is too unstable, and the pressures on it are too great, for College Sports Inc. to continue in its current form to the end of this decade.

The crucial question, however, is how will the changes—some now being proposed by the NCAA Presidents' Commission, others soon to be put on the table by the Knight-Ridder Commission—affect American higher education? The hundreds of athletic directors and coaches whose careers will be disrupted will not quietly pack their gym bags and leave. They will do anything to preserve their present power and wealth, even if it means harming their host institutions. If the fight becomes bloody enough, no trustee, no administrator, no faculty member, and no student at the schools involved will remain untouched. The fiscal and academic integrity of many American colleges and universities could rest on the outcome.

William Atchley was president of Clemson University in the early 1980s when a college sports scandal shrouded that school. Rather than allow him to investigate fully, the Clemson Board of Trustees demanded his resignation. He is president of the University of the Pacific in Stockton, California. In an interview, he summed up the tension between College Sports Inc. and American higher education: "When academics takes a back seat to athletics, you have a problem. You no longer have an institution where people with integrity want to teach, or where people with common sense and good values want to send their children to learn."

Unless American higher education solves this problem, College Sports Inc. will continue to corrupt it—and with increasing speed.

Notes

1. For the statistics on Knight's graduation rate, see Tom Witowsky, *Des Moines Register*, 25 March 1990 and 24 June 1990; and "NCAA Academic Reporting Form [for the Athletic Department of Indiana University]." Additional information was supplied by the Indiana University Office of Afro-American Affairs. Excluding his current players and beginning with his 1980 group of recruits, during the last decade Knight had 17 black recruits, and only two of them graduated from Indiana University.
2. Patricia Edmonds, *Chicago Tribune*, 6 June 1990.

Sport Participation and Women's Personal Empowerment: Experiences of the College Athlete

Elaine M. Blinde
Diane E. Taub
Lingling Han

As a result of gender-role socialization, women are often discouraged from viewing themselves as strong, competent, and self-determining individuals. Becoming empowered at the personal level would represent a foundation from which women could counteract these limiting self-perceptions as well as gain control over their lives. We explore the potential of sport participation to provide women with this increased sense of power. Telephone interviews were conducted with 24 women athletes in three Division I intercollegiate sport programs in the United States. Athletes' responses suggest that sport participation related to the development of three empowering qualities women traditionally lack: (a) bodily competence, (b) perceptions of a competent self, and (c) a proactive approach to life. Despite participating in a sport context that is largely governed by men and where male notions of power prevail, the nature of power discussed by these women athletes was generally consistent with feminist reconceptualizations.

In a society characterized by rigid gender-role socialization and institutional discrimination, women are often denied opportunities to develop the knowledge and skills necessary for advancement (Brown, 1981; Coll, 1986; Schur, 1984; Staples, 1990).

Internalization of traditional gender norms discourages women from viewing themselves as competent, autonomous, strong, and self-determining individuals (Cantor & Bernay, 1992; Schur, 1984). Such socialization deters women from gaining a sense of control over their lives and generally perpetuates women's lack of power. Unless this condition of powerlessness is reversed, women will remain in a disadvantaged position and continue to be disempowered (Swift & Levin, 1987).

One means to reverse this "empowerment deficit" (Swift & Levin, 1987) is for women to become active participants in constructing the course of their lives. The process by which individuals in a disadvantaged social group develop skills and abilities to gain control over their lives and to take action to improve their life situation has been termed empowerment (Gutierrez, 1990; McWhirter, 1991; Rappaport, 1983-1984). Critical to this process is the development of potential that a person already possesses; individuals empower themselves rather than being recipients of power bestowed by others (Staples, 1990). The effects of empowerment can occur at various levels—personal, group, and institutional (Hartsock, 1983; Theberge, 1987). These levels are interrelated and hierarchically structured; the personal component represents the foundation for subsequent empowerment at the group and institutional levels (Gutierrez, 1990; Hartsock, 1983).

Reprinted from Blinde, Taub, and Han, 1993.

Emphasizing the development of "participatory competence" (Kieffer, 1983-1984), empowerment at the personal level is related to perceived control over life events (Kieffer, 1983-1984; Rappaport, 1985). Central to gaining this control is the attainment of such qualities as self-efficacy, perceived competence, internal locus of control, and self-esteem (Conger & Kanungo, 1988; Rappaport, 1985; Simmons & Parsons, 1983; Staples, 1990). Qualities associated with personal empowerment are often those that women lack; attaining such skills allows women the opportunity to overcome attributes and self-perceptions that limit their potential (Polk, 1974; Stromquist, 1988; Swift & Levin, 1987). Personal empowerment thus represents a foundational base from which women can eventually challenge their disadvantaged position (Brown & Ziefert, 1988).

The process of empowerment for women may occur in a variety of settings, ranging from nonformal education (Stromquist, 1988) and feminist movement organizations (Riger, 1983-1984) to women's experiences in such settings as churches, clubs, and voluntary organizations (Rappaport, 1983-1984, 1985). Along with these settings, it has been suggested that women's advancement into institutions traditionally dominated by men may be empowering. By learning attributes and skills which have generally been denied, women can gain a greater sense of control in their lives (Cantor & Bernay, 1992; Messner & Sabo, 1990).

Sport may represent one arena in which women can gain valued qualities and abilities at the personal level (Cantor & Bernay, 1992). In particular, two characteristics of sport suggest its empowering capability. First, the focus of sport on physicality and the body could enhance women's understanding of their bodily potential (Lenskyj, 1986; MacKinnon, 1987). Second, as sport occurs in a competitive environment, women participants can develop skills that not only lead to success in sport (e.g., persistence, competitiveness), but which can be applied to a variety of life situations (Cantor & Bernay, 1992).

Although participation in sport may possess the potential to empower women, many scholars have argued that sport is male-dominated and perpetuates patriarchal power and privilege. Uncritical acceptance of these male structures and values contributes to the oppression of women participants (Beck, 1980; Messner & Sabo, 1990). Moreover, feminists associate the form of competition found in male-controlled sport settings with such patriarchal values as aggression, power, and domination (Theberge, 1987). An overemphasis on competition and winning may instill values in women that run counter to feminist ideals (Birrell & Slatton, 1981; Hall, 1990).

These concerns about women's participation in male sport contexts have received some empirical support. For example, the movement of women athletes into intercollegiate sport programs resembling those of men (i.e., post-Title IX period) has been associated with various forms of conflict, including value alienation, role strain, role conflict, and exploitation (Blinde & Greendorfer, 1992). Despite these outcomes, women's continuation in sport may be influenced by the positive skills and qualities that sport participation provides. In one of the few works discussing the empowerment outcomes of sport participation, Theberge (1987) concentrates on woman controlled sport organizations, feminist sport leagues, and lesbian teams. In such contexts, women developed outcomes such as a positive sense of self, enhanced attitudes about their bodies, self-actualization, and a spirit of cooperation.

This paper represents one aspect of a larger project investigating the experiences of women athletes in Division I intercollegiate sport programs. Unlike the woman-centered sport structures discussed by Theberge (1987), the sport setting in our study is primarily controlled and dominated by men. We examine whether such a context, despite previously cited negative outcomes for athletes, is capable of providing women with qualities and experiences that can assist in challenging their disadvantaged position in society.

Relative to the different levels at which empowerment can occur, the present work explores ways in which sport facilitates the personal empowerment of women athletes. In particular, our focus is on the potential contribution of sport participation to the development of personally empowering skills and attributes women traditionally lack. Such an analysis represents the foundation for subsequent study examining the empowerment potential of sport at the group and institutional levels. Research at these higher levels should provide insight into athletes' understanding of sport as a gendered institution as well as women's ability to effectively utilize the empowering qualities developed at the personal level. Taken as a whole, studies investigating these three levels can suggest whether athletes develop skills and gain experiences through sport that enable them to challenge those forces that contribute to women's subordination.

Method

Sample

Varsity women athletes were selected from lists provided by athletic directors at three Division I universities (two Midwestern and one Southern) representing three major athletic conferences. These rosters consisted of all women athletes participating in the school's intercollegiate sport program during the 1990-91 school year and who had completed at least one year of athletic eligibility. Different universities were chosen to reduce the possibility that findings might reflect the uniqueness of a particular institution.

A final sample size between 20 and 30 athletes was desired since it was manageable for telephone interviews, yet diverse enough to permit a wide range of sport experiences. As it was anticipated that not all athletes would agree to participate in the study, a larger number of names than needed were randomly drawn from the lists provided by the three universities. Seventy-eight athletes (twenty-six from each school) were mailed a letter explaining the importance and general purpose of the study. We indicated our interest was in learning athletes' viewpoints about various dimensions of their sport experience. Those willing to be included returned an informed consent form and were later contacted by telephone to establish a convenient interview date and time. Since specific interview topics were not mentioned in the cover letter, there was little reason to suspect that nonrespondents would be notably different from participants on issues central to this research.

Twenty-four athletes (10-5-9 from each school) agreed to participate in the study and granted permission for a tape-recorded telephone interview. Women athletes in the sample were currently involved in a variety of sports—basketball (n=5), track and field (n=4), volleyball (n=3), swimming (n=3), softball (n=3), tennis (n=2), diving (n=2), and gymnastics (n=2). With an average age of 20.2 years and overwhelmingly white (92%), the sample contained 2 freshmen, 9 sophomores, 5 juniors, and 8 seniors. The majority of athletes (n=22) were recipients of an athletic scholarship. Due to limited variation in both ethnic composition of the sample and scholarship status of the athletes, results are primarily generalizable to white female athletes with athletic scholarships.

Procedures

Data reported in this paper are part of a larger interview study examining several aspects of the college sport experience of women athletes. A significant portion of the interview focused on the relationship between women's sport participation and various types of empowerment, including that at the personal, group, and societal levels. The present work explores what respondents perceived as outcomes of sport participation at the personal or individual level. For example, athletes were asked general questions about such issues as what they personally gain or lose from sport participation, how sport makes them feel and what it means to them, what they learn about themselves from sport participation, ways sport might assist or hinder their interactions outside of sport, and the extent to which sport participation affects them differently than other activities. Rather than targeting specific outcomes of sport in our questioning, we allowed the athletes' responses to guide the analyses. Probing techniques were utilized to encourage athletes to elaborate on their responses.

Given the geographical distance between the three universities, telephone interviews were the most feasible data collection technique. Two trained females conducted the interviews with the 24 athletes. Efforts were made to establish rapport and trust between the interviewer and athlete. For example, the gender of the interviewers, their past participation in intercollegiate sport, and their understanding of the sport context facilitated open and empathic interaction. Interviews were tape-recorded and lasted approximately 50 to 90 minutes. In order to encourage athletes to fully discuss topics most salient to their lived experiences, interview questions were open-ended.

Data Analysis

Verbatim transcriptions of the telephone interviews were prepared. To protect the confidentiality of respondents, code names and numbers were assigned to each transcription. Three individuals independently performed a content analysis of the interview data in order to identify common personal outcomes of sport participation. Results of this task yielded a very high level of consistency among the researchers. Upon completion of this analysis, the investigators mutually agreed upon a set of coding categories depicting various concepts, themes, and patterns (Bogdan & Biklen, 1982).

Relative to this paper, the focus was on outcomes that women as a group traditionally have not experienced. Summary sheets were developed and all relevant comments from the interviews for each of these categories were noted. For example, summary sheets were created for personal empowerment outcomes such as sense of accomplishment, body image, independence, mastery, sense of control, self-efficacy, confidence, determination, and assertiveness.

Rather than constructing a profile representative of all athletes, data reflect both commonalities and variations in responses. However, given the small sample size, findings are not differentiated by subgroup membership (e.g., sport team, ethnicity, grade level). In addition, the results concerning personal empowerment represent a portion of the total interview and only one aspect of the overall sport experience of women athletes.

Result

Athletes' responses to items related to outcomes of sport participation were generally positive in nature, suggesting that these individuals felt sport was beneficial. In interpreting these results, two points should be kept in mind. Although not the focus of this paper, there was evidence in athletes' responses that disempowering forces coexist in college sport (e.g., homophobia, discrimination, pressure to win). These forces may work in opposition to the empowering outcomes discussed in this paper. Also, given the positive outcomes often emphasized by the sport culture in which athletes are socialized (Adler & Adler, 1991; Sage, 1990), these women may not fully understand how the sport system can disadvantage them. However, since the purpose of this paper concerned empowering outcomes that challenge traditional socialization patterns for women, the presence of disempowering and/or unrecognized outcomes of sport does not detract from the findings.

Analysis of athletes' comments suggests three main outcomes of sport participation reflecting personal empowerment. These were (a) bodily competence, (b) perceptions of a competent self, and (c) a proactive approach to life.

Bodily Competence

One empowering theme emerging from the comments of these athletes concerned a positive perception of their bodily competence. Development

of such a perspective is particularly critical for women given the historical neglect of women's potential for physicality (Vertinsky, 1987). Since females have neither been provided opportunities nor been encouraged to achieve their bodily potential, they are often not in accord with their bodies. Contributing to this lack of harmony is the internalization of body norms for women defined by men (Hall, 1990; Vertinsky, 1987). Such standards perpetuate women's weakness and dependency as they focus on a small, petite, and fragile body (Lenskyj, 1986).

When questioned about the general outcomes of sport participation, the majority of respondents mentioned factors related to the development of a strong and competent body. Several comments of athletes emphasized the health benefits of sport involvement. Participation in physical activity increased the health consciousness of athletes and enhanced understanding of how to care for the body (e.g., knowledge about nutrition, role of exercise, amount of sleep). As one track and field athlete stated, "If I wasn't involved in sport, I wouldn't care as much about my health." A swimmer added, "I think your body is really very important . . . I don't think a lot of women [nonathletes] understand how important your body is and keeping it in sense of personal control over their bodies."

A second aspect of bodily competence was related to the emergence of body mastery. Sport allowed these women a unique context in which to experience a strong and capable body and to maximize physical potential. Through sport, respondents learned how to use and control their bodies, as well as the means to keep the body in good physical condition. For example, a tennis player indicated that through sport she learned "the different ways your body will move and stretch . . . and how much you can lift." When asked if sport provided the athlete with something that she could not obtain in other contexts, several women mentioned the physical nature of sport participation. As one basketball player commented:

> The physical element . . . is very important . . . working through exhaustion, working through preseason conditioning, and forcing your body to do things that your mind thinks it can't . . . there's a lot of things the physical element can teach you.

Such a sense of body mastery encourages the development of independence and control in their lives.

Viewing one's body as strong and capable can empower women by emphasizing the enabling aspects of the body. This perception challenges prevailing patriarchal depictions of women's bodies as objects and shifts the focus to women's bodies as subjects (Hall, 1990). A competent and healthy body can help women feel confident in meeting other challenges and tasks, as well as enhance their sense of security, mastery, and control. Not only does such a view of the body encompass instrumental aspects, but it also facilitates the development of the expressive and creative dimensions of the body (Theberge, 1987).

Competent Self

Another major theme emanating from the responses of athletes related to their self-perceptions of competence. Conceptually consistent with Cantor and Bernay's (1992) "competent self," such a characteristic is premised on the existence of a strong sense of self. Women traditionally have relied upon others' definitions of themselves and have seen most life events as outside their control (Cantor & Bernay, 1992). Alternatively, the competent self entails a view of self based on both a positive personal definition and an internal locus of control. Central to the development of a competent self is an individual's ability to see challenges as possibilities rather than obstacles (Cantor & Bernay, 1992). When self-perceptions are both positive and stable, individuals do not feel threatened by situations involving risk or challenge. Moreover, negative situational outcomes (e.g., failure, losing) are not powerful enough to destroy secure self-identities.

Athletes' responses indicated several ways in which sport helped to develop this notion of the competent self. An essential foundational component underlying this construct related to an athlete's feeling of self-efficacy. Frequently underdeveloped in women, self-efficacy refers to an individual's belief in her ability to exercise control over given events (Ozer & Bandura, 1990). Athletes reported the feeling of being able to achieve goals through hard work and persistence. An example of self-efficacy is reflected in the response of the following track and field athlete when asked how sport participation impacted her life outside of sport:

> You are the one making it happen. And you are the one in the driver's seat. It's whatever you decide, whatever you do that is going to make it happen and consequently you take the credit or you take the consequences.

Further, a volleyball player stated that sport "gives me a sense of satisfaction when I see a problem and . . . I can learn how to do it and learn how to do it well."

The notion of "being in control" was common throughout the interview responses. As a result of their sport participation, athletes "learned to make decisions," believed they could "set their own limits," and were willing to "go for it" when they desired something. Control over self was often evident in athletes' responses. As one track and field participant remarked, "What it [sport] gives me is a self-assurance of my own . . . capabilities, and my own self-strength and self-power." Other respondents indicated that sport provided a feeling of security not experienced in other realms of their lives, as well as helping them control emotions in stressful situations. For example, a track and field athlete attributed sport with "keeping me levelheaded."

In addition to self-efficacy, athletes frequently credited sport involvement with the development of a high level of self-esteem. When asked how sport participation made them feel, athletes expressed high self-esteem in such comments as "sport made me feel confident," sport provides a "source of pride" and a "keen sense of your inner strength," "sport enhances who I am," and "I have a feeling of self-worth." Athletes also discussed the increased self-esteem they developed not only in a sport context, but in life in general. As one track and field athlete commented:

> Sport is the most important thing in my life right now . . . it is the thing that I am getting the most positive feedback from in a lot of aspects, mentally and physically . . . A lot of things I learn I can transfer and try to make myself feel as confident in my personal life as I do in athletics.

Another factor contributing to the emergence of a competent self was the ability of sport participation to facilitate independence in the individual. As a swimmer stated:

> I would say that we [athletes] are a lot stronger than the average female . . . because we are more dependent on ourselves and don't depend on someone else to get us through.

Others added that sport participation developed independence earlier than what would have been the case without sport. This independence contrasts with the feelings of dependency often experienced by women. Being an athlete also instilled a sense of specialness or uniqueness since people look up to athletes. As one volleyball player expressed, "It's something not everybody can be; it takes a lot of dedication and hard work. "When asked how she feels at the time she actually participates in her sport activity, a swimmer indicated, "You don't feel like an ordinary person. You feel above the rest."

Athletes also frequently mentioned the contribution of sport participation to enhancing their feelings of competency and accomplishment. Respondents expressed pride and satisfaction in the commitment, motivation, and dedication that they drew upon to succeed in the sports world. These sentiments were reflected in the response of a swimmer who commented:

> I've really accomplished something with my life . . . just looking back on how much time and effort I put into it [sport], it just makes me feel good.

Such feelings of accomplishment were not limited to the sport context, however; athletes often noted that the sport experience assists them in handling difficult situations outside of sport. As one softball player remarked when asked about the impact of sport, "I think I can make it through tougher situations within life now." A tennis player added:

> If I participate like I do in tennis in the classroom and towards friends and other things, then I have a feeling I am going to do good.

Finally, sport participation provided women athletes with a sense of self-actualization. Respondents indicated satisfaction knowing that they had used their ability "to its fullest." A feeling of self-fulfillment resulted when athletes realized that they had worked hard to meet the challenges of sport. As a diver stated:

> It takes a special kind of person to put that much time into something, to work that hard at something . . . I try to be the best at it . . . I've tried to do that and I think I've succeeded.

Further, discussing how the challenge of sport participation impacts her life, one track and field athlete commented:

> Athletics has really been a kind of growing process . . . facing things head on, and not only just working on being physically fit, and being ready for competition . . . but also being mentally fit.

Based on the voices of these athletes, sport participation was related to the development of a competent self. Such a view of self is empowering for women in that it encourages individuals to see themselves as capable and competent, as well as possessing the ability to control events in their lives. This view of self lays the foundation for women's proaction.

A Proactive Approach to Life

A final theme underlying the comments of women athletes concerned the adoption of a proactive approach to life. Similar to Cantor and Bernay's (1992) "creative aggression," proaction includes the ability to seek challenge and take risks, set goals and establish strategies for achieving them, and feel comfortable being assertive and competitive. Women traditionally have not been encouraged to develop such qualities; in fact, these abilities are often considered unfeminine or unacceptable to display (Cantor & Bernay, 1992). If a passive rather than a proactive approach is adopted, women will likely remain in a subordinate position and continue to lack control over life events.

Responses of athletes revealed ways sport participation related to a proactive approach to life. Given the goal-oriented nature of sport, athletes frequently mentioned how sport provided them with experience in formulating goals. Not only did this goal setting assist them in the sport domain, but athletes were able to apply this ability to other aspects of their lives (e.g., academic, career, personal). For example, one swimmer illustrated the importance of the goal setting learned in sport when she commented:

> I just have to sit down and tell myself I've planned it (the swimming race) and I want to do it this way . . . and it's the same in the class, I just have to make up my mind that I'm going to study hard and do well in the class too.

Respondents also remarked that sport participation assisted them in developing strategies for obtaining their goals in nonsport situations (e.g., getting good grades, making decisions). When asked what sport participation means to her, a gymnast indicated:

> It [sport] has helped me throughout my life in other areas . . . it helps . . . as far as determination in my school work . . . whenever I want something I have a pretty big desire to go for it. And I think that's from participating in sport.

A second example of proaction mentioned by athletes was a willingness to seek challenge and take risks. Sport participation encouraged women to approach a variety of situations, including those in which success was not guaranteed. Athletes felt that their experiences in confronting challenge and risk in sport assisted them in adopting an assertive approach to life. Due in part to the strong sense of self (i.e., competent self) developed as a result of sport, athletes generally did not fear failure and thus were able to separate lack of success from their self-worth. As a tennis player stated, "I can handle losing if someone beats me." Similarly, a diver commented that she learned "it is alright to fail but you always have to get back up and try again no matter what happens to you." One swimmer added that "if things do get stressful, I can handle the situation better just because I've had more experience (dealing with stress)."

Another indicator of proaction discussed by respondents concerned the adoption of a competitive orientation. Such a focus enables women to develop a more assertive approach to life events. Sport provided numerous opportunities for women to test their capabilities and to compare themselves with others. Several respondents indicated that sport provided training in competition that they could not obtain in other activities. When one volleyball player was asked what sport did for her, she replied:

> I just love the competition. It's fun . . . I love any kind of challenge. And through sport, that's one way to fulfill that.

A softball player added that "it [sport] helps you . . . because the real world is very competitive. So I think sports definitely help you with that edge."

A final proactive dimension related to sport participation was persistence and determination. Such an orientation is critical once goals and strategies are identified and implementation begins. Since sport consists of numerous situations that entail pressure, obstacles, and frustration, athletes credited sport participation with learning how to overcome such challenges. As a swimmer stated, "I realize that I am a hard worker and can really dedicate myself to something that is very time-consuming and stressful and I can get through it." Others indicated sport taught them to "accept failure," "realize that not everything comes easy," and "not to quit and give up." Athletes also commented that they learned to cope with failure through their sport and not to let defeat deter their efforts in achieving goals.

Sport participation was thus empowering to women in that it provided athletes the opportunity to gain experience in the process of goal attainment. Through the sport context, women learn how to set goals, develop strategies to achieve goals, and persist in the pursuit of goals. Such skills help women to take an active role in controlling and determining the direction of their lives and not to retreat from challenges or obstacles. Experiencing themselves as effective actors rather than reactors encourages women to differentiate themselves from others (Kieffer, 1983–1984) and transforms women's view of self as object to that of subject (Stromquist, 1988).

Discussion

Results from this study suggest that sport represents one vehicle for enhancing the control a woman athlete has over her life. Although interview questions were open-ended, respondents generally mentioned positive outcomes of their sport experience at the personal level. In particular, sport participation assists these athletes in developing an increased sense of bodily competence, a competent self, and a proactive approach to life. Since women have traditionally lacked such qualities, acquisition of these skills can personally empower women by facilitating opportunities for advancement.

Relative to the experiences of women intercollegiate athletes, two aspects of the empowerment process are noteworthy—the sport context in which the empowerment occurs and the nature of the empowerment itself. First, unlike the context found in woman-controlled sport organizations, including feminist or lesbian sport teams, college sport generally has a male-dominated sport structure that is product-oriented, competitive, and professionalized (Blinde, 1989a). Further, this setting is controlled by men and dominated by notions of masculinity (Messner, 1990; Theberge, 1987). Such a context, however, provides athletes the occasion to develop skills and attributes often denied women, thus giving them a greater opportunity to gain control over their lives.

Second, concerning the interpretation of athletes' comments, the type of power relayed in the responses of these athletes is significant. Despite participating in a sport structure often replete with male values, women athletes rarely mention empowering outcomes consistent with traditional (or male) notions of power. The traditional conceptualization of power emphasizes the ability to control or dominate others, focusing on such traits as authority, strength, aggression, and forcefulness (Cantor & Bernay, 1992; Gross, 1985; Theberge, 1987).

Conversely, the type of power that athletes in this study generally discuss is creative and enabling. When an athlete alludes to feelings of power or control, the focus is usually in reference to herself rather than to others. For example, women comment about gaining mastery over their own bodies and lives instead of demonstrating control over others.

The nature of power primarily discussed by women athletes is consistent with feminist reconceptualizations of power (Cantor & Bernay, 1992; Hartsock, 1983; Theberge, 1987; Wartenberg, 1988). As opposed to more traditional male notions, feminists have emphasized the capacity, potential, and creativity of power. This form of power is enabling in that it accentuates one's potential and self-actualization as opposed to controlling others. Rather than achieving personal betterment at the expense of others, power is gained through altering one's perceptions of self.

Although it may appear that certain athletes' comments are consistent with male notions of power (e.g., "forcing your body to do things that your mind thinks it can't," "you are the one in the driver's seat"), it is important to remember the relative position of men and women in both the sport structure and the larger society. As a disadvantaged group, women are not in the same position as men to use power to dominate others. Thus, similar comments by male and female athletes regarding such qualities as control and assertiveness may not constitute identical forms of power.

Men and women may experience power differently due to contrasting gender-role socialization, differences in gender identity formulation, and varying lived experiences due to their position in the social structure (Chodorow, 1974; Gilligan, 1982; Hartsock, 1983; Wartenberg, 1988). Moreover, different notions of power may relate to the value system that emerges from the more commercialized and professionalized sport form found in men's programs. The conceptualization of power as relayed by women athletes is not necessarily consistent with that associated with the experiences of male athletes in intercollegiate sport programs (Messner & Sabo, 1990; Whitson, 1990). Often emphasizing the more traditional notion of power, sport encourages males to "experience their bodies, and therefore themselves, in forceful, space-occupying, even dominating ways" (Whitson, 1990, p. 23).

Although the women athletes in this study acquired skills that enhance their sense of perceived control, it should be emphasized that these empowering gains coexist with forces that can be disempowering in nature. For example, the presence of both homophobia within the women's sport structure and an overemphasis on winning may interfere with the effective utilization of these empowering outcomes (Blinde, 1989b; Blinde & Taub, in press; Lenskyj, 1990). Also, fear of being labeled lesbian often leads women athletes to disassociate from many qualities previously identified as empowering (e.g., reluctance to develop a muscular body, hesitant to be aggressive, feeling a lack of control; see Blinde & Taub, in press). In addition, a win-at-all-cost philosophy may counter athletes' perceptions of being in control of their body when they are encouraged to play with pain as well as reach unrealistic weight standards (Blinde, 1989b). Such outcomes may perpetuate alienation rather than accordance with one's body.

The empowering outcomes identified in this paper (i.e., a positive view of one's body, a sense of personal competence, and a willingness to act) do not necessarily assure an understanding of the structural context or existing framework in which the skills are to be used (Hicks, 1990). Moreover, personally empowering qualities could become counterproductive if women have a false sense of control or power, or internalize belief systems that disadvantage certain groups. In order to maximize usage of these newly gained qualities, women must be able to critically analyze the institutionalized structures and power relations that maintain patriarchal privilege (Brown & Ziefert, 1988; Hicks, 1990). The formulation of strategies to effect change (Kieffer, 1983–1984; Rappaport, 1985) and the linkage of personal competence with the political realm (Brown & Ziefert, 1988) strengthen one's participatory competence. Development of this consciousness in women then provides the impetus for empowerment at the group and institutional levels. Attainment of such levels of consciousness may be difficult since women athletes as a group generally do not possess a feminist perspective (Boutilier & SanGiovanni, 1983).

Although intercollegiate athletics is not an empowered institution in terms of women's position in this structure, it may nevertheless represent an empowering institution at the personal level. Even with the presence of counterforces that disempower women, sport allows athletes the opportunity to "get in touch" with their bodies and to develop a sense of bodily competence. Along with this change of bodily perception, women begin to view themselves as competent beings and thus feel secure in adopting a proactive approach to life situations. Women displaying such a perspective respond to obstacles and structural barriers with increased determination rather than passive acceptance. Through the process of personal empowerment, women athletes are thus in a better position to take control of their lives.

Conclusion

This research has provided evidence that sport may have the potential to empower women athletes at the personal level. To extend the findings of this study, future research should examine the dynamics of the empowerment process in greater detail, including differential experiences of subgroups within the female athlete population. Beyond identifying commonalities and variations in the experiences of the overall sample, as was done in the present work, attention needs to be given to the uniqueness that may differentiate various groups. For example, diversity in ethnicity, scholarship status, grade level, sexual orientation, social class, and athletic divisional level should be incorporated into a sample design. Moreover, since research on women athletes has indicated both empowering and disempowering outcomes from sport, more focus needs to be placed on the conflict that characterizes women's sport participation. Understanding the net effect of these contradictory outcomes should provide additional insight into the lived experiences of women athletes.

References

Adler, P.A., & Adler, P.(1991). *Backboards & blackboards: College athletes and role engulfment.* New York: Columbia University Press.

Beck, B. (1980). The future of women's sport: Issues, insights, and struggle. In D.F. Sabo & R. Runfola (Eds.), *Jock: Sports and male identity* (pp. 299–314). Englewood Cliffs, NJ: Prentice-Hall.

Birrell, S., & Slatton, B. (1981, November). *The embarrassment of competition: Why feminists avoid sport.* Paper presented at annual meetings of the North American Society for the Sociology of Sport, Fort Worth, TX.

Blinde, E.M.(1989a). Participation in a male sport model and the value alienation of female intercollegiate athletes. *Sociology of Sport Journal, 6,* 36–49.

Blinde, E.M. (1989b). Unequal exchange and exploitation in college sport: The case of the female athlete. *Arena Review, 13*(2), 110–123.

Blinde, E.M., & Greendorfer, S.L. (1992). Conflict and the college sport experience of women athletes. *Women in Sport & Physical Activity Journal, 1,* 97–113.

Blinde, E.M., & Taub, D.E. (in press). Homophobia and women's sport: The disempowerment of athletes. *Sociological Focus.*

Bogdan, R.C., & Biklen, S.K. (1982). *Qualitative research for education.* Boston: Allyn and Bacon.

Boutilier, M.A., & SanGiovanni, L.(1983). *The sporting woman.* Champaign, IL: Human Kinetics.

Brown, K.S., & Ziefert, M. (1988). Crisis resolution, competence, and empowerment: A service model for women. *Journal of Primary Prevention, 9*(1/2), 92–103.

Brown, P. (1981). Women and competence. In A. N. Maluccio (Ed.), *Promoting competence in clients: A new/old approach to social work practice* (pp. 213–235). New York: Free Press.

Cantor, D.W., & Bernay, T. (1992). *Women in power: The secrets of leadership.* Boston: Houghton Mifflin.

Chodorow, N. (1974). Family structure and feminine personality. In M. Z. Rosaldo, L. Lamphere, & J. Bamberger (Eds.), *Woman, culture, and society* (pp. 43–66). Stanford, CA: Stanford University Press.

Coll, R. (1986). Power, powerlessness, and empowerment. *Religious Education, 81,* 412–423.

Conger, J.A., & Kanungo, R.N. (1988). The empowerment process: Integrating theory and practice. *Academy of Management Review, 13,* 471–482.

Gilligan, C. (1982). *In a different voice: Psychological theory and women's development.* Cambridge, MA: Harvard University Press.

Gross, S.J. (1985). Personal power and empowerment. *Contemporary Education, 56,* 137–143.

Gutierrez, L.M. (1990). Working with women of color: An empowerment perspective. *Social Work, 35,* 149–153.

Hall, M.A. (1990). How should we theorize gender in the context of sport? In M.A. Messner & D.F. Sabo (Eds.), *Sport, men, and the gender order: Critical feminist perspectives* (pp. 223–239). Champaign, IL: Human Kinetics.

Hartsock, N.C.M. (1983). *Money, sex, and power: Toward a feminist historical materialism.* New York: Longman.

Hicks, L. E. (1990). A feminist analysis of empowerment and community in art education. *Studies in Art Education, 32,* 36–46.

Kieffer, C.H. (1983–1984). Citizen empowerment: A developmental perspective. *Prevention in Human Services, 3*(2/3), 9–36.

Lenskyj, H. (1986). *Out of bounds: Women, sport, and sexuality.* Toronto: Women's Press.

Lenskyj, H. (1990). Power and play: Gender and sexuality issues in sport and physical activity. *International Review for Sociology of Sport*, **25**, 235–245.

MacKinnon, C.A. (1987). *Feminism unmodified: Discourses on life and law.* Cambridge, MA: Harvard University Press.

McWhirter, E.H. (1991). Empowerment in counseling. *Journal of Counseling & Development*, **69**, 222–227.

Messner, M. (1990). Boyhood, organized sports, and the construction of masculinities. *Journal of Contemporary Ethnography*, **18**, 416–444.

Messner, M.A., & Sabo, D.F. (1990). Toward a critical feminist reappraisal of sport, men, and the gender order. In M.A. Messner & D.F. Sabo (Eds.), *Sport, men, and the gender order: Critical feminist perspectives* (pp. 1–15). Champaign, IL: Human Kinetics.

Ozer, E.M., & Bandura, A. (1990). Mechanisms governing empowerment effects: A self-efficacy analysis. *Journal of Personality and Social Psychology*, **58**, 472–486.

Polk, B.B. (1974). Male power and the women's movement. *Journal of Applied Behavioral Science*, **10**, 415–431.

Rappaport, J. (1983–1984). Studies in empowerment: Introduction to the issue. *Prevention in Human Services*, **3**(2/3), 1–7.

Rappaport, J. (1985). The power of empowerment language. *Social Policy*, **16**(2), 15–21.

Riger, S. (1983–1984). Vehicles for empowerment: The case of feminist movement organizations. *Prevention in Human Services*, **3**(2/3), 99–117.

Sage, G.H. (1990). *Power and ideology in American sport. A critical perspective.* Champaign, IL: Human Kinetics.

Schur, E.M. (1984). *Labeling women deviant: Gender, stigma, and social control.* New York: McGraw-Hill.

Simmons, C.H., & Parsons, R.J. (1983). Empowerment for role alternatives in adolescence. *Adolescence*, **18**, 193–200.

Staples, L.H. (1990). Powerful ideas about empowerment. *Administration in Social Work*, **14**(2), 29–42.

Stromquist, N.P. (1988). Women's education in development: From welfare to empowerment. *Convergence*, **21**, 5–17.

Swift, C., & Levin, G. (1987). Empowerment: An emerging mental health technology. *Journal of Primary Prevention*, **8**(1/2), 71–94.

Theberge, N. (1987). Sport and women's empowerment. *Women's Studies International Forum*, **10**, 387–393.

Vertinsky, P. (1987). Body shapes: The role of the medical establishment in informing female exercise and physical education in nineteenth-century North America. In J.A. Mangan & R.J. Park (Eds.), *From 'fair sex' to feminism: Sport and the socialization of women in the industrial and post-industrial eras* (pp. 256–281). London: Frank Cass.

Wartenberg, T.E. (1988). The concept of power in feminist theory. *Praxis International*, **8**, 301–316.

Whitson, D. (1990). Sport in the social construction of masculinity. In M.A. Messner & D.F. Sabo (Eds.), *Sport, men, and the gender order: Critical feminist perspectives* (pp. 19–29). Champaign, IL: Human Kinetics.

The College Life Experiences of African American Women Athletes

Robert M. Sellers
Gabriel P. Kuperminc
Alphonse Damas Jr.

The present study provides a descriptive analysis of four areas of African American women student athletes' college life experiences: academic performance; alienation and abuse; perceived social advantage as the result of athletics; and life satisfaction. Multivariate comparisons were made between the four areas of college life experiences of 154 African American women student athletes and 793 white women student athletes, 250 African American women nonathletes, and 628 African American men student athletes from a national sample of 39 NCAA Division I universities. Overall, African American women student athletes are performing adequately academically, integrating socially within the university, perceiving some social advantage as the result of being athletes, and are fairly satisfied with their life. Their experiences seem most consistent with African American women nonathletes. Results are discussed in the context of potential policy recommendations as well as the need for more research on this particular population.

Key Words: African American; athletics; black; sport; student athlete, women.

Introduction

Three important tenets of community psychology research are (a) to include groups who have historically been ignored in the research process; (b) to investigate how the person and the social ecology interact to influence behavior; and (c) to use research to inform social policy in hopes of making a change in the lives of the people which we study. The present study attempts to accomplish all three goals by investigating the college life experiences of African American women athletes. The present study presents an empirical, descriptive analysis of their socioeconomic and educational backgrounds as well as four areas of their college life experiences. The four areas examined include academic performance, alienation and abuse, perceptions of social advantage, and satisfaction.

Dearth of Research on African American Women Student Athletes

Studies of the life experiences of African American female athletes are virtually nonexistent. Although African American female athletes are often included within the samples of studies focusing on African American athletes and female athletes, results of these studies are seldom interpreted with the African American female athlete in mind. Our literature review revealed only two empirical studies that focused specifically on the college life experiences of African American women student athletes (see Evans & Quarterman, 1983; Prakasa Rao & Overman, 1984). Studies of African American athletes' collegiate experiences have typically focused on African American men. When studies include both

Reprinted from Sellers, Kuperminc, and Damas, 1997.

male and female, there is a tendency to ignore gender differences (e.g., Center for the Study of Athletics, 1989a). Similarly, studies of women athletes' life experiences have typically focused on white women. Those studies that have used a racially diverse sample have tended to ignore race differences in the experiences of women athletes (e.g., Center for the Study of Athletics, 1989b). Thus, the current research literature represents a *de facto* assumption that the life experiences of African American female athletes do not differ in meaningful ways from either African American male athletes or white female athletes. However, some researchers question this assumption of uniformity of athletic experience across gender and race (see Bird & Cripe, 1986; Corbett & Johnson, 1993; Duda & Allison, 1990).

College Life Experience and Academic Perfomance

Consistent with the conceptual work of Bell (1986), Bronfenbrenner and Crouter (1982), and Seidman (1991), the present research views student athletes' college life experiences as a mediating factor in the relationship between protective/risk factors (such as gender, race, socioeconomic background) and important social outcomes (such as graduation, upward social mobility, and psychological well-being). The college life experience represents the ecological context that student athletes encounter during their stay on campus. Although research examining student athletes' college life experience is sparse, there is a substantial body of research investigating the relationship between nonathletic students' perceptions and experiences on campus and their academic performance. A number of investigations have linked college life experiences outside of the classroom to college students' persistence rates and overall academic performance (e.g., Defour & Hirsch, 1990; Nettles & Johnson, 1987; Stage, 1988, 1989; Stoecker, Pascarella, & Wolfle, 1988; Terenzini & Pascarella, 1978; Tracey & Sedlacek, 1984). Within this literature, a number of theoretical and empirical models have been presented to explain students' present college experiences as well as their academic background in determining academic outcomes. Within this research, evidence of gender and race differences with regard to college experiences and their influence on students' academic performance has been found (e.g., Nettles & Johnson, 1987). For example, social and academic integration in the university community seem especially critical to the academic success of African American students (Allen, 1985; Loo &

Rolison, 1986). To fully understand the impact the ecological context has on the academic and psychological functioning of African American women student athletes, an examination of their on-campus life experiences is needed.

Social Policies Affecting African American Women Student Athletes

African American women student athletes are at the center of the two most important issues facing intercollegiate athletics in the 1990s: (a) the enforcement of Title IX, a federal regulation prohibiting sex discrimination in educational institutions; and (b) the academic reform movement within the National Collegiate Athletic Association (NCAA). Pressure from Congress and the Justice Department has forced institutions to ensure that their intercollegiate athletic programs comply with Title IX. Title IX mandates that any educational institution receiving federal funds must provide equal educational opportunities, including intercollegiate athletics, for both men and women. The enforcement of Title IX should provide greater opportunities for women in athletics. Meanwhile, a reform movement within the National Collegiate Athletic Association (NCAA) has attempted to enforce the academic viability of student athletes by raising initial eligibility requirements (i.e., SAT and high school grade point average) for potential student athletes. African American student athletes are disproportionately excluded from the opportunity of an athletic scholarship as a result of the reform legislation (McArdle & Hamagami, 1994; NCAA, 1991).

It is an open question as to which social policy has the greatest impact on African American women student athletes. The dearth of research on African American women student athletes makes evaluation of the impact of both gender equity and academic reform legislation on African American women student athletes' experiences tenuous. A baseline description of the social ecological experience of African American student athletes provides an important reference from which to evaluate the impact of future social policy.

Review of Literature on Race, Gender, and Athletic Status Differences in College Experiences

Although there is little research directly examining the college experiences of African American women student athletes, researchers have found important race, gender, and athletic status differences in experiences. This research provides direction for the present investigation on four areas of college life experience.

Academic Performance

The research literature on precollege predictors of student athletes' academic performance has reported gender and race differences in overall academic performance. There are significant race differences in both academic background and college academic performance for student athletes. African American student athletes come from poorer educational backgrounds than their white counterparts (Center for the Study of Athletics, 1989a; Sellers, Kuperminc, & Waddell, 1991), and once in college, they perform less well academically (e.g., Ervin, Saunders, Gillis, & Hogrebe, 1985; Kiger & Lorentzen, 1986; Purdy, Eitzen, & Hufnagel, 1982; Sellers, 1992; Shapiro, 1984). With respect to gender differences, female athletes achieve higher grade-point averages (Center for the Study of Athletics, 1989b; Kiger & Lorentzen, 1986) and graduate at a higher rate than male athletes (NCAA, 1995). Graduation data specifically on African American women athletes are consistent with previous findings of race and gender differences in academic performance. African American women student athletes graduate at a rate of 49% which is considerably lower than the graduation rate of 69% for white women athletes (NCAA, 1995). On the other hand, African American women athletes graduate at a significantly higher rate than both African American men athletes (42%) and African American women nonathletes (41%).

Isolation and Alienation

Consistent with the person-environment fit conceptual framework, researchers have consistently delineated integration within the university setting as an important component of successful college student development (e.g., Bean & Bradley, 1986; Nettles & Johnson, 1987; Terenzini & Pascarella, 1978; Tinto, 1975, 1987). Integration within the university community has been positively associated with academic performance for minority college students (Gosman, Dandridge, Nettles, & Thoeny, 1983; Stoecker, Pascarella, & Wolfle, 1988) as well as African American graduate students (Defour & Hirsch, 1990). For African Americans, the racial climate of the environment significantly impacts their feelings of integration and subsequent behavior and well-being (Beckham, 1988; Rutledge, 1982;

Sedlacek, 1987). Unfortunately, for many African American students the college environment can be both hostile and alienating. Suen (1983) found that African American college students report experiencing greater levels of alienation than white college students. Similarly, Allen (1988) noted that nearly half of his sample of African American students at six predominantly white universities reported feelings of alienation from the general campus life. Experiences with sexism may result in African American women having very different perceptions of the racial climate of their universities than African American men (Smith & Stewart, 1983).

Along with being at risk for alienation and abuse as a result of their status as African American students, African American women student athletes also have to deal with the additional demands associated with participating in intercollegiate athletics. For instance, women student athletes spend approximately 25 hours a week in athletic-related activities (Center for the Study of Athletics, 1989b). Some researchers argue that these demands can help isolate student athletes from the rest of the campus environment (Adler & Adler, 1991; Davis, 1990; Sellers, 1993). The time demands associated with intercollegiate athletics make it difficult for athletes to become involved in student activities outside of athletics which has been associated with positive student development (Boyer & Sedlacek, 1988; Sedlacek, 1987). Feelings of isolation from the rest of the student body can result in poorer social and emotional development. As a result, student athletes' emotional and social development are often hampered (Petitpas, 1981).

Perceptions of Social Advantage As the Result of Athletics

Although the time demands associated with intercollegiate athletics may result in feelings of alienation, participation in intercollegiate athletics has also been related to positive personal development (Danish, Petitpas, & Hale, 1990; Duke, Johnson, & Nowicki, 1987; Iso-Aloha & Hatfeld, 1986; Picou & Curry, 1974; Ryaii, 1989; Sonestroem, 1982). Participation in intercollegiate athletics provides the opportunity to develop a number of skills which may enhance the personal competence of the student athlete (Danish, 1983). Benefits that athletes report receiving from their participation in intercollegiate athletics include learning to make a commitment, the opportunity to travel, self-control, learning patience, and becoming disciplined (Danish, 1983). Also, Ryan (1989) found in a national sample of college students that those who participated in intercollegiate athletics reported greater motivation to earn a college degree, stronger interpersonal and leadership skills, as well as greater satisfaction with their overall college experience. With respect to women athletes, the Center for the Study of Athletics (1989b) reported that the majority of women student athletes feel that it is easier for them as the result of being an athlete to learn new skills, learn about themselves, take on leadership responsibilities, and set and achieve personal goals. Participation in sports may result in the development of skills and competencies that are important in later life. In fact, some psychologists have trailed athletics as an important intervention for preventing and/or reducing at-risk behavior in youths (e.g., Agnew & Peterson, 1989; Burling, Seidner, Robbins-Sisco, & Krinsky, 1992; Cusson, 1989; Reppucci, 1987).

Satisfaction

Another potentially important area of the African American student athletes' college life experience is the extent to which she is satisfied. Because college athletes are required to perform the duties of both student and athlete, any assessment of their life satisfaction should include domain-specific assessments as well as an assessment of their overall satisfaction with life. With respect to measures of global satisfaction, the research literature suggests that athletes tend to report higher levels of satisfaction than nonathletes (Pascarella & Smart, 1991; Ryan, 1989; Sellers et al., 1991). Sellers and his colleagues found that African American student athletes reported being more satisfied with life in general than African American nonathletes. In contrast, Pascarella and Smart's (1991) study of male college athletes and nonathletes did not find a significant difference for African American student athletes and nonathletes in life satisfaction. However, they did find an overall difference in satisfaction between athletes and nonathletes. The discrepancy between the Pascarella and Smart (1991) and the Sellers et al. (1991) findings may result from the inclusion of African American women student athletes in the Sellers et al. study.

In sum, the research literature suggests that student athletes experience college in ways that are different from nonathletes. Many of these experiences are beneficial such as perceptions that they receive important inter- and intrapersonal competence as a result of their athletic participation. They also report that they are more satisfied than other college students with their lives. The research literature also suggests significant race and gender differences in the way in which student athletes experience college. With respect to academic performance whites and women perform better than African Americans and men. Exposure to racism and sexism also differentially impact student athletes' experiences of social isolation and alienation. Unfortunately, as noted above, these findings do not directly address the experiences of African American women. It is the intent of the present study to address this oversight in the literature. An empirical descriptive analysis is utilized to investigate two interrelated questions. First, how do African American female student athletes experience college life? Second, do the life experiences of African American student athletes vary meaningfully as a function of gender and race? In other words, do African American female student athletes experience college differently from white female student athletes and African American male student athletes? A national sample consisting of African American female athletes, white female athletes, African American female nonathletes, and African American male athletes from 39 predominantly white institutions are employed.

Method

Sample

The present study utilizes data from a 1987 survey of a national representative sample of 5,123 full-time undergraduate student athletes and students at Division I institutions commissioned by the President's Commission of the NCAA. The students were from 42 of the 291 Division I schools in 1987-1988 randomly sampled institutions. The national survey, conducted by the American Institutes for Research (AIR), also included two comparison groups of nonathletes: a sample of African American students and a sample of students involved in extracurricular activities. (For a more complete description of the sample, see Center for the Study of Athletics, 1988.) The present study examines only students from predominantly white institutions (39 of the 42 institutions sampled). Although there may be important differences between student athletes' experiences at these institutions and at predominantly African American institutions, the fact that approximately 95% of the 302 NCAA Division I institutions are predominantly white institutions justifies a focus on these institutions as an initial investigation. An examination of differences by racial composition of the institution is also prohibited by the small number of predominantly African American institutions (3) that are included in the data set.

The sample for the present study consists of subsamples of African American female student athletes ($n = 154$), white female student athletes ($n = 793$), African American female nonathletic students ($n = 250$), and African American male athletes ($n = 628$) from the original study. The AIR data set does not report response rates by race and gender groups, thus we are unable to report a specific response rate for the subsample of the AIR data set which comprises the sample for the present study. However, the response rate for the entire AIR data set was reported as 75% (Center for the Study of Athletics, 1988).

In the present sample, approximately 75% of the African American female athletes were women's basketball players and the other 25% participated in nonrevenue-producing sports. For white female athletes, the proportions were almost reversed: Approximately 35% participated in women's basketball and 65% participated in nonrevenue sports. The distribution of sport participation is very different for African American and white athletes regardless of gender. African American athletes participate in the revenue-producing sports of football and men's and women's basketball at a rate that is greatly disproportionate to their population on campus, whereas they are underrepresented in the other nonrevenue sports (Center for the Study of Athletics, 1989a).

Procedures and Measures

Upon obtaining the informed consent of all respondents, students were administered questionnaires. The questionnaires for both the athletic and nonathletic groups were nearly identical in content but differed in their wording to correspond to respondents' group membership. The questionnaires elicited information on a variety of topics, including academic preparation, social background, personal and interpersonal experiences at college, expectations and attitudes regarding educational and career goals, and mental health. The present study investigates academic preparation, social background and four groups of variables reflective of the college life experiences of African American female athletes: These four groups of variables consist of academic performance; social isolation and alienation; perceived growth; and academic, athletic, and college life satisfaction. Factor analysis and principle components analysis were used to reduce data on various aspects of college life experience

and to construct multiitem measures of students' college life experiences. Composite variables were constructed and analyzed using both raw scores and standardized scores. Because both methods yielded results that did not differ substantively from one another, the raw score composites are reported in order to simplify interpretation of the results.

Academic Preparation and Social Background

Two measures of academic preparation were used in the present study: students' self-reported high school grade point average (HSGPA) and scores on the Scholastic Aptitude Test (SAT). HSGPA was rated on an 8-point scale in which 1 represented a grade of C- or below and 8 represented an A or A+ average. Students' combined verbal and math SAT scores were gathered from transcripts (SAT equivalent scores were computed for students who had only taken the ACT). Family income, occupational prestige, and parental education were standardized and averaged to construct a single composite measure of socioeconomic status (SES). When available, father's occupation level was coded using prestige scores from U.S. census codes; otherwise, mother's occupation was used. Students reported their parents' education levels on a 6-point scale in which 1 represented less than high school graduation and 6 represented having earned a postbaccalaureate degree (e.g., MA or PhD) (see Center for the Study of Athletics, 1988, for further details).

Academic Performance

Two indicators of collegiate academic performance were used. First, students' cumulative college grade point averages (college GPA) were collected from students' transcripts. Grades were calculated on a 4-point scale. The second indicator of academic performance was a composite variable encompassing three types of academic difficulties: whether students had been placed on academic probation; repeated a class; or received an incomplete course grade since entering college. The total number of these incidents experienced were summed to create a measure of Academic Difficulties (the range of this scale was 0–3). Examination of these variables revealed weak to moderate negative correlations with college GPA ($r = -.15$ for incomplete grades, $r = -.24$ for repeating classes, and $r = -.32$ for academic probation, all $p < .01$), and a moderate multivariate relationship ($R^2 = .12$, $p < .01$). The composite variable of academic difficulties was moderately correlated with college GPA ($r = -.28$, $p < .01$). The moderate relationships between these variables and college GPA suggest that it may be meaningful to view the construct of academic performance as multidimensional.

Isolation and Alienation

Isolation and alienation were measured as the extent to which students reported feelings of negative experiences on campus. High scores on these variables were seen as contributing to higher levels of isolation and alienation. Two composite variables were derived through principal components analyses of seven items in the questionnaire. The first composite variable was labeled Alienation/abuse (Cronbach's $\alpha = .65$) and measured the extent to which students reported feeling a lack of control, feeling isolated, feeling sexual discrimination, feeling mental abuse and physical abuse. The second composite variable was labeled Racial tension (Cronbach's $\alpha = .85$) and measured the degree to which students experienced feelings of racial isolation and racial discrimination. Because reports of feeling racial isolation and racial discrimination were likely to have different meanings for African American versus white students, we did not examine comparisons across race (i.e., comparisons of African American women athletes vs. white women athletes) for the racial tension variable. Both composite scores were based on a response scale of 1 (never) to 4 (frequently).

Perceptions of Social Advantage As the Result of Athletics

Student athletes rated the extent to which it was easier or harder for them as an athlete to experience 20 activities associated with personal growth on a 5-point scale ranging from 1 (much easier) to 5 (much harder). Maximum likelihood factor analysis of the subsample included in the present study yielded a similar three-factor solution to an earlier analysis derived from the entire sample (see Sellers et al., 1991); thus the earlier composites were used in this study. Social skills ($\alpha = .83$) measures student athletes' perceived difficulty or ease with items such as exercising self control, taking on leadership responsibilities, and learning from mistakes as a result of being an athlete. Opportunities ($\alpha = .74$) includes items such as the student athletes' perception of the ease or difficulty in gaining opportunities to travel, displaying one's talents, earning praise, and interacting with people of other races. Finally, Assertiveness ($\alpha = .72$) measures students' perceived ease or difficulty with making decisions, getting dates, getting to know other students, and speaking one's mind. Comparisons between student athletes and nonathletes were not included

because of differences in the wording of questions. Specifically, whereas student athletes were asked to rate the perceived personal development items with regard to their experiences as athletes, the African American nonathletes responded with regard to their experiences as students.

Academic, Athletic, and College Life Satisfaction

Principal components analysis was used to construct composite indices of satisfaction with three aspects of college life. Four items rated on a 4-point scale from 1 (dissatisfied) to 4 (satisfied) comprised a measure of Academic Satisfaction ($\alpha = .65$). These items included students' satisfaction with their choice of major, with their courses, with their current course performance, and with their overall academic performance. Two items measuring satisfaction with coaching staff and satisfaction with sport personality ($r = .49$) loaded on a factor labeled Athletic Satisfaction and scored on a 4-point scale from 1 (dissatisfied) to 4 (satisfied). (Note that athletic satisfaction was not examined in the comparison including African American women nonathletes.) Life Satisfaction was represented by a single item that elicited students' satisfaction with life in general ranging from 1 (dissatisfied) to 4 (satisfied).

Plan of Analysis

Analyses were performed to examine mean differences between the target group of African American women athletes and each of the three comparison groups. Comparisons of African American women athletes versus white women athletes emphasize race differences in women student athletes' college life experiences. Comparisons of African American women athletes and nonathletes emphasize differences in the collegiate experiences of African American women who differ in athletic status. Finally, comparisons of African American female versus male athletes accentuate gender differences among African American student athletes. A series of multivariate analyses of variance (MANOVAs) were used to compare African American women athletes with the three comparison groups on SES, HSGPA, and SAT. Next, a series of multivariate analyses of covariance (MANCOVAs) were performed to compare African American women athletes' experiences in the four areas of college life with the experiences of the three comparison groups while partialling out the effects of the precollege variables of SES, HSGPA, and SAT by including them and all of their two-way interaction terms as covariates in all analyses. The influence of sport (revenue vs. nonrevenue) is partialled out by including such a variable as an independent variable in the race comparison analyses. Revenue sports were defined as women's basketball, men's basketball, and football. In all cases, race, athletic status, and gender differences on dependent variables are examined only when the multivariate F for each MANOVA is significant at the $p < .01$ level.

Results

College Life Experiences of African American Women Student Athletes

Table 13.1 summarizes African American women student athletes' academic and demographic background as well as their college life experiences. The mean cumulative GPA for African American women athletes is 2.32. On average, African American women athletes report experiencing about one academic difficulty. African American women athletes' responses to Alienation/abuse suggest that they almost never feel alienated or abused. Similarly, African American women athletes report almost never experiencing racial isolation or incidents of racial discrimination. With regard to their perceived personal development, African American women athletes, on average, feel that it is somewhat easier for them to learn social skills, gain opportunities, and be more assertive as a result of their athletic

status. African American women athletes seem somewhat satisfied with their academic and athletic situation. They also report being more satisfied than dissatisfied with their life in general.

Demographic and Academic Background of African American Women Athletes and Comparison Groups

Table 13.2 summarizes the results of analyses of demographic and academic background variables. African American women athletes' demographic and academic background differed from all three comparison groups. Compared to white women athletes (Multivariate $F = 80.38$, $p < .01$), African American women athletes came from poorer social backgrounds ($p < .01$). African American women athletes' average score of 759.55 on the SAT was 166.19 points lower than white women athletes ($p < .01$), and the average HSGPA reflected a B average, compared to a B+ average for white women athletes ($p < .01$). A similar pattern of results emerged in comparing African American women athletes to African American women nonathletic students (Multivariate $F = 12.71$, $p < .01$). African American women athletes had a lower mean SES level ($p < .05$), earned lower high school grade point averages ($p < .05$), and had SAT scores that were more than 100 points lower than African American women nonathletes ($p < .01$). Compared to African American men athletes, however, a different pattern

Table 13.1   Description of African American Women Athletes' College Life Experiences

	M	SD	Response range
Academic performance			
College GPA	2.32	0.49	0.00–4.00
Academic difficulties	0.99	0.93	0.00–3.00
Alienation and isolation			
Feel alienation/abuse	1.98	0.58	1=never to 4=frequently
Feel racial tension	1.89	0.80	1=never to 4=frequently
Perceived personal growth			
Social development	2.48	0.56	1=much easier to 5=much harder
Opportunities	2.07	0.56	1=much easier to 5=much harder
Assertiveness	2.67	0.66	1=much easier to 5=much harder
Satisfaction			
Academic satisfaction	2.88	0.52	1=dissatisfied to 4=satisfied
Athletic satisfaction	2.76	0.59	1=dissatisfied to 4=satisfied
Life satisfaction	3.22	0.54	1=dissatisfied to 4=satisfied

Reprinted from Sellers, Kuperminc, and Damas, 1997.

Table 13.2   Results of MANOVA and ANOVA Analyses of Demographic and Academic Background Variables by Group[a]

	Black women athletes $n = 154$	White women athletes $n = 793$	Black women nonathletes $n = 250$	Black men athletes $n = 628$
SES	45.30 (7.34)	52.41 (7.20)	47.15 (7.98)	–
HSGPA	4.93 (1.70)	5.98 (1.54)	–	4.16 (1.63)
SAT	759.55 (160.50)	925.74 (163.80)	889.14 (238.71)	–
Wilks's λ Multivariate F	–	.80 ($F = 80.38$)	.91 ($F = 12.71$)	.96 ($F = 9.53$)

[a]Only means (SD) are reported for comparisons in which the main effect for group (race, gender, or athletic status) is significant at the $p < .05$ level and the overall F for the ANOVA model is also significant at the $p < .01$ level.

Reprinted from Sellers, Kuperminc, and Damas, 1997.

emerged (Multivariate $F = 9.53$, $p < .01$). African American women athletes were similar to African American men athletes in terms of their social background and SAT scores, but differed in their HSGPA ($p < .01$). African American women athletes earned higher high school grades (B) than did African American men athletes (B-).

African American Female Athletes Versus White Female Athletes

The results in table 13.3 indicate that African American women athletes differed from their white counterparts on three of the nine comparisons that were examined (Multivariate $F = 6.98$, $p < .01$).

Academic Performance

African American women athletes differed from white women athletes on both indices of college academic performance. African American women athletes carried lower grades than white women athletes ($F_{total} = 21.95$, $p < .01$). While the covariates (SES, HSGPA, SAT composite score, participation in revenue sports, and their two-way interactions) accounted for a substantial proportion of the variance in college GPA ($F_{covariates} = 21.31$, $p < .01$), race differences persist after accounting for these effects ($F_{race} = 23.32$, $p < .01$). Examination of the academic difficulties composite revealed a similar pattern. African American women athletes reported experiencing 0.99 of three indices of academic difficulties, compared to 0.42 for white women athletes ($F_{race} = 12.72$, $p < .01$). Once again, the covariates accounted for a significant proportion of the variance in academic difficulties ($F_{covariates} = 18.24$, $p < .01$).

Isolation and Alienation

African American and white women athletes reported similar levels of alienation/abuse. Both groups reported that experiences of alienation/abuse had occurred "rarely (about 1 to 5 times since being at school)." Feelings of alienation/abuse were significantly related to the covariates ($F_{covariates} = 4.33$, $p < .01$). No group comparisons were examined for feeling racial tension (see above).

Perceptions of Social Advantage as the Result of Athletics

Generally, both African American and white women athletes reported that their experiences as athletes facilitated their personal development. These groups did not differ in the extent to which they reported ease with gaining social skills or in the extent to which they reported that it was easier for them to gain opportunities as a result of their status as athletes. Both groups reported that as athletes it is "easier/no difference" to develop social skills and to gain opportunities as a result of being an athlete. African American women athletes reported that it was easier to gain assertiveness skills than did white women athletes ($F_{race} = 8.89$, $p < .01$). The covariates also explained a significant proportion of the variance in perceptions of gaining assertiveness skills as a result of participation in athletics ($F_{covariates} = 2.50$, $p < .01$).

Academic, Athletic, and Life Satisfaction

Although there appear to be some observed differences in the levels of satisfaction that African American and white women athletes report, these differences appear to be a function of race differences in the covariates used in the analysis. Race was not a significant main effect for any of the three areas of satisfaction. However, the covariates were significant predictors of academic satisfaction ($F_{covariates} = 9.74$, $p < .01$), athletic satisfaction ($F_{covariates} = 10.42$, $p < .01$), and life satisfaction ($F_{covariates} = 2.43$, $p < .01$), respectively.

African American Female Athletes Versus African American Male Athletes

Table 13.3 also summarizes the results of the comparison of African American women versus men athletes. African American women athletes differed from African American men athletes on 3 of the 10 areas of college life experiences that were examined (Multivariate $F = 5.65$, $p < .01$).

Academic Performance

African American women athletes differed from African American men athletes on one of the two indicators of academic performance. African American women athletes had higher college GPAs than their male counterparts ($F_{gender} = 8.17$, $p < .01$). However, no gender differences were found in the number of academic difficulties. Also, the covariates (SES, HSGPA, SAT composite score, and their two-way interactions) accounted for a significant proportion of the variance in student athletes' college GPA ($F_{covariates} = 9.64$, $p < .01$) and academic difficulties ($F_{covariates} = 7.41$, $p < .01$).

Isolation and Alienation

The covariates were significant predictors of alienation/abuse ($F_{covariates} = 2.58$, $p < .05$); however, no gender differences were found in alienation/abuse. With regard to racial tension, gender differences were found ($F_{gender} = 9.14$, $p < .01$). Although both groups reported "rarely" feeling racial tension, African American men athletes reported feeling racial tension more often than African American women athletes. The covariates did not account for a significant proportion of the variance in racial tension.

Perceptions and Social Advantage As the Result of Athletics

Men and women African American athletes perceived similar levels of ease with social development and gaining opportunities as a result of being athletes. For gaining social skills and opportunities,

both groups felt that being an athlete made no difference in these aspects of their personal development. However, gender differences were found with respect to their perception of the ease to which they could obtain assertiveness skills as a result of being an athlete ($F_{gender} = 20.10$, $p < .01$). African American women athletes were less likely to report that being an athlete made gaining assertiveness skills somewhat easier than African American men athletes. The covariates were not significant predictors of any of the three perceived personal development indicators.

Academic, Athletic, and Life Satisfaction

African American men and women athletes reported similar levels of academic, athletic, and life satisfaction. Women athletes and men athletes reported being "more satisfied than dissatisfied" with life in general. Mean scores for both groups on academic and athletic satisfaction suggest some ambivalence, falling slightly below the response range for "more satisfied than dissatisfied." The covariates were not significant predictors of any of the areas of satisfaction.

African American Female Athletes Versus African American Female Nonathletes

Table 13.3 summarizes the results of the comparison of African American women athletes and African American women nonathletes. Although there was a significant multivariate effect for the models comparing African American women athletes and nonathletes (Multivariate $F = 6.40$, $p < .01$), this effect seems to be driven by the relationship between the covariates (SES, HSGPA, SAT composite score, and their two-way interactions) and the dependent variables. There was no significant group differences for any of the individual dependent variables when the effects of the covariates were partialled out. The covariates were significant predictors of both college GPA ($F_{covariates} = 4.31$, $p < .01$) and academic difficulties ($F_{covariates} = 4.70$, $p < .01$).

Discussion

The present study had two objectives. The first was to provide a descriptive analysis of the life experience of African American women student athletes. Our results suggest that in terms of academics, African American women athletes are performing

Table 13.3 Results of MANOVA and ANOVA Analyses of College Life Experiences by Group[a]

	Black women athletes M (SD)	White women athletes M (SD)	Black men athletes M (SD)	Black women nonathletes M (SD)
Academic performance				
College GPA	2.32 (0.49)	2.80 (0.56)	2.14 (0.44)	–
Academic difficulties	0.99 (0.93)	0.42 (0.72)	–	–
Alienation and isolation				
Feel alienation/abuse	1.98 (0.58)	–	–	–
Feel racial tension	1.89 (0.80)	na	2.22 (0.94)	–
Perceived personal growth				
Social development	2.48 (0.56)	–	–	na
Opportunities	2.07 (0.56)	–	–	na
Assertiveness	2.67 (0.66)	2.81 (0.58)	2.38 (0.73)	na
Satisfaction				
Academic satisfaction	2.88 (0.52)	–	–	–
Athletic satisfaction	2.76 (0.59)	–	–	–
Life satisfaction	3.22 (0.54)	–	–	–
Wilk's lambda for group		.94 (F = 6.93)	.93 (F = 5.61)	.91 (F = 6.40)

[a]Only means (SD) are reported for comparisons in which the main effect for group (race, gender, or athletic status) is significant at the $p < .01$ level and the overall F for the ANOVA and MANOVA models are also significant at the $p < .01$ level.

Reprinted from Sellers, Kuperminc, and Damas, 1997.

adequately considering the time demands associated with athletics and their poorer academic preparation. Although there is certainly room for improvement, African American women athletes perform, on average, above most institutions' minimal GPA requirements (2.0) for good academic standing. They also do not experience multiple academic problems such as repeating courses, receiving incomplete grades, or being placed on probation. On average, African American women athletes reported almost never experiencing alienation or abuse. Although they reported more racial isolation than white women athletes and lower than African American men, the level of racial isolation reported also was in the "rarely" range of response. Of course, one could argue that experiencing incidents of racial tension only rarely is still too often.

With regard to their perceived personal development, African American women athletes seem to believe that their athletic status provides them with a greater opportunity to learn social skills, gain opportunities, and be more assertive. Their perceptions of enhanced social advantage as a result of athletics are consistent with the work of Danish and his colleagues (Danish, 1983; Danish et al., 1990) who suggest that participation in organized athletics may actually enhance the development of personal competence. It should be noted that although African American women athletes view athletic participation as facilitating their personal development, the present study did not measure whether they actually had a relatively easier time developing or the extent of development that actually occurred. We measured only their perceptions of growth. Consistent with their somewhat positive profile in other areas of college life, African American women athletes seem to be satisfied with their college experience. Their satisfaction with their academic performance appears to be linked to relatively high expectations and reasonable assessments of their current academic status. They also seem to be somewhat satisfied with their athletic performance. As a whole, African American women athletes seem to enjoy a somewhat positive collegiate experience.

Our second objective was to examine whether African American women athletes' college life experiences differ significantly from white women athletes and African American men athletes. Our results suggest that even after accounting for background differences, African American women student athletes' college life experiences differ in meaningful ways from both white women student athletes and African American men student athletes.

With regard to academic performance, African American women student athletes perform less well than white women student athletes but achieved higher GPAs than African American men student athletes. African American and white women athletes report similar experiences with regard to social integration. Both African American and white women athletes report relatively low levels of alienation and abuse.

African American women athletes also reported experiencing less racial tension than their African American men counterparts. This finding is consistent with those of Fleming (1983, 1984), who concluded that African American women college students were able to fair better academically and interpersonally on a predominantly white campus than their African American men counterparts. Some authors have argued that African American men are perceived as posing a greater threat to the white social structure than African American women and therefore, are at greater risk within the current social structure (Staples, 1991). Although we did not directly test this hypothesis, our findings that African American women student athletes performed stronger academically and reported lower levels of perceived racial tension than their African American men counterparts are consistent with such an interpretation.

With regard to perceptions of social advantage, African American women athletes perceive that their athletic status is more beneficial to learning assertiveness skills than do white women athletes, but they do not report as great a benefit as African American men athletes. One interpretation of this finding is that assertive behavior has traditionally been viewed as more socially appropriate among males than among females. African American women athletes, being a "double minority," may be more sensitive compared to white women athletes to the notion that the role of athlete affords a greater opportunity for their assertive behavior to be viewed as socially appropriate. Fleming (1983, 1984) found that African American women college students were more assertive on a predominantly white campus than on a historically African American campus as a result of there being fewer African American men around. Thus, the African American women take on more assertive roles that are usually fulfilled by African American men when there is a dearth of men. Meanwhile, another interpretation argues that because African American females have traditionally played a more assertive role in all facets of family life (Albert & Porter, 1988; Myers, 1989), they may be more

familiar than white females with the increased opportunities to be assertive that may be afforded by the role of athlete.

Interestingly, the college life experiences of African American females seem to be comparable regardless of whether or not they participate in intercollegiate athletics. Although African American women athletes and African American women nonathletes come from different backgrounds, they reported similar experiences across the three areas of college life which were examined. Whereas African American women athletes had significantly lower college GPAs and more academic problems than the African American women nonathletes, these differences were accounted for by academic preparation and demographic background differences. An interesting question is whether or not African American women athletes and nonathletes perceived similar levels of personal development. As mentioned previously, the items used in the questionnaire do not allow such an analysis. Nonetheless, the similarities in the other areas of college life experience suggest that participation in athletics for African American women athletes does not seem to influence their experiences as much as race and gender. However, further research is needed before a definitive statement regarding the relative importance of race, gender, and athletic status can be assessed.

There are limitations to the present study which suggest that the results should be interpreted with caution. First, all the data in this study were collected from self-reports. The extent to which participants' responses were influenced by social desirability is unknown. Also, the study represents student athletes' experiences, attitudes, and beliefs at only one period of time. Thus, it is impossible to capture the potential dynamic nature of their experience. For instance, it is plausible that the African American women athletes may have a different developmental trajectory during their college tenure than other groups of students. Longitudinal data are needed before such an analysis can occur. Despite these limitations, the present study provides an important foundation upon which further research can build. It focuses on a population that has been virtually ignored by the research literature.

Policy Implications

The present study serves as a baseline from which to evaluate the impact of potential policy changes in the future. The present results also speak tangentially to the current debate regarding increased academic standards for incoming first-year student athletes. In general, African American women athletes are doing relatively well academically in comparison to African American men athletes. Despite the differences in college GPA, African American women athletes have similar SAT scores and come from similar socioeconomic backgrounds as African American male student athletes. These results call into question the predictive value of the SAT composite score for the academic performance of African American student athletes (Sellers, 1992). The present results suggest that the use of HSGPA as a criterion for initial athletic eligibility may be preferential to the use of SAT composite score (Sellers, 1992). However, more in-depth analyses are needed before a definitive policy recommendation can be made.

The high concentration of African American women athletes in the revenue-producing sport of women's basketball has implications for the enforcement of Title IX at the collegiate level. Many institutions have added women's sports and cut men's sports as a way of complying with Title IX. Most of these sports tend to have very few African American women who participate (e.g., women's crew). There is some concern that African American women athletes will not benefit from the increased opportunities that may occur as a result of the enforcement of Title IX at the collegiate level unless they are provided with greater access and exposure to these "new" sports at the high school and recreational level (Corbett & Johnson, 1993). Nonetheless, African American women still have less access to collegiate athletics than African American men as evidenced by the far smaller percentage of African American women receiving athletic scholarships (2%) as compared to African American men receiving athletic scholarships (11%: NCAA, 1995).

In conclusion, the present study represents an effort to examine the ecological experiences of the African American women student athletes. Such an effort is consistent with Sellers' (1993) argument that policy makers interested in improving the academic performance of student athletes should focus more on the college life experiences of student athletes. The present study also provides baseline data on the unique experiences of African American women athletes from which to evaluate the impact of potential policy changes. Finally, we hope that the present study will spur other investigators to recognize that African American women athletes are a sample population worthy of study in and of itself.

Note

The present study was made possible through the cooperation of the National Collegiate Athletic Association. However, all conclusions and recommendations are made solely by the authors and do not represent the views of the officers, staff, or the membership of the NCAA. The authors also express their gratitude to all of the students who participated in the studies.

References

Adler, P., & Adler, P. (1991). *Back boards and blackboards: College athletics and role engulfment.* New York: Columbia University Press.

Agnew, R., & Peterson, D.M. (1989). Leisure and delinquency. *Social Problems,* **36**, 332–350.

Albert, A.A., & Porter, J.R. (1988). Children's gender-role stereotypes: A sociological investigation of psychological models. *Sociological Forum,* **3**, 184–210.

Allen, W.R. (1985). Black student, white campus: Structural, interpersonal, and psychological correlates of success. *Journal of Negro Education,* **54**, 134–147.

Allen, W.R. (1988). Black students in U.S. higher education: Toward improved access, adjustment and achievement. *Urban Review,* **20**, 165–188.

Bean, J.P., & Bradley, R.K. (1986). Untangling the satisfaction-performance relationship of college students. *Journal of Higher Education,* **57**, 393–412.

Beckham, B. (1988). Strangers in a strange land: The experiences of Blacks on White campuses. *Educational Record,* **68**, 74–78.

Bell, R.Q. (1986). Age specific manifestations in changing psychosocial risk. In D.C. Farran & J.D. Mckinney (Eds.), *Risk in intellectual and psychosocial development* (pp. 169–183). New York: Academic Press.

Bird, A.M., & Cripe, B.K. (1986). *Psychology and sport behavior.* St. Louis: Times/Mosby.

Boyer, S.P., & Sedlacek, W.E. (1988). Noncognitive predictors of academic success for international students: A longitudinal study. *Journal of College Student Development,* **29**, 218–223.

Bronfenbrenner, U., & Crouter, A.C. (1982). Work and family through time and space. In S.B. Kamerman & C.D. Hayes (Eds.), *Families that work: Children in a changing environment of work, family, and community.* Washington, DC: National Academy of Science.

Burling, T.A., Seidner, A.L., Robbins-Sisco, D., & Krinsky, A. (1992). Relapse prevention for homeless veteran substance abusers via softball team participation. *Journal of Substance Abuse,* **4**, 407–413.

Center for the Study of Athletics (1988). *Report No. 2: Methodology of the 1987-88 national study of intercollegiate athletes.* Palo Alto, CA: American Institutes for Research.

Center for the Study of Athletics (1989). *Report No. 3: The experiences of black intercollegiate athletes at NCAA division I institutions.* Palo Alto, CA: American Institutes for Research.

Center for the Study of Athletics (1989). *Report No. 4:Women in intercollegiate NCAA division I institutions.* Palo Alto, CA: American Institutes for Research.

Corbett, D., & Johnson, W. (1993). The African-American female in collegiate sport: Sexism and racism. In D. Brooks & R. Althouse (Eds.), *Racism in college athletics: The African American athlete's experience.* Morgantown, WV: Fitness Information Technology, Inc.

Cusson, M. (1989). Disputes over honor and gang aggression. *Revue Internationale de Criminologie et de Police Technique,* **42**, 290–297.

Danish, S.J. (1983). Musings about personal competence: The contributions of sport, health and fitness. *American Journal of Community Psychology,* **11**, 221–240.

Danish, S.J., Petitpas, A.J., & Hale, B.D. (1990). Sport as a context for developing competence. In T.P. Gullotta, G.R. Adams, & R. Montemayor (Eds.), *Developing social competency in adolescence.* Newbury Park, CA: Sage.

Davis, J.A. (1990). *Researcher issues and strategies in regard to the educational treatment of the black athlete.* Paper presented at the meeting of the Southern Association for Institutional Research and the Society for College and University Planning, Fort Lauderdale, FL.

Defour, D.C., & Hirsch, B.J. (1990). The adaptation of black graduate students: A social network approach. *American Journal of Community Psychology,* **18**, 487–503.

Duda, J.L., & Allison, M.T. (1990). Cross-cultural analysis in exercise and sport psychology: A void in the field. *Journal of Sport and Exercise Psychology,* **12**, 114–131.

Duke, M., Johnson, T.C., & Nowicki, S. Jr. (1987). Effects of sport fitness camp experiences on locus of control orientation in children ages 6-14. *Research Quarterly,* **48**, 280–283.

Ervin, L., Saunders, S.A., Gillis, H.L., & Hogrebe, M.C. (1985). Academic performance of student athletes in revenue-producing sports. *Journal of College Student Personnel,* **26**, 119–124.

Evans, V., & Quarterman, J. (1983). Personality characteristics of successful and unsuccessful black female basketball players. *International Journal of Sports Psychology,* **14**, 105–115.

Fleming, J. (1983). Black women in black and white college environments: The making of a matriarch. *Journal of Social Issues,* **39**, 41–54.

Fleming, J. (1984). *Blacks in college.* San Francisco: Jossey-Bass.

Gosman, E.J., Dandridge, B.A., Nettles, M.T., & Thoeny, A.R. (1983). Predicting student progression: The influence of race and other student and institutional characteristics on college student performance. *Research in Higher Education,* **18**, 209–236.

Iso-Aloha, S., & Hatfield, B. (1986). *Psychology of sports: A social psychological approach.* Dubuque, IA: Wm. C. Brown.

Kiger, G., & Lorentzen, D. (1986). The relative effect of gender, race, and sport on university academic performance. *Sociology of Sport Journal,* **3**, 160–167.

Loo, C.M., & Rolison, G. (1986). Alienation of ethnic minority students at a predominantly White university. *Journal of Higher Education,* **57**, 59–77.

McArdle, J.J., & Hamagami, F. (1994). Logit and multi-level logit modeling of college graduation rates for 1984–85 freshman student athletes. *Journal of the American Statistical Association,* **89**, 1107–1123.

Myers, L.W. (1989). Early gender role socialization among black women: Affective or consequential? *Western Journal of African American Studies,* **13**, 173–178.

National Collegiate Athletic Association (1991). A statistical analysis of the predictions of graduation rates for college student athletes. *NCAA Research Report #91-02.* Overland Park, KA: Author.

National Collegiate Athletic Association (1995). *1995 NCAA division 1 graduation-rates report.* Overland Park, KA: Author.

Nettles, M.T., & Johnson, J.R. (1987). Race, sex and other factors as determinants of college students' socialization. *Journal of College Student Personnel,* **28**, 512–524.

Pascarella, E.T., & Smart, J.C. (1991). Impact of Intercollegiate Athletic Participation for African American and Caucasian Men: Some Further Evidence. *Journal of College Student Development,* **32**, 123–129.

Petitpas, A. (1981). *The identity development of the male intercollegiate athlete.* Unpublished doctoral dissertation, Boston University.

Picou, J.S., & Curry, E.W. (1974). Residence and the athletic participation-educational aspiration hypothesis. *Social Science Quarterly*, **55**, 768–776.

Prakasa Rao, V., & Overman, S. (1984). Sex-role perceptions among Black female athletes and nonathletes. *Sex Roles*, **11**, 601–614.

Purdy, D., Eitzen, D.S., & Hufnagel, R. (1982). Are athletes also students? The educational attainment of college athletes. *Social Problems*, **29**, 439–448.

Reppucci, N.D. (1987). Teen-age pregnancy, child sexual abuse, and organized youth sports. *American Journal of Community Psychology*, **15**, 1–22.

Rutledge, E.M. (1982). Students' perceptions of racism in higher education. *Integrated Education*, **20**, 106–111.

Ryan, F.J. (1989). Participation in intercollegiate athletics: Affective outcomes. *Journal of College Student Development*, **30**, 122–128.

Sedlacek, W.E. (1987). Black students on White campuses: 20 years of research. *Journal of College Student Personnel*, **28**, 484–495.

Seidman, E. (1991). Growing up the hard way: Pathways of urban adolescents. *American Journal of Community Psychology*, **19**, 173–201.

Sellers, R.M. (1992). Racial differences in the predictors of academic achievement of Division I student athletes. *Sociology of Sport Journal*, **9**, 48–59.

Sellers, R. M. (1993). Black student athletes: Reaping the benefits or recovering from exploitation? In D. Brooks and R. Althouse (Eds.), *Racism in College Athletics*, Morgantown, WV: Fitness Information Technology.

Sellers, R.M., Kuperminc, G.P., & Waddell, A.S. (1991, Fall). Life experiences of African American student athletes in revenue-producing sports: A descriptive empirical analysis. *Academic Athletic Journal*, 21–38.

Shapiro, B.J. (1984). Intercollegiate athletic participation and academic achievement: A case study of Michigan State University student athletes, 1950-1980. *Sociology of Sport Journal*, **1**, 46–51.

Smith, A., & Stewart, A.J. (1983). Approaches to studying racism and sexism in Black women's lives. *Journal of Social Issues*, **39**, 1–15.

Sonestroem, R.J. (1982). Exercise and self esteem: Recommendations for expository research. *Quest*, **33**, 124–139.

Stage, F.K. (1988). Reciprocal effects between the academic and social integration of college students. *Research in Higher Education*, **30**, 517–530.

Stage, F.K. (1989). Motivation, academic and social integration, and the early dropout. *American Educational Research Journal*, **26**, 385–402.

Staples, R. (1991). Black male genocide: A final solution to the race problem in America. In B.J. Bowser (Ed.), *Parenting and education in community context.* Lanham, MD: University Press.

Stoecker, J., Pascarella, E.T., & Wolfle, LM. (1988). Persistence in higher education: A 9-year test of a theoretical model. *Journal of College Student Development*, **29**, 126–209.

Suen, H.K. (1983). Alienation and attrition of Black college students on a predominantly White campus. *Journal of College Student Personnel*, **24**, 117–121.

Terenzini, P.T., & Pascarella, E.T. (1978). The relation of students' precollege characteristics and freshman year experience to voluntary attrition. *Research in Higher Education*, **9**, 347–366.

Tinto, V. (1975). Dropout from higher education: A theoretical synthesis of recent research. *Review of Educational Research*, **45**, 89–125.

Tinto, V. (1987). *Leaving college: Rethinking the cause and cures of student attrition.* Chicago: University of Chicago Press.

Tracey, T.J., & Sedlacek, W.E. (1984). Noncognitive variables in predicting academic success by race. *Measurement and Evaluation in Guidance*, **16**, 171–178.

UNIT VI

Race, Ethnicity, and Sport

Objectives

The unit illustrates and examines how discriminatory practices manifest themselves in the world of sport.

Sport sociologist Jay Coakley (1998) defines race as "a category of people regarded as socially distinct because they share genetically transmitted traits believed to be important in a group or society" (p. 249), and he defines ethnicity as ". . . the cultural heritage of a particular group" (p. 250). Whereas race is commonly associated with genetically determined physical traits, an ethnic group "is a category of people regarded as socially distinct because they share a way of life associated with a common cultural background" (Coakley, p. 250). For example, according to the U.S. Census Bureau, Hispanic is not a "racial category but instead, refers to an ethnic group consisting of all people whose roots can be traced to Spanish-speaking countries" (Coakley, 1998).

Conventional wisdom has it that American sport is a "color-blind," ethnically diverse, equal-opportunity employer in which the assignment of valued positions and roles is determined solely on the basis of ability, skill, and hard work. The general public has typically viewed sport as a meritocratic, egalitarian social institution that judges not on the basis of skin color or cultural heritage but on performance ("if you can play the position, you get the position"). These popular beliefs are reinforced by the success many African American athletes have had in college and professional basketball, college and professional football, major-league baseball, college and professional track, and the boxing ring. The average baseball salaries of top African American players like Mo Vaughn of the Anaheim Angels ($13.3 million), Albert Belle of the Baltimore Orioles ($13.0 million), and Ken Griffey Jr. of the Cincinnati Reds ($12.9 million) provide additional proof that skin color matters little in professional sports ("Baseball's Top Contracts," 2000).

Similarly, Chinese Americans take special satisfaction in the figure-skating magic of Nancy Kwan and the outstanding athleticism of professional tennis player Michael Chang, and Japanese Americans point with pride to the artistry of figure skater Kristi Yamaguchi and the successes of major-league baseball pitchers Hideki Irabu and Hideo Nomo. Youthful Notah Begay III, the only Native American currently playing on the Professional Golf Association tour, surely inspires his followers with his promising game.

The multicultural, multiethnic character of American sport can be easily documented. For example, 37 international players from 25 different countries were included on National Basketball Association opening rosters for the 2000 season ("Basketball Goes Global," 2000). Approximately 17 percent of major-league baseball players are of Hispanic ancestry (Lapchick, 1999).

Although some members of some racial and ethnic groups have had considerable success in American sports, it must be recognized that racial desegregation has occurred selectively. The white majority continues to dominate several sports (e.g., ice hockey, automobile racing, tennis, golf, gymnastics, swimming, soccer, field hockey, skiing, volleyball). Although genuine humanitarian interests may well have motivated some sports to open their previously closed doors to racial and ethnic minority participation, it would be naive to believe that this was the sole motivation. As Sage (1998) astutely observed, "It was in those team sports in which spectator appeal was strong and growing and in which the profit motive was foremost, that African Americans were given a chance . . ." (p. 93).

The question of whether racial progress has meant racial equality in American sports is a difficult one to answer. Some would argue that sport, perhaps more than any other social institution, has done an excellent job of providing racial and ethnic minorities with opportunity and access (the "glass is half full" perspective). Others are quick to point out that an underlying racism has denied minorities full and equal opportunities on and off the field (the "glass is half empty" perspective). Sage (1998) takes the position that "sport has simultaneously been a powerful reinforcer of racist ideology and an instrument of opportunity for African Americans" (p. 88). He argues that ". . . the ideology underlying racism has not been incompatible with African American sport participation . . ." (p. 88). That is, African American participation in American sports, regardless of their participation rates, has done little to change race-based power relations in society or alter racial stereotyping and racialized thinking. The racial ideology of white superiority continues to perpetuate racial inequality in sport and accounts for the many discriminatory practices directed at racial and ethnic minorities.

Sport sociologists have sought to document the institutional consequences of racial ideology in American sports by focusing their attention on both on-the-field and off-the-field practices. On the playing field, researchers have noted that entry-level barriers in some sports (e.g., baseball, basketball) appear to be higher for some minorities than they are for whites. This pattern of racial inequality has been referred to as the "mediocrity is a white luxury" phenomenon. Also of interest to sport researchers is the apparent racial segregation by playing position in some team sports (the "stacking" phenomenon). For example, we find that in baseball, football, volleyball, and soccer, African Americans are statistically overrepresented in noncentral, peripheral playing positions (positions requiring speed, quick reactions, jumping ability, and excellent hand-eye coordination). The data indicate that whites are overrepresented in central playing positions requiring decision-making ability, dependability, and intelligence (e.g., quarterback in football). Sport sociologists continue to debate whether these patterns are the result of nondiscriminatory social forces (e.g., socialization effects, role modeling, imitative behavior), the result of deliberate discriminatory processes (e.g., racial and ethnic stereotyping), or the result of a joint act involving both the athlete and the coach or management.

Although the presence or absence of racial ideology on the field continues to be a contentious issue, discriminatory practices directed at minorities away from the playing field are much easier to substantiate. Minorities are conspicuously absent in head coaching and managerial positions, as well as administrative, executive, entrepreneurial, and media-related roles within the organizational structures of sport. Of course, notable exceptions exist. The former owner of the Continental Basketball Association, Isiah Thomas, is an African American and a former NBA all-star for the Detroit Pistons. Michael Jordan, former basketball superstar, holds the dual titles of part owner and president of basketball operations for the Washington Wizards of the NBA. Although the general public has a tendency to generalize based on isolated cases, sport sociologists seek evidence in patterns of institutional behavior. Here the record could not be more clear. As Sage notes,

> Access for black athletes has expanded greatly in recent years, but very few African Americans—men or women—have been hired for positions high in the sport hierarchy. Blacks now account for less than 5 percent of the important management positions in professional and intercollegiate sports. (p. 94)

For example, of the past 30 new head coaches hired in the NFL, a league where 68 percent of the players are African American, only one was black (King, 2000).

Given the real presence of race bias in the larger society (e.g., public schools still fail to provide minorities with the same quality of education that whites receive; Henry, 2000), the reader should not be surprised to find racial discrimination within the sport institution. If racial prejudice and injustice exist in other sectors of American life, why should sport be any different?

In the first selection, González investigated the "stacking" of Latino players by playing position in major-league baseball for the years 1950 to 1992. Of special interest is the fact that the pattern of position allocation that emerges is diametrically opposed to stacking findings involving African American baseball players. Clearly, traditional stacking theories are inadequate for explaining such results. Does this mean that Latino players are not discriminated against in professional baseball? González has some perceptive observations to share on this question.

In the second selection, Sigelman examines the public's reaction to racially insensitive team names by focusing on what a national survey sample and a sample of residents living in the Washington, D.C., area and northern Virginia think about the NFL team name Washington Redskins. These findings reveal the extent to which Americans dissociate themselves from offensive racial stereotypes. This is important information because racially insensitive stereotypes are strongly related to racial prejudice and discrimination, not just in sport but in the larger society as well.

In the third selection, Evans uses the term "key functionaries" (e.g., "positions within a social system that are capable of influencing and performing crucial activities") to study racial stratification in professional sport. By focusing on the presence or absence of black sportscasters, executives, and managers, Evans makes the reader painfully aware of a new "color line" that has been drawn in American sport. How formidable a barrier this demarcation line will prove to be in the future deserves serious thought and debate.

References

Baseball's top contracts. (2000, February 7). *USA TODAY*, p. 5B.

Basketball goes global. (2000, February 2). *USA TODAY*, p. 1B.

Coakley, J.J. (1998). *Sport in society: Issues and controversies.* New York: McGraw-Hill.

Evans, A. (1997). Blacks as key functionaries: A study of racial stratification in professional sport. *Journal of Black Studies, 28,* 43-59.

González, G.L. (1996). The stacking of Latinos in Major League Baseball: A forgotten minority? *Journal of Sport and Social Issues, 20,* 134-160.

Henry, T. (2000, March 1). Survey finds continued race bias in U.S. schools. *USA TODAY*, p. 1A.

King, P. (2000, February 7). The NFL's black eye. *Sports Illustrated,* p. 30.

Lapchick, R. (1999). *1999 racial report card.* Boston: The Center for the Study of Sport in Society.

Sage, G.H. (1998). *Power and ideology in American sport.* Champaign, IL: Human Kinetics.

Sigelman, L. (1998). Hail to the Redskins? Public reactions to a racially insensitive team name. *Sociology of Sport Journal, 15,* 317-325.

Discussion Questions

G. Leticia González

1. What is meant by the term "stacking"? What does a review of the "stacking" literature in sports reveal?
2. Describe the overall picture of the distribution of Latinos in core, peripheral, and noncentral playing positions.
3. What happened to the pattern as the percentage of Latinos in the major leagues grew between 1950 and 1992? Discuss and explain.
4. How are Latino "stacking" patterns different from traditional "stacking" patterns for blacks? Discuss and explain.
5. How does the researcher explain the "stacking" patterns of Hispanic major-league baseball players? Explain.
6. If playing a core position is related to managerial recruitment, why are there so few Hispanic baseball managers? Discuss and explain.

Lee Sigelman

1. Is the call for racially sensitive team names just another example of the "political correctness police" sticking their noses where they do not belong? Discuss and explain.
2. How does team management defend its use of so-called racially insensitive team names?
3. Describe the research methodology employed in this study.
4. Describe in detail the Washington, D.C., survey findings.
5. Do the Washington, D.C., survey findings indicate that management has anything to fear from the public about objectionable or insensitive team names? Explain.
6. Why do you think the general public "just doesn't get it"? Discuss and explain.
7. What do you think the public's reaction would be if a professional team were called the San Diego Caucasians, the Cincinnati Jews, or the Indianapolis Irish?

Arthur Evans Jr.

1. What is a "key functionary" position?
2. In what ways are conflict and functionalist theories useful in explaining the social inequality that blacks experience in American sports? Discuss and explain.
3. How successful have blacks been in occupying "key functionary" positions in professional sports? Explain. In particular, comment on the racial integration of the following sport roles: (a) sportscasters, (b) team executives, (c) head coaches and managers.
4. How successful have black athletes been at making personal appearances and promoting commercial products? Explain.
5. What are the prospects of black fans becoming a power base in professional sports? Explain.
6. Why is it that blacks are nearly absent from "key functionary" positions in professional sports? Discuss and explain.
7. What is the relationship between rationalization and stratification?
8. Do you believe that things will be different in professional sports 20 years from now? Explain.

The Stacking of Latinos in Major League Baseball: A Forgotten Minority?

G. Leticia González

The theory of stacking, or the disproportionate relegation of athletes to specific sport positions on the basis of ascribed characteristics such as race or ethnicity, was first developed by Loy and McElvogue about 25 years ago and implies that minorities are assigned to playing positions on the basis of what they are, not what they have achieved. As a result, stacking is usually seen as a negative phenomenon because it is a discriminatory process. The present study examines the stacking of Latinos in major league baseball from 1950 to 1992. The results show that Latinos are stacked in the central positions of shortstop and second base, a finding that is diametrically opposed to traditional stacking theories.

The theory of stacking, or the disproportionate relegation of athletes to specific sport positions on the basis of ascribed characteristics such as race or ethnicity, was first developed by Loy and McElvogue (1970). Their classic study, which combines Blalock's (1962) proposition that "there will be less discrimination where performance of independent tasks is largely involved" (Loy and McElvogue, 1970, p. 7) with Grusky's (1963) concept of spatial location within the formal structure of organizations, hypothesizes that "racial segregation in professional team sports is positively related to centrality" (Loy and McElvogue, 1970, p. 7). The theory implies that minorities are assigned to playing positions on the basis of what they are, not what they have achieved. Whereas Loy and McElvogue's stacking theory is still being used today as the foundation for many studies, the validity and usefulness of Grusky's theory of "centrality" has been questioned when applied to the players on the field. This is due to the fact that it does not take the role of coaches and managers into account. As they make decisions regarding position alignments and responsibilities, the centrality of positions on the field may become irrelevant. Nevertheless, stacking plays an important role in the assignment of players to designated playing positions.

As a result, stacking is usually seen as a negative phenomenon because it is a discriminatory process. For example, according to existing research, stacking moves minority players to a supporting rather than a leading role. In addition, stacking causes minorities to compete with each other for specific or limited playing positions, which reduces the number of minorities on the playing field (e.g., Dubois, 1980; Eitzen and Yetman, 1977; Jiobu, 1988; Pattnayak and Leonard, 1991; Phillips, 1983).

For about 25 years, sociologists and other scholars have worked to find explanations for the occurrence of stacking in sports organizations (see Curtis and Loy, 1978, for an excellent overview of early studies). Most stacking theories are based on one of several alternative perspectives that may be labeled as biological, psychological, or sociological. Empirical evidence for each of these perspectives varies. The biological explanations focus on the genetic differences between whites and blacks but appear to have the weakest scientific foundation of the three perspectives (Jordan, 1969; Malina, 1965). The psychological justifications for stacking are

Reprinted from González, 1996.

based on two theories: the idea that blacks are better at reactive tasks whereas whites excel at self-paced tasks (Worthy and Markle, 1970) and the idea that blacks and whites have different personalities (Jones and Hochner, 1973). Finally, the majority of proposed explanations for stacking fall under the sociological perspective. Under this perspective, there are two groups of three interpretations each. In the first group of interpretations, discriminatory processes consist of stereotyping (Eitzen and Furst, 1989), interaction and discrimination (Loy and McElvogue, 1970), and outcome control dynamics (Edwards, 1973). The second group of interpretations can be labeled as "levels of socialization" and includes hypotheses dealing with prohibitive cost (Medoff, 1976, 1986), differential attractiveness of positions (Eitzen and Yetman, 1977; Scully, 1974), and role modeling (McPherson, 1974). Sociological explanations are the predominant focus of contemporary scholars.

As a result, there is a substantial amount of stacking literature available covering a wide variety of sports such as baseball (e.g., Eitzen and Yetman, 1977; Guppy, 1983; Jiobu, 1988; Leonard, Pine, and Rice, 1988; Medoff, 1976, 1977, 1986; Pattnayak and Leonard, 1991; Scully, 1974), football (e.g., Brower, 1972; Eitzen and Sanford, 1975; Eitzen and Yetman, 1977, 1982; Madison and Landers, 1976), basketball (e.g., Berghorn, Yetman, and Hanna, 1988; Eitzen and Yetman, 1977; Leonard, 1987), ice hockey (e.g., Lavoie, 1989; Marple, 1975; Marple and Pirie, 1978; Roy, 1974), volleyball (e.g., Eitzen and Furst, 1989), and soccer (e.g., Maguire, 1988).

The vast majority of the stacking studies explore the stacking phenomenon as a black and white issue. However, an issue that must not be overlooked in today's multicultural society is the absence of studies that analyze the situation with regard to races and ethnic groups other than black and white (see, e.g., Leonard, 1977; Leonard et al., 1988; Pattnayak and Leonard, 1991). The lack of available research concerning the positional occupancy patterns of Latinos is especially noteworthy because Latinos have played (and still play) a prominent role in professional baseball. What makes an in-depth analysis of this ethnic group important is the impression that Latinos are overrepresented in central positions, thereby defying the traditional stacking theory that minorities are found mostly in noncentral playing positions. Phillips indicated in 1983 that Latinos are stacked just like blacks and whites, but there was insufficient evidence to support this idea at the time. However, Phillips's argument did point out that the stacking of baseball

players involves more than a simple division between black and white.

Finally, stacking is more than a mere cross-tabulation of specific player positions by race. Consequences of stacking are often felt outside the domain of sport itself, both during and after an athlete's career. Examples of these consequences are differences in leadership recruitment (e.g., Fabianic, 1984; Grusky, 1963; Kjeldsen, 1981; Klonsky, 1977; Loy, Curtis, and Hillen, 1987; Loy, Sage, and Ingham, 1972; Roy, 1974), endorsements (e.g., Eitzen and Yetman, 1977), career length (e.g., Berghorn et al., 1988; Curry and Jiobu, 1984), and retirement benefits (e.g., Curry and Jiobu, 1984; Eitzen and Sage, 1978).

Data and Methods

Within this theoretical framework, positional occupancy patterns as a function of ethnicity were analyzed and evaluated for Latinos in major league baseball for the years 1950-1992.

Sample

In 1947, baseball was "integrated" by Jackie Robinson, and racial and ethnic minorities began to enter the major leagues with some regularity. Because of this, the time period sampled for this study was set at 1950-1992. The justification for this time frame is the argument that only after integration had been achieved did minorities (including Latinos) enter professional baseball in large enough numbers to expect the sample to be reliable.

The time frame was then broken down by year. This assisted in identifying any trends such as underrepresentation or overrepresentation and increases or decreases in the positional distribution of Latino athletes in major league baseball during the 43 years studied. Whereas previous studies have limited their samples to one playing season (e.g., Maguire, 1988) or different years at regular intervals (e.g., Leonard et al., 1988), the present study covers a continuous time period spanning more than four decades.

Stacking research has relied mainly on data that are readily available in printed form. Sources that have been used include press brochures and media guides (Berghorn et al., 1988; Eitzen and Yetman, 1977), record book data (Dubois, 1980), and even team photographs (Fabianic, 1984). This study followed in the footsteps of earlier studies in that it used *The Baseball Encyclopedia* (Wolff, 1993) as its main reference source.

Procedures

The subjects of the sample are all major league baseball players who could be identified as Latino or non-Latino and were active in the major leagues between 1950 and 1992. A database was created, using Microsoft Works and Claris Works databases and spreadsheets, in which each player was entered as a separately coded case and categorized according to country of birth, position, number of games played, years played, and ethnicity. The second step was to separate the eligible players from the ineligible players in this database. This was done according to the criteria that are listed in this subsection. The database was cross-checked with another reference guide, *Total Baseball* (both in book form [Thorn and Palmer, 1993] and on CD-ROM), to verify numbers and correct any possible mistakes.

The third step was to cross-check the list of eligible players with various other sources to determine the ethnicity of all players. This was done by using lists of Latino players such as those published in *Hispanics in the Major Leagues* (Evans, 1992, 1993), *The International Pastime* (Bjarkman, 1992), various lists and articles from *Nuestro* magazine, and the help of Mario Longoria, an independent historian from San Antonio, Texas, whose field of study is the presence of Latinos in professional sports. Thus ethnicity was the last variable coded.

To make valid comparisons and draw valid conclusions with regard to existing stacking studies, criteria were set that follow patterns and trends found in existing studies as much as possible. However, as a result of the inconsistencies and limited availability of stacking literature on Latino baseball players, some criteria that are unique to the present study had to be set.

The following criteria were used to set the parameters of the data sample and increase reliability:

1. A player was considered a Latino if he is "from North and Central America (such as Mexico, Guatemala, Nicaragua, El Salvador), South America (such as Argentina, Brazil, Uruguay), and the Spanish-speaking Caribbean (such as Puerto Rico, Dominican Republic, Cuba). The term also includes Chicanos (Mexican Americans). The term LATINO refers to a shared cultural heritage (Black, Native American, and Spanish), a history of colonization by Spain, and a common language (Spanish)" (Lapchick and Benedict, 1993, p. 23). Therefore, persons originating from Spain are also included in this term.
2. For a player to be counted in a season, he needs to have played at least 50 games in that particular season (see Jiobu, 1988; Loy and McElvogue, 1970).
3. If a player played more than one position, he was assigned to the position in which he played the most games.
4. When categorizing positions as core, peripheral, and noncentral, the core positions are catcher, second base, and shortstop; peripheral positions are first base and third base; noncentral positions are in the outfield.
5. Pitchers and designated/pinch hitters were considered separately and were not included in this study.

Descriptive Analysis

The research problem consisted of the questions where Latinos tend to be stacked and whether this stacking increases as the number of Latinos in major league baseball rises. To answer these questions satisfactorily, the analysis was broken down into several steps. The first step was to determine the ethnic composition (Latino, non-Latino) by playing positions in major league baseball for the years mentioned under study as well as the distribution by ethnicity across the various playing positions. The second step was to analyze and interpret the data according to the stacking model and centrality concept for the following:

1. The total sample, by year (positions were divided by position and as core/peripheral/noncentral)
2. The Latino segment of the data sample, by year (positions were categorized by position and as core/peripheral/noncentral)
3. Answers to the question whether Latinos are stacked by position as a function of ethnicity
4. Answers to the question that if Latinos are stacked by position as a function of ethnicity, in what positions do they appear most?

The final step was to determine whether any substantial changes in the ethnic composition of playing positions have taken place between 1950 and 1992. If this was the case, the changes were analyzed and interpreted.

The following procedures were followed:

1. For every year, every player was identified by position and ethnicity.
2. The totals and percentages of Latino and non-Latino players were calculated by year, both by position and for the overall population of players.
3. The totals and percentages of Latino and non-Latino players were calculated, comparing the core, peripheral, and noncentral categories.
4. Finally, the information was used to make analyses, interpret possible patterns, and draw conclusions.

Results

According to the existing stacking literature, the results of this study are expected to show that Latino baseball players are stacked in noncentral positions and that this trend becomes more pronounced as increasing numbers of Latinos enter the major leagues every year. These expectations are based on the fact that another minority group in professional sports (i.e., blacks) has shown a similar pattern.

First, the total number of Latinos was calculated for each year from 1950 to 1992. Next, it was determined what percentage of the total number of players these numbers constituted.

Table 14.1 and figure 14.1 demonstrate that even though there was a slump during the 1970s and early 1980s, there has been a steady increase in the percentage of Latinos who play professional baseball. This increase was almost sevenfold over the 43-year period, from 3.0% in 1950 to 19.9% in 1992.

Distribution of Latino Players by Position As a Percentage of All Players

Table 14.2 shows the percentage distribution of Latino baseball players as a percentage of all players by position. The data show that Latino players tend to be stacked in the infield (especially at the core positions of shortstop and second base), not in the outfield as was predicted. This argument is strengthened by the fact that, in table 14.2, the category of outfield encompasses three positions (left field, center field, and right field), unlike all other categories in the same table. This is a finding that is diametrically opposed to the prevailing stacking theories.

Distribution of Latino Players by Position As a Percentage of All Latinos

To verify the finding that Latinos tend to be stacked in the infield when they are studied as a percentage of all players, the distribution of Latino players by position as a percentage of all Latinos was studied

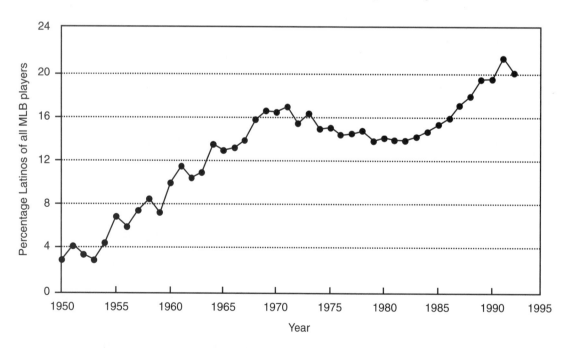

Figure 14.1   Latino major league baseball players as a percentage of all major league baseball players (1950-1992), by year.
Reprinted from González, 1996.

Table 14.1   Totals and Percentages of Latino Major League Baseball Players (1950-1992), by Year

Year	Number of Latino players	Total number of major league players	Percentage of total
1950	6	198	3.0
1951	9	213	4.2
1952	7	201	3.5
1953	6	203	3.0
1954	9	205	4.4
1955	14	205	6.8
1956	12	205	5.9
1957	16	217	7.4
1958	18	214	8.4
1959	15	208	7.2
1960	21	213	9.9
1961	27	236	11.4
1962	28	269	10.4
1963	29	268	10.8
1964	35	261	13.4
1965	35	272	12.9
1966	35	267	13.1
1967	37	268	13.8
1968	42	268	15.7
1969	54	328	16.5
1970	52	318	16.4
1971	52	308	16.9
1972	48	314	15.3
1973	49	303	16.2
1974	46	309	14.9
1975	48	321	15.0
1976	45	314	14.3
1977	51	354	14.4
1978	51	346	14.7
1979	46	336	13.7
1980	48	344	14.0
1981	39	282	13.8
1982	45	328	13.7
1983	49	348	14.1
1984	51	354	14.4
1985	54	358	15.1
1986	55	353	15.6
1987	58	342	17.0
1988	59	331	17.8
1989	67	348	19.3
1990	69	357	19.3
1991	76	356	21.3
1992	69	347	19.9

Reprinted from González, 1996.

(table 14.3). When looking at all positions by year, it becomes apparent that the positions of second base and shortstop have the highest percentages overall, that is, proportionately more Latinos have been playing these positions than have been playing other positions. This is a pattern that can be detected throughout the period studied.

Based on these results, a rank order of the stacking of Latinos in major league baseball would be as follows (high to low): shortstop, second base, outfield, first base, catcher, third base. The same conclusion remains: Latino baseball players are overrepresented in the core positions, especially at second base and shortstop.

Table 14.2 Latinos As a Percentage of All Major League Baseball Players (1950-1992), by Position and by Year

Year	Catcher percentage (*n*)	First base percentage (*n*)	Second base percentage (*n*)	Shortstop percentage (*n*)	Third base percentage (*n*)	Outfield percentage (*n*)
1950	7.4 (2)	0.0	3.9 (1)	4.8 (1)	4.8 (1)	1.3 (1)
1951	9.1 (3)	0.0	8.3 (2)	3.3 (1)	0.0	3.7 (3)
1952	0.0	0.0	4.0 (1)	7.1 (2)	4.2 (1)	4.0 (3)
1953	0.0	0.0	3.7 (1)	9.5 (2)	0.0 (1)	4.0 (3)
1954	0.0	0.0	3.9 (1)	8.3 (2)	5.0 (1)	6.6 (5)
1955	0.0	3.9 (1)	5.0 (1)	13.6 (3)	7.1 (2)	8.5 (7)
1956	0.0	4.1 (1)	3.9 (1)	21.1 (4)	4.0 (1)	6.3 (5)
1957	0.0	7.1 (2)	4.2 (1)	21.7 (5)	7.1 (2)	7.3 (6)
1958	0.0	9.4 (3)	13.0 (3)	20.0 (5)	0.0	8.6 (7)
1959	0.0	9.7 (3)	12.5 (3)	12.5 (3)	4.8 (1)	6.7 (5)
1960	0.0	9.1 (3)	19.1 (4)	21.7 (5)	4.2 (1)	10.1 (8)
1961	3.3 (1)	15.6 (5)	14.8 (4)	30.8 (8)	0.0	9.5 (9)
1962	7.5 (3)	6.1 (2)	6.7 (2)	32.3 (10)	6.1 (2)	8.8 (9)
1963	5.3 (2)	5.7 (2)	12.9 (4)	25.0 (8)	4.0 (1)	11.2 (12)
1964	2.6 (1)	13.3 (4)	6.1 (2)	28.6 (8)	10.7 (3)	16.5 (17)
1965	4.7 (2)	11.8 (4)	15.2 (5)	31.3 (10)	0.0	13.6 (14)
1966	5.1 (2)	11.1 (3)	15.2 (5)	21.4 (6)	16.3 (5)	12.7 (14)
1967	5.6 (2)	12.9 (4)	25.7 (9)	17.9 (5)	6.5 (2)	14.0 (15)
1968	11.4 (4)	10.7 (3)	22.9 (8)	27.6 (8)	12.9 (4)	13.6 (15)
1969	15.2 (7)	8.6 (3)	30.0 (12)	19.4 (7)	17.5 (7)	13.7 (18)
1970	11.6 (5)	2.9 (1)	28.9 (11)	28.2 (11)	17.1 (6)	14.0 (18)
1971	12.5 (5)	5.1 (2)	26.3 (10)	25.7 (9)	15.6 (5)	16.9 (21)
1972	6.7 (3)	5.4 (2)	33.3 (13)	27.3 (9)	8.3 (3)	14.5 (18)
1973	10.0 (4)	7.7 (3)	35.9 (14)	25.7 (9)	6.3 (2)	14.4 (17)
1974	7.1 (3)	4.4 (2)	35.9 (14)	27.0 (10)	6.9 (2)	12.8 (15)
1975	8.7 (4)	7.9 (3)	32.4 (12)	25.0 (11)	9.7 (3)	12.0 (15)
1976	6.4 (3)	10.8 (4)	22.5 (9)	25.0 (9)	5.9 (2)	15.1 (18)
1977	4.0 (2)	9.3 (4)	25.6 (11)	19.5 (8)	14.3 (5)	14.8 (21)
1978	7.1 (3)	15.4 (6)	18.0 (7)	23.3 (10)	4.8 (2)	16.3 (23)
1979	8.7 (4)	13.5 (5)	16.3 (7)	24.4 (10)	10.5 (4)	12.2 (16)
1980	8.2 (4)	8.9 (4)	14.6 (6)	35.9 (14)	2.8 (1)	14.2 (19)
1981	8.3 (3)	11.9 (5)	21.4 (6)	18.8 (6)	5.7 (2)	15.6 (17)
1982	11.6 (5)	10.3 (4)	17.1 (6)	25.6 (10)	10.8 (4)	11.9 (16)
1983	15.6 (7)	8.7 (4)	23.7 (9)	25.6 (11)	19.1 (8)	7.5 (10)
1984	10.9 (5)	11.9 (5)	15.8 (6)	31.1 (14)	15.6 (7)	10.1 (14)
1985	13.3 (6)	11.6 (5)	18.4 (7)	40.0 (16)	4.7 (2)	12.1 (18)
1986	9.6 (5)	10.3 (4)	18.9 (7)	48.7 (18)	2.4 (1)	13.7 (20)
1987	11.8 (6)	9.1 (3)	22.5 (9)	38.1 (16)	7.1 (3)	15.4 (21)
1988	9.8 (5)	17.1 (6)	27.3 (12)	39.4 (13)	7.1 (3)	15.9 (20)
1989	9.3 (5)	13.5 (5)	25.6 (10)	41.5 (17)	15.4 (6)	17.4 (24)
1990	17.0 (9)	17.1 (7)	36.8 (14)	34.2 (13)	12.5 (6)	14.4 (20)
1991	15.1 (8)	26.3 (10)	33.3 (14)	38.1 (16)	14.6 (6)	15.7 (22)
1992	16.0 (8)	21.1 (8)	27.0 (10)	36.4 (16)	12.2 (5)	16.1 (22)

Reprinted from González, 1996.

Table 14.3 Percentage Distribution of Latinos (1950-1992), by Position, As a Percentage of All Latinos

Year	Catcher	First base	Second base	Shortstop	Third base	Outfield[a]	Total n
Expected[b]	12.5	12.5	12.5	12.5	12.5	37.5	
1950	33.3	0.0	16.7	16.7	16.7	16.7	6
1951	33.3	0.0	22.2	11.1	0.0	33.3	9
1952	0.0	0.0	0.0	42.9	14.3	42.9	7
1953	0.0	0.0	16.7	33.3	0.0	50.0	6
1954	0.0	0.0	11.1	22.2	11.1	55.6	9
1955	0.0	7.1	7.1	21.4	14.3	50.0	14
1956	0.0	8.3	8.3	33.3	8.3	41.7	12
1957	0.0	12.5	6.3	31.3	12.5	37.5	16
1958	0.0	16.7	16.7	27.8	0.0	38.9	18
1959	0.0	20.0	20.0	20.0	6.7	33.3	15
1960	0.0	14.3	19.1	23.8	4.8	38.1	21
1961	3.7	18.5	14.8	29.6	0.0	33.3	27
1962	10.7	7.1	7.1	35.7	7.1	32.1	28
1963	6.9	6.9	13.8	27.6	3.5	41.4	29
1964	2.9	11.4	5.7	22.9	8.6	48.6	35
1965	5.7	11.4	14.3	28.6	0.0	40.0	35
1966	5.7	8.6	14.3	17.1	14.3	40.0	35
1967	5.4	10.8	24.3	13.5	5.4	40.5	37
1968	9.5	7.1	19.1	19.1	9.5	35.7	42
1969	13.0	5.6	22.2	13.0	13.0	33.3	54
1970	9.6	1.9	21.2	21.2	11.5	34.6	52
1971	9.6	3.9	19.2	17.3	9.6	40.4	52
1972	6.3	4.1	27.1	18.8	6.3	37.5	48
1973	8.2	6.1	28.6	18.4	4.1	34.7	49
1974	6.5	4.4	30.4	21.7	4.4	32.6	46
1975	8.3	6.3	25.0	22.9	6.3	31.3	48
1976	6.7	8.9	20.0	20.0	4.4	40.0	45
1977	3.9	7.8	21.6	15.7	9.8	41.2	51
1978	5.9	11.8	13.7	19.6	3.9	45.1	51
1979	8.7	10.9	15.2	21.7	8.7	34.8	46
1980	8.3	8.3	12.5	29.2	2.1	39.6	48
1981	7.7	12.8	15.4	15.4	5.1	43.6	39
1982	11.1	8.9	13.3	22.2	8.9	35.6	45
1983	14.3	8.2	18.4	22.5	16.3	20.4	49
1984	9.8	9.8	11.8	27.5	13.7	27.5	51
1985	11.1	9.3	13.0	29.6	3.7	33.3	54
1986	9.1	7.3	12.7	32.7	1.8	36.4	55
1987	10.3	5.2	15.5	27.6	5.2	36.2	58
1988	8.5	10.2	20.3	22.0	5.1	33.9	59
1989	7.5	7.5	14.9	25.4	9.0	35.8	67
1990	13.0	10.1	20.3	18.8	8.7	29.0	69
1991	10.5	13.2	18.4	21.1	7.9	29.0	76
1992	11.6	11.6	14.5	23.2	7.3	31.9	69

Note: Pitchers and designated hitters are excluded.

a. These percentages should be divided by three when making comparisons by position because this category includes three positions: left field, center field, and right field.

b. These percentages should be expected if all positions were to have an equal distribution of Latino players.

Reprinted from González, 1996.

Distribution of Latino Players by Centrality As a Percentage of All Players

Table 14.4 represents the distribution of Latino and non-Latino players (1950-1992) by centrality. Although there is no significant pattern in the percentages of Latino players for each of the three categories until about 1960, during the period from 1960 to 1992 there was a gradual but nonlinear growth of Latinos in the core positions, from 15.7% in 1961 to 25.9% in 1992, with a low of 11.0% in 1964 and a peak of 27.9% in 1990. The peripheral and noncentral positions show a similar pattern of growth, but the percentages lag behind those for the core positions. Both categories started from a lower percentage in 1950 (2.2% for peripheral and 1.3% for noncentral positions, as compared to 5.4% for core positions) and ended with a lower percentage in 1992 (14.6% for peripheral and 14.4% for noncentral positions, as compared to 27.9% for core positions).

In conclusion, the following overall picture of the distribution of Latinos in core, peripheral, and noncentral positions is evident. All three categories show signs of increased Latino representation. However, whereas the core positions show the strongest signs of growth (figure 14.2), the peripheral positions are more varied (figure 14.3), and the noncentral positions indicate a steady but slower increase in the percentage of Latinos (figure 14.4).

The most recent decades seem to show the most dramatic changes.

Distribution of Latino Players by Centrality As a Percentage of All Latinos

From table 14.5, the conclusion can be drawn that, of the total number of Latinos in major league baseball, there is a large representation in the core positions. For most years, the percentages are in the 40%–60% range, and this surpasses the percentages for the other two categories for most years studied. When compared to the expected percentages (in the ideal situation in which no stacking exists, each of the eight positions being given an equal share of 12.5%), the importance of these percentages surfaces. Whereas 37.5% of Latinos are expected to occupy the core positions, the observed percentages are generally substantially higher. On the average, the percentage of Latinos playing core positions between 1950 and 1992 was 47.2%. This is 9.7% higher than expected, thus indicating the possibility of stacking.

The percentages for first and third base (peripheral positions) are substantially lower. For most years, the percentage of Latinos in these two positions varies from 10% to 20% with a few minor exceptions. The expected percentage is 25.0%, but on average only 15.0% of all Latino players are in

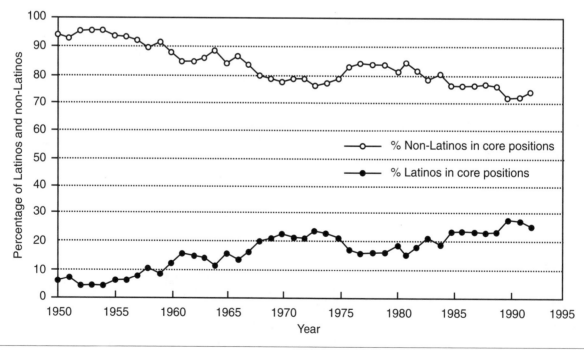

Figure 14.2 Latinos and non-Latinos in core positions (1950-1992).
Reprinted from González, 1996.

Table 14.4   Latinos in Core, Peripheral, and Noncentral Positions As a Percentage of All Major League Baseball Players (1950-1992), by Year

Year	Core percentage (n)	Peripheral percentage (n)	Noncentral percentage (n)
1950	5.4 (4)	2.2 (1)	1.3 (1)
1951	6.9 (6)	0.0 (0)	3.7 (3)
1952	3.8 (3)	2.2 (1)	4.0 (3)
1953	4.0 (3)	0.0 (0)	4.0 (3)
1954	3.8 (3)	2.0 (1)	6.6 (5)
1955	5.8 (4)	5.6 (3)	8.5 (7)
1956	6.5 (5)	4.1 (2)	6.3 (5)
1957	7.6 (6)	7.1 (4)	7.3 (6)
1958	10.1 (8)	5.6 (3)	8.6 (7)
1959	8.2 (6)	7.4 (4)	6.7 (5)
1960	11.7 (9)	7.0 (4)	10.1 (8)
1961	15.6 (13)	8.6 (5)	9.5 (9)
1962	14.9 (15)	6.1 (4)	8.8 (9)
1963	13.9 (14)	5.0 (3)	11.2 (12)
1964	11.0 (11)	12.1 (7)	16.5 (17)
1965	15.7 (17)	6.6 (4)	13.6 (14)
1966	13.0 (13)	14.0 (8)	12.7 (14)
1967	16.2 (16)	9.8 (6)	14.0 (15)
1968	20.2 (20)	11.9 (7)	13.6 (15)
1969	21.3 (26)	13.3 (10)	13.7 (18)
1970	22.5 (27)	10.1 (7)	13.9 (18)
1971	21.2 (24)	9.9 (7)	16.9 (21)
1972	21.4 (25)	6.9 (5)	14.5 (18)
1973	23.7 (27)	7.0 (5)	14.4 (17)
1974	22.9 (27)	5.4 (4)	12.8 (15)
1975	21.3 (27)	8.7 (6)	12.0 (15)
1976	17.1 (21)	8.3 (6)	15.1 (18)
1977	15.7 (21)	11.5 (9)	14.8 (21)
1978	16.1 (20)	9.9 (8)	16.3 (23)
1979	16.2 (21)	12.0 (9)	12.2 (16)
1980	18.6 (24)	6.2 (5)	14.2 (19)
1981	15.6 (15)	9.1 (7)	15.6 (17)
1982	18.0 (21)	10.5 (8)	11.9 (16)
1983	21.4 (27)	13.6 (12)	7.5 (10)
1984	19.4 (25)	13.8 (12)	10.1 (14)
1985	23.6 (29)	8.1 (7)	11.9 (18)
1986	23.8 (30)	6.2 (5)	13.7 (20)
1987	23.7 (31)	8.0 (6)	15.4 (21)
1988	23.4 (30)	11.7 (9)	15.9 (20)
1989	23.9 (32)	14.5 (11)	17.4 (24)
1990	27.9 (36)	14.6 (13)	14.4 (20)
1991	27.7 (38)	20.2 (16)	15.7 (22)
1992	25.9 (34)	16.4 (13)	16.0 (22)

Note: Pitchers and designated hitters are excluded.

Reprinted from González, 1996.

peripheral positions, a finding that expresses underrepresentation.

For the noncentral positions, Latinos follow the expectations. Whereas 37.5% of all Latinos are expected to play in the outfield, the real percentage is 37.8%, or only 0.3% above what is expected.

However, whereas the percentage of all Latinos in the core positions continues to increase and the percentage of peripheral players appears to be fairly stable, there seems to be a slow decline in the percentage of Latinos playing in the outfield.

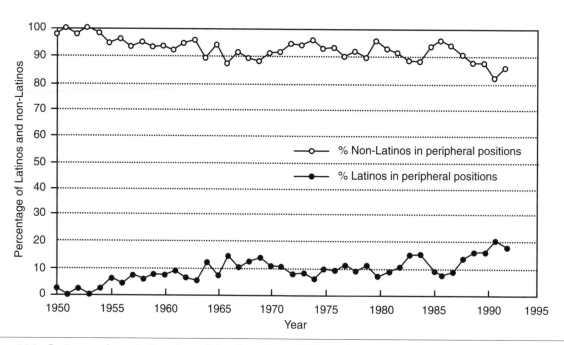

Figure 14.3   Latinos and non-Latinos in peripheral positions (1950-1992).

Reprinted from González, 1996.

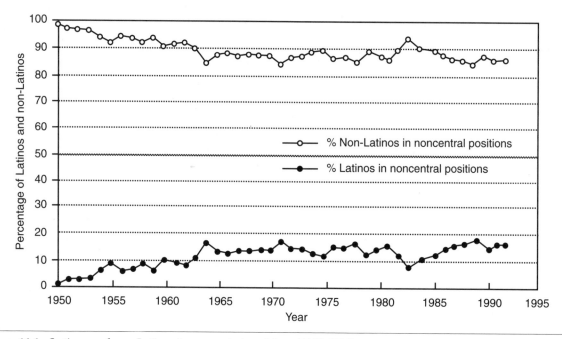

Figure 14.4   Latinos and non-Latinos in noncentral positions (1950-1992).

Reprinted from González, 1996.

Positions in Which Latinos Are Stacked

The data have established that Latino players tend to be stacked in the core positions. To determine in what particular position(s) they are stacked within this category, the positions of catcher, second base, and shortstop were studied separately. The data reveal that shortstop is the most heavily populated by Latinos in core positions, followed by second base and catcher. Even though the sample is relatively small during the early years of the period studied here, this need not be a barrier in a longitudinal analysis of the stacking phenomenon. Thus it can be concluded that the more recent the years,

Table 14.5   Latinos in Core, Peripheral, and Noncentral Positions As a Percentage of All Latinos (1950-1992), by Year

Year	Core	Peripheral	Noncentral	Total *n*
Expected[a]	37.5	25.0	37.5	
1950	66.7	16.7	16.7	6
1951	66.7	0.0	33.3	9
1952	42.9	14.3	42.9	7
1953	50.0	0.0	50.0	6
1954	33.3	11.1	55.6	9
1955	28.6	21.4	50.0	14
1956	41.7	16.7	41.7	12
1957	37.5	25.0	37.5	16
1958	44.4	16.7	38.9	18
1959	40.0	26.7	33.3	15
1960	42.8	19.1	38.1	21
1961	48.2	18.5	39.1	27
1962	53.6	14.3	32.1	28
1963	42.3	10.3	41.4	29
1964	31.4	20.0	48.6	35
1965	48.6	11.4	40.0	35
1966	37.1	22.9	40.0	35
1967	43.2	16.2	40.5	37
1968	47.6	16.7	35.7	42
1969	48.2	18.5	33.3	54
1970	51.9	13.5	34.6	52
1971	46.2	13.5	40.4	52
1972	52.1	10.4	37.5	48
1973	55.1	10.2	34.7	49
1974	58.7	8.7	32.6	46
1975	56.3	12.5	31.3	48
1976	46.7	13.3	40.0	45
1977	41.2	17.7	41.2	51
1978	39.2	15.7	45.1	51
1979	45.7	19.6	34.8	46
1980	50.0	10.4	39.6	48
1981	38.5	18.0	43.6	39
1982	46.7	17.8	35.6	45
1983	55.1	24.5	20.4	49
1984	49.0	23.5	27.5	51
1985	53.7	13.0	33.3	54
1986	54.6	9.1	36.4	55
1987	53.5	10.3	36.2	58
1988	50.9	15.3	33.9	59
1989	47.8	16.4	35.8	67
1990	52.2	18.8	29.0	69
1991	50.0	21.1	29.0	76
1992	49.3	18.8	31.9	69

Note: Pitchers and designated hitters are excluded.

a. The expected percentages were calculated as follows. There are eight positions, and if the distribution is equal for all positions, they account for 12.5% each. The core positions are catcher, second base, and shortstop (3 × 12.5% = 37.5%); the peripheral positions are first base and third base (2 × 12.5% = 25%); and the noncentral positions are left field, center field, and right field (3 × 12.5% = 37.5%).

Reprinted from González, 1996.

the more balanced and pronounced the stacking of Latinos in core positions becomes.

This observation helps to substantiate the theory that states that the increasing number of Latinos in the major leagues results in an increase in the stacking of Latinos by position as a function of ethnicity. To test this, a comparison of the growth patterns of each of the stacked positions was made (see table 14.6).

The position of shortstop is the most stacked position; even during the years in which the total percentage of Latinos dropped (mid-1970s; see table 14.1 and figure 14.1), the percentage of Latinos playing shortstop increased. The position also showed strong growth during periods of increasing Latino participation in major league baseball (e.g., 1958-1961, 1980-1986). The positions of second base and, to a lesser extent, catcher show a similar pattern, although the percentages are lower. Overall, then, overrepresentation does increase at certain positions when the percentage of Latinos in the major leagues grows.

Discussion and Conclusion

Racial and ethnic discrimination is deeply embedded in American society. In the realm of professional sports, this phenomenon is often described as stacking and is usually measured in terms of centrality, or relative distance to the center of the action on the playing field. In this case, minorities are often seen as being stacked in noncentral positions, that is, those positions that require the smallest amounts of leadership qualities, interaction, and decision making.

Over time, historical data have shown a distinctive pattern of distribution of professional baseball players by position and by race. Black players have tended to occupy positions in the outfield, whereas white players have been concentrated in the infield. This distribution pattern has been accounted for by various stacking theories. Such theories purport to account for the segregation by position that is evident in the empirical data.

In addition, Latino stacking patterns tend to be different from traditional stacking patterns for blacks, as developed in the landmark study of Loy and McElvogue (1970). According to the existing stacking literature, minorities should be underrepresented in central positions and overrepresented in noncentral positions. Generally speaking, data for Latino baseball players for the 1950-1992 period reveal that Latinos are stacked in central positions, especially the core positions of second base and shortstop.

Thus the traditional stacking theories do not explain the positional occupancy patterns of Latino players. As Phillips (1983) argued,

It would seem unlikely that prejudiced white coaches and managers would place foreign, colored players who do not speak English well in positions requiring interaction and control. But they do, and the "stereotyping" version of the centrality theory does not explain this. (pp. 13–14)

The data show that "blackness" or color does not necessarily put Latinos in the outfield. Why this is the case is uncertain, and when considering the overall stereotypes, which may play a role in positional distribution of different racial and ethnic groups, this is not a satisfactory explanation for the stacking of Latinos in the infield. Latinos range from black to white; they represent an ethnic group, not a racial group, and so far only one study has been done that uses a five-level classification of the color of black faces, ranging from light to dark (Scully, 1974). Obviously, classifying Latinos by the color of their skin to determine whether darker Latinos tend to be positioned in the noncentral positions is tricky because pictures of players do not always show their true color due to age and differences in printing procedures. However, skin color remains an important issue in stacking.

The traditional stacking theory is premised on the biological view that blacks are strong athletes whose speed and strength make them good outfielders, whereas Latino players are considered to be better infielders because they are relatively short, are more agile, and have better hands. Latinos are not seen as having the power or the speed to be outfielders. This is illustrated by a statement made by Pittsburgh Pirates scout Angel Figueroa, who argued in an interview for *USA Today* that it is very rare to find Mexican players with speed or power. But, he added, because of their Indian blood, Mexicans could run to the city of New York without stopping; they just could not do it very fast (Beaton and Myers, 1993, p. C1).

In addition, the psychological explanations for stacking are based on the idea that blacks and whites are different. According to supporters of these explanations, whites possess an orientation toward the team, success, and competition—qualities that are needed to play in the central positions. By contrast, blacks supposedly express the characteristics of the noncentral positions, which include a focus on the

Table 14.6 Totals and Percentages of All Latino Players in Catcher, Second Base, and Shortstop Positions (1950-1992), by Year

Year	Catcher n (percentage)	Second base n (percentage)	Shortstop n (percentage)	Total n
1950	2 (50.0)	1 (25.0)	1 (25.0)	4
1951	3 (50.0)	2 (33.3)	1 (16.7)	6
1952	0 (0.0)	1 (33.3)	2 (66.7)	3
1953	0 (0.0)	1 (33.3)	2 (66.7)	3
1954	0 (0.0)	1 (33.3)	2 (66.7)	3
1955	0 (0.0)	1 (25.0)	3 (75.0)	4
1956	0 (0.0)	1 (20.0)	4 (80.0)	5
1957	0 (0.0)	1 (16.7)	5 (83.3)	6
1958	0 (0.0)	3 (37.5)	5 (63.5)	8
1959	0 (0.0)	3 (50.0)	3 (50.0)	6
1960	0 (0.0)	4 (44.4)	5 (55.6)	9
1961	1 (7.7)	4 (30.8)	8 (61.5)	13
1962	3 (20.0)	2 (13.3)	10 (66.7)	15
1963	2 (14.3)	4 (28.6)	8 (57.1)	14
1964	1 (9.1)	2 (18.2)	8 (72.7)	11
1965	2 (11.8)	5 (29.4)	10 (58.8)	17
1966	2 (15.4)	5 (38.5)	6 (46.2)	13
1967	2 (12.5)	9 (56.3)	5 (31.3)	16
1968	4 (20.0)	8 (40.0)	8 (40.0)	20
1969	7 (26.9)	12 (46.2)	7 (26.9)	26
1970	5 (18.5)	11 (40.7)	11 (40.7)	27
1971	5 (20.8)	10 (41.7)	9 (37.5)	24
1972	3 (12.0)	13 (52.0)	9 (36.0)	25
1973	4 (14.8)	14 (51.9)	9 (33.3)	27
1974	3 (11.1)	14 (51.9)	10 (37.0)	27
1975	4 (14.8)	12 (44.4)	11 (40.7)	27
1976	3 (14.3)	9 (42.9)	9 (42.9)	21
1977	2 (9.5)	11 (52.4)	8 (38.1)	21
1978	3 (15.0)	7 (35.0)	10 (50.0)	20
1979	4 (19.1)	7 (33.3)	10 (47.6)	21
1980	4 (16.7)	6 (25.0)	14 (58.3)	24
1981	3 (20.0)	6 (40.0)	6 (40.0)	15
1982	5 (23.8)	6 (28.6)	10 (47.6)	21
1983	7 (25.9)	9 (33.3)	11 (40.7)	27
1984	5 (20.0)	6 (24.0)	14 (66.0)	25
1985	6 (20.7)	7 (24.1)	16 (55.2)	29
1986	5 (16.7)	7 (23.3)	18 (60.0)	30
1987	6 (19.4)	9 (29.0)	16 (51.6)	31
1988	5 (16.7)	12 (40.0)	13 (43.3)	30
1989	5 (15.6)	10 (31.3)	17 (53.1)	36
1990	9 (25.0)	14 (38.9)	13 (36.1)	36
1991	8 (21.1)	14 (36.8)	16 (42.1)	38
1992	8 (23.5)	10 (29.4)	16 (47.1)	34

Reprinted from González, 1996.

individual, style, and play. In short, blacks and whites are seen as having different sports personalities and motivational systems, which account for racial stacking (Jones and Hochner, 1973).

Both the biological and the psychological explanations for stacking have been heavily criticized, and rightly so. In addition, for the purposes of this study, they do not apply given that Latinos are classified as an ethnic group, not a racial group. Therefore, another explanation for the stacking of Latinos needs to be developed.

The sociological explanations, which have come to the foreground as a third source of explanation for stacking, seem to hold their ground a little bit better when applied to Latino players. Even though this third group of explanations is based primarily on race, most of them can be applied to an ethnic group such as Latinos. However, the category of "discriminatory processes" seems to be stronger than the explanations falling under the header "levels of socialization."

A possible explanation for this could be the fact that the focus of the two categories is completely different. Whereas the discriminatory processes tend to focus on the perspective of management and the players of the majority group in a sports organization, the levels of socialization theories are centered around self-selection of members of the minority group.

Although there is something to say for the latter category, an explanation for the stacking of Latinos will probably be based on the decisions of the management of major league organizations. Managers, and especially scouts, seem to have preconceived notions that are based on their knowledge and beliefs regarding biology, culture, experience, and, above all, organizational needs. These beliefs then play a role in the decision-making process as to what type of players the scouts will seek.

The levels of socialization theories may play a minor role, but they are definitely overshadowed by the theories mentioned previously. Role modeling, cost, and opportunities to play in a certain position may have some effect, but in the end it is the major league organization that decides who will be signed and what position they will play. In the case of baseball, a unique feature that plays an important role in this respect is the existence of major league baseball academies in the Dominican Republic. These academies train prospects to play certain positions, a decision that is based on the preconceived notions mentioned earlier.

The fact that minorities are stacked in certain positions has profound implications. The most important of these is that minority players have to face heightened competition with one another for a limited number of positions, that is, the positions in which they tend to be stacked (see, e.g., Eitzen and Yetman, 1977, p. 4). For Latino players, this means that they will mostly compete for the positions of second base and shortstop. As a result, talented Latino players may not be drafted as second basemen or shortstops due to an overabundance of Latinos for those two positions. Further, often they are not considered for any other infield positions even though they are quite adept in these positions. Research has shown that white bench (reserve) players tend to be chosen over minority bench players (see, e.g., Phillips, 1983, p. 3). In short, competition among Latinos, or for that matter all minorities, is fiercer than it is among whites because minorities are competing among themselves and for fewer positions as a result of stacking. Whites, by contrast, compete more equally for all positions.

Finally, even though Latinos tend to be stacked in the positions from which coaches and managers are recruited most often, there is an obvious lack of Latinos in these nonplaying positions. Thus, parallel to the argument that traditional stacking patterns do not apply to Latino baseball players, neither does the present mobility theory, which holds that career advancement is related to former playing positions. It seems that for Latinos, holding an infield position may not be sufficient to lead to advancement from a player to a managerial position.

If the current research on managerial recruitment cannot explain the gross underrepresentation of Latino managers, what might be the necessary conditions leading to a managerial position? What accounts for the virtual absence of Latinos from managing positions? One possible explanation is that upward movement from player to manager is an infrequent occurrence (a 1 in 15 chance) even for whites. Between 1980 and 1992, there were 115 different managers, 22 of whom never played in the major leagues. The remaining 93 are but a small fraction of the total number of players who populated the major leagues during the same time period. If Latinos were to advance at the same rate as whites, they would do so in smaller numbers than those of whites (63% of all players excluding pitchers) given the much smaller base of Latino players (16.6% of all players excluding pitchers). Consequently, the lack of Latino managers might be alleviated only by drastically increasing the number of Latino players.

Another possible explanation is that Latinos may not be part of the relevant networks of social contacts. Latino players tend to bond together (because of a common language or cultural background) and associate primarily within a Latino community of players. As a result, they may lack the social connections (i.e., mostly with whites) that could be a necessary factor in the hiring of managers. This is an especially convincing argument for those who believe that managers are hired by a so-called "old boys" network in which the right connections, in addition to qualifications, are crucial.

Moreover, Latinos who are foreign born may return to their countries of origin, families, and friends after their playing days are over. Consequently, they would not be available to be considered for managing positions. This would lead to a diminishing basis of Latino players available for postplaying careers. However, it remains to be determined whether denial of a postplaying career as a manager leads to a return to the country of origin or vice versa.

Along the same lines, networking might be a factor as well. A large percentage of Latinos are foreign nationals, which is not the case for whites. As a result, Latino players may not be able to make the same important career contacts that are afforded to whites early in their careers, through influential coaches in high school and college or even in the minor leagues. These coaches may be highly networked within the professional baseball world and may act as mentors or role models for the native white players. A counterargument could be that foreign-born Latinos have the option of entering baseball academics (e.g., in the Dominican Republic), but several things need to be kept in mind. First, baseball academies do not exist in every Latin American country. Second, prospects are picked by the academies, not vice versa. Networking is irrelevant in this situation.

One can also speculate that Latinos are not hired as managers because of the color of their skin. If this is the case for Latinos, then Afro-Latinos should have a smaller chance of getting hired than non-Afro-Latinos, and all Latinos should have a smaller chance of getting hired than whites.

Finally, it is possible that Latinos are held to a higher standard of play than are others (consider the firing of Tony Perez as manager of the Cincinnati Reds in 1993 after only a few months on the job). Maybe they are expected to perform better simply because they are Latinos. This appears to be similar to the argument that Latino players have been held to a higher standard ever since they entered the major leagues, which would explain the theory that good (not superior) white players are considered for playing positions before good Latino players are. Both skin color and higher standards imply that discriminatory hiring practices are at work.

In sum, even though the data in this study show that Latinos are overrepresented in core positions, there are virtually no Latino managers. So far, no plausible explanation for this phenomenon has been proposed. Even though there is a wide range of possible explanations, the necessary research has yet to be conducted to support one or another of these explanations.

References

Beaton, R., and Myers, J. (1993, February 25). Scouts say players lack speed, power. *USA Today*, pp. C1, C7.

Berghorn, R., Yetman, N.R., and Hanna, L. (1988). Racial participation and integration in men's and women's intercollegiate basketball: Continuity and change, 1958–1985. *Sociology of Sport Journal*, 5,107–124.

Bjarkman, P. (Ed.). (1992). *The international pastime: A review of baseball history*. Cleveland: Society for American Baseball Research.

Blalock, H.M. (1962). Occupational discrimination: Some theoretical propositions. *Social Problems*, 9, 240–247.

Brower, J. (1972). *The racial bias and the division of labor among players in the National Football League as a function of racial stereotypes*. Paper presented at the Pacific Sociological Association meetings, Portland, OR.

Curry, T.J., and Jiobu, R.M. (1984). *Sports: A social perspective*. Englewood Cliffs, NJ: Prentice Hall.

Curtis, J.E., and Loy, J.W. (1978). Race/ethnicity and relative centrality of playing positions in team sports. In R. Hutton (Ed.), *Exercise and sport sciences review*, 6, 285–313.

Dubois, P.E. (1980). The occupational attainment of former college athletes: A comparative study. *International Review of Sport Sociology*, 15, 107–126.

Edwards, H. (1973). *Sociology of sport*. Homewood, IL: Dorsey.

Eitzen, D.S., and Furst, D. (1989). Racial bias in women's collegiate volleyball. *Journal of Sport and Social Issues*, 13, 46–51.

Eitzen, D.S., and Sage, G.H. (1978). *Sociology of American sport*. Dubuque, IA: William C. Brown.

Eitzen, D.S., and Sanford, D.C. (1975). The segregation of Blacks by playing position in football: Accident or design? *Social Science Quarterly*, 55, 948–959.

Eitzen, D.S., and Yetman, N.R. (1977). Immune from racism? *Civil Rights Digest*, 9, 3–13.

Eitzen, D.S., and Yetman, N.R. (1982). Racial dynamics in American sports: Continuity and change. In *Social approaches to sport*. Rutherford, NJ: Associated University Press.

Evans, H. (Ed.) (1992). *Hispanics in the major leagues: Hispanos en las grandes ligas* (Vol. 2; bilingual annual yearbook). New York: R. Panaguia.

Evans, H. (Ed.) (1993). *Hispanics in the major leagues: Hispanos en las grandes ligas* (Vol. 3; bilingual annual yearbook). New York: R. Panaguia.

Fabianic, D. (1984). Minority managers in professional baseball. *Sociology of Sport Journal*, 1, 163–171.

Grusky, O. (1963). The effects of formal structure on managerial recruitment: A study of baseball organizations. *Sociometry*, 26, 345–353.

Guppy, N. (1983). Positional centrality and racial segregation in professional baseball. *International Review of Sport Sociology*, 18, 95–109.

Jiobu, R.M. (1988). Racial inequality in a public arena: The case of professional baseball. *Social Forces, 67,* 524–534.

Jones, J.M., and Hochner, A.R. (1973). Racial differences in sports activities: A look at the self-paced versus reactive hypothesis. *Journal of Personality and Social Psychology, 27,* 86–95.

Jordan, J. (1969). Physiological and anthropometrical comparisons of Negroes and Whites. *Journal of Health, Physical Education, and Recreation, 40,* 93–99.

Kjeldsen, E.K. (1981). The rise to leadership in major league baseball: Playing background and early career influences. In A. Dunleavy, A.W. Miracle, and C.R. Rees (Eds.), *Studies in the sociology of sport.* Fort Worth, TX: Texas Christian University Press.

Klonsky, B. (1977). *The effects of formal structure and role skills on coaching recruitment and longevity: A study of professional basketball teams.* Paper presented at the 72nd annual meeting of the American Sociological Association, Chicago.

Lapchick, R.E., and Benedict, J.R. (1993). *1993 racial report card.* Boston: Northeastern University, Center for the Study of Sport in Society.

Lavoie, M. (1989). Stacking, performance differentials, and salary discrimination in professional ice hockey: A survey of the evidence. *Sociology of Sport Journal, 6,* 163–166.

Leonard, W.M. II. (1977). An extension of the Black, Latin, White report. *International Review of Sport Sociology, 12,* 85–96.

Leonard, W.M. II. (1987). Stacking in collegiate basketball: A neglected analysis. *Sociology of Sport Journal, 7,* 294–301.

Leonard, W.M. II, Pine, J., and Rice, C. (1988). Performance characteristics of White, Black, and Hispanic major league baseball players: 1955–1984. *Journal of Sport and Social Issues, 12,* 31–43.

Loy, J.W., Curtis, J.E., and Hillen, J. (1987). Effects of formal structure on managerial recruitment: Comparisons on Japanese and North American professional baseball clubs. *Sociology of Sport Journal, 4,* 1–16.

Loy, J.W., and McElvogue, J.F. (1970). Racial discrimination in American sport. *International Review of Sport Sociology, 5,* 5–24.

Loy, J.W., Sage, J.N., and Ingham, A.G. (1972). *The effects of formal structure of organizational leadership: An Investigation of collegiate baseball teams.* Paper presented at the 85th national convention of the American Association for Health, Physical Education, and Recreation, Seattle, WA.

Madison, D.R., and Landers, D.M. (1976). Racial discrimination in football: A test of the "stacking" of playing position hypothesis. In D.M. Landers (Ed.), *Social problems in athletics: Essays in the sociology of sport.* Urbana, IL: University of Illinois Press.

Maguire, J. (1988). Race and position assignment in English soccer: A preliminary analysis of ethnicity and sport in Britain. *Sociology of Sport Journal, 5,* 257–269.

Malina, R.M. (1965). Anthropology, growth, and physical education. In R. Singer et al. (Eds.), *Physical education: An interdisciplinary approach.* New York: Macmillan.

Marple, D.P. (1975). Analyse de la discrimination que subsissent les Canadians Français hockey professionel. *Movement, 10,* 7–13.

Marple, D., and Pirie, P. (1978). *The French Canadian ice hockey player. A review of evidence and suggestions for further research.* Paper presented at the Canadian Sociology and Anthropology Association meetings, Fredericton, New Brunswick.

McPherson, B.D. (1974). Minority group involvement in sport: The black athlete. In J. Wilmore (Ed.), *Exercise and sport science reviews* (Vol. 2, pp. 71–101). New York: Academic Press.

Medoff, M.H. (1976). Racial segregation in baseball: The economic hypothesis versus the sociological hypothesis. *Journal of Black Studies, 6,* 393–400.

Medoff, M.H. (1977). Positional segregation and professional baseball. *International Review of Sport Sociology, 12,* 49–56.

Medoff, M.H. (1986). Positional segregation and the economic hypothesis. *Sociology of Sport Journal, 3,* 297–304.

Pattnayak, S.R., and Leonard, J. (1991). Racial segregation in major league baseball. *Sociology and Social Research, 76,* 3–9.

Phillips, J.C. (1983). Race and career opportunities in major league baseball: 1960–1980. *Journal of Sport and Social Studies, 7,* 1–17.

Roy, G. (1974). *The relationship between centrality and mobility: The case of the National Hockey League.* Unpublished master's thesis, Department of Kinesiology, University of Waterloo.

Scully, G. (1974). Discrimination: The case of baseball. In R. Noll (Ed.), *Government and the sports business* (pp. 221–273). Washington, DC: Brookings Institution.

Thorn, J., and Palmer, P. (Eds.). (1993). *Total baseball: The ultimate encyclopedia of baseball.* New York: Harper Collins.

Wolff, R. (Ed.). (1993). *The baseball encyclopedia.* New York: Macmillan.

Worthy, M., and Markle, A. (1970). Racial differences in reactive versus self-paced sports activities. *Journal of Personality and Social Psychology, 7,* 439–443.

Hail to the Redskins? Public Reactions to a Racially Insensitive Team Name

Lee Sigelman

The use of American Indian team names, mascots, and symbols has stirred considerable controversy over the last decade. This paper focuses on public attitudes toward the most frequently objected-to team name, the Redskins, Washington, DC's professional football team. Data from two surveys, one local and the other national, establish that very few members of the general public see any need to change Redskins to another name. Support for a name change is significantly higher among racial or ethnic minorities; the more highly educated; and those who are not fans of professional football in general or the Washington team in particular. However, even in those parts of the public, support is far outweighed by opposition. These findings stand in stark contrast to the idea that Americans now routinely disassociate themselves from ideas and stereotypes that might convey the impression that they are racially insensitive.

On the night of Saturday, November 15, 1997, Washington, DC's professional basketball team lost 102-91 to the Orlando Magic, preserving its winless record at home under its new team name, the Wizards. The team had abandoned its former name, the Bullets, after the 1996-1997 season in order to disassociate itself from negative imagery.

On the same night, Washington's professional ice hockey team, the Capitals, defeated the Montreal Canadiens 3-2. This was Washington left-winger Chris Simon's first game back in uniform after be-

ing suspended for three games for directing a racial epithet at Edmonton Oilers right-winger Mike Grier, an African American.

The next day, Washington's professional football team suffered a disappointing 17-14 loss to its hated rivals, the Dallas Cowboys. Following the game, no team names were altered, no suspensions were announced, and no commentator mentioned and presumably few fans paused to reflect upon the questionable propriety of a team name, Redskins, that the National Congress of American Indians has condemned as "pejorative, derogatory, denigrating, offensive, scandalous, contemptuous, disreputable, disparaging, and racist" (Goldberg, 1993, p. D1).

The Issue of Racially Insensitive Team Names

How racial and ethnic minority groups refer to themselves—as *colored*, *Negro*, *black*, or *African American*; *Mexican American*, *Chicano*, *Hispanic*, or *Latino*; *Indian* or *Native American*, for example—matters a great deal to many members of these groups (Smith, 1992). How *others* refer to them not only serves as a litmus test of the tenor of intergroup relations, but can literally be a matter of life and death. Racial and ethnic slurs, whether born of deeply rooted hostilities or of unthinking stereotypes, generate ill will and often escalate into violence.

Public concern about racial stereotyping and scholarly analyses of the phenomenon are concentrated

Reprinted from Sigelman, 1998.

primarily on deleterious stereotypes of African Americans. Thus, for example, it would be unthinkable for a professional sports franchise to have a name even as ostensibly unstigmatizing as the "New York Negroes," let alone a name that smacks of blatant racism. But although levels of consciousness have been raised concerning the stereotyping of African Americans, the same consciousness has not carried over to all other groups. Thus, as Pace (1994, p. 7), building on the "New York Negroes" example, asks, "Why would it be socially repugnant to name a team the 'New York Negroes' but not to name one the 'Cleveland Indians'? Worse yet, could there be a team named the 'New York Niggers'? Isn't that just the racial equivalent of the 'Washington Redskins'?"

In an attempt to demonstrate greater cultural sensitivity, a number of colleges and universities—Eastern Michigan, Marquette, Miami of Ohio, St. John's, and Stanford among them—have abandoned their traditional American Indian-related team names. In many instances, critics have decried these actions as proof positive that political correctness is running wild on college campuses. The *Chicago Tribune* charged as much in an editorial titled, "Will the 'Fighting Irish' Be Next?" (1993) that blamed "the correctness police" for riding roughshod over collegiate athletic departments.

Though frequently criticized for lingering racism even decades after official or unofficial color lines have been broken, professional sports leagues have come a long way in recent years. Much remains to be done to overcome the underrepresentation of all minorities in management positions and of some minorities in most sports, and the stacking of some minorities in certain positions (e.g., African Americans in positions requiring speed and quickness rather than leadership and poise; Eitzen and Sage, 1989). However, the professional leagues now take pains to avoid the appearance of discrimination based on race or ethnicity. In this context, it is especially striking that no major league team has yet dropped its Indian-related team name, the most objectionable of which is clearly the "Redskins," a name that even the *Chicago Tribune*, in the editorial just cited, condemned as "patently offensive." Team management defends this name as "reflecting positive attributes of the American Indian such as dedication, courage and pride" (Goldberg, 1993, p. D3). The grain of truth underlying this defense is that the contemporary stereotype of Native Americans, embodied in the prevalence of Indian imagery in American popular culture and consumer products and in the ongoing public demand for Native American crafts and artifacts, contains many elements that

would be considered "positive," such as bravery, wisdom, spirituality, and closeness to nature. As a consequence, it may never even have occurred to millions who cheer for a team with an Indian name or mascot that they are engaging in racial stereotyping or, if they do recognize this, they may see nothing wrong with this particular form of stereotyping.

Others recognize that racial stereotyping per se, whether "positive" or "negative," is harmful, and scoff at the idea these team names "honor" Native Americans, reserving special fire for a team name as blatant as "Redskins." Writing in the *Village Voice*, Alex Heard (1992, p. 148) notes that "The Redskins 'honor' American Indians by having a black man gallivant on the sidelines in buckskins and a headdress. Reverse that image and you'll see the Indians' point. Imagine an Indian in blackface and a Zulu warrior outfit, as a mascot for a team called the 'Black Savages'." "Redskins," the publisher of America's largest Indian-owned newspaper has written, "is a word that should remind every American there was a time in our history when America paid bounties for human beings. There was a going rate for the scalps or hides of Indian men, women and children. These 'redskins' trophies could be sold to most frontier trading posts. Along with coon skins, beaver skins and bear skins, the selling of 'redskins' was also profitable" (Giago, 1994, p. 9). As *Washington Post* columnist Colman McCarthy (1991, p. A23) puts it, "'Redskins' is a slur name that smells with the stench of racism." Most of the team's current fans are not old enough to recognize the historical context of their team's racial insensitivity: The "Redskins," never noted for progressive race relations, were the last National Football League team to sign African American players and did so only under the duress of the 1957 Stadium Act.

Full consideration of the arguments both for and against team names like "Braves" and "Indians," let alone "Redskins," would go well beyond the purpose of this article; these arguments and counterarguments are nicely summarized elsewhere (Davis, 1993; Kelber, 1994; Loving, 1992). Here the underlying issue is why professional sports teams in general and the Washington team in particular have made no move to scrap their racially insensitive team names. By their inaction are they not swimming against a tide in which they are expected at least to pay lip service to racial and ethnic tolerance? By clinging to such names, are they not risking a public relations fiasco, alienating their fans and the general public through their apparent racial insensitivity?

Thus framed, the issue of racially insensitive team names carries echoes of a debate among students of race relations concerning what has been called "symbolic racism" (Kinder and Sears, 1981), "modern racism" (McConahay, 1986), "aversive racism" (Gaertner and Dovidio, 1986), or "racial resentment" (Kinder and Sanders, 1996). The basic and highly controversial idea underlying the symbolic racism thesis is that white racism endures but is now less crude and less openly articulated than it used to be. As Sniderman and Piazza (1993), who reject this idea, see it:

> A mythology has grown up around the problem of racial stereotypes. . . . Perhaps the most crucial of these myths expresses itself in the ubiquitous assumption that whites no longer will openly express a frankly derogatory characterization of [minorities]. . . . What has changed, it is suggested, is not how [whites] feel . . . but what they feel free to say. . . . Who, it is asked . . . will openly make remarks that could give the impression they are racists?

> . . . But if one goes out into American society and talks with taxi drivers or nurses or transportation executives or schoolteachers or a host of others about problems of race in American life, one would have to put blinders on one's eyes and cotton batten in one's ears not to see and hear the negative characterizations routinely expressed about [minorities]. . . . [C]ontrary to the conventional wisdom, these negative racial characterizations are openly and routinely expressed. (Sniderman and Piazza, 1993, p. 36)

Two aspects of this issue are addressed here. First, when the question is directly put to them, do most Americans try to distance themselves from the "Redskins" team name, as a symbolic politics-based interpretation would lead one to expect? Or is the American public sufficiently insensitive on racial matters (or especially insensitive on, or at least unattuned to, matters involving American Indians) that relatively few people feel the need to disassociate themselves from a name like "Redskins"? Second, do reactions to this name tend to follow the same lines that have emerged in prior research on racial attitudes? For example, are more highly educated Americans and members of racial and ethnic minority groups less likely to condone it?

Analysis

These questions are addressed here through analysis of data from two random-digit dialing–based telephone surveys by Chilton Research Services. One of these surveys, commissioned by ABC News and the *Washington Post* and conducted in January 1992, focused on the upcoming Super Bowl game between Buffalo and Washington (ABC News–*Washington Post*, 1992). The other survey, conducted in August of 1992, was commissioned by the *Washington Post* to probe support in the Washington, DC, metropolitan area and Northern Virginia for the proposed construction of a new football stadium (*Washington Post*, 1992). There were 810 interviewees in the national survey and 1,244 in the local one.[1] In each survey, interviewees were asked the same question about the Redskins' team name: "Some people say that the Washington Redskins should change its team name because it is offensive to Native American Indians. Others say the name is not intended to be offensive, and should not be changed. What about you? Should the Redskins change their team name, or not?"

These appear to be the only surveys in which opinions concerning the "Redskins" team name have been elicited. Of course, these surveys are now somewhat dated. The time at which they were conducted marked a highpoint of media and public attention to the issue of racially insensitive team names and mascots, reflecting the successes of the Atlanta Braves, Florida State University Seminoles, and Washington Redskins during 1991 and 1992 and the protests these names and mascots engendered (Loving, 1992). Since then, the issue of racially insensitive team names has attracted little public notice. Accordingly, it seems safe to assume that insofar as the mass public is concerned, this issue is currently less salient than it was in the early 1990s, and it is highly unlikely that public opposition to these symbols is much more widespread now than it was then. It also warrants mention that even though the "bottom line" of the focal question ("Should the Redskins change their team name or not?") was straightforward, negative answers to it could have stemmed from various considerations. One could, for example, have opposed a name change because one saw "Redskins" as honoring Native Americans rather than derogating them, or because one thought of Native Americans as quaint cultural artifacts, or because one had no strong feelings one way or the other and thus preferred to maintain the status quo, or because one was unsympathetic to anything that smacked of "political correctness." Thus, it is not entirely clear what negative answers to this question mean. It is, however, abundantly clear that they do not signify a racially progressive stance.

Virtually everyone who was asked this question was willing to venture an opinion about whether a name change was called for, and these opinions were overwhelmingly negative (see table 15.1). In the Washington area, only about 1 in 6 interviewees thought the team should change its name, and 80% thought it should not. Scarce as support was locally for abandoning the "Redskins" name, it was even rarer nationally: Almost 9 out of every 10 of those polled around the country opposed a name change, and only 7.4% said they favored it. These results convey an unambiguous answer to the first set of questions posed above. In stark contrast to the notion that most Americans avoid voicing sentiments that might smack of racial insensitivity, the vast majority of those interviewed in these two surveys indicated that they saw no reason to abandon the "Redskins" name. That Washington-area residents were somewhat less resistant than Americans nationwide to a name change reflects, in large measure, the heavy minority composition of the Washington area. To anticipate a point that will stand out in table 15.2, non-Hispanic whites were much more likely to oppose a name change than were members of racial and ethnic minority groups, presumably because the latter were more attuned to the negative impact of racial and ethnic stereotyping.

To address the second set of issues, that of the patterning of opinion, table 15.2 summarizes the results of a pair of logistic regression analyses of support for or opposition to a name change (coded 1 and 0, respectively). The independent variables in these models were an interviewee's age (in years), gender (*male = 0, female = 1*), educational attainment (in years of school completed), minority status (0 = *non-Hispanic whites*, 1 = *all others*), and status as a football fan (in the local survey, 1 = those who considered themselves fans of the Washington team, 0 = those who did not; in the national survey, those who said they follow professional football 3 = *very closely*, 2 = *fairly closely*, 1 = *not too closely*, and 0 = *not closely at all*). The expectations underlying the analyses were, first, that support for a name change would be more widespread among younger interviewees, the more highly educated, and women among whom levels of racial and ethnic prejudice have often been shown to be lower (e.g., Kluegel and Smith, 1986; Sigelman and Welch, 1991). Members of racial ethnic minority groups were also expected to be more sensitive to the use of stigmatizing group labels and therefore to be more positively disposed toward a name change. On the other hand, football fans in general and Washington fans in particular were expected to be more likely than others to resist the idea of a name change—Washington fans because of their greater investment in the team and its current name, foot-

Table 15.1 Public Opinion About Changing the Name of the Washington Redskins

	DC area	Nation-wide
Should change team name	16.2%	7.4%
Should not change team name	80.6%	88.0%
Don't know, no opinion, refused	3.2%	4.6%

Reprinted from Sigelman, 1998.

ball fans nationwide because they had grown accustomed to and would be more likely to accept without question the "Redskins" name.

According to table 15.2, there were no significant age- or gender-based differences in these responses. These unexpected null results might reflect, first, the lack of attention that has been paid to stereotyping of Native Americans in recent public discourse, and perhaps a sense that the stereotyping embodied in Indian teams is not as objectionable as that seen in traditional stereotypes of African Americans. Each of the remaining hypothesized effects did emerge in both surveys. That is, as expected, more highly educated interviewees, members of racial-ethnic minority groups, and those who were not fans of the Washington team or who did not follow professional football were significantly more likely to express support for a name change. The last column in the table details these effects. The coefficients for level of education mean that, controlling for the effects of the other predictors in the model, for every year of education an interviewee had, the odds that he or she favored a name change increased by 26% in the local survey and by 21% in the national one; thus the odds would double if one of two otherwise-identical interviewees had 4 or 5 more years of schooling than the other.[2] For minorities, the counterpart coefficients signify that the odds of supporting a name change more than doubled in comparison to the odds for non-Hispanic whites. And for fans of the Washington team in particular or professional football in general, these coefficients signify odds only two thirds or three fourths as high as those observed among those who were not followers of the Washington team or of pro football.

Of course, none of these comparisons implies that the odds of supporting a name change were very great in an absolute sense. Indeed, few interviewees of any sort—highly educated or not, minorities or not, football fans or not—said that the "Redskins" name should be changed. For example, even among college graduates, only 14% nationwide and 22%

Table 15.2   Sources of Support for and Opposition to a Name Change

Predictor	b	SE	Wald	$\mathrm{Exp}(b)$
Results from the DC area survey				
($N = 1167$)				
Age	−.003	.006	0.175	0.998
Gender	−.062	.006	0.117	0.940
Minority	1.023	.194	27.848*	2.782
Education	.236	.041	33.447*	1.266
Redskins fan	−.425	.185	5.303*	0.654
Constant	−5.124	.711	51.970*	
Results from the national survey				
($N = 773$)				
Age	−.001	.009	0.008	0.999
Gender	−.299	.279	1.146	0.742
Minority	.809	.300	7.265*	2.245
Education	.191	.051	14.152*	1.210
Pro football fan	−.303	.135	5.078*	0.738
Constant	−4.710	.894	27.715*	

Note: $\chi^2 = 58.243$

*$p < .05$.

Reprinted from Sigelman, 1998.

locally called for a name change, and the comparable figures for racial-ethnic minorities were 12% and 23%. Clearly, then, the results reported in table 15.2 must be interpreted within the context of the widespread lack of support for a name change that is so evident in table 15.1. Within that context, the odds that someone would say that the "Redskins" name should be changed were much higher within certain segments of the public (the more highly educated, minorities, and those who did not follow football or the Redskins), but the fact remains that the odds were not very high within any segment of the public.

Conclusion

Professional teams like the "Redskins," the Atlanta "Braves," the Cleveland "Indians," and the Kansas City "Chiefs" have attracted considerable criticism from Indian activists. For example, in 1993 Ben Nighthorse Campbell, the only Native American member of the U.S. Senate, introduced legislation to force the Washington team to change its name before federal land would be transferred to build a new stadium. That same year, a state legislator in Ohio sponsored a bill designed to block the use of public money for a new stadium for the Cleveland "Indians" unless the club dropped its mascot, "Chief Wahoo." However, if the findings reported here are

any guide, these teams have little to fear from the general public in terms of objections to or campaigns against their names, or even in terms of sympathy for the cause of those who do object or threaten action. Simply put, the general public "just doesn't get it" with respect to these team names.

Especially since actual Indians are a virtually invisible minority for most Americans, stereotypical images of Native Americans have long been widespread in American popular culture. As a consequence, a name like "Redskins" seems unlikely to become a source of widespread public outrage—far less likely than would be the case if a team had an unflattering name (or any name at all) signifying, say, blacks, Asians, or Jews. Many white Americans who understand that terms like "nigger" and "spic" are derogatory and who even know something about the history of such terms may not recognize "redskin" as a derogatory term. On the other hand, repeated attempts to raise public consciousness on this issue, especially around the time the surveys analyzed here were conducted, have fallen flat. Not only has the general public failed to rally to this cause, but even those segments of the general public that are most positively disposed remain overwhelmingly unconvinced of the necessity for change. Many Americans may have learned to distance themselves from unflattering stereotypes of various minorities, but in the case examined here that lesson has obviously not taken hold.

The unpopularity of the move to get professional teams to abandon Native American names has not been lost on Indian activists, who for the most part have recognized the futility of attempting to sway public opinion on this issue. Accordingly, in recent years they have pursued a quieter but potentially more effective strategy. Failing to spark a public outcry that would force team owners to abandon the objectionable team name, they have concentrated on the courts, as did African Americans in the 1950s and 1960s. Their legal challenge has been directed not at the Washington team's right to use the "Redskins" name, but to enjoy federal trademark protection for it, in apparent violation of Section 2(a) of the Federal Trademark Act, which denies protection to any mark that "consists of or comprises immoral, deceptive, or scandalous matter; or matter which may disparage or falsely suggest a connection with persons, living or dead, institutions, beliefs or national symbols, or bring them into contempt, or disrepute." The idea underlying the trademark challenge has been that the threat of potential lost revenue may cause the team to abandon its name voluntarily (see Claussen, 1996; Kelber, 1994; Likourezos, 1996; Loving, 1992; Pace, 1994).

Whether this challenge will ultimately bear fruit will not be known until it has worked its way fully through the federal courts. What seems certain at this point is that the courts are a more promising venue for fighting this battle than are the media. As one legal scholar has written, "Due to the size of the Native American population, and the inability of many Americans to relate to the problem, the movement opposing the use of Native American team names has failed to apply significant political pressure on team owners. Without judicial intervention, the notion that more speech, more talking, more preaching, and more lecturing can counter this practice is appealing, lofty, romantic—and wrong" (Kelber, 1994, p. 534).

References

ABC News–*Washington Post*. (1992). ABC News–*Washington Post* Super Bowl poll, January 1992 [Computer file]. Radnor, PA: Chilton Research Services [producer]. Ann Arbor, MI: Inter-University Consortium for Political and Social Research [distributor].

Claussen, C.L. (1996). Ethnic team names and logos: Is there a legal solution? *Marquette Sports Law Journal*, **6**, 409–421.

Davis, L.R. (1993). Protest against the use of Native American mascots: A challenge to traditional American identity. *Journal of Sport and Social Issues*, **17**, 9–22.

Eitzen, D.S., and Sage, G.H. (1989). *Sociology of North American sport* (4th ed.). Dubuque, IA: Brown.

Gaertner, S.L., and Dovidio, J.F. (1986). The aversive form of racism. In J.F. Dovidio and S.L. Gaertner (Eds.), *Prejudice, discrimination, and racism* (pp. 61–89). Orlando, FL: Academic Press.

Giago, T. (1994, March 13). Drop the chop! Indian nicknames just aren't right. *New York Times*, pp. 8–9.

Goldberg, K. (1993, July 10). Ethnic team names draw new attacks. *Washington Times*, pp. D1, D3.

Heard, A. (1992, January 28). Hail to the racists? *Village Voice*, pp. 148, 102.

Kelber, B.C. (1994). "Scalping the Redskins": Can trademark law start athletic teams bearing Native American nicknames and images on the road to racial reform? *Hamline Law Review*, **17**, 533–588.

Kinder, D.R., and Sanders, L.M. (1996). *Divided by color: Racial politics and democratic ideals*. Chicago: University of Chicago Press.

Kinder, D.R., and Sears, D.O. (1981). Symbolic racism versus racial threats to the good life. *Journal of Personality and Social Psychology*, **40**, 414–431.

Kluegel, J.R., and Smith, E.R. (1986). *Beliefs about inequality: Americans' views of what is and what ought to be*. New York: Aldine de Gruyter.

Likourezos, G. (1996). A case of first impression: American Indians seek cancellation of the trademarked term "Redskins." *Journal of the Patent and Trademark Office Society*, **78**, 275–290.

Loving, P.E. (1992). Native American team names in athletics: It's time to trade these marks. *Loyola of Los Angeles Entertainment Law Journal*, **13**, 1–44.

McCarthy, C. (1991, November 2). No feathers, no drums. *Washington Post*, p. A23.

McConahay, J.B. (1986). Modern racism, ambivalence, and the modern racism scale. In J.F. Dovidio and S.L. Gaertner (Eds.), *Prejudice, discrimination, and racism* (pp. 91–125). Orlando, FL: Academic Press.

Pace, K.A. (1994). The Washington Redskins case and the doctrine of disparagement: How politically correct must a trademark be? *Pepperdine Law Review*, **22**, 7–57.

Sigelman, L., and Welch, S. (1991). *Black Americans' views of racial inequality: The dream deferred*. New York: Cambridge University Press.

Smith, T.W. (1992). Changing racial labels: From "colored" to "Negro" to "black" to "African American." *Public Opinion Quarterly*, **56**, 496–514.

Sniderman, P.M., and Piazza, T. (1993). *The scar of race*. Cambridge, MA: Harvard University Press.

Washington Post. (1992). *Washington Post* District of Columbia Stadium Poll, August 1992 [computer file]. Radnor, PA: Chilton Research Services [producer]. Ann Arbor, MI: Inter-university Consortium for Political and Social Research [distributor].

Will the "Fighting Irish" be next? (1993, November 7). *Chicago Tribune*, p. 4, p. 2.

Notes

1. These data were obtained from the Inter-University Consortium for Political and Social Research. Chilton Research Services, the *Washington Post*, ABC News, and the ICPSR bear no responsibility for the findings and interpretations presented here.

2. The coefficient would equal 1 if the odds of supporting a name change were exactly the same for those with $n + 1$ years of education as for those with n years of education; it would be greater than 1 if the odds were higher among those with $n + 1$ years of education than those with n years; and it would be less than 1 if the odds were lower among those with $n + 1$ years of education than those with n years. Thus, these coefficients are simply ratios of odds.

Blacks As Key Functionaries: A Study of Racial Stratification in Professional Sport

Arthur S. Evans Jr.

Key functionaries are positions within a social system that are capable of influencing and performing crucial activities (Olsen, 1978, pp. 25–26). As a result of their location, these positions are centers of power and control (Buckley, 1966, pp. 8–18). Some key functionaries control inputs and outputs with outside environments, whereas others serve as channels for the flow of messages among the system's parts. Still others are responsible for directing the flow of system activities. Because each social system must depend on the adequate performance of these positions for its overall operations, key functionaries are capable of wielding considerable power.

The scarcity of blacks in key functionary positions in professional sport is the major concern of this article. Because sport reflects society, it is reasonable that the question of the acceptance of blacks in these roles is relevant. For example, before 1946, blacks were denied full participation with whites in professional baseball, football, and basketball. Today, this barrier has dissipated and is no longer a factor restricting the participation of the black athlete. Blacks now participate in major sports (i.e., baseball, football, and basketball) in numbers disproportionate to their percentage of the larger population (Edwards, 1973, pp. 213–245; Leonard, 1988, pp. 214–255). However, discriminatory barriers toward blacks have not been entirely abolished in professional sport. Indeed, new and formidable barriers involving key functionary positions have appeared to replace the old ones. The new barriers entail institutional practices extending to nonathletes and are not as easily remedied as rights re-

lating to athletic participation (Ball, 1973, pp. 97–113; Grusky, 1963, pp. 345–353). Thus, although blacks have overcome the problem of gaining admittance to professional sport as players, they face the issue of securing proportional representation in positions of control within this milieu.

The first section of this article examines the theoretical origins of beliefs and attitudes that have functioned to impede blacks' mobility into key functionary positions within professional sport. The second portion of this article provides examples from professional sport to demonstrate the lack of acceptance of blacks in key functionary positions.

Racial Inclusion and Exclusion

The Calvinist experiment of the 16th and 17th centuries is alive today, but the religious emphasis (see, e.g., Abrahamson, 1990, pp. 174–176; Collins and Makowsky, 1989, pp. 118–140; Erikson, 1966, pp. 33–64; Ritzer, 1988, p. 134; Takla and Pope, 1985, pp. 74–88; Weber, 1958, pp. 30–98) has been replaced by a racial one. For example, current efforts at social reform for blacks must confront this ethic as a major obstacle. As was true for the poor in general who were considered by the Calvinists to be unworthy and lacking the requisites for citizenship, blacks today are perceived in a similar manner. Whether the issue is to assist blacks through needs-based financial assistance or through affirmative-action programs, Americans and their elected representatives tend to question whether the recipients are

Reprinted from Evans, 1997.

"deserving" (Wilson, 1987, pp. 109–139). In general, the latent effects of Calvinism have encouraged the perception that blacks do not possess the requisites to be equal citizens or to occupy key functionary positions.

One sphere of society appearing free of this negative portrayal is professional sport (Luschen, 1980, pp. 315–347; Nixon, 1984, pp. 34–84; Snyder and Spreitzer, 1973, pp. 249–255). Today in professional sport, blacks are making progress in gaining access to key functionary roles (e.g., sportscaster, executive, coach, or paid endorser of commercial products) that were formerly denied them. This upward mobility has been encouraged by the civil rights movement of the 1960s, greater specialization and efficiency within the professional sports sphere, industrialization, better education of blacks, sympathetic whites, and affirmative-action programs. Yet, as blacks take their newly acquired places in positions of power and control, one senses that among the larger population, there exists concern and doubt over whether or not they are qualified to occupy these positions. There are two explanations, both of which explain in part this apprehension.

On one hand, conflict theory suggests that such attitudes toward blacks stem from this nation's long history of prejudice and institutional discrimination. This theory explains that although slavery ended more than 100 years ago, many Americans still consider blacks as immoral, lazy, undependable, and undeserving of positions of higher authority (Lenski, 1966, pp. 40–82). This theory, however, fails to account for the fact that despite negative attitudes against them, some blacks do experience upward mobility and occupy key functionary roles in society.

On the other hand, functionalist theory suggests that apprehension toward blacks in key functionary positions results from the important responsibilities and uniqueness of these roles. This theory argues that key functionary positions are crucial to an organization's survival. Consequently, these roles should be enacted by qualified persons in an adequate manner. In general, these roles require higher qualifications and more extensive training than do other less powerful positions. In addition, key functionary roles are frequently demanding in terms of their duties, time, and responsibilities. Inferring from this theory, if professional sport is to survive and continue as an ongoing entity, it must be able to ensure that key functionary positions be enacted by qualified persons in an adequate manner. This theory also suggests that because blacks historically have lacked access to knowledge and training for the specific skills and abilities needed

when enacting key functionary positions, it is not surprising that important questions regarding their qualifications in these positions arise (Davis and Moore, 1945, pp. 242–249). The functionalist theory reflects the Calvinist notion of rugged individualism. More important, its greatest weakness is its failure to appreciate and account for structural constraints such as institutional discrimination and prejudice.

Although neither the conflict nor the functional theories appear to be adequate by themselves to explain all social inequality that blacks experience gaining access to key functionary positions, the existing empirical data do suggest that each of the above theories is relevant to some aspects of this process. Hence, the two theories should be viewed as complementary, rather than as competing explanations of social stratification.

Blacks As Key Functionaries in Professional Sports?

Today, blacks comprise about 12.2% of the U.S. population, but they are overrepresented on professional sport rosters in the National Basketball Association (NBA; 75%), the National Football Association (63%), and in major-league baseball (33%) (Coakley, 1986, pp. 143–160). Although the black community has triumphed in its efforts to gain initial entrance into the world of sports, it now faces a more difficult barrier of acquiring access to key functionary positions. For example, today few blacks are in posts that determine where a stadium will be located or in choosing the managers and/or coaches of a team. Furthermore, although blacks are overrepresented as players, they are underrepresented in other salient categories of the world of sports. For example, today in professional sports, few blacks are fans, referees, head coaches, sportswriters, and broadcasters. In those areas of sports (outside the role of player) where the serious money is made, most individuals are white. Roles such as program producers, directors, senior executives, those who control the point spread, key executives, shareholders, companies that buy TV time, printers of programs and tickets, waste management companies, agents, attorneys, parking concessionaires, and vendors all have extremely low black representation (Hoose, 1989, p. 24).

The key functionary positions mentioned above generally require their occupants to have a proven record of prerequisites or necessities before acquiring them (Massengale and Farrington, 1977, pp. 107–115; Scully, 1974, p. 246). For example, sports broadcasters who are charged with analyzing the game tend to be ex-coaches, and athletes who have played at specific positions tend to become coaches. Because blacks until recently have not been head coaches and have until this decade been limited in the type of playing positions they frequent (Eitzen and Sage, 1986, pp. 263–283), they are less likely than are whites to have the essentials deemed necessary to occupy these posts. In addition, the history of race discrimination against blacks has placed the majority of them in a disadvantaged position when seeking employment in upper level jobs requiring skills in writing, speaking, negotiating, and the like (Kjeldsen, 1980; Lapchick, 1984, p. 58).

Some key functionaries, who maintain the real power and wealth in sports, do not perceive of most blacks as possessing the "necessities" for roles other than as players of the game. Their perception of blacks as "unfit" to hold positions other than as players can be observed in remarks made by Al Campanis—at the time the third ranking executive in the Los Angeles Dodgers organization. In a nationally televised interview in commemoration of the 40th anniversary of Jackie Robinson's first year in major-league baseball, Campanis was asked by host Ted Koppel "Is there still that much prejudice" in sports? Campanis responded that he did not believe prejudice was a major factor in professional sports. Rather, he blamed blacks' low representation on their lack of "necessities" to fulfill key roles and statuses within the sports (Phillips, 1993, p. 179).

The sentiments expressed by Campanis are not merely the feelings of an isolated person but extend throughout the world of sports. Campanis' remarks are important theoretically because they support Blumer's notion that the basis of racial discrimination has subtly shifted from criteria based on ascription (i.e., race) to achievement (or holding the proper necessities for the job). What is not noted by Campanis, however, is that previous discrimination against blacks resulted in them being limited in their ability to acquire the necessities that are essential for occupying key functionary positions. In professional sports, blacks are numerous and highly visible, but their role in the world of sports is for the most part relegated to that of performer—a role that often receives publicity and celebrity. However, unlike some other sports roles, it rarely affords its occupants entry to the corridors of real power and wealth in professional sports.

Black Sportscasters

The bulk of research addressing professional black athletes confirms that they face systematic discrimination throughout their playing careers. There is evidence that such differences between the races in part reflect the paucity of black athletes in central playing positions (central positions in football are quarterback, center, and middle linebacker; in baseball, these positions are catcher, pitcher, shortstop, and second baseman). For example, in 1988, more than three fourths of all black baseball players played first base or in the outfield (Hoose, 1989, p. 65). Eitzen and Sage (1986, pp. 84–107) have demonstrated that blacks are further relegated to an inferior status even when their playing careers are finished. One indication of this is seen in the scarceness of blacks in radio and television broadcasting. National broadcasting jobs are mostly reserved for ex-coaches, most of whom are white, and/or ex-players who starred in controlling positions where blacks until very recently were least likely to play. For example, in most cases broadcasters like Joe Garagiola, Tony Kubek, Tim McCarver, and Jim Palmer played in the middle infield, as pitchers and/or catchers. Only a very select number of blacks (e.g., Sugar Ray Leonard, Bill Russell, Oscar Robertson, O.J. Simpson, Reggie Jackson, and Maury Wills) broadcast games. In its 15-year history of covering NBA basketball, Columbia Broadcasting System (CBS) hired only five blacks to announce its games (Leonard, 1988, pp. 214–253). At the network level it is not uncommon for blacks to cover only the losing team, to interview the losing coach, or to flag down an injury report and relay it to the booth. Still other blacks from the network report only scores of games that whites have broadcast (Hoose, 1989, p. 37). Indeed, as of 1987, only one black person held a broadcasting job doing other than providing the "color" commentary (Leonard, 1988, p. 225).

The aforementioned situation may change for black sportscasters in the immediate future. One might expect that the number of black sportscasters will increase as blacks gain greater access to coaching and central playing positions on the field. On the other hand, if this should occur, then there could be serious negative ramifications. For example, those blacks in the sportscaster "pipeline" might face the possibility that their aspirations and occupation of these roles could generate conflicts and hostile competition with whites over valuable resources such as wealth, power, and prestige. Such a struggle would introduce the variable of race at the individual level once again as the barrier between the respective groups. Such conflict if left unchecked could extend to the group level.

Black Executives and Managers

Blacks are also a rarity in executive positions in sport (see, e.g., Chu and Segrave, 1980, pp. 13–22; Edwards, 1973; Massengale and Farrington, 1977, pp. 107–115; Scully, 1974, p. 246). Edwards (1984, pp. 11–12) has demonstrated that there are no blacks with administrative authority in the National Football League (NFL) commissioner's office, and that only five blacks held executive positions (although none were general managers) among the NFL teams. Edwards (1984, pp. 11–12) showed that in 1984, of the 913 front office positions on baseball teams, only 32 were occupied by blacks and 26 of these were secretarial positions. Professional basketball has the best record of hiring blacks in leadership posts, but even there, most key functionary positions remain in predominantly white hands (Eitzen and Sage, 1986). Exactly 1 year after Al Campanis made his appearance on Night Line, baseball commissioner Peter Uberroth presented data showing that 180 new minority employees had been hired during the previous year. This figure represented almost one third of all employees hired during that period. What Uberroth failed to mention, however, was that most of these new hires were placed in jobs having almost no decision-making authority (e.g., instructor, public relations, special assistant to an executive, minor-league coach, trainer, and scout). In this same year six major-league managers were fired and replaced. Not one of these was replaced by a black (Hoose, 1989, pp. 20–36). Recently, the plight of blacks in professional sport seems to have taken a turn for the better. For example, in February 1989, Bill White, a black ex-first baseman and local broadcaster, was named to replace Bartlett Giamatti as president of baseball's National League. White's position, however, has little control relative to key functionary positions because it is largely confined to disciplinary actions, such as ruling on fines, implementing suspensions, and settling disputes between managers and umpires. Blacks attempting to gain social power through professional sport must often first seek the approval of team owners, general managers, field managers, and key executives—almost all persons occupying these roles are white (Hoose, 1989, p. 23).

No black except for those who owned in the Negro League has ever owned a share of a major-league sports team in the United States. This is ironic, given that the black athlete is the product that is being sold. Even when one considers the large salaries that some black athletes earn, there are individuals (usually whites) who are nonathletes who earn even more from their performance. These include key functionaries such as the owners of the stadiums, arenas, and concessions, contract negotiators, and boards of companies that buy TV time. It is very difficult to find blacks among this group of individuals (Lapchick, 1984, p. 58).

Within baseball's 100-year history there have been no more than six black managers. Almost all the blacks who have been hired as baseball coaches have been hired as hitting instructors or have coached first base. Currently, there are only two black managers and one black third base coach—the second person who is in command and who is responsible for relaying the manager's strategy to the players. Throughout baseball's history and even today, there exists a small group of white managers who throughout their careers have held more managing jobs than the number held by all black managers combined within the history of the game (Hoose, 1989, pp. 57–59).

With respect to the other sports, there is one black head coach in professional football, and only a small percentage of NBA head coaches are black. Assistant coaching positions also tend to be occupied by whites. For example, in 1984, blacks in the NFL comprised 52% of all players. Despite this, there were only 31 blacks among the 258 assistant coaches, and only 2 were offensive or defensive coordinators (the most responsible and prestigious assistant coaching positions). In 1988, only 15% of assistant coaches in basketball were black, as were only 11% in major-league baseball (Leonard, 1988, p. 83). Even when blacks are hired as coaches it has usually been in those situations where most players on a team were black. In some cases, the hiring of a black coach was logical from a dominant perspective, because the coach would have power over only a few white players and motivate black players more positively than would white coaches (Eitzen and Sage, 1986, p. 48).

The small percentage of blacks in coaching positions is mostly the result of them being denied access to central, leadership, and decision-making positions during their playing careers. For example, Scully (1973, pp. 67–84) has shown that in baseball, 68% of all the managers from 1871 to 1968 were former infielders. Because black athletes were historically excluded from playing these positions, they tended not to possess the infield experience necessary for a management position. Even though things have changed in the past decade, that nearly 100-year legacy cannot be dismissed. Massengale and Headman (1981, pp. 111–118) suggest that this argument also holds true for football. For example, they found that 65% of head coaches at major universities played at central positions (e.g., quarterback, offensive center, guard, or linebacker) during their playing days. They also argued that about one third of the playing positions produce two thirds of professional coaching positions. The same pattern has been found to exist in basketball, where two thirds of professional and college head coaches played at guard (the most central position). One's racial background persists as a salient factor that determines the percentage of blacks who reach and/or remain in coaching positions. Even when blacks are deemed qualified to become coaches, they are more likely than are whites to be labeled *insolent* or *arrogant* by white coaches and teammates. As these labels are applied, they function to restrict future opportunities in the coaching field. Because coaching jobs are more often than not obtained through the sponsorship of other coaches, qualified blacks who are labeled negatively probably will not receive the sponsorship needed to secure these positions (Eitzen and Sage, 1986, pp. 143–86).

Blacks and Advertisement

Another area of unequal opportunity for black athletes is in making personal appearances, promoting commercial products, or both. In 1968, the Equal Employment Opportunity Commission showed that in 1966, only 5% of 351 commercials associated with New York sports events had black athletes in them (Leonard, 1988, p. 246). Yetman and Eitzen (1984, pp. 88–95) demonstrated that this trend continued—they showed that of the starters for one professional football team in 1971, 8 out of 11 whites (73%) in comparison with 2 out of 13 blacks (15%) held advertising and media positions. In a 1988 survey, a firm that rates the attractiveness of celebrities found that all seven of the most appealing athletes in the world were black. Despite this, only one of the highest paid athletes in terms of commercial endorsements (i.e., Michael Jordan) was black. Only a few superstars such as Michael Jordan and Bo Jackson seem able to overcome the racial stigma when it comes to commercial endorsements.

According to C. Grantham, former executive vice president of the NBA Players Association, advertisers fear the potential negative reaction of whites to a black face promoting a product (Hoose, 1989,

p. 29). Hence, in Calvinist fashion, blacks are deemed as lacking the necessities to make products appealing to whites. As a consequence, black athletes are usually relegated to promoting those products that are especially appealing to members of the black community. According to Grantham's observations, "The market for endorsements by black athletes is very limited" for either print or TV ads. The lack of blacks in advertising interrelates with earlier discrimination: In his survey of 65% of teams in the three major sports, Leonard (1988, p. 254) found that 75% of media advertising slots were held by athletes who played central positions.

Perhaps the most lucrative areas for the professional black male athlete are the footwear and sportswear industries. In 1990, these industries expect to gross over $5.5 billion from name brand shoes and more than $2 billion in sweatpants, sweatshirts, and warm-up suits. The footwear industry heavily advertises its products on TV, radio, and in print ads at a cost of $200 million annually (Phillips, 1993, p. 57). Nike alone spent $26 million to promote its shoes in 1983 (its sales were $867 million) and most of that came from basketball sneakers. In 1990, however, Nike's advertising costs are expected to exceed $60 million. Many companies have shoes retailing for considerably more than $100; the "Reebok Pump" shoe being the highest at $170. Vogler and Schwartz (1993, p. 85) charge that the shoe and sportswear industries specifically target young black males through the use of seductive, macho-loaded sales pitches, mainly by black professional athletes. This argument, if true, suggests that these industries are using subtly racist tactics to manipulate young blacks into buying their products.

Black female athletes find the advertising business even less promising. Janis (1985) notes that professional black female endorsements for products are almost nonexistent. This is because there are few professional black female athletes and the fact that the bigger ad markets tend to use male athletes to endorse their products, which usually consist of alcoholic beverages. To date, the only black female athletes having any measurable success in endorsements are Florence Griffith Joyner, Zina Garrison, Lisa Leslie, and Leslie Allen (Vogler and Schwartz, 1993). Grantham suggests that because advertisers are very cautious, the long-range future for additional black female athletes in advertising is not good. If what happened to Zina Garrison and Lori McNeil portends anything, it is that a business career in advertising for minority women does not look promising. For example, in 1987, the top two black women's tennis players, Zina Garrison (no. 7) and Lori McNeil (no. 12) failed to obtain a clothing company's endorsement, a rarity among the Top 15. However, Pony (who failed to renew its contract with Garrison) has Anne White—no. 46—a white American, promote merchandise on its behalf (Phillips, 1993, p. 65).

Black Fans

Finally, one major area where blacks lack significant influence is in the role of the professional sports fan. After all, it is the fan who spends considerable time and money to support the sport enterprise. However, the prospect of black fans becoming a power base within professional sport— as is true for middle-class whites—is not promising. For example, currently in the NBA, NFL, and major-league baseball, blacks account for a small percentage of total fans relative to their proportion of the population in the larger metropolitan areas (i.e., 17%, 7.5%, and 6.8%, respectively). Don Newcombe (director of community relations for the Los Angeles Dodgers) estimates that there are no more than 50 blacks among the Dodgers' 27,000 season ticket holders (Coakley, 1986, p. 37). Al Harazin (Senior Vice President of the New York Mets) reports that in 1982, the last year racial demographics were taken, about 6% of the fans were black, although they represented 25.2% of the city's population that year. Thus, although more blacks are playing professional sport, it is the affluent white who has easier access to the stadiums and the expensive seating therein (Staples, 1987, pp. 26–58). In sport, network sponsorship and ticket sales, not necessarily winning, generate revenue. Most of the fans who attend professional games are white and middle-class with children. Thus, owners may believe that they will make more profit by catering to only white fans. Calvin Griffin, the former owner of the Minnesota Twins, moved his team there from Washington, DC, in 1978. In part, he made the move because there were few blacks in Minnesota, and consequently, he did not have to depend on blacks for fan support. In his view, blacks would not pay to support a ball team (Hoose, 1989, p. 38).

That opinion of black fans today is not surprising, given their history. Black fans started attending white major-league sports contests in significant numbers in 1946 when Branch Rickey signed Jackie Robinson to the Brooklyn Dodgers. The fact that Robinson was a black as well as a superior athlete encouraged people to come to the ball park. Dur-

ing his rookie year, the attendance of blacks at Ebbets Field in Brooklyn increased by 400%, and almost 2 million people watched the Dodgers play during that season, setting a new record. Actually, it was the promise of gate receipts that sold desegregation to major-league baseball, not Robinson's performance (Coakley, 1986, p. 45). The Robinson experiment led to other successes elsewhere in the nation. For example, it led to the desegregation of spectator seating patterns. During a Cardinal game in St. Louis, so many blacks came to the stadium that all could not be seated in the very small segregated sections reserved for them. Immediately afterward, the St. Louis management realized that the discriminatory treatment of black spectators hurt their business, because it cost them considerably. They eliminated this restrictive policy and allowed blacks, like their white counterparts, to buy any seats they could afford (Baker, 1982, pp. 13–15). During this same year, both the National and American Leagues set up a body to study the "race" question in response to the vast numbers of black fans turning out to see Robinson play. Under Larry MacPhail, this major steering committee concluded that increasing black attendance upon Robinson's arrival could frighten white fans away and therefore endanger the viability of major-league baseball in America (Hoose, 1989, p. 26).

Under the harsh conditions to which some blacks were subjected in many stadiums, it is difficult to determine how MacPhail perceived them as threatening. Hoose (1989, pp. 52–65) explains that even as late as 1962, all blacks were forced to sit together at Grayson Stadium (a minor-league stadium in Savannah, Georgia) in distant seats down the left field line. A brick wall separated them from white fans. Blacks relieved themselves in their own rest rooms, bought food from only black vendors at their own concession stand, drank from their own fountains, bought tickets at their own windows, and entered through gates reserved for them. The practice of segregating black and white spectators in professional sport was not in force in all stadiums and arenas, but it occurred often enough to demonstrate that blacks alone were to be a sign of damnation and something to be avoided if possible. Paraphrasing from the Calvinist doctrine, one might argue that black fans were perceived as persons not touched by God's grace and who, therefore, could not share equally with white fans in the enjoyment of professional sport. Segregated seating, then, was imposed as a color line to ensure that those unworthy did not mix with those deserving.

Conclusion

In American society there is a persistent belief that sports are a promising avenue of upward mobility for black Americans. This belief is bolstered by those (i.e., coaches, athletes, mass media, and so on) who have an economic interest in assuring that sports are perceived positively by the larger society. The major finding of this work is that although blacks have achieved great success in integrating professional sport as players of the game, they have failed to secure key functionary positions in proportions comparable to their percentage in the larger society; much less in comparison to their representation as athletes. The theories used in this article suggest that blacks today are nearly absent from key functionary positions in professional sport because past discrimination made it considerably difficult for them to acquire the necessities or prerequisites to occupy these positions. The struggle to gain access to these positions is the new color line, which will be contested for years to come. Blacks must oppose this color line because it impedes their mobility in professional sport. It is the effect of the Calvinist ideology made manifest today that considers blacks as lacking the necessities for serious consideration for positions outside the role of athlete. Much of the exclusion of blacks from key functionary positions also results from feelings of white hostility stemming from the Calvinist ethic, which suggests that it is improper to give them an opportunity to participate in and/or man control positions because they are unworthy.

The dilemma that blacks face with respect to control positions in professional sport may shift to their favor within the near future. It is well-known that the socioeconomic status of the most disadvantaged members of the black population has deteriorated rapidly since 1970. However, because of the processes of industrialization and rationalization, the plight of more advantaged blacks has significantly improved. Indeed, during the past 10 years blacks have improved at a relatively faster rate than their white counterparts. According to Wilson (1987, p. 75), the most notable gains have occurred in professional employment, income of married-couple families, higher education, and home ownership. Thus, a broad array of evidence suggests, at least to this writer, that better placed blacks have simply been able to take more advantage of the opportunities created in the last decade than those mired in the underclass.

In the future, as these social processes play a greater role in the professional sport order, one might expect the position of blacks to improve significantly. Hence, in professional sport, I believe that upwardly mobile blacks will have more of an equal chance with whites to obtain key functionary positions than will blacks of lower status. This expectation is based on Weber's (1958, pp. 160–165) belief that rationalization is a positive and necessary component of industrialization because it replaces ascriptive judgments with explicit and abstract procedures that are detached from specific persons. For example, he argued that rationalization, at least in the long run, is intolerant of social bonds based on affective feelings, group emotions, loyalty, and alliances. Rationalization, then, modifies the process of racial stratification by weeding out most ascriptive considerations for social mobility. Thus, as rationalization continues to affect professional sport, blacks should expect the historical color line that impedes their social mobility into key functionary positions to be slowly removed. However, as this line dissipates, it will be important for blacks to keep in mind that only the better trained, talented, and educated segments of this group will be able to attain authoritative positions. The competitive resources developed by advantaged blacks will result in their benefiting disproportionately from the process of rationalization, by removing artificial barriers to their acquiring key functionary roles in professional sports.

References

Abrahamson, M. (1990). *Sociological theory: An introduction to concepts, issues and research.* Englewood Cliffs, NJ: Prentice-Hall.

Baker, W.J. (1982). *Sports in the Western world.* Totowa, NJ: Rowman and Littlefield.

Ball, D. (1973). Ascription and position: A comparative analysis of stacking in professional football. *Canadian Review of Sociology and Anthropology,* **10,** 97–113.

Buckley, W. (1966). *Sociology and modern systems theory.* Englewood Cliffs, NJ: Prentice-Hall.

Chu, D.B., and Segrave, J.O. (1980). Leadership recruitment and ethnic stratification in basketball. *Journal of Sport and Social Issues,* **4,** 13–22.

Coakley, J.J. (1986). *Sport in society: Issues and controversies.* St. Louis: C.V. Mosby.

Collins, R., and Makowsky, M. (1989). The discovery of society (4th ed.). New York: Random House.

Davis, K., and Moore, W.E. (1945). Some principles of stratification. American Sociological Review, **10,** 242–249.

Edwards, H. (1973). Sociology of sport. Homewood, IL: Dorsey.

Edwards, H. (1984). The collegiate arms race: Origins and implications of "Rule 48" controversy. *Journal of Sport and Social Issues*, **8**, 11–12.

Eitzen, S.D., and Sage, G.H. (1986). *Sociology of North American sport*. Dubuque, IA: William C. Brown.

Erikson, K.T. (1966). *Wayward puritans: A study in the sociology of deviance*. London: Wiley.

Grusky, O. (1963). The effects of formal structure on managerial recruitment: Study of baseball organization. *Sociometry*, **26**, 345–353.

Hoose, P.M. (1989). *Necessities: Racial barriers in American sport*. New York: Random House.

Janis, L. (1985). Annotated bibliography on minority women in sport. *Sociology of Sport Journal*, **2**, 266–274.

Kjeldsen, E. (1980, October). *Centrality and leadership recruitment: A study of their lineage*. Paper presented at the meetings of the North American Society for the Sociology of Sport, Denver, CO.

Lapchick, R. (1984). *Broken promises: Racism in American sports*. New York: St. Martin's.

Lenski, G.E. (1966). *Power and privilege: A theory of social stratification*. New York: McGraw-Hill.

Leonard, W.M. (1988). *A sociological perspective of sport* (3rd ed.). New York: Macmillan.

Luschen, G. (1980). Sociology of sport: Development, present state and prospects. *Annual Review of Sociology*, **6**, 315–347.

Massengale, J.D., and Farrington, S.E. (1977). The influence of playing position centrality on the careers of college football coaches. *Review of Sport and Leisure*, **2**, 107–115.

Massengale, J.D. and Headman, R.J. (1981). The centrality phenomenon in football: Senior bowl, 1975–1981. *Journal of Sport Behavior*, **4**, 111–118.

Nixon, H.L (1984). *Sport and the American dream*. New York: Leisure.

Olsen, M.E. (1978). *The process of social organization: Power in social systems* (2nd ed.). Dallas: Holt, Rinehart and Winston.

Phillips, J.C. (1993). *Sociology of sport*. Boston: Allyn and Bacon.

Ritzer, G. (1988). *Sociological theory*. New York: Knopf.

Scully, G.W. (1973). Economic discrimination in professional sports. *Contemporary Problems*, **38**, 67–84.

Scully, G.W. (1974). Discrimination: The case of baseball. In R.G. Noll (Ed.), *Government and the sports business* (pp. 223–254). Washington, DC: Brookings Institution.

Snyder, E.E., and Spreitzer, E. (1973). Family influence and involvement in sports. *Research Quarterly*, **44**, 249–255.

Staples, B. (1987, May 17). Where are the Black fans. *New York Times Magazine*, pp. 26–49.

Takla, T., and Pope, W. (1985). The force imagery in Durkheim: The integration of theory, metatheory and method. *Sociological Theory*, **3**, 74–88.

Vogler, C.C., and Schwartz, S.E. (1993). *The sociology of sport: An introduction*. Englewood Cliffs, NJ: Prentice-Hall.

Weber, M. (1958). *The Protestant ethic and the spirit of capitalism*. New York: Scribner.

Wilson, J.W. (1987). *The truly disadvantaged: The inner city, the underclass and public policy*. Chicago: University of Chicago Press.

Yetman, N., and Eitzen, S.D. (1984). Racial dynamics in American sport: Continuity and change. In S.D. Eitzen (Ed.), *Sport in contemporary society* (2nd ed., pp. 88–95). New York: St. Martin's.

The Body in Culture and Sport

Objectives

The unit focuses on the social construction of the body and examines the implications of this process for sport.

In reflecting on the study of the body in sociology of sport, Theberge (1991) observed that "in its quest to establish the social significance of sport . . . this field has had little to say about the body. It is ironic that in studying sport, where the body is essential to the experience, we have largely missed its meaning and importance" (p. 124). It is not just the sociology of sport that has failed to recognize the body as a socially significant marker; it is the whole of the social sciences! As Hargreaves (1987) observed, "Until quite recently, the body has been almost entirely evacuated from social and political theory: a built-in resistance prevents its role in the constitution of power relations from being analyzed" (p. 139). Rather than allow the body to become the sole property of the natural sciences, Turner (1996) has argued that the body should be the focus of sociological analysis.

Why should the sport sociologist take an interest in the body? Hargreaves offers the following:

Although the degree of physical input varies from sport to sport, the primary focus of attention in sport overall, is the body and its attributes . . . it is the body that constitutes the most striking symbol, as well as constituting the material core of sporting activity. (p. 141)

A growing number of sport sociologists now fully recognize that sport sociology has for too long been a "disembodied" subfield. They argue that what is needed today is an "embodied sociology of sport," one that takes full advantage of an impressive corpus of empirical and theoretical work on the subject. Rather than having to choose sides between a "sociology of sport" and a "sociology of the body," Hall (1993) argues a natural relationship exists between the two, a connection that deserves much more attention from sport scholars.

Loy, Andrews, and Rinehart (1993) suggest that sport sociologists have overlooked the body because they have been influenced by the nonbody bias of general sociology and the proclivity of Western culture to separate the mind from the body. Hargreaves adds that the mind has been assigned greater primacy because "in contrast, the body belongs to nature, the kingdom of desire, the source of threatening, irrational impulses and dangerous appetites . . ." (p. 139).

Until recently, the only sport researchers who have shown a primary interest in the body were those motivated by performance considerations. For example, the exercise physiologist is interested in the exercising body because of a desire to learn how the various physiological systems adjust to increasing levels of aerobic and anaerobic work. For the biomechanist, the moving body is a wondrous assemblage of levers, pulleys, and forces that propel it through space in mechanically efficient ways. Given the increasing scientization of sport performance throughout the world and the co-option of the body by "hard" sport scientists, it becomes clear why sport sociologists have chosen to pay so little attention to the corporeal self. However, several factors account for the recent interest in the body in sociology of sport. Foremost among them are feminist analyses that view the body as "a central locus of the construction of femininity and of gender" (Theberge, 1991, p. 125) and the influential writings of French social critic Michel Foucault. In commenting on the theoretical relevance of Foucault's writings for critically examining homophobic discourse in sport, Veri (1999) observed that "Foucault recognizes the function of the body as both an object and a target of power throughout history and focuses a great deal of his work on the docile body as a means of demonstrating how those in power are able to manipulate and dominate others" (pp. 357-358).

The study of the body as a social and cultural phenomenon extends well beyond a feminist, poststructural interest in issues of domination, control, and gender relations. As Coakley (1998) points out, how bodies are socially defined or "constructed" has "implications for how people think about sex, sex differences, sexuality, ideals of beauty, self-image, body image, fashion, hygiene, health, nutrition, eating disorders, fitness, body-building, racial classification systems, disease, drugs and drug testing, violence, and power, and many other things that affect our lives" (p. 11).

The notion that the body is a socially constructed entity is an important one for sport sociologists who seek to understand its social and cultural significance. As Coakley argues, "social definitions of the body are grounded in social relations and heavily influenced by those with the power to promote agreement about what should be considered 'natural' when it comes to the body" (p. 8). A dramatic example of how those with power influence definitions of the body is seen in the way influential artists of their day portrayed female beauty. Contrast the female nudes of Reubens, Renoir, and Picasso and you will see startling differences in their interpretations of what is "natural" with respect to the female form, female beauty, and femininity. That is, each artist's rendering of the female form on canvas is a "social construction" in the sense that it reflects the gender definitions and gender relations characteristic of the sociocultural context in which the artist lived and labored.

With respect to the body as "cultural," Coakley observed that the body is cultural in the sense that it is "read" and understood in terms of a particular set of historical, social, and cultural circumstances. The bodies of athletes today are likely to be "read" as specialized machines geared to deliver maximum performance rather than as sources of personal pleasure and satisfaction.

Although slow to be recognized as a subject worthy of scholarly attention, the body has now become, for a growing number of sport sociologists, a focal point for inquiry into the social significance of sport. Loy, Andrews, and Rinehart, in their extensive review of research related to the body in sport, identify and discuss the following lines of scholarly activity.

1. The communicative body refers to research that examines how sport participants use body techniques to manage impressions.
2. The disciplined body reflects on research focused on how "body work" associated with personal fitness and athletic training is related to the reproduction of class, gender, and ethnic divisions.
3. The dominating body research endeavors to explicate how the male body contributes to the subjugation of females and the construction and confirmation of gender identities in sport.
4. The mirroring body speaks to efforts by researchers interested in how the athletic body serves as both a vehicle of pleasure and an instrument of desire.

Because the sporting body is socially constructed and historically and culturally situated, we can expect it to continue to remain an ideological battlefield, a contested terrain where dominant and subordinate groups vie for definitions and interpretations that maximize their advantage, influence, and power within the larger social order. Hargreaves makes the point well when he writes, "The body then, constitutes a major site of social struggles and it is in the battle for control over the body that types of social relation of particular significance for the way power is structured—class, gender, age, and race—are to a great extent constituted" (p. 140).

In the first selection, Trujillo examines the ways in which ABC's *Monday Night Football* sportscasters and the network production team present images of the male body that reproduce masculine hegemony. By showcasing the male body as tool, weapon, and object of gaze, televised football does important "gender work" by marginalizing, subordinating, and symbolically annihilating women. The reader is encouraged to challenge the repressive and oppressive images of masculinity reproduced in sports such as football, rugby, boxing, and ice hockey.

In the second selection, Markula employs ethnographic fieldwork, interviews, and media analysis to expose several contradictory messages associated with aerobicizing female bodies. Based on a Foucaultian perspective, the author is able to demonstrate how the media discourse surrounding the female body image contributes to the patriarchal ideal. We see that women's relationship with the ideal is contradictory. On the one hand, they desire to conform to the ideal, but on the other hand, they find the whole process ridiculous. That is, how can the aerobicizing female be both muscular and petite at the same time? Strong but thin? Shapely but slender? By giving these women's private voices a public stage, Markula hopes to initiate a dialogue about the use of power in postmodern consumer society.

In the third selection, King also uses Foucaultian concepts to analyze the discourse that surrounded former NBA all-star Magic Johnson's public announcement that he was HIV positive. We learn how Johnson, a likable, personable sports hero, was presented by the media in ways that helped maintain his heroic stature. His body was used to generate media communications that clearly distanced him from conventional images associated with AIDS victims. How the media attempted to disassociate Johnson from gay men and drug use makes fascinating reading. We also discover that in helping construct a healthy, heterosexual body for Johnson, the media also contributed to reproducing and reinforcing dominant messages supporting homophobia and misogyny.

References

Coakley, J.J. (1994, 1998). *Sport in society: Issues and controversies.* New York: McGraw-Hill.

Hall, M.A. (1993). Feminism, theory and the body: A response to Cole. *Journal of Sport & Social Issues,* **17**, 100-101.

Hargreaves, J. (1987). The body, sport and power relations. In J. Horne, D. Jarry, & A. Tomlinson (Eds.), *Sport, leisure and social relations* (pp.139-159). London: Routledge & Kegan Paul.

King, S. (1993). The politics of the body and the body politic: Magic Johnson and the ideology of AIDS. *Sociology of Sport Journal,* **10**, 270-285.

Loy, J.W., Andrews, D.L., & Rinehart, R.E. (1993). The body in culture and sport. *Sport Science Review,* **2**, 69-91.

Markula, P. (1995). Firm but shapely, fit but sexy, strong but thin: The postmodern aerobicizing female bodies. *Sociology of Sport Journal,* **12**, 424-453.

Theberge, N. (1991). Reflections on the body in the sociology of sport. *Quest,* **43**, 123-134.

Trujillo, N. (1995). Machines, missiles and men: Images of the male body on ABC's *Monday Night Football. Sociology of Sport Journal,* **12**, 403-423.

Turner, B.S. (1996). *Body and society.* London: Sage.

Veri, M.J. (1999). Homophobic discourse surrounding the female athlete. *Quest,* **51**, 355-368.

Discussion Questions

Nick Trujillo

1. What is the purpose of this research study? Describe and explain.
2. Which theoretical perspective does the researcher employ in this investigation? Explain.
3. What does Foucault mean when he observes that the body always has an ideological function in a society? Discuss and explain.
4. What does the term "hegemonic masculinity" mean? Explain.
5. Identify the three dominant images of the male athlete body in televised football.
6. Discuss and describe some serious costs to women that may result from the masculine hegemony reproduced on *Monday Night Football.*
7. Does the hegemonic masculinity reproduced in televised football have any serious consequences for men? Discuss and explain.
8. Would you be in favor of eliminating the sport of football? Debate the issue in class.

Pirkko Markula

1. Why are feminist scholars opposed to the way females are presented in popular women's magazines? Discuss and explain.
2. Is bodybuilding liberating or oppressing for women? Discuss and explain.
3. What is the "aerobicizing female body" in postmodern society? Explain.
4. Briefly describe the research methods employed by the author.
5. Identify some of the major themes the researcher discovered in her investigation of the female body image in aerobics.
6. How does the present image of the perfect female body serve masculine ideology? Discuss and explain.

7. According to the author, how does the women's fitness movement ultimately serve patriarchal interests? Discuss and explain.

8. In what sense is a woman's relationship with the body ideal contradictory? Discuss and explain.

Samantha King

1. In what sense is the body "an important sociocultural entity"? Explain.

2. Do you agree with the author that the bodies of male sports stars are "marketable commodities"? Explain.

3. Define HIV and AIDS. Which groups in society are statistically most vulnerable to HIV? Discuss and explain.

4. Identify the "irreconcilable schism" that was created when Magic Johnson went public with the news that he was HIV positive.

5. Was Johnson able to maintain his hero image? Explain. Why was it important for Johnson to assure the public that he was a heterosexual? Explain.

6. Why were AIDS activists angry about the public's response to Johnson's condition? Discuss and explain.

7. Speculate about the possible public response if a well-known female athlete publicly announced that she was HIV positive.

8. In what ways did the handling of Johnson's condition by commercial and professional sports interests help reinforce homophobia and misogyny? Discuss and explain.

Machines, Missiles, and Men:
Images of the Male Body
on ABC's *Monday Night Football*

Nick Trujillo

This paper examines how images of the male body are reproduced in media coverage of professional football. Specifically, it examines television coverage of football games broadcast during the 1993-1994 season on ABC's *Monday Night Football,* paying special attention to the discourse of sportscasters Al Michaels, Frank Gifford, and Dan Dierdorf and to the production techniques (e.g., camera angles, slow-motion replays, etc.) of the program. Guided by a critical orientation, the paper examines how three patriarchal images of the male body and football, and the resulting paradoxes, are reproduced on *Monday Night Football,* including (a) the body as tool: football as work, (b) the body as weapon: football as war, and (c) the body as object of gaze: (watching) football as pleasure.

Last week, [Thurman] Thomas gets hurt early on, has bruised ribs, he has trouble breathing the rest of the game, and he winds up carrying the ball 30 times. (Al Michaels)

[Greg Lloyd] just catapulted himself into [Bobby] Hebert. Take a look at this. This is a man-sized hit. (Frank Gifford)

[Steve Young] played with it, even though it was swollen, as he said, "like a sausage." It's still a little swollen. Now he's calling it "a cocktail frank." Well, Steve Young's cocktail frank is doing pretty well. (Dan Dierdorf)

Reprinted from Trujillo, 1995.

American football has been called "a brutal sport" (Pronger, 1990, p. 21), a "rite of gender reproduction" (Foley, 1990, p. 118), and "a reflection of our society's capitalist order" (McMurtry, 1985, p. 241). The purpose of this article is to examine how images of the male body are reproduced in media coverage of professional football. Specifically, I examine television coverage of football games broadcast on ABC's *Monday Night Football (MNF),* paying special attention to the discourse of sportscasters and to the production techniques of the show. In this article, I discuss the critical perspective that guided this analysis, examine three images of the male body discussed by sport scholars, and show how these images, and their resulting paradoxes, are reproduced on *MNF.* I conclude with some remarks about the costs of hegemonic masculinity to men and women.

A Critical Perspective on Sport, Media, and the Body

When interpreted from a critical perspective, sport, media, and the body intersect in interesting ways. In recent years, some critical scholars who study sports have turned their attention to how the body is used ideologically in sports (see Andrews, 1993; Cole, 1993; Hargreaves, 1986, 1987; King, 1993). Applying the work of Foucault, as well as literature in feminism and cultural studies, these theorists argue that sport and media function hegemonically to reproduce and reinforce dominant ideologies of American culture including, among others, capitalism and the gender order.

From this perspective, the athletic body is interpreted as a key resource in reproducing a preferred ideology. As Foucault (1977) argued, the body always has an ideological function in a society because it is "invested with power and domination" as an instrument of production, while, at the same time, it is controlled by "a system of subjection" (pp. 25–26). However, the ideological function of the athletic body in sport is more subtle (and perhaps more potent), because its use appears to be more "natural" and less connected to politics, economics, and other institutions (see Cole, 1993).

In this study, I discuss how the mass media reproduce certain ideologies, as they produce images of the athletic body in competition. After all, as King (1993) advised,

> The political, social, economic body in and of itself means little until it is reproduced through the discourse of the mass media. . . . Through frames, values, and conventions they actively define, construct, and reproduce images of our society. . . . The media work in the same way to reproduce our bodies and the meanings attached to them. (pp. 271–272)

Sport and the Media

The relationship between professional sport and the mass media in American society has been characterized as a "symbiotic" one, in which sports and media organizations have provided mutual resources and experienced complementary growth. Although the relationship is sometimes a rocky one in which, as Klatell and Marcus (1988, p. 26) described, "mutual back-scratching occasionally draws blood," the relationship has produced substantial dowries for both parties.

This relationship has also reproduced particular ideologies of American culture. And critics argue that televised sport has played a particularly powerful role in reproducing these ideologies. As Sage (1990) put it, "Sportscasters and their entire apparatus involved in producing programs have become the definers of the subculture of sport, the interpreters of its meaning, and most important, a crucial means by which hegemonic ideology is propagated and reproduced" (p. 129).

Scholars who study gender have pointed out that televised (and other mediated) sports have empha-

sized men's sports over women's sports. As Sabo and Jansen (1992) reported, "Although women have been involved in organized sports in the United States for more than a century . . . the media spotlight remains firmly fixed on the male athlete" (p. 174). Despite this emphasis on men's sports, however, "limited attention . . . has been paid to media representation of male athletic bodies" (White & Gillett, 1994, p. 19).

In this study, I examine media representations of the male athletic body in professional football. In particular, I analyze how these media representations reinforce an ideology of masculinity that has been called hegemonic masculinity. "Hegemonic masculinity," as Hanke (1990) defined it, "refers to the social ascendancy of a particular version or model of masculinity that, operating on the terrain of 'common sense' and conventional morality, defines 'what it means to be a man'" (p. 232). Specifically, it is "the culturally idealized form of masculine character" that emphasizes "the connecting of masculinity to toughness and competitiveness" as well as "the subordination of women" and "the marginalization of gay men" (Connell, 1990, pp. 83, 94). As a form of hegemony, though, hegemonic masculinity is not a unitary form of male domination that is simply imposed on viewers by the media; rather, it is a somewhat incomplete and an ultimately contested form of male domination, open to potential contradiction, ironies, and paradoxes.

In sum, this analysis of the male athletic body is guided by a critical approach. I assume that the male athletic body is a political and economic instrument used for production. I also assume that in using the body in this fashion, sports organizations and athletes reproduce patriarchal ideologies regarding masculinity, capitalism, and sports in American culture. Finally, I assume that by presenting particular visual and verbal images of the male athletic body, the mass media function hegemonically, reinforcing patriarchal ideologies while at the same time providing subtle opportunities for contesting those ideologies.

Studying Images of the Male Body on *Monday Night Football*

American football is one of the most appropriate sports in which to find reproductions of hegemonic masculinity. As Sabo and Panepinto (1990) observed, "Football's historical prominence in sport media and folk culture has sustained a hegemonic model of masculinity that prioritizes competitiveness, asceticism, success (winning), aggression, violence, superiority to women, and respect for and compliance with male authority" (p. 115). Indeed, as Real (1975) concluded, "If one were to create from scratch a sport to reflect the sexual, racial, and organizational priorities of the American power structure, it is doubtful that one could improve on football" (p. 191).

This study examines NFL football games broadcast on ABC's *Monday Night Football*. *MNF* began in 1970 as a seemingly high-priced experiment by ABC to gain ground on rival networks NBC and CBS in prime-time ratings (cf. Chandler, 1991). It differed from its counterparts because it offered football at night rather than during the traditional Sunday morning/afternoon time slot. It also differed because ABC used far more cameras and an extra production truck (for isolated coverage of individual players on the field and spectators in the stands) in an effort to make the game an entertainment experience for attracting bigger and broader audiences. Howard Cosell summarized the need to make *MNF* an entertainment experience in the early years: "Look, there is no damn way you can go up against Liz Taylor and Doris Day in prime-time TV and present sports as just sports" (quoted in Rader, 1984, p. 132). Although some TV critics predicted its early demise, *MNF* has won several Emmy awards for live sports shows and completed its 24th consecutive year on prime-time TV in the 1993-1994 football season.

Methods

The sample for this study included all 18 regular-season games broadcast on *MNF* during the 1993-1994 season. These games were videotaped, from the pregame music videos through the closing credits. As such, it is a complete sample of one full season, representative of the recent era of *MNF,* with announcers Frank Gifford (23 seasons), Al Michaels (8 seasons), and Dan Dierdorf (7 seasons), though it obviously is not representative of the 24-year history of *MNF.*

The critical approach used to analyze the sample is described by VandeBerg and Wenner (1991) as "gender ideology criticism": "By examining various devices such as language, character, settings, narrative structure, camerawork, laugh tracks, and musical soundtracks, gender ideology critics evaluate how television texts maintain or deconstruct existing cultural definitions of masculinity and femininity" (p. 35). Accordingly, the general research question that guided this analysis was, How are cultural definitions of masculinity maintained and/

or reproduced in television texts of professional football produced by *MNF?*

More specifically, this study analyzed how *MNF* productions use verbal and visual images of the male athletic body to maintain and/or critique cultural definitions of masculinity. First, like Bryant, Comisky, and Zillmann (1977), I focus on the discourse (the verbal images) of televised sports, analyzing the language used by *MNF* commentators to describe the athletic body (as well as the language used by musicians in pregame videos and by athletes or officials in live or taped interviews). I transcribed all discourse explicitly related to body size, appearance, motion, injuries, and so on. Second, like Birrell and Loy (1979), I also focus on the technology (the visual images) of televised sports, analyzing how the production techniques (e.g., camera angles, slow-motion replays, graphics, etc.) present the male athletic body to viewers.

In this study, as in most critical studies, the development of analytical categories involved some deduction and some induction.[1] That is, based on an examination of the sociological literature on the athletic body and an analysis of the discourse and technology used in this sample, three interrelated categories of images of the male athletic body were developed, together with some of the resulting ideologies and contradictions of masculinity, that are reproduced on *MNF.* There appear to be three dominant images of the male athletic body in football: (a) the body as tool: football as work, (b) the body as weapon: football as war, and (c) the body as object of gaze: football as pleasure. As Duncan (1990) wrote, "Responsible textual studies do not assert with absolute certainty how particular texts are interpreted . . . but they suggest . . . *likely* interpretations of the persuasiveness and logic of the researcher's discussion" (p.27). The following considers each of these analytical categories in detail.

The Body As Tool: Football As Work

[Mike Golic, defensive lineman for Miami] is a bear-down kinda guy. This is a guy who comes to work every day, brings his lunch box, and over the course of the season, he'll contribute in a lot of ways. (Dan Dierdorf)

"In the guise of a game which is supposed to freely develop the strengths of the individual," wrote Brohm (1978), "sport in fact reproduces the world of work" (pp. 55–56). Sage (1990) concurred: "Even the language of the bureaucratic work world has become prominent in sport—productivity, hard work, sacrifice, loyalty. Some critics of modern sport contend that it has increasingly come to resemble a workplace" (p. 109).

There are at least two related senses of the body as an instrument of work reproduced in sport, and each one is reproduced on *MNF*: sport as industrial labor, where the body is treated as a machine, and sport as capitalism, where the body is treated as a commodity.

The Body As Machine: Football As Industrialized Labor

Critical scholars have argued that in its organization and mediation, much of the work of sport is in the form of industrialized labor. For example, Hargreaves (1982) argued that sport exhibits features of industrial production such as "a high degree of specialization and standardization," "bureaucratized and hierarchical administration," and an "increased reliance on science and technology" (p. 41).

When industrial principles are applied to sport, the athletic body becomes a tool—a machine—to be used for industrialized production. "Sport is basically a mechanization of the body," wrote Brohm (1978), "treated as an automaton, governed by the principle of maximizing output," and he went so far as to suggest that the industrialization of sport requires a "Taylorization of the body" (pp. 55, 57). Sage (1990, p. 111) concurred, writing that sports organizations treat "individual athletes as machines, or as though they ought to be machines," and they use "training methods [that] are designed to achieve maximum performance from the human body" (cf. King, 1993; Rigauer, 1981).

MNF reproduced the mechanization of the body in several ways. *MNF* commentators often described the rigorous training techniques of the respective teams (and the benefits of those techniques), as Dan Dierdorf did during the first regular-season game on *MNF* between the Dallas Cowboys and the Washington Redskins in early September, when he told us about the importance of practice (and of the right kind of practice): "I'm not sure there's a team in the National Football League that does as much live tackling during practice both in-season and pre-season as the Dallas Cowboys. It's really reflected in how aggressive their secondary and linebackers are and how well they execute the open-field tackle. They're very good at it."[2]

Additionally, *MNF* commentators often described the hard work and training of individuals in preparation for games and season. For example, during a game between the Washington Redskins and Miami Dolphins, Frank Gifford described 15-year Washington linebacker Monte Coleman: "There have been 15 superb years for Monte Coleman, who concentrated as much as any player, I know, on keeping that body in shape. He's worked so hard."

During a game between the New Orleans Saints and the San Francisco 49ers in November, Dierdorf preached more explicitly about how every individual, no matter how talented, needs to and should practice. Specifically, he described the work habits of the 49ers talented wide receiver, Jerry Rice: "Remember last night when we came out to watch the 49ers practice? . . . A lot of 49ers were back under the tunnel, waiting to come out for the start of practice. The only player who was outside doing anything was Jerry Rice, who was running up and down the sidelines, having somebody throw the ball." And he concluded his sermon with the lesson: "It's a great lesson for you kids out there that hard work is really the only way to get there. And if anybody embodies the work ethic the way it oughta be in any sport, it's Jerry Rice. He not only has the God-given talent, he outworks everybody else as well." In this description of Jerry Rice, a black player, Dierdorf not only affirmed an image of football as labor, but he also went against the documented tendency of broadcasters to label black players as "natural athletes" and white players as "hard workers" (cf. Messner, Duncan, & Jensen, 1993).

Finally, *MNF* sportscasters reproduced the mechanization of the body when they commented on how individual players use (or should use) their bodies. For example, when Kansas City quarterback Joe Montana ran and dove out of bounds for a first down against Denver, Frank Gifford announced supportively, "Fifteen years later, he's still willing to waste that body." Dan Dierdorf was more blunt when he made it known that he thought Pittsburgh Steeler tight end Eric Greene should be used more during a game against the Dolphins, saying "I'd use that guy till his legs fell off."

The Body As Commodity: Football As Capitalist Enterprise

Critical scholars have also argued that American sport reaffirms principles of capitalism. For example, sport has been used to reinforce the idea that

American work is supposed to be a meritocracy. As Sabo and Jansen (1992) put it, "Based upon skill, discipline, training, strategy, competition, and rules of fair play, the sporting event is a pure articulation of the values of a meritocratic system. . . . The real-world analogue is, of course, capitalist ideology. . . . Hence, within the changing structure of the postindustrial capitalist order, sport rituals are likely to be just as much a source of achievement ideology as of gender order" (p. 183).

This achievement ideology reproduced in sport has been subject to much criticism because it has been narrowly defined in terms of games and championships won. As Sage (1990) argued, "The spontaneous, creative motive to participate in sport for the love of the game has been overshadowed by an obsession with victory above all else. Broadcast sports tend to be unbridled odes to winning. . . . Almost any action in the pursuit of victory is justified" (p. 128). This achievement ideology transforms the athletic body into a commodity, as an instrument with value only if it can help the team win games. On *MNF,* this image of body was perhaps stated the clearest in a pregame opening quote by San Francisco quarterback Steve Young: "It's about performance, and not only how you perform, but that you win every game too. . . . As a player, you're always proving that you can perform and do well and that you can lead your team to championships."

Players—especially certain "star" players—who are important resources for earning team victories enjoy higher values as commodities. As King (1993) argued,

> For sports stars, mainly male sports stars, their bodies have also become marketable commodities that on the one hand are sold to sponsors, advertisers, and the consuming public to generate profit, and on the other hand are used to maintain interest and a pool of upcoming talent for their sports. (p. 272)[3]

On *MNF,* the value of the football player as commodity was often reproduced in discourse about the salaries of players, free agency, the new salary cap that was to take place in the 1994–1995 season, and other aspects of the NFL business. For example, during halftime of the second game of the season, Al Michaels interviewed Dallas running back Emmitt Smith, who was still holding out at the time for a bigger contract. As Smith revealed in that interview, "If the situation does not occur where Jerry [Jones, owner of Cowboys] makes a better offer to myself, I feel like I'm going to remain firm and per-

haps sit out the season and take my chances next year in the restricted free agent market." In this example, Smith not only illustrated how the athletic body is commodified but also revealed how athletes contest the domination of owners by refusing to employ their bodies as instruments of work unless the price is right.

Some Paradoxes of the Body As Instrument of Work

Several paradoxes arise when the male athletic body is treated as an instrument of work, two of which are noted here. First, work in general, and sports work in particular, places workers in situations where they are defined as valuable not if they have produced in the past but if they keep producing in the present and future. As Fiske (1987) argued, this is true for men in capitalist America: "Men are cast into ceaseless work and action to prove their worth. . . . Masculinity becomes almost a definition of the superhuman, so it becomes that which can never be achieved" (p. 210). In sport, the cliché that epitomizes this paradox is, "You're only as good as your last game." This paradox was reflected on *MNF* when quarterback Steve Young told the viewing audience, "As a player, you're always proving that you can perform and do well and that you can lead your team to championships." The problem (and the paradox) is that only one team can win a championship, meaning that players on all other teams are ultimately reproduced as failures who will have to work harder next season.

Second, all machines, especially human bodies, eventually break down. And, ironically, the type of work that football players perform increases the likelihood that their bodies will break down, preventing them from a full season and from having lengthy careers. "No workplace matched football for either the regularity or severity of injury," reported Young (1993). "In a 4-month NFL season, all players can expect to be injured at least once. By mid season, 1992, an average 17 players per team had been 'hurt seriously enough to miss at least one game'" (p. 377). Sage (1990), too, reported that "injuries have cut short the playing careers of many professional athletes, and for a few injury has brought permanent physical disability" (p. 159). Thus, when a football player does his work well, he increases the likelihood that he will no longer be able to work.

In sum, when sport is treated as work, the sporting body is transformed from a human organism into an instrument of industrialization and a commodity of capitalism. With respect to football, this transformation results in serious injuries that prevent players from continued work and that reduce their value as commodities. As Young (1993) pointed out, the athletic injury associated with football is not only a result of the "organization (ownership, management) and supervision (coaching) in a venal occupational culture designed to produce profit"; it is also a result of "the nature of forceful sports work itself" (p. 377). The next section discusses the unique forceful nature of football work in more detail.

The Body As Weapon: Football As War

> [Steeler linebacker] Greg Lloyd is a terminator-type player. . . . We'll see him make more than just a couple big hits. And we're talking about earthquake-type collisions." (Dan Dierdorf)

In all sports, the body is an instrument of production. But in American football, that instrument is a weapon, and its production is a reproduction of war. Some researchers have argued that militarism is a structural trait in football itself (Arens, 1976; Guttmann, 1978, Real, 1975). "The similarity to war is unmistakable," wrote Phillips (1969): "Each game is a battle with its own game plan, each season is a campaign, the whole thing a series of wars. . . . There is even a general draft" (p. 48). Others have pointed out that because of football's inherent militarism, it has actually been used by military and educational institutions to teach military concepts to young men (Brohm, 1978; Dunning, 1986).

If sport is interpreted as war, then the body is transformed into a weapon, into an instrument of violence and aggression. As Messner (1990) summarized, "It seems reasonable to simply begin with the assumption that in many of our most popular sports, the achievement of goals (scoring and winning) is predicated on the successful utilization of violence—that is, these are activities in which the human body is routinely turned into a weapon to be used against other bodies, resulting in pain, serious injury, and even death" (p. 205). Although all sports have some amount of violence and aggression, there are few games as violent and aggressive as American football. "Football far surpasses . . . most other sports, except for boxing, in extent of physical violence," argued Real (1989, p. 192). As

Stade (1966) put it, football is a sport "whose mode is violence and whose violence is its special glory" (p. 173).

The militarism and violence of football were represented on *MNF* in several ways. There were many direct comparisons to war, as when Buffalo linebacker Bruce Smith said, "All out war, baby," to begin one *MNF* opening. Rap artist Johnny Grill opened another by singing, "Put all the kiddies in bed, 'cause this mean war," before he rapped, "Steelers gonna roar, Falcons gonna soar, Bodies gonna hit the floor, Rock 'em to the core, Too tough to ignore, Ain't gonna be no more, Bodies gonna hit the floor."

The discourse that *MNF* sportscasters used to describe players and plays also reproduced the imagery of war and weaponry in football. During the season, players were described as "weapons," "missiles," "shields," "rockets," "hitting machines," and other instruments of violence. And these "weapons" engaged in an impressive array of offensive and defensive maneuvers. For example, among the terms used by *MNF* commentators to describe what these offensive and defensive weapons (bodies) did on the football field were attack, blow away, break through, burst, catapult, club, crash, cripple, crunch, decapitate, decimate, destroy, dislocate, dislodge, dismantle, drill, explode, fire, fly, hammer, hit, hurdle, jackhammer, kill, launch, mortar, mug, penetrate, plug, pop, pound, push, ram, rifle, rip, shoot, shred, slam, slash, smash, smoke, snap, spin, steamroll, tattoo, tomahawk, toss, twist, unload, upend, whack, whip, wound, and wreck.

Especially violent impacts were shown in multiple, slow-motion replays and were narrated in ceremonial detail. For example, as viewers watched several replays of a violent tackle by Steeler linebacker Greg Lloyd, Gifford and Dierdorf talked admiringly about the hit:

Gifford: That's almost worth a look again. (A second replay is shown.)

Dierdorf: Uhmm. Uhmmm.

Gifford: He just catapulted himself into Hebert. Take a look at this. (Another replay is shown.) This is a man-sized hit.

Dierdorf: Here he comes!

Gifford: Watch Lloyd, 95. Watch this. He launches himself into him. Hebert went one way, and the ball went another way.

On another occasion, Dierdorf commented on a violent hit made by Vinny Thompson of the Chiefs, as viewers watched several replays: "Watch this shot. He never sees that coming. Vinny Thompson just jackhammers Brooks. Brooks is a fortunate young man that he could get up and make it back to the Packers' sideline." As we watched one more time, this time at regular speed, Dan concluded, "That's just a brutal shot by Vinny Thompson."

The Battered Body: Football Violence and Injuries

These violent impacts on the playing field often resulted in injuries. As Young (1993) explained, "We find high levels of cultural tolerance of danger related to paid work [in sport]. . . . This is an occupational context where the requirements of masculinity entail routinely doling out and incurring injury, and where self-esteem and power derive from doing violence to the bodies of coworkers" (p. 379). And the workplace known as the National Football League is one of the most dangerous in all of sports. Sage (1990) wrote that "injuries are so numerous in the NFL that the league publishes a weekly list of injured players—a casualty list" (p. 159). And he added some alarming details: "In a [1988] survey of 440 former NFL football players, 78% said they suffer continuing football-related disabilities, 54% admitted to having psychological adjustment problems, and 66% said that they believe that playing has shortened their life expectancy" (p. 159).

Not surprisingly, multiple injuries occurred on every *MNF* game *without exception*, and as the season progressed, a regular feature of each broadcast was the injury report for each team. Among the injuries reported during the 1993–1994 season were torn Achilles tendons, broken wrist, broken arm, fractured hand, torn up knee, torn ligament, concussion, sprained ankle, knee surgery, broken thumb, shoulder surgery, groin pull, broken fibula, fractured hip, dislocated finger, pulled hamstring, back spasms, sore thigh, shoulder separation, cervical vertebrate fusion, bruised ribs, rolled ankle, sore lower leg, cut toe, and a screw in the foot. And descriptions of these injuries were often graphic, as when Dierdorf told Michaels about how a torn Achilles tendon appears to the eye: "When it's torn, it rolls all the way up the back of your leg like a Venetian blind."

Players who played with injuries, especially those who played in pain, were complimented as tough, as reflected in Al Michaels's description of what Buffalo running back Thurman Thomas did the previous week: Thomas "gets hurt early, has bruised ribs, he has trouble breathing the rest of the game,

and winds up carrying the ball 30 times." In a game between Kansas City and Green Bay, Michaels mentioned Packer player Johnny Holland, prompting a story from Dierdorf: "Boy, great story, Johnny Holland being back on the field in the NFL. Here's a guy who had to have a serious back operation, had a cervical vertebrate fusion, and yet, back on the fields in the National Football League!" As Sabo and Panepinto (1990) suggested, this ability of football players to play in pain "appears to cement hierarchical distinctions between males, fuse the players' allegiances to one another, set men apart from and above women, and solidify the coach's authority within the intermale dominance hierarchy" (p. 124).

Some Paradoxes of the Body As Weapon

Several paradoxes arise when the male athletic body is treated as an instrument of violence. First, the aggressive and violent acts that the male body must perform in sport are transformed from dangerous ones that result in injuries to others and self, to legitimate, even natural and safe ones performed in the normal course of doing one's job. As Messner (1990) argued, "Aggression, 'within the rules,' is considered legitimate and safe" (p. 210). Similarly, the injuries that result from this violence are legitimized and naturalized because they, too, "are considered part of the job" (Sage, 1990, p. 112).

MNF broadcasters legitimized player violence often, as when Dierdorf described a punishing blow levied against a Buffalo Bill wide receiver by a Pittsburgh Steeler defensive back: "That's a good clean legitimate shot by Jones. Beebe's in the field of play, he's not spearing, he saw what he hit, and he hit it hard." On other occasions, the commentators would even question a referee's call of unnecessary roughness, as when Dierdorf said, "There's nothing wrong with that hit," after the refs called a penalty.

MNF broadcasters also legitimized player injuries, as when New York Giants coach Dan Reeves told a viewing audience in a halftime interview that injuries were "just a part of the game." And Dierdorf described one player, after taking a hit to the knee, as "lucky that he didn't blow out his knee," though it may be more accurate to say that he is unlucky to be in an occupation where getting your knee blown out is a distinct probability every time you report to work.

Second, in football (and other violent sports), an athlete subjects himself to rigorous disciplinary training and uses advanced technology that transforms the body from a naturally athletic (and healthy) one into an artificial (and unhealthy) one. And, just as in the case of violence and aggression, the artificial quality of the athletic body is naturalized and legitimated. This paradox was reproduced elegantly during one *MNF* regular feature on sport and science, sponsored by AT&T. The narrator described new leg pads that would be used by NFL players during the 1993–1994 season: "The Air Armor system adds protection to the lateral thigh and the upper shin, while leaving room for the mandatory soft knee pad. The laminate-composite shell, air bladder, padding system, and support mechanisms all work in combination to permit free, natural, and dynamic movement of the legs, while providing more protection than previously possible." The contradiction was obvious: There simply is nothing free, natural, or dynamic about legs being protected by padding systems and support mechanisms so they can be hit by large and fast men wearing helmets. Yet the report used science and technology to neutralize the contradiction.

The final, and perhaps ultimate, paradox that occurs when the body is treated as an instrument of violence in sport is "the alienation from one's own body—the tendency to treat one's body as a tool, a machine to be utilized (and 'used up') in the pursuit of particular ends" (Messner, 1990, p. 62). In football, this alienation from the body is revealed most vividly in the fact that a player is likely to suffer pain and injury to his own body by using his body as a weapon to injure others on the field. Indeed, Messner (1990) put it best when he described "one of the ultimate paradoxes of organized combat sports":

> Top athletes, who are often portrayed as the epitome of good physical conditioning and health, are likely to suffer from a very high incidence of permanent injuries, disabilities, alcoholism, drug abuse, obesity, and health problems. The instrumental rationality which teaches athletes to view their own bodies as machines and weapons with which to annihilate an objectified opponent ultimately comes back upon the athlete as an alien force: the body-as-weapon ultimately results in violence against one's own body. (p. 212)

MNF dramatizes this point symbolically before every game, as animated helmets of the two opposing teams for the night crash into each other; predictably, both helmets explode into fragments, foreshadowing the broken bones and pulled muscles that are about to occur during the game.

Perhaps one of the most interesting ironies is that the discourse and technology of television transform these violent and aggressive acts into aesthetically pleasing performances. The next section considers how the male athletic body as an instrument of violence is reproduced as an object of pleasure, and how television enhances that pleasure.

The Body As Object of Gaze: (Watching) Football As Pleasure

> If the old saying holds true that you can really undress the guy across from you with some good moves, [New York Giant] Vince Buck would be naked right now. (Dan Dierdorf)

When measured simply by the quantity and nature of announcer comments, the two dominant images of the male athletic body on *MNF* are the tool and the weapon. However, a third, and more subtle, image—the body as object of gaze—is also reproduced on *MNF*, especially in slow-motion replays and pregame music videos. "If athletic bodies are the commodity of sport," argued Morse (1983), "the *look* at the image of male bodies in motion is what television has to offer the viewer" (p. 59). There are two forms of scopophilia or specular pleasure that can be seen in *MNF* when the male athletic body is presented as an object of gaze: fetishism and voyeurism.

Fetishism: The Body As Object of Fascination

Duncan and Brummett (1989) defined "fetishism" as a form of scopophilia involving "the pleasure of fascination directed toward a spectacle, an object of frank, even invited, viewing pleasure" (p. 198). They suggested that televised sport creates fetishes by producing sport as spectacle, by unifying the thousands of camera shots into a coherent game, by explicitly telling viewers to look at certain plays and players, and by commodifying athletes' bodies and actions.

In her critical analysis of televised football, Morse (1983) claimed that televised sport is "the only situation in which [the male body] is a legitimate object of the male gaze" and that televised sport "can license such a gaze and render it harmless" (p. 45). Morse argued that the production techniques of television, especially slow-motion replays and the commentators' narration of the action, transform the male body from a sexual object to be desired into an athletic instrument to be admired. As she explained, "It is the dual nature of the slow-motion technique itself, scientific and dreamlike, which is reiterated in the commentary of the color-man, allowing the image of the male body to be displayed and the look at it to be disavowed" (p. 52). According to Morse, this transformation allows heterosexual men to derive pleasure from watching the male body without embracing the homosexual orientation that normally would be associated with such a fascination with the male body, though gay men may not embrace this sexual denial (cf. Pronger, 1990).

In addition, the violence performed by the male body in football is transformed from dangerous, if sanctioned, aggression—which produces serious injuries, sometimes to favorite players—into graceful movements that can be appreciated aesthetically. Indeed, Morse pointed out that the technique of slow motion makes accessible body motions that are usually imperceptible to the naked eye, and, in so doing, it "transforms a world of speed and violent impacts into one of dance-like beauty" (p. 49). Both of these sources of fetishism—the male body and its actions—are featured prominently on *MNF.*

The Football Body

The most striking feature of the male body in football is its size on the field. The players themselves are larger than average men, and the football uniform, as Morse (1983) pointed out, "inflates its already large bearers to gigantic proportions; it is a mask which not only serves the purpose of protection, but also of creating the phantasmatic body of a titan, which, when in slow motion, is uncannily like that of the first moon-walker" (p. 50).

After analysis of an entire season of *MNF,* it is safe to assert that color commentator Dan Dierdorf (and perhaps Frank Gifford as well) has a serious fetish for large football bodies and large body parts. For example, when country-and-western singer Billy Ray Cyrus joined the trio in the booth at half-time during one game, Dan asked Billy Ray, "When you're down on the field for warm-ups, can you believe how big they are? Can you believe the size of the people who play this game?" Billy Ray laughed and told Dan about how the tunnel shook as players ran through. Over the course of the season, Dierdorf described several large players as "big hunks of men," as he did when he called Miami running-back Keith Byers "a big hunk of man who is stable in his legs."

Dierdorf also spent the season admiring the various body parts of the big men who play this game. On one occasion, he expressed admiration for the arm of New Orleans Saints defensive lineman Terry Kennard: "Look at the arms on this guy. Is there a nozzle on that thing or what?" He then asked Gifford, "Frank, did you ever play with anybody who had arms that big?" Gifford muttered, "He isn't normal," as Dierdorf laughed again.

During a game between Pittsburgh and Buffalo, Gifford and Dierdorf admired the legs of Steeler tight end Eric Greene, indicating that his legs were so big and muscular he did not need to wear leg pads. Later in the same broadcast, they reminded viewers again of Greene's legs in a way that invited scopophilia:

Gifford: "As we said earlier, Dan and I were looking at him clasp, and [he wears] no [leg] pads at all. I don't think he even wears hip pads."

Dierdorf: "I don't think he could get them in his pants."

Football Bodies in Motion

Throughout the season, Dierdorf and Gifford also expressed admiration for the movements of the big football bodies. Seemingly nonimpressive plays were described as pleasing, as when Dierdorf said, "That's as good-lookin' a four-yard run as you can find." The best plays, of course, were replayed several times and were described with words such as *beautiful, brilliant, stunning, marvelous,* or other superlatives. For example, after Vance Johnson caught a touchdown pass from John Elway against the Chiefs, Dierdorf described the catch with hyperbole as the viewer saw several replays: "What footwork by Vance Johnson, getting his toes down on the red in the end zone for a Denver touchdown! What a spectacular play. Watch this, and watch him extend his feet and get them inbounds. That is brilliant by Vance Johnson."

Predictably, the vast majority of these "beautiful" plays are performed by running backs and wide receivers who run with and catch the football. Given the fact that a majority of these two positions are held by black men, the discourse used to describe their bodies in motion, and the slow-motion replays used to present their bodies in motion, indirectly reinforce the stereotype of the black man as a natural athlete (cf. Messner et al., 1993).

Voyeurism: The Body As Sex Object

Another form of specular pleasure derived from televised sports is voyeurism, a form of scopophilia that involves "the pleasure of illicit looking, of watching some object (usually another person) without being invited or allowed to" (Duncan & Brummett, 1989, p. 198). There are many forms of voyeurism in televised sport, but one of the most interesting is sexual voyeurism. As Duncan and Brummett (1989) argued, "Sexually motivated voyeurism, while not openly encouraged by television producers, is always possible" (p. 203).

When seen voyeuristically, the athletic male body becomes a sex object. "Sport," as Segal (1990) suggested, "provides the commonest contemporary source of male imagery" inasmuch as "the acceptable male image suggests—in its body pose, its clothes, and general paraphernalia—muscles, hardness, action" (p. 89); she added that this sporting image of the male is "active, able to penetrate, and not passive" such that "it conveys the phallic function" (p. 88). Morse (1983) and Pronger (1990) suggested that female and gay viewers eroticize the bodies of male athletes, directing a gaze that "is ultimately scopophilic and [for men] homoerotic" (Morse, pp. 58-59).

Dundes (1978) demonstrated that the discourse of football is replete with sexual references, such as "tight end," "penetration," "scoring," and others, and he concluded that "American football is an adolescent masculinity ritual in which the winner gets into the loser's end zone more times than the loser gets in his" (p. 85). Similarly, Pronger (1990) described the potential homoeroticism of the football ritual:

> A group of men get together in . . . a locker room and take off their clothes. In various states of undress, they stand around talking to each other. . . . Ritual garments are donned. . . . Then a coalition of pads and suspenders work together to dramatize and accentuate the masculine form. The men pull themselves into tight pants that closely adhere to the shapes of their buttocks. . . . [Then] one man bends over, while another, behind him, puts his hands between the inclined man's legs, grasps a ball that's shaped like a large testicle, and attempts to throw it to another man. . . . Unless the ball goes out of bounds, each play climaxes with men lying on top of each other, the testicle-shaped ball forming the nucleus of this masculine clutch. . . . When time is up, the boys go back to the locker room, take their clothes off again, and shower together. (p. 179)

Although commentators on MNF used many of the suggestive terms discussed by Dundes (1980) dur-

ing live broadcasts of games, this ABC program, like most other network productions of sports, does not openly encourage sexually motivated voyeurism, and it does not openly objectify football players as sex objects. However, in an unusual pregame music video segment recorded by a different group each week on MNF, the male body was often objectified sexually.[4] This pregame music video segment is a "safe" place for the sexual objectification of male bodies, since such objectification has come to be expected in music videos on MTV. It is also a place where MNF—as a prime-time entertainment program—reveals its intent to attract female as well as male audiences.

The most explicit sexual objectification of the male body on these MNF music videos came before a December game between Pittsburgh and Miami, when two members of the female rap group known as Salt N' Pepa performed a variation of their hit "Whatta Man." The two black women, decked in tight athletic tops (with the logos of the two teams) and tight exercise pants, did their rap from a gym where male athletes, presumably members of the two teams, were pumping iron. The two women fondled the white and black muscular men appreciatively and suggestively, as they strutted around the gym rapping lines such as, "My man likes pushin' / That's why I call him killer"; "He takes a big hit / Why? / 'Cause he's a real man"; and the chorus, "Whatta man / Whatta man / Whatta mighty good man." Quick images of male athletes from the teams were used throughout the video, and two of these shots—both of a black Miami linebacker in his uniform—were explicitly sexual; one showed him swinging his pelvis suggestively, whereas the other showed his buttocks swaying as he ran off the field.

This Salt N' Pepa rap was a powerful, if unusual, display of the sexual objectification of the male athletic body. The women rappers swung their pelvic areas suggestively throughout the video, marking the sexual nature of the video explicitly; the first and last scenes of the video showed the two women directly fondling their crotches. Of course, it was the women who sexualized the male bodies as objects that they desired. In this way, the male athletic body was objectified as a sex object, but it was sexualized in a traditional (and hence "safe") heterosexual context.

Moreover, the Salt N' Pepa rap also reinforced racial stereotypes of black men as sexual performers. The images of the black player swaying his hips and buttocks on the field may have been representative of the so-called "cool pose" discussed by Majors (1986), whereby the black male athlete challenges the societal constraints imposed on him by adopting a uniquely expressive style in athletic performances. However, by inserting those images of the black athlete in an overtly sexual music video, and by juxtaposing those images with images of a white player walking off the field holding hands with his son and daughter, the Salt N' Pepa rap not only objectified football players as sex objects but also reinforced stereotypes of black men as sexual performers and white men as loving fathers.

Some Paradoxes of the Body As an Object of Pleasure

There are several paradoxes inherent in reproducing the male athletic body as an object of heterosexual pleasure. First, although voyeurism suggests that the male athletic body can be seen as a sex object, there are forces that, ironically, transform that body into an asexual instrument. For football players, there is the inevitable paradox of having a muscular body that stands as a symbol of male sexuality but using self-disciplinary practices that keep the body from engaging in (and sometimes from being able to engage in) healthy sexual relations. As Brohm (1978) described it, "Sport is a powerful factor of sexual repression" (p. 179) because it "turns the 'love-body' into a 'labouring body'" (p. 57). For example, Connell (1990) demonstrated that Australian iron men, like football players, must spend a great deal of time developing the physicality of their bodies and, thus, have little time to enjoy their bodies in sexual encounters. Ironically, many of the techniques for developing muscular bodies and for using them in violent games in fact reduce their ability to perform sexually (i.e., serious injuries, steroids, etc.).

In addition, certain male athletes so exaggerate their masculinity and heterosexuality that they reveal their insecurities as men and become less attractive to women. This irony is revealed eloquently when the lyrics of Salt N' Pepa's *MNF* rap are compared to the original lyrics of their hit song "Whatta Man." For example, in the *MNF* version, the female artists rapped that their man "likes pushin'," "spends quality ball with the fellas," and "takes a big hit, 'cause he's a real man." However, in the original version of their hit "Whatta Man," they rapped that their man "gives real lovin'," "spends quality time with his kids," and is "secure in his manhood, 'cause he's a real man." Thus, the Salt N' Pepa rap can be reinterpreted, unexpectedly, as a critique of the hypermasculinity associated with combat sports such as football. In-

deed, although Salt N' Pepa objectified football players as sex objects on *MNF*, the original lyrics suggest that they would rather be with the men who don't play football and are "more secure in their manhood."

A final contradiction occurs for male athletes who adopt explicit heterosexual orientations (and often attack homosexual orientations) but then confine themselves to homosocial environments and engage in actions that, in most other situations, would be interpreted as homosexual. As Arens (1976) suggested, "Dressed in this manner [with their uniforms], the players engage in hand holding, hugging, and bottom patting, which would be ludicrous and disapproved in any other context" (p. 9). This contradiction may occur for viewers who adopt heterosexual orientations but then engage in fetishistic gazes of the male body on the field and in the locker room. As noted, though, the potential homosexual connotations of the male athletic body can be disavowed by players and spectators when the body is transformed into a machine that is analyzed (and appreciated) scientifically and that is used (and appreciated) for violence and aggression. Messner (1990) explained the apparent paradox:

> The salience for gender relations of the image of male power and grace lies not in identification with violence . . . but rather in the opportunity to engage in an identificatory male gaze which is both narcissistic and homoerotic. [But] . . . rather than concluding that the violence has no meaning, it is reasonable to speculate that if men are using sports spectatorship to narcissistically identify with the male body as a thing of beauty, perhaps the violence is an important aspect of the denial of the homoerotic element of that identification. (p. 214)

Despite the apparent denial of homoeroticism, however, gay men may in fact eroticize *MNF* and other combat sports. Pronger (1990) suggested that "televised sports spectacles are a deeply disguised form of homoerotic pornography" (p. 182), and he explained bluntly, comparing combat sports to homosexual intercourse,

> Although they are often portrayed by the media as adversaries, competitive athletes are actually erotic accomplices . . . because men's sports is a bodily, carnal experience . . . Just as in fucking there is an ecstatic meeting . . . so too in sports there is an exhilarating coalescence of equal bodies devoted to the carnal working out of manly struggle. (p. 181)

Ironically, then, the technology of television (especially slow-motion replays) may invite heterosexual men to adopt an asexual gaze of male athletic bodies as instruments of violence, while simultaneously inviting gay men to adopt an overtly sexual gaze at the same athletic bodies.

Concluding Remarks

Some sport sociologists and historians have theorized that in eras when women gain power in society, sports that emphasize traditional images of masculinity gain popularity (Connell, 1978; Nelson, 1994; Whitson, 1990). As Whitson (1990) argued, "Men who are threatened by these larger changes in gender relations talk loudly about the importance of all-male institutions and defend the importance of confrontation in 'men's games'" (p. 25).

Although progress may not be as swift as most feminists would prefer, American society has witnessed a rise in power for women and a change in the dynamics of gender relations in the 1990s. Not surprisingly, then, we have also witnessed a rise in the popularity of American football in the 1990s, with the expansion of the National Football League, the expansion of the Canadian Football League into America, and the continued survival of the Arena Football League. As Nelson (1994) put it in the title of her book, "The stronger women get, the more men love football."

This paper has examined how traditional images of masculinity are reproduced in *Monday Night Football* broadcasts. Specifically, the paper showed how three images of the male body—as instrument, weapon, and object of gaze—are reproduced in *MNF*. It should be noted that these three images are not mutually exclusive but work together to define hegemonic masculinity. Football is a kind of work, organized in accordance with military images, that requires the body to be used as an instrument of sanctioned aggression and violence. Television transforms these weaponlike bodies into objects of fascination and the aggressive and violent acts they perform into graceful gestures that can be appreciated aesthetically, even erotically. It should also be noted that there are other images of the male body and of football, such as the body as temple (football as religion), the body as form of influence (football as politics), the body as organism (football as open system), and others. In the final analysis, though, American football reproduces hegemonic masculinity by demonstrating that the male body is most powerful when it is used for work and vio-

lence, and when it performs in a homosocial (but heterosexual) environment.

The hegemonic masculinity reproduced in televised sports like football has serious costs for both men and women. Clearly, these televised sports marginalize, subordinate, and symbolically annihilate women. As Messner (1990) explained,

Football, based as it is on the most extreme possibilities of the male body (muscular bulk, and explosive power used aggressively) is clearly a world apart from women, who are relegated to the role of cheerleader/sex object on the sidelines, rooting their men on. In contrast to the bare and vulnerable bodies of the cheerleaders, the armored male bodies of the football players are elevated to mythical status, and as such, give testimony to the undeniable "fact" that here is at least one place where men are clearly superior to women. (p. 213)

Messner (1990) concluded that the violence of football is important to hegemonic masculinity because, "ultimately, men's control of women rests on violence" (p. 204).

The hegemonic masculinity reproduced in televised football also has serious consequences for men. Such televised sports marginalize nontraditional images of masculinity, especially nonwhite and nonheterosexual images. As noted in this article, televised sports may reproduce images of black men as natural athletes and even sexual performers and may reinforce an avowedly heterosexual gaze despite seemingly homosexual content. Perhaps more importantly, though, hegemonic images of men may have the highest cost on the very men—black and white, and gay and straight—who adopt such images as their own. Indeed, men who accept the image of men as violent and aggressive are most likely to subject themselves to this violence and aggression. As Messner (1990) argued, "Within the world of organized sport, men are almost exclusively the perpetrators as well as the victims of violence" (p. 206). Although some might argue that anyone who adopts such an outdated image deserves to pay the price, for the men who adopt it on the football field and in other violent work contexts, it is a very high price to pay.

As a form of hegemony, however, the hegemonic masculinity reproduced in American football is subject to contestation. Accordingly, sociologists and other critics of combat sports must take every opportunity to challenge the repressive and oppressive images of masculinity reproduced in such sports. With respect to football, the public attention that has been paid recently to concussions and other serious injuries in the NFL is one opportunity to make our critical voices heard. In addition, we should attempt to direct public attention to the stories of former football players who still suffer health problems long after their retirement. Although the NFL will undoubtedly be with us well into the 21st century, sport sociologists must continue to look for opportunities to critique its repressive and oppressive features.

References

Andrews, D.L. (1993). Desperately seeking Michel: Foucault's genealogy, the body, and critical sport sociology. *Sociology of Sport Journal, 10,* 148–167.

Arens, W.H. (1976). Professional football: An American symbol and ritual. In W.H. Arens and S.P. Montague (Eds.), *The American dimension: Cultural myths and social realities* (pp. 3–15). Port Washington, NY: Alfred.

Birrell, S., and Loy, J.W., Jr. (1979). Media sports: Hot and cool. *International Review of Sport Sociology, 1,* 5–19.

Brohm, J-M. (1978). *Sport: A prison of measured time* (I. Fraser, Trans.). London: Inks Links.

Bryant, J., Comisky, P., and Zillmann. (1977). Drama in sports commentary. *Journal of Communication, 27,* 140–149.

Chandler, J. (1991). Sport as TV product: A case study of "Monday Night Football." In P.D. Staudohar and J.A. Mangan (Eds.), *The business of professional sports* (pp. 48–60). Urbana, IL: University of Illinois Press.

Cole, C.L. (1993). Resisting the canon: Feminist cultural studies, sport, and technologies of the body. *Journal of Sport and Social Issues, 17,* 77–97.

Connell, R.W. (1978). *Gender and power: Society, the person, and sexual politics.* Stanford, CA: Stanford University Press.

Connell, R.W. (1990). An iron man: The body and some contradictions of hegemonic masculinity. In M.A. Messner and D.F. Sabo (Eds.), *Sport, men, and the gender order: Critical feminist perspectives* (pp. 83–96). Champaign, IL: Human Kinetics.

Duncan, M.C. (1990). Sports photographs and sexual difference: Images of women and men in the 1984 and 1988 Olympic Games. *Sociology of Sport Journal, 7,* 22–43.

Duncan, M.C., & Brummett, B. (1989). Types and sources of spectating pleasure in televised sports. *Sociology of Sport Journal, 6,* 195–211.

Duncan, M.C., Messner, M.A., & Williams, L. (1990). *Gender stereotypes in televised sports.* Los Angeles: Amateur Athletic Association of Los Angeles.

Dundes, A. (1978). Into the end zone . . . American football. *Western Folklore, 37,* 75–88.

Dunning, E. (1986). Sport as a mate preserve: Notes on the social sources of masculine identity and its transformations. In N. Elias & E. Dunning (Eds.), *Quest for excitement: Sport and leisure in the civilizing process* (pp. 224–244). New York: Basil Blackwell.

Fiske, J. (1987). *Television culture.* London: Methuen.

Foley, D.E. (1990). The great American football ritual: Reproducing race, class, and gender inequality. *Sociology of Sport Journal, 7,* 111–135.

Foucault, M. (1977). *Discipline and punish: The birth of the prison.* New York: Pantheon.

Guttmann, A. (1978). *From ritual to record: The nature of modern sports.* New York: Columbia University Press.

Hanke, R. (1990). Hegemonic masculinity in *Thirtysomething. Critical Studies in Mass Communication, 7,* 231–248.

Hargreaves, J. (1982). Sport, culture, and ideology. In J. Hargreaves (Ed.), *Sport, culture, and ideology* (pp. 30–61). London: Kegan Paul.

Hargreaves, J. (1986). Schooling the body. In J. Hargreaves (Ed.), *Sport, power and culture* (pp. 161–181). Cambridge, UK: Polity Press.

Hargreaves, J. (1987). The body, sport, and power relations. In J. Horne, D. Jary, and A. Tomplinson (Eds.), *Sport, leisure, and social relations* (pp. 139–159). London: Routledge & Kegan Paul.

King, S. (1993). The politics of the body and the body politic: Magic Johnson and the ideology of AIDS. *Sociology of Sport Journal, 10,* 270–285.

Klatell, D.A., & Marcus, N. (1988). *Sports for sale: Television, money, and the fans.* New York: Oxford University Press.

Majors, R. (1986). Cool pose: The proud signature of black survival. *Changing Men: Issues in Gender, Sex, and Politics, 17,* 5–6.

McMurtry, J. (1985). The illusions of a football fan: A reply to Michalos. Reprinted in D.L. Vanderwerken and S.K. Wertz (Eds.), *Sport inside out* (pp. 241–244). Fort Worth, TX: Texas Christian University Press.

Messner, M.A. (1990). When bodies are weapons: Masculinity and violence in sport. *International Review of Sport Sociology, 25,* 203–219.

Messner, M.A., Duncan, M.C., and Jensen, K. (1993). Separating the men from the girls: The gendered language of televised sports. *Gender and Society, 7,* 121–137.

Morse, M. (1983). Sport on television: Replay and display. In E.A. Kaplan (Ed.), *Regarding television: Critical approaches—An anthology* (pp. 44–66). Los Angeles: The American Film Institute.

Nelson, M.B. (1994). *The stronger women get, the more men love football: Sexism and the American culture of sports.* New York: Harcourt Brace.

Phillips, W. (1969). A season in the stands. *Commentary,* **48,** 66.

Pronger, B. (1990). *The arena of masculinity: Sports, homosexuality, and the meaning of sex.* New York: St. Martin's Press.

Rader, B. (1984). *In its own image: How television has transformed sports.* New York: Free Press.

Real, M.R. (1975). The Super Bowl: Mythic spectacle. In M.R. Real (Ed.), *Mass-mediated culture* (pp. 170–203). Englewood Cliffs, NJ: Prentice Hall.

Real, M.R. (1989). Super Bowl football versus World Cup soccer: A cultural–structural comparison. In L.A. Wenner (Ed.), *Media, sports, and society* (pp. 180–203). Newbury Park, CA: Sage.

Rigauer, B. (1981). *Sport and work* (A. Guttmann, Trans.). New York: Columbia University Press.

Sabo, D., & Jansen, S.C. (1992). Images of men in sport media: The social reproduction of gender order. In S. Craig (Ed.), *Men, masculinity, and the media* (pp. 169–184). Newbury Park, CA: Sage.

Sabo, D.F., & Panepinto, J. (1990). Football ritual and the social reproduction of masculinity. In M.A. Messner and D.F. Sabo (Eds.), *Sport, men, and the gender order: Critical feminist perspectives* (pp. 115–126). Champaign, IL: Human Kinetics.

Sage, G.H. (1990). *Power and ideology in American sport: A critical perspective.* Champaign, IL: Human Kinetics.

Segal, L. (1990). *Slow motion: Changing masculinities, changing men.* New Brunswick, NJ: Rutgers University Press.

Stade, G. (1966, Fall). Game theory. *Columbia Forum,* pp. 173–175.

Staudohar, P. (1986). *The sports industry and collective bargaining.* Ithaca, NY: ILR Press, Cornell University.

VandeBerg, L.R., and Wenner, L.A. (Eds.) (1991). *Television criticism: Approaches and applications.* New York: Longman.

White, P.G., & Gillett, J. (1994). Reading the muscular body: A critical decoding of advertisements in *Flex* magazine. *Sociology of Sport Journal,* **11,** 18–39.

Whitson, D. (1990). Sport in the social construction of masculinity. In M.A. Messner and D.F. Sabo (Eds.), *Sport, men, and the gender order: Critical feminist perspectives* (pp. 19–30). Champaign, IL: Human Kinetics.

Young, K. (1993). Violence, risk, and liability in male sports culture. *Sociology of Sport Journal,* **10,** 373–396.

Notes

1. I would argue that all research involves some deduction and some induction. Researchers who produce studies under a traditional social science framework may develop hypotheses deductively, but they invariably discover unexpected results that may be tested in subsequent studies. By the same token, interpretive researchers never analyze their data *tabula rasa* to find totally unique results that "emerge" from the data but rather use the literature to help guide their interpretations.

2. Since Dan Dierdorf and Frank Gifford provided the color commentary in this sample of *MNF* programs, their comments—especially those of the more dramatic Dierdorf—are featured more extensively than the comments of play-by-play announcer Al Michaels.

3. Staudohar (1986) pointed out that players are valuable assets for franchise owners who enjoy unique tax advantages because "only sports businesses are allowed to depreciate their human assets" (p. 18).

4. During the 1993-1994 season, a different musical artist performed a variation of a hit song, with references to *MNF* and the opponents of the night. This format of the different musical guests replaced the previous opening performed by Hank Williams, Jr. that was played before every game during the 1992-1993 season.

Firm but Shapely, Fit but Sexy, Strong but Thin: The Postmodern Aerobicizing Female Bodies

Pirkko Markula

This paper aims to reconstruct the cultural dialogue surrounding the female body image in aerobics. To do this I have used several methods: ethnographic fieldwork, interviews, and media analysis. I found that the media ideal is a contradiction: firm but shapely, fit but sexy, strong but thin. Likewise, women's relationships with the media image are contradictory: They struggle to obtain the ideal body, but they also find their battles ridiculous. I interpret my findings from a Foucaultian perspective to show how the discourse surrounding the female body image is part of a complex use of power over women in postmodern consumer society. In addition, I assume a feminist perspective that assigns an active role to the individual aerobicizers to question the power arrangement.

Introduction: The Feminine Beauty Ideal

She is fit . . . she's got an incredible body, she is completely tight, she has no fat on her body. (Anna)

Popular women's magazines are saturated with images of beautiful, thin, and tight models. These polished images are often accompanied with advice on how we readers can achieve a body that resembles these images. When the magazines motivate us to work toward the model look, they provide us with an opportunity for a positive change: to obtain our best body ever.

Many feminist scholars, however, consider this glossy festival of feminine beauty a disservice to women. They point out that women's bodies come in a variety of shapes and weights. Paradoxically, the media portray only thin and tight models. Therefore, these scholars conclude, this fashion ideal is oppressive precisely because of its singularity: If only slim and toned women are attractive, most women with normal figures are classified as unattractive (e.g., Bartky, 1988; Bordo, 1990; Coward, 1985; Martin, 1987; Spitzack, 1990; Wolf, 1990). Consequently, to look attractive in this society, the majority of us have to engage in activities—like dressing, applying makeup, dieting, exercising, or, most drastically, reconstructive surgery—to mask or alter our body shapes. Because the sole purpose of these practices is to change our bodies to resemble the narrowly defined beauty ideal, many feminists deem them as vehicles of oppression (e.g., Bartky, 1988; Bordo, 1989; Cole, 1993; Martin, 1989; Wolf, 1990).

Regardless of the feminist opposition to such practices, many women still engage in these potentially degrading activities. For example, they continue to read women's magazines for beauty tips or exercise to lose weight. Can one simply assume that most women are unaware of how they contribute to their own suppression through their everyday behavior? Or is a woman's everyday life a more

Reprinted from Markula, 1995.

complex phenomenon? Perhaps one's behavior is not purely a function of ignorance or lack of education. Although several researchers have examined the discourses surrounding feminine practices, few studies examine how individual women experience their bodies in everyday life. In this paper, therefore, I plan to investigate how women encounter and sense the body ideal in one potentially oppressive female activity, aerobics. I map women's body experiences within aerobics through an ethnographic study. Similar to other feminist scholars, I examine the body ideal, but I limit myself to the exercise context. Furthermore, I am interested in how women react to this body ideal. Are women single-mindedly occupied with improving their bodies in aerobics classes? Or do they celebrate their own figures ignoring the ideal imposed on them by the mass media? Or do they struggle to disregard the image but, at the same time, exercise to reshape their bodies?

First, however, I survey the literature examining women's need to become thinner by dieting and to become tighter by exercising. This journey will lead to my analysis of what kind of body ideal aerobics promotes and an interpretation of what some aerobicizing women think of this ideal.

"No Fat on Her Body"

Several writers have examined women's dieting in today's society (Arveda, 1991; Bordo, 1989, 1990; Chernin, 1981; Imm, 1989; Spitzack, 1990). Their findings suggest that women in general are more obsessed with dieting, body weight, and slimness than men are and that women's ideal slenderness also seems to be more narrowly defined than men's (Arveda, 1991; Bordo, 1990; Cole, 1993). Women diet to obtain the desired extremely slender body rather than accept the natural dimensions of their own bodies. Pamela Imm (1989) suggests that many women participate in aerobics because they are unhappy with their body shape and feel fat. She points out that particularly women who exercise excessively (6 or more hours per week) view their bodies negatively although they are not heavier than the other participants. Why are women required to be so thin? Why do we submit to rigid, constant dieting regimes?

Carol Spitzack (1990) examines women's dieting practices from a Foucaultian perspective. She locates women's body reduction within the net of disciplining discursive power. Her main argument is that women accept the disciplining body control (diet) because it is masked under promises of liberation. In other words, women are persuaded to believe

that after they lose weight their lives suddenly change and they can pursue new challenges, unobtainable earlier due to their excess weight. However, Spitzack (1990) proceeds, this voice of liberation only masks a continuous control over women by the dominant patriarchal and capitalist powers. This control process starts with individual confession that one has excess weight. After realizing her problem, a woman is capable of improvement; now she is ready to lose weight. This change requires, thus, individual initiative and willingness to take control of one's life. This confession mentality, Spitzack (1990) argues, also necessitates an ongoing surveillance and monitoring of one's own body. For example, women keep constantly looking for the excess fat that needs to be eliminated. The female body has become a site of constant self-scrutiny. Therefore, instead of liberating their lives, dieting practices increase the body discipline required from women. In this way, the dominant practice, without openly suppressing women, invisibly controls them.

Margaret Duncan (1994) applies Spitzack's formula to analyze women's body image in two issues of *Shape* magazine. She focuses her analysis on the text of "Success Stories," a recurring feature that introduces *Shape* readers to women who have successfully lost weight through diet and exercise. Duncan (1994) traces a similar pattern to Spitzack's (1990) study: *Shape*'s text urges individual readers to confess that they have a problem, advises them to take the initiative to change from fat and unhealthy to thin and healthy, and advocates how good they will feel after such a body change. Through the "Success Stories," Duncan (1994) concludes, *Shape* practices oppressive disciplinary control over women.

"She Is Completely Tight"

Dieting, thus, is an important part of the disciplinary practices designed to oppress women in this society. The desire to lose weight is maintained through the unobtainable female body ideal: Women are expected to be thin to be considered attractive and accepted in this society. Susan Bordo (1990) adds another component to this ideal: Now it is not enough to eliminate the excess, soft fat from our bodies; we are also required to achieve an athletic, tight look as well. Therefore, women must become more disciplined: In addition to dieting to lose weight, we now exercise to build muscle.

This new requirement—the tight, athletic look—creates a paradoxical body ideal that oscillates "back and forth between a spare 'minimalist' look and a solid, muscular athletic look" (Bordo, 1990, p. 90). Slenderness, Bordo (1990) suggests, can be associated with reduced power and femininity, whereas muscularity symbolizes strength, control, willfulness and masculinity. Therefore, these two ideals, Bordo (1990) continues, can promote different ideas about femininity in the same body: The muscularity could indicate women's liberation from the narrow definition of the female body as frail, whereas the thinness of this ideal restores the connotation to traditional femininity. This observation of such coexisting, disparate images characterizes many so-called postmodern studies examining the women's body ideal. If the women's body ideal simultaneously expands and limits the notions of femininity, it is no longer enough to label women's body practices only as disciplining or as empowering. Rather, in Helen Lenskyj's (1994) words, "a particular social practice cannot be understood purely as conformity or rebellion: rather, the ambiguities and contradictions need to be considered" (p. 258). Women's bodybuilding lends itself well to an analysis in which the disciplined exercise routine is interpreted both as oppressive and liberating (Lenskyj, 1994).

The Bodybuilding Body

Women's bodybuilding has captured many researchers' attention, because the bulging muscles of these competitors so clearly oppose the traditional frail feminine body ideal. These women lift weights to become visibly big. Hence, bodybuilding has clear potential to challenge the traditional notion of femininity. However, some research demonstrates that this emergent resistance has turned to serve the dominant power by sexualizing and objectifying the transgressive female bodybuilder body (Balsamo, 1994; MacNeill, 1988). Particularly, filmed or televised bodybuilding competitions that closely resemble beauty contests contribute to such an oppressive practice.

Other scholars have disengaged from debating whether bodybuilding is liberating or oppressing women. Rather, they argue that women's bodybuilding is a contradiction in itself: It simultaneously complies with and resists the dominant powers in the society (Bolin, 1992a, 1992b, 1992c; Daniels, 1992; Guthrie and Castelnuovo, 1992; Miller and Penz, 1991). Sharon Guthrie and Shirley Castelnuovo (1992) observe that women bodybuilders are compliant with the dominant discourse of feminine beauty in that they worry about their body shapes and invest tremendous energy to body care. In addition, their pink posing costumes, their blond, fluffy hair styles, and their feminine posing routines and music choices are in line with the traditional femininity. However, women bodybuilders resist the same femininity by actively creating a new female body shape. As a result, they do not feel compelled to model themselves after the more traditional feminine body form.

Anne Bolin (1992a, 1992b, 1992c) expands this analysis by locating the more compliant practices on the public—front stage—arena and the more resistant practices on the private—backstage—arena. When on the front stage during a competition, the women bodybuilders use the feminine accessories to comply with the judges' requirements of proper femininity. This, Bolin (1992a) demonstrates, is necessary if one wants to win the competition, and bodybuilders are there to win. Therefore, enforced notions of femininity for them are simply a necessary means to a higher goal: a victory. On the backstage, outside of the competition, women bodybuilders do not worry about looking feminine. They train seriously to build more muscle mass in the hard-core gyms devoted only to bodybuilding. They wear training gear far from skimpy posing outfits: sweat pants, sweat shirts, baggy tee shirts, and shorts. Bolin (1992b) concludes,

> Theirs is a transformative experience. . . . The presentation of an appearance that the judges will regard as feminine is just a matter of strategizing one's training, diet, and accessorizing with insignias of femininity. This exposes femininity as a cultural construction with boundaries, while femininity as a lived attribute knows no such limits. (p. 395)

What about the aerobicizing body? Some bodybuilders consider that aerobics supports the dominant oppressive beauty ideal. For example, they regard "the aerobics instructor body" as a derogatory term when they discuss women bodybuilders like Cory Everson, who deliberately keeps her muscles smaller and softer to comply with the traditional femininity required by the media (Bolin, 1992a). Nevertheless, some scholars argue that aerobics, similar to bodybuilding, creates a double image that embodies traditional conceptions of both feminine and masculine characteristics.

The Aerobicizing Body

Margaret MacNeill (1988) observes that although aerobics helps to uphold a feminine look, it also promotes healthy life and vitality that assumes a tight, thin, and muscular body. Regina Kenen (1987) characterizes such an aerobics image as a "hybrid" of a patriarchal image (the feminine look) and a feminist image (strong, muscular look). Interestingly, Kenen (1987) argues that women need to obtain the feminine look to successfully manipulate the power source—the men. This form of resistance has provoked lively discussion among feminist scholars. They observe that instead of initiating open resistance women effectively obtain power through similar manipulation of the traditional channels (e.g., Abu-Lughod, 1990; Bolin, 1992a; Dubisch, 1986; Gottlieb, 1989; Strathern, 1981). Therefore, what looks like oppression to the researcher's eye might serve as a means for power for the women involved. Kenen (1987) also points out that the media equate the feminist image with sex appeal and turn it to serve the patriarchal powers. Here the aerobics image is truly ambiguous: The traditional feminine image is resistant, but the strong "feminist" image sexualizes women.

In their approach to the double image, Elizabeth Kagan and Margaret Morse (1988) place the aerobicizing body in the postmodern context. They concentrate on the images in Jane Fonda's exercise videotapes. Like Kenen (1987), they contend that Fonda's body incorporates the slender femininity with a new powerful self-determining subject in motion. However, these writers assume that women participate in aerobics basically to fight against their aging and sagging bodies. This preoccupation results in a compromising aerobics body image: The subjectivity and its will are delegated to shape the body to a commercially supported ideal of femininity. Like those who studied women's bodybuilding (Balsamo, 1994; MacNeill, 1988), Kagan and Morse (1988) conclude that the emergent potential for liberation is revisited to serve the purposes of patriarchy by linking women's physical activity to attractiveness.

Kagan and Morse (1988) like MacNeill (1988) focus on the body discourse transmitted through media. What about the everyday practice in aerobics classes? Do the aerobicizers there struggle to confront a contradictory body image? To find answers to these questions I set myself to listen to the voices of the aerobicizing women.

Method

Like Kagan and Morse (1988), I locate my research of aerobics within the postmodern cultural condi-

tion. Central to my study is the view that this culture is communication between different voices. Michael Bakhtin's (1981) examination of the dynamics of cultural dialogue serves as a foundation for my analysis.

In every dialogue, Bakhtin (1981) argues, several voices, some more dominant than others, struggle over each other to give meanings to cultural phenomena. Cultural dialogue, therefore, implies a certain authority and assumes certain power relations in its exchange. Bakhtin (1981) locates dominant voices in the public, official sphere, from where they claim the rights for the correct interpretation of the phenomenon at hand. For example, the magazines and aerobics videotapes are claiming the rights for public representation of the perfect female body image. The private voices, like the aerobicizers', must use other channels available to them to replace the official interpretation with their own meaning. I believe, therefore, that the meaning of aerobics in this culture is created by many voices that contradict with each other and work to replace each other. All these meanings, the public as well as the private, are produced within cultural discourses.

For example, our understanding of the body is formed within such discourses as health, medicine, and femininity. However, I believe it is insufficient to examine the discursive construction of the body ideal at the public arena. Like Spitzack (1990), I aim to examine how the discursive dialogue of the public arena materializes in the women's everyday experiences. To find out, I have to listen to the voices of the individual women. I assume, along with many other feminists, that women actively make sense out of their social world and construct different meanings in different social contexts. In this paper, individual women engage in a dialogue with the discursive representations: They strive to make sense of the "fit body ideal." Here I focus on the ambiguities and contradictions in women's body experience (Lenskyj, 1994), as I do not believe that any experience can be classified as purely empowering or purely oppressive. However, I believe, following Spitzack (1990), that aerobicizers' critical voices have the potential to alter the course of dominant practices.

I also assign an active role for myself when I aim to uncover women's meanings about the aerobicizing body. The reported meanings are my subjective interpretations based on my fieldwork within aerobics. In this study, therefore, the aerobicizers and I have negotiated a shared understanding of the aerobicizing body in American culture. I also acknowledge that I am a human observer whose personal, social, and historical background structures research considerably (e.g., Bruner, 1993; Clifford and Marcus, 1986; Denzin, 1992; Rosaldo, 1989).

Fieldwork

I used several methods to reconstruct the dialogue surrounding the body image in aerobics: fieldwork, interviews, and media analysis. My research derives predominantly from my ethnographic fieldwork among aerobicizers from 1990 to 1992. Although ethnography is most often associated with anthropology, today its methods have been increasingly used to study the state of Western society as the minutiae of everyday life (de Certeau, 1984) have attracted researchers across the social sciences. Many taken-for-granted, commonplace phenomena like aerobics are now considered especially fruitful topics, because they, in their popularity, unveil central aspects of our culture to a critical inquiry (Dunn, 1991; Featherstone, 1988; Foley, 1992; Johnston, 1986; McRobbie, 1994).

Aerobics handed itself quite easily to ethnographic fieldwork because aerobicizers gather regularly together in a public, yet well-defined place—the gymnasium. My field was mainly the university community in a small Midwestern town: Most aerobics classes were organized by the university and the participants were in some way associated with the university. This is only one context for aerobics classes. Kenen (1987) has found that the setting influences the aerobics praxis. For example, commercial health clubs exacerbate the negative, oppressive practices more than do public-sector classes like the YMCA. I do not intend to generalize my findings over the private aerobics sector (the health clubs) or different geographical regions of the U.S., although I attended private health clubs in the community and in other parts of the country to complete my ethnography. In this study I focus on women's experiences within a university community. On average, I participated in seven 1-hour classes weekly.

In addition to my field observations, I conducted both informal and formal interviews to closely trace the individual experiences. I interviewed the aerobicizers informally whenever possible: before and after classes, in the locker rooms, in the street, in coffee shops, in the classes, or any other time I met one of the participants. The formal interviewing technique used in this study can be characterized after Michael Quinn Patton (1980) as openended topical interviews. I had prepared a list of topics instead of setting up detailed questions. I selected the topics—the structure and nature of an aerobics class, the body image, health, and nutrition—based on findings in the literature (Kagan and Morse, 1988; Kenen, 1987; MacNeill, 1988; Martin, 1987), an earlier pilot study, and my ongoing participant observation. Therefore, the discussion regarding the body was only one part of my larger research project on aerobics (Markula, 1993b). I wanted to adopt a conversational model (e.g., Spitzack, 1990) in which both the researcher and respondent assume equal responsibility for the discussion. Basically, we discussed the abovementioned topics during each interview, but the conversation could also follow a particular concern of the interviewee. Body matters were such a concern for many of the aerobicizers, and we usually discussed body image extensively. The length of each interview varied from 30 minutes to 2 hours. I interviewed most participants once, but certain "informative" or verbal participants were interviewed twice. All the interviewees assumed anonymity, and I refer to them here by their pseudonyms. I interviewed 35 exercisers (33 women and 2 men). This imbalanced gender ratio was common in the aerobics classes I participated in; the vast majority of the participants were women. Consequently, in this paper I focus on women's views. The exercisers in my study were mostly students but also were secretaries, staff members, and researchers. This research, therefore, is based on the experiences of a select group. The typical aerobicizer in my study was a white, well-educated, 18- to 45-year-old female, a description which—according to nationwide surveys—also characterizes an average aerobics exerciser around the U.S. (Rothlein, 1988).

In addition to recording the aerobicizers' private voices, I wanted to record the public voice constructing the aerobics body. Therefore, to support my investigation, I analyzed how aerobics was presented in the media. My research drew from images in aerobics videotapes but mainly I examined exercise images in such magazines as *Health, Women's Sport and Fitness, Shape,* and *Self.* I selected *Health* and *Women's Sport and Fitness* because they were likely to contain frequent articles on women's exercise. In addition, because they were available since 1979 I had a chance to examine the change in media representation of the female body through these magazines. I selected the other two monthly magazines, *Shape* and *Self,* because of their self-proclaimed specialization in women's fitness matters. For example, *Shape,* published by bodybuilding tycoon Joe Weider, promised to provide "mind and body fitness for women" (*Shape,* March 1994, p. 2). Moreover, individual aerobicizers I spoke with recommended these two magazines for me. I investigated issues of both magazines starting from 1986. In these magazines I focused specifically on articles about aerobics or women's exercise. Their topics varied from aerobics shoe and video guides to articles advising strength and toning exercises. I read the text of each article and examined the accompanying pictures, which I also compared to the text.

Several of the women I interviewed also exercised using videotapes. I have, therefore, included the women's views about the video bodies in my study. Among the numerous exercise tapes available the women talked most about Jane Fonda's "Workout" series and Kathy Smith's exercise videos.

To analyze how the contradictory body image evolves in aerobics, I first look at the meanings the magazines construct around the female body image. I then proceed to identify how these meanings materialize in aerobicizers' everyday experiences: How do the media discourses structure women's ideas about their bodies? In addition, I am interested in women's responses to the dominant media discourses: Do women question the media representation of the body? To conclude, I will explain why the media portray a certain female image and why women react to this ideal the way they do. I will start by sketching the ideal body of the exercising female in the media.

Shapely, Slender, and Softly Curvy

Since the early days of aerobics, women's bodies seem to occupy a central space in the fitness discourse. For example, in the 1960s the father of the aerobics running program, Kenneth Cooper, felt that women's exercise should primarily improve bodily appearance: "The way it works out, women earn a double payoff from aerobics; they go to the program to improve their looks and they get fitness and health as fringe benefits" (Cooper, 1970, p. 134).

In the 1970s and early 1980s women were increasingly urged to exercise to take care of their bodies. In addition to light aerobic activities such as jogging, swimming, or tennis, calisthenics, light strengthening exercises, and stretching were often recommended. The ideal feminine body was described as shapely, slender, and softly curvy (Fairclough, 1980; Hoover, 1980; Lenskyj, 1986). Muscles did not fit with this image: Muscle bulk was seen as masculine and unsuitable for the

"proper" feminine look. Fear of visible muscle growth and the fear of lost femininity due to physical activity were commonly addressed in the exercise articles. One way of countering the muscle bulk was to exercise correctly: Magazines advised slow, controlled repetitions. Women were also blessed with another way of avoiding bulging muscles. Magazines comforted their readers that female hormones prevented any extensive muscle development despite engagement in physical activity. It was, therefore, a physiological fact that women had soft, small muscles and curvy bodies. Conversely, it was naturally unfeminine to display well-defined muscles. The following quote summarizes the sentiment that surrounded women's conditioning:

> Today, the leg to strive for embodies the virtues of predecessors—it should be shapely, smooth and supple—but it also must be strong. . . . No, we are not talking about big, muscular legs like Richard Gere's. A woman's legs can have power without having bulk. . . . The way to strength without mass is to exercise against low resistance, but with a higher number of repetitions. . . . Muscles will increase a bit in size, but combining the resistance/repetition formula with your body's female hormones will prevent your legs from becoming locker room curiosities. (Farah, 1984, p. 38)

The whole concept of a muscular woman was redefined when Jane Fonda published *Jane Fonda's Workout Book* in 1981. Jane Fonda aimed for a fit, trim, and muscular body, and a new ideal stepped into the aerobics movement. If the idea of women having muscles was "just abhorrent" (Tucker, 1990, p. 97) earlier, muscles now became acceptable, even a desired part of the ideal female body. Starting from the 1980s "fashion magazines were abuzz with the news that muscles were chic" (Tucker, 1990, p. 97). Muscles are still a central feature of the ideal female body. Exercise reserves, therefore, a prominent place in women's lives: The only way to obtain the desired, trim muscles is to exercise. The magazines sensed a need for exercise advice. Special workout articles, which encouraged women to develop their muscle tone, started to appear in the magazines. For example, in 1990 *Shape* began its "Spot Training" columns, which focused on training for muscle tone with free weights or machines. Muscle tone is also a prominent part of aerobicizers' everyday exercise experience. In what follows, I discuss the discourses surrounding women's toning exercises.

Toned and Trim

When toned muscles became an important part of the ideal feminine body, special shaping exercises became an integral part of the aerobics class. Some aerobicizers call these exercises "toning"; others refer to them as "floorwork" (most of the training is done while lying on the floor). This muscle work resembles the spot training exercises depicted in *Shape* and *Self*. The most important principle underlining these exercises is to focus on one muscle group—or body "spot"—at a time. This focus ensures that the participant effectively tones the intended, isolated body part. This is how one gets the best results: The particular muscle is toned without wasting time and energy to condition the unintended muscles. Aerobicizers' comments reflect this philosophy:

> I don't see how you can really work the abs and do a good job if you are doing something else. (Sheila)

> When you are toning, you concentrate on one muscular area; I think it's the best way to do it, because . . . it's kind of hard to the mind to do two things at once. (Trisha)

> You can concentrate more in one area, if you are only working one area, that makes sense. (Anna)

Aerobicizers have faith in toning exercises: These workouts do, indeed, effectively tone the body. At the same time, many of them view toning as hard, repetitious, and boring:

> Toning is boring to me, period. I hate toning, the worst part of the class. (Trisha)

> Boring, body toning is intensely boring . . . with these little boring ah, ah, ah, sit-up aerobics . . . they are doing body toning grimacing and looking unhappy. (Antoinette)

Although it is torturous, hard, and horrible, most exercisers would incorporate toning into their class. They find it a necessary yet uncomfortable and difficult way to achieve muscle tone. Some of the exercises are particularly difficult as they are aimed for muscles infrequently used in everyday life. These muscles have to be trained in strange positions, which adds to the discomfort. Sheila talks about the so-called "doggy lifts," also referred to as "elbows and knees":

> I really don't like the elbows and knees, I don't know why it is . . . we always do it, maybe it's just a strange way to do it . . . I think people don't like it because it's just an abnormal way to do things, we don't sit like that or do anything like that. I feel like I'm walking around like a dog; it's just not very comfortable feeling.

Sheila points out a contradiction: "elbows and knees" (which is designed to train the gluteus maximus) is frequently done in her class although it's an abnormal move. The whole exercise makes her feel uneasy and she wonders why it is included in her class. Kagan and Morse (1988) explain this contradiction. They argue that exercises like "elbows and knees" do not improve functionality: We do not need these movement patterns to perform everyday chores. Rather, these exercises are designed to improve our appearance. Thus, toning in aerobics class dissociates body parts from their functional roles. Sheila was right when she pointed out that doggy lifts are abnormal because she never does such a movement in "real" life. The meaning of such exercises, Kagan and Morse (1988) believe, is to change the body to look like the ideal, toned body. In this way women are assigned to manipulate their body parts for the sake of appearance. Apparently, not all the exercisers are prepared to work only for their "looks": Sheila questioned the rationale for performing "elbows and knees" because that exercise did not have a functional meaning for her. In addition, many aerobicizers lined at the water fountain to avoid this uncomfortable exercise. Paradoxically, in the line we complained about our problematic body parts that needed more tone.

"Hot Moves to Shape Your Trouble Spots"

Magazines deepen the fragmented image when they assign special parts of our bodies as problem spots. Problem areas—abdomen, thighs, underarms, and the "butt"—are particularly resistant to manipulative toning, albeit they need it the most. Already in 1980, one article pointed out that "the main areas of concern for most women are the upper arms (batwings), abdomen (stretch marks and flab) and outer thighs (saddlebags)" (Stallings, 1980, p. 49). Fifteen years later these particular parts still trouble women. Jane Fonda, for example, advertised her 1992 video "Lower Body Solution" as "designed especially for the #1 problem areas for women: abs, buns, and thighs" (e.g., *Self*, March 1992, p. 178). In every issue magazines introduce workouts to "hit" one or more of these parts. A myriad of special exercises such as abdominal tighteners, waist cinchers, lower belly flatteners, back-of-the-thigh hardeners, seat shapers, bottom lifters, fanny firmers, hip slimmers, and front-of-the-thigh definers are designed to firm women's problematic body parts. These movements are promoted as simple, effective, and easy to perform. Therefore, even the busiest women can manage to fit exercise into her daily schedule.

Magazines advocate these workouts based on one assumption: Women need to look good. They assume further that their readers presently find their bodies imperfect. This imbalance results in great anxiety, which only their workout program can cure. In this sense, the magazines see themselves contributing to women's well-being.

> If you balk at pool-party invitations; if you lie awake at night wondering how to cover your thighs while keeping cool and looking great; if you seriously consider moving to Antarctica as soon as the hot weather sets in—this workout is for you. (Sternlicht, 1990c, p. 34)

> Weak triceps can make wearing a sleeveless shirt or evening dress an embarrassment. By adding triceps exercises to your workout, you can make the back of your arms shapely and strong. (Sternlicht, 1990a, p. 46)

> Both women and men alike are self-conscious of their derrieres, whether their buttocks are large or flat, high or low, round or saggy. But relax. It's fairly easy either to develop this area and give it more roundness or to firm it up and give it more sleekness. (Sternlicht, 1990b, p. 38)

One participant in my study also confirms that women exercise because their bodies are flawed:

> I think everyone there has a certain area that they want to work on; it's obvious to them or it's obvious to you, they wouldn't be there if they hadn't a complex about [some area]. They don't like something . . . like a stereotype, we don't like our arms, that's why we signed up . . . we are trying to get rid of our arms. (Sarah)

In the magazine texts, the problem spots cause the biggest anxieties; the thighs, the triceps (underarms), and the butts are what women are most embarrassed about. Are their predictions well placed? When I asked the aerobicizers to identify any problematic parts of their bodies, their answers resonate with the magazine discourse. The problem spots

trouble the aerobicizers the most. For example, Jane, Cecilia, and Laura quickly identified their problem parts:

> *Pirkko:* Do you feel that you have certain problem areas in your bodies?

> *Jane:* My lower half, I sit all day.

> *Cecilia:* My stomach, that's the hardest part.

> *Laura:* After having a baby, stomach muscles are the worst.

Many aerobics classes I participated in included exercises for these particular parts. The instructors, like the magazines, presumed that women want to tackle those particular areas. I asked Becky, an aerobics instructor, to describe a typical toning session. She found that "a lot of them [the participants] want to work on their sides, the outer thighs or . . . the seats more. . . . I think stomachs are probably one [problem area], hips, outer thighs, those are the main ones." When questioned why these areas are so problematic, she explained, "That's where we have most of our fat cells, that's where we store most of the fat." Obviously, storing fat is a highly undesirable, yet natural, process. The storage places are the problem spots whose fat levels women carefully monitor. These areas require special toning as they appear especially prone to excess fat and flab.

As other scholars, I contend that these spots "where we store most of the fat" are the very parts of our bodies that identify us as females: the rounded bellies, the larger hips, the thighs, the softer underarms. These "female parts" are also the ones we hate the most and fight the hardest to diminish. Logically then, we hate looking like women. Bordo (1990) argues that women grow up despising their feminine form, because the ideal feminine shape in this society resembles that of a young boy: wide shoulders, tight muscles, narrow hips (also Bartky, 1988; Chernin, 1981; Coward, 1985). The majority of women, regardless how hard they try, can never achieve this type of body. Most women simply are not born with male bodies. Kim Chernin (1981) adds that the unattainable boyish ideal is one of the major causes for women's anxieties with their bodies. The dissatisfaction with one's feminine shape can lead to an extreme fear of fat and, consequently, a distorted body image. Ronda Gates (1991) reports that devoted aerobicizers and fitness professionals, more than anyone, have a distorted understanding of their bodies. They are afraid of fat: "If 22 percent of fat is optimum, 18 percent is better" (Gates, 1991, p. 28), these exercisers conclude (see also Imm,

1989). According to Chernin (1981), this attitude generates desperate attempts to control one's body weight that precede serious eating disorders like anorexia nervosa and bulimia nervosa.

Magazines advocate muscle tone as a vital feature of an ideal female body, and the aerobicizers seem to accept this model. Paradoxically, although they work hard to "sculpt" their trouble spots into the desired tone, they also question the meaning of the uncomfortable toning exercises. I examine next what is meant by toned muscles: What kind of muscle definition is desirable?

Sleek and Sexy

Although a "good female body" is a muscular body, the magazines discourage extreme muscularity. Exercise articles primarily promote a toned and shapely look. Magazine workouts, thus, aim to "tone" one's muscles, not to build muscles. One article puts a clear limit on female muscle size: "Strong muscles mean more shape in arms and shoulders, definition in the legs and a flat, but not concave middle" (Kaufman, 1989, p. 124). The ideal body is layered with long, sleek, unbulky muscles. Such muscles are also defined as "sexy." For example, workouts are advertised with such slogans as "The Ultimate Guide to Sexy Muscles" (*Self*, March 1991, cover), "Three Easy Ways to a Strong and Sexy Stomach" (*Self*, February 1991, cover), "Sculpted and Sexy" (Rover, 1992, p. 48), "Shoulders are Sexy" (Laurence, 1992, p. 103).

"Is It All Right for Women to Have Muscular Arms?"

Evidently, muscles—particularly the problem spots—need to be toned, tight, and firm. Most problem spots are located in the lower body. Toning the upper body in general and arms in particular is a more complex enterprise. Magazines encourage upper body workouts: "Firm Triceps and Shapely Biceps are in Vogue" (Sternlicht, 1991, p. 48) and "It's all right for women to have muscular arms" (Sternlicht, 1991, p. 48). For women in aerobics classes, however, muscular arms are not "all right." Many women fear large arm muscles if they do upper body workouts in their classes. Arm toning is complicated, because one of the problem areas is the triceps region, under the upper arm. Aerobicizers want firm triceps without bulking up. Sarah, for example, trains her arm muscles, but says, "I am afraid that I bulk up when I do arms. . . . I used to swim and I was huge, like bulky and I hated it." Sarah continues to explain why women hate "big arms":

Girls don't really work out their arms, because if you work your arms, you get big arms, you look like a guy. It seems to be okay if you have strong legs, but if you are athletic and you have big arms, it's like she looks like a guy. It's more socially acceptable to have big legs than the arms.

Women do not want to look masculine, Sarah explains, and that is what muscular arms do to you: You end up looking like a guy. Considering that the ideal female body nowadays "looks like a young guy" more than a woman, this distaste of big arms seems unjustified. Apparently, although women should possess broad shoulders, they should not be muscular.

Not only muscle size but also the location of the muscles defines the exerciser's femininity. Sarah in her earlier quote points out that muscular legs—firm thighs—are socially acceptable, unlike muscular arms. Kathy adds that tight legs are not only acceptable but desirable:

I personally would like to work on my arms more, but it seems that a lot of girls would rather work on their thighs, their outer, inner thighs and their butt, but they don't feel that they need their arms built up. . . . The thing that guys look at or a lot of women are concerned, tends to be your butt or their thighs. They don't say, "I have fat arms" . . . and you don't have guys going by and saying, "Look at those sexy arms."

Well-toned legs are sought after because men notice them. Women do not urgently shape their arms because men do not care about seeing them. Obviously, arms are not as vital a part of an attractive woman as legs are. In addition, Kathy implies that women are exposed to a gaze that sets the standards of the desirable female form. We shape our bodies to please that gaze. Kathy clearly identifies the gaze as male; other aerobicizers do not really recognize a source for the controlling gaze. They are objects of a gaze that is just ubiquitously "societal": "It's a product of society" (Colleen); "It's socially acceptable" (Sarah). The preferences of this gaze often contradict the exercisers' own will, but they feel pressured to please the gaze. Most exercisers comply with, as Kelly puts it, what "most people presumably think women are . . . softer lines," and she continues, "which is too bad." Kelly indicates, hence, that she does not agree with such definitions of femininity. She weight trains herself, as do Andrea, Becky, Colleen, and Trisha. Trisha has even tried bodybuilding, and Kelly would like to start:

> I would like to do bodybuilding myself and we've [she and her bodybuilder husband] actually been in bodybuilding competitions . . . and I would like to do that. But I think I am a minority; a lot of women feel that's not the way a woman should look, but I wouldn't mind looking like that. (Kelly)

Interestingly she adds, "within reason, of course. I don't want to look like Arnold Schwarzenegger. I would like to build my muscles a little more than they are [now]." None of the women in my study desires to have big muscles, not even the exercisers who work out with weights. All the weight trainers also indicate that women cannot become too muscular even with the help of weights and definitely not without serious commitment and work. Becky and Colleen rely on a biological explanation: "I don't think women should worry about getting too muscular, because they just don't have the hormone" (Colleen), which Becky specifies as testosterone. Trisha reflects her own experience:

> It takes so much, I didn't realize . . . it's just really, very disciplined sport. . . . I think a lot of women have a misconception that if I go to the gym and lift weights I'll look like Rachel McLish, Cher or somebody, [but] it takes a lot. This one lady spent 40 hours a week in the gym—that's a career—but that is ridiculous and I think there are lot of people who think if you lift like six weeks you can see the difference. . . . I think women see men going do situps, 100 sit-ups every day and their stomachs look like Rambo's: the women can do 100 sit-ups the rest of their lives and their stomachs still wouldn't took like that.

Although women do not want big muscles, everybody admires toned muscles. Most aerobicizers also admit needing more tone, also in their upper bodies. Kathy and Kelly indicate that they want to include more arm work in their classes but find themselves different from the majority of the women in this matter. Others, like Helen and Sarah, acknowledge that they benefit from arm exercises, although they prefer toning their legs to upper body work. Maria's comment summarizes the feelings of many exercisers in my study: "I just want my legs to be more toned and the upper arms, when you get older, you know, the little wonderful thing that flabs down here (points at her triceps area)." Maria is 21 years old, but already worries about how her aging body is changing. I discuss this concern more in depth later in this paper.

Some women, like Antoinette, Becky, Colleen, or Christy do not want appear muscular but still want to be strong. Antoinette reasons that it is good to be strong,

> because if I'm physically strong, I can do things that I want to do: I can unscrew jam jars—I don't have to ask some guys to do it for me—I can put the trash out; I can lift things. I don't like feeling weak and helpless and end up asking other people to do things for me.

Maria and Molly want to be strong to excel in the sports they love. For these women, it's not the appearance, the muscle size, that matters but the actual functionality of the muscles. Christy, a former competitive swimmer, likes to be strong and to have strong arms but believes that "you don't have to have muscle definition to have good strong muscles." Therefore, the aerobicizers might conform with the toned look of the ideal body, but for functionality, not only for looks.

"I Was Bulky and I Hated It!"

The aerobicizers admire other participants or instructors with tight and firm muscles, but built, big muscles are disliked. The muscle size, therefore, is an intricate matter. The women I interviewed define toned muscles quite differently from built muscles. For example, Kelly points out that "when you are toning you are just keeping the muscle firm and when you are bodybuilding you are actually enlarging the muscle and building what they call definition, when you can see one muscle from the other." To the aerobicizers, toned muscles can be visible but not big and massive. Toned muscles are lean, in use, and tight. But when exactly does the tone turn into bulk? This, apparently is a hard question to answer. Trisha considers that "there is a real fine line between looking good and being too muscular." Many women are perplexed: They begin to work out their muscles but end up feeling ashamed of their bodies. Andrea tells a story of a confused friend who started weight training but is not sure about the results:

Andrea: We were going to go out and she was wearing a dress and she was like "I can't take off my jacket" . . . they [the arms] were definitely tight, but I don't think they were that unattractive, but she said she is always used to having great, thin arms, not the actual muscle, so I guess for some girls, maybe for the majority, it just is not very attractive.

Pirkko: Why did she start lifting weights?

Andrea: I'm not sure. I think she did it because she was working on her upper body more, she just tried to get rid of her arm fat. I think eventually she started to work more on the arms, so she wouldn't overwork her legs.

Andrea's friend felt that she was unattractive; the never-resting eyes of society glanced at her arms disapprovingly. Some of the exercisers sense a contradiction here: They recognize that they want to be strong—it is good to be strong—but concurrently they feel bad about it. For example, Melissa is struggling with her feelings about being strong:

> It is really contradictory, because the very things that I do in aerobics, like my class always has this long session of push-ups, I'm strong and I feel uncomfortable with that, but at the same time I'm proud of that, not proud, that makes me feel good about myself to be strong, but I don't know. . . . I'm not satisfied and I don't know what I want to look better; it doesn't make sense.

Feeling simultaneous pride and shame does not make sense to Melissa. Many of these women can, thus, see the unfair expectation placed on them. It is, however, almost impossible to resist the societal pressure to conform. Aerobics does not seem to help women to expand the boundaries of the ideal feminine body to the same extent as, for example, women's bodybuilding does. However, Helen and Sarah compare aerobics to ice skating and ballet, physical activities they have been involved in earlier. They prefer aerobics because, unlike ice skaters or ballet dancers, aerobicizers can be proud of their muscles:

> I've been in ballet forever, and I prefer aerobics to it, because in ballet you are supposed to be skinny and have no muscles. I mean, muscles are not valued, just flexibility. In aerobics muscles are valued, because it shows that you've been doing aerobics for a while and if

you have big calves . . . [they think], "Oh, she is dedicated." (Sarah)

For these women, aerobics has been a liberating experience, because they no longer feel ashamed of their well-defined leg muscles. Both, however, express an added desire "to look thinner" (Helen). Therefore, along with the refined regulations regarding ideal tone, the perfect female body is also required to be thin.

"I Like to Be Sort of Petite"

The connection between women's exercise and slimness dates back to the advent of aerobics. When aerobics began, its initial purpose was to facilitate weight loss (Cooper, 1968, 1970; Sorensen, 1979). Presently, weight loss is always listed as an advantage of a regular exercise program. Occasionally strength training is also sold to the audience by linking it with weight loss. Theoretically, increased muscle mass burns calories even at rest. Therefore, a muscular person will consume more calories in everyday life than her or his weaker counterpart (e.g., Barrett, 1991). This logic implies that women should build muscles to assist weight loss, not to increase strength.

Weight loss is important for the exercisers in my study, more so than the firm muscles. For example, one should first worry about being thin; once sufficiently thin, one can work on muscle tone. Cari's comment illustrates this sentiment:

> I'm trying to burn out some fat and just stay in shape, maybe if I got down to when I was satisfied [with my weight], maybe then I worked on shaping, but I'm a long way from there; right now, I'm just trying . . . to burn out some of those fat cells.

Cari supposes that shaped muscles are something slim exercisers work on; for her the ideal body is thin, and tone is a fringe benefit. The present body ideal is definitely slim. However, slimness does not mean soft, meatless flesh but requires firm, tight, and sleek muscle tone. Bordo (1990) confirms that "unless one goes the route of muscle building, it is virtually impossible to achieve a flab-less, excessless body unless one trims very near to the bone" (p. 90). Consequently, Cari could not achieve a fashionably small body by only losing weight. Jiggling flesh, even on a thin body, feels loose—like fat. Hence, without toning one will always feel big.

Magazine texts appeal to similar reasoning: They construct their strengthening exercises to reduce women's bodies like their diet regimens are designed to downsize their female readers. For example, Laurence (1992) reasons,

> Broad shoulders, squared and relaxed, create a regal, imposing carriage that signifies power and presence. They can also make your waist seem smaller, more delicate, and the sight of silk sliding over a creamy shoulder carries its own potency. (p. 103)

Although broad shoulders signify "power and presence," above all, they make one's waist appear smaller. Some aerobicizers complete their toning exercises based on this rationale: Toned muscles actually will make one smaller. Even the much-feared arm exercises become acceptable when they, instead of strengthening, diminish women's arms. Eileen defends the arm exercises done in her aerobics class: "It's not that their arms are going to get bigger [by doing toning], they are just going to be tighter, they actually will look smaller, because they'll be tighter and not flabby."

Apparently, women do not want to be associated with big anything: Big muscles, big bones, and big bodies are generally feared. Somehow, we ought to fight the big body. This struggle to reduce the body is problematic. Sheila discusses a dilemma she has faced:

Sheila: I tend to build muscle pretty fast, especially when I do biking. . . . I like to slim down my legs, most slim down the muscle. I do have a lot of muscle I could slim down.

Pirkko: By doing what?

Sheila: I don't know, it's hard. When I was a freshman, I managed to do it. I have a slow metabolism; I have to not eat, and I have to do more exercising. When I did I was only eating dinner as a meal, and I was trying to make it light and have a few snacks during the day.

Pirkko: It didn't bother you to get more muscles by doing all those exercises?

Sheila: You have to eat enough less, so that you are using more calories. It's hard to do for me. You have 50 pounds of equipment [when you play ice hockey] and you go skating around, it's going to build up my muscles unless I don't eat anything, so, I try to keep a balance so that I don't gain weight but it's hard, it's a battle. . . . I mean, I have a petite frame, I just don't have petite muscles.

Sheila tries to control her rebellious body—prevent it from becoming any bigger—by dieting and exercising, which creates a predicament: Her muscles tend to develop due to her workout. She is trapped in a vicious cycle where only a strict diet, as she believes, can free her. An ascetic diet regime is the only way to reveal her petite frame. Her hobby, however, is ice hockey, which is not a sport for small and frail females. A hockey player, like Sheila, needs strong muscles. She, therefore, has to be strong and delicate, big and small all at the same time.

It is evident that aerobicizers' lived experiences reflect the double body image detailed by the scholars studying the aerobics image in the media (Kagan and Morse, 1988; MacNeill, 1988). Earlier studies also debated whether this image resists or complies with those in power. I believe that, like the bodybuilding body, it is an ambiguous image: It embraces potential for both empowerment and oppression. Similar to the women bodybuilders (Bolin, 1992a, 1992b), the aerobicizers aim to challenge the traditional beauty ideal by toning their muscles, but they also engage in oppressive feminine practices like dieting. Unlike bodybuilders, however, the aerobicizers dislike big muscles, especially in the upper body. Moreover, the aerobicizers aim to become smaller: They tone their muscles to look smaller when bodybuilders even diet to appear more muscular (Bolin, 1992b). Many aerobicizers think bodybuilders are disgusting:

> I've seen women's bodies that I find repulsive, because they are so muscular. (Cari)

> They have this huge bulging muscle that I think is really unattractive. (Molly)

> Women bodybuilders, that looks bad. (Eileen)

> I don't like . . . the women bodybuilders, to lift weights to become big, I personally don't like that. (Daedra)

The magazines support the aerobicizers' views regarding bodybuilding. For example, although the fitness articles promote upper body work, they clarify that their weight training will not result in bulging arm muscles (Barrett, 1991; Brick, 1990). Why this fear of big muscles?

Feminist research explains that such rejection of big muscles serves women's oppression in society. Namely, patriarchal domination over women is based on the assumption that men are naturally—biologically—stronger and bigger than women. Physically stronger males are also alleged to be naturally determined, intellectual, active leaders who should dominate the weak, passive, and small women. To retain this power arrangement in patriarchal society, it is necessary, thus, to define the female body differently from the male body: ideally, the weak female's muscles are sleek and firm, whereas the powerful male's muscles are visible and big. The aerobics body fits in this scheme nicely, whereas the bodybuilding body challenges this gender dichotomy, because it resembles the big, muscular male body and minimizes the biological gap separating the sexes (Holmlund, 1989). A simple conclusion would be that aerobics supports the patriarchal ideology but bodybuilding resists it. However, Bolin (1992b) adds an interesting dimension to this discussion.

She points out that not only bodybuilding but other sporting lifestyles can challenge and minimize the biological differences between the sexes. She uses triathlon, long-distance running, and rock climbing as examples in which there is a considerable overlap in the contours of male and female physiques. It is noticeable that these athletic male bodies are small. Therefore, the resistant female body does not have to be bulky to challenge the patriarchal, dualistic definitions of gender. In this light, a well-toned aerobicizer's body could be seen to resemble a male athlete's body and defy the dominant patriarchy over the female body.

In addition to having toned muscles, the aerobicized body is thin. The aerobicizers accordingly are afraid of fat, more than they are afraid of big muscles. For example, Becky explains that she appreciates muscles, because they make "the person look very fit." However, when asked why she exercises, she answered, "I was once fat. I don't ever want to be fat again." Being overweight was a bigger concern for more of the aerobicizers than extensive muscles. As we know, bodybuilders also need to be unnaturally thin to show their muscle development. Therefore, even women bodybuilders, although challenging femininity through developing big muscles, do not aim to overcome the requirement of feminine thinness. Being fat is still probably the furthest from the ideal feminine body of the 90s. A strong, overweight woman, theoretically, would offer the most direct resistance to the patriarchal notions of femininity in this society, as her body would directly oppose the toned and thin ideal. If we define resistance only through clear binary oppositions like this, aerobics—or any other physical activity—would never offer an avenue for true resistance. I believe that instead of classifying women's practices exclusively into resistance or oppression, it is more fruitful to concentrate on the richness of everyday experiences.

Women in aerobics classes keep struggling to make sense of the contradictory requirements of the female body. There is an additional element in the ideal female body that needs to be analyzed. This ideal implies that besides being thin and toned, our bodies must stay young. This adds another component to our bodywork load.

"I Am Not Sure If It's Too Late"

The ideal female body is also a youthful body. Women over 30 seldom appear in fitness magazines. The flabless, firm muscles do not cover an old, wrinkly, bent, gray-haired body. Nevertheless, everyone will grow older, and the natural signs of aging are opposite to the requirements of the beautiful body. Some women in my study have turned to aerobics to specifically fight the effects of age: "I have this cellulite and these fat cells. I'm not sure if it's too late; at least I'm attempting to do something" (Cari). Cari feels somewhat optimistic about the power of exercise to overcome her aging body, although her late start worries her. Others feel that age exacerbates the problems they have with their body shapes. Some exercisers become desperate when their bodies show signs of old age. When the aging progresses, women have to work incredibly hard to obtain the ideal figure. Particularly, the problem areas—underarms, thighs, hips, and abdomen—seem to get flabbier and more resistant to shaping. This experience is tangible for some aerobicizers. Colleen, Ann, and Rosi describe their bodies:

> When you get older . . . your muscles aren't that dividing any more. . . . It seems relatively easy when you are a young person to have toned muscles. (Colleen)

> My body is getting older, it's harder to keep my weight in control, and I get really fat if I don't exercise. (Ann)

> You gain so much weight, you don't know how to get rid of it. (Rosi)

Why do we have to fight the naturally aging body so hard? To explain our urge to remain youthful, Mike Featherstone (1991) locates the body in the context of so-called consumer culture. He argues that in present consumerism the perfect body—youthful, physically beautiful, and healthy—makes its owner more marketable. For example, "good looks" increase a person's exchange value in the job market: A physically attractive person gets hired before someone else. Like the aerobicizers, Featherstone (1991) observes that the desired body shape can be achieved only with effort and body work. Cosmetic, beauty, fitness, and leisure industries have emerged to guide people in their quest for perfection. Sagging flesh, for example, should be treated in exercise programs provided by the fitness industry. But even with the help of specific programs, the consumer has to work hard for the results. Video queen and marketing master Jane Fonda (1981) emphasizes individual hard work as a means to a better body:

> Notice I've said "vigorous" and "exercise hard." I don't use these words idly. Namby-pamby little routines that don't speed up your heart beat and make you sweat aren't really worth your while. (p. 49)

> If you are serious about wanting to lose weight once and for all, about changing the shape of your body, about improving your self-image and your morale, you must get over being soggy. There are not short cuts. No sweatless quickies. You must be committed to working hard, sweating hard and getting sore. . . . You have to work for it. (pp. 55-56)

Fonda's own body demonstrates how effective vigorous work is. She, although over 50, displays the ideal young boyish body discussed earlier: broad shoulders, narrow hips, long legs. Her body is "reminiscent of adolescence" (Coward, 1985, p. 41) in late middle age; it is a "version of an immature body" (Coward, 1985, p. 41) possessed by a mature woman. Spitzack (1990) reads two meanings in Fonda's fantastic teenager body. First, many women view Fonda in hopeful terms: Her body suggests that women over 50 can be viewed as attractive and can have a "good body." Consequently, older women are still attractive and maintain their marketability in consumer society. But second, women fear that this means an ongoing attention to appearance. Some had looked forward to middle age because of less focus on "looks," but now women need to continue monitoring their bodies to maintain an adolescent body, like Fonda's body, to a mature age.

In consumer society, we need to invest in body care to secure our positions in the market. Featherstone (1991) adds that this creates an expanding market for commodities that aid body work. Looking after one's body, he illustrates, is like looking after a car. As a car needs a whole array of things to function, the body needs products from soaps to diet teas to keep its shape. Such products as cosmetic surgery, diet pills, or cosmetic devices (Coward, 1985; Spitzack, 1990) are marketed particularly at women. I would place aerobics in this line of products: It is advertised to help women battle their aging, bulging, and sagging bodies in a manner similar to other body industry products. Evidently, if women start worrying about their bodies growing old at 20, and aerobics is one of the solutions to discipline such a body, aerobics classes will be securely filled with customers, because we all will age and our bodies will need more and more work to resemble the ideal body.

Featherstone (1991) also points out that good looks are promoted by the media. Fitness magazines, TV programs, and exercise videos portray a stylized image of the body in consumer culture. Feminist research (Kagan and Morse, 1988: MacNeill, 1988) has found that these media images sexualize and objectify women as they emphasize appearance rather than fitness. The aerobicizers have obviously come face to face with the perfect media bodies in these sources. How do they find the media representation of the exercising women?

"You Don't See Them Sweating"

Women's ideas about exercise often resonate with the fitness discourse in the media: They work on their problem spots; they long for a toned body, but not for visible muscle definition; they struggle to fight fat and age, exactly as urged by the media texts. However, the same aerobicizers criticize the portrayal of exercisers in the media. Many women are consciously suspicious of this representation. To illustrate, Eileen, Anna, and Andrea consider the media exercisers unreal, even irritating:

> TV doesn't seem realistic; it's like they go out and get models to do it, because they are all tall and very skinny, in shape and kind of disgusting in a way; they have their hair perfectly done and their make-up is perfect; you don't see them sweating. It's the same image they project, very thin, lean . . . they are just generally thin, they are just models.

This portrayal makes the exercisers doubt the expertise of the demonstrators. They suspect that these "models" are there because of their looks, not because they know something about exercise. Christy verbalizes her skepticism: "They [the demonstrators] don't have to be necessarily fit, they could just be someone who looks good in a leotard and who are told, 'Put your body in this position.'" Christy refers to the way many exercises are presented in the magazine pictures: The demonstrator is in a still pose waiting for the camera to capture the moment. Often a series of these pictures is arranged on the page to illustrate a continuous exercise routine. The real-life aerobicizers feel, therefore, that even unfit, thin models can pose a couple of seconds for a beautiful picture, but they would not be able to follow a continuous aerobics class.

If my interviewees are skeptical of the magazine representations, they view exercise videotapes with an even stronger suspicion. Unlike the static pictures, a video shows a continuous aerobics class lasting 30 to 60 minutes. The video exercisers should, thus, demonstrate a good fitness level. The aerobicizers I interviewed are distrustful: The videotapes are a media trick because the video exercisers appear too perfect to be real. Sarah, for example, is annoyed with the exercise videos:

It kind of makes me mad because I keep hearing that they stop, put on more make-up and jump another five minutes and then come back, wipe off the sweat, and you never see them really ugly; there is something wrong.

While being disturbed, women have also accepted that the media display only perfect bodies. For example, Daedra explains,

I expect that anyone demonstrating any exercise in any magazine is going to have to be close to that ideal body. I don't think I expect anything but that.

Flawless models do not irritate all the aerobicizers. For some women, the perfect media exercisers are a positive incentive that keeps them exercising.

Regardless, many women in this study like to see "normal people" demonstrating the exercises. Or they prefer to follow a fitness expert who knows what she or he is doing. The body size is not as important as fitness level and professional instruction. These exercisers welcome a larger-size leader or participant in exercise class. Actually, a little "chunkiness" makes the person more human and easier to relate to. Therefore, the media class should resemble more closely the "real-life" classes they participate in. Sarah summarizes her requirements for an instructor:

You can be an aerobics teacher and not have a body. My only requirements for an aerobics teacher are that they can do the routines with us and that they've got energy doing that. . . . I don't care if they are like 200 pounds, but if they can jump as high and are energetic. . . . There is this picture in our minds like Jane Fonda, perfect body, [but] like [our teachers], they've got nice bodies, but are not beautiful, but as long as they can keep up with us, lead us, that's fine.

Sarah notices the discrepancy between the media images of an aerobicizer ("there is this picture in our minds like Jane Fonda, perfect body") and her instructors. She still prefers her instructors. Some exercisers have discovered that the recent exercise videos include different types of people in their model classes. For example, Fonda instructs some "overweight" exercisers in one of her latest tapes; in Kathy Smith's video class exercisers in different fitness levels aerobicize together. However, my interviewees regard these tapes as exceptional.

The interviewees do not like the thin and toned media ideal: It is too perfect, it is no longer real. This conscious rejection seems odd as the women keep working toward the same ideal in their aerobics classes. Therefore, women's relationship with the contradictory body ideal is ambiguous: Against their own judgment, many aerobicizers still desire to look like the flawless models. It seems a lot easier to judge the body image at the intellectual level than engage in the resistant action in real life. Recall how aerobicizers like Melissa or Sheila struggle to keep weight training. They choose to be strong, but when their bodies grow more muscular and less feminine, they find it hard to face the judgment of the policing gaze without shame. Likewise I, a feminist researcher, am petrified that I will become fat regardless of my knowledge that the ideal thinness is an unrealistic goal designed to keep women dieting. One has to be extremely secure to be able to confront the everyday challenges put forward by the dominant discourses and even more confident to engage in an openly resistant action. We struggle to resist the body ideal but are not able to ignore it or achieve it. Our bodies remain imperfect.

Many of my interviewees feel that they are continuously required to improve some part of their bodies. Occasionally—like Antoinette here—they reflect their unhappiness with a touch of irony: "We talk about it [the body] a lot. My roommates and I sit around all the time, which is hilarious, because we are all in pretty good shape . . . but we think we are overweight or out of shape or we have too much fat." Antoinette and her friends realize that they actually look acceptable, but they still want to work on their bodies. Considering that the same women criticize the present body ideal for being unrealistically thin, their desire for change appears quite contradictory. Daedra is aware of her problematic relationship with the ideal body:

> I think it's [the body ideal] really unhealthy, but . . . the ideal body is the perfect woman . . . with no fat, a beautifully shaped body. . . . You have to work your butt off for that type of body . . . and a lot of people can just never look that way because of the way they are. I think a lot of girls have fallen into a trap that they have to look certain way. . . . I'm falling into that trap.

She recognizes how "unhealthy" and unrealistic the body ideal is but admits, at the same time, that she longs to have such a body herself. She is trapped into a false fight with her body. Why do we fall into the illusionary body ideal? Why do we need to change our bodies that really do not need a change? Why do women drive themselves for the image they find fallacious? In her discussion of dieting practices Spitzack (1990) connects the present beauty ideal to health. This connection provides a starting point for my discussion of women's antagonistic relationships with their bodies.

The Panoptic Power: Be Positive and You Can Change!

Spitzack (1990) first locates the body image in patriarchal consumer society. Her discussion confirms my notions that the present image of the perfect female body jointly serves visions of traditional femininity—women's muscles are toned and firm but not "hulkish," visible, or big—and the economic interest of consumer society. However, Spitzack (1990) argues further that the influence of these powerful agencies on the female body becomes more obvious when discussed in connection with the discourse of health.

Spitzack's key to understanding women's situation in society is the "aesthetics of health." Women's present beauty standard is defined through health: The "healthy look" and "natural beauty" are now fashionable, albeit culturally constructed, descriptions of a good-looking woman. Basically, a beautiful body in this society is a healthy body, not only a slender body as 10 years ago. This shift away from thinness should provide more diverse models for women, but most descriptions of the healthy look still center on the requirements of physical attractiveness. In reality, the healthy body "mandates even greater restrictions on female bodies" (Spitzack, 1990, p. 37). For example, toned muscles now cast the required healthy glow on the slender women. Bradley Block's (1988) article in *Health* magazine can serve as a case in point. He proclaims that the great body today is a healthy body and, therefore, there is no single great body "look." The article introduces six women who demonstrate the growing diversity. However, when we take a closer look at these women, we find that they are all thin, young, and toned. The only variable is their height. Therefore, the healthy body is only a new, fashionable rubric for the physically attractive body.

Spitzack (1990) adds high self-esteem, self-confidence, and increased assertiveness to the measures of "the healthy took." This connection is evident in aerobics. Many women in aerobics classes assert that exercise makes them feel better not only about their physique but also about "themselves," much like the *Shape* "Success Story" heroines in Duncan's (1994) study. For example, Eileen tells how aerobics boosts her self-confidence:

> When I do aerobics, I feel toned; if I'm not even any more toned, at least I feel my muscles are tighter and I feel better about myself.

In this sense, aerobics indirectly makes the participants' self-confidence grow, which at first glance seems to empower the exercisers. Eileen, however, connects positive feelings about herself to her looks: When one looks better, one feels better. Here a conversation by Sarah and Helen further reveals how good looks and positive self-image are inevitably linked with each other:

> *Helen:* It feels better, when the jeans fit looser.

> *Sarah:* You can loosen your belt buckle . . . and you feel more confident . . . you can look better, you feel better . . . you look skinnier, you feel more confident about your body.

> *Helen:* The reason [to go to aerobics] is to look better, not just for a better body, but for self-image . . . you definitely see a difference in your body, maybe other people don't but you feel a lot better.

> *Sarah:* You just feel like you are doing your best for the body; this is straining, but it's also good for us, so you feel better.

Helen obviously believes that good looks consist not only of a "skinny" body but also of a good self-image, which again is a result of the improved body. Therefore, better self-confidence derives from an attractive body.

Similar to the aerobicizers, magazine texts connect self-confidence with good looks. Many articles claim that a better body ignites positive self-esteem. Magazines describe confidence and self-esteem to characterize the beauty ideal of the 90s. Now women who have confidence and a positive attitude look good. Furthermore, the new beauty reflects our growth and self-acceptance; women now "want to look and feel good" (Lazarus, 1991, p. 62). In one article Rita Freedman (1991), a psychologist, points out the unquestionable link between a woman's self-esteem and her body image: "Improving your body image is quite likely to improve your self-esteem—so, working on self-esteem will usually improve your body image also. Body-loathing leads to self-loathing, while body-love leads to self-love" (p. 98). Consequently, women should not try to turn themselves into something they are not. Instead, magazines encourage readers to find their normal, healthy body weights and accept their current measurements. For example, magazines advise women to focus on the positive points of their mirror reflections, not the flawed parts (Freedman, 1991; Wise, 1990). In addition, exercise clothing—although quite revealing—can be designed to accentuate the positives about one's body: "Magicians do it with smoke and mirrors, but bodywear designers use lines, stitching, nips and cuts to improve upon reality. These exercise pieces perform their own magic to accentuate your positives" (p. 92) writes Kathleen Riquelme (1994) in *Shape* to introduce "the latest and greatest in figure-flattering bodywear" (p. 92). The article is named ironically "Grand Illusions" as if to acknowledge that women have to trick themselves to feel positive with bodywear magic. Women need magic to mask the real body like magicians need to create an illusion by hiding the traces of their tricks.

Partly, such a discourse sounds quite strange after readers are advised to accept themselves as they are. Why do we need illusions if we are to accept our "real" bodies? Is it something to do with the models wearing these clothes that create "larger-than-life" illusions? Their perfectly thin bodies are not imaginary; they are real. We readers know we don't look like them, but with the right clothing we can at least make the best of our "bottom-heavy figures" (Riquelme, 1994, p. 92).

Partly, this discourse is very encouraging: Every woman should accept her body, feel confident about it, and derive increased self-esteem from her appearance even if it is achieved through clothing magic. These positive feelings and increased powerfulness can free women from the regulative mechanism of the masculine ideology and consumerism. Spitzack (1990) argues, however, that this seemingly liberating discourse is in itself an illusion.

Illusions surrounding the women's fitness movement have been tackled previously by other feminist researchers (Kagan and Morse, 1988; Lenskyj, 1986; MacNeill, 1988; Theberge, 1987). According to these scholars, as pointed out earlier, the potentially liberating impulses in aerobics have been turned to serve the masculine ideology by cementing the effects of exercise with an improved appearance. Spitzack (1990) agrees that such claims of liberation only "mask increasing control with a rhetoric of freedom" (p. 42). For example, to maintain a healthy body, women are required to detect their bodily flaws more carefully. While constantly scrutinizing, one has to appear assertive and confident about one's body. Rather than being free, women are prisoners of more detailed regulations of beauty. Why do women accept this controlling discipline?

Spitzack (1990) believes that this control is implemented over women through a confession that women have secret problems. As I demonstrated earlier, the magazine texts were indeed convinced that their readers all possessed hidden body anxieties. Similar to Duncan's (1994) and Spitzack's (1990) dieters, exercisers were urged to admit that their bodies are imperfect and then take action to change for the better. One article advises the reader to follow these exact steps: "The most important thing I have learned is that you have to accept the way you look now in order to make a change . . . you have to think positively about yourself, your appearance and your ability to accomplish your goals" (Glenn, 1992, p. 13). Another article assures us that we women are not helping ourselves by self-disgust, which only "creates a feeling of punishment" (Weaver and Ruther, 1991, p. 81) and defeats our attempts to change through exercise or weight loss programs. To successfully change our female bodies, we have to enjoy the process.

In sum, self-acceptance in exercise discourse promotes only bodily change; feeling positive about oneself is a necessary precondition for a model body. One is to accept one's body shape only to reform it. Focus on women's psychological well-being disguises increased attention to women's appearance and makes a deeper obsession with the body possible. This practice, Spitzack (1990) observes, is analogical to the treatment of another obsession, alcoholism. For instance, similar to Alcoholics Anonymous (AA), Overeaters Anonymous (OA) is patterned to help overeaters overcome their addiction. Exercise discourse advocates similar logic. Curiously, unlike other addictions, the confession of body problems does not free one from the obsessive behavior. On the contrary, it precedes a more thorough internalization of the addiction. To further implement the logic of confession, magazines, as I interpret them, urge women to take responsibility for their change. The Foucauldian concept of panoptic power explains some meanings embedded in this discourse.

In his analysis of contemporary society, Foucault (1979) argues that the body is a target of subtle disciplinary practices that seek to regulate its existence. Different disciplinary practices—which Foucault ties to modern forms of the army, the school, the hospital, the prison, and the manufactory—produce "docile bodies" ready to obey the regimes of power in society. Each person has internalized the control mechanisms through the body discipline. Individual citizens are, therefore, governed not by visible and openly repressive power sources, but by themselves. Foucault (1979) illustrates this power arrangement with an analogy to the Panopticon, a model prison whose circular design leaves all inmates in their individual cells permanently visible for the invisible supervisor in the center tower. Each prisoner is disciplined through his or her awareness of the supervisor rather than the supervisor's actual presence. The inmates are controlled by their own awareness of power. Spitzack (1990) finds dieting practices effectively disciplining women's bodies. She adds that the power over them is the most effective and captivating when the dieting discourse persuades the individual women to control their bodies on account of society. This logic is evident in aerobics.

Individual aerobicizers have taken the responsibility to control their bodies. They, sometimes questioningly, aim to change to resemble the ideal body. In addition, women feel good when their body shapes begin to approximate the ideal. However, societal standards, not women's own standards, define this ideal. Therefore, even the heightened self-esteem derived from a better body ultimately serves the purposes of the powerful to continue the oppression of women in society. Aerobics, like dieting, is part of a complex use of power over women in postmodern consumer society. The panoptic power arrangement, whereby the individuals control themselves on behalf of the powerful while the power source itself remains invisible, ensures that women are so occupied with obtaining the healthy look that they do not have time to wonder why they are doing it. Such a conclusion sounds quite depressing. Is the power over us so extensive and does it penetrate so deeply into our lives that whatever we think we are doing for our own benefit is actually harnessed to serve the purposes of an invisible power?

Conclusion

The invisible discursive power seems to effectively shape our thoughts and our behavior regarding our bodies. But if this grip were complete, women would passively follow the confessional logic without ever questioning it. Aerobicizers in this study have an active voice. They do not quietly dedicate their lives to body reconstruction, but they question the body ideal and are particularly skeptical about the media presentation of exercising women. This questioning leaves many women puzzled: They want to conform with the ideal, but they also find the whole process ridiculous. As a result, women's relationship with the body ideal is contradictory. This awareness, nevertheless, demonstrates that women have not internalized the panoptic power arrangement entirely. Aerobicizers do not, however, visibly resist the patriarchal body ideal by actively aiming to build transgressive bodies like the women bodybuilders. Aerobics does not offer an avenue for a large-scale revolution, at least not in the public arena. Nevertheless, in aerobics, much like women's bodybuilding (Bolin, 1992a), the private setting is quite different from the official discourse and does not necessarily follow the practices set by the dominant powers.

Although many aerobics classes revolve around body shaping (e.g., the toning moves are designed to improve appearance rather than functionality; the muscles are built to increase the caloric expenditure, not to gain strength), many aerobicizers participate for reasons other than improving their bodies. For example, aerobics is a source of enjoyment and not only because of the improved body (Markula, 1993a, 1993b, in press); it provides a safe environment for being physically active (Markula, in press); it supplies women with increased energy to carry on with their work (Markula, 1993b); it allows women to spend time on themselves (Markula, 1993b); and it is an opportunity to meet and make friends (Markula, 1993b). All these reasons, whose resistant potential I have discussed in detail in other contexts, demonstrate that aerobics does not entirely serve as a vehicle for the oppressive dominant body discourses. Furthermore, the real-life aerobics class does not appear similar to the video classes. For instance, the instructors are not all picture-perfect (recall Sarah's earlier comment about her instructor); the aerobicizers themselves do not wear skimpy clothes like the video or magazine exercisers (Markula, 1992); and not all classes include nonfunctional moves geared around body shaping (Markula, 1993b).

Central to my examination of the body in aerobics has been the view that culture consists of communication between different voices. In this paper, individual aerobicizers' voices engage in a dialogue with the media voices of aerobics. Following Bakhtin (1981) I assume that cultural dialogue implies certain power relations: Some voices are public and more dominant than other, private, voices. For example, the voices of the magazines and aerobics videotapes can dominate the public representations of the perfect aerobics body. It seems obvious that this public discourse around the aerobics body is a voice of oppression. However, individual aerobicizers struggle to give different meanings to the ideal aerobicizing body. Like Spitzack's (1990) dieters, aerobicizers privately question the logic of this discourse whose contradictory beauty requirements leave many of these women confused. This leads me to ask, if the public voice authoritatively shapes the meaning of women's exercising bodies, are women's private voices heard? Bakhtin (1981) believes that individual voices can use alternative channels to replace the official meanings with their own meanings. I believe this study is one attempt to bring women's private voices to a public stage and give them the lines in the body dialogue they deserve. I hope these voices are loud enough to ignite a change.

References

Abu-Lughod, L. (1990). The romance of resistance: Tracing transformations of power through Bedouin women. *American Ethnologist,* **17**(1), 41–55.

Arveda, K.E. (1991). One size does not fit all, or how I learned to stop dieting and love the body. *Quest,* **43,** 135–147.

Bakhtin, M.M. (1981). Discourse in novel. In M. Holquist (Ed.), *The dialogical imagination* (pp. 259–442). Austin, TX: University of Texas Press.

Balsamo, A. (1994). Feminist bodybuilding. In S. Birrell and C.L. Cole (Eds.), *Women, sport, and culture* (pp. 341–352). Champaign, IL: Human Kinetics.

Barrett, E. (1991, March). The ultimate guide to sexy muscles. *Self,* pp. 137–143.

Bartky, S.L. (1988). Foucault, femininity, and the modernization of patriarchal power. In I. Diamond and L. Quinby (Eds.), *Feminism and Foucault: Reflections on resistance* (pp. 61–86). Boston: Northeastern University Press.

Block, B.W. (1988, July). Great American body. *Health,* pp. 27–35.

Bolin, A. (1992a). Beauty or beast: The subversive soma. In C. Ballerino Cohen (Ed.), *Body contours: Deciphering scripts of gender and power* (pp. 54–77). New Brunswick, NJ: Rutgers University Press.

Bolin, A. (1992b). Flex appeal, food, and fat: Competitive bodybuilding, gender and diet. *Play and Culture,* **5,** 378–400.

Bolin, A. (1992c). Vandalized vanity: Feminine physiques betrayed and portrayed. In F. Mascia-Lees (Ed.), *Tattoo, torture, adornment and disfigurement: The denaturalization of the body in culture and text* (pp. 79–99). Albany, NY: State University of New York Press.

Bordo, S. (1989). The body and the reproduction of femininity: A feminist appropriation of Foucault. In A.M. Jaggar and S.R. Bordo (Eds.), *Gender/body/knowledge: Feminist reconstructions of being and knowing* (pp. 13–33). New Brunswick, NJ: Rutgers University Press.

Bordo, S. (1990). Reading the slender body. In M. Jacobus, E. Fox Keller, and S. Shuttleworth (Eds.), *Body/politics: Women and the discourse of science* (pp. 83–112). New York: Routledge.

Brick, L. (1990, May). The get set for summer workout. *Shape,* pp. 81–87.

Bruner, E. (1993). Introduction: The ethnographic self and the personal self. In P. Benson (Ed.), *Anthropology and literature* (pp. 1–26). Urbana, IL: University of Illinois Press.

Chernin, K. (1981). *The obsession: Reflections on the tyranny of slenderness.* New York: Harper and Row.

Clifford, J., and Marcus, G.E. (1986). *Writing culture: Poetics and politics of ethnography.* Berkeley: University of California Press.

Cole, C. (1993). Resisting the canon: feminist cultural studies, sport, and technologies of the body. *Journal of Sport and Social Issues,* **17,** 77–97.

Cooper, K. H. (1968). *Aerobics.* New York: Simon and Schuster.

Cooper, K.H. (1970). *New aerobics.* Philadelphia: Lippincott.

Coward, R. (1985). *Female desires: How they are sought, bought and packaged.* New York: Grove Weidenfeld.

Daniels, D.B. (1992). Gender (body) verification (building). *Play & Culture, 5,* 370–377.

de Certeau, M. (1984). *The practice of everyday life.* Berkeley, CA: University of California Press.

Denzin, N. (1992). *Symbolic interactionism and cultural studies: The politics of interpretation.* Cambridge, MA: Blackwell.

Dubisch, J. (1986). Introduction. In J. Dubisch (Ed.), *Gender and power in rural Greece* (pp. 3–41). Princeton, NJ: Princeton University Press.

Duncan, M.C. (1994). The politics of women's body images and practices: Foucault, the panopticon, and *Shape* magazine. *Journal of Sport and Social Issues, 18,* 49–65.

Dunn, R, (1991). Postmodernism: Populism, mass culture, and avant-garde. *Theory, Culture & Society, 8,* 111–135.

Fairclough, E. (1980, May). Legs. *Women's Sports,* pp. 34–53.

Farah, A.D. (1984, January). Legs. *Health,* pp. 38–42.

Featherstone, M. (1988). In pursuit of the postmodern: An introduction. *Theory, Culture & Society, 6,* 195–213.

Featherstone, M. (1991). The body in consumer culture. In M. Featherstone, M. Hepworth, and B.S. Turner (Eds.), *The body: Social process and cultural theory (pp. 170–196).* London: Sage.

Foley, D.E. (1992). Making the familiar strange: Writing critical sports narratives. *Sociology of Sport Journal, 9,* 36–47.

Fonda, J. (1981). *Jane Fonda's workout book.* New York: Simon and Schuster.

Foucault, M. (1979). *Discipline and punish: The birth of the prison.* New York: Vintage Books.

Freedman, R. (1991, July). Mind over mirror. *Shape,* pp. 66–68.

Gates, R. (1991, March). Body image: The problem with trying to be perfect. *IDEA Magazine,* pp. 28–29.

Glenn, J. (1992, March 2). Healthy mind, healthy diet. *The Daily Illini,* p. 13.

Gottlieb, A. (1989). Rethinking female pollution: The Beng of the Cote D'Ivoire. *Dialectical Anthropology, 14,* 65–79.

Guthrie, S.R., and Castelnuovo, S. (1992). Elite women bodybuilders: Models of resistance or compliance. *Play & Culture, 5,* 401–408.

Holmlund, C.A. (1989). Visible difference and flex appeal. *Cinema Journal, 28*(4), 38–51.

Hoover, S. (1980, January). Exercise and all that jazz. *Women's Sports,* pp. 10–18.

Imm, P. (1989). *Exercise habits and perceptions of body image in female exercisers.* Paper presented at fourth Annual IDEA Conference, Los Angeles, CA.

Jacobs, C. (1991, March). Winning at the losing game. *Shape,* pp. 74–77.

Johnston, R. (1986). The story so far: And further transformations? In D. Punter (Ed.), *Introduction to contemporary cultural studies* (pp. 277–313). London: Longmans.

Kagan, E., and Morse, M. (1988). The body electronic: Aerobic exercise video. *The Drama Review, 32,* 164–180.

Kaufman, E. (1989, December). Put some muscle into it. *Self,* pp. 123–128.

Kenen, R.L. (1987). Double messages, double images: Physical fitness, self-concepts, and women's exercise classes. *Journal of Physical Education, Recreation, and Dance, 58*(6), 76–79.

Laurence, L. (1992, January). Shoulders are sexy. *Self,* pp. 102–105.

Lazarus, J. (1991, September). Beauty and the best. *Shape,* pp. 62–64.

Lenskyj, H. (1986). *Out of bounds: Women, sport and sexuality.* Toronto: Women's Press.

Lenskyj, H. (1994). Sexuality and femininity in sport contexts: Issues and alternatives. *Journal of Sport and Social Issues, 18,* 356–376.

MacNeill, M. (1988). Active women, media representations, ideology. In J. Harvey and G. Cantelon (Eds.), *Not just a game.* (pp. 195–212). Altona, MB: University of Ottawa Press.

Markula, P. (1992, November). *Bodywear that lets the body speak: Pleasures of fitness fashion in aerobics.* Paper presented at the Thirteenth Annual Conference of the North American Society for Sociology of Sport, Toledo, OH.

Markula, P. (1993a). Looking good, feeling good: Strengthening mind and body in aerobics. In L. Laine (Ed.), *On the fringes of sport* (pp. 93–99). Sankt Augustin, Germany: Akademia Verlag.

Markula, P. (1993b). *Total-body-tone-up: Paradox and women's realities in aerobics.* Unpublished doctoral dissertation, University of Illinois, Urbana-Champaign.

Markula, P. (in press). Postmodern aerobics: Contradictions and resistance. In A. Bolin and J. Granskog (Eds.), *Athletic intruders.* Newbury Park, CA: Sage.

Martin, E. (1987). *The woman in the body: Cultural analysis of reproduction.* Boston: Beacon Press.

Martin, E. (1989). The cultural construction of gendered bodies: Biology and metaphors of production and destruction. *Ethos, 3–4,* 143–159.

McRobbie, A. (1994). *Postmodernism and popular culture*. London: Routledge.

Miller, L., and Penz, O. (1991). Talking bodies: Female bodybuilders colonize a male preserve. *Quest, 43,* 148–163.

Patton, M.Q. (1980). *Qualitative evaluation methods*. Beverly Hills, CA: Sage.

Riquelme, K. (1994, March). Grand illusions. *Shape,* pp. 92–97.

Rosaldo, R. (1989). *Culture and truth: The remaking of social analysis*. Boston: Beacon Press.

Rothlein, L. (1988, May). Portrait of an aerobic dancer. *Women's Sports and Fitness,* p. 18.

Rover, E. (1992, January). Biceps strengthener. *Self,* p. 48.

Sorensen, J. (1979). *Aerobic dancing*. New York: Rawson, Wade.

Spitzack, C. (1990). *Confessing excess: Women and the politics of body reduction*. Albany, NY: State University of New York Press.

Stallings, J. (1980). Fantasy, fact. *Women's Sports,* p. 49.

Sternlicht, E. (1990a, January). Testing your triceps. *Shape,* pp. 46–48.

Sternlicht, E. (1990b, February). Behind every great shape . . . is a great behind. *Shape,* pp. 38–40.

Sternlicht, E. (1990c, July). Try this for thighs. *Shape,* p. 34.

Sternlicht, E. (1991, May). Up in arms. *Shape,* pp. 48–50.

Strathem, M. (1981). Culture in a netbag: The manufacture of a subdiscipline in anthropology. *Man,* **16**(4), 276–292.

Theberge, N. (1987). Sport and women's empowerment. *Women's Studies International Forum,* **10,** 387–393.

Tucker, S. (1990, July). What is the ideal body? *Shape,* pp. 94–112.

Wolf, N. (1990). *The beauty myth*. London: Vintage.

Weaver, G., and Ruther, K. (1991, March). Learning to love exercise. *Shape,* pp. 81–86.

Wise, E. (1990, July). Feeling fat. *Shape,* pp. 20–21.

Acknowledgments

I would like to thank Jim Denison and the two anonymous reviewers for their helpful comments and suggestions. I am also grateful for the support of M.K. Howard and K.S.W. Davidson during the preparation of this paper.

The Politics of the Body and the Body Politic: Magic Johnson and the Ideology of AIDS

Samantha King

This paper analyzes the discourse surrounding AIDS and HIV in the light of Magic Johnson's public announcement that he was HIV positive. In the context of the New Right backlash of the 1980s, the bodies of Johnson and others have been used to (re)produce specific, narrowly defined messages about the meaning of AIDS and the HIV virus. Commercial and professional sports interests have used this event to enter into a well-established discourse that reproduces and reinforces the dominant messages of homophobia and misogyny surrounding the syndrome.

On November 8, 1991, headlines across the world told the same story, the story that Earvin "Magic" Johnson, professional basketball player, sports hero, and media personality, had contracted the HIV virus and was to retire immediately. While the cultural politics of this virus, and specifically of the AIDS syndrome, stands at the intersection of many different histories—histories of medicine, media, gay liberation, feminism, racism, injected drug use, and so on (Watney, 1989b)—sport as a cultural activity is also a site where definitions of the social world are constructed. Hence, the Magic Johnson story presents a unique opportunity to analyze many different but interconnected sets of social relations.[1]

Using Foucauldian concepts, within a broadly feminist cultural studies approach, the discussion considers how the process of sports hero creation relies on the subjugation of athletes' bodies in order that they may carry specifically produced messages. The press conference at which the news of Johnson's HIV status was broken supposedly "told all" and set the record straight. However, it actually served to disguise the reality of HIV further by using a powerful figure to convey specific, narrowly defined images of AIDS and HIV. In the Magic Johnson story, with the lead player (re)constructed as a sports hero with HIV, the dominant and most significant messages serve to reproduce and reinforce the homophobia and misogyny that have shaped both the dominant discourse surrounding AIDS in the 1980s and 1990s and the standard image of sports heroes for many years.

The subject of analysis is complex because it involves numerous conflicting ideas and forces. It is not simply a matter of comparing the portrayal of Magic, the HIV-positive, body-positive hero, with that of the "gay AIDS victim." Nor is it enough to recognize the way in which women specifically, and gender relations in general, have been overlooked in the discourse surrounding the Johnson case. One must also consider how Johnson has acted (consciously and unconsciously) to reproduce certain power relations while obscuring others, and how the women who had sex with him have done the same. Further, it is necessary to recognize that the public can only conceive of Johnson and the women, and that they might partly recognize themselves in relation to the circulation of available images in our society. Finally, such an analysis must recognize and

Reprinted from King, 1993.

avoid the danger of promoting myths about African-American hypersexuality and other naturalized constructions.

Sports Heroes: Productive Bodies/ Subjugated Bodies

The work of Michel Foucault, particularly his conceptualization of the body as an important sociocultural entity, is particularly useful to an analysis of the Magic Johnson story. In *Discipline and Punish* (1979a), Foucault argues,

> The body is directly involved in a political field; power relations have an immediate hold upon it: they invest it, train it, torture it, force it to carry out tasks, to perform ceremonies and to emit signs. The political investment of the body is bound up, in accordance with complex, reciprocal relations, with its economic use; it is largely as a force of production that the body is invested with power and domination; but, on the other hand, its constitution as labour power is possible only if it is caught up in a system of subjection . . . the body becomes a useful force only if it is both a productive body and a subjugated body. (pp. 25–26)

Hence, the major social, political, and economic institutions in society constantly pressure us to subjugate our bodies—in the various (conflicting) names of sport, health, beauty, strength, masculinity, femininity, motherliness, respectability, and so on. These notions are vested in a set of power relations that includes (among others) class, race, sex, and gender. They are almost inscribed onto the body, which acts as a vehicle for the playing out of these forces and, at particular conjunctures, serves as a battleground for the conflicting tensions that exist among these relations.

The political, social, economic body in and of itself means little until it is reproduced through the discourse of the mass media. The role of the mass media in shaping public perceptions of "reality" has been widely documented. Newspapers and television in particular produce news, not truth; through frames, values, and conventions they actively define, construct, and reproduce images of our society and, using various methods of legitimation, present them as fact. The media work in the same way to reproduce our bodies and the meanings attached to them (Birrell and Cole, 1990; Glasgow

University Media Group, 1976, 1980; Theberge and Cronk, 1986).

According to Winterson, Abrams, Weeks, Coward, and Wilson (1989), our bodies have never before "been so available for inspection, comparison, enjoyment and violation" (p. 31). As members of the public, we are constantly bombarded with images of our bodies on advertising billboards, in magazines, on film, and on television. While in the last decade female bodies have continued to appear painfully thin, fragile, and vulnerable (see, for example, Bartky, 1988), a particular version of the male "body beautiful" has emerged in the media in capitalist societies that forms part of a more general fitness cult connected with conspicuous commodity consumption.[2] The male sports image is fashionable and profitable, having been commercialized through the mass marketing of sporting goods and services (Hargreaves, 1986).

For all athletes, their bodies are their tools of production and as such have great significance. For sports stars, mainly male sports stars, their bodies have also become marketable commodities that on the one hand are sold to sponsors, advertisers, and the consuming public to generate profit, and on the other hand are used to maintain interest and a pool of upcoming talent for their sports.

What Johnson represented until the watershed press conference was a "marketable physicality" in two senses. Because he was an outstanding athlete on the basketball court, sponsors attached themselves to him to sell their products. But in order for him to be as profitable as possible, it was also necessary to construct him as an ideal typical hero. On the one hand, Johnson could be used to sell products unrelated to basketball and, along with Larry Bird, rescue the National Basketball Association (NBA) from the doldrums of boredom and possible financial collapse. On the other hand, as a successful athlete, business person, and millionaire (see, for example, Hoffer, 1990; Pascarelli, 1992), Johnson was seen as a role model for aspiring basketball players, to maintain the NBA as a legitimate goal for young African Americans to reach for (Smith, 1991).

The following sections briefly examine the construction of Johnson as a larger-than-life sporting hero. This analysis is relevant because it exposes some of the methods used to enhance Johnson's marketability prior to his announcement. More importantly, this construction warrants investigation because it continues to shape his image as a person with AIDS, and therefore continues to reinforce certain social, cultural, political, and economic structures and power relations.

Constructing Sports Heroes

Magic Johnson was born in Lansing, Michigan, in 1959. By the end of his high school career he was the most highly regarded player of his age in the country (Pascarelli, 1992). The renaissance of the NBA began in 1979 when Johnson and Larry Bird met as college players in the NCAA finals. This infamous clash between Michigan State and Indiana State presented a prime opportunity for the NBA and the media to revive the appeal of basketball and to create a national identity for Johnson and Bird, as two of the most "fascinating personalities and performers ever" (Pascarelli, 1992, p. 25). Following Michigan's victory, Johnson was drafted to the Los Angeles Lakers, with whom he enjoyed an outstanding career. His unofficial designation as an ambassador for the NBA and his commercial and charitable interests have further enhanced his public profile (Pascarelli, 1992).

According to R.C. Crepeau,

> Sport as social myth is often found embodied in the heroes of sport, who are really purveyors of myth rather than heroes of sport.... A hero in any society will embody some of the attributes of the myth: He will affirm the myth; he will illustrate its reality. (1981, p. 60)

Therefore, sport is a particularly significant arena for the construction of gender relations because it appears to be outside real life. For example, one of the central, socially constructed "commonsense" lessons of sport is that sexual differences are "natural" and that men are naturally superior to and naturally different than women (Willis, 1974). It is primarily the body that acts as a site on which rival and incompatible forces and values are involved in the ceaseless struggle to define these supposedly universal "human" truths (Birrell and Cole, 1990). Therefore, as the epitome of the naturalizing ideologies or myths that inform representations of the male athletic body, specifically the construction and naturalization of masculinity and heterosexuality in the male sporting body, and the myths surrounding the "innate" ability of black athletes, Magic Johnson has always been a suitable candidate for hero status.

The following are descriptions that typify the mystification and charisma generated by the discourse of hero creation, and specifically the process of image building and characterization surrounding Johnson:

> The Public Johnson . . . possesses a different order of reality. This is the Olympian Magic, the guy who thrills us on the court, who beguiles us with the most famous smile since the Mona Lisa, who behaves with such generosity and charity, such warmth and sweetness, that these qualities become magnifications of the spirit, just as his sports feats become magnifications of the physical. ("Magic's Message," 1991, p. 70)

> They dreamed of being like him. He was their idol and he was sensitive to their worship, regardless of how good they really were. ("Johnson's Influence," 1991, p. B13)

In these descriptions, Johnson is a glowing, godlike figure who towers above his adoring followers. His nickname "Magic" (given to him by a local sports reporter during his high school career) only adds to the mystique and power that surround him.

The aura created around Johnson obviously worked well. He ranked fourth in a recent consumer survey on the appeal of athletes as commercial endorsers ("AIDS Virus," 1991). His success as a role model for young basketball players was demonstrated in the emotional reactions of so many of them to the news of his retirement and described in the eulogylike media coverage of this aspect of the story (see, for example, "When AIDS Taps Hero," 1991).

AIDS and Cultural Representations

To link this analysis of Johnson as a sports hero to an analysis of the portrayal of Johnson as a person with AIDS makes sense only in the context of the history of the syndrome. Disease is not merely a biological phenomenon, manifesting itself in the body. It is also shaped by powerful behavioral, social, and political forces that affect the way we come to understand disease and the interventions we undertake. In this view, disease is socially constructed with the body as the prime site of construction and representation.

The appearance of AIDS in the early 1980s coincided with the emergence of the New Right, on the "threshold of its decade of triumph" (Winterson et al., 1989, p. 36). In this context its timing was perfect, for "what better judgement on the moral failures of the past than a virus that seemed to affect disproportionately those already targeted for punitive action—the sexually, culturally and racially marginal" (Winterson et al., 1989, p. 36). The moral absolutist ideology of this period has constructed a cultural agenda for AIDS that relies upon a limited set of overdetermined words and images. These proceed from the initial notion of "the AIDS virus," itself an ideological condensation, as opposed to a medical construction. HIV (human immunodeficiency *virus*) is an *infection* transmitted in body fluids.[3] AIDS is one of the possible results of HIV infection and is therefore a syndrome. The phrase "AIDS virus" obscures the distinction between a virus and a syndrome and at the same time establishes a basis from which the equally inaccurate notion of "the AIDS carrier" can be advanced.

Thereafter a discourse comes into being that summons up imagery of contagion and plague, and the crucial distinction between infectious and contagious diseases is obscured: AIDS is presented as a miasmatic condition that can be caught by casual contact. The commentary thereby effects a sinister reversal; instead of being regarded as threatened, people with AIDS become threatening (Watney, 1989a).

To understand the force of this slippage, it is necessary to examine the ways that the cultural agenda surrounding AIDS has consistently presented the syndrome as if it were an intrinsic property of social groups—a symbolic extension of all imagined inner essence of being—therefore equating the source of the epidemic with its cause. It is commonplace in medical history that epidemics proceed from an initially vulnerable community. In this case HIV manifested itself in groups already marginalized and feared: gay men, people of color, and intravenous drug users. In this context, those first affected are held to be directly responsible for its emergence. Thus the dominant agenda invites us to regard AIDS as a well-deserved punishment and a justification for punitive actions (Watney, 1989a).

Such people are also constructed as the "guilty" victims of the disease, who are continually distinguished from "innocent" sufferers, such as hemophiliacs, babies, and white, middle-class, "respectable" people. Johnson's announcement prompted some explicit examples of this division of the world into elect and damned: "What we have lost can only be matched by what we can no longer deny: That this is not a disease for other people, for the weird, the perverse, the drug addicted, people who somehow deserve it" ("Life Will Go On," 1991).

Hollands (1988) has described the way in which fictional sports heroes are developed by contrasting them with a major antagonist. This is glaringly apparent in the discourse surrounding Magic

Johnson, in which the major antagonists, gay men, have been long established. It is important to emphasize explicitly the social construction of the homosexual body in order to demonstrate the power of the contrast with Johnson's heterosexual body.

The abjection of the bodies of gay men is repeated throughout history under a variety of guises.[4] The persecution of gay men is based on the threat that they pose to so-called normal symbolic and social life, particularly their transgression from the restriction of sex to heterosexual coupling (Gagnon and Folland, 1992). In order to reaffirm social definitions of sanctified norms (or correct behavior), transgressive behavior is identified and isolated (as "otherness"). Foucault (1979b) argued that homosexuality has been constructed as a biological category or "species" since 1870. As such, it is the physical bodies of gay men upon which social and political attention and control are focused (Gagnon and Folland, 1992).

According to Watney (1987), the most high-profile antagonists in the AIDS crisis, that is, gay men, are portrayed through the discourse of "punitive fidelity" in three ways: as AIDS victims abandoned by their families, friends, and lovers; as irresponsible men stalking the streets at night to put other gay men at risk; and as broken men with whispered voices, talking in terms of self-recrimination, disclosed in lonely apartments and hospital isolation wards. Such images stand in stark contrast to the rousing headlines telling of Johnson's illness. According to the *Vancouver Sun* ("Tragic Johnson," 1991), the "whole world (was) applauding Johnson's heroics. . . . Israelis reacted with dismay. Newspapers from Madrid to Tokyo hailed him as a hero" (p. D12). The *Toronto Star* ("Magic's Brave Disclosure," 1991) told us that "In Los Angeles . . . Johnson is a hero to the masses" (p. B5). *El Pais* (November 8, 1991) carried the headline, "The Magic Man: A Legend and a Myth in the Sports World." Johnson's physical appearance, both on television and in newspaper photographs, further reinforces these ideas. He is always smiling, standing tall and muscular, radiant with the markers of health. In this way, his body is literally being used to produce messages, messages that distance Johnson from the conventional pictures of AIDS "victims" displaying all the markers of sickness—wasted bodies, thinning hair, and blemished skin (Zita Grover, 1989).

The (re)creation of Johnson as a hero with AIDS is also important because it clearly demonstrates the power (and, to some extent, the function) of sport in culture. On the one hand, Johnson is still an African-American male and therefore a member of the "guilty" category. On the other hand (as noted subsequently), he has taken great pains to establish his hypermasculinity and heterosexuality in the aftermath of his announcement. So although he participated in his own "getting caught" with the virus, he escapes blame because he is a sports hero. This speaks volumes to the role of sport in the reproduction of relations and representations of gender, race, and sexuality, both as they relate to AIDS and in general.

Central to the media portrayal of people living with AIDS (PLWA) is the assumption that newspapers and television are addressing a certain type of audience. To ensure that advertising space will be sold, the media industry constructs an abstract general public that is categorized into broad bands of potential purchasing power. "Good" journalism therefore consists of persuading this audience to recognize itself with pleasure and reassurance as individual members of a white, patriarchal, heterosexual, and above all family-oriented general public, whose values and institutions must at all costs be regarded as threatened rather than threatening (Watney, 1987). The family, as a primary site of economic consumption as well as a moral entity, is positioned as central in media discourse and as such serves to establish a fixed agenda of values and interests to the virtual exclusion of all other approaches to the construction of family life (Watney, 1987). Therefore, fixed categories of gender, race, and sexuality are orchestrated together to isolate audiences from the diversity of social and sexual life and to deny them any identification with marginalized groups.

Watney (1987) has noted, "AIDS has been used to articulate profound social fears and anxieties, in a dense web of racism, patriotism and homophobia. It is this web . . . which hangs across the entire media industry of the Western world and beyond" (p. 8). The anxieties constructed through sex, gender, and sexuality, and reconstructed in media discourse, reside ultimately in the body and our attitudes toward our own bodies as well as the bodies of others.[5] A fear of disease is articulated in a similar way and, according to Winterson et al. (1989), "has been matched by a fetishisation of fitness." Therefore as a body-destructing "disease" related to sex, AIDS has become symbolic of a "healthy body beautiful undermined by a viral invader" (p. 36).

In this context, it would appear that when Magic Johnson, a seemingly invincible hero creation whose image centered around his "body beautiful," came face to face with the terrible history of the construc-

tion of the AIDS epidemic, an apparently irreconcilable schism was created. The power of sport to define and structure dominant societal beliefs and practices has meant that such a fear has not been realized. Johnson has been hailed anew as hero, for displaying the courage to disclose his condition, and for assuming the role as a national spokesperson for "safe sex" (Smith, 1991).

To understand the paradox of this situation, it is necessary to analyze how Johnson is represented as a hero with AIDS. Watney (1987) writes, "AIDS is not only a medical crisis on an unparalleled scale, it involves a crisis of representation itself, a crisis over the entire framing of knowledge about the human body and its capacities for sexual pleasure" (p. 9). The representation of Magic Johnson as person with AIDS, and the messages produced through him, have served to further deepen this crisis of representation and, in doing so, have reinforced existing stereotypes and social relations based on the oppression of certain sectors of society.

Magic Johnson: (Heterosexual) Hero With AIDS

When Johnson discovered that he was HIV positive, he had to decide whether or not he should retire. Knowing that his condition could not be kept secret forever, he could choose to acknowledge it early and end his career or try to hide it until (or if) he developed AIDS. Since the dominant discourse surrounding AIDS tends to label those who hide their status (such as Rock Hudson) as "guilty victims," Johnson probably made a wise decision by "coming out" as an HIV-positive heterosexual and therefore avoiding such stigma. And while the fears that are continually expressed about the transmission of the virus during the playing of contact sports are exaggerated, such potential risk probably added to pressures placed on him in the name of "living life at a slower pace" and "preserving energy."[6]

In our society, heroes usually fall because their seemingly heroic characteristics are brought into question. They may be involved in a scandal (the marriage of Jerry Lee Lewis to his teenage cousin, for example). They may be found guilty of being like the rest of us, that is, ordinary human beings with personal shortcomings (alcohol and drug abuse are most often cited). Less commonly, they might die, symbolically as when a sports star retires, or literally as in the case of people like Lou Gehrig or Howie Morenz, both of who died at the peak of their sporting careers. In all instances there is a moment of crisis for the athlete and his (not usually "her") image as a commodity and a vehicle for the sale of other products.

The commercial interests that surrounded Johnson during his playing career could not risk being labeled as traitorous and uncaring by deserting him when he made his momentous announcement. For the mass media that rely upon him as a newsworthy personality, AIDS was good news because it promoted sales. At first the solution for these interests was to support Johnson in his campaign—at least for the time being, and at least until he might become visibly sick. (Some commentators argued that if he became symptomatic, support might fade and racism grow; "Magic's Message," 1991.)

Johnson, at the time of his announcement, had contracts worth $10 million annually with Pepsi, Converse, KFC, Spalding, Nintendo, and NBA Properties. All these contracts were subject to renewal in 1992, and immediately following his announcement several companies were noncommittal when asked about their plans to continue working with him ("AIDS Virus," 1991). Subsequently it became clear that the majority of Johnson's major endorsements were not going to be renewed ("Advertisers Shying," 1992). Nestle left on the shelf a completed campaign, and Johnson only reappeared for Pepsi when his place in the Olympic team was confirmed. So despite his hero status, corporate America was pushing him to the margins, along with thousands of other people with AIDS who no longer belong in the mainstream of society.

Converse, however, announced that it was to begin airing public service announcements featuring NBA stars, working under the title "Magic's Athletes Against AIDS" ("AIDS Ads," 1992). Commercial motives aside, the key phrase in the Converse ads, "Anyone can get the AIDS virus," is a subtle way of saying, "Watch out heterosexual, drug-free Americans, the AIDS virus has now reached us, too." This response is typical of the way that social institutions such as the media, governments, schools, and health services, as well as the heterosexualized general public, have only taken AIDS seriously since it is no longer seen as a gay disease and is seen to also threaten "us." This extract from the *Toronto Sun* ("Life Will Go On," 1991), exemplifies the attitude:

People . . . are looking for an answer to this most awful question. Why? Those who believe in fate might say he [Johnson] was chosen in some horrible fatalistic way, to become the

floodlight on this disease, which if allowed to run rampant, could kill us all. (p. C1)

In order to sustain the hero image of Magic Johnson and therefore keep him profitable, and in order for him to gain legitimacy for his campaign, it has been necessary to maintain his connections to basketball through appearing in All-Star games and the Olympics. But more importantly it has been necessary to distance him and his socially constructed healthy, heterosexual body, from the anxiety and loathing that usually accompany AIDS because of its connection with gay men and drug use.

So the big question at the Los Angeles news conference centered on how Johnson contracted the virus; posed timidly, it remained unanswered. Only later that evening, as he continued his drive for "safe sex" on "The Arsenio Hall Show," did he reveal that he had picked up the virus while "living the life of a bachelor" (Smith, 1991); he continued, "I am far from being a homosexual." The audience applauded, and the media, the corporations, and the government breathed a sigh of relief, once more able to continue along the path of heterosexism and homophobia.

Despite Johnson's attempts to appear unbiased—"I sympathize" he wrote in *Sports Illustrated,* "with anyone who has to battle AIDS"—such words are always qualified with the firm reiteration, "But I have never had a homosexual encounter" (Johnson, 1991, pp. 19–20). The sports officials and businessmen who surround Johnson have also made a conscious effort to reaffirm his heterosexual status. In a statement to the press on the day of the announcement, Laker's physician Michael Meliman said, "This is a heterosexual individual who was infected through heterosexual activity" ("Stricken," 1991). These statements serve to construct boundaries between straight society and gay people. As Watney (1987) writes, "Straight society needs us. We are its necessary 'Other'. Without gays, straights are not 'straight' " (p. 27). Not only does the Johnson story reinforce "otherness," it serves to further reinforce the idea that gays brought AIDS upon themselves.

Anger has been intensified among AIDS activists by the way Johnson has been so warmly embraced, not only by the media, some commercial interests, and the public, but also by those in government. Then President of the United States, George Bush, interrupted his news conference at the NATO summit in Rome, to praise Johnson:

He's a hero to me, to everybody that loves sports. I just can't tell you the high regard I have for this athlete. I saw the heartbreak of some of the kids who idolize him. I think he's a gentleman who has handled his problem in a wonderful way. ("Tragic Johnson," 1991, p. D12)

Bush's positive and supportive reaction to Johnson's announcement stands in stark contrast to his response to AIDS in general. Bush's conspicuous silence on this matter had allowed AIDS to virtually disappear from his administration's agenda ("Magic Johnson," 1991).

Johnson was swiftly asked by Bush to fill a vacancy on the National AIDS Commission. In a letter to Bush, Johnson stressed the importance of his remaining an independent voice on the commission; however, he also clearly defined the audience he would be talking to, namely "the heterosexual community, African Americans and young people" ("Honoured," 1991). Had Johnson acquired HIV through gay sex or through needles, it is unlikely that this appointment would have been made.

Johnson subsequently resigned from the commission claiming that Bush repeatedly turned down requests for funding and that he was placed on the commission as a popular figurehead, rather than as a serious activist. His concerns are certainly valid, although it is clearly not only government officials who are using him in this way. The mass media and commercial endorsers have also found in Johnson a perfect body through which to produce the messages that they want transmitted. This is not to portray Johnson as a passive dupe, for he has certainly been active in this process. At the same time, Johnson would likely not have received any institutional or commercial support had he taken a pro-gay, pro-feminist approach.

From Homophobia to Misogyny

It was concerns such as these that prompted Martina Navratilova to speak out against the double standards being reinforced by Johnson's campaign. In an interview with the *New York Post*, Navratilova said that the response to a woman athlete testing positive would be very different from the sympathy Johnson generated. She referred to Johnson's announcement of his HIV status and to his claim of (heterosexual) promiscuity; "The corporations would drop, them like a hot balloon [*sic*]," she said, "and she [*sic*] would be called a slut . . . they would not be a hero" ("Navratilova's View," 1991). Later,

on the "Donahue" talk show (November 27, 1991), Navratilova said that her homosexual preference has prevented her from obtaining endorsements outside tennis and public service announcements. Navratilova's interjections are significant in that they brought attention not only to the homophobia in professional sport but also to the position of women in this saga, who in every chapter of the history of AIDS have been overlooked and obscured.

While persecution of gay men with AIDS has continued through the late 1980s and into the 1990s, it was only in 1986-87 that the Western world began to acknowledge the existence of the female with AIDS. With this acknowledgment came a further reassertion of male power. There is nothing surprising about homophobia and the reassertion of male power operating in tandem—they always have. Both are defenses of the dominant form of heterosexual masculinity enshrined in marriage, a masculinity that oppresses women and gay men alike (Segal, 1989).

Gagnon and Folland (1992) write that the current abjection of the gay body, produced across a variety of institutions, finds a precedent in the general subjection and abjection of the woman's body. This is evidence of the way in which fear and fascination are simultaneously evoked in confrontation with one another, by bodies that are (to be) marked by difference. Gagnon and Folland claim that while the specific constructions involve different motivations, operations, and effects, "these are bodies bound and confined by the language of Western patriarchy, and therefore related to fields outside of the sanctified, white, heterosexual terrain. Outside but strictly managed and therefore dominated" (p. 56).

Both in the popular imagination and in academic writings, AIDS is regarded as preeminently an infection of men (predominantly gay men), and therefore women are viewed as of interest not so much for their own sake but by virtue of their connection with men and children who may be infected. As a result "the social construction of the AIDS crisis provides a dramatization and reinforcement of stereotypical gender constructs about women, particularly with respect to women's procreative and sexual activities" (Overall, 1991, p. 28). In AIDS discourse women are important "not as individuals but merely as vectors of virus transmission" (Mitchell, 1988, p. 50). It is commonplace for feminist scholarship to claim that medical and popular discourse represents women's bodies as pathological and contaminated (Gallagher and Laqueur, 1987;

Suleiman, 1986; Treichler, 1993). Unfortunately, these representations bear complex historical burdens. Women have long been regarded as the reservoirs of disease, and the contemporary Right, many in the medical profession, and the media have readily taken up this notion to describe women as the "vessels" of procreation, which gives men an additional stake in this control.

Since HIV transmission is often interpreted in terms of innocence and blame, and sexually active people as vectors of transmission, in typical patriarchal *either/or* terms, women must be regarded as either the innocent recipient or the guilty transmitter of infection. Women are portrayed as either nurturers and mothers or as seductresses and prostitutes, the former good and natural, the latter bad and unnatural; these images serve only to limit the autonomy of women. The good women are those who care for the HIV positive, the faithful wives of infected husbands. They are also those seen as passive victims of HIV transmission from men, that is, pure virgins or faithful wives contaminated by sexually deviant husbands. The bad women are those seen as actively evil transmitters (prostitutes or stereotypically loose women) of disease to men.[7]

Such representations are nowhere manifested more clearly than in relation to the Magic Johnson case. His wife Cookie is always "his college sweetheart," and "pregnant." As a future mother with an HIV-positive husband, Cookie was of concern not so much for her own sake as for the sake of the child she was carrying. She and their baby are also HIV free at present; if either becomes a carrier, Johnson's position will certainly be undermined. As for the women from whom Johnson allegedly caught the virus, fitting conveniently into the "evil transmitter" category of woman, nobody, it seems, has even stopped to consider how many of them are HIV positive, how many of them Johnson has exposed to the virus (that is, until 1 year later, see Note 1).

It is also interesting to consider that only 2.2% of HIV cases are thought to have resulted from transmission via women to men during heterosexual intercourse. Although I wish to avoid entering into the very discourse that this case study attempts to deconstruct and critique, I believe this statistic is extremely significant as an illustration of the need to consider the unstated or hidden agenda of media discourse. In this case, the stated agenda is based on the unstated assumption that because Johnson is represented as a heterosexual and a hero, he cannot and must not be associated with "others" (IV drug users, gay men, and so on). The blame (for blame must be placed in AIDS discourse) is therefore displaced onto the bodies of a readily available "other." Because groupies are categorized as prostitutes and therefore as evil carriers of HIV, it is "obvious" that they infected Johnson, the innocent recipient.

Also underlying this discourse is the common assumption that women's illnesses and women themselves are less important than men. The deeply rooted fear and hatred of "other," communicated by the images of these groupies, construct them as existing outside of public health and public concern (in contrast to infected fetuses, hemophiliacs, and so on). For them, like gay men, HIV is a punishment for their "evil debauchery," and like gay men, as soon as they are labeled, they can be forgotten. Hence there has been a conspicuous absence of these women from public discourse since the day of the announcement. Like prostitutes in wider discourse, they are constructed as much by their absence from media commentary as through it.

It is also striking, but not surprising, that little has been said about groupies as a significant and permanent feature of the NBA (and all professional sport leagues in North America). No serious effort has been made to question the assumption that groupies are present because male sport greatness warrants sexual reward. One *Sports Illustrated* article (Swift, 1991) on groupies completely overlooked issues of gender and power and instead provided descriptions of the sex lives of various players and vicious criticisms of the groupies. Take for example Clippers forward Ken Norman, who expressed his disgust for groupies and said he wanted "to distinguish them from the women who do have moral values and do have self respect about themselves and are not real busy chasing jocks" ("Running Scared," 1991, p. B1).

All of these stories convey paradoxical messages. On the one hand, these male athletes are portrayed as victims and targets of loose women who prey on male athletes. On the other hand, such reports contain the message that male sexual desire, as a "natural object not a product" (Mohr, 1988, p. 45), should be regarded as irrepressible and uncontrollable: "Believe me, the sky is the limit out there. Women, drugs, every vice you could want, any time of the day or night," said Dodgers player Brett Butler ("Running Scared," 1991, p. B1).

In a similar vein, the Johnson campaign has assumed a nonexistent "level playing field" for women and men that obscures both the public and private inequalities in power that define women and men in their relationships (Overall, 1991). The emphasis on safer sex overlooks the fact that women exist in a sexual economy where they have unequal power in relationship to their potential sex partners and has served to endorse rather than question the most macho and heterosexist conceptions of sexuality; the focus of safe sex seems to rest solely on persuading young men to use condoms with the help of young women. This "penetration propaganda" (Campbell, 1987, p. 9) helps to maintain an "exaggerated respect for male desire and an unquestioning acceptance of penetration" (Richardson, 1989, p. 56).

Johnson's campaign and AIDS discourse in general could provide good reason and space to rethink the powerful symbol of the male sexual beast, a "myth so central to maintaining existing ideologies and practices of male domination" (Richardson, 1989, p. 56); unfortunately this has not been the case so far. Hence the irony in Johnson's words that he was "only joking" when he wrote in *Sports Illustrated* (Johnson, 1991) that he "tried to accommodate as many women as possible," and that he "respects women to the upmost" and will handle his predicament "like a man" (p. 19).

Concluding Remarks and Further Questions

As this discussion has demonstrated, in our society one way of dealing with what cannot be contemplated, that is, homosexuality, predatory women, people of color in positions of power, and so on, is to turn the repressed into an "other." According to Davis (1990), "The quest to distinguish self (i.e., the white, Christian, heterosexual, middle- to ruling class, male self) from all others is embedded in Western thought. 'Others' . . . are seen as needing to be explained and rendered distinct from and inferior to the self" (p. 182). What is particularly threatening about AIDS is that it threatens to break down the border between "other" and self; its threat is not only one of disease but one of dissolution, the contamination of categories (Williamson, 1989). These threats are conveyed through the body and representations of the body, hence the need for the media to create a complex system of checks and balances.

In this respect, the Magic Johnson chapter in the history of AIDS provides an intriguing twist to the tale. While, as we have seen, Johnson has clearly defined boundaries between himself and certain "others," he as a black American also represents an "other." As a white, middle-class woman, with all my privileges and biases, I find it extremely difficult to identify with Johnson's "safe sex" campaign; perhaps this is how it is supposed to function.

Johnson can talk to members of the African-American urban underclass culture, while white middle-class America can sit back and look on with smug approval. At the same time Johnson's story may "through the selective lens of age old bigotry, feed the myths about the hypersexuality of African Americans" (Smith, 1991).

The assumptions surrounding the "natural" genesis of black athletes' sexuality and athleticism have not been dealt with adequately in this paper. Also, as yet, issues of race and racism have been noticeably absent from coverage of and debate over the Johnson story. Because racial myths are so taken for granted, this silence is far from reassuring. And while popular assumptions are probably being reinforced, vital questions pertaining to the disproportionate number of black men and women (along with other people of color) affected by the HIV virus, inequalities in access to health care, and other effects of socioeconomic oppression are being ignored.

Johnson's work is probably having some positive effects. But by reinforcing particular social relations, myths, and stereotypes and concealing and naturalizing others, the construction of Johnson as a "hero with AIDS" and the representation of dominant ideologies of AIDS through the bodies of him and others in the story have caused more harm than good. To quote Richard Dyer (1982),

> The political chances of different groups in society—powerful or weak, central or marginal—are crucially affected by how they are represented, whether in legal and parliamentary discourse, in educational practices, or in the arts. The mass media in particular have a crucial role to play, because they are a centralised source of what people are like in any given society. How a particular group is represented determines in a very real sense what it can do in society. (p. 43)

The representation of AIDS has been used by a wide variety of groups to articulate a whole array of issues and concerns. So while the syndrome has brought to the fore long-ignored issues in gay politics, feminism, and black activism, it has at the same time been used to justify people's fears and prejudices and intensify the marginalization of oppressed groups. The Magic Johnson story exemplifies such contradictions and, at a time when the importance of issues surrounding the body and its investment with social, political, economic, and sexual power is becoming increasingly recognized, points to a need for sports sociologists to take more seriously the study of popular heroes and culture as they intersect with representations and relations of race, power, gender, sexuality, and the body.

Acknowledgments

I would like to thank Rob Beamish, Cheryl Cole, and Hart Cantelon for their careful readings and incisive critiques of earlier drafts of this essay.

References

Advertisers shying from Magic's touch. (1992, January 1). *New York Times*, p. 44.

AIDS ads to feature NBA. (1992, January 2). *Montreal Gazette*, p. C1.

AIDS virus admission may end Magic's endorsements. (1991, November 9). *Toronto Star*, p. C3.

American Academy of Pediatrics. (1991). Human Immunodeficiency Virus [Acquired Immunodeficiency Syndrome (AIDS) Virus] in the athletic setting. *Pediatrics*, **88**(3), 640–641.

Bartky, S. (1988). Foucault, femininity and patriarchal power. In I. Diamond and L. Quinby (Eds.), *Feminism and Foucault: Reflections on resistance* (pp. 61–86). Boston: Northeastern University Press.

Birrell, S., and Cole, C. (1990). Double fault: Renee Richards and the construction and naturalization of difference. *Sociology of Sport Journal*, **7**(1), 1–21.

Campbell, B. (1987, December). Taking the plunge. *Marxism Today*, p. 9.

Crepeau, R. (1981). Sports, heroes and myth. *Journal of Sport and Social Issues*, **5**(1), 23–31.

Davis, L. (1990). The articulation of difference: White preoccupation with the question of racially linked genetic differences among athletes. *Sociology of Sport Journal*, **7**(2), 179–187.

Dyer, R. (1982, April–June). The celluloid closet. *Birmingham Arts Lab. Bulletin*, p. 43.

Foucault, M. (1979a). *Discipline and punish: The birth of the prison*. New York: Vintage.

Foucault, M. (1979b). *History of sexuality: Vol. 1. An introduction*. London: Penguin.

Gagnon, M., and Folland, T. (1992). The spectacular ruse. In A. Klusacek and K. Morrison (Eds.), *A leap in the dark. AIDS, art and contemporary cultures* (pp. 96–108). Montreal: Vehicule Press.

Gallagher, C., and Laqueur, T. (Eds.) (1987). *The making of the modern body: Sexuality and society in the nineteenth century*. Berkeley, CA: University of California Press.

Glasgow University Media Group. (1976). *Bad news*. London: Routledge and Kegan Paul.

Glasgow University Media Group. (1980). *More bad news*. London: Routledge and Kegan Paul.

Hargreaves, J. (1986). *Sport, power and culture: A social and historical analysis of popular sports in Britain*. New York: St. Martin's Press.

Hoffer, R. (1990, December 3). Magic's kingdom: Laker star Magic Johnson owns LA, and someday he plans to own a lot more. *Sports Illustrated*, pp. 106–122.

Hollands, B. (1988). English Canadian sports novels and cultural production. In J. Harvey and H. Cantelon (Eds.), *Not just a game* (pp. 213–226). Ottawa: University of Ottawa Press.

"Honoured" Johnson agrees to serve on U.S. AIDS commission. (1991, November 16). *Montreal Gazette*, p. C2.

Johnson, E. (1991, November 18). I'll deal with it. *Sports Illustrated*, pp. 16–27.

Johnson's influence: A study of class. (1991, November 12). *New York Times*, p. B13.

"Life will go on": Magic. (1991, November 8). *Toronto Star*, pp. C1, C7.

Magic Johnson, as president. (1991, November 9). *New York Times*, p. 22.

Magic's brave disclosure may save a lot of lives. (1991, November 9). *Toronto Star*, pp. B1, B5.

Magic's message in the AIDS war. (1991, November 18). *Newsweek*, pp. 58–62.

Miles, R. (1989). *The women's history of the world*. London: Paladin.

Mitchell, J. (1988). Women, AIDS and public policy. *AIDS and Public Policy Journal*, **3**(2), 50–52.

Mohr, R. (1988). *Gays/justice: A study of ethics, society, and law*. New York: Columbia University Press.

Navratilova's view on Magic. (1991, November 21). *New York Times*, p. B16.

Overall, C. (1991). AIDS and the women: The (hetero)sexual politics of HIV infection. In C. Overall and W. Zion (Eds.), *Perspectives on AIDS: Ethical and social issues* (pp. 27–33). Toronto: Oxford University Press.

Pascarelli, P. (1992). *The courage of Magic Johnson*. New York: Bantam.

Richardson, D. (1989). *Women and the AIDS crisis*. London: Pandora.

Running scared. (1991, December 1). *Chronicle Herald*, pp. B1, B10.

Segal, L. (1989). Lessons from the past: Feminism, sexual politics and the challenge of AIDS. In E. Carter and S. Watney (Eds.), *Taking liberties: AIDS and cultural politics* (pp. 133–146). London: Serpant's Tail.

Smith, G. (1991, November 19). Magic moment: Mirror of American culture. *Kingston Whig Standard*, p. 4.

Sontag, S. (1989). *AIDS and its metaphors.* New York: Farrar, Straus and Giroux.

Stricken Lakers star to be a father, doctor confirms. (1991, November 9). *Montreal Gazette*, p. A14.

Suleiman, S. (Ed.) (1986). *The female body in western culture.* Cambridge, MA: Harvard University Press.

Swift, E.M. (1991, November 18). Dangerous games. *Sports Illustrated*, pp. 40–43.

Theberge, N., and Cronk, A. (1986). Work routines in newspaper sports departments and the coverage of women's sports. *Sociology of Sport Journal*, **3**, 195–203.

Tragic Johnson. (1991, November 8). *Vancouver Sun*, p. D12.

Treichler, P. (1993). AIDS, gender and biomedical discourse: Current contests for meaning. In L. Kauffman (Ed.), *American feminist thought at century's end: A reader* (pp. 281–354). Cambridge, MA: Blackwell.

Watney, S. (1987). *Policing desire: AIDS, pornography, and the media.* London: Methuen.

Watney, S. (1989a). Introduction. In E. Carter and S. Watney (Eds.), *Taking liberties* (pp. 11–58). London: Serpant's Tail.

Watney, S. (1989b). AIDS, language and the Third World. In E. Carter and S. Watney (Eds.), *Taking liberties* (pp. 183–192). London: Serpant's Tail.

When AIDS taps hero, his "children" feel pain. (1991, November 9). *New York Times*, p. 1.

Williamson, J. (1989). Every virus tells a story: The meaning of HIV and AIDS. In E. Carter and S. Watney (Eds.), *Taking liberties* (pp. 69–80). London: Serpant's Tail.

Willis, P. (1974). Performance and meaning: A sociocultural view of women in sport. *Stencilled Occasional Papers, 19.* University of Birmingham, Centre for Contemporary Cultural Studies.

Winterson, J., Abrams, P., Weeks, J., Coward, R., and Wilson, E. (1989, December 22–29). Revolting bodies. *New Statesman and Society*, **2**, 81.

Zita Grover, J. (1989). Constitutional symptoms. In E. Carter and S. Watney (Eds.), *Taking liberties* (pp. 147–160). London: Serpant's Tail.

Notes

1. The story continues to unfold. This paper focuses on developments up until the 1992 Olympics. Since then, Johnson has retired again, apparently as a result of fears of infection expressed by fellow players. This is in the midst of public debate about his sexual orientation and an impending lawsuit from an infected former partner.

2. Such bodies are seen in the infamous Calvin Klein advertisements, for example.

3. The fact that HIV transmission often occurs through sexual contact greatly enhances the stigma attached to the disease. According to Sontag (1989), this stigma is powerful because it draws upon meanings historically associated with cancer, a biological "invasion," and venereal disease, a "form of pollution."

4. Rosalind Miles in her *Women's History of the World* (1989), for instance, describes the burning of gay men at the stake of witches.

5. As this discussion progresses it will become clear that these anxieties, while residing in the body, are at the same time manifested in, and recreated by, the "othering" of marginalized groups such as women (both lesbian and heterosexual), people of color, gay men, the elderly, and so on.

6. According to the American Academy of Pediatrics (1991), the risk of infection from skin exposure to the blood of a person with HIV is unknown, but apparently it is minute and much less than the risk of HIV infection by needlesticks from infected patients. Although it is theoretically possible that transmission of HIV could occur, there are no reported cases to date.

7. It is important to recognize that lesbian women do not fit into this sexist and homophobic categorization. This is reflected in the conspicuous invisibility of lesbian women in the majority of AIDS discourse.

Gender and Sport: Constructions of Femininity and Masculinity

Objectives

The unit examines the various ways sport produces and reproduces the gender order to maintain masculine hegemony.

Solomon (1982) defines a gender role as consisting of "those behaviors, expectations, and role sets defined by a society as masculine or feminine which are then embodied in the behavior of the individual man or woman." Gender roles are not biological givens, something we have at birth. Rather, gender is a dynamic component of the self which develops across the life cycle, is occasionally confronted by crises, and which is subject to redefinition and modification as individuals continually interact with their social environment (Messner, 1990).

The ways in which the gender roles of masculinity and femininity, as social constructions, are defined, learned, reinforced, and sometimes resisted within the social world of sport is a subject that has attracted the attention of many sport scholars. Clearly, sport sociologists can no longer avoid the issue, as Coakley (1998) puts it, of "why half the world's population traditionally has been excluded or discouraged from participating in many sports . . ." (p. 211). With the exception of a small number of "sex-appropriate" sports (e.g., figure skating, gymnastics, tennis, golf, swimming) and the always beckoning role of cheerleader, the sports arena has traditionally been an uninviting, sometimes hostile environment for girls and women with "no trespassing" signs posted at any number of entry points.

In recent years, sport sociologists have shown a keen interest in the ways in which participation in organized sports contributes to the social construction of "feminine" and "masculine" behaviors. It is clear that organized sports are not only a "gendered institution" but a "gendering" one as well. That is, sports actively, and sometimes aggressively, contribute to the continual reproduction of the gender order and maintenance of masculine hegemony. From a profeminist perspective, modern sports are viewed as ". . . reinforcing the sexual division of labor, perpetuating inequality between the sexes, and contributing to the exploitation and repression of both males and females" (Kidd, 1987).

Interest in gender-related sport issues has generally been twofold. Some researchers choose to focus on participation and equity issues (e.g., the effects of the 1972 Equal Education Amendments Act on female sport participation rates) while others are more interested in the ideological and structural issues underlying the treatment of girls and women in sports. But as sport sociologist George Sage (1998) perceptively observed, the two sets of issues cannot be neatly separated. To be sure, sex discrimination and sexism are supported by several institutional structures (e.g., political, economic, educational) and practices, but it is the ideology of patriarchy (e.g., "a structured and ideological system of personal relationships that legitimate male power over women and the services they provide"; Sage, 1998, p. 58) that helps sustain and perpetuate gender inequities in sport and the larger society. The very constructs of "femininity" and "masculinity" reinforce patriarchal culture. As long as men and women continue to be socialized into, and conform to, their respective "gender scripts," males will continue to be viewed as dominant and superior and females as subordinate and inferior.

The contribution of organized, competitive sports to patriarchy (Sage, 1998), gender logic (Coakley, 1998), masculine hegemony (Bryson, 1994), or the "discourse of femininity" (Foucault, 1984) requires a careful analysis of the ways femininity and masculinity are constructed and reified within sport. Commonsense notions and beliefs associated with females and males in general, and female and male athletes in particular ("gender sense"), as in "You throw like a girl," reflect the ideological underpinning that maintains and supports a gender-based system of social stratification in American society.

One of the consequences of "acting out" feminine and masculine gender scripts is the way both sexes perceive their bodies. Although many American men and women are likely to express some dissatisfaction with their physical selves in a society obsessed with "flat abs, tight buns, and toned thighs," it is males who are much more likely to desire to be taller, heavier, stronger, and larger (e.g., arms, pecs, quads, calves). Women, on the other hand, are much more likely to desire bodily changes that make them thinner, smaller, less muscular, and simply "not so big." The physical traits and characteristics American society typically associates with traditional notions of femininity and masculinity are likely to encourage girls and women to spend the better part of their lives trying to become as small as they can (i.e., "take up as little space as possible") while encouraging boys and men to get as large as they can ("take up as much space as possible"). The implications of these "ideal" body types for both sexes are obvious in terms of having an interest in sports, participating in particular sports, committing oneself to serious athletic training, and desiring to be the best athlete one can be.

Although traditional gender prescriptions for females and males appear to favor the latter, men need to recognize the price they pay for conforming to dominant definitions of masculinity. British sport sociologist Jennifer Hargreaves makes the point that not only do traditional gender notions restrict and oppress women, they also "damage men." Coakley (1998) also observed that male participation in sports that emphasize aggression and domination (traditional masculine traits) can lead to chronic, serious injuries, an inability to relate to women, an inordinate fear of intimacy with other men, homophobia (e.g., "an irrational fear or hatred of those who love and/or sexually desire those of the same sex," Veri, 1999, p. 357), and a constant need to compete with and outdo other men.

In the first selection, Anderson investigates the emerging sport of snowboarding to demonstrate how male snowboarders construct their sport as a masculine practice. Although the methods they choose differ somewhat from those commonly used in more traditional male sports, the net effect is the same, namely, support of male dominance and the marginalization and sexualization of female participants. Of special interest to the reader should be the author's discussion of the ways in which class, race, ethnicity, and age influence the creation of the masculine snowboarding "script."

In the second selection, Klein analyzes, in his ethnographic assessment of a Mexican League baseball team, the North American notion that Latino and American men are one-dimensional machos. He notes interesting differences in the way Anglo and Mexican players express vulnerability and hurt, react to children, and express their physicality. Most important, we discover that machismo exists along a continuum, extending from an aggressive, womanizing masculinity at one end to tender, gentle behavior at the other. The reader interested in the sport-gender nexus should find the presence of "tender machos" in baseball especially intriguing.

In the third selection, Theberge analyzes the production (construction) of gender in women's ice hockey by drawing from fieldwork and interviews with elite-level ice hockey players and coaches. In the players' accounts of their physicality and the ways in which they respond to injury, we see sport's potential for empowering female athletes and challenging masculine hegemony. The reader also learns, however, that the sport of female ice hockey is not without its contradictions, as evidenced by its construction as a "milder version of the sport that really counts" (e.g., men's ice hockey).

References

Anderson, K.L. (1999). Snowboarding: The construction of gender in an emerging sport. *Journal of Sport and Social Issues,* **23**, 55-79.

Bryson, L. (1994). Sport and the maintenance of masculine hegemony. In S. Birrell & C.L. Cole (Eds.), *Women, sport, and culture* (pp. 47-64). Champaign, IL: Human Kinetics.

Coakley, J.J. (1998). *Sport in society: Issues & controversies.* New York: McGraw-Hill.

Foucault, M. (1984). *The Foucault reader.* (P. Rabinow, ed.) New York: Pantheon Books.

Kidd, B. (1987). Sports and masculinity. In M. Kaufman (Ed.), *Beyond patriarchy: Essays by men on pleasure, power, and change* (pp. 250-265). New York: Oxford University Press.

Klein, A.M. (1995). Tender machos: Masculine contrasts in the Mexican baseball league. *Sociology of Sport Journal,* **12**, 370-388.

Messner, M. (1990). Boyhood, organized sports and the construction masculinity. In M.A. Messner & D.F. Sabo (Eds.), *Sport, men, and the gender order* (pp. 19-29). Champaign, IL: Human Kinetics.

Sage, G. H. (1998). *Power and ideology in American sport.* Champaign, IL: Human Kinetics.

Solomon, K. (1982). The masculine gender role. In K. Solomon & N.B. Levy (Eds.), *Men in transition: Theory and therapy* (pp. 45-76). New York: Plenum Press.

Theberge, N. (1997). It's part of the game: Physicality and the production of gender in women's ice hockey. *Gender & Society,* **11**, 69-87.

Veri, M.J. (1999). Homophobic discourse surrounding the female athlete. *Quest,* **51**, 355-368.

Discussion Questions

Kristin Anderson

1. What does the author mean when she writes "gender is created"? Explain.
2. What do we know about the construction of gender in alternative and emerging sports? Discuss and explain.
3. Offer a brief social and historical context for the sport of snowboarding.
4. Identify some of the social practices snowboarders engage in to give their sport a masculine identity.
5. What role, if any, does violence and aggression play in snowboarding? Discuss and explain.
6. How do attitudes about heterosexuality and homosexuality help in the construction of the snowboarder's masculine image? Explain.
7. How is it that age, race, and social class support as well as constrain the construction of masculinity among snowboarders? Discuss and explain.
8. How are "girl snowboarders" treated? Explain.
9. To what extent is the street-punk image of male snowboarders resisted? Identify the sources of resistance and then comment on how successful they have been at challenging the image.

Alan Klein

1. Why are the Owls of the Two Laredos, a baseball team in the Mexican League, a perfect subject for doing cross-cultural analysis? Explain.
2. What does the term "machismo" mean? Explain.
3. Briefly describe the author's ethnographic study.
4. Identify the "masculine continuum" that the author used to locate the displays of behavior he observed.
5. Did the author observe expressions of machismo among the Teco players? Explain.
6. (a) Did the Mexican and American players differ in terms of emotions and behavior? (b) Why were the Mexican players better able to express physical affection among themselves? Discuss and explain.
7. Identify an American sport in which one is likely to encounter "tender machos." Explain.

Nancy Theberge

1. Identify the focus and research methodology employed by the researcher.
2. Identify the most popular topics of conversation among the players.
3. Identify the essential features of the "community" constructed by the players.
4. Comment on the bonding and group identification that took place among the players.
5. Compare and contrast this group of female ice hockey players with, for example, a college

sorority. In what ways are the two groups likely to be similar and in what ways are they likely to be different? Discuss and explain.

6. Comment on the importance of physicality within this sport community and the extent to which it challenged traditional notions of femininity.

7. To what extent do sports like women's ice hockey successfully challenge the "gender order"? What is the author's position on this question? Discuss and explain.

Snowboarding: The Construction of Gender in an Emerging Sport

Kristin L. Anderson

Previous research has identified sport as a practice that creates and legitimizes notions of male dominance. However, gender is constructed and resisted differently within various sporting activities. This article addresses the diversity of masculinities in sport through an exploration of the construction of gender in an emerging sport—snowboarding. The analysis identifies four social practices used by male snowboarders to construct their sport as a masculine practice: (a) appropriation of other cultural masculinities, (b) interaction and clothing styles, (c) violence and aggression, and (d) emphasized heterosexuality. The findings indicate that the historical context of snowboarding and the social class, race-ethnicity, and age of snowboarding participants influence the social practices used to create masculinity. Although snowboarders rely on different social practices to construct masculinity than those used in organized sports, these practices also serve to support notions of male dominance and difference from women.

I guess it's kind of like controlled chaos . . . controlled anarchy with a cause behind it. The cause? Is to go bigger and fatter than everybody, or spin the most or whatever you're doing at the time that you want to do it. And you want to do it better than everybody else.

—Male snowboarder, age 16

In U.S. culture, doing it "bigger and fatter" is one means of exhibiting masculinity. He who earns more money, owns a bigger house, and drives a faster car is thought to possess the masculine qualities of strength, skill, aggression, and competitive drive. One of the most common ways for men to "do it better" is in sport. Through their attempts to run faster, to hit harder, to jump higher, or to throw farther, men can demonstrate strength and superiority. Past research has emphasized the importance of sport in creating and maintaining notions of male dominance and difference from women (Hall, 1985; Hargreaves, 1986; Messner, 1992a; Oglesby, 1989; Sabo, 1985). Within organized sports, the exclusion of women, hierarchical and regulated structure, and violence help to create a particular form of idealized masculinity that becomes part of men's identities through their participation as athletes or fans (Messner, 1992a). Moreover, as spectators celebrate the "masculine" qualities of the athletes, they legitimize the notion that men are naturally suited to "do it better" in institutions other than sport (Messner, 1989; West and Zimmerman, 1987).

However, sport is not a monolithic structure; gender is created and resisted differently in the many activities considered sport. The various constructions of masculinity within the institution of sport have received little attention in the literature on gender and sport. The masculinities of the runner, football player, and rock-climber are qualitatively different; each sport combines various symbolic discourses to create a masculinity particular to the sport. Most of the sociological study of sports

Reprinted from Anderson, 1999.

275

and masculinity has focused on organized sports such as football, baseball, and basketball—sports that have a history of excluding (and more recently separating) women. Little is known about the construction of gender in alternative and emerging sports, such as mountain biking, in-line skating, and disc golf. Unorganized and highly individualized, emerging sports may be sites for new constructions of masculinity.

This article addresses the diversity of sporting masculinities through an exploration of the construction of gender in an emerging sport—snowboarding. Recent theories of gender emphasize that masculinity and femininity are idealized cultural symbols rather than individual qualities or traits and that gender is collectively constructed through social practice (Connell, 1987; Segal, 1990; West and Zimmerman, 1987). Moreover, the social practices that form the gender power structure simultaneously reflect and recreate structural inequalities (Connell, 1987; Messerschmidt, 1993). Age, social class, sexual preference, and race support or constrain individual opportunities to "do gender" through exhibiting the dominant and idealized masculine or feminine qualities (Collins, 1991; hooks, 1989; West and Zimmerman, 1987).

As cultural practice, gender is not unified or cohesive but contradictory and contested (Bordo, 1993). Many competing versions of masculinity and femininity appear in a culture at a given point in time, but power structures influence which constructions of gender become dominant and which are subordinated (Connell, 1987). Because there are competing versions of masculinity, dominant notions of masculinity must be formed in relation to what Connell (1987) calls "subordinated" masculinities and in relation to women (p. 183).

Despite this emphasis on the active construction of gender within feminist theory, few studies have focused on the role of sport in creating and sustaining idealized images of masculinity and femininity. As Whitson (1990) notes, "Theoretically informed studies of the place of sport in the social construction of masculinity remain exceptional and isolated, not forming part of a focused scholarly dialogue" (p. 19). The exceptions, however, have expanded our understanding of how and why sport serves to create notions of male dominance and difference from women (see Cahn, 1990; Messner, 1992a; Sabo and Messner, 1993). Recent analyses of alternative sports such as the Triathalon and body building have revealed contradictions athletes face while trying to embody masculine ideals (Connell, 1990; Klein, 1990, Wacquant, 1995). Other research

has shown that race and class influence men's ability and choices to "do masculinity" through sport (Messner, 1989).

As an inchoate sport, snowboarding is a good case for analyses of the ways in which new sporting practices become gendered. In the following analysis, I focus on the processes of gender construction within snowboarding and the contradictions that emerge from these processes. Initially, I describe the social and historical context of this emerging sport. Second, I discuss the strategies that snowboarders use to create a masculine image for snowboarding. I then explore the ways in which social class, race, and age influence the construction of gender within snowboarding, and how female snowboarders both resist and accommodate these masculinizing strategies.

Method

The following analysis is informed by a combination of methods: (a) in-depth interviews conducted with 10 snowboarders, (b) a content analysis of the 1993 and 1994 editions of the two largest snowboarding magazines: *Snowboarder* and *TransWorld Snowboarding,* and (c) participant observation at a snowboarding shop and several ski resorts in Southern California. I interviewed six men and four women who had been involved in snowboarding for at least 2 years. Respondents were located through a voluntary sign-up sheet at a snowboarding shop in Southern California and through a snowball technique.

Table 20.1 provides demographic information about the respondents and pseudonyms through which the snowboarders are referenced in the following analysis. Five of the snowboarders were European American, two African American, one Cuban American, one Mexican/Native American, and one Asian/European American. Their ages ranged from 16 to 29 years. All of the respondents reported a heterosexual orientation. Although the majority of snowboarders are young White men (TransWorld Publications, 1994), I purposely conducted interviews with a diverse group of snowboarders to gain information about the perceptions of snowboarders on the margins of this new sport. The interviews with women, snowboarders older than 25, and with both men and women of color were especially useful in illuminating the interactions and contradictions of race, class, and gender in snowboarding. All interviews were conducted by the author in cafés and restaurants near the snowboarding shop. The interviews lasted about 1 hour, and they were tape-recorded and transcribed for analysis. I asked open-ended questions about the respondents' initial involvement and current experiences in snowboarding; participation in other sports; attitudes about riding with, and competing against, men and/or women; and the political aspects of snowboarding.

The content analysis focused on how women and men are portrayed within the snowboarding media and the gender issues that appear in the media text. However, to describe the media presentation of snowboarders, I coded all photographs of snowboarders in the seven 1994 issues of *Snowboarder* and calculated the percentages of representation by race and gender. *TransWorld Snowboarding,* the largest snowboarding magazine, has a distribution of more than 165,000 copies (TransWorld Publications, 1994). *Snowboarder* has a circulation of around 80,000 ("A look," 1994). Four of the snowboarders interviewed subscribed to *TransWorld Snowboarding,* two subscribed to *Snowboarder,* and three others reported that they purchased and read one or both magazines on occasion.

In addition, I worked as a salesperson in the snowboarding shop during the period the interviews were conducted and observed snowboarders for an average of 20 hours a week for a 5-week period. I also observed snowboarders on several occasions as I attempted snowboarding. My interaction with snowboarders in these contexts facilitated the analyses of interview and magazine data.

Social and Historical Context

Snowboards were first marketed in 1977, after two East Coast surfers wanted to practice surfing in the winter and created "snurfers" to ride on the snow ("Battle of the Piste," 1993). Since this inauspicious beginning, snowboarding has become "the fastest growing winter sport" (Battle, 1993, p. 96). In 1988, snowboarders made up around 6% of those actively involved in downhill snow sports, whereas skiers made up the other 94%. By 1992, snowboarders constituted 24% of those active on the slopes (TransWorld Publications, 1994).

The rapid growth of this new sport is largely due to the interest of young, middle-class men. The median age of snowboarders is 15.5 years, about 70% come from households with annual incomes above $35,000, and 80% are male (TransWorld Publications, 1994). Although information on race and ethnicity for the general market of snowboarders is not available, my content analysis of the 1994 issues of *Snowboarder* revealed that snowboarders receiving media coverage are overwhelmingly young, white, and male. More than 86% of the images (both features and advertisements) depicted white men, whereas only 5% of the photos portray Latino, African American, or Asian men. White women were pictured in 9% of the shots, and images of minority women were entirely absent.

Like organized sports, snowboarding is currently dominated by men. However, it is developing in a very different social and historical context than did

Table 20.1   Description of Respondents

Pseudonym	Sex	Age	Race	Education (years)	Occupation	Years participation
Adam	M	20	European American	15	College student/ snowboard shop	4
Ben	M	20	European/Asian American	14.5	College student/ snowboard shop	4
Chris	M	27	African American	12	Electronics	2
Debbie	F	20	European American	15	College student/ waitress	3
Eric	M	16	Cuban American	10	High school student/ food service	3
Fern	F	29	European American	15	Office manager	3
Gina	F	24	Mexican/Native American	24	Office manager/esthetician	3
Holly	F	21	European American	21	College student/retail clerk	5
Irving	M	29	African American	29	General contractor	2
John	M	16	European American	11	High school student	5

Reprinted from Anderson, 1999.

organized sports. Women's increasing sport participation in past decades has meant that sport is no longer an exclusively male institution (Cahn, 1990). Within snowboarding, the norms and rules of participation are actively debated and the images and identities of the "snowboarder" are in a state of flux. In response to my question about how her male friends view snowboarding, Debbie replied, "I don't know if they really think of it as a guy thing. I think it's so new it hasn't been labeled anything yet." Furthermore, the data suggest that women's participation is increasing. All of the snowboarders interviewed had noticed more women riding in the 1994 season than in previous years. In addition, female snowboarders are beginning to receive some media attention and a few are sponsored by snowboarding corporations. The 1994 snowboarding magazine issues contained more references to, and images of, female riders than the 1993 issues. Thus, unlike most organized sports, snowboarding is emerging in a context of women's sport participation and is not automatically considered a masculine practice.

Part of the reason for women's rising participation may be the unorganized nature of the sport. In contrast to the exclusive and competitive nature of organized sport participation, snowboarding is open to those that can afford the lift tickets and equipment. Moreover, few snowboarders participate in competitions. Only one respondent, Holly, had participated in a snowboarding competition, and this was a local competition sponsored by a ski resort and open to anyone wishing to compete. Some respondents said that they liked the individualistic practice of snowboarding in contrast to the organized team sports in which they had participated in previous years. Adam noted that he did not like team sports because they have "kind of the one-for-all attitude. If one person screws up, the whole team gets punished. I didn't like being responsible for other people." Thus, the practice of snowboarding does not involve the sex-segregated teams and emphasis on group effort that characterizes organized sports.

In practice, riding a snowboard involves little that conforms to the dominant ideals of the sporting masculinity, such as strength, aggression, and teamwork (Segal, 1990). It involves binding one's feet onto a 4- to 6-foot oblong board and "riding" the board down the mountain by shifting one's weight such that the board glides through the snow on its edges. Snowboarding looks similar to surfing or skateboarding to an observer. Chris described it as "the sensation of floating on powder." Also, snowboarders create "tricks," which involve "airs"

(jumps and turns), and construct obstacles and half-pipes in the snow to facilitate these tricks. Riding the board downhill is termed *carving,* whereas riding in the half-pipe or jumping obstacles is *jibbing.* Those riders who prefer carving are "old school," whereas those who prefer the jib style are the "new schoolers." Several respondents emphasized that snowboarding requires balance and flexibility as well as strength. Ben said that "girls are probably more, they are better suited for snowboarding and skateboarding because their center of gravity is in their hips, it's not like in their shoulders." Thus, the physical practice of snow boarding does not require the "masculine" strength and aggression that legitimize the exclusion of women in some sports (Young and White, 1995).

Snowboarding's contextual differences from most organized men's sports influence the ways in which snowboarders construct gender. Snowboarding does not have the regulated structure, standard competitions, organized recruitment strategies, and exclusive participation practices that have facilitated the construction of masculinity within organized sports (Messner, 1992a). However, snowboarding has come to be a means of masculinity construction for its young male participants. Through several social practices, snowboarders can make the practice of riding a board down a mountain into something that conveys their masculine status.

Street Punks, Skaters, and Gangstas

How are meanings about the appropriateness of snowboarding for men or women created? My interviews, content analysis, and observations suggest that male snowboarders engage in social practices that help to construct this emerging sport as a masculine activity. In the following section, I argue that these practices combine to form a masculinity signified by the image of the "street punk."

Appropriation

Male snowboarders and the snowboarding media have appropriated elements of two existing cultural versions of masculinity—the "skater kid" and the "gangsta"—in creating the stereotypical snowboarding image. The skater kid image is borrowed from skateboarding, which has become a major influence on snowboarding in recent years. According to Ben, to be a good snowboarder, you have to have some kind of skateboarding skill too, because like, I'd say 95 percent of the tricks I do—no, 100 percent of the tricks I do are skateboard related, and I think that if you don't skate, it's going to be really hard for you.

By stressing that a skateboarding background is an essential requirement for success in snowboarding, male participants connect snowboarding to an almost exclusively male sport and diminish women's belief that they can be as successful (Fize, 1990–1991). Fern stated the following: "I don't know any other women that snowboard . . . I think most of the girls that I know don't have any kind of a skating background, and I didn't either, and it helps you so much. The guys who started skating just like stepped on a board and rode it." In addition, the appropriation of skateboarding style helps male snowboarders construct snowboarding as a tough, street punk activity, as Debbie suggests:

Most snowboarders were skateboarders, or a good percentage in California of snowboarders were skateboarders, and then there are surfers and all that, and that is all male-dominated things. And because it, in California it's kind of a scrappy thing. It's supposedly not a thing that a girl should do.

The term *scrappy* suggests that snowboarding is aggressive and violent; women may appear unfeminine or even be harmed if they try to participate. By appropriating elements of skateboarding, snowboarders can affiliate with a male-dominated sport and construct snowboarding as "not a thing that a girl should do."

Snowboarders also co-opt elements of another masculinity—that of the urban "gangsta." Ben reported that "snowboarders buy all of this stuff that makes them look like a gangsta even though they're not." In discussing conflict between snowboarders and skiers, Eric said: "I guess in a way it's like a gang, the snowboarders and the skiers. You know, skiers get in a fight and some other skiers will help them and boarders' friends help them." The gangsta is popularly represented as a fearless, aggressive, and heterosexual man. Gangsta rap, one medium through which the gangsta image is transmitted, has been criticized by feminist groups for its sexist lyrics, which degrade and objectify women (Alston, 1994; Holland, 1994; but see hooks, 1994a, for a discussion of the ways in which this music reflects the values of the dominant white culture).

The snowboarding media blatantly appropriates the gangsta image. One ad describes a trip to the mountain as "another day in da hood" when snowboarders "go hike with da boyz" ("Fifty One Fifty," 1994). A *Snowboarder* feature article compares snowboarders to urban gangstas:

It's weird to note that those things society immediately fears invariably become mainstream. Rap is no longer a fad, it is an integral part of American youth culture. The jib style is no longer an isolated phenomenon; ski areas build entire structures just for this kind of expression session. The concept of a "posse" or extended informal family bonding together for protection and a sense of belonging runs through both inner-city dwellers and snowboarders. (Graves, 1994, p. 79)

This passage constructs snowboarding as a parallel to gangsta culture, yet it also suggests that snowboarders' forms of "expression" may be more legitimate than those of gangstas. The term *posse* conjures the image of white men gathering to protect the domain of "civilized" society from outlaws (e.g., Native Americans displaced from the land or black men accused of raping white women), in fascinating contrast to the illegitimate and criminal acts of "gangstas." Yet, by drawing on the gangsta image, boarders construct the mountain as dangerous and suggest that snowboarding requires courage and strength.

In cultural imagery, both the "skater kid" and the "gangsta" are young male delinquents who vandalize, tag, and loiter on city streets. By appropriating these images, snowboarders can construct the practice of riding down the mountain as a 'street punk' activity. Ben said that

snowboarders go a different way, they zigzag across the mountain looking for things like obstacles, they ride on railings and wood and whatever, you know, rocks. Things that skiers would traditionally scorn because it ruins your equipment. But snowboarders don't care because they're mostly punks from the street.

This co-optation helps male snowboarders construct their sport as masculine practice. Both skateboarding and gangs are largely homosocial male environments, in which women are discouraged or prevented from full participation. Through their identification with the "street punk" image of skateboarders and gangstas, snowboarders can make the practice of snowboarding appear more masculine and "scrappy"—an aggressive activity in which women should not participate.

Street-Punk Style

In many youth subcultures, "style [is] the message and the means of expression" (Fox, 1987, p. 345). Style becomes a means of distinguishing group membership, declaring agreement with a belief system, and distinguishing the "posers" from the "pro's" (Donnelly and Young, 1988; Fox, 1987; Lowney, 1995). Snowboarders exhibit street-punk style through their appearance and social interaction. The respondents described this interactional style as exhibiting "attitude," a buzzword in the snowboarding media at the time the interviews were conducted. Fern said that "the attitudes seem to be a lot worse now. [I: What's the attitude?] I don't care about anybody, get out of my way. Indifferent and aggressive I'd say. Self-absorbed, that's a good word." Ben also emphasized that the snowboarding "attitude" is aggressive and superior:

> The snowboard attitude is, it's pretty bad kind of, you know, it is bad. Most people have this attitude like "I'm better than you," as in "you" in general. As in "you suck, look at you, you don't know how to ride."

The snowboarding "attitude" conforms closely to the traditional masculine ideals of aggression, stoicism, and confidence. By acting indifferent and superior, male boarders attempt to convey that they can "do it better" than others on the mountain.

Clothing constitutes an important symbolic marker of membership in the snowboarding "posse." Respondents agreed that the snowboarding "look" combines elements of skater and gangsta style. According to Ben, the snowboarding look is "like a street punk, like a skater, baggy jeans, wallet chains." Irving described the origins of the street punk image:

> There's so many clothes now that are baggy and that's the look that people are trying to fit into. And whether it's, you know, people wanting to be like gangstas or people wanting to be like skateboarders, and whoever wants to claim that they had it first, that's where everybody's trying to get into.

Yet, beyond distinguishing snowboarders from skiers or other sporting participants, the street punk style identifies snowboarding as a masculine activity. By wearing oversized clothing, snowboarders can look like skaters and/or gangsta's—like men who are part of an exclusively male group. In addi-

tion, male boarders exhibit stoicism and strength when they wear clothing that does not protect them from the snow and cold temperatures. Holly noted that male riders obtain street punk style at the expense of comfort:

> [I: Is there a specific look that goes with snowboarding?] Definitely like flannels and . . . See, I think snowboarders are crazy. I see snowboarders up there who are wearing pants that sag down to their knees and flannels that are just covered in snow. . . . I just look at them and think it's so stupid, they care more about the way they look than if they are freezing their butt off.

Although she has been riding for 5 years, Holly refers to snowboarders as "they" rather than "we." She wears warmer clothing when riding but adheres to the snowboarding style elsewhere. When asked whether her description was a stereotype for a male snowboarder, she replied, "yeah, and girls kind of go along with it. Because if you look in my closet, I probably own about 20 flannels." This suggests that although she can copy the street punk image, Holly does not perceive herself as having an active role in its construction. None of the female respondents reported that they wore the baggy, oversized pants that were the style at the time the interviews were conducted. By adopting the clothing style of skater kids and gangstas—a style most women do not wear—male boarders can look like they are part of an exclusively male group of aggressive, indifferent street punks.

Violence and Aggression

The street punk snowboarder likes danger, risk taking, and aggression according to many respondents. Four of the male snowboarders mentioned participating in, or observing, fights while snowboarding. One particularly colorful recollection from Eric typifies other fights male snowboarders described:

> [I: Tell me about the fights you just had.] As a matter of fact, there was one last night. We were about to get in the lift lines, and some skiers came and ran over all our boards. And they didn't say anything, you know, there wouldn't have been a problem if they would have said, "Hey, I'm sorry about that." My brother, my brother and I are both Cuban and we have not very good temperaments, it's a

Cuban trait, we're, "Hey man, you ran over our boards, bro, that's not really cool." He came up to us with an attitude about it, "Well, you guys shouldn't have been standing [there] . . ." And my brother has no patience, none. We went off on the guy. We were smart though, we made sure he took the first swing. And then about five of his friends jumped me and my brother and then all my friends came down the mountain. . . . It just turned into a big brawl.

Violence, threats, and intimidation are common within snowboarding according to the male snowboarders interviewed. Ben reported his experience with a snowboarder with "attitude":

One guy threatened me from the lift line, from the actual lift. There was a snow-blower and I did a trick over it, didn't touch it or anything, and it was fine and I rode away. He's all "do that again and I'll kick your ass."

Historically, violence has been a means of exhibiting masculinity in sport (Messner, 1992b; Smith, 1983). Within street-punk snowboarder culture, as in other sports, violence is glamorized and a means of gaining status and prestige. The conflicts described by the respondents were often caused by perceived challenges to status. The media reinforce this image; a recent magazine article published a list of snowboarders who had been thrown out of a nightclub in a popular snowboarding resort, stating that "invariably, it seems, where there is drink, snowboarders, and dance, there will also be altercations" (Galbraith, 1994, p. 24).

Emphasized Heterosexuality

Along with many mainstream sport participants, male snowboarders construct masculinity through asserting heterosexuality and subordinating homosexuality (Curry, 1991; Messner, 1992a; Pronger, 1990). Ben said that "skiers are fags" when asked how snowboarding differs from skiing, and he described snowboarding style as "wearing dark clothes to try to look, to offset skiers, don't be a pretty boy." As Eric put it, "I ain't down with no pink type clothing." In response to the question of why snowboarding is not an Olympic sport, a magazine columnist stated that it was probably because a snowboarder would steal the torch and chase the male figure skaters around with it (SBIA Minister,

1994b). Heterosexuality is constructed antonymously—as the absence of homosexuality (Sedgwick, 1990). To assert their heterosexual masculinity, boarders imply that other sports are "gay."

Furthermore, women who excel in snowboarding may be called lesbians, as "real" (e.g., heterosexual) women cannot expect to be as good as men. Ben described the sanctions against talented female snowboarders: "Obviously, a woman's not going to really power as high as a man. If they do look all burly and buff like a man, then people say they're a lesbian." However, several male respondents said that they would like to form a relationship with a female snowboarder. When asked if he ever rode with women, Chris said that "someday I'd like to meet somebody up there who snowboards to hang out with." Ben, who was teaching his girlfriend to snowboard at the time of the interview, said that he encouraged his girlfriend to learn: "I got her a board and everything. She, ah, she expressed a wish to try it. She knew I was super interested and that was the reason she became interested." Adam expressed his disappointment that his current girlfriend did not want to learn and said that he would like to find a girlfriend with whom he can ride. These comments suggest that women are accepted within snowboarding if they do not try to compete with men and if they are involved in a heterosexual relationship with a male snowboarder—in essence, if they reinforce the masculine image of the sport. The objectification of women within the snowboarding media also reinforces heterosexual masculinity (see below). Within snowboarding as in other men's sports, "heterosexual masculinity is collectively constructed through the denigration of homosexuality and femininity as 'not male'" (Messner, 1992a, p. 96).

In contemporary society, the "sporting male" epitomizes the masculine attributes of strength, aggression, speed, and skill (Segal, 1990). Snowboarding adds the element of a deviant subculture to the construction of masculinity within this emerging sport, creating a "street punk" masculinity that connects indifference and image to ideals of strength and skill. Snowboarders do not have the team jersey, the stands full of fans, or the participation in an exclusively male group to evidence their masculine status. Thus, male boarders create a masculine street punk image through copping an attitude, wearing street punk style, emphasizing the violence and danger within snowboarding, and asserting their heterosexuality. These exaggerated social practices provide male snowboarders with an image that sets them apart from skiers and female snowboarders and expresses their masculine difference and superiority.

Not all of the male respondents engaged in all masculinizing practices. The street punk image is an idealized version of masculinity. Yet, because the stereotypical snowboarder is an indifferent, aggressive, masculine "street punk," male boarders can convey their masculinity through snowboarding. Masculinity is embodied in the image of the street punk, and this idealized image legitimizes the notion that male boarders naturally "do it better" than skiers and female riders (see Messner, 1989, p. 79). However, like all cultural constructions of masculinity, this construction of a street punk masculinity within snowboarding is fraught with paradox.

Age, Race, and Social Class

Structures of age, race, and class interact in complex and paradoxical ways with the creation of masculinity within snowboarding. Previous research suggests that race and class may support or constrain men's opportunities to engage in social practices that convey their masculinity (Majors, 1990; Messner, 1989). The majority of snowboarders are young, male, and upper/middle class (TransWorld Publications, 1994). These structural circumstances provide male snowboarders with considerable freedom in developing an image for their sport. As young, white, and affluent men, snowboarders are able to construct a rebellious, aggressive version of masculinity with little fear of experiencing discrimination or retribution.

In attempting to be like "street punks," some male snowboarders and the snowboarding media have rejected the emphasis on professional employment, social responsibility, and personal ambition that characterize middle-class masculinity (Segal, 1990). The gangsta image is associated with young, inner-city, black men who are denied opportunities and resources to gain professional employment. Thus, gangsta culture involves a rejection of middle-class notions that masculinity is linked to corporate or professional success, and instead measures masculinity in terms of aggression and fearlessness. In appropriating the gangsta image, the creators of the snowboarding image similarly reject the connection between masculinity and professional success. In media representations, the snowboarder is presented as a rebel who needs neither material comfort nor professional aspirations. The freedom of snowboarders in contrast to professional men is exalted. For instance, one magazine feature de-

scribed the difference in the day of a corporate man and a snowboarder:

> "Get a real life!" was the comment from some suit on the phone early one deep powder morning. . . . Arriving at my office, to the sight of 3-4 feet of fresh pow [snow], slapping fives with the homies, and waiting for the chairs to begin loading, all of us were forced with the difficult decision of which lines to poach first. Meanwhile that same suit grabbed the boss his first cup of morning coffee and pondered who else he was to brown nose the rest of the day. (Valenzuela, 1993, p. 25)

According to Debbie, the anticorporate image of snowboarding is rebellious: "It's kind of defiant. It's a defiant attitude. It's just against corporations being . . . snowboarders don't want to have to wear a suit and tie." Snowboarders who become sponsored by big corporations risk being labeled "sellouts." One ad pictured an unclothed Ken Barbie doll and the following text: "Some riders are nothing but corporate barbie dolls. Some riders have no balls. Tonawawa. We sell clothes, we don't sell out" (Tona-Wawa, 1994). The ad suggests that to be corporate is to be less masculine, rejecting the link between masculinity and professional success.

Because of their youth and privileged class position, few snowboarders are concerned about presenting the middle-class cultural capital required for professional employment. Unlike older men, they can adopt a street punk image without concern that this will harm their employment opportunities. However, this rejection of middle-class notions of masculinity creates contradictions for snowboarders. Although their privileged class position enables snowboarders to adopt this rebellious masculinity, at the same time it will provide most snowboarders with the opportunity to achieve professional employment in the future. The media may glorify the antiestablishment rebel, but it is not in the interests of most snowboarders to reject the corporate masculinity that sustains the power they may someday possess. Most snowboarders stand to benefit from the dominance of men in high-paying corporate positions. One letter to the editor exemplifies this paradox. A college freshman wrote to the *Snowboarder* advice columnist, questioning the wisdom of staying in school when he would rather be working in the snowboarding industry. He received the following response:

> Finishing college is the best way to get a job in the snowboarding industry. Even I, the Min-

ister, have a college degree. Stay in school and have fun while you can. It's in the snowboarding industry, for sure, but it's still work. (SBIA Minister, 1994a, p. 16)

In this case, the media columnist drops the "anticorporate" image and counsels the snowboarder to pursue a path toward professional employment. Moreover, this passage reveals the paradox of an anticorporate image promoted by the clearly corporate media. The creators of the snowboarding media are generally college-educated corporate men, who do not fit the street punk image.

In addition, street punk masculinity is challenged by ski area operators, skiers, and older snowboarders, as the following letter to the editor in *Snowboarder* demonstrates:

I represent a small, relatively unrecognized group. During the week we can be seen shredding the halls of corporate America. . . . We're the educated, over 30, high-powered, silent snowboarding minority. We are the original snowboard bad-asses. We walk taller, talk louder, spit further, screw longer, drive faster, earn higher, party harder, and recover quicker. . . . Our sport's image has been created by loud-mouthed, disrespectful, lazy, pimple-popping, pre-adolescents. Is it any surprise most resorts dislike snowboarders? . . . Keep up that image you've worked so hard to create, and keep pissing off skiers. Soon you will not be able to snowboard at any resort. As for us, don't worry, we'll always be able to afford to snowboard . . . maybe we'll buy our own resort. (Dondo, 1994, p. 10)

Asserting his greater economic, physical, and sexual power, the author conveys the superiority of his corporate masculinity and challenges snowboarders to compete. As this letter implies, snowboarders do not have the power to construct a rebellious image without consequence. *Snowboarder* magazine published "An Open Letter to Our Readers" due to a growing concern that more and more ski resorts may be closing their lifts to snowboarders:

It seems, my friends, that ski area operators are not happy with us. It seems that many of them are strongly considering the idea of bucking us off their mountains, regardless of our massive numbers and our money. And, it seems, they blame us, the magazines, for encouraging and glorifying your alleged bad attitudes and gutterish life styles. The source

of their contention varies: too much cussing . . . too much attitude . . . too many skiers complaining. (Palladini, 1994, p. 51)

Thus ski resorts, which rely on the business of middle-/upper-class patrons, are threatening to prohibit snowboarding due to the complaints of their regular customers. Ben expressed his concern that "attitude" would lead ski resorts to ban snowboarding:

Hopefully, we don't get kicked off all the mountains, you know, from attitude and from, I guess, riding styles, you know—ruining all the fixtures at resorts, rails and running into skiers and telling them to screw off, fuck off, whatever.

Ski-area operators and skiers challenge the construction of the street punk image, yet they simultaneously provide validation of this construction. Snowboarders invoke the threat of censor by ski-area operators to foster their image as aggressive gangsta outlaws.

However, the idealized street punk image contradicts the real-life situation of most snowboarders. The rejection of middle-class values is inherently contradicted by the actual class status of most snowboarding participants. Snowboarding is an expensive sport that requires extensive equipment, transportation to the mountain, lodging, and access to ski lifts. As he described how to look like a snowboarder, Ben clearly expressed this contradiction:

You go get like Ben Davis, or like Dickies clothing—like baggy, it's really for poor people or like workmen, you know, gas station jackets and shirts . . . if you have a couple hundred bucks you can become like instant snowboarder.

Structures of class and age, then, both support and constrain the construction of a street punk image within snowboarding. The youth and middle-/upper-class status of most boarders provides them with the freedom and resources to construct a rebellious image. However, these structures also constrain male snowboarders' attempts to be like street punks. As young men, snowboarders are challenged by the older ski-area operators and patrons who dislike the aggression and "attitude" associated with the street punk image. Furthermore, the privileged class position of most boarders inherently contradicts their lower-class street punk image.

The co-optation of the "gangsta" image within snowboarding is similarly contradictory. In one respect, this appropriation represents an attempt to gain access to the extreme version of masculinity created by urban black youth. Because the physical practice of snowboarding does not require obvious strength, violence, and aggression, snowboarders must use other practices, such as language, fashion, and "attitude," in creating a masculine identity. Clothing, hairstyles, language, and musical preferences are important topics in the snowboarding media, where there is continuous debate about the appropriate subcultural signifiers of the "snowboarder." Like the African American men who create a "cool pose" masculinity through "unique, expressive and conspicuous styles of demeanor, speech, gesture, clothing, hairstyle, walk, stance, and handshake" (Majors, 1990, p. 111), snowboarders rely on exaggerated and elaborate social practices to exhibit their masculine status.

Yet, taking on a gangsta image has different implications for white, middle-class snowboarders than for the inner-city black youths who created the image. The dominant race and class position of most snowboarders allows them to appropriate gangsta style with little fear that they will experience the discrimination and hostility faced by black youths who adopt this image. Interestingly, both of the African American male snowboarders rejected gangsta style although they recognized its importance within snowboarding. The following exchange with Chris demonstrates a contradiction experienced by an African American snowboarder. In reply to a question about how the typical snowboarder dresses, Chris replied,

> baggy, yeah, baggy. I made a vow to not be baggy. . . . See my look—like when I first got into it—I wanted to go with the Ninja look, you know, all black scuffy—the scuff look. . . . But, I don't have a problem with it. I mean, I can't say that I'm not gonna look that way, because I might wake up one morning and say, "I'm gonna go get me some baggies and go boarding," but I can't see how you could be warm in them.

When asked about the stereotypical snowboarder, Irving responded in a similar fashion:

> The major baggies, let's see, long hair, flannel top. That's the way it is. . . . And you know, me personally, I don't wear the baggy pants as far as the jean look, I go for the board pants with the pads on them, because, I want something that's going to give me protection. And I'm not into the baggy pants hanging down your butt kind of look. You know, I want something that is gonna keep me warm.

Although both boarders define their choice not to be baggy in terms of physical comfort, later in the interview Chris reveals that he does not want to be associated with the baggy image. "[I: So how come you made a vow not to be baggy?] Probably because to me it kind of has that punk attitude, you know, and, well it's like, gossip, that's the only reason." These comments suggest that, for Chris and Irving, adopting gangsta style may have different implications than it does for white snowboarders, who are less likely to experience discrimination or hostility from the predominantly white ski-area operators and patrons. When asked if he had ever experienced discrimination on the mountain, Chris noted that he has been cut off in lift lines or ignored by skiers: "It's mainly skiers. I don't know if it's because of my color or what, but I think it's a combination of that and the board, for the skiers." If he appeared on the mountain in gangsta style, it is likely that skiers may respond negatively; perhaps watching him carefully and steering clear of him on the mountain. Thus, race may constrain the choice of black snowboarders to adopt the current snowboarding look.

The half-Asian and Latino male boarders, Ben and Eric, were less rejecting of the street punk image and said that they did not feel that race mattered in the sport. However, their ethnicity was less visually apparent. Gina, the Mexican/Native American respondent, occupied a minority position within the sport in terms of ethnicity, class, age, gender, and marital status. She clearly rejected the street punk image for herself. "I hate it though—it's just real trendy and it makes me sick. It really does, you know. Because there's a lot of spoiled rich kids out there, you know, and we worked hard to be able to snowboard." As Gina notes, the privileged class and the youth of snowboarders enable the co-optation of street punk masculinity. Moreover, the emphasis on style and trends in the sport makes her participation less enjoyable, and she does not feel involved in the creation of snowboarding style.

However, the privileged class and racial/ethnic status that allows white snowboarders to adopt gangsta style simultaneously contradicts some of the "masculine" elements of the image. Black youths created the gangsta style in response to a context of poverty, discrimination, and inequality (hooks, 1994b). Snowboarding "gangstas" do not face the dangers that are common within the daily lives of inner-city African American gang members and do not perform the acts of violence and aggression that give the gangsta image its extreme masculine status. Within snowboarding, the privilege of white race and middle-class position that allows for this appropriation also calls it into question. Segal (1990) writes that

> the closer we come to uncovering some form of exemplary masculinity, a masculinity which is solid and sure of itself, the clearer it becomes that masculinity is structured through contradiction: the more it asserts itself, the more it calls itself into question. (p. 123)

The more money and effort exerted by snowboarders to create a street punk masculinity, the clearer it becomes that they are not really street punks. This irony was most clearly expressed by John in response to a question about the drawbacks of snowboarding:

> The drawbacks are that you're labeled as an outlaw, you're looked at differently by society. You're looked at as more of a radical, you're not going to get as much respect. . . . [I: Have you ever felt that you're treated differently because of that?] No, not yet, not yet. I've yet to experience that yet.

John suggests that snowboarders are outlaws who face societal discrimination, but his position becomes questionable when he notes that he is not treated as an outlaw. His race and middle-class status provide him with the resources to adopt an outlaw image but also ensure that he will not be treated like a rebel and thus call his image into question.

In sum, the age, race, and class position of most male snowboarders both supports and constrains their ability to construct a street punk image within their sport. As young, middle-class, white men, snowboarders possess the resources to purchase the music, media, clothing, equipment, and other paraphernalia that signify that they are "street punks." They can compare their activities with those associated with gangstas and emphasize that violence and aggression are required in their sport. However, contradictions of race and class are embedded within this appropriation of the street punk gangsta image.

"Girl-Boarders"

Like other cultural constructions of gender, street punk masculinity is formed in relation to various idealized and subordinated masculinities within U.S. culture. The indifferent "skater kid," the aggressive "gangsta," and competitive "sporting man" are appropriated as masculine ideals, whereas the corporate "suit" and the "pretty boy" skier are rejected versions of masculinity. Yet, as Connell (1987) contends, constructions of masculinity must also be formed in relation to women. The successful construction of a street punk masculinity depends in part on how snowboarding handles the presence of "girl-snowboarders."

Women's entry into organized sports during the past century has been controlled and regulated by physical educators and sports promoters, who developed different rules, clothing, and time and spatial dimensions for women's sports than for men's sports (Cahn, 1990). These practices, as Cahn (1990) suggests, "preserved the masculine identity of sport and made women's continued presence a marginal and contradictory phenomenon" (p. 395). Within snowboarding, such overt control strategies are less available due to the unorganized, individual nature of the sport. Male snowboarders, however, use several strategies to define the acceptable and appropriate ways of being a "girl-snowboarder." Within snowboarding as in other sports, female snowboarders are constructed as the "other" against which masculinity is defined. The data suggest that male snowboarders and the snowboarding media rely on two general strategies to differentiate female boarders and retain the sport's masculine image: (a) sexualization and (b) devaluation.

(Hetero) Sexualizing Female Riders

As defined by male riders and the media, the most legitimate place for women within snowboarding is with a man. In media features of snowboarding trips, if a woman is present, the text often notes that she is the heterosexual partner of a male rider, even is she is featured as a snowboarder (e.g., England, 1994; Kelly, 1994; Zellers, 1994). One letter to the editor succinctly described the "appropriate" place of female riders: "A lot of men assume that any girl on a board is either: A: looking for a guy, B: there because her guy is there, or C: trying to be 'one of the guys!'" (Blum, 1994, p. 9). As this boarder notes, if women are not viewed as snowboarding due to heterosexual interests, they are constructed as women who want to be men. My observations of snowboarders and the interview data suggest that women often learn to snowboard from a male partner. On the mountain, the most commonly observed patterns were women riding in small groups or pairs and larger groups of male riders with a single woman. Thus, female snowboarders are defined as being there for men, and those who resist this construction risk being labeled unfeminine or lesbian.

Moreover, the snowboarding media depicts female riders (and women generally) in a sexualized manner. Several female boarders criticized the objectification of women in snowboarding films and magazines. According to Debbie,

> The ads are very condescending, not condescending but very sexist. [I: How so?] Just really fleshy. Portraying women as not so concerned with snowboarding. . . . You know, there's this one ad I thought was interesting; it was a really small ad advertising woman snowboard wear, like girls snowboard wear . . . but it has got the picture of the girl and she doesn't have a shirt on and she's looking over her shoulder . . . and I'm like, this is made for women? . . . I don't care if she has a big chest. At least half the ads have got girls in them draping themselves over snowboards.

The advertisements of one snowboarding company place the company name, "Joyride," and text such as "experience" over photos of women in sexually suggestive poses, sometimes with snowboards representing a phallus (Joyride, 1994). The graphic on the top of a 1993 snowboard (on which the snowboarder stands) pictures a woman standing in a suggestive pose, wearing only a garter and high heels. These ads suggest that women should be "ridden" upon, in both a literal and a sexual sense.

When female snowboarders are featured in the magazines, they are often sexualized. Debbie described one feature: "They had all these, they had four or five girl snowboarders. They were all sponsored, and it was equal amounts of them doing all these Charlie's Angels poses in all these funky clothes and then of them snowboarding." In this case, female snowboarders were pictured in sexualized poses as often as in action shots. Through privileging sexualized images of women and suppressing images of women as active and talented riders, the snowboarding media emphasizes gender difference, a difference that helps to reproduce the masculine image of snowboarding (Cohen, 1993; Duncan, 1990).

Devaluating Female Riders

In addition to emphasizing women's difference from male boarders as heterosexual objects, the masculinization of snowboarding involves constructing female riders as "naturally" weaker and less skillful than men. Male boarders use several strategies to suggest that women are essentially different from men. First, in both the media and in the interviews, the neutral "snowboarder" is male, whereas women are called "girl-snowboarders." Such gender marking serves to infantilize women and distinguish them as "other," thus supporting the construction of snowboarding as a masculine practice (Messner, Duncan, and Jensen, 1993; Richardson, 1987). In addition, female boarders receive less media attention than male riders. Fern stated that the magazines rarely show women snowboarding:

> Like you look at any snowboarding mag and there are hardly any pictures of women and the pictures you do get they are not doing anything. . . . I asked [a top female snowboarder] about why you never see any pictures of women and she said because the mags won't print them. She said she actually took pictures herself and would submit them to mags but they would just never show up.

Male boarders sometimes overtly devalue women. In a magazine interview, an "up-and-coming" rider said that he was sorry he "ever missed a day of riding to hang out with a girl" (Wright, 1993, p. 36). Fern recalled hearing comments such as "pretty good for a chick" from male riders on the mountain. Each of these practices devalues female snowboarders and helps to maintain male snowboarders' positions as different and superior.

The devaluation of female boarders extends into the few organized aspects of snowboarding. Perhaps the most telling example of gender construction within snowboarding came from Holly's description of her attempt to compete in a snowboarding competition:

> [I: What were the competitions like that you were in?] Oh, they were so small, it's hard for me to even say I really competed in them. . . . I didn't do very well because there were no other girl snowboarders so they just put me in with the skiers, and so. [I: Instead of the guy snowboarders?] They put me with just the girl category with the skiers. So, I mean, I didn't place or anything because the skiers

went down first. [I: So you were competing against the skiers?] Right, because there were enough guys for a guys snowboard competition, but since I was a girl they just wanted to put me in with the girls rather than the guys.

Holly's story illuminates a crucial masculinizing strategy within sport. Through separating Holly from the male boarders, the competition organizers emphasized Holly's "difference," constructing her as "other" on the basis of her sex. The competition became a gendered practice in which the male competitors were assumed to "do it better" than Holly and could participate in an exclusively male event. West and Zimmerman (1987) note that "once differences have been constructed, they are used to reinforce the essentialness of gender" (p. 137). Thus, when female riders are not given equal attention and sponsorship support within snowboarding, it is because they are "naturally" the weaker riders. A snowboarding filmmaker's comments in response to criticism that his films exclude female riders exemplify this process: "Women have not achieved the same level as men in snowboarding due to body structure, mental attitude, etc." (Dugan, 1993, p. 10). The filmmaker justifies his exclusion of women by essentializing a gender difference that is first constructed through practices of separation and exclusion. Holly's story suggests that, as in other sports, greater organization in snowboarding will lead to gender separation.

Female snowboarders sometimes reinforce the masculine construction of snowboarding through their acceptance and support of gender differences. Holly did not find it problematic that she was not allowed to compete against male snowboarders: "I think I would have rather been with the girls just because I knew the guys would just blow me out of the water anyway." Several of the female snowboarders interviewed supported the construction of snowboarding as a masculine domain. Holly described her perception of a magazine feature on female riders who are sponsored by snowboarding companies:

I think anybody can be that good if they decide, practice with guys, because guys will push them. And I, when I was sitting there reading it, I was sitting there thinking "I bet each one of those girls rides with a guy"—you know—that's really good.

This view of male riders as more aggressive and skillful snowboarders was common in interviews with both male and female riders. Debbie stated that "I would go to a guy to talk about snowboarding before I'd go to a girl. Because you think that more guys do it and more guys know about it." This theme was repeated in a letter to an editor from a woman arguing that the media

will probably always be that way [sexist]. I mean, I know I can learn easier by watching a guy boarder! My advice: it does absolutely no good to sit and complain, go out and show the guys on the snow, and if you can rip it hard in a bikini, better luck to ya! (Sobeteer, 1993, p. 13)

Some female snowboarders, then, participate in their domination by supporting gender difference. These women feel privileged by their access to male power, through which they can gain some of the status of this masculinity (Benjamin, 1988). This is sometimes done through constructing differences between women: Several female snowboarders stated that only some women can snowboard, women who, like themselves, are able to handle the pain and difficulty of learning to ride. Debbie expressed her desire that her female friends learn to snowboard but stated that "there's a certain type of girl I'd want to take. Like, they couldn't be a sissy at all." Thus, only some women are deserving of participation in this masculine sport. The presence of "girl-snowboarders," then, in some ways facilitates the construction of snowboarding's streetpunk masculinity. However, many women (and some men) also resist this gendered construction.

Because gender is ideology that is formed, shaped, and reinforced through innumerable social institutions and cultural practices, it can also be challenged, resisted, and changed (Bordo, 1993). Currently, female snowboarders are forcing the media to recognize gender as an issue. Women are writing letters to magazine editors questioning the lack of coverage on female boarders and the objectification of women in the magazines and films. Two of the female snowboarders interviewed, Fern and Debbie, expressed indignation about the lack of media representation for female riders.

Female snowboarders have also begun to form women's snowboard camps, creating spaces where women can come together to learn in an environment free from objectification and devaluation. In a magazine article describing five women's snowboard camps, the author described her experience: "We never would've [sic] ridden like we did without the confidence we'd developed from riding together. With the support of other women, old inhibitions faded fast" (Gasperini, 1994, p. 28). The creation of camps for women challenges the masculine image of the sport and validates female riders' identities as snowboarders, which may aid women in confronting sexism when they ride in other settings.

Moreover, the practices used to construct female riders as "other" contain inherent contradictions. Each of the respondents offered some support for the notion that male boarders are "naturally" better riders, but this construction was also resisted in some ways in all of the interviews. For example, many respondents expressed uncertainty when asked whether male and female riders should compete against each other in snowboard competitions. Eric expressed his contradictory position:

[I: Do you think that male and female riders should compete against each other?] I don't know really. I think that because males usually have the stronger bodies, you know, I think it would be kind of unfair. You know if you're stronger you're going to be able to go higher and a bit farther and that gives women the disadvantage. But I don't know, I've seen some women who can just shred guys.

Fern also expressed both support and resistance to the gendered construction of snowboarding within the same response:

I've often thought it would be really interesting if you took a woman and disguised her as a man and had her compete and see what would happen. And I wish I could get good because I would shave my hair and do it. And I wonder what you would find, because in all the other sports men have stronger times and I don't know, but I think in snowboarding it would be closer. But I do think there's like a mental edge that men have with aggression because women do not seem to be as aggressive and I think it has to do with the risk taking. You look at that stuff, the airs [jumps] and things like that. I think there is—it's almost intangible—but men seem to have an edge.

Within this passage, Fern moves from the position that women are not given an equal chance to compete to one of explaining reasons for gender differences in snowboarding skill. The contradiction inherent within the gendered structure is revealed; women are not given equal opportunity to compete

so we do not know if they are different, yet women must be different in some way because they are not allowed to compete.

Conclusions

This research suggests that there are different ways of constructing gender within the institution of sport, resulting in many sport masculinities. Sport is often depicted as an institution that creates and maintains male dominance, but the construction of gender differs greatly in the various activities that constitute sport. Snowboarding is developing in a different social and historical context than did organized men's sports, and these contextual differences are salient to the particular ways in which it becomes gendered. The unorganized, individual practice of snowboarding and a context of greater female sport participation have inhibited the ability of male snowboarders to define the sport as an exclusively male practice. Because snowboarding does not involve the sex-segregated teams, regulated structure, and exclusive participation policies of organized sports, male snowboarders must rely on different practices in developing a masculine image than those used in organized sports. To make snowboarding a practice that endows its participants with a masculine status, snowboarders use a variety of exaggerated social practices to create a masculinity symbolized by the "street punk." Through adopting the street punk style, copping an aggressive and superior attitude, emphasizing the violence and danger of their sport, and stressing their heterosexuality, male snowboarders and the snowboarding media attempt to construct snowboarding as a masculine practice.

This street punk masculinity must be formed in relation to other cultural versions of masculinity and to women (Connell, 1987). Snowboarding's version of masculinity is formed in relation to a variety of images of masculinity—the corporate "suit," the "fag" skier, the "sporting man," the "skater-kid" and the "gangsta"—and in relation to the "girl-boarder." The age, race, and class position of most snowboarders influences which masculine images are co-opted and which are rejected. As young, privileged, white males, snowboarders possess the financial and social resources to appropriate extreme versions of masculinity, such as the "gangsta" masculinity, without fear of retribution or discrimination. They have the economic resources to purchase cultural signifiers of the image such as clothing, music, and equipment. They can define snowboarding as aggressive and violent through references to the danger and physical confrontations that they produce through their activities on the mountain. They can construct female riders as "other" through processes of objectification and devaluation.

Yet, as with other cultural constructions of masculinity, this attempt to link snowboarding to the street-punk image is continually resisted. The rebellious construction is challenged by the ski-area owners and predominantly middle-/upper-class skiers, who have the power to prohibit snowboarding at the resorts if riders do not conform to their rules. Female snowboarders also resist this gendering of their sport, through their presence as well as their voices, which increasingly challenge the dominance of male riders. Furthermore, contradictions between the street punk masculine image created by snowboarders and the actual class, race, and gender of the participants continuously call this masculinity into question.

These findings suggest that, like organized sports, some emerging sports are constructed in ways that reinforce notions of gender difference and masculine hegemony. Snowboarders rely on different practices in creating masculinity than those that appear in organized sports, yet these social practices also serve to legitimize male dominance. The use of extreme strategies to masculinize snowboarding demonstrates the resilience and strength of young men's need to construct a masculine identity. However, gender is a symbolic construct that becomes paradoxical when translated into real-life practices. Sports that take on an idealized gendered form, such as snowboarding, must continually work to perpetuate this image in the face of resistance.

Acknowledgments

Paul Sterling and Christine Williams provided assistance throughout the project, and I am especially grateful for their suggestions. I would like to thank Kirsten Dellinger, Jeffrey Jackson, Livia Pohlman, Tracey Steele, and Debra Umberson for their comments on an earlier draft of this article.

References

Alston, W. (1994). NOW dis's gangsta rap. *National NOW Times*, **26**(3),1–2.

Battle of the piste. (1993, April 24). *Economist*, p. 96.

Benjamin, J. (1988). *The bonds of love: Psychoanalysis, feminism, and the problem of domination*. New York: Pantheon.

Blum, M. (1994, August). PC girl: Take one (letter to the editor). *Snowboarder*, p. 9.

Bordo, S. (1993). *Unbearable weight: Feminism, western culture, and the body*. Berkeley, CA: University of California Press.

Cahn, S.K. (1990). *Coming on strong: Gender and sexuality in women's sport, 1900–1960*. Ann Arbor, MI: University Microfilms International.

Cohen, G.L. (1993). Media portrayal of the female athlete. In G.L. Cohen (Ed.), *Women in sport: Issues and controversies* (pp. 171–184). Newbury Park, CA: Sage.

Collins, P.H. (1991). *Black feminist thought: Knowledge, consciousness and the politics of empowerment*. New York: Routledge.

Connell, R.W. (1987). *Gender and power: Society, the person and sexual politics*. Stanford, CA: Stanford University Press.

Connell, R.W. (1990). An iron man: The body and some contradictions of hegemonic masculinity. In M.A. Messner and D.F. Sabo (Eds.), *Sport, men and the gender order: Critical feminist perspectives* (pp. 83–95). Champaign, IL: Human Kinetics Books.

Curry, T. (1991). Fraternal bonding in the locker room: A profeminist analysis of talk about competition and women. *Sociology of Sport Journal*, **8**, 119–135.

Dondo. (1994, Summer). Bonfire of vanity (letter to the editor). *Snowboarder*, p. 10.

Donnelly, P., and Young, K. (1988). The construction and confirmation of identity in sport subcultures. *Sociology of Sport Journal*, **5**, 223–240.

Dugan, J. (1993, Spring). Response to letter to the editor. *Snowboarder*, p. 10.

Duncan, M.C. (1990). Sports photographs and sexual difference: Images of women and men in the 1984 and 1988 Olympic Games. *Sociology of Sport Journal*, **7**, 22–43.

England, D. (1994, November). 81: Syracuse to Knoxville. *Snowboarder*, pp. 61–76.

Fifty one fifty. (1994, November). Advertisement. *Snowboarder*, p. 20.

Fize, M. (1990–1991). Ce monde où l'on skate. *Revue de L'Institut de Sociologie*, pp. 259–278.

Fox, K.J. (1987). Real punks and pretenders: The social organization of a counterculture. *Journal of Contemporary Ethnography*, **16**(3), 344–370.

Galbraith, J. (1994, January). Club get out, eh? *Snowboarder*, p. 24.

Gasperini, K. (1994, Spring). No boys allowed. *Snowboarder*, p. 28.

Graves, T. (1994, January). Midwest. *Snowboarder*, p. 79.

Hall, A. (1985). How should we theorize sport in a capitalist patriarchy? *International Review for the Sociology of Sport*, **20**, 109–116.

Hargreaves, J. (1986). Where's the virtue? Where's the grace? A discussion of the social production of gender relations in and through sport. *Theory, Culture and Society*, **3**, 109–121.

Holland, B. (1994). Gangsta rap protesters stage second demonstration at D.C. Sam Goody (National Political Congress of Black Women). *Billboard*, **106**, 5–6.

hooks, b. (1989). *Talking back: Thinking feminist, thinking Black*. Boston: South End.

hooks, b. (1994a). *Outlaw culture: Resisting representations*. New York: Routledge.

hooks, b. (1994b). The Ice opinion: Who gives a fuck? (book review). *Artforum*, **32**, 57–59.

Joyride. (1994, September). Advertisement. *Snowboarder*, p. 39.

Kelly, J. (1994, Spring). Japan. *Snowboarder*, p. 118–124.

Klein, A. (1990). Little big man: Hustling, gender narcissism, and bodybuilding subculture. In M.A. Messner and D.F. Sabo (Eds.), *Sport, men, and the gender order: Critical feminist perspectives* (pp. 127–139). Champaign, IL: Human Kinetics Books.

A look inside *Snowboarder* ('94 Media Kit). (1994). *Snowboarder Magazine*. San Juan Capistrano, CA: Snowboarder Magazine.

Lowney, K.S. (1995). Teenage satanism as oppositional youth culture. *Journal of Contemporary Ethnography*, 23(4), 453–484.

Majors, R. (1990). Cool pose: Black masculinity and sports. In M.A. Messner and D.F. Sabo (Eds.), *Sport, men and the gender order: Critical feminist perspectives* (pp. 109–114). Champaign, IL: Human Kinetics Books.

Messerschmidt, J.W. (1993). *Masculinities and crime: Critique and reconceptualization of theory*. Lanham, NY: Rowman and Littlefield.

Messner, M.A. (1989). Masculinities and athletic careers. *Gender and Society*, **3**, 71–88.

Messner, M.A. (1992a). *Power at play: Sports and the problem of masculinity*. Boston: Beacon.

Messner, M.A. (1992b). When bodies are weapons: Masculinity and violence in sport. *International Review for the Sociology of Sport*, **25**, 203–220.

Messner, M., Duncan, M.C., and Jensen, K. (1993). Separating the men from the girls: The gendered language of televised sports. *Gender and Society*, **7**, 121–137.

Oglesby, C. (1989). Women and sport. In J.H. Goldstein (Ed.), *Sports, games and play: Social and psychological viewpoints* (pp. 124–145). Hillsdale, NJ: Lawrence Erlbaum.

Palladini, D. (1994, Holiday). An open letter to our readers. *Snowboarder*, p. 51.

Pronger, B. (1990). *The arena of masculinity: Sports, homosexuality and the meaning of sex*. New York: St. Martin's.

Richardson, L. (1987). *The dynamics of sex and gender: A sociological perspective*. New York: Harper and Row.

Sabo, D. (1985). Sport, patriarchy and male identity: New questions about men and sport. *Arena Review*, **9**, 1–30.

Sabo, D., and Messner, M. (1993). Whose body is this? Women's sports and sexual politics. In G.L. Cohen (Ed.), *Women in sport: Issues and controversies* (pp. 15–23). Newbury Park, CA: Sage.

SBIA Minister. (1994a, Spring). Response to letter. *Snowboarder*, p. 16.

SBIA Minister. (1994b, October). Response to letter. *Snowboarder*, p. 22.

Sedgwick, E.K. (1990). *Epistemology of the closet*. Berkeley, CA: University of California Press.

Segal, L. (1990). *Slow motion: Changing masculinities, changing men*. New Brunswick, NJ: Rutgers University Press.

Smith, M. (1983). *Violence and sport*. Toronto: Butterworths.

Sobeteer, K. (1993, September). One more PC girl (letter to the editor). *Snowboarder*, p. 13.

Tona-Wawa. (1994). Advertisement. *Transworld Snowboarding*, **7**, 12.

TransWorld Publications. (1994). *Four year comparative reader survey: 1991 through 1994*. Oceanside, CA: TransWorld Publications Research.

Valenzuela, I.J. (1993). Get a real life! *Choice*, **1**, 25.

Wacquant, L.J.D. (1995). A body too big to feel. *Masculinities*, **2**(1), 78–86.

West, C., and Zimmerman, D.H. (1987). Doing gender. *Gender and Society*, **1**, 125–151.

Whitson, D. (1990). Sport in the social construction of masculinity. In M.A. Messner and D.F. Sabo (Eds.), *Sport, men and the gender order. Critical feminist perspectives* (pp. 19–29). Champaign, IL: Human Kinetics Books.

Wright, A. (1993, October). Next. *Snowboarder*, p. 36.

Young, K., and White, P. (1995). Sport, physical danger, and injury: The experiences of elite women athletes. *Journal of Sport and Social Issues*, **19**(1), 45–61.

Zellers, J. (1994, January). The brucemeister's Alaska. *Snowboarder*, pp. 94–100.

Tender Machos: Masculine Contrasts in the Mexican Baseball League

Alan M. Klein

This study examines the social and cross-cultural aspects of masculinity through an ethnographic assessment of a Mexican League baseball team. The institution and meaning of "machismo" are examined along three indices of emotion: expression of vulnerability and hurt, reactions to children, and expression of physicality. The view widely held by North Americans that Latino and Latin American men are one-dimensional machos is critiqued. It is argued that, rather than comprising a single category, machismo exists along a continuum of masculinity from more to less macho. Cross-cultural comparisons of masculinity between Mexican and Anglo baseball players were also observed, with Mexican players shown as more capable of exhibiting "tender" emotions than their North American teammates. Finally, the study of emotions is shown to also have social consequences for nationalism.

For two years, 1993 to 1994, a Mexican League team, The Owls of the Two Laredos, was the subject of an ethnographic and historical study that sought to explore the way in which nationalism is constructed on the Texas-Mexican border (Klein, in press). This team is binational, consisting of a social core of players, the majority of whom are Mexican, along with contingents of North American players, called *importados* or "imports." This setting is ideal for cross-cultural and cross-national comparisons. In working up the ethnography, one of the compari-

sons observed had to do with the ability to express gentler emotions. Despite widespread perceptions of Mexican players as *machos*, their ability to verbalize and express emotions that the typical North American athlete finds difficult was noted. Differences between these two groups of players were expressed at a variety of levels, but the subject studied here involves emotional differences that underwrite masculinity.

Making Sense of Machismo

Latino and Latin American men have long been characterized as machos. The term *machismo* has come under continuous scrutiny since the early 1980s, but Octavio Paz began the dialogue 20 years earlier. He defined machismo dramatically, as male aggression: "There are two possibilities in life for the Mexican macho. He either inflicts actions implied by 'chingar' (Spanish infinitive: to fuck) or he suffers them himself" (1962, p. 77). After Paz, most definitions of machismo are toned down, yet they continue to engage in rhetoric centering on the male need to dominate and control through sexuality, fighting, and other forms of competitive behavior. A whole range of related behavior such as joking or posturing (e.g., Limón, 1989; Mirandé, 1988) has also been shown to operate along lines of male aggression to the point where one can, following Lancaster (1992), clearly point to machismo as a full-fledged societal institution.

Reprinted from Klein, 1995.

Most often seen as domination of women, machismo runs the gamut from simple monopolizing of all marital and familial decision making, to regularized marital infidelity, to abuse of women (Lancaster, 1992). Likewise there is a strong cultural component that drives men to prove themselves against other men (Limón, 1994). Acceptable forms include, but are not limited to, competition of a social, political, or linguistic nature (Brandes, 1980; Gutmann, 1994b). In this view of machismo there is no room for reason, softness, compromise, or subordination.

The writings of Paz (1962), Ramos (1962), and Peñalosa (1968) contain an implied critique of machismo, but these works have also inadvertently reinforced negative views of Mexican men long held by segments of North American Anglos and social scientists. According to this view, the Mexican macho, and by extension all Latin American men, are forever aggressively posturing, irresponsible to family, philandering to a fault, and abusive of women and substances (e.g., Madsen, 1973). Whether perceived as completely involved in this gender role, or as a reaction to lack of power, machos become, according to this view, negative characters. These masculine profiles fit quite neatly with views of Mexicans held by racist segments of the population at large.

Beginning in the 1970s, Chicano(a) scholars launched a series of studies and critiques against what they asserted was an ethnocentric depiction of Latino/Latin American men as machos. While differences between Mexican and Chicano men exist, machismo is shared. Care was taken by Baca Zinn (1975, 1982) to distinguish between cultural notions of machismo that can act as magnifiers of behavior and structural relations that more directly bear on actual behavior. The Chicano community Baca Zinn studied, for instance, was shown to distinguish between cultural ideals of machismo and structural relations between men and women in the family. The relations studied evinced a greater degree of egalitarianism than one might presume based on widely disseminated cultural assertions about Latino machismo.[1] In these studies egalitarian relations are pronounced: Fathers and husbands are responsible, sober, and caring (Mirandé, 1988).

While there are times when Latinos (Hispanic-Americans such as Chicanos) and Latin Americans are fused in analyzing machismo, it is important, nevertheless, to distinguish between them when discussing the range of machismo. Matthew Gutmann, an Anglo anthropologist (hence not part of the Chicano challenge), studied working-class men in a Mexico City neighborhood. He found that Mexican institutions are undergoing change, some of which have fostered a decline in importance of traditional machismo (1994a). A goodly number of the Mexican men studied seemed to eschew traditional machismo and its opposite (*mandilónes:* female-dominated men). "Ni macho, ni mandilón [neither macho nor mandilón]" they declared, as they searched for a new identity. As a function of the increased necessity for women to work, this "third" category lends credence to works like Baca Zinn's (1975, 1982). Still others in the colonia Gutmann studied continued to hold onto traditional views of machismo, underwriting the contested nature of Mexican male identity rather than one-dimensional stereotypes (Gutmann 1994b).

Relevant Sport Studies of Masculinity

Sport sociologists have addressed issues of machismo primarily through critiques of masculinity and hypermasculinity in athletes, and almost exclusively in Western society. While sport sociologists have arrived a bit late to the debate on machismo's form and function, an argument can nevertheless be made that sport sociologists, who specialize in the study of masculinity, have been at the vanguard of the sociology of masculinity studies. Certainly, the substantial efforts of Sabo (1985, 1986), Sabo and Runfola (1980), Messner (1985, 1992), and Messner and Sabo (1991) place them in the company of pioneers in the field. Other sport sociologists have contributed to the study of sport and masculinity as well (e.g., Curry, 1991; Donnelly and Young, 1985; Elias and Dunning, 1986; Fine, 1987; Foley, 1990; Klein, 1993; Pronger, 1991).

By and large these views of the American male athlete are critical, showing him shooting himself in the proverbial foot. The American male's limited range of acceptable gender behavior and attitudes hamper his ability to promote gender security, as well as attempts to live a more rewarding life. That men sicken and die more readily than women has been linked, among other things, to male views of his body and to his ability to respond to illness and stress (see Messner and Kimmel, 1989). This is mute testimony to how men in pursuit of masculinity often wind up harming or killing themselves. Kidd (1991) summarized some of these shortcomings as the inability of males to express feelings of vulnerability or concern for others. Sabo (1986) pointed up male inability to admit to physical injury (a kind of vulnerability). Others (Connell, 1991; Klein, 1993) have discussed the homophobically fueled inability except through highly visible macho rituals—of men to show physical affection to each other. The present study seeks to further these efforts.

Sociology of Emotions

It is in the confluence of sport sociology and masculine behavior that we find an area which has to date been poorly studied. I refer to the sociology of emotions, an area of study which most of us traverse but few pay formal attention to. While this branch of sociology has its own set of issues and controversies (e.g., Kemper, 1990), I find that part of it which bears a close resemblance to symbolic interactionism (e.g., Hochschild, 1979, 1983) is particularly appropriate to the ethnographic study below. Of particular value is Hochschild's notion of emotion management through the "social constructionist" perspective, emphasizing people's responses to themselves and others through their social milieu. Relations between Anglo and Mexicano members of the team are shown as a series of differences in the way gender emotions are manifested, differences Hochschild would term "emotion lines."

In the course of looking at the Tecos, the tender macho concept formulated here is also seen as an outgrowth of cultural construction of emotions (Rosaldo, 1993) in addition to the social positions that individual Tecos share with each other. The conclusions place their sense of machismo between hypermasculine macho and nonmacho styles; that is, these men exhibit machismo at times and not at others. Determining which contexts and settings invoke which behavior and emotions is part of the task involved.

The Study

An ethnographic study of Los Tecolotes de los dos Laredos [The Owls of the Two Laredos] was conducted over two baseball seasons, 1993 and 1994. The larger goal of the project was to study the formation of kinds of nationalism on the U.S.–Mexican border and the role of baseball in this process (Klein, in press). The "Tecos" (as they are known locally) are one of the oldest teams in the Mexican League, the only foreign league formally affiliated with Major League Baseball. Aside from the relatively ancient pedigree of the team (going back to the beginnings of the league in 1940), the Tecos are unique in that they are the only binational sports team in the world. The Tecos represent both Nuevo Laredo, Tamaulipas, and Laredo, Texas: one team affiliated with two countries. The team is structurally binational in that it is comprised of men from both countries, has two home stadiums, and splits its home games between the Texas and Mexican ball parks. Further, the team is owned by a resident of Nuevo Laredo but is run by a Laredan, and while it is a Mexican League franchise, the team has a structural bond with the Atlanta Braves in the major leagues.

The Mexican League consists of 16 teams divided evenly into a northern zone and a southern zone. They play a 132-game annual schedule, followed by a playoff series and a championship series. Each team's roster is comprised of 29 players: 24 Mexicans and a supplement of 5 importados (foreign imports). For the Tecos, the first few weeks of the season have been unusual of late because their working agreement with the Atlanta Braves precludes the arrival of the importados as the season starts. Unlike other Mexican League clubs, Teco importados attend Atlanta's spring training. While placing the Tecos at an obvious disadvantage, it nevertheless also makes the entrance of the importados more sociologically significant (e.g., their assimilation into the team and Mexico is more dramatic because the imports have to accelerate the process). As has been shown (Klein, in press), the ability of the players to bond across national lines is further impaired by this process. The imports are preferentially treated by the owners of these Mexican teams. North American players also demand better treatment, partially because many have previously played in the major leagues and expect better treatment, partly because they feel culturally superior to the Mexicans they are playing with. The result is that although players work together to win ball games, there is a good deal of tension on these teams (Klein, in press).

The Tecos players come from all parts of Mexico, but particularly the baseball-rich areas of Veracruz, Sonora, Sinaloa, and the Yucatan. The racial makeup of the team also reflects Mexico's history, with most players being mestizo (mixture of Spanish and Indian). Some, however, are of Afro-Caribbean background found in the state of Vera Cruz, and some are of pure Indian background (one Cora and one Yaqui). There is less heterogeneity when we come to class makeup of the team. Only 2 of the Mexican players come from more educated and well-heeled families; the other 22 come from the classes of working poor and struggling lower middle class.

In carrying out the study I used a variety of methods. Field observation was the basis of the study. Seven field trips, made up of stays ranging from 1 to 6 weeks during every part of the two seasons with the Tecos, were made. I traveled with the team on the road, sharing a bit of the life of the itinerant player in hotels, restaurants, and nightspots. I was there before and after games (pitched some batting practice) and attended the social functions held by the team. I dropped in steadily at the offices of the club and occasionally at some of the players' homes. In that time, I went from tolerated outsider to friend, welcomed by some, respected by most.

Observations were buttressed by both formal and field interviews. The formal interviews focused on gathering life histories of all the frontline players as well as detailing specific team issues. The larger project also included the history of baseball in the region, to which end I gathered the few living players from the earliest days (the 1930s), moving up to the contemporary period with even larger numbers of ex-players. Archival material was also critical in this part of the study. Some use was made of surveys, as people in both cities were canvassed regarding specific issues, and a content analysis was made of the newspapers in each city as well (see Klein, 1991).

Constructing the Teco ethnography involved several departures from methodological conventions. The use of names, both of the site studied and of the players, is not typically advocated. While someone might find it easy to conceal the identity of the Two Laredos in a study of, say, drug trafficking, trying to conceal their identity as the site of the only binational sports franchise in the world is pointless, particularly to the people who are most knowledgeable on the topic. Conversely, for academic colleagues, both the team and the cities are so far removed from the academic experience that naming the team and players does not impair their anonymity. As for maintaining anonymity to protect the vulnerable, I have taken great care to do so on sensitive topics. Finally, the people of the Laredos area have not had much of a voice, and the ethnography was my way of projecting that voice.

Making Teco Sense of Machismo

For many Latino(a) and Latin American scholars, working with machismo is sort of like living with an embarrassing relative: Everyone is forced to accept his presence, but no one wants to embrace him or be publicly seen with him. The efforts to show that machismo does not represent all sectors of society are a valuable corrective, but we cannot deny its existence.

Mirandé's (1988) efforts are instructive in this regard because he attempts to show that machismo is varied, that it can represent the bullying, pejorative form, as well as the masculine ideal of an earlier, more noble time (e.g., valuing bravery, honor, responsibility). In dichotomizing, Mirandé has carried forward the distinction made by Mendoza (1962) and Paredes (1993) between "false" machismo and "genuine" hombria, or masculinity. For these scholars, machismo is capable of being either negative or positive. The problem, however, remains that holding onto any form of machismo forces the scholar studying it to assess it as more progressive than he or she might be comfortable with.[2]

Machismo as constituted in this study exists along a male-to-male line. Male–female relations are also discussed and are obviously important in assessing machismo; however, most of the data collected came from baseball-related contexts and, so, deal with men.[3] Male–female relations in Mexican society are typically viewed as heavily male-dominant.

Machismo and hypermasculinity occupy the more extreme end of the masculine continuum, which shades off in macho attributes into its opposite, that is, tenderness and gentle displays.[4]

Bullying macho—Tender macho—Androgyny—
More feminine—Transvestite

I looked at displays of behavior that were conventionally macho as well as at departures from masculine convention. The latter included men's displays of physical affection, their dealings with children and other people at the park who are less well off, and their ability to express hurt and/or vulnerability. I confined these observations to the ballpark (primarily dugout behavior, but also including dressing rooms). Space permits only a few of the more representative examples.

With 10 straight playoff appearances since 1983 and two league championships since 1977, the Tecos are a force to be reckoned with: Their signature, appropriately enough, is power. Andres Mora, who retired in 1994, is the number two all-time home run hitter in the league with 426. Another Teco, Alejandro Ortiz, has 320 and, at 32 years of age, can potentially pass Mora. Both are Teco legends. Coming up quickly are tough, younger hitters like 26-year-old Marco Romero. These men prefer the unshaven look, cut off the sleeves of their uniforms, and routinely pound their cups with bat handles because, as they sometimes declare, *tenemos muchos huevos* [We have a lot of balls (eggs)]. Their penchant for power hitting and macho is further demonstrated in the way the Tecos tend to perform as a team: seemingly doing everything to hamstring themselves, then putting on a last-minute power surge that catapults them into the zone's lead. While speed is valued, there is little effort to acquire it. As the sine qua non of the macho, power is expressed in the trademark Mexican League hitter who either powers the ball for a 430-ft. home run or a 400-ft. single. The Teco hitters, or at least half the lineup, swing with the idea of gulfing one out of the park. When they succeed and round the bases meeting their fellows they, like their American counterparts, choreograph a group macho fist-slamming-fist exchange, except that the Mexicans cap theirs off with a mutual Mexican salute (hand sideways chopped out from chest).[5]

On the day-to-day baseball level there are many other expressions of macho posturing. Machismo is not designed to be subtle. Paz notes that the macho's aggressiveness "provokes a great sinister laugh," even turning humor into "an act of revenge" (1962, p. 91). In the very first Tecos series I watched in the summer of 1992, I witnessed an illustration of the fusion of aggression, joking, and macho in a game against the Leones from Merida.

The plate umpire was calling the kind of game that brought on murderous cries from the Tecos fans. He was consistently "squeezing" both pitchers (calling borderline pitches "balls" rather than "strikes"), but since this was a home game, the Tecos fans were convinced he was doing it only to their pitcher. This umpire, a huge rotund man, when viewed from behind, completely obscured the catcher. In about the third inning the Teco battery retaliated by having the catcher call for a fast ball then shift to the side, allowing the pitch to come through and hit the umpire. This worked much better than expected, and the umpire took a 90-mile-per-hour pitch in the groin. He instantly went down on all fours, and the fans roared their approval, screaming "Burro!" and "Check the ball," and whistling their derision. Lying on the ground, the umpire fought to catch his breath, while the fans continued their merciless foot stamping and cheering. Finally, he stumbled to his feet, face red and sweating. A huge malevolent sneer spread across his lips, and he turned to face the crowd. Holding up both arms as if signifying a halt to the game, his voice shouted for all to hear, *Chingen sus madres!*

Pendejos! [Fuck your mothers, jerks!]. The stadium went momentarily silent in response to his unexpected behavior, and, understanding the impact he had, the bear-of-an-umpire laughed aloud. Though the fans rebounded within seconds and began heaping abuse upon him, which lasted right through the game, it was for naught as he had already bested them.

That laugh is also the signature of the story or joke that puts people down. Often the veterans who nightly hold court before the game recall someone's faux pas or recount someone's colossal failure, but the humorous story has an edge to it that comes out not so much in the narrative as in the inflection and laughter that punctuate the tale.

One set of field notes will have to suffice on this matter. Romero was one of the most macho of the Tecos. He cultivated the look. His thick jet-black hair combed straight back from his forehead and bushy Vandyke beard, forever setting off a 2-day growth of the rest of his beard, fit predictably upon a powerful beer-swilling body that swaggered. But what one remembers most is his laugh: gravelly, loud, explosive, and always capable of being used as a bludgeon. The following entry from my field notes chronicles some of this. In the early part of my fieldwork, when I was very much an outsider and not trusted, I sought to chronicle some of this behavior but it spilled over to engulf me:

March 12, 1993, Reynosa: This afternoon the veterans were giving a workshop on Teco-lore in the dugout. Seeking respite from the midday heat they straggled in one by one until a small group had gathered. Then each of the veterans (Mora, Romero, Ortiz) would hold center stage talking to the rest of some encounter with other players (usually involving besting someone). Always sentences are punctuated with *Chinga!* or *Pinche*, or any of the standard swearing that passes for an exclamation mark. Romero recounts a time when he took off after an opposing pitcher, mimicking the feeble, cowardly way the latter ran around the diamond trying to avoid Romero and his bat. Ballistically imitating his fury with a scowl and raised gloved fist on an overly hairy ham-of-a-hand, Romero flew into the face of one of the players. Then, that menacing laugh of his boomed from his goatee'd face, joined by a chorus of laughter. . . . Turning his attention to me (he noticed me listening), Romero's smile slid smoothly to a sneer, and he used what limited English he knew to refer to my book, making it clear that he does not welcome my presence. He used the English word, *"book"* in his otherwise Spanish diatribe, "Look it this one, the barbón (bearded one), writing a *book . . . fuckin' book."* Always the sneer-smile. The others were keenly interested in seeing my response. They smiled at me in a thinly veiled friendliness which clearly called attention to my foreignness.

Romero bested me. I was constrained by my role as both anthropologist and Teco/cultural outsider. In time he began to sense that I was neither a sports writer (whom he disdained) nor a front office lackey (whom he mistrusted). By 1994 he even began to trust me to the point of occasionally asking for help in a very different way than characterized in the above description.

In a related set of events occurring about the same time, some of the veterans were challenging the stewardship of the Tecos' new manager, Dan Firova. Issues at the heart of their resistance had to do with nationalism, but the style of the challenge was pure macho. Firova is a *Pocho* (a Mexican-American) who acts more like the classic tight-lipped Texan that he is than like a Mexican. Marco Romero, more than others, seemed to be in Firova's face. On the surface there was no real reason for the reaction to Firova. He was relatively young (38 years old), an ex-Teco himself who had played with many of the Tecos he was now managing. The anti-Firova sentiment was also felt by the fans and press of Nuevo Laredo and was directed at his style of managing, which was not Mexican (e.g., he refused to coach third base), and his being American.

Romero was the one whose actions seemed most designed to offend. One of his (and many others') weapons was the transparent comment or joke, where the meaning of a statement exists at two very different levels: the benign and malevolent. For instance, the term *Cachucha* means "baseball cap," but it can also mean "expendable woman," "because like a hat you can put it on or take it off whenever you want." Or consider the oft-heard refrain *Sacala!* meaning "take it out (of the ball park)," as in a home run. It also means "take it (penis) out of your pants."

Romero, however, only occasionally used these linguistic devices in dealing with the Teco manager. He preferred to be a bit more direct, stopping short of a direct confrontation. His intentions were clear, however, as in one pregame episode in which the players were out taking fielding drills and doing light running. Firova entered the dugout, where Romero had come to drink some water.

Firova (joking): "Hey Romero, what's this? Let's get out there." Grabbing a bat, Firova turns and goes onto the field to hit grounders, standing about forty feet from Romero. Romero commences to growl to others in the dugout, but loudly enough for Firova to hear: "Fuck! Go out and do what? I need water, not more work, Damn!" Firova turns ever so slightly, deliberating for a second whether or not to confront this, and then goes on hitting grounders. Others in the dugout make eye contact with each other and Romero, saying nothing yet saying everything. (March 7, 1993)

This is the kind of quasi-challenge that is often uttered and, in the macho Mexican world of men, demands some sort of response. The manager, however, is very much a Texan ready to respond to a direct challenge (which this stopped just short of being). For the North American there are options for handling a borderline insolent player like Romero, but not so for the Mexican. In head-to-head encounters like this, Firova's handling of it was not the most manly and cost him some measure of respect.

Relations with their wives and girlfriends also tend to reflect macho attitudes. Only one Teco wife held a job, and she was Mexican–American. There was a marked gender hierarchy, with men dominant in matters of decision making, authority, and economic control. Attempts to look at the wife as controlling the household realm, suggesting the public/private division of authority (Rosaldo and Lamphere, 1974), do not obviate the fact that men are in a position of control. The wife of one of the players, herself a veteran of many years in Mexican baseball, summed up her husband's macho in general:

He has to be tough. He has to be the head. What he says goes with his girlfriend or his family. He has to be in control. My husband had to be tough. His no's were no's. His yes was yes. If he wanted to go out he'd go out. It wasn't a matter of asking. They'd call each other mandilon (feminine-dominated) if the wife said no and you listened.

Machismo also involves having extramarital sexual relations with women, and there are any number of Tecos who comply with that norm. One wife claims that 95% of the players do, but in this regard Mexican players differ little, if at all, from their North American counterparts. "We go back to our hotel. We get showered and get our adrenaline going cuz there's gonna be some women from the game at a bar. We're baseball players, so of course we're gonna score." Infidelity is certainly not the exclusive province of the Mexican player, but it does function easily as part of the demonstration of the macho-as-bully profile. The wives and girlfriends understand this as well and attempt as best they can to prevent it:

> I do see their [wives] going to the park, going through a few insecurities. They're always there after the games taking care of their husbands to make sure they come home after the game. I did that. . . . I know some Mexican [players'] wives confront their husbands [about infidelities on the road]. What's unbelievable is that they [husbands] would deny everything. You'd think there was a script and you hand it out from one generation to the next. You call a guy 2 o'clock in the morning and he's not in his room [when they are on the road], and he says "I went out to eat." [Wife asks] "At two in the morning?" "Well, hon, the game went 14 innings." The other excuse, "I was in Solano's room playing cards." And you feel like a fool. They all use those lines, and nobody plays cards.

However easily she sees through these excuses, the wife most often stops well short of calling her husband's bluff. She knows that trying to force the issue his team would test her husband's sense of macho vis-à-vis his teammates, resulting in hardening his position.

Tender Machos

Three areas were observed: interactions with children and fans, expressions of feelings and vulnerability, and physical affection with each other. Space permits only representative examples of each, but these behaviors and views recurred frequently enough to be considered normative.

The relationships between the Tecos and their fans, and particularly children, were filled with instances of two-way social intimacy and concern. In relations with children one also sees the affection, as in the way players complied with the constant requests for signing of balls or scraps of paper (as many as 50 requests for team autographs on balls and other objects per game).

> April 4, 1994 [West Martin Field, Laredo]: Romero, with his three-day growth looks like central-casting's choice for a Mexican bandito. He laughs like a three-pack-a-day convict, but when he holds his little baby girl and zooms her around like a little pink dirigible [she was wearing a pink head band], he's the warmest most comforting man imaginable. Each time he stops, she cries to be picked up and zoomed, and so he and the others continue to take turns spinning her.

Another time Ortiz, having struck out, returns to the dugout ready to explode:

> July 24, 1993 [Parque La Junta]: Ortiz storms over to the "Time Out" corner of the dugout [my term for a place in the dugout where players vent], curses loudly, and slams his bat against the bat rack. Without losing a step he moves to the other side of the dugout still glowering, his cleats clicking angrily up the stairs to the chain-link fence that separates the players from the fans, spots the baby of one of the fans he knows sitting on her mother's lap. Not missing a beat he sweeps from fury to smile losing twenty years in the bargain, and voice piping up perhaps two full octaves, pleads, "Give me a kiss, Alexis."

Ortiz's actions are noteworthy in that the "time out zone" represents complete isolation. So furious is the individual in this state of mind that others will avoid even eye contact with him. In this instance, Ortiz's ability to readily melt from anger to affection exemplifies the close proximity of macho and tenderness in these players. To some extent this can be explained as a different view of professionalism, yet its difference lies in culture, and it is simultaneously a cultural difference in masculinity. Anglo players, while friendly, were (with two observed exceptions) nowhere nearly as emotive and spontaneous as the Mexicanos.

In direct contrast to the macho image of either Mexican or American players is the ability of Mexican players to express vulnerability. Just as easily as some of these men seek to intimidate and dominate, they also beseech one another for help or voice fear and hurt. The following example came from the 1993 Championship Series between the Tecos and Olmecas, after a Teco loss. Third baseman Ortiz had made an error that cost the game. He was beside himself with anger and drank all night. The following morning it was a haggard Ortiz that appeared at the office of the manager Firova's wife (the two families are very close and she is an executive at a hotel). What makes this particularly telling is that he goes beyond the emotional rules (Hochschild, 1979) that apply to Mexican machos both by asking for help and by doing so from a woman. She describes the meeting:

> He comes to my office, practically gets on his knees and wants me to tell him that he's doing okay, that he didn't make a mistake, that he's gonna snap out of his slump. He went to *my* office. He hadn't gone to sleep. He'd been drinking all night, and like, "God, where have you been?" And he sits down, puts his head down, grabs his forehead, and says, "I let the team down. I let my friends down." He was really emotional. He said, "I tried! I lost the ball and I couldn't make up for it with a hit. I let Dan [manager] down and you don't know how much that hurts me. I'm really trying. What am I doing wrong?" He kept asking me, practically crying. He was in my office for two hours, and I'm thinking, "Man, this macho guy? And him coming to a woman?"

Oftentimes, in their dealings with the gringo imports or other representatives of the U.S. baseball establishment, these Mexican players are insulted and/or hurt. Yet here, as well as in other areas, they can express their feelings as hurts (not simply as anger) with a mixture of sadness and incredulity, mixed with pity for *norteamericanos*. This was the case with one of the younger players when he went to Atlanta's spring training facility. He was angry at the way he was treated, but unlike so many North American athletes Moreno could delve beneath it and talk of his wound:

> I had a good spring training here, then got an invitation to West Palm Beach with the Braves. They paid for my ticket, food, everything. And they wanted me to stay there. They told me they wanted to send me to the Rookie League. They wanted to pay me $40 a week. Then I got that problem that my dad died last year and now I have to send money to my mom; cuz we owe money to the bank and I'm helping her. I told them, "I'll stay here if you send $200 a month to my mom. Don't give me nothing, just send it to her." And they said they couldn't do that. They said all you can do is call Laredo [the Tecos front office] and have them send the money. Then I called here to Laredo and they never talked to me. And I said, "Okay, I'm gonna sacrifice this and go back to Mexico." And J. [a pitching coach for the Braves] said to me, "We want you here. If you go back to Mexico you're not coming here no more." I said, "I'm sorry. I appreciate that you invited me." I told him that I have the certificate of my Dad's death and I'd show it to him. He didn't care. What kind of a man is this that doesn't care about family?

It is difficult to think of this as an expression of someone overly concerned with seeming impenetrable or irresponsible or with being tough. Anglo players rarely talked about such things in a vulnerable way. When, for instance, Willie Waite talked about this being his last chance to get promoted, it was in an angry way: "Fuck it. I only got one or two more fuckin' years left."

For all of its male bonding qualities, the expression of physical affection between North American players (and by extension, males) is most carefully legislated. The fear of being labeled homosexual is part of the socialization of young men in North America, and the category of behavior that is considered suspect extends to include showing signs of physical affection (Connell, 1991; Kaufman, 1987; Messner, 1992). In a column of the nationally syndicated Sunday magazine *Parade* (August 14, 1994) the question was posed, "Why Can't Guys Hug Each Other?" The two young men whose responses were printed had internalized the homophobia in our society. One wrote,

> A lot of times, when you're confused and stuff, and you feel lonely, just to hug somebody— the human touch—would be nice. But if I'm with guy friends, I can't say, "I'm feeling down right now. Would you hug me?" They'd be like, "what?" And if I went over and hugged a friend, like to give him support, I would immediately be called gay. (Travis Neal, 14, Oakland, CA)

Public affection is limited to moments following success or victory. A no-hitter or a touchdown run warrants hugs, a slap on the behind, even a macho kiss on the top of the head in front of 25 million viewers. That same hug in the parking lot could get someone punched. As pointed out by Curry (1991), and White and Vagi (1991), who studied North Americans, touching is tolerated in the locker room if it is accompanied by a good deal of homophobic joking. Anglos on the team tended to mediate feelings of genuine affection for each other with masculine protest and excess, so that when Boi talked to Eric about how well he was hitting, it had to be with a macho ritualistic high fiveing/slapping and a dose of homophobic joking, "You fucked him bad man! [Meaning he was hitting that pitcher well]. He's gonna be walking tight [as if having been anally penetrated]." The Tecos offered stark contrasts here as well.

Early on I noticed that the Mexican players expressed physical affection more easily and without the need for the cover of a joke. It was not at all uncommon for men to watch events on the field with one using the other as a leaning post; players could be seen standing on the steps of the dugout arms around each other's waist watching the game. There was no self-consciousness about these acts or looks of any sort from the other players. Sometimes the affection was fused with more conventional macho forms. On one occasion I saw two of the Tecos play-boxing in the dugout.

April 2, 1994 [Parque La Junta]: It started out typically enough with each man circling around throwing phantom punches at the other and moved into a flurry of body slamming. As they dodged and ducked and flicked jabs that barely missed, the thought ran through my head that this could escalate into something serious. A headline flashed through my brain, "Play Fighting Turns Deadly for Two Tecos." Instead, these two moved from their Mexican version of Capuera (Brazilian martial arts dance) to gliding around the dugout in a waltz-like embrace and finally settling into watching the game with arms around each other's waist. One punctuated this choreographed event by pinching the other's behind. Headline in my brain altered to read, "Play Fighting Turns Dearly."

Somewhat later I observed an even more striking incident that triggered my questioning of conventionally perceived machismo. At one game in May 1994, the Teco players were sitting, as usual, in a row of plastic seats placed in front of the dugout so that they could take advantage of any cooling breezes. The row was filled and everyone seemed preoccupied with the man out on the mound pitching against them. He was vexing with his array of forkballs and curves, and as of the sixth inning no one had gotten a hit off of him. The Tecos were busily trying to unlock the riddle of his pitching, and everyone was caught up in the discussion. Two or three additional Tecos were standing behind the row also in the conversation. I noticed that one of the players standing behind the row was talking animatedly about a short slider and simultaneously stroking, as if grooming, the hair of the player seated

in front of him. Again, this was as public as one could get (in front of other players and fans), yet no one seemed even the slightest bit struck by this action, except the anthropologist.

It was at this point that I thought I would try to determine just how many on the team engaged in various forms of physical affection and how often it occurred. For two 1-week periods (separated by 2 months) I tried to count the number of times I saw players showing physical affection for each other. I wrote down their names and the context and form the affection took. Not all of the Tecos are so given to demonstrating physical affection. These are, after all, men from widely different cultural and regional backgrounds within Mexico. The two men who are Indian, while warm and genuine, are not given to showing physical affection, for instance. Andres Mora, the macho hero of the Mexican League, always had a socioemotional moat around him, and while he was friendly, there was only baseball to be talked about with him.

Of the 24 Mexicanos on the team, I could count 9 whom I saw somewhat regularly being physically affectionate (holding each other, leaning on each other, etc.); another 7 touched or were touched occasionally. Those exhibiting affection could be married or single, rookies or veterans. The only pattern I found was that 7 of the 9 players who exhibited regular affection were pitchers and catchers. Perhaps these two positions involve a degree of mutual dependency that encourages such familiarity. The total number of physical acts I counted in those two week-long periods were 11 and 14. Of the 25 total affectionate acts, 21 were in and around the dugout area or bullpen, and the other 4 were in the clubhouse.

These represent only the players and acts I was able to pick out, and not at all the total numbers that would make it more widespread. I detected no homophobic joking to legitimate the acts. In fact, I conclude that these men are not even conscious of these acts. Finally, I told one of the players that I was impressed with how easily Mexican men showed affection, that in the U.S. men are worried about doing this for fear of being considered homosexual. He looked somewhat surprised and puzzled, then, after a moment, seemed to come to a realization. "When I went to spring training in the States," he recalled, "I remember once putting my arm around one of the gringos who was a good guy. He looked at me like [head showing a recoil in horror]. I thought he just didn't like me and I was surprised because we got along good, but now maybe I understand this thing better."

The 9 North American players who played during the two seasons were also observed. While gringos exhibited social and psychological differences among themselves, they functioned similarly on the indices examined here. Gringo players were less likely to talk about their vulnerabilities, and when they did so they would more likely discuss issues angrily or with deflective humor, keeping their masculinity intact. North Americans would be affectionate with children and those of other players, but they were never seen gushing emotionally over children, especially if they had their "game face" on (Gallmeier, 1987). This was not lost on the Mexican players and their families and prompted one of the Teco wives to comment, "In our culture a gringo, we know, is cold. They may be good guys—not mean, not machos—but they're also not gonna be emotional." On the key issue of showing physical affection, with one exception I never witnessed North Americans behaving as emotionally open as I saw the Mexicans behave.[6] Above all, gringo players never touched each other except in carefully scripted ways (e.g., high fives, or in the rush of emotional highs).

It is in the area of masculine behavior which revolves around homophobia that some of the greatest differences lie. While Mexican players were antigay, their homophobia did not extend as far as their North American counterparts. There was far less overt homosexual joking in the locker room than one would find in North America, due to a fear associated by North Americans with showing emotion or physical affection to other men that could be construed as homosexual. Attributes associated with effeminacy such as being emotional, expressing emotion, or physically touching other men are, by Anglos, scrupulously avoided or socially choreographed. Mexican players also insist on being perceived of as very masculine but don't seem to associate physical affection or expressing emotions to other men as violating the masculine charter. While homophobia may partially account for these social and psychological differences between the Mexican and Anglo players, society and culture play large roles in framing homophobia as well. For Mexicans, like other Latin Americans, homosexuality is less associated with issues of effeminacy than it is with the idea of being passive or submissive (see Lancaster, 1992; Parker, 1991).

Regarding male–female behavior, however, the North Americans held decidedly less authoritarian views on their wives working (all approved of it), on the role of women in society in general, or on their wives having a social life apart from their husbands (7 of 9 had no problem with it). In short, both axes—male/male and male/female—reveal macho attitudes on the part of the Mexican males, but the present study shows that Mexican players may be less macho vis-à-vis each other than previously thought.

Discussion

In order to more fully comprehend the meaning of the emotions of these tender machos, "one must consider the subject's position within a field of social relations" (Rosaldo, 1993, p. 2). The structural study of the team and of the interrelations between groups becomes as important as the cultural differences that each of these groups brings to their relation. Some unique features of the subculture of the Tecos also foster the strong sense of community. Through the development of a large nucleus of returning players, over the years the Tecos have encouraged feelings of family and community among teammates that mirror Mexican kin-based values around *familia, compadrazgo*. Almost all of the Mexican players live in Nuevo Laredo and tend to reside in clusters, which increases the amount of interdependence between men and their families. There is an atmosphere of trust that makes it easy for them to ask for help. I have often seen these Tecos waiting for each other to go to supermarkets or assist each other's families. Unlike most professional athletes, the Tecos have come to take for granted their seasonal gathering. As with many of the more accomplished Mexican players, the summer season in the Mexican League is supplemented by their playing in Mexico's "other league," the Pacific Coast League, which plays in the winter. One of the Tecos who plays in both leagues underscored both his introspection and the unique camaraderie of the Tecos:

> Over there [in Mexicali] they have a lot of big-name players and when they talk they don't make it easy for others. It's like they're the main people and we're less. Here [among the Tecos] there is a solidarity that allows everyone to feel like they belong. I can talk with others about anything. There, all I talk about is baseball.

This explanation was not delivered in a boastful way: rather, it was soft and straightforward. It was also delivered by someone who was at the social center (i.e., not marginal). Whether we want to consider these departures from traditional macho a "value stretch" (Rodman, 1965), or something akin to Goffman's "front stage v. back stage" distinction (Goffman, 1959), or a function of culturally held emotions, what strikes me as impressive is the fact that these Mexican men, most of whom were uneducated, could verbalize fears, concerns, and tenderness in front of and to outsiders, strangers, or their own. The ethnographic observations of the players' behavior show the nonmacho behavior acting as a kind of brake against a runaway view of Latin American men as macho. Díaz, Romero, Cuevas, and others are machos who claim to live by the code of machismo, but as one wife reminds, "they also bend the rules. They wash dishes. They carry the baby. They change diapers. So, that's not a real macho." Luis Fernando Díaz, right fielder, provides a final instance of a man considered a macho behaving in a most unmacho way. When a call went out to the Tecos to take part in a fashion show, Díaz was the only Teco who appeared. The others wouldn't hear of such an unmacho thing:

> I invited him [and others] to take part in a fashion show, and thought "They're never gonna buy this." But he showed up with his family. He wanted to come and he took his wife to pick out his clothes. And I'm like, "What?" This is one of the last guys I expected to show. His wife picks out his clothes and he comes out of the dressing room and asks, "Is this okay?" She's dressing him! (Laredo, July 12, 1994)

Although many players illustrated a level of gentleness, we cannot assign the whole team to a single category. Some Tecos exist closer to the bullying macho end of the scale (e.g., one player reputed to have three families scattered about and a drinking habit that he feels makes him macho). Others appear as real machos in their womanizing and bragging about conquests but also exhibit tenderness. And still others rarely exhibit bullying features of macho; instead they are machos only on the field but not off of it. I have tried to show that in the normal course of professional baseball, the Tecos players have ample opportunity to demonstrate machismo's competitive, aggressive, showy side. Nevertheless, these players—at least the Mexicanos—also share a level of softness that is noteworthy and impressive both relatively (to Anglos) and absolutely (even in comparison to other players in the league).

Machismo is a "system," but it is not unilaterally oppressive. Rather, machismo is complex enough that it can contain within itself a dialogue around more and less hypermasculine traits. This view is in keeping with Connell's (1987, 1991) "hegemonic masculinity" as coexisting and contrasting forms of masculinity existing both within society and within individuals in society. Even in cultures marked by significant gender hierarchy, machismo can be mediated by culture, class, and situational factors, prompting a more nuanced construction of identity. Guttman's admonition to rethink Mexican machismo within changing social–cultural institutions is well taken and, to one degree or another, confirmed in the Tecos data. Among other things, the present validation of social–cultural findings through sports should serve as a reminder to our colleagues in sociology and anthropology to examine sport as they would economics, politics, or household division of labor.

Differing emotional responses are socially and culturally constructed (Hochschild, 1979; Rosaldo, 1993) and, so, offer us dimensions of cross-cultural comparisons. In this instance, social structural factors combined with cultural differences to create emotional differences but also social consequences. The ways in which Anglo players are preferentially treated by the owners of these Mexican teams in terms of travel and pay, for instance, exacerbate the consequences of differing emotional complexes. A two-class system is fostered on the team with all of the attendant resentment. The latter is, however, muted as much as possible since its expression might undermine the collective goals. At the level of interaction and social bonding, the differences in emotional makeup tend to become exhibited in creating exclusionary social principles, in this instance through nationalist antagonism between the two groups. Social structural factors, then, play a role as preconditions for differences between the groups, as well as the consequences of these differences (i.e., nationalism). North Americans may be teammates but they are not part of the social or emotional community formed by members who play for the same organization. Cultural construction of emotions promotes separation between the two groups.

Machismo has been shown as a locus of emotions and behaviors. Mexican males exhibit a greater range of emotions and behaviors that should facilitate a new view of Latin American masculinity as *ni macho, ni mandilón*. Differences between Anglos and Mexicanos along indices of masculine emotions were shown to exist as well. These do more than reflect cultural differences; the different emotional complexes act to maintain social segmentation among the team members on the basis of national identity. Hence, Mexicans and North Americans often coexist in a state of nonverbalized hostility, which on occasion surfaces.

References

Baca Zinn, M. (1975). Political familism: Toward sex role equality in Chicano familism. *International Journal of Chicano Studies Research, 6,* 13–26.

Baca Zinn, M. (1982). Chicano men and masculinity. *Journal of Ethnic Studies, 10*(2), 29–44.

Brandes, S. (1980). *Metaphors of masculinity: Sex and status in Andalusian folklore.* Philadelphia: University of Pennsylvania Press.

Connell, R.W. (1987). *Gender and power.* Sidney, Australia: Allen and Unwin.

Connell, R.W. (1991). An iron man: The body and some contradictions of hegemonic masculinity. In M. Messner and D. Sabo (Eds.), *Sport, men, and the gender order.* (pp. 83–96). Champaign, IL: Human Kinetics.

Cromwell, R.E., Corrales, R., and Torseillo, P.M. (1973). Normative patterns of marital decision-making power and influence in Mexico and the United States. *Journal of Comparative Family Studies, 4*(3), 175–196.

Curry, T. (1991). Fraternal bonding in the locker room: A profeminist analysis of talk about competition and women. *Sociology of Sport Journal, 8,* 119–135.

Donnelly, P., and Young, K. (1985). Reproduction and transformation of cultural forms of sport. *International Review of the Sociology of Sport, 20*(1), 19–38.

Elias, N., and Dunning, E. (1986). *Quest for excitement.* London: Blackwell.

Fine, G. (1987). *With the boys: Little League baseball and preadolescent culture.* Chicago: University of Chicago Press.

Foley, D. (1990). *Learning capitalist culture: Deep in the heart of Tejas.* Philadelphia: University of Pennsylvania Press.

Gallmeier, C. (1987). Putting on the game face: The staging of emotions in professional hockey. *Sociology of Sport Journal, 4,* 347–363.

Goffman, I. (1959). *Presentation of self in everyday life.* Garden City, NJ: Doubleday.

Gutmann, M. (1994a). *Machismo and Lo Mexicano: An ethnohistorical appraisal.* Paper delivered at the annual meeting of the Latin American Studies Association, Atlanta, GA.

Gutmann, M. (1994b). The meanings of macho: Changing Mexican male identities. *Masculinities, 2*(1), 21–33.

Hochschild, A. (1979). Emotion work, feeling rules, and social structure. *American Journal of Sociology, 85*(3), 551–575.

Hochschild, A. (1983). *The managed heart: Commercialization of human feeling.* Berkeley, CA: University of California Press.

Hondagneu-Sotelo, P. (1992). Overcoming patriarchal constraints: The reconstruction of gender relations among Mexican immigrant women and men. *Gender and Society, 6*(4), 398–415.

Hondagneu-Sotelo, P., and Messner, M. (1994). Gender displays and men's power: The 'new man' and the Mexican immigrant man. In H. Brod (Ed.), *Theorizing masculinities* (pp. 200–218). Newbury Park, CA: Sage.

Kaufman, D. (1987). *Beyond patriarchy: Essays by men on pleasure, power, and change.* Toronto: Oxford University Press.

Kemper, D. (Ed.) (1990). *Research agendas in the sociology of emotions.* Albany, NY: State University of New York Press.

Kidd, B. (1991). The men's cultural centre: Sports and the dynamic of women's oppression/men's repression. In M. Messner and D. Sabo (Eds.), *Sport, men, and the gender order* (pp. 31–44). Champaign, IL: Human Kinetics.

Klein, A. (1983). The political-economy of gender: A 19th century Plains Indian case study. In P. Albers and B. Medicine (Eds.), *The hidden half: Studies of Plains Indian women* (pp. 143–175). Washington, DC: University Press of the Americas.

Klein, A. (1991). *Sugarball: The American game, the Dominican dream.* New Haven, CT: Yale University Press.

Klein, A. (1993). *Little big men: Bodybuilding and gender constitution.* Albany, NY: State University of New York Press.

Klein, A. (in press). *The Owls of the Two Laredos: Nationalisms and baseball on the Texas–Mexican border.* Princeton, NJ: Princeton University Press.

Lancaster, R. (1992). *Life is hard: Machismo, danger, and the intimacy of power in Nicaragua.* Berkeley, CA: University of California Press.

Limón, J. (1989). Carne, carnales, and carnivalesque: Bakhtinian batos, discourse and narrative discourse. *American Ethnologist, 16,* 471–486.

Limón, J. (1994). *Dancing with the devil: Society and cultural poetics in Mexican–American south Texas.* Madison, WI: University of Wisconsin Press.

Madsen, W. (1973). *The Mexican–American of south Texas.* New York: Holt, Rinehart, Winston.

Mendoza, V. (1962). El machismo en Mexico a traves de las canciones, corridos y cantares [Machismo in Mexico through songs, ballads, and singing].

In *Cuadernos del Instituto Nacional de Antropologia III* (pp. 11–25). Buenos Aires: Ministerio de Educacion y Justica.

Messner, M. (1985). The changing meaning of male identity in the life course of the athlete. *Arena Review,* **9,** 31–60.

Messner, M. (1992). *Power at play: Sport and the problem of masculinity.* Boston: Beacon Press.

Messner, M., and Kimmel, M. (1989). *Men's lives.* New York: Macmillan.

Messner, M., and Sabo, D. (Eds.) (1991). *Sport, men, and the gender order: Critical feminist perspectives.* Champaign, IL: Human Kinetics.

Mirandé, A. (1982). Machismo: Rucas, chingasos, y chingaderas [Machismo: "Home-girls," punches, and nonsense]. *De Colores,* **6**(l), 17–47.

Mirandé, A. (1988). Que gacho es ser macho: It's a drag to be a macho man. *Aztlan,* **17**(2), 63–89.

Paredes, A. (1967). Estados Unidos, Mexico y el machismo [United States, Mexico and machismo]. *Journal of Inter-American Studies,* **9,** 65–84.

Paredes, A. (1993). *Folklore and culture on the Texas–Mexican border.* Austin: University of Texas Press.

Parker, R. (1991). *Bodies, pleasures, and passions: Sexual culture in contemporary Brazil.* Boston: Beacon Books.

Paz, O. (1962). *Labyrinth of solitude.* New York: Grove Press.

Peña, M. (1991). Class, gender and machismo: The "treacherous woman" folklore of Mexican male workers. *Gender and Society,* **5**(l), 30–46.

Peñalosa, F. (1968). Mexican family roles. *Journal of Marriage and the Family,* **30,** 680–689.

Pronger, B. (1990). *Sport and the arena of masculinity.* Toronto: University of Toronto Press.

Ramos, S. (1962). *Profile of man and culture in Mexico.* Austin, TX: University of Texas Press.

Rodman, H. (1965). The lower class value stretch. In L. Ferman (Ed.), *Poverty in America* (pp. 75–92). Ann Arbor, MI: University of Michigan Press.

Rosaldo, M., and Lamphere, L. (Eds.) (1974). *Women, culture, and society.* Stanford, CA: Stanford University Press.

Rosaldo, R. (1993). *Culture and truth: The remaking of social analysis.* Boston: Beacon Press.

Rudoff, A. (1971). The incarcerated Mexican–American delinquent. *Journal of Criminal Law, Criminology, and Police Science,* **62**(4), 224–238.

Sabo, D. (1985). Sport, patriarchy, and male identity. *Arena Review,* **9,** 1–30.

Sabo, D. (1986). Pigskin, patriarchy, and pain. *Changing Men: Issues in Gender, Sex, and Politics,* **16**(Summer), 24–25.

Sabo, D., and Runfola, R. (Eds.) (1980). *Jock: Sports and male identity.* Englewood Cliffs, NJ: Prentice Hall.

White, P., and Vagi, A. (1991). Rugby in the 19th century British boarding school system: A feminist psychoanalytic perspective. In M. Messner and D. Sabo (Eds.), *Sport, men, and the gender order* (pp. 67–78). Champaign, IL: Human Kinetics.

Ybarra, L. (1982). When wives work: The impact on the Chicano family. *Journal of Marriage and the Family,* **44**(February), 169–178.

Notes

1. See also Cromwell, Corrales, and Torseillo (1973), Mirandé (1982, 1988), Ybarra (1982), Hondagneu-Sotelo (1992), and others who have shown that Chicano families are not terrified appendages of authoritarian males but are extremely varied.

2. Indeed Chicana(o) scholars have repeatedly pointed to the sexism and paternalism of even benevolent forms of macho.

3. Relations of men with their wives and/or lovers were observed primarily around games. Occasionally I would be at the homes of players. Conversations and interviews with some of these women took place occasionally.

4. Public displays of emotion and vulnerability as noted by Hondagneu-Sotelo and Messner (1994) were interpreted as obscuring gender hierarchy with a token show of egalitarian behavior. The displays of affection dealt with in this study were not public presentations but rather an outgrowth of intragroup relations.

5. Mexican players don't stand at the plate to admire their home runs, but they do like to punctuate these dramatic blows with the shout of the victor, a uniquely Mexican tremolo.

6. Upshaw was somewhat unusual for an import. He had played on the Tecos a few years earlier, spoke some Spanish, and was interested in developing closer ties with the Mexican players off of the field (e.g., family interactions). This was relatively rare. Mexican and North American players tended to live in communities on either side of the border and function along parallel lines while playing together (see Klein, in press).

Acknowledgments

I would like to thank Arnie Arluke, Maxine Baca Zinn, Heide Dobratt, Esther Firova, Matthew Gutmann, Pierrette Hondagneu-Sotelo, and the *SSJ* reviewers for their help in preparing this article.

"It's Part of the Game": Physicality and the Production of Gender in Women's Hockey

Nancy Theberge

Contemporary developments in sport pose a powerful challenge to the historical connections between gender, physicality, and power. This process is examined through an analysis of the production of gender in women's ice hockey. Drawing from fieldwork and interviews with players and coaches who participate at elite levels, the author considers the place of physicality in the practice of women's hockey. The analysis suggests that while women's hockey provides an important challenge to historical constructions of gender, the challenge to masculine hegemony is weakened by its construction as an alternative to men's hockey, the version of the sport that "really counts."

Competitive sport is one of the most important arenas for the production and expression of gender. Connell (1987, 85) writes that "images of ideal masculinity are constructed and promoted most systematically through competitive sport," in which "the combination of skill and force" in athletic experience becomes a defining feature of masculine identity. This experience is variable and for some men, one of frustration and disappointment (Klein 1993; Messner 1992). Nonetheless, as Klein (1993, 4) notes, all men must "make peace" with the symbolism of male musculature, and the relationship between masculinity and power.

The contribution of sport to ideologies of femininity has been no less powerful. Historically, sport has been a setting in which gender differences were established and celebrated (Cahn 1994; Lenskyj 1986). When women were admitted, it was on restricted terms and according to an adapted model whereby events were adjusted (races shortened; rules altered, as in six-person basketball) to conform to a view of women as fragile and weak. In contrast to the experience of empowerment that constituted sport for men, the contribution of sport to the "myth of female frailty" (Theberge 1989) has been a lasting legacy of the history of women's exclusion or admission on restricted terms.

Perhaps as much as any social setting in the contemporary period, the world of sport is seeing considerable change regarding the condition of women and gender relations. To be sure, professional sport remains largely a male preserve in which the majority of opportunities and rewards go to men. In other contexts, including school and university sport and international competitions including most notably the Olympics, opportunities for women are expanding, performances are improving, and public interest is rising. These developments pose a challenge to ideologies of gender and to the historical association between gender, physicality, and power.

A particularly significant challenge to gender ideologies is the increased involvement of women in sports that Bryson (1990, 174) calls "flag carriers" of masculinity. These are sports that "quintessentially promote hegemonic masculinity and to

Reprinted from Theberge, 1997.

which a majority of people are regularly exposed" (Bryson 1990, 174). Writing from an Australian setting, Bryson cites as examples cricket and football (i.e., soccer). In the North American context, the best examples are football and ice hockey. In these sports, which celebrate force and toughness and involve direct confrontation between competitors, it is "dominate or lose" (Whitson 1994, 359).

The ideological significance of contact sports such as football and ice hockey is heightened in the contemporary period of shifting gender relations. The historical grounding of masculine hegemony in force and power has been eroded by the willingness of the legal system to intervene in domestic violence, increasing automation and the growth of the service sector in the economy, and the declining importance of physical work (Whitson 1994, 359). Whitson (1994, 359) notes that "body contact sports are one of the few areas of public life in which force and intimidation are still allowed to triumph, where men who love to hit can still enjoy doing so, and others will celebrate their toughness and willingness to pay the price." The movement of women into these sports is thus a particularly important instance of the shifting terrain of contemporary gender relations.

This article provides an analysis of challenges to hegemonic masculinity posed by women's participation in the "flag carrier" sport of ice hockey. Data are taken from fieldwork and interviews with players and coaches participating at the highest levels of the sport in Canada. The analysis begins with a discussion of the satisfaction players derive from the physicality of sport. This is followed by a detailed examination of the material and ideological conditions that structure the experience of physicality. A key determinant of the practice of women's hockey is rules that limit—but by no means eliminate—body contact. Debates about the place of contact in women's hockey and its relationship to injury occur within a framework in which men's sport is positioned as the "real" thing. The conclusion contrasts the transformative potential of sports organized within the dominant model of masculine sport with possibilities presented by activities organized outside the framework of institutionalized sport.

Data and Methodology

Women's hockey is now experiencing a period of growth and development, with the most notable event in this regard being its inclusion in the Olympic program for the 1998 games in Nagano, Japan. The first World Championships were held in 1990, with subsequent events in 1992 and 1994. Canada has won all three of these competitions.

In Canada, the sport is growing; the number of female players registered with the Canadian Hockey Association increased from 8,146 in 1990-91 to 19,050 in 1994-95. These figures do not include girls playing on boys' teams, for which there are no reliable statistics (Etue and Williams 1996). While school and university programs are expanding, the sport is primarily organized in clubs that are affiliated with provincial associations, which in turn are affiliated with the national governing body, the Canadian Hockey Association.

The analysis presented here is part of a broader study of women's ice hockey in Canada. The primary focus of the research is a team I call the Blades, which plays in a league located in a large Canadian metropolitan area. The league in which the Blades play is generally considered to be the strongest in the country. As an indication of this strength, several players from the Blades and from other teams in its league were members of one or more Canadian national teams that won World Championships in 1990, 1992, and 1994.

The research began when I attended the Annual General Meeting of the Provincial Women's Hockey Association in May 1992, where I met a woman who plays on the Blades and also operates a girls' hockey camp. In July I spent several days at the camp, where I met the Blades coach and told him of my interest in doing research in women's hockey. He was supportive, and in November, shortly after the start of the season, I attended a practice during which the coach introduced me to the team. I then met with the players in the coach's absence, explained my interests, and asked for permission to spend time with the team for the purpose of doing research.

Following this meeting, I began to attend games, practices, and other events such as the annual Christmas party. The fieldwork continued from November 1992 until the completion of the season in April 1993 and through the following season, from October 1993 until April 1994. I had complete access to team activities, including access to the team change room where I spent time with the players before and after games and practices. I also accompanied the team to out-of-town tournaments, including the provincial and national championships. Following each game, practice, or other event, I wrote field notes. The field notes cover a range of issues concerned with the practice and organization of the sport, team activities, and team dynamics.

In the first year of my research there were 18 players on the Blades; in the second year this was reduced to 15 with the departure of 5 and addition of 2 players. Players ranged in age from 16 to 30. The team included students and women who worked in a variety of occupations, including health professions, teaching, financial services, office work, and recreational management. I interviewed all but 1 of the women who played on the team during the two-year period, or 19 members. Most of these interviews took place between the first and second seasons of the research. Two interviews were conducted during the first season, and three took place after the second season. These interviews covered many of the same issues as the field notes, as well as topics related to individual players' careers.

To provide some perspective on experiences of players from elsewhere in the sport, I interviewed an additional eight players from three provinces, all of whom played at an elite level. I also interviewed 11 coaches from three provinces, all of whom also have experience at the highest levels of women's hockey. These additional interviews, conducted between 1993 and 1995, focused on the practice of the sport and the organization of women's hockey in Canada. All of the interviews were tape-recorded and transcribed.

There is no professional women's hockey in Canada, and the women who are the subjects of this research have "day jobs" or are students. Their involvement in hockey is nonetheless of a very high caliber, and they are committed athletes. For the purposes of the analysis provided here, it is important to note that the data are taken from athletes who participate at the highest level of the sport.

Players' Accounts of Physicality in Their Games

In an effort to construct a profile of players' athletic identities, respondents were asked to discuss their "games," specifically their strengths (and weaknesses) as hockey players. Descriptors covered a broad range: being unselfish, committed to team play, hard working. Others cited being a digger, having desire, having a good shot, being a fast or strong skater. In the midst of this variety, a striking commonality was the use of the term "aggressive," in some cases by players who otherwise characterize their styles and abilities quite differently.

The following are several players' descriptions of being aggressive on the ice. Notable about these statements is the manner in which these women convey a sense of taking initiative, of being powerful and fearless. One player said:

> I like to be first to get to the puck. If the other person gets the puck, I want to make sure I get them off the puck. And sometimes that's physically aggressive but it's always within the rules. Well, . . . usually [laughs]. I will never let another person physically overpower me.

Q.: Never?

> Okay, I guess I should say I never want another person to physically overpower me. . . . One of the things I think is my strength is being able to get there first, be the stronger one able to manipulate my base of support. Like just to be able to manipulate the body to be able to beat them to the puck.

A second woman, who also described her playing style as aggressive, indicated:

> I've always been a stronger player. I've always had the satisfaction of being on top of people . . . It's hard to describe. How can I say it? It's just knowing that the other person's helpless. She can't do anything. She's totally out of the play. You've just won . . . I mean it's great satisfaction.

This sense of satisfaction was echoed by another player: "It's great to go into a corner and come out standing when someone else is on the ground. You've done your job. You've got them." Later in the interview this player spoke of another skill she felt she had, which is to "keep your cool better than your opponent. . . . I can get people to do something stupid to take a penalty when I know I'm not going to retaliate." She was then asked to discuss the satisfaction she derives from these different abilities. Both, she noted, are important to the game, but

> I think the most satisfying is the physical. When you run into somebody and you stand up and they're down, that makes you feel a lot better than if you outsmarted somebody. It makes you feel better, the physical part.

For the women quoted above, the experience of sport is one of testing and extending their physical capacities. Additional accounts of the experience of sport and athleticism as empowering for women are provided in Blinde, Taub, and Han (1994), Miller and Penz (1991), and Young and White (1995). While the experience of personal empowerment is significant for the lives of individual women, the political potential of sport rests on its ability to challenge dominant ideologies and structures of gender relations (Young and White 1995). The remainder of the article examines the potential for political transformation embodied in women's ice hockey through an analysis of the construction and practice of the sport.

Playing the Game: The Construction of Women's Hockey

One of the major determinants of the expression of physicality in sport is the rules and regulations, formal and informal, surrounding the practice of the game. The rules of play in men's and women's ice hockey are substantially the same, with one major difference: the rules of women's hockey prohibit intentional body checking—that is, intentional efforts to hit, or "take out," an opposing player. To be sure, there is still considerable use of the body and body contact in women's hockey, both intentional and unintentional—as indicated by the player accounts above. To watch a game is to see players constantly try to outmaneuver and outmuscle one another. At the same time, women's games are noticeably different from the full contact game played at the higher levels of the men's sport. Without body checking, the forceful collisions that are a defining feature of men's hockey at these levels are largely absent (Theberge 1995).[1]

Interviews with players and coaches reveal a variety of views about the elimination of body checking from women's hockey. Respondents generally agree this results in a game in which speed, strategy, and playing skills are featured more prominently than in a full-contact game, which emphasizes power and force. Beyond this point of agreement, however, lies greater debate about the construction of women's hockey, with contrasting assessments of the relation of women's and men's hockey.

Until the late 1980s, the rules regarding body contact in women's hockey varied across Canada. The sample of women interviewed for this research includes a number who have played both full contact and the current game, which prohibits body checking. These players see advantages to both versions. While most acknowledge the attraction of the game that favors speed and playmaking, a number of these same players also express a sense of pleasure and accomplishment in playing the full-contact game and in receiving and taking a body check well. In interviews, these women describe body checking as "part of the game," "the way it should be," and "part of the fun." In this view, body checking is a skill, one among a repertoire of abilities that players can master. The following statement by a player is a representative account:

> It's a certain aggressiveness. You're putting your strength against, your technique against. It's still a technique. It's not somebody, to me it's not go and kill that person, they hurt me, I'm going to get them back. It's nothing like that. It's a technique that you've learned and you can complete, and maybe you can complete it better than they can. You can prove your flexibility and your stamina, your stability on the ice.

This player's reference to checking as "killing," "hurting," and "getting back" alludes to the view, held by some, that body checking is uncontrolled aggression often regarded as an occupational requirement in the National Hockey League (NHL), the professional men's league. As her comments indicate, it is a view she rejects.

Other players support the limitations on contact. One woman, who has never played the full-contact game, said:

> I prefer it without. Maybe just because I've always played without. You know the women's game being a bit different from the men's game, it may actually be better without it. I like to think of it as more of a finesse game. And I don't know if body contact has any part in it, really if it would enhance it in any way. I mean I think maybe the reason for having the body contact in the men's game is possibly just to make it more exciting to watch. I don't know. It's hard to say when you haven't really played that much.

Coaches also express a range of views. Some indicate that the women's game as it is played today is ideal—it is physical, sometimes very physical, and "just right" in this regard. Some see the inclusion of body checking as the "wedge" that leads to the unacceptably rough play that characterizes men's hockey. One coach offered the following comments:

> I ask myself sometimes, "Would body contact be a good thing?" It could be good if they stay

within the limits, which seems very hard to do. And if the guys didn't do it, we're not smarter than the guys. . . . Women's hockey, if you were allowed body contact, to me, we'll end up as guys' hockey with slashing and cross checking. In my head, it's hard to believe it won't happen.

Other coaches have reservations about, or actively disagree with, the current formulation. Like some players, these coaches say checking is "part of the game" and a skill that can be—and should be—taught and used effectively. The argument that body checking is responsible for the violence that plagues the men's game is also disputed. Several respondents noted that women's hockey already has severe penalties—usually suspension for several games—that limit the incidence of dirty play. So long as these sanctions are in place, it is argued, introducing body checking will not lead to an increased incidence of other, undesirable features of men's hockey.

Efforts to promote women's hockey often emphasize that it is not only different from but superior to the men's game. The superiority, it is argued, lies in the emphasis on speed and playmaking and in the absence of the violence characteristic of the men's game and most dramatically displayed in the fighting that seems a routine feature of the National Hockey League. The construction of women's hockey as different and the effort to promote the game on this basis is an important aspect of the contemporary ideological struggle surrounding the construction of sport (Theberge 1995).

A number of players recognized the dilemma of playing an alternative version of the sport. The player quoted above on the technique of body checking had extensive experience playing boys' hockey before moving to women's hockey in late adolescence. She commented on the women's game:

It is a different game and there are different rules . . . I think a lot of women think it's better. But I prefer the game where you're allowed contact. I grew up playing that game. I just think it's different and why make it different . . . I want to be able to say I play hockey and [people] understand it's the same hockey. But now I have to say I play girls' hockey. It's not the same game as boys' hockey. . . . They're changing the game.

Another player, whose only experience is in women's hockey, offered further commentary. She described her reaction to a seminar she attended during which an official from the Canadian Hockey Association emphasized the uniqueness of the game:

When you're playing a sport, you don't go out there saying, "OK, I'm a woman. OK, I have to play like one." You go out there and you play aggressive, you play your game and that's that, whereas people are trying I think to give the image that it's just an all-skill game and it's a woman's game kind of thing. Basically they were saying that you know women don't compare to men. Which is true, when you get to the older ages, I mean there's no NHL calibre women in the game right now and that's fine. Strength factor and everything, I mean people are going to know that no matter what. But you don't have to go around saying that this is a woman's sport, there's no contact, it's totally skill, and make it sound like it's a nothing sport either. I think that's part of the reason why women's hockey went nowhere for so many years.

A third player, who played women's hockey when body checking was allowed, also expressed cynicism about efforts to de-emphasize the physical aspects and to promote women's hockey on the basis of its difference from the men's game. This player explicitly acknowledged a connection between the rules of play in women's hockey and concerns about its image:

It doesn't make any sense to me. If they want to say, I don't know, the words feminine, I don't like those types of terms, masculine, feminine, all that crap. If they want to do it [promote women's hockey], that's not the way to do it, for my view. Hitting doesn't make you any more of a boy than nonhitting. I just don't know what they are trying to do.

Officiating and the Construction of the Game

The practice of the game depends not only on how the rules are written but also on how they are interpreted and enforced. This points to the importance of officiating. In most quarters of women's hockey, an effort is made to have female referees for games. This is done to increase the involvement of women, to provide role models, and, most important for the practice of the sport, to insure that games are called by officials who are familiar with the women's game.

The effects of this effort are evident on occasions when the policy cannot be followed. The most common examples are in large tournaments, in which dozens or hundreds of games are played over a course of several days. On these occasions, the limited pool of referees in women's hockey often is supplemented by officials brought over from boys' and men's hockey (who are always men). My observations lead me to suggest that on these occasions complaints about referees increase. The most common explanation for poor officiating is that the "borrowed" referees do not know how to interpret and apply the rules of women's hockey, particularly the rules regarding body contact. Players often are frustrated by the inferior refereeing, wherein penalties are called for practices normally allowed or play that is normally restricted is allowed. In either case, the result is a diminished experience for players and spectators alike. In these instances, the limited development of women's hockey, evident in the need to reach out to men's hockey for officials, is one factor affecting the practice of the game.

Refereeing is also implicated directly in the debate around body checking. The interview sample for this study includes a number of coaches in areas of the country where there is little history of women playing full contact. When asked about reasons for prohibiting body checking, two (of five) respondents from one such jurisdiction volunteered that one reason is to make the game easier to officiate. These coaches indicate that because officials in women's hockey are less familiar with this aspect of the sport, eliminating contact has the advantage of improving the quality of the refereeing.

A coach from another jurisdiction, one of the most experienced in the country with extensive involvement in the highest levels of women's hockey, offered a contrasting perspective. This respondent argued that players today are bigger, stronger, and more skilled, such that at higher levels, they are routinely pushing the limits of rules on contact. In deference to "allowing the game to be played," officials must rely too heavily on judgments, rather than a clear interpretation of the rules. In this coach's view, the rules should be reviewed and rewritten to better reflect and accommodate both players' abilities and the game itself as they evolve. In contrast to the argument that the difficulty of refereeing the game is a basis for removing full contact, this respondent believes that the challenges posed to officiating by the development of the game require a reexamination of the rules, and by extension, the training of officials.

Injury and Pain in the Lives of Women Hockey Players

A concern that figures prominently in discussions of physicality in women's hockey is the risk of injury. During the first year of my fieldwork, the Blades benefited from the services of a therapist who worked with the team on a volunteer basis. Before games and practices, he ministered to players in the manner of taping, massaging, applying ice, and otherwise attending to their bodies—shoulders, legs, knees, ankles, hips, backs, and necks. This ministering was part of the regular change-room activity before the players went on the ice.

The need for a therapist or some other health professional in the everyday lives of the players was clarified in their accounts of their hockey careers. In interviews, players were asked to discuss their "history" of injuries. The collective responses provide a lengthy list of conditions. Profiles of five players include the following: Player A, age 27, has had back problems that she is certain will lead to arthritis, a separated shoulder, and a broken arm, ankle, and fingers; Player B, age 27, who considers her career to be largely injury free identifies only hip and knee injuries in addition to "the odd bruise" and groin pulls; Player C, age 26, who also sees her career as largely injury free, suffers a chronically sore back due to a vertebra that is permanently out of alignment; Player D, age 28, and one of the few players who sees her career as marked by injuries, has had separated shoulders, a broken thumb and other thumb injuries, a hyperextended elbow, shoulder tendinitis, a kneecap fracture, a "blown-out knee," and a neck injury; Player E, age 30, has had a herniated disk that kept her on her back for six weeks and a knee injury requiring arthroscopic surgery, in addition to muscle pulls, sore knees, and turned ankles.

When asked to discuss their injuries, most players initially responded with a partial account that was limited to "major" concerns like broken bones. Players also routinely experience bruises, sore joints, muscle pulls, and cuts. Often, these were omitted from their initial response, and when asked about them, players would indicate, as one did, that these are "minor stuff' and "you just warm up and play."

During the course of my two years with the team, injuries were a regular occurrence, and at any given time, one or more players were dealing with major injuries and others were managing less serious conditions. The following is an account of this aspect of team life over the course of a weekend. At a game one Saturday night, I noted injuries that were serious enough to be a topic of discussion in the change room before the game. One player injured a shoulder playing earlier in the week and intended to play that evening but avoid taking a slap shot (the shot taken with a big windup) for fear it would cause further damage. Playing was itself a matter of some risk, as she chanced being hit and further damaging the shoulder. Another player was not dressed for the game because of an injured knee that would later require arthroscopic surgery. A third player, nursing a pulled groin muscle for some time, had come out for her first skate in several weeks and was testing the muscle. Yet another player was tending a sore wrist, from a play involving a teammate, that occurred a week earlier. As they dressed before the game, these two players spent considerable time discussing how the injury had occurred and trying to reconstruct exactly what had happened. There was no sense of blame or guilt from either woman; rather, the play was clearly understood as something that "just happens" in hockey.

The picture developed further in a game the following night. The player who was already suffering from a groin pull took a skate blade in the same area and left the game for some minutes but returned. She was not cut but badly bruised and would be walking and skating very tentatively for more than a week to follow. Another player was blindsided (hit hard while looking the other way) by an opposing player and for a few moments lay immobile on the ice. She left the game but later returned, reporting that she only had the wind knocked out of her. The player with the sore shoulder played extensively and took several slapshots. When later asked about this, she said it was too hard to hold back once she started playing. In addition, she was preparing for an upcoming tryout for the Canadian national team that would compete at the 1994 World Championships and was eager to get her game up to par.

There is an important relationship between the players' experience of injury and pain and their sense of themselves as skilled athletes. Injury and pain are not an excuse for less-than-full effort or best performance. Rather, a measure of a player's ability is her capacity to play and play well despite these concerns. One player was asked, "What's it like to play when you're injured?" She responded:

In between shifts and before and after the game, you're very conscious of it. If you're in the game and you're thinking of the game, you should not realize you're injured. It could kill you like anything when you stop skating, but when you're playing you shouldn't realize it.

Q.: Does it affect your game?

If you're capable of playing, then it shouldn't.

Q.: Are there times when it does?

Well, then you shouldn't be playing.

Another player discussed her approach to playing with an injury. Player D, quoted above as one of the few who sees her career to be marked by getting hurt, said of most of her injuries,

I played through those. I was able to. I try mostly to, if I can play without really doing that much more damage then I usually try and play.

Q.: Do you play often with pain then?

I wouldn't say often. I'd say enough. . . . Especially now that I'm older [she was 28 at the time] it's a little more consistent.

Hughes and Coakley (1991, 308) have characterized the acceptance of pain in sport as "positive deviance," which they suggest is "caused by an unqualified acceptance of and an unquestioned commitment to a value system framed by . . . the sport ethic." The sport ethic is what athletes "have come to use as the criteria for defining what it means to be a real athlete." This ethic prominently features in the Blades' value system. Playing through pain is an indication of a player's ability and an affirmation of her commitment to her team and her sport.

Injuries and the Construction of the Game

The relationship between the risk of injury and the place of body checking is one of the contested features of the debate about the construction of women's hockey. Some coaches and players believe that a main reason for eliminating body checking is to reduce the risk of injury. Others dispute this association and believe that eliminating body checking has actually increased the risk of injury.[2] The explanation is that without checking, there is more illegal contact and stick work. One player who said, "I think I've had more injuries with the no intentional body checking rule in," explained the effect of this rule on the practice of the game:

I think because [with no body checking] I'm not expecting some of the hits that I'm getting because some people don't play within the rules. And if they can hit you or hurt you and hit you and put you into the boards or whatever when you're not expecting it, which usually I don't, because I think, no, we play within the rules, they don't want to get a penalty, they don't want to hurt me. You know I'm a nice person [she laughs]. So I don't expect it.

Another player offered further explanation:

I think most of the players at first liked the idea of no checking, no intentional body checking. Some of them I think have come around and said, "hey, yeah, less stick work." So okay, say you get frustrated out there and you hit somebody clean and you know it's coming, like if you know it's coming you're not going to get hurt. That's the way I always feel. If . . . there's body checking I know I'm going to get hit. Fine. I know how to go into the boards a little differently. . . . So with that in mind, yeah, I prefer the body checking, myself. It's the game.

When asked why players seem to see an inevitable trade-off between checking and illegal stick work, she explained:

Well because you've got to slow them down somehow. You've got to get in front of them somehow and usually if you can't hit them or at least take a piece of them, that's the only thing left. And that's your stick to slow them down. Myself—unless you can outskate them. Well, that's not me.

This player's comments speak to the view that checking is part of the repertoire of a hockey player's skills. When it is not available, players resort to other tactics to accomplish their task. These tactics include illegal and sometimes dangerous practices.

Other players who spoke of the risks of body checking attributed these risks to the fact that players are not taught to receive and take checks. One player said that when there was body checking:

It wasn't clean at all. Girls aren't taught how to hit. 'Cause you don't hit all the way up. Then all of a sudden you get to senior A and there's contact. No one knows how to hit; sticks are up, hands are up.

A second player provided a similar analysis. When asked about playing the game when there was body checking, she said:

Well to be honest with you checking was fine but I believe that the women weren't taught properly how to check. And there was a lot of injuries, like I was pretty scared of a few people out there just because I know, they were going to hit you like this [demonstrates], with their fists up or whatever. If checking had been taught, you know properly at a young age, just like the boys, they learn checking at a young age up, then maybe it wouldn't be so bad. Like you know, to take a hit on the boards is fine. It's just, I don't think women know how to check properly.

Medical Support and the Treatment of Injuries

The experience of injury is also conditioned by the availability of medical and therapeutic support. In interviews conducted between the two seasons I spent with the team, players were asked about the importance of having regular access to the services of a qualified therapist or other health professional. Most indicated this was important, in light of the level and intensity of play and the injuries and conditions that players contend with over a season. Some cited instances in their own biographies when such treatment was essential to their ability to play.

This assessment took on a new meaning in the following year, when there was a personnel change. The therapist who worked with the team on a volunteer basis did not return, and another was unable to maintain a regular commitment. Reliance on volunteers meant that at most games and practices there was no qualified person on site to tend to injuries as they occurred and to the players' ongoing conditions.

The absence of a therapist in the second year brought little notice or discussion among the players. Conversations with players revealed that like bruises and injuries, the women saw lack of onsite medical care as a reality of the sport they play. That is, they understand that in most quarters of women's hockey, players cannot expect to have regular access to the services of a qualified therapist or other health professional (whereas the reality of injuries was a feature of hockey generally, women's as well as men's).

This point was remarked on by one of the more senior players, during a period in which back problems forced her to miss part of the season. In an earlier interview this player indicated that when the same condition plagued her in a previous season, the regular services of the therapist were essential to her ability to play. When asked to comment on not having a therapist with the team in the current year, she indicated she was not surprised, that every season is new and has different circumstances. She then volunteered that if this were a men's team, there likely would be three trainers or therapists to work with players.

Conclusion: Women's Hockey and the Challenge to Masculine Hegemony

This discussion has focused on two aspects of the debate around physicality in women's hockey: the risk of injury and the appeal of a full-contact version of the sport versus one that prohibits body checking but is nonetheless very physical. Debate over these issues occurs within a material and ideological context that conditions the practice of the sport.

Suggestions that a "problem" with body checking is that girls are not taught this skill complement the observation that eliminating checking improves the game by making it easier to officiate. Both imply that the "problem" with checking is not the practice, per se, but limitations in the organization of the sport regarding training and skill development of athletes and officials.

The discussion of injuries also offers a critique of material conditions. Players identified the availability of medical and therapeutic support as important conditions of their participation, in light of the intensity of the game and the injuries they incur over the course of a season. Yet, among the teams that competed in the league reported on here—which offers the highest caliber of competition below the international level—the presence of qualified medical and therapeutic personnel was the exception rather than the rule.

Some respondents linked their support for the inclusion of body checking in women's hockey to the professionalization of the sport. When asked about reasons for the prohibition of body checking, a coach and a player both responded, "these people [we] aren't being paid to play" and "they [we] have to get up and go to work the next day." Another coach who endorsed the inclusion of body checking went on to note that it would only be feasible if the game were organized professionally and women could earn a living by their efforts. In effect, he was arguing for a structure that offers material rewards to athletes commensurate with their own investment and commitment.

Gender equality has received increased attention in many sports, including hockey, in recent years (Williams 1995). Calls for better training of players, coaches, and officials, and improved material conditions, including medical support, are an important aspect of the struggle within women's hockey to gain legitimation. At the same time, this struggle heightens the significance of the debate around the construction of the sport. As women players become bigger, stronger, and more skilled and as the practice of the game becomes more intense and physical, the question "How should women play hockey?" raises the ideological stakes.

Women's hockey is played in a cultural context in which men's sport is hegemonic. This view that body checking is an integral "part of the game" is emblematic of hockey as it has historically been conceptualized, practiced, and epitomized by the National Hockey League. Debates about what version of the game is most appealing, and the relation between physicality and the incidence of dirty play, occur in a context in which this version has been positioned as the "real" game and the model against which others have been compared and evaluated (Theberge 1995).

The dominance of the "NHL model" of hockey is under challenge today not only from women's hockey but also from within boys' hockey, about which parents and officials have expressed concern. Targets of criticism in boys' hockey are the style of play, which emphasizes intimidation and domination, and the competitive and elitist system that eliminates boys by early adolescence who are unable to perform by these standards. In response to these concerns, some provincial and local hockey associations have implemented programs that prohibit body checking, reduce the emphasis on winning, and stress the enjoyment of participation (Gruneau and Whitson 1993). Other alternatives to the dominant model are recreational men's leagues that prohibit body checking in the interests of safety and make the game more attractive to participants.

As Gruneau and Whitson (1993, 162) note, however, "NHL-style customs and values remain those ones that really 'count' in the subculture of Canadian hockey."

The dominance of men's hockey provides the background to much of the debate over the construction of the women's game. Against this background, to argue that women's hockey need not be the same as men's is to position the women's game as not only different from but inferior to the "real" game. Alternatively, to argue women should play the same game as men is to capitulate to the violence and other problems that plague men's hockey. Within the confines of a debate structured by the model of the "NHL style" of play, the challenge posed by women's hockey to dominant views of how the game should be played is severely diminished.

As noted, some of the players and coaches interviewed for this research dispute the contention that playing by the same rules as men will inevitably lead to the reproduction of the problems in men's hockey. They argue that women's hockey can be constructed, and the rules enforced, in a way that eliminates the violence and other unacceptable features of the men's game while including full body contact. Some contest the view that body checking increases the rate of injury. These views are significant because they suggest that debate about the construction of the women's game should not be contained by the practices and experiences of men's hockey. These arguments, however, are rarely part of the public discussion of women's hockey.

The prohibition of body checking is central to a strategy to promote women's hockey by emphasizing its differences from the men's game.[3] While the game clearly is different from men's hockey in the absence of body checking, evidence of troubling similarities is provided in the discussion of pain and injury in women's hockey. A growing body of literature examines the violence inflicted on athletic bodies through the routinization of pain and injury in sport. Initial interest in this issue focused on male athletes (Curry 1993; Messner 1990; Young 1993; Young, White, and McTeer 1994). More recent work has extended the discussion to women. Young and White (1995) examined experiences of pain and injury among a sample of elite women athletes who had incurred a variety of injuries, including broken bones, separated shoulders, dislocated knee caps, and herniated disks. These athletes normalized the presence of pain in their lives, through strategies of denial and "disrespect" or indignation toward painful injuries. Citing comparisons with earlier work they conducted with male athletes, Young and

White (1995, 51) identify similarities in the acceptance of physical danger and injury and conclude that "if difference exists between the way male and female athletes in our projects appear to understand pain and injury, it is only a matter of degree." In a study of university students, Nixon (1996) found higher pain thresholds among athletes than nonathletes and no significant gender differences in their acceptance of pain.

Injury and pain were routine features of the lives of the hockey players examined here. For these athletes, overcoming injury and pain is a measure of both ability and commitment. Like the athletes Young and White (1995) studied, the hockey players in this study showed little critical awareness of the physical dangers of their sport participation. In interviews, players were asked to comment on the element of risk in women's hockey. Most denied that it was risky, often following this assessment with rationalizations about the presence of danger in everyday life, for example, the possibility of being hit by a car while crossing a street. The increasing evidence that women athletes readily accept violence inflicted on their bodies in competitive sport suggests an incorporation of, rather than resistance to, the dominant model of men's sport.

Testimony provided at the outset of this discussion indicates the satisfaction and sense of accomplishment women hockey players derive from their sport participation. These sentiments are directly tied to the physicality of sport and the possibility for the exercise of skill and force in athletic competition. A number of writers (MacKinnon 1987; Theberge 1987; Whitson 1994) have identified these features as the basis of sport's potential to challenge traditional ideologies of gender and empower women. While women hockey players experience empowerment from their sport participation, the challenge to masculine hegemony posed by the sport is diminished in two key ways.

The transformative possibilities of women's sport are seriously compromised by the uncritical adoption of a "sport ethic" (Hughes and Coakley 1991) that celebrates toughness in the face of physical violence. One of the troubling ironies of improved material resources in women's hockey is that players now have greater affinities with a system that normalizes injury and pain.

Ideologically, the challenge to masculine hegemony is weakened by the location of the debate about the practice of women's hockey within a framework that positions men's hockey as the "real" game. While women's hockey provides clear and compelling refutation of the myth of female frailty, the potential of the sport to challenge traditional ideologies of gender is diminished by its construction as a milder version of the sport that "really counts."

The analysis presented here suggests the complexities inherent in women's involvement in "flag carrier" sports such as ice hockey. Drawing from Connell's (1983) observation that every sport involves a balance between force and skill, Whitson (1994) suggests that the more force is decisive, the more a physically dominating hegemonic masculinity can be celebrated and the more likely it is that the culture of sport will be part of the defense of the existing gender order. Whitson acknowledges that sports such as hockey and football do allow for empowerment in the absence of domination and cites testimony from former NHL player Eric Nesterenko (in Terkel 1974) on the pleasure of performing the skills required in ice hockey. This pleasure, however, was never allowed to be the central purpose of participation and usually was subordinated by the quest for victory, a quest that demanded an emphasis on force and domination. This quest, Whitson argues, becomes the norm in organized male sport at an early age.

Empowerment is perhaps more readily available through activities separate from the dominant model of masculine sport. The most well-known examples are activities engaged in outside organized sport, such as running and cycling. Another important example is aerobics. From its beginnings in the fitness boom of the 1970s, aerobics has been promoted mainly among women. For some women, aerobics has provided a safe space in which to pursue physical activity in an all-female setting, free from the competitive pressures of institutionalized sport (Hargreaves 1994).

Possibilities for challenge to masculine hegemony also exist within the context of team sports. An example is provided in Birrell and Richter's (1987) account of a women's recreational softball league. The women Birrell and Richter interviewed consciously rejected the view that the dominant model of sport, which many referred to as the "male model," is the only "real" version. Informed by this belief, they rejected an excessive emphasis on winning and domination and an ethic of endangerment that values performance over safety. Instead, they actively worked to construct and practice their own vision of sport, which emphasized the pleasure and satisfaction of participation and the development of physical skills in a supportive context.

In an analysis of the historical significance of sport for the politics of gender relations, Messner (1988) argues women's increasing athleticism represents a genuine quest for equality. This quest, however, is marked by contradictions and ambiguities over the socially constructed meanings of sport and gender. Messner concludes that in the contemporary period the woman athlete is "contested ideological terrain." This ideological struggle occurs across a variety of settings. The above brief accounts of aerobics and recreational softball suggest possibilities for challenge to masculine hegemony in contexts removed from institutionalized sport. The transformative power of each, however, is limited. In many aerobics classes and videos, the idealized version of feminine athleticism is "firm but shapely, fit but sexy, strong but thin" (Markula 1995). The sexualization of women's physicality counters the progressive possibilities contained within aerobics.

While the vision of sport realized in women's recreational softball is a genuine challenge to masculine hegemony, its marginalization within women's communities diminishes its impact on broader ideologies and gender relations. Nonetheless, in its commitment to an ethic of care and personal empowerment, this vision is important as a model for change in the world of sport and beyond.

The cultural struggle in women's hockey also is conditioned by its relation to the dominant model. Unlike the recreational softball community studied by Birrell and Richter (1987), in which participants consciously challenged the "male model," the struggle within elite-level women's hockey occurs largely within a value system regulated by this model. While women's hockey provides participants with pleasure and a sense of personal empowerment, it does so in a context that reproduces the problems of institutionalized sport. A more fully transformative vision of hockey would offer empowerment in a setting that rejects violence and the normalization of injury in favor of an ethic of care.

Notes

1. As indicated, while there is considerable contact in women's hockey, the rules prohibit *intentional body checking*. The distinction between *body checking* and *contact* is often blurred in discussions, including some of the interview excerpts provided here, in which the women's game is described as "noncontact."
2. Interviews with women who played full contact hockey during the 1980s reveal that part of collective memory of the league in which

the Blades compete is stories of particular hits and players who had an especially forceful game. While these stories are an important part of the history of the sport, there are no data to test the relationship between playing full-contact hockey and rates of injury. Some believe that to the extent body checking increases injuries, this is "limited" to serious injuries such as broken bones.

3. The main challenge to the prohibition against body checking comes not domestically but within the International Ice Hockey Federation, in which some countries argue for the inclusion of body checking in international women's hockey. Proponents of the rule change generally are from countries where development lags behind that in Canada and the United States, the dominant countries in the sport. Because the inclusion of body checking is generally agreed to slow the game down and reduce the advantage of superior playing skills, body checking is thought to offer an advantage to weaker teams. (My thanks to Elizabeth Etue for information on this issue.) It should be noted that it is unlikely that Canadian support for prohibiting body checking arises out of a concern for a loss of competitive dominance should the rules be changed. The first World Championships in 1990 were played with body checking. Canada won this tournament, as well as subsequent tournaments in 1992 and 1994 played without body checking.

References

Birrell, S., and D. Richter. 1987. Is a diamond forever? Feminist transformations of sport. *Women's Studies International Forum* 10: 395–409.

Blinde, E., D. Taub, and L. Han. 1994. Sport as a site for women's group and social empowerment. *Sociology of Sport Journal* 11: 51–9.

Bryson, Lois. 1990. Challenges to male hegemony in sport. In *Sport, men and the gender order,* edited by Michael Messner and Donald Sabo. Champaign, IL: Human Kinetics.

Cahn, Susan. 1994. *Coming on strong.* New York: Free Press.

Connell, R. W. 1983. Men's bodies. In *Which way is up?* Sydney: Allen & Unwin.

——. 1987. *Gender and power.* Stanford, CA: Stanford University Press.

Curry, Timothy. 1993. A little pain never hurt anyone: Athletic career socialization and the normalization of sport injury. *Symbolic Interaction* 16: 273–90.

Etue, Elizabeth, and Megan Williams. 1996. *On the edge: Women making hockey history.* Toronto: Second Story.

Gruneau, Richard, and David Whitson. 1993. *Hockey night in Canada.* Toronto: Garamond.

Hargreaves, Jennifer. 1994. *Sporting females: Critical issues in the history and sociology of women's sports.* London and New York: Routledge.

Hughes, Robert and Jay Coakley. 1991. Positive deviance among athletes: The implications of overconformity to the sport ethic. *Sociology of Sport Journal* 8: 307–25.

Klein, Alan M. 1993. *Little big men: Bodybuilding subculture and gender construction.* Albany, NY: State University of New York Press.

Lenskyj, Helen. 1986. *Out of bounds: Women, sport and sexuality.* Toronto: Women's Press.

MacKinnon, Catherine. 1987. Women, self-possession, and sport. In *Feminism unmodified.* Cambridge, MA: Harvard University Press.

Markula, P. 1995. Firm but shapely, fit but sexy, strong but thin: The postmordern aerobicizing female bodies. *Sociology of Sport Journal* 12: 424–53.

Messner, Michael. 1988. Sports as male domination: The female athlete as contested ideological terrain. *Sociology of Sport Journal* 5: 197–211.

——. 1990. When bodies are weapons: Masculinity and violence in sport. *International Review for the Sociology of Sport* 25: 203–18.

——. 1992. *Power at play.* Boston: Beacon.

Miller, Lesley, and Otto Penz. 1991. Talking bodies: Female bodybuilders colonize a male preserve. *Quest* 43: 148–63.

Nixon, Howard. 1996. The relationship of friendship networks, sports experiences, and gender to expressed pain thresholds. *Sociology of Sport Journal* 13: 78–86.

Terkel, Studs. 1974. *Working.* New York: Avon Books.

Theberge, Nancy. 1987. Sport and women's empowerment. *Women's Studies International Forum* 10: 387–93.

——. 1989. Women's athletics and the myth of female frailty. In *Women: A feminist perspective,* 4th ed., edited by Jo Freeman. Mountain View, CA: Mayfield.

——. 1995. Sport, caractere physique et differenciation sexuelle. *Sociologie et Societes* 27: 105–16.

Whitson, David. 1994. The embodiment of gender: Discipline, domination, and empowerment. In

Women, sport, and culture, edited by S. Birrell and C. Cole. Champaign, IL: Human Kinetics.

Williams, Megan. 1995. Women's hockey: Heating up the equity debate. *Canadian Woman Studies* 15: 78–81.

Young, Kevin. 1993. Violence, risk, and liability in male sports culture. *Sociology of Sport Journal* 10: 373–97.

Young, Kevin, and Philip White. 1995. Sport, physical danger, and injury: The experiences of elite women athletes. *Journal of Sport and Social Issues* 19: 45–61.

Young, Kevin, Philip White, and William McTeer. 1994. Body talk: Male athletes reflect on sport, injury, and pain. *Sociology of Sport Journal* 11: 175–94.

Author's Note

I would like to thank the editor of *Gender & Society* and the reviewers for their comments on earlier drafts of this article. Thanks also to Margot and Don Page for their support for my work in women's hockey. The research reported here was funded by grants from the University of Waterloo—Social Sciences and Humanities Research Council of Canada Small Grants Program and the Sport Canada Applied Sport Research Contribution Program.

Sport and the Mediated Image

Objectives

The unit examines how the media portray sport figures and influence our perception of race, class, and sexuality in sport.

When social scientists refer to the mass media they have in mind all technically organized means of communication used to reach large, geographically dispersed audiences quickly and effectively (Sage, 1998). This powerful social institution includes both print (newspapers, magazines, books) and electronic (radio, television, movies, videos, Internet) media. In total, the sector of the United States economy involved in the "production and distribution of knowledge" accounts for 29 percent of the gross national product and 31 percent of the labor force. The mass media link practically all major parts of society to one another and are involved "in virtually every major process of conflict, change, integration, and control that power seekers, communities, states, and whole societies face" (Ball-Rokeach & Cantor, 1986).

Of all the media, television is by far the most pervasive and powerful. Approximately 98 percent of all U. S. households own at least one television, which means that more American households have televisions than indoor plumbing! Television accounts for a majority of the words consumed each day by the average American, and approximately 50 percent of the population say television is their

primary source of news (compared with newspapers at 25.5 percent and radio at 11 percent) ("Where Do Americans Get Most of Their News," 2000). Further, 67 percent of all American households receive basic cable and spend a total of 61 hours and 22 minutes per week watching television ("Weekly Viewing Habits," 2000). Young people are especially heavy consumers as evidenced by the fact that by the end of high school, the average American youth will have spent 22,000 hours in front of the television set versus only 11,000 hours in the classroom (Kottack, 1990).

The economic relationship between sport and television is well established. As Pat Bowlen, owner of the NFL Denver Broncos, observed, "Leagues and teams could not exist without TV revenues. But where would television be without sports?" (cited in Hall, Slack, Smith, & Whitson, 1992, p. 134). Sport sociologist George Sage (1998) put the matter succinctly in noting that "sport and television have become mutual beneficiaries in one of capitalism's most lucrative associations" (p. 169). Organized sport benefits from the national exposure it receives, not to mention the hefty rights fees it commands from television networks. The networks profit from the association by using sports events to pack their programming schedules and by selling precious advertising seconds to corporate America (e.g., the average 30-second commercial aired during Super Bowl XXXIV cost $1.9 million). Lastly, corporate sponsors and advertisers profit because their association with popular sport events like college football bowl games, the NCAA's men's basketball championships, and the World Series guarantees them access to huge viewing audiences.

Given that males ages 18 through 49 are especially heavy sport consumers, the above arrangement is particularly attractive to advertisers who depend on male consumers for their profitability (e.g., beer, automobiles, electronics, financial services, insurance). Although the financial arrangements among leagues, television networks, and corporate advertisers are not without risk, the synergy between television and sport is likely to remain strong into the 21st century. As Rowe (1996) astutely observed, the "culture of pleasure" will continue to be centered in the private home.

The scholarly study of sport and the mass media is a relatively recent phenomenon (see Wenner, 1989). According to Hall et al. the study of the mass media and their relationship to sport has essentially taken two directions. The empirical tradition has been characterized (some would say preoccupied) by a positivistic, quantitative, more social-psychological approach to documenting the nature of media effects on individual audience members. The motives, behaviors, perceptions, values, and reactions of media-sport consumers have served as the major thrust of this line of inquiry. Overlapping the empirical tradition in recent years has been a more critical orientation with an emphasis on understanding how "ideologies become embedded in the media, and how the media organize their representations in a way that reflects the dominant ideologies of the culture" (Hall et al., 1992, p. 140).

Understanding how the media's portrayal of sport reinforces and reaffirms existing social and power arrangements is one of the key tasks confronting critical researchers as they seek to "crack the codes" (Gruneau, 1988) contained within media images and messages. Thus the reader needs to understand that mediated sport does important "ideological work" because the "makers and shapers" of media content (e.g., reporters, editors, producers, directors, photographers, writers, commentators, technicians, etc.) assign preference to the images and messages that are consistent with dominant ideologies, ideologies that best serve the interests of the powerful and influential (Coakley, 1998).

The selection, or "filtering process," conducted by media personnel is designed with one purpose in mind—to make the sport event as entertaining and engaging as possible. When a television viewer observes that "the game is much better on television," what he or she is saying is that the "edited" or "mediated" version of the game is superior to watching the game in person.

Among the preferred images and messages media producers are likely to favor are those that emphasize heroic action, fierce competition, high-level performance, aggressive play, statistics and records, the spectacular, heated rivalries, and the dramatic ("the thrill of victory, the agony of defeat"). The authors who have contributed to this unit all embrace, in one form or another, the critical tradition previously alluded to. Each in his or her own way has used textual analysis research methodology to "deconstruct" sport media messages (text) and images (pictures) to discover specific "themes"—political, moral, racial, gender, or class based—that reinforce the established social order and help promote dominant meanings and ideas (Sage, 1998).

In the first selection, Messner, Duncan, and Wachs combine both empirical and critical traditions to analyze the ways in which CBS's pregame, game, and postgame coverage of the women's and men's 1993 NCAA championship basketball tournaments helped construct an "audience preference" for the men's competition. We discover that the consequences of this gender-driven, audience-building process was to assign the men's game an aura of importance and reduce the women's game to a nonevent.

In the second selection, researchers McCarthy and Jones use hermeneutics ("the science and methodology of interpretation") to analyze the verbal messages that television commentators use to describe English soccer league play. Although no blatant racial bias or racist intent was discovered, it will become evident to the reader that performance evaluations, descriptions of physical characteristics, and psychologically based commentary differed sharply between black and white players. The reader is encouraged to consider how the racial stereotyping of athletes in general supports a corporate, white, male-dominated race ideology.

In the third selection, Jamieson uses textual analysis of selected Anglo and Latino-Latina print media to "decode" representations of Nancy Lopez, the only Latina on the Ladies' Professional Golf Association Tour. Her analysis reveals several important "themes" centered on Lopez's sexuality and ethnicity. This analysis of selected "Lopez texts" offers powerful evidence of how the print media choose to represent Lopez in racialized, classed, and sexualized gender forms.

References

Ball-Rokeach, S.J., & Cantor, M.G. (Eds.). (1986). *Media, audience, social structure.* Beverly Hills, CA: Sage.

Coakley, J.J. (1998). *Sport in society: Issues & controversies*. New York: McGraw-Hill.

Gruneau, R. (1989). Television, the Olympics, and the question of ideology. In R. Jackson (Ed.), *The Olympic movement and the mass media* (pp. 723-734). Calgary, Alberta: Hurford Enterprises.

Hall, A., Slack, T., Smith, G., & Whitson, D. (1992). Mass media and ideology. In A. Hall, T. Slack, G. Smith, & D. Whitson (Eds.), *Sport in Canadian Society* (pp. 134-153). Toronto: McClleland & Steward.

Jamieson, K.M. (1998). Reading Nancy Lopez: Decoding representations of race, class, and sexuality. *Sociology of Sport Journal, 15*, 343-358.

Kottack, C.P. (1990). Television and cultural behavior. In C.P. Kottack (Ed.), *Prime-time society: An anthropological analysis of television and culture* (pp. 87-95). Wadsworth, CA: Wadsworth.

McCarthy, D., & Jones, R. (1997). Speed, aggression, strength and tactical naivete: The portrayal of the black soccer player on television. *Journal of Sport Social & Social Issues, 21*, 348-362.

Messner, M., Duncan, M., & Wachs, F.L. (1996). The gender of audience building: Televised coverage of women's and men's NCAA basketball. *Sociological Inquiry, 66*, 422-439.

Rowe, D. (1996). The global love-match: Sport and television. *Media, Culture & Society, 18*, 562-582.

Sage, G.H. (1998). *Power and ideology in American sport*. Champaign, IL: Human Kinetics.

Weekly viewing habits (2000, February 21). *USA TODAY*, p. 8B.

Wenner, L. A. (1989) (Ed.). *Media, sports, and society*. Newbury Park, CA: Sage.

Where do Americans get most of their news (2000, February 10). *USA TODAY*, p. 11B.

Discussion Questions

Michael Messner, Margaret Carlisle Duncan, and Faye Linda Wachs

1. Do television producers simply respond to what the audience wants to see? Discuss and explain.
2. (a) In what ways are audiences "built" for major men's sporting events? (b) Do you believe this practice "serves to bolster the ideological hegemony of masculine superiority?" Discuss and explain.
3. What is meant by the statement, "A media text is never completely open." Explain.
4. Discuss and explain the ways in which male and female college basketball fans are "prepared" for the Final Four and championship games.
5. Discuss and explain the differences in the visual and aural game-day coverage of the women's and men's games.
6. To what extent have the authors convinced you that the television industry deliberately builds audiences for men's games but not women's games? Discuss.
7. In what ways might capitalist interests undercut patriarchal interests? Discuss and explain.

David McCarthy and Robyn Jones

1. Do you agree with the authors that "televised sport has a powerful role in creating and maintaining images and stereotypes"? Discuss and explain.
2. Why is television considered the most powerful of all the mass media? Explain.
3. Define a stereotype. How is the black athlete stereotyped on television? Discuss and explain.
4. How did commentators portray the physical characteristics, psychological attributes, and performances of white and black athletes? Discuss and explain.
5. Based on their findings, what did the researchers conclude about the racial stereotyping of black soccer players on television? Do you agree with their conclusions?
6. What do you think the researchers would have found if they had done a verbal content analysis of the commentary associated with televised National Football League games? Discuss and speculate.

Katherine Jamieson

1. Identify the purpose of the study.
2. Identify the data sources for this textual analysis of the media's representation of professional golfer Nancy Lopez.
3. Why do you think the media choose to represent Lopez as a symbol of racial equality in the United States? Discuss and explain.
4. Why do dominant or powerful groups frequently choose sport to do their "ideological work"? Discuss and explain.
5. How do Anglo print media represent Mexican culture? Discuss and explain.

6. How did the Anglo and Latino-Latina print media deal with Lopez's ethnicity? Explain.

7. In what sense do the print media "construct" Lopez as a heterosexual woman? What are their possible motives? Discuss.

8. In what ways does "reading Nancy Lopez" help us better understand the dynamics of white-male superiority in American society? Discuss.

The Gender of Audience Building: Televised Coverage of Women's and Men's NCAA Basketball

Michael A. Messner
Margaret Carlisle Duncan
Faye Linda Wachs

This article, based upon a comparative analysis of televised coverage of the "Final Four" of the women's and men's 1993 NCAA basketball tournaments, sheds light on some of the mechanisms through which an "audience preference" is socially constructed for men's sports over women's sports. First, we examine the temporal framing of the women's and men's tournaments by the sports/media complex. Next, we present a comparative description of the visual and verbal televised presentation of the women's and men's games. On the basis of these comparisons, we argue that the sports/media complex actively constructs audiences that are likely to see the men's Final Four as a dramatic, historic event that they simply "must" watch, while fans are likely to see the women's Final Four as a nonevent or, at best, as just another game. This, we argue, serves to situate viewers of men's sports at a nexus of power and pleasure, while simultaneously containing the potential challenge that female athleticism poses to hegemonic masculinity. Finally, we discuss, in light of socialist-feminist theory, the potentially contradictory outcomes of recent hints of increased televised coverage of women's basketball.

Since the passage of Title IX in 1972, girls' and women's participation in sports and fitness activities has skyrocketed in the United States (Cahn 1994; Snyder 1993). And although equity for women athletes is still far from a reality (Lopiano 1993), this numerical increase in women's athletic participation has been accompanied by dramatic improvements in female athletic performance and by a broadening of public support for girls' and women's sports (Nelson 1991; Wilson and the Women's Sports Foundation 1988). But one would never know these facts simply by looking at televised sports, which is consistently presented as an almost entirely male-only world (Kane and Disch 1988; Kane and Greendorfer 1994). Sport sociologists have argued that by ignoring, marginalizing, or trivializing girls' and women's sports, the media serve to bolster the ideological hegemony of masculine superiority (Messner 1988; Kane and Greendorfer 1994).

When confronted with pleas or demands to expand coverage of women's sports, editors and producers often respond simply that they are "giving the public what they want to see." To support this position, they could easily point to the Neilson Ratings for the 1993 Final Four (the games that form the basis of this study), which indicated that the two men's semifinal games garnered a 14.4 audience rating, compared with only a 3.8 rating for the women's semifinal games. The men's championship game had a 22.2 rating, while the women's championship managed only a 5.5 rating. Although such measures of audience consumption of various athletic events seem to support the industry view, we will argue that this supply-and-demand, market-driven argument is merely an ideological

Reprinted from Messner, Duncan, and Wachs, 1996.

justification for what is in fact a socially constructed "audience preference" for men's sports. In fact, television producers do not simply respond to what the audience wants to see. Rather, they attempt to actively build audiences for specific program events. Part of this audience building is a result of a rational, planned attempt to deliver a targeted market group (e.g., 35- to 49-year-old men) to advertisers (Ang 1991; Comstock 1980). And part of this audience building results from the everyday operations of what Sut Jhally (1984) calls the "sports/media complex," (which includes newspaper and electronic sports news). In this article, we will present our analysis of televised coverage of the 1993 NCAA women's and men's basketball Final Four as an example of how, through conscious choices about where and how to deploy resources, and through the day-to-day conventional practices of the sports/media complex, audiences are built for major events like the men's NCAA Tournament, the NBA playoffs, the World Series, or the Super Bowl, while audiences are not similarly built for major women's sporting events.

We want to emphasize that in focusing our analysis on the production end of the text of televised women's and men's basketball, we are limited in our ability to assess the ways that audiences might variously read or interpret this text. A recent popular trend in media studies has been to stress the "openness of the text," and the ability of audience members to "modify or deflect" the hegemonic ideologies that may be encoded in the text (Fiske 1987, p. 64). Surely, people do tend to consume and interpret a text in at least somewhat different ways: nevertheless, a text is never completely open, like "an imaginary shopping mall in which audience members could wander at will, selecting whatever suits them" (Murdock 1989, p. 36). Rather, a media text contains a "preferred reading" that is "structured in dominance" (Hall 1973, p. 13). As David Morley (1992) argues, "The moment of encoding thus exerts, from the production end, an over-determining effect (though not a fully determined closure) on the succeeding moments in the communication chain" (p. 52).

Thus, although we believe it is important to conduct ethnographic studies of audiences, our concern here is with how the choices of televised sports producers and commentators might serve to actively build audiences in ways that support masculine hegemony while undercutting any potential challenge posed by women's sports. After analyzing the text of televised coverage of the 1993 NCAA basketball women's and men's Final Four, we will

conclude with some speculative points about how, from the production end, audiences are actively built for men's sports in ways that combine viewing pleasure with masculine power. For women's games, we will argue, this combination of pleasure and power is undermined by several factors.

The Study

There are two general issues that should be addressed in discussions of televised coverage of women's and men's sports: (1) *Which athletic events are covered?* Television producers, editors, and sports news broadcasters engage in information gatekeeping, which is "the process by which billions of messages that are available in the world get cut down and transformed into the hundreds of messages that reach a given person on a given day" (Shoemaker 1991, p. 1). (2) *How are athletic events covered?* Once gatekeepers decide to cover an event, numerous decisions are made as to how an event should be covered: How much time, human resources, and money should be devoted to producing an event (Creedon 1994; Duncan 1993; Theberge and Cronk 1986)? How should a news story or live athletic event be framed by broadcasters? What parts of a story or an event should be covered or not covered; what should be emphasized, de-emphasized, or ignored (Messner and Solomon 1993; Sabo and Jansen 1992; Theberge 1989)?

In 1993, we explored these questions in our study of televised sports (Amateur Athletic Foundation of Los Angeles 1994) that served as a follow-up to a study we had conducted in 1989 (Amateur Athletic Foundation of Los Angeles 1990). Both studies addressed both quantitative and qualitative aspects of televised coverage of women's and men's sports. As with the 1989 study, our major questions concerned the quality of actual coverage of women's versus men's athletic events. Therefore, we examined televised sports programs in which men's and women's coverage could be analyzed comparatively. First, we analyzed three two-week segments of televised sports news coverage on each of three local (Los Angeles) network affiliates. Second, we analyzed the women's and men's singles, women's and men's doubles, and mixed doubles matches of the 1993 U.S. Open tennis tournament. And third, we analyzed the Final Four of the women's and men's 1993 NCAA basketball tournaments. In this article, we will focus on the third of these categories (though we will draw from our TV news data insofar as it reflects upon coverage of the NCAA basketball tournaments).

The Temporal Frame: Preparing the Audience for Game Day

We have identified two ways that television, as a whole, builds audiences in advance of the playing of the men's NCAA Final Four basketball tournament, while largely failing to do so for women's Final Four: (1) showing far more regular season and postseason men's games than women's games; and (2) covering regular-season and postseason men's games on nightly news broadcasts while mostly ignoring women's games.

Broadcasts of Regular-Season and Postseason Games

As table 23.1 indicates, an examination of the television listings in the *Los Angeles Times* for the entire 1992-1993 basketball season (November 24, 1992-April 5, 1993) revealed that far more regular-season men's games than women's games were televised.

Although CBS showed the women's and men's Final Four, these numbers indicate that nearly all of the women's regular-season games were on cable, not on network television. Moreover, women's games were far more likely than men's to be tape-delayed (i.e., usually late-night) broadcasts, a practice that virtually ensures a small audience. The numbers for televised coverage of postseason NCAA Division I games were similar, as indicated in table 23.2.

Again, the numbers for postseason broadcasts indicate that far fewer women's games were televised, most were on cable (the only three women's postseason broadcasts on network television were the two semifinal games and the championship game), and nearly half were tape-delayed.

Coverage of NCAA Basketball on Nightly News Broadcasts

During the six weeks that we examined televised sports news on three network affiliates, we found almost no coverage of women's sports. The numbers (94% of the time devoted to coverage of men's sports, 5% to women's sports, 1% to gender-neutral topics) were almost identical to the proportions we found in our 1989 study. Two weeks of our TV news sample, for March 15-28, occurred during the First Round, Second Round, and Regional Championships of the women's and men's NCAA basketball tournament. During this 2-week period, the three stations combined devoted a total of 22 minutes to women's sports, compared with 254 minutes to men's sports. During the 42 broadcasts that we analyzed during this 2-week period, there were a total of 10 stories on the women's NCAA basketball tournament and 41 stories on the men's tournament. Visuals accompanied 39 of the men's stories (usually taped action shots), but only 6 of the women's. The men's stories averaged 2 minutes, 16 seconds, while the women's stories averaged 36 seconds each.

These statistics actually tend to *understate* the extent to which serious women's athletic events such as golf, distance running, tennis, or basketball were either ignored or quickly glossed over in the nightly news reports. Instead, when a choice was made to focus on a women's event or a female athlete, it was often a gag feature or a story on a marginal (but visually entertaining) sport. For example, on a March 28 Sunday night sports news broadcast, 1 minute, 19 seconds was spent covering nuns playing with bikini-clad women in a celebrity volleyball game. The footage included smirking comments by the broadcaster ("Meet 75-year-old Sister Matilda Gerber . . .") and comical shots of the nuns making various bloopers, with the "Chariots of Fire" theme song playing in the background. The same broadcast featured a 2-minute, 19-second piece on a female "sky gymnast" or "aerial free-stylist." This relatively unknown sport obviously

Table 23.1   1993 Televised NCAA Division I Regular-Season Basketball Games, by Sex

	Total games	On cable	Non-cable	Tape-delayed
Men's games	370	311	59	71 (19%)
Women's games	29	26	3	11 (38%)

Reprinted from Messner, Duncan, and Wachs, 1996.

Table 23.2   1993 Televised NCAA Division I Postseason Basketball Games, by Sex

	Total games	On cable	Non-cable	Tape-delayed
Men's games	68	40	28	3 (4%)
Women's games	14	11	3	6 (43%)

Reprinted from Messner, Duncan, and Wachs, 1996.

requires superior athletic skills and courage, but the broadcasters undercut the woman's athleticism with sarcastic remarks. In the remainder of the show, they squeezed in 8 seconds of women's tennis (with verbal coverage only), 6 seconds of women's basketball (with verbal coverage only), and 13 seconds of women's golf (with verbal coverage and with a film clip). Thus, of 4 minutes, 5 seconds of coverage of women's sports, 3 minutes, 38 seconds consisted of snide, condescending coverage of a gag feature and of a relatively unknown sport. Twenty-seven seconds were shared by women's golf, tennis, and basketball.

In addition, news stories on women athletes were far less likely than those on men athletes to be accompanied by interviews with athletes or coaches (13 of the 41 men's basketball stories were accompanied by interviews, while only 1 of the 10 women's stories was). A typical example of how this was played out occurred on a March 27 broadcast. The report opened with a 2-minute, 10-second story of the men's NCAA basketball tournament games, complete with action film clips from the games, discussions of the statistical performances of the star players, an interview with Indiana coach Bobby Knight, and mention of the upcoming tournament semifinal matchup. This dramatic, in-depth report was followed immediately by the following: "In the women's tournament, Iowa beat Tennessee, 72-56; Ohio State beat Virginia 75-73." This report, which ran for 8 seconds and was accompanied by no film footage or interviews, conveyed none of the excitement of the games (particularly the Ohio State vs. Virginia cliffhanger) and did not mention the upcoming tournament semifinal matchups.

When women athletes were interviewed, the quality of the interviews was usually at best uneven and ambivalent; at worst the interviews were condescending. An example of the latter was a March 21 live studio interview with college basketball star Lisa Leslie. The first comment that the interviewer made had nothing to do with Leslie's performance or women's basketball at all; instead, he turned to the topic of the *men's* game: "I know you're a big men's basketball fan; you didn't get a chance to see the Bruins. I saw when the guys walked off you told them congratulations, which was very nice of you." Later in the same interview, after Hill brought the discussion back to women's basketball, he declared, "And you've also seen yourself, Lisa, mature, not only as a lady, but as a basketball player on the court, taking more of a role of leadership." These two interview fragments illustrate two tendencies in the ways women athletes

are commonly interviewed and reported on. First, even during the rare focus on a woman athlete, priority somehow is given to men's sports as the standard. And second, sportscasters seem rarely to be able to talk to women athletes or discuss their skills without referring to their femaleness.

Game Day: Tightening the Frame

Our analysis of the actual broadcasts of the three women's and three men's games revealed two general categories of qualitative difference: (1) the visual and aural framing of the contests; and (2) the gendered nature of the verbal commentary. In the descriptions that follow, we will deploy numbers when appropriate, but will rely mostly on textual descriptions.

Visual and Aural Framing of the Contests

As in the 1989 study, the visuals and the sound in the three men's 1993 contests were consistently of the highest quality. The camera angles and the editing of visuals were technically sophisticated. Graphics were sophisticated, stylish, and frequent. The commentators were "high-profile," experienced, and skillful. The sound was clear. Throughout the games, the shot clock and the game clock appeared on screen frequently and appropriately. We noted in the 1989 study that by contrast, the three women's contests were characterized by poor sound quality, periodic mistakes in editing, generally less skillful and colorful commentary, far less frequent appearance of game and shot clocks on screen, and the use of fewer camera angles. Graphics were used less frequently, and occasionally incorrectly. In the 1993 study, we identified some notable improvements in the visual and aural framing of the women's games, but the production quality of the women's games tended to be uneven and, overall, still lagged behind that of the men's games.

Pregame Framing of the Contests

Verbal and cinematic clarity, combined with some form of either emotional, intellectual, or narrative development, are key elements in the creation of an opening sequence capable of instigating and maintaining audience participation. To accomplish this, camera operators choose well-composed, focused, and ideally evocative shots. The editors combine the shots in a meaningful, continuously evolving fashion, choosing bits of interview that add excitement, poignancy, or information. Just as in the 1989 study, the openings for the men's 1993 games offered a model of these techniques. The openings for the women's 1993 games—though better than the 1989 openings—again tended to ignore these tenets.

Pregame Shows for Men's Games

Hip, entertaining, and enhanced by many of the filmic conventions of contemporary music videos, the opening segment of the men's Final Four gets the contest off to a great start. A catchy Paul Simon song provides both the music and theme for the opening. The song, with chorus lyrics "I'm on my way, I don't know where I'm goin' . . . seeing me and Julio down by the schoolyard" accompanies black and white, hand-held footage of two teenage boys playing a game of HORSE in an urban schoolyard. Each player goads the other to try increasingly difficult shots, made famous by their heroes in college basketball: "Do my man, Billy McCaffry's move, now a Daryl Hancock reverse shot," and so forth. Exciting NCAA clips are intercut with slow-motion footage of the schoolyard game, filmed in such a way as to make the teenage boys' moves appear professional, and at times superhuman. Sound effects such as the sound of a rocket emanating from a flying basketball and the excited commentary of NCAA announcers played over the playground HORSE game add to drama. The last fantasy basketball shot of the HORSE game works as a transition to the main event, taking the audience and the ball "off the building, down Bourbon street, and across the river" to the Louisiana Superdome. An opening of this quality easily captures and maintains the interest of the audience. In mythologizing college players, and fostering the dreams of boys and young men playing high school pickup games, the opening further increases interest in the upcoming games and in men's basketball in general.

Next, the tone changes with a super-wide-angle aerial zoom-out from the Superdome, a cut to a closer shot of the dome, a dissolve to a wide, high-angle shot from the dome interior, then to a courtside shot, shots of spectators, and finally to announcer Pat O'Brian, whose voice we've been hearing speaking with excitement about sellout crowds. The stylistic change keeps our attention from straying.

The contest is set up with commentary, laced with words that feel as though they must be capitalized, that lends an epic dimension to the event. "Each [team] banged their way through two games in four cities. They've all gathered in the Crescent City for what is clearly a Basketball Classic called the Final Four. What a show this Final Four will be—three #1 seeds and one #2—Elite Teams." Pat O'Brian then talks briefly about stars in both of the semifinal games and shows footage from a breakfast interview held earlier with one of them, Eric Montross. Lesley Visser follows from the floor with an update on injured players and descriptions of particular matchups. More excitement is then created with archival footage from earlier championship games—famous game-ending shots by players wearing #23, set to music, then dissolving to contemporary footage of this year's #23, Rex Walters. Will we see the same quality of play from one of this year's stars? Interviews and footage shot in the apartment of the "odd couple," Kansas stars Rex Walters and Adonis Jordan, follow this introduction, allowing us access into their private lives.

Finally, Georgetown coach John Thompson joins O'Brian and James Brown for an intricate game analysis illustrated with an electronic chalkboard—enhancing the sense of elaborate strategizing—and a look ahead to the second semifinal game. A five-point graphic and verbal game analysis precedes each of the men's games as well.

The pregame show for the men's championship game was perhaps even more dramatic. The 40-minute show, entitled "Prelude to a Championship," underlined the momentous nature of the upcoming game. The segment included numerous interviews with members of both teams, sophisticated and entertaining graphics, various statistics on the players and the teams, and more interviews and expert commentary on what it would take for each team to win the game.

Pregame Shows for the Women's Games

Although more coherent than the introduction to the 1989 women's games, the introduction to the 1993 semifinal women's games seemed to express a lingering ambivalence regarding women athletes. The theme of the women's opening was not a schoolyard game of HORSE (with a direct relationship to a sporting event) but, instead, a concept pulled from the television show "Designing Women": Our players, too, are "women with designs, designs on a national championship." A clip from the show's title sequence begins the opening program with the image of a red rose. A series of dissolves between images of individual players and images of flowers, backed up by the slow-paced

"Georgia, Georgia," gets the show off to a sentimental, sappy start. Commentary about the upcoming games is intercut with clips from the TV show that act as transitions. For example, a shot of players arriving at the station is followed by a character from the show excitedly exclaiming, "It's hootenanny time!" The theme music from the show playing under the clips has as much drive as something heard in a dentist's office. The sequence ends with a character from the show exclaiming, "We made it!" followed by an uneven zoom to reveal the stadium interior. The program probably cost very little to make.

Iowa coach Vivian Stringer had recently lost her husband to a heart attack, and a fair amount of attention was given to the many "heartaches this season" that made "Vivian Stringer's team the sentimental choice." Next, announcer Mary Carillo built up some excitement outside of the stadium as she spoke about the record-breaking sellout crowds: "You know you've really arrived as a big-time sport when for the first time tickets are being scalped outside your event. That's what's been happening here outside the Omni Arena all morning. . . . The Omni seats 16,000 for the women's Final Four, and it's been sold out for over a week. . . . Another first ever for the Women's Final Four, a Las Vegas betting line on the game—boy, all the sport needs now is a couple of juicy scandals, some dope testing, point shaving, and it'll be just as big as the guys! Well, hopefully it'll never get *that* big."

The rest of the pregame show consisted of an interview with one of the coaches. Pregame discussion of strategies was hampered by the lack of an expert commentator. Whereas all of the men's games included at least one expert commentator, such as Georgetown coach John Thompson, the first women's semifinal game had no expert commentator (though the subsequent two games did).

The pregame show for the women's championship game consisted entirely of a 1-minute, 30-second montage of highlight footage from earlier games, edited to a medium tempo song with slightly ridiculous lyrics: "You better run or you hide, now you slip, now you slide, you say you will but you won't, you really do or you don't"—repeated several times. This very brief, low-budget prelude to the women's national championship stood in stark contrast to the dramatic 40-minute "Prelude to a Championship" that preceded the men's game.

The Half-Time Shows

There was a striking difference in the quality of the men's and women's half-time shows. The half-time shows of the women's games constantly cut back and forth between discussion and analysis of the women's game and discussion and pregame hype of the upcoming *men's* games. For instance, the half-time show of the women's semifinal game between Ohio State and Iowa begins with a brief interview with Marsha Sharp, coach of the victorious Texas Tech team, followed quickly by a "peek at the scene" [of the men's games] in New Orleans, where, we are told, "a modern-day battle" will soon be fought. This "peek" includes seven clips from interviews with male players in which they tell us what it means to them to have made it to the Final Four. We then return to the women's game, where Marsha Sharp and guest commentator and Stanford coach Tara Vanderveer offer their predictions concerning the outcome of the men's games. Overall, this half-time show allotted about two-thirds of its time to a discussion of the men's game, players, and teams. By contrast the men's half-time shows concentrated almost entirely on the men's games, including statistical overviews of the first half, graphic shot charts, and expert discussions of strategy and tactics for the upcoming second half. During the half-time shows of the men's semifinal games, there was a single mention of the women's games: "The women had their national semifinal games."

The same gender differences occurred in the half-time shows of the championship games, where considerable time was spent during the women's half-time show in interviews of the two coaches of the men's teams. There was no analogous set of interviews with the coaches of the women's teams during the men's half-time show.

The Postgame Shows

The postgame shows of the women's and men's championship games also showed contrasts in their respective production values. The men's game ends with dramatic camera cuts back and forth between celebrating, victorious players and weeping female cheerleaders. Next we see the ritual championship net cutting with the announcer's voice-over intoning that the net cutting "has to be one of the defining moments of a young man's life." The importance and drama of the moment is further underlined by interviews with some of the winning players and an interview with the losing coach, Steve Fisher. By contrast, as the women's game ended, the cameras cut back and forth between the celebrating winning team to lingering close-ups of the tear-streaked faces of the losing players. And although announcer Tim Ryan stated positively that the game was "a dandy," and "all that a championship game should be," there were no postgame interviews on the floor or in the locker room, and no coverage of the net cutting. The postgame wrap-up for the women's national championship game took only 2 minutes, 25 seconds, and that included a 9-second plug for the upcoming men's championship game and pregame show.

Those Little Extras

The men's games were also characterized by several "extras" that indicated a policy of greater investment in the production of men's games than of women's.

- The pregame introductions of the players and coaches. When a male player was introduced, an on-screen graphic showed his name, position, year in school, height, and weight. By contrast, when a woman player was introduced, an on-screen graphic showed only her name and position. Similarly, when a coach in the men's games was introduced, an on-screen graphic showed the coach's number of winning seasons and his lifetime win-loss statistics. When a coach in the women's games was introduced, this information was not supplied to viewers.
- In the men's games, after nearly every time-out or commercial break there was a statistical graphic or a slow-motion replay. This was not the case in the women's games.
- In the men's games, after every basket the score and the game clock were shown, adding excitement and emphasizing the pace of the game. This was not the case in the women's games.
- During the men's pregame and half-time shows, and at times throughout the men's games, sophisticated on-screen graphics and expert commentators' frequent use of the telestrator added both pizzazz and important information about on-court strategies to the viewing experience. These sorts of graphics and telestrator use were far less frequent in the women's games.

Undercutting Women, Glorifying Men: The Verbal Commentary

Just as in the 1989 study (see Messner, Duncan, and Jensen 1993), we identified numerous gender differences in the ways that the commentators spoke of women and men athletes.

Gender Marking

In the 1989 study, we noted that announcers and on-screen graphics in women's basketball constantly gender-marked women's games (e.g., "Welcome to the women's national championship game") and women athletes (e.g., "She holds the women's record for the most points in a game"). By contrast, the men's games and the male players were always referred to verbally and in graphics as the universal norm (e.g., "Welcome to the national championship game" and "He holds the record for the most points in a game"). We suggested that this practice tends to make women's events seem derivative and inferior to men's contests.

As in 1989, we found in the 1993 study that gender marking in women's tennis was roughly equivalent to that in men's tennis. This parity likely reflects a need to equally mark men's and women's events for the sake of clarity, given the fact that the women's and men's tennis matches take place in the same venue and are somewhat overlapping in terms of the timing and sequence of the matches. In basketball, where the events are taking place in a different venue, with different announcers, we again found dramatic differences in the amount of gender marking in the women's and men's games, as table 23.3 indicates. In women's basketball, verbal gender marking remained constant in 1993, but graphic gender marking rose dramatically in comparison with 1989. Men's basketball was gender-marked four times verbally in 1993, an increase from zero in 1989. But we see this increase as insignificant. Once again, men's basketball was consistently referred to as the universal (e.g., "The National Championship Game"), with women's basketball gender-marked constantly (e.g., "The Women's National Championship Game").

Table 23.3   Instances of Gender Marking in TV Reporting of Basketball, 1989 and 1993

	Graphic	Verbal	Total
Men, 1993	0	4	4 (1.3/game)
Men, 1989	0	0	0 (0/game)
Women, 1993	229	47	276 (92/game)
Women, 1989	28	49	77 (25.7/game)

Note: Observations made for three men's and three women's games in each year.

Reprinted from Messner, Duncan, and Wachs, 1996.

Table 23.4   Instances of Gender Marking in TV Reporting of Basketball, Including Mention of Team Names

	Graphic	Verbal	Team names	Total
Men, 1993	0	4	0	4 (1.3/game)
Men, 1989	0	0	0	0 (0/game)
Women, 1993	229	47	55	331 (110.3/game)
Women, 1989	28	49	102	179 (59.7/game)

Note: Observations made for three men's and three women's games in each year.

Reprinted from Messner, Duncan, and Wachs, 1996.

In the above tabulations, we did not include the use of team names (e.g., "The Lady Techsters"), as we wanted to underline the gender-marking choices made by the commentators and producers of the show. However, as table 23.4 shows, if we add the number of times that gendered team names were mentioned or included in graphics, we can see that the viewers of the women's games were once again subjected to a constant barrage of verbal and visual reminders that they were watching *women's* basketball and *women* athletes.

Verbal Attributions of Success and Failure

In the 1989 study, basketball and tennis announcers tended to describe women's and men's action differently. For instance, basketball and tennis commentators appeared to hold two formulas for success: one for men, the other for women. Men appeared to succeed through a combination of talent, instinct, intelligence, size, strength, quickness, hard work, and risk taking. Women also apparently succeeded through talent, enterprise, hard work, and intelligence. But commonly cited with these attributes were emotion, luck, togetherness, and family. Women were likely to be framed as failures because of some combination of nervousness, lack of confidence, lack of "being comfortable," lack of aggression, and lack of stamina. Men were far less often framed as failures—men appeared to miss shots and lose matches not so much because of their own individual shortcomings (nervousness, losing control, etc.), but because of the power, strength, and intelligence of their (male) *opponents*. This framing of failure suggests that it is the thoughts and actions of the male victor that win games, rather than that the loser's lack of intelligence or ability is responsible for losing games.

In the 1993 study, we found greater respect for women athletes' abilities and less ambivalence about their strengths, but this change was especially evident in the women's tennis commentary. By contrast, we noted in comparison with the 1989 commentary more lingering (though perhaps more subtle) gender differences in the basketball commentary about errors in play and failures (Duncan, Aycock, and Messner 1994). When women basketball players made errors in play, the commentators pointed them out repeatedly and meticulously and attributed them directly to the player who made them (e.g., "She missed that shot"). Comparable errors in the men's games tended to be disguised or redefined by commentators in one of four possible ways: (1) Errors were not spoken of at all (e.g., no comment was made about a missed shot); (2) an error by one player was attributed to the superior ability of an opponent (e.g., after a bad pass: "I think he surprised Jalen Rose with his defensive ability to stop what normally Rose throws over the top of guards' heads"); (3) errors were minimized by commentators' noting that they didn't reflect the player's true skills (e.g., "It's kind of unusual to see Jordan throw that one away") or that the error was caused by factors beyond the player's control (e.g., "It was a tough ball to catch, though, 'cause the backboard was causing some problems"); and (4) errors were described using descriptive words that seemed to attribute the cause of the error to chance, rather than to a player's actions (e.g., "The ball hits the rim and bounces off").

Sport Media and the Contested Meanings of Gender

Through a comparison of the televised coverage of the women's and men's NCAA basketball Final Four, we have demonstrated some of the ways that the television industry actively builds audiences for men's games, while failing to do so for women's games. There are two general but interrelated levels of this audience building. First, in terms of the larger (industry-wide) temporal frame, producers decide to show large numbers of men's regular-season games on television and very few women's games. Meanwhile, televised nightly news echoes this cacophony of words and images about men's games while virtually ignoring the women's games. As a result, it is reasonable to assume that when the men's NCAA Final Four arrives, fans have been actively constructed into the picture—indeed, they are "part of the game." Very likely they already know a great deal about the men's teams, the players, coaches, and even the announcers. During an exciting and crucial game situation, the fans will recall (and be reminded by the announcers) previous games in the season (or in seasons past) where a player made (or failed to make) the big play, or when a coach made a winning or disastrous strategic move. Moreover, they are likely to be remarkably familiar with these individuals to the point of knowing intimate, non-sports-related biographical information that adds poignancy and drama to watching the "big game." By contrast, most fans tuning in to the women's Final Four could not be expected to have been familiar with the teams or the players. Although on game day networks introduced the audience to one or two women star players "up close and personal," since few regular-season games had been aired and electronic and print media had given so little attention to women's sports, very few, if any, of the star women basketball players or coaches were known by name in advance by most sports fans. The televised sports news contributed to the women's Final Four being seen as a trivial nonevent by affording the games only token coverage, and by affording regular-season women's games almost no coverage at all.

We are arguing, then, that the sports/media complex actively constructs audiences that are likely to see the men's Final Four as a dramatic, historic event that they simply "must" watch, while fans are likely to see the women's Final Four as a nonevent or, at best, as just another game. On game day the actual presentation of the contests serves dramatically to reinforce this difference. As we have shown, the pregame, half-time, and postgame shows are indicators of a dramatically greater investment in the men's games than in the women's. This inequity was most glaring in the ways that the women's games were used to build audience interest for men's games.

Finally, the verbal commentary, though improved since our 1989 study, still tended consistently to mark women athletes and the women's games as the derivative, inferior, gendered "other," while framing men athletes and their games as the universal, superior (nongendered) standard. The verbal commentary framed men as powerful, active subjects, in control of their own historic destinies, and women as reactive objects, verbally denied of their strength, status, and ability (Duncan and Hasbrook 1988).

It is important to reiterate the point we made at the outset concerning the limits of a study that analyzes a text, without taking into account the actual "readings" of that text by audiences. Yet we would like to speculate about the possible outcomes, for audiences, of the encoded gender differences we have pointed to in the text. First, we speculate that the gendered differences discussed above operate to situate fans of men's basketball in a nexus of power and pleasure that gives them the feeling of being part of an exciting event of historic import. As Duncan and Brummett (1989) have argued, there are various sources of viewing pleasure for fans of televised sports. Our research suggests that sports programmers intertwine these viewing pleasures with dominant ideologies of hegemonic masculinity (heterosexuality, physical power, violence, winning at all costs, etc.). We suspect that this is a key to understanding the current state of play of mediated men's and women's sports in the construction and possible contestation of gendered power relations. Second, our observations suggest that not only has television failed, thus far, to build audiences for women's basketball; it has actively undermined the possibility of the development of such an audience. The sports media complex gives audiences no reason to be interested in, much less excited about, tuning in to view a women's Final Four tournament that may seem to descend into their living rooms from virtually nowhere. For those who did tune in, the event was likely to have been experienced as lacking in historical depth, and lacking in the kind of technical razzle-dazzle that builds knowledge, interest, and emotional connection. As a result, the viewer is likely to have experienced the women's games as somewhat disorienting, perhaps even boring.

But is television in the mid-1990s, led by corporations like Nike (Cole and Hribar 1995), beginning to discover and actively build audiences for women's sports? Since we conducted the study that this article is based upon, a potentially meaningful change has taken place. In 1995 ESPN began to broadcast a significant number of women's regular-season NCAA basketball games. An unsystematic viewing of ESPN news during the 1995 season suggests that ESPN at least incrementally increased their news coverage of women's NCAA basketball, perhaps in a conscious attempt to build audiences for their own broadcasts. Though this cable sports network's increase in coverage of women's basketball has not had any apparent spillover into network sports news coverage of women's NCAA basketball, it does raise some important theoretical and political questions. First, in simply leaving the discussion of the relative quantity of coverage of women's and men's sports within the context of an assessment of market rationality, advocates of equality are conceding a significant political terrain. Socialist-feminist analyses have long shown how capitalism has historically used gender inequalities to control and reproduce the labor force, to produce markets for consumption, and ultimately to maximize profits. But clearly, the dominant interests of capitalism and patriarchy are not always in accord. For instance, it could be argued that industrial capitalism, while exploiting women's unpaid labor and utilizing women as a reserve army to undercut men's wages, also created the structural basis for the creation of the women's liberation movement. Moreover, it is also apparent that when it is seen to be in accordance with corporate and/or state interests, elites can move affirmatively (at least partially and sometimes temporarily) to undermine gender divisions and inequalities (e.g., the undercutting of the gendered public/domestic split and the creation of daycare centers for working mothers during World War II).

Given this institutional flexibility, it is apparent that the post-Title IX surge of female athleticism has created a potentially huge market for the sports industry. But the sports/media complex has been very slow to build audiences aimed at exploiting this potential market, owing perhaps to the fact that the sports media are so thoroughly dominated by men who have been raised in a system that has taught them to equate sports with men and masculinity (Nelson 1994; Messner and Sabo 1994). But what if, as the recent moves by ESPN suggest, some leaders in the sports/media complex have begun to recognize and take affirmative moves toward tapping this potential market? What will it mean if the larger sports/media complex follows ESPN's lead, and we see dramatic increases in the quantity of coverage of—and active audience building for—women's sports, as we approach the turn of the century? We speculate that such a change would result, simultaneously, in several related and contradictory outcomes. On the one hand, a dramatic increase in the quantity of coverage of women's sports could lead to increased profits for the sports/media complex, increased revenues for girls' and women's sports, and thus a dramatic undercutting of the current role of sports in providing ideological "proof" of the "natural superiority" of men over women. In other words, this is an example of an area in which capitalist interests might undercut patriarchal interests. On the other hand, as our study suggests, even a roughly equal quantity of coverage of women's and men's events can be undercut by subtle (and not so

subtle) differences in the quality of production and framing of the events, and in the gendered language of the commentators. Moreover, if significant numbers of men in the population still look to sport as an arena in which they symbolically bond with other men as superior to women, it is possible that increased quantity and quality coverage of women's sports will lead to an increased interest in the kinds of men's sports that celebrate the most extreme possibilities and expressions of powerful, aggressive, and violent male bodies. In other words, the sports/media complex is perfectly capable of building audiences for women's sports—thus undercutting one basis of masculine hegemony—while at the same time responding to the new "needs" of a threatened male audience by providing increasingly violent sports that continue to "separate the men from the girls."

Endnote

The research for this article was funded by the Amateur Athletic Foundation of Los Angeles. We thank Wayne Wilson of the AAF for his support in this project. We also thank Kerry Jensen for her primary data collection. The article benefited from suggestions by Bob Dunn and Bill Solomon.

An earlier version of this article was presented at the 1995 American Sociological Association meetings in Washington, D.C.

References

Amateur Athletic Foundation of Los Angeles. 1994. "Gender Stereotyping in Televised Sports: A Follow-up to the 1989 Study." Los Angeles: Amateur Athletic Foundation.

Amateur Athletic Foundation of Los Angeles. 1990. "Gender Stereotyping in Televised Sports." Los Angeles: Amateur Athletic Foundation.

Ang, Ien. 1991. *Desperately Seeking the Audience*. London and New York: Routledge.

Cahn, Susan K. 1994. *Coming on Strong: Gender and Sexuality in Twentieth-Century Women's Sports*. New York: Free Press.

Cole, Cheryl L., and Amy Hribar. 1995. "Celebrity Feminism: Nike Style, Post-Fordism, Transcendence, and Consumer Power." *Sociology of Sport Journal* 12: 347-369.

Comstock, George. 1980. *Television in America*. Beverly Hills, CA: Sage.

Creedon, Pamela J. 1994. "Women, Media and Sport: Creating and Reflecting Gender Values." Pp. 3-27 in *Women, Media and Sport: Challenging Gender Values,* edited by Pamela J. Creedon. Thousand Oaks, CA: Sage.

Duncan, Margaret Carlisle. 1993. "Beyond Analyses of Sport Media Texts: An Argument for Formal Analyses of Institutional Structures." *Sociology of Sport Journal* 10: 353-372.

Duncan, Margaret Carlisle, Alan Aycock, and Michael A. Messner. 1994. "Engendering the Language of Sport: NCAA Basketball, Foucault and Formulas of Exclusion." Paper presented at the meetings of the North American Society for the Sociology of Sport, Savannah, Georgia, November.

Duncan, Margaret Carlisle, and Barry Brummett. 1989. "Types and Sources of Spectating Pleasure in Televised Sports." *Sociology of Sport Journal* 6: 195-211.

Duncan, Margaret Carlisle, and Cynthia A. Hasbrook. 1988. "Denial of Power in Televised Women's Sports." *Sociology of Sport Journal* 5: 1-21.

Fiske, John. 1987. *Television Culture.* London: Methuen.

Hall, Stuart. 1973. "Encoding/Decoding in Television Discourse." In *Culture, Media, Language,* edited by S. Hall et al. London: Hutchinson.

Jhally, Sut. 1984. "The Spectacle of Accumulation: Material and Cultural Factors in the Evolution of the Sports/Media Complex." *Insurgent Sociologist* 12(3): 41-57.

Kane, Mary Jo, and Lisa J. Disch. 1988. "Media Coverage of the Female Athlete Before, During, and After Title IX: *Sports Illustrated* Revisited." *Journal of Sport Management* 2: 87-99.

Kane, Mary Jo, and Susan L. Greendorfer. 1994. "The Media's Role in Accommodating and Resisting Stereotyped Images of Women in Sport." Pp. 28-44 in *Women, Media and Sport: Challenging Gender Values,* edited by Pamela J. Creedon. Thousand Oaks, CA: Sage.

Lopiano, Donna A. 1993. "Political Analysis: Gender Equity Strategies for the Future." pp. 104-116 in *Women in Sport: Issues and Controversies,* edited by Greta L. Cohen. Thousand Oaks, CA: Sage.

Messner, Michael A. 1988. "Sports and Male Domination: The Female Athlete as Contested Ideo-logical Terrain." *Sociology of Sport Journal* 5: 197-211.

Messner, Michael A., Margaret Carlisle Duncan, and Kerry Jensen. 1993. "Separating the Men from the Girls: The Gendered Language of Televised Sports." *Gender and Society* 7: 121-137.

Messner, Michael A., and Donald F. Sabo. 1994. *Sex, Violence and Power in Sports: Rethinking Masculinity.* Freedom, CA: Crossing.

Messner, Michael A., and William S. Solomon. 1993. "Outside the Frame: Newspaper Coverage of the Sugar Ray Leonard Wife Abuse Story." *Sociology of Sport Journal* 10: 119-134.

Morley, David. 1992. *Television, Audiences and Cultural Studies.* London and New York: Routledge.

Murdock, Graham. 1989. "Critical Inquiry and Audience Activity." In *Rethinking Communication,* Vol. 2, edited by B. Dervin et al. Newbury Park and London: Sage.

Nelson, Mariah Burton. 1991. *Are We Winning Yet? How Women Are Changing Sports and Sports Are Changing Women.* New York: Random House.

Nelson, Mariah Burton. 1994. *The Stronger Women Get, the More Men Love Football: Sex and Sport in America.* New York: Harcourt Brace.

Sabo, Donald F., and Sue Curry Jansen. 1992. "Images of Men in Sport Media: The Social Reproduction of the Gender Order." Pp. 169-184 in *Men, Masculinity, and the Media,* edited by Steve Craig. Newbury Park, CA: Sage.

Shoemaker, Pamela J. 1991. *Gatekeeping.* Newbury Park, CA: Sage.

Snyder, Marjorie A. 1993. "The New Competition: Sports Careers for Women." Pp. 264-274 in *Women in Sport: Issues and Controversies,* edited by Greta L. Cohen. Thousand Oaks, CA: Sage.

Theberge, Nancy. 1989. "A Feminist Analysis of Responses to Sports Violence: Media Coverage of the 1989 World Junior Hockey Championship." *Sociology of Sport Journal* 6: 247-256.

Theberge, Nancy, and A. Cronk. 1986. "Work Routines in Newspaper Sports Departments and the Coverage of Women's Sports." *Sociology of Sport Journal* 3: 195-203.

Wilson Sporting Goods Co. and the Women's Sports Foundation. 1988. *The Wilson Report: Moms, Dads, Daughters and Sports.* New York: Women's Sports Foundation.

Speed, Aggression, Strength, and Tactical Naivete: The Portrayal of the Black Soccer Player on Television

David McCarthy
Robyn L. Jones

The aim of the study was to analyze whether the language used by television commentators during the coverage of domestic English soccer matches differed according to the race of the player. It was hypothesized that the English television medium constructed negative images of the black domestic soccer player through the descriptive narratives and metaphors adopted. The methodology was composed of a verbal content analysis (as used by Sabo and colleagues). The analysis centered on the identification and categorization of positive and negative commentator remarks. The categories were (a) players and their performances, (b) physical characteristics of players, and (c) psychological characteristics of players. Although black players were depicted positively in each of the defined categories, evidence of covert racial stereotyping was found in the excessive positive depictions related to the physicality of the black players and the psychological characteristics of the white players.

The relationship between professional sport and the mass media has been characterized as a "symbiotic" one (Leonard, 1993) in which "sport and television have become mutual beneficiaries in one of capitalism's most lucrative associations" (Sage, 1990, p. 123). Thus, television uses sport to increase viewing figures, whereas sport uses television as an avenue to increase income.

Within this symbiotic relationship, televised sport has a powerful role in creating and maintaining images and stereotypes. Thus, it contains the potential to shape the images we receive of people and to construct information that reproduces underlying values in a society (McPherson, Curtis, & Loy, 1989). Whannel (1992) supported this suggestion, making note of the many different stereotypes of foreigners that have unfolded partly around images of sport, whereas Sabo and Jansen (1994) were even more explicit in their belief that the sports media have great power in shaping the images we receive of people, particularly from different racial groups.

Coverage of televised sport in England has escalated in the 1990s with growing penetration into homes by the BSkyB and Eurosport satellite services (Key Note Publications, 1995), whereas the traditional terrestrial channels of the BBC and ITV also are devoting more of their prime-time slots to covering sports events, in particular football (soccer) (Key Note Publications, 1995). Mass exposure is the result of this escalation, transmitting and reflecting images of televised soccer to an increasing number of viewers. Indeed, the power of the mass media today stems in many ways from their ability to be "in more or less instantaneous, continuous touch with the majority of the population" (Hargreaves, 1986, p. 138) and, consequently, have the ability to impose stereotypical images on millions of people. Sabo and Jansen (1994) referred to such a status as

Reprinted from McCarthy and Jones, 1997.

the capacity to create and shape "pictures in our heads" with all the resultant implications.

The growth of electronic media, and in particular television, has been central to the development of this potential. Indeed, according to Birrell and Loy (1979), television, above all other media forms, best meets the affective (pleasurable and emotional experiences) and escapist (tension release and escape from normal roles) needs of the sports consumer. Thus, it is little wonder that television has been considered by many as Western culture's most potent instrument of interpretation (Sage, 1990), which, together with huge sporting audiences, makes the mediated sports event a very powerful agency through which meanings are constructed.

An integral part of this process, the announcers and commentators are carefully selected to command credibility (Sage, 1990). Although the media rely heavily on the personas of all the individuals involved here, a hierarchy of relations between commentator and the accompanying expert summarizer, in terms of credibility of comment, often is seen to exist. The accredited experts usually are former athletes who, in turn, possess high name recognition and whose statements are perceived to convey knowledge and authority. Thus, whereas the commentator has the prime responsibility for description, it is the view of the expert that serves to legitimize media interpretation (Hargreaves, 1986). In investigating this phenomenon further, Sage (1990) contended that such former sports stars are "models of the competitive meritocracy. . . . [Thus,] their social consciousness is congruent with dominant value perspectives" (p. 130). Consequently, the finding that they espouse the "commonsense" hegemonic perspectives and interpretations of mainstream society should not come as a surprise.

In the domain of race relations, Cashmore (1994) noted, "A stereotype is often defined as an overgeneralization about the behavior or other characteristics of members of particular groups" (p. 323). Racial stereotypes can thus be positive and/or negative, whereas apparently positive stereotypes often can imply a negative evaluation. For example, to say that blacks are athletically gifted comes close to the negative stereotype of the lazy black athlete in that he or she does not have to work hard to obtain athletic excellence. Similarly, Sage (1990) highlighted a trend in the American mass media of attributing black athletes' achievements to their natural abilities. Such media reporting and commentary often possess a commonsense authenticity, thus reproducing racist stereotypes of blacks as natural athletes. Sage (1990) made note of a trend in the

American sports media toward attributing white athletes' achievements to their intelligence.

Earlier research studies (Jackson, 1989; Rainville & McCormick, 1977), in examining the representation of black athletes in televised sport, have generally supported Sage's (1990) contention regarding the existence of commonsense stereotypical images. By contrast, a recent study undertaken by Sabo, Jansen, Tate, Duncan, and Leggett (1995) found that the television production techniques adopted (e.g., narratives, framing devices) provided racially unbiased treatment of all athletes.

The aim of this study was to investigate whether the language used by television commentators during the coverage of domestic English soccer games differed according to the race of a player. It aimed to investigate whether the English sporting television medium constructed negative images of black domestic soccer players through the narrative used.

Taking as a guideline Birrell's (1989) definition of race as "a category popularly constructed along assumptions of biological distinctions indexed by color and then naturalized through cultural practices," the term *black* within the context of the present study refers to all non-white players. To include all mixed-race players within the black category also would be in line with the cultural commonsense assumption made regarding the aforementioned racial group within the wider British society, thus reinforcing the construction of racial categorization as a social rather than biological phenomenon. Finally, the terms *football* and *soccer* are used interchangeably within the study to describe the commentary of the sport under investigation, as is customary in the United Kingdom.

The significance of the work is grounded in an investigation into how sport continues to contribute to the "reproduction of particular configurations of racial relations" (Birrell 1989, p. 218). An acknowledgment for the need to move beyond a descriptive study of race is thus recognized with an investigation of how race relations are produced and reproduced through sport.

In addition, contradictory findings in previous research (Jackson, 1989; Rainville & McCormick, 1977; Sabo et al., 1995) have suggested the need for further study to determine whether the narrative adopted by television when covering domestic soccer games differed according to the race of a player. Furthermore, because there currently is a relative paucity of information on this issue in relation to English sport, no meaningful cross-cultural comparison with American or other televised sport can be conducted at this time. The lack of such research thus further provides a basic premise on which the significance of the present study is based.

Messner's (1988) conviction is that the entire mediation of the sporting event is based on invisible, taken-for-granted assumptions and values of dominant social groups such as event "framing," be it conscious or subconscious. This should be revealed so that future productions may reflect a more egalitarian outlook. It is within these confines that the real significance of such research lies.

Literature Review

Sports events experience a change when they are presented in the media (Hall, Slack, Smith, & Whitson, 1992; Hargreaves, 1986). According to Hargreaves (1986), media sport does not just present the world as it is; rather, it re-presents the world through its own interpretative framework, creating events with their own features. Through their consequent ability to create definitions of reality, the media help shape the individual's perceptions of the social world (Hall et al. 1992). For example, the language used in mediated sport has the ability to impose ideological viewpoints on the coverage of a game (Kinkema & Harris, 1992), consequently suggesting the hegemony of one group over another. In the context of sport, white male dominant ideology may be supported by using "natural physical ability" to explain a black athlete's success (as opposed to intelligence and hard work or commitment). Thus, the individual thinks that he or she "hears and sees it like it is" when, in reality, television coverage gives only one of many possible sets of images and messages (McCarthy, 1996).

The production codes used to create particular images or messages during a televised sporting event include camera angles, close-ups, slow-motion replays, commentators' play-by-play descriptions, and the postgame analysis (Coakley, 1994). These techniques of production, whether visual or auditory codes, can be selectively used or "filtered." They provide a distinct portrayal of the sporting world that usually is in line with dominant ideological viewpoints (Clarke & Clarke, 1982; Coakley, 1994; Gruneau, 1989; Kinkema & Harris, 1992).

Although sport offers a hoard of positive images of talented black athletes succeeding, it also assists in the proliferation of instances of racial stereotyping. Furthering this point, Whannel (1992) suggested that one of the principal ways in which this stereotyping is articulated on television has been in terms of the "natural ability" of the black athlete.

Similarly, Dewar (1993) suggested that, in explaining the success of blacks in sport, natural ability has been promoted to reinforce stereotypes so as to assimilate "the facts," or explanations as to why blacks are successful in sport, into existing frameworks without challenging hegemonic representations. By making commonsense assumptions as to why the black athlete is so successful (i.e., by suggesting that the black athlete has natural ability), the mass media can covertly make positive excuses as to why the white athlete is not so successful. In relation, Ellison (1964), as cited by Sabo and Jansen (1994), made the interesting observation that the object of the stereotype (in this instance) is not so much to crush the black man as it is to console the white man. However, as Hargreaves (1986) pointed out, by portraying blacks as successful in sports and failing to portray them as successful elsewhere, the media reproduce the stereotype that blacks, being naturally better at physical pursuits and less so at intellectual ones, are closer to nature and, therefore, less civilized than whites.

In a similar vein, Sage (1990) stated that where a black athlete's achievements have been attributed to his or her natural ability to run fast, a white athlete's achievements typically have been attributed to his or her intelligence. Thus, physicality is suggested by Birrell (1989) as "the key to the construction of dominant images of racially defined groups" (p. 222) with a belief that the black is better at sport because of a natural physical advantage. The stereotypical image of the physically powerful black in contrast to the intelligent white results in an image of the black athlete gaining any superiority in sport only because of a commonsense belief that the black is a better athlete because he or she "was made that way."

Recent research (Sabo & Jansen, 1994) has suggested that producers of sports media are becoming more conscious about the ways in which they portray differing racial groups and can project more positive images of blacks. However, excessive exposure of, as well as exposure to, black athletic success could aggravate the problem rather than act as a remedy, with such achievements only reinforcing traditional stereotyped images about blacks being adept at physical pursuits but inept at intellectual ones.

Methodology

The basic method of research was a verbal content analysis of Premier and Endsleigh League soccer coverage, screened on ITV, BBC, and BSkyB satellite television during a 2-week period of the 1995-1996 domestic soccer season, to determine whether verbal descriptions of players varied according to race. An explanatory point to note is that the Premier League is composed of the apex of the professional soccer pyramid throughout England and Wales, whereas the Endsleigh League is composed of three divisions inclusive of automatic promotion and relegation between each other and to/from the Premier League.

The following programs devoted to soccer provided the data for the study: live Premiership games on the Sky Sports satellite station, live Endsleigh League games on ITV, *Match of the Day* on the BBC (incorporating Premiership highlights), and *Goals on Sunday* (a program showing extended highlights of the previous day's Premiership matches) on the Sky Sports satellite station. It was believed that a sample of programs from a variety of channels would provide more reliable and representative data. The aforementioned programs were videotaped from the opening sequences through the closing credits.

In total, 37 hours of football footage screened on satellite and terrestrial television were recorded, which corresponded to the samples used in similar studies (Jackson, 1989; Rainville & McCormick, 1977). The specific programs examined included the following:

- Six screenings of *Match of the Day*, making a total of 7 hours of footage, shown on the BBC. *Match of the Day* predominantly screened highlights of Premiership games. However, included in the 7 hours of analysis was the exclusive live coverage of the 1996 F.A. (Football Association) Cup semifinal between Manchester United and Chelsea.
- A total of 3 hours of *Goals on Sunday* (three screenings), a program screened on the Sky Sports satellite station that showed highlights of the previous day's Premiership games.
- Six live matches, focusing on the Premiership and F.A. Cup competitions, screened on the Sky Sports satellite station. Each of these six programs had a duration of between 3 and 4 hours. In addition to the featured live game, Sky's soccer coverage featured highlights of other matches already played during these broadcasts. In total, 22 hours of football footage screened on Sky Sports' *Monday Night Football* and *Super Sunday* were analyzed.
- Two live Endsleigh League Division 1 games screened on ITV. In total, *The Sunday Match*

contributed to 5 hours of footage. Highlights of other Endsleigh League games were shown. The comments made about these highlights also were included in the results of this study.

In line with previous research (Sabo et al., 1995; Trujillo, 1995), commentator dialogue was transcribed, with various elements of the verbal content taken as units for analysis. The verbal descriptors used by commentators to portray and characterize players were put into three analytical categories. The first category was composed of evaluations of players and their performances, the second related to the physical characteristics of players, and the third concerned psychological descriptors of the players.

Positive and negative evaluations within each of these three categories were counted to determine whether any difference of frequency occurred in the number of times positive and negative remarks were made about black and white players. A positive and negative evaluation in each category used by a commentator when describing a player was taken as a single unit in the counting of verbal descriptors to determine any variations in frequency of use between black and white players.

In the study, the term *commentator* referred to any individual talking about, or making reference to, a player during the actual footage of a game, whether live or recorded. No distinction was drawn between the play-by-play commentator and the expert summarizer in this regard. The verbal descriptors used in pre- and postmatch analyses of clips of action taking place in the studio, or in the broadcasting booth at the venue, were thus defined as commentator remarks and, consequently, contributed to the findings of the study. Comments made in pre- and postmatch discussions also were included in the study.

In relation to the first category of the verbal content analysis, positive and negative commentator evaluations of players' past achievements, as well as present performance, were defined and counted. From earlier pilot work, it was anticipated that positive evaluations would include phrases and sentences such as "one of the most exciting players on the pitch," "technically an excellent player," "having a good game," "one of the best finishers in the game," "a player who always seems to perform well on the big occasion," and "always seems to have plenty of time on the ball." It was similarly anticipated that negative evaluations would include phrases and sentences that suggested criticism or disapproval such as "he's having a terrible game," "he's very inconsistent," "poor effort on goal," "a very one-footed player," "bad pass," he's not really made an impact on today's game," and "poor clearance."

Positive and negative commentator remarks referring to physical characteristics of players also were defined and counted. Anticipated examples of positive physical descriptors included "so strong," "very athletic player," "strong in the tackle," "tremendous running," "strong running," "great leaping ability," "so strong in the air," "an imposing physical figure," "shielded the ball well," and "very quick over the first 5 yards." It was similarly anticipated that negative remarks referring to physical characteristics of players would include "weak on the ball," "not the quickest," "easily knocked off the ball," and "not the biggest player on the pitch."

Finally, psychological descriptors referred to phrases or sentences that described or called attention to the inner emotional state or personality characteristics of a player. It was anticipated that psychological descriptors would include "he's just not thinking," "did not use his head," "focused on the task at hand," and "not concentrating on his job."

To ensure accuracy of interpretation, interobserver agreement was sought throughout the categorization process. As a result of a high degree of consequent correlation between two observers, the validity and reliability of the findings were further increased. In addition, the production techniques used and the consequent visual images broadcast during the footage covered also were analyzed. Thus, the programs' opening sequences were examined to establish whether images emphasized racial diversity and whether the types of images portrayed on-screen reflected established racial stereotypes.

Results

The findings illustrated in table 24.1 provide no evidence to suggest that English football commentators criticized black players, in terms of evaluating the players and their performances, more than white players. Indeed, of the 772 comments that were made in regard to the evaluation of black players' performances, 26% were negative, which compared equally with the 423 (25%) negative evaluations made in the 1,717 comments about white players' performances. Thus, from a chi-square analysis of the data, it was concluded that no significant difference in the number of positive and negative evaluatory comments between black and white players existed.

Black players were indeed depicted positively as opposed to negatively by commentators in all three analytical categories, thus providing no explicit evidence to suggest that commentators constructed negative representations of black players. However, closer examination of the results reveals discrepancies in the verbal descriptors used to depict the two racial groups.

Although both blacks and whites were depicted positively in the category referring to the physical characteristics of players, it is notable that blacks were praised more often in physical terms. Indeed, 115 of the 120 comments (96%) made about the physical characteristics of black players made positive references (e.g., "quick," "strong," "well built"). Of equal significance was the fact that only 4% of the comments made in this category were negative. This suggests commentators' perpetual use of the stereotype of the strong black athlete, whether overtly or covertly, when referring to the physical characteristics of a black player. Conversely, only 38% of the positive comments made about physical

Table 24.1   Comments Made About Players in Each of the Three Categories as Interpreted Along Racial Lines

	Evaluation of players and their performances			Physical characteristics of players			Psychological descriptors		
	Total	Negative	Positive	Total	Negative	Positive	Total	Negative	Positive
Black	772	197 (26)	575 (74)	120	5 (4)	115 (96)	57	26 (46)	31 (54)
White	1,717	423 (25)	1,294 (75)	74	29 (39)	45 (61)	167	35 (21)	132 (79)

Note: Percentages are in parentheses.

Reprinted from McCarthy and Jones, 1997.

characteristics in the footage analyzed referred to white players, adding further support to this stereotyping suggestion.

In addition, of the 74 comments made about the physical characteristics of white players, only 45 were positive (61%), in stark contrast to the figure for black players. A significant difference in the number of positive and negative comments in relation to the physical characteristics between black and white players was revealed from chi-square analysis of the data.

The findings illustrate that both white and black players were depicted positively in psychological terms. However, it should be noted that 79% of the comments made about white players fell into the positive category, whereas only 54% of the comments about black players fell into the positive category. Thus, a higher percentage of black players were depicted negatively in a category that makes reference to the thinking ability of an individual, from significantly fewer commentator remarks. Indeed, of the 57 commentator remarks that described the psychological state of black players, 46% were negative. When comparing this to the percentage of negative commentator remarks for white players in the category (21%), taken from a significantly larger number of comments, a discrepancy between black and white players is apparent. Although not represented negatively, compared to comments made about white players, a significantly larger percentage of comments made about black players suggested a demeaning psychological state. Thus, from a final chi-square analysis of the data, a significant difference was found in the numbers of positive and negative comments made in relation to the psychological characteristics between black and white players.

After viewing the opening sequences of the programs that constituted the study, it was found that the images generally emphasized racial diversity. However, four images portrayed in the opening sequences of *Match of the Day* can be questioned in terms of stereotyped racial representation. These particular images seem to evoke the stereotypes of the "unintelligent," "foolish," "happy," "laid back," and "athletically gifted" black and are discussed more fully in the next section.

Discussion

Akin to the findings of Sabo et al. (1995), no evidence was found that commentators composed negative representations of black players when reference was made to players and their performances. These findings are in contrast to those of Rainville and McCormick (1977), who found that the language used by commentators in the coverage of American football aided the construction of negative reputations in relation to the technical ability of black players.

Within the confines of the present study, in terms of technical ability, black players were praised as profusely as were their white counterparts. Positive messages describing blacks as extremely talented individuals were constantly dispatched from the footage covered. Whannel (1992) outlined this apparent vogue sport has for portraying the black athlete in a positive light by noting that "an analysis of representations of black people on television suggests that, in contrast to the images of social problems, inner-city riots and the racist discourses of crime and immigration, sport coverage offers a striking contrast" (p. 130).

Echoing this, many positive images of black players as "good soccer players" (John Barnes, Les Ferdinand, Paul McGrath, and Peter Ndlovu, to name only a few) were clearly evident within the data, with these individuals being expressly described as talented people. Injecting a note of caution here, however, Sabo and Jensen (1994) suggested an underlying agenda to the praise in that "in effect, media images of black men as physically adept and economically successful athletes tend to obscure Blacks' and Whites' historical relationship of oppression" (p. 153).

In agreement with the earlier work of Jackson (1989), the results of the present study reveal that 62% of all the comments made about the physical characteristics of players were made about blacks. It can be argued that this language and the stereotype it suggests feed the "pictures in our heads" of the physically gifted black. Similarly, it is noteworthy that in the category examining psychological descriptors, almost half the total comments made referring to black players were negative. Consequently, if the findings within this latter category are considered with those referring to physical characteristics, it also could be argued that an image of the physically powerful, athletic, but unintelligent black athlete was being covertly suggested.

Of equal significance is the fact that such a massive proportion of comments referring to the physical characteristics of blacks were positive. Examples from the footage analyzed included "[Sol] Campbell, a powerhouse of a figure," "[Michael] Duberry, such a strong player in defense," and the most overt example, with Les Ferdinand, Newcastle United's black center forward, being referred to as "big, strong, quick, powerful, with the ability to hang in the air" in a prematch discussion. Similarly, according to Sage (1990), subtle racial stereotyping also has been present in the reporting of black athletes' performances in the American sports media, with the most blatant example being "the frequent attributions of black athletes' achievements to their 'natural' abilities to run fast" (Sage, 1990, p. 134).

Continuing on from the suggestion made by Sage (1990), by excessively portraying the black soccer player in positive physical terms, it is being implied that any success achieved is due to an inherent physical advantage the black player has over the white player. Here, an ostensibly positive stereotype could imply a negative evaluation (Cashmore, 1994), with the picture of achievement being distorted. Consequently, however much success the black athlete gains, when his or her performance is being associated with natural ability, the implicit suggestion remains that it should be remembered that the white athlete is competing without the natural ability possessed by the black athlete. Thus, in a bizarre way, the covert suggestion is made that the white athlete still is superior. Within this context, Dewar (1993) made the point that in explaining the success of blacks in sport, natural ability is popularized to underline stereotypes so as to assimilate "the facts" into existing frameworks without challenging hegemonic representations of blacks. According to Cashmore (1982), the view that black success in certain sports is not due to hard work but rather due to an intangible capacity called natural ability holds sway among coaches, managers, and even athletes themselves. If this is the case, then it can only be expected that those indirectly associated with sport, in addition to those in wider society, will have beliefs in a similar stereotypical image.

That stereotypes regarding the black player and the associated concepts of "stacking" and "centrality" exist in English football is beyond doubt (Maguire, 1991; Norris & Jones, in press). However, when hearing the descriptions of players occupying noncentral positions that traditionally are associated with strength, speed, and reactive capabilities, a question emerges as to whether the description is of the player or the position, the race of the player being incidental. It thus could be argued that commentary emphasizing physical attributes merely reflects the needs of the position and is therefore not a reflection of the race of the player. Nevertheless, taking this into account, the over-

representation of blacks in noncentral roles created largely by the stereotypes relating to their physical attributes ensures that the perceived need of the position and the image of the black athlete are locked into a mutually reinforcing set of constraints. Thus, the racial hegemony as manifest through the prevailing stereotype is maintained.

As indicated in table 24.1, this study found that black players received a significantly higher percentage of negative commentator remarks concerning psychological descriptors than did white players. Comments made in this category often made reference to the thinking ability of players. Clear examples of positive remarks made about white players in this category included "[Dennis] Berkamp's intelligent runs" and "[Eric] Cantona's intelligence took him into that position." No such blatantly positive remarks were made about black players.

A large proportion of the negative comments made about black players in this category referred to players being "too casual" or "overconfident" with "a little too casual by [Gary] Charles" and "overconfidence from [Faustino] Asprillia" being two examples. These comments call forth images that feed the racial stereotypes of blacks as "too casual in their approach" or as having a "couldn't care less" facade (Cashmore, 1982). However, Cashmore (1982) counters the suggestion of the black athlete as laid back, making note of the attempt by black athletes to transmit an impression of themselves as cool in that "they like people to believe they are always relaxed and unflustered. In other words, they work at it, which is a quite different thing from saying they are psychologically predisposed to remain relaxed under pressure" (p. 51). Cashmore (1982) continues by suggesting that, if anything, the psychological condition of the black athlete should be tension packed given the social circumstances surrounding his or her involvement, with sport providing a possible avenue out of his or her everyday existence.

Although the results of the study indicate that reference was made to the intelligence of the black player, it was not made to the extent of the "intelligent play" and "general awareness" referred to the white player. Thus, it can be concluded that one racial group was expressly favored over the other when being described as executing intelligent play, with instances of illiberal language evident that could be interpreted as reflecting the stereotypical image of the black athlete. Nevertheless, although such a tendency was evident, the findings generally are in contrast to those emanating from the research of Rainville and McCormick (1977) and Jackson (1989), who found specific evidence of overtly negative representations of the black athlete as unintelligent.

According to Cashmore (1994), images of backwardness and stupidity have become associated with blacks, which in turn have become unquestioningly accepted as part of commonsense assumptions. Such an "ideology's strength rests on people's failure to unmask it and examine alternative ways of viewing reality" (p. 136). Sabo et al. (1995) further supported this viewpoint by suggesting that race remains an indisputable social fact because people continue to assign attributes to groups based on presumed physical differences. Furthermore, the continuation of socially structured silences around these attributes historically has served the status quo of racial inequality (Sabo et al., 1995).

In further examining the function of the image of the body in sport, Trujillo (1995) argued that the athletic body is a key resource in reproducing a preferred political and cultural ideology. Similarly, Foucault (1977) concluded that the body and its image are vested with power and domination and that its use as an ideological conduit is "more subtle [than others] because its use appears more 'natural' and less connected to politics and other institutions" (Trujillo, 1995, p. 404).

Birrell's (1989) related concept of physicality is closely linked to such hegemonic masculinity and can be seen in the spheres of race and gender alike. Within the latter field, American media studies since the 1970s have revealed that women athletes were more likely to be overtly trivialized, infantilized, and sexualized through coverage (Boutilier & San Giovanni, 1983; Duncan, 1990; Dyer, 1987; Felshin, 1974), thus continually emphasizing female physical inferiority as compared to male athletes. Thus, the masculinist hegemony is reproduced through the manipulation of images of natural physicality and interpreted physical inferiority.

According to Birrell (1989), a comparable analysis "could also be brought to race relations and sport if we focus on physicality as the key to the construction of dominant images of racially defined groups" (p. 222). Such images relate to the naturally talented black athlete and the consequent commonsense assumption regarding the inherent physical advantage possessed by the black athlete. Consequently, in an examination of sport, and of sports coverage in particular, as an area for increasing gender and racial equality, Hargreaves (1993) noted that caution is well founded. Thus, although recent studies (e.g., Elueze, 1996) show that media recognition of

female athletes and athletic events is increasing, by progressively partaking in male-defined sports and consequently allowing increasingly direct comparisons to male athletes, further evidence of the "natural superiority" of male athletes is represented with cultural stereotypes being reinforced. Similarly, through continuing positive emphasis on the physical attributes of black athletes at the expense of the cognitive attributes, a picture of the physically gifted black athlete as opposed to the cognitively gifted white athlete is produced. The hegemony of physicality is thus applicable to race and gender alike.

Such a hegemony, however, never has been absolute (Hargreaves, 1993) and is in constant need of reproduction and reinforcement. It is within this context that the media play a crucial role in that their "general definition of reality promotes the dominant political-ideological agenda" (Elueze, 1996, p. 21). Furthermore, the credibility of the media as the objective authoritative interpreter of events is maintained by the apparent lack of agreement on all issues. Thus, the granting of increased coverage time to female athletes and athletic events, and the portrayal of black athletes in almost unequivocally positive terms, could be viewed as a reflection of the continued reinforcement of commonsense assumptions and stereotypes by the media, whose credibility and legitimacy are enhanced through an illusion of neutrality.

Through observation of the media, people piece together a commonsense picture of reality and, by accepting this picture, make themselves available for exploitation by those who dominate society (Cashmore, 1994). A crucial feature of this situation is that those accepting the commonsense picture remain unaware of their exploitation. The language used in mediated sport has the capacity to impose ideological viewpoints, and, although no outright reference was made to blacks as "stupid" or "unintelligent" within the confines of the study, the covert instances of stereotypical images identified may serve this purpose. As Messner (1988) noted, the entire mediation of the sporting event is based on invisible assumptions and values of dominant social groups. As such, presentation of the event tends to support corporate, white, and male-dominant ideologies.

In addition to racial diversity, the images generally portrayed in the opening sequences of the programs analyzed did not reflect the stereotypical image of the black athlete. This result resonates the earlier findings of Sabo et al. (1995). Yet, it can be argued that a number of particular images in the opening sequences of *Match of the Day* clearly called forth images that reflected and fed racial stereotypes.

The first shows a white player, Eric Cantona, using extravagant skill to completely "fool" and "trick" a black player, Carlton Palmer. The second shows the "speed" of Les Ferdinand, a black center forward, and the third depicts Dwight Yorke, Aston Villa's black center forward, as smiling. Such images could be taken to reflect the physicality, coolness, or happy black figure, all stereotypical images of the black person. Indeed, in further exploring the image of the happy or "comical" black, in the extreme, it could be argued that *Match of the Day* producers in this instance were using "recycled racial stereotypes inherited from black face minstrelsy" (Dates & Barlow, 1993, p. 196). Finally, and most overtly in this regard, a white player, David Platt, is depicted in the clear role of "organizer" and "director" of play on the field. Platt is shown pointing teammates into position while "mouthing" instructions. This image is all the more questionable when it is noted that Platt, although an experienced international player, is not even the captain of his team, thus providing no obviously identifiable reason to portray him in this way. In a similar vein, Michener (1976), cited in Cashmore (1990), described the Harlem Globetrotters' comical antics as deepening the stereotype of the loveable, irresponsible black. Within the present context, it can be suggested that, to a certain extent, the visual image of a smiling Dwight Yorke is doing the very same thing.

Conclusion

Although black players were depicted more positively than negatively in all three categories analyzed, instances of covert stereotyping were found in the way that black players were portrayed and described. The findings thus support Whannel's (1992) assertion that "while sport offers a fund of positive images of talented Black athletes succeeding, it also serves to reproduce elements of stereotypical attitudes" (p. 129). Consequently, although no unfeigned racially structured language was evident from the footage covered, it appears that the image of the black player depicted, to a considerable degree, continues to be "filtered through the racial misconceptions and fantasies of the dominant White culture" (Dates & Barlow, 1993, p. 523).

No evidence emerged that those commentating on the soccer footage analyzed were guilty of blatant racial bias in the language used, which tended to echo the earlier findings of Sabo et al. (1995). However, a difference in the number of positive and negative comments made relating to the psychological descriptors and physical characteristics between black and white players was evident. Thus, although the language adopted by commentators in this study may not have been made with any racist intent, racial ideology is so deeply rooted within Western culture that no doubt racism sometimes exists without awareness (Coakley, 1994).

References

Birrell, S. (1989). Racial relations theories and sport: Suggestions for a more critical analysis. *Sociology of Sport Journal, 6*, 212-227.

Birrell, S., & Loy, J. (1979). Media sport: Hot and cool. *International Review of Sport Sociology, 14*(1), 5-19.

Boutilier, M.A., & San Giovanni, L. (1983). *The sporting woman.* Champaign, IL: Human Kinetics Books.

Cashmore, E. (1982). *Black sportsmen.* London: Routledge & Kegan Paul.

Cashmore, E. (1990). *Making sense of sport.* London: Routledge.

Cashmore, E. (1994). *Dictionary of race and ethnic relations* (3rd ed.). London: Routledge.

Clarke, A., & Clarke, J. (1982). Highlights and action replays: Ideology, sport and the media. In J. Hargreaves (Ed.), *Sport, culture and ideology* (pp. 62-87). London: Routledge & Kegan Paul.

Coakley, J. J. (1994). *Sport and society: Issues and controversies* (5th ed.). St Louis, MO: C.V. Mossy.

Dates, J. L., & Barlow, W. (1993). *Split image: African Americans in the mass media* (2nd ed.). Washington, DC: Howard University Press.

Dewar, A. (1993). Sexual oppression in sport: Past, present, and future alternatives. In A.G. Ingham & J.W Loy (Eds.), *Sport in social development* (pp. 147-165). Champaign, IL: Human Kinetics Books.

Duncan, M.C. (1990). Sports photographs and sexual differences: Images of women and men in the 1984 and 1988 Olympic Games. *Sociology of Sport Journal, 7*, 22-40.

Dyer, G. (1987). Women and television: An overview. In H. Baeher & G. Dyer (Eds.), *Boxed in: Women and television* (pp. 6-16). New York: Pandora.

Ellison, R. (1964). *Shadow and act.* New York: Random House.

Elueze, R. (1996). *A quest for equality: A gender comparison on the BBC's TV coverage of the 1995 World Athletic Championships.* Unpublished dissertation,

Brunel University College, Isleworth, United Kingdom.

Felshin, J. (1974). The social view. In E.W. Gerber, J. Felshin, P. Berlin, & W. Wyrick (Eds.), *The American woman in sport* (pp. 179-279). Reading, MA: Addison-Wesley.

Foucault, M. (1977). *Discipline and punish: The birth of the prison* (A. Sheridan, Trans.). New York: Pantheon.

Gruneau, R. (1989). Making spectacle: A case study in television sports production. In L.A. Wenner (Ed.), *Media, sports and society* (pp. 134-154). Newbury Park, CA: Sage.

Hall, A., Slack, T., Smith, G., & Whitson, D. (1992). *Sport in Canadian society*. Toronto: McClelland & Stewart.

Hargreaves, J. (1986). *Sport, power and culture*. Oxford, UK: Polity.

Hargreaves, J. (1993). Gender on the sports agenda. In A. Ingham & J. Loy (Eds.), *Sport in social development* (pp. 167-186). Champaign, IL: Human Kinetics.

Jackson, D.Z. (1989, January 22). Calling the plays in Black and White. *Boston Globe*.

Key Note Publications. (1995). *UK sports market, December, 1994*. London: Author.

Kinkema, K.M., & Harris, J.C. (1992). Sport and the mass media. *Exercise and Sport Sciences Reviews*, **20**, 127-159.

Leonard, W.M. (1993). *A sociological perspective of sport* (4th ed.). New York: Macmillan.

Maguire, J. (1991). Sport, racism and British society: A sociological study of England's elite male Afro/Caribbean soccer and rugby union players. In G. Jarvis (Ed.), *Sport, racism and ethnicity* (pp. 102-123). London: Falmer.

McCarthy, D. (1996). *The portrayal of the Black soccer player on television*. Unpublished dissertation, Brunel University College, Isleworth, United Kingdom.

McPherson, B.D., Curtis, J.E., & Loy, J.W (1989). *The social significance of sport*. Champaign, IL: Human Kinetics.

Messner, M. (1988). Sport and male domination: The female athlete as contested ideological terrain. *Sociology of Sport Journal*, **5**, 197-211.

Michener, J. (1976). *Sports in America*. New York: Random House.

Norris, J., & Jones, R.L. (in press). Toward a clearer definition and application of the centrality hypothesis in English professional association football. *Journal of Sport Behaviour*.

Rainville, R.E., & McCormick, E. (1977). Extent of covert racial prejudice in pro football announcers' speech. *Journalism Quarterly*, **54**(1), 20-26.

Sabo, D., & Jansen, S.C. (1994). Seen but not heard: Images of Black men in sports media. In M.A. Messner & D.F. Sabo (Eds.), *Sex, violence and power in sports: Rethinking masculinity* (pp. 150-160). Freedom, CA: Crossing.

Sabo, D., Jansen, S.C., Tate, D., Duncan, M.C., & Leggett, S. (1995). *The portrayal of race, ethnicity and nationality in televised international athletic events*. Los Angeles: Amateur Athletic Foundation of Los Angeles.

Sage, G. H. (1990). *Power and ideology in American sport*. Champaign, IL: Human Kinetics.

Trujillo, N. (1995). Machines, missiles, and men: Images of the male body on ABC's Monday Night Football. *Sociology of Sport Journal*, **12**, 403-423.

Whannel, G. (1992). *Fields in vision: Television sport and cultural transformation*. London: Routledge.

Reading Nancy Lopez:
Decoding Representations
of Race, Class, and Sexuality

Katherine M. Jamieson

As though it were unfolding today, the Lopez story provides a fertile field for analyzing the varied consequences of interlocking inequalities of race, ethnicity, class, and sexuality. Lopez is constructed through the print media as a symbol of assimilation, as well as a body co-opted in the project of Latino-Latina pride and social justice. The selected "Lopez texts," which include *Sports Illustrated*, *Nuestro*, and *Hispanic* magazines, offer powerful and complex examples of the authority of the media to construct and reconstruct the events surrounding Lopez's career. The purpose of the paper is to apply feminist insights regarding racialized, classed, and sexualized forms of gender to examine the complexity and salience of Nancy Lopez's presence on the Ladies Professional Golf Association tour.

Much like the recent rise of PGA golfer, Tiger Woods, Nancy Lopez burst onto the Ladies Professional Golf Association (LPGA) tour with a bang. Nancy Lopez began playing golf at the age of 8 and by age 12 had won the New Mexico Women's Invitational (Chavira, 1977). In 1975, prior to graduating high school, Lopez tied for third in the U.S. Women's Open golf tournament, and in the same year, accepted a scholarship to the University of Tulsa, where she won the intercollegiate golf title and was named collegiate athlete of the year (Chabran & Chabran, 1996). After two successful years as a col-

legiate athlete, Lopez joined the LPGA tour. During her first year on the tour (1978), Lopez won nine tournaments, including an unprecedented five in a row, was named Rookie of the Year, Rolex Player of the Year[1] (also won in 1979, 1985, & 1988), Vare Trophy Winner[2] (also won in 1979 & 1985), Golfer of the Year, and Female Athlete of the Year. In 1985, Lopez set an all-time record at the Henredon Classic, recording a 20-under-par tournament total (268), including 25 birdies (LPGA homepage, 1997). Lopez has amassed 47 LPGA victories and in 1987 became the youngest inductee to the LPGA Hall of Fame. Now 20 years after Lopez joined the LPGA, she continues to compete, consistently draws large crowds, and remains the only U.S. Latina on the tour (LPGA home page, 1997).

Moreover, the arrival of Lopez was pivotal for the LPGA, which at that time was experiencing the popularity problems that face tennis today. Similar to the rhetoric about Tiger Woods, Lopez's presence supposedly marked an opening up of golf to the masses, especially to "young people" and other unlikely golf fans (Deford, 1978). Although this paper centers on the cultural significance of Nancy Lopez's public prominence, Tiger Woods is mentioned to illustrate the continued currency of race, class, sexual, and gender ideologies that operate in U.S. society and permeate all forms of media. Despite two decades of scholarly, political, and institutional progress toward race relations and gender equity, both the Lopez and Woods stories stand out

---

An earlier draft of this paper was presented at the Symposium on Women in Sport and Education, Baltimore, Maryland, 1996.

Reprinted from Jamieson, 1998.

as symbols of persistent, yet shifting inequalities in the lives of all women and men, but especially women and men of color. Clearly public stories such as these provide cultural material from which we may make sense of our everyday social worlds.

The purpose of this work is to reveal the social significance of media constructions of Nancy Lopez. The analysis of these specific texts is based in multiple feminist agendas that are best consolidated in what Baca Zinn and Dill (1994, 1996) have labeled *multiracial feminism*. Ultimately, the analytic goal is to reveal several ways that Lopez was upheld as the ideal, assimilated Mexican woman. The paper begins with a discussion of the selected texts and method of analysis. An outline of multiple inequalities in sport is provided and an argument made for the usefulness of multiracial feminism for making sense of Lopez's experiences. The analysis of the selected media representations of Lopez follows, calling attention to constructions of race and ethnicity, as well as constructions of sexualities. Throughout the analysis, the texts are located in particular historical, social, and political contexts within which they were constructed. Specifically, it is argued that dominant narratives about Lopez's family of origin have been constructed out of a deficiency model[3] (Baca Zinn, 1992; Zavella, 1994) and toward a myth of racial equality, while upholding assimilationist ideals. Moreover, this paper illustrates how the Latino-Latina print media contested the dominant constructions of Lopez's family of origin and paid little attention to her roles as mother and wife. The paper concludes with a statement about the usefulness of decoding texts from varied and shifting standpoints, as well as the significance of using multiple historical and political discourses to uncover widely varied meanings of a singular event.

The Lopez Texts

It is generally accepted that the media construct and reconstruct particular events in multiple ways and for a variety of purposes (Birrell & Cole, 1994a; Duncan, 1994; Kane & Greendorfer, 1994). Although the power of the media is pervasive (television, radio, print, and electronic options) consumers—real people—make their own meaning of the texts with which they engage (Birrell & Cole, 1994a; Duncan, 1994). Curiously, non-dominant popular texts seldom have been examined regarding the varied meanings they may be constructing about particu-

lar events in the U.S. social and political landscape (Messner, 1993; Williams, 1994). The selected "Lopez texts," which include *Sports Illustrated*, *Nuestro*, and *Hispanic* magazines, offer powerful and complex examples of the authority of the media to construct and reconstruct the events surrounding Lopez's career. The objective is to apply feminist insights regarding racialized, classed, and sexualized forms of gender to examine the complexity and salience of Nancy Lopez's presence on the LPGA tour.

The focus is on two significant time frames in Lopez's career as a professional golfer: her bold entry onto the Ladies Professional Golf Association tour (1977-1978) and her pregnancy years (1983-1991). These particular periods of media interest in Lopez do not tell an entire story, but they do offer several texts that construct Lopez in specific racialized, classed, sexualized, and gendered ways. This analysis rests on three articles from *Sports Illustrated*, a cover story and an additional feature article that appeared in *Nuestro*, a popular Latino-Latina news magazine, and a feature article from *Hispanic*, also a popular Latino-Latina news magazine. *Sports Illustrated* was selected due to its vast readership, national visibility, and status as a perpetrator of hegemonic ideological story lines. The *Nuestro* publication was selected in part because it claims to be a magazine for Latinos. Additionally, *Nuestro* seems to market itself to middle-class Latino-Latina readers, many of whom may also be readers of *Sports Illustrated*. Similarly, *Hispanic* offers a middle-class Latino-Latina take on Lopez's stories and portrays itself as a magazine "for and about Hispanics." Furthermore, *Hispanic* offered one of very few Lopez texts from the Latino-Latina popular print media long after her celebrated entry onto the tour. Thus, while these magazines have their unique characteristics, they also may meet at the axis of class with regard to the narrative themes that they have pursued.

The exclusion of some texts and inclusion of others in this analysis appropriately delimits the work, and in some cases reflects a lack of media attention to particular Lopez story lines. For example, it is curious that Lopez's marriages and pregnancies did not fill as many Latino-Latina print media pages as they did *Sports Illustrated* and other publications. Moreover, not one of 40 texts that were reviewed made a connection to her "inter-racial" marriages and her own racial-ethnic heritage. This particular text may have worked well within an assimilationist argument. Perhaps these authors and publishers felt the effect of marrying non-Latino men made a strong enough statement on its own and required no further textual posturing or deserved no additional attention. This omission is both puzzling and intriguing; however, a detailed critique is beyond the scope of this paper. Nevertheless, the selected texts seemed to be most content-rich and best timed to make sense of the significant events in Lopez's career.

Making Sense of Multiple Inequalities

As though it were unfolding today, the Lopez story provides a fertile field for analyzing the varied consequences of interlocking inequalities. Lopez may be seen as a symbol of false racial equality in the U.S., as well as a body co-opted in the project of Latino-Latina pride and social justice. Lopez symbolically straddles several social and cultural borders in the daily-ness of her life, as do all women and men, but especially women and men of color (Anzaldua, 1987, 1990a, 1990b; Baca Zinn & Dill, 1994; Pesquera & de la Torre, 1995). More to the point, Baca Zinn and Dill (1994) have suggested that for racial-ethnic women, lesbians, older women, disabled women, and lower social class women, gender is but one part of a larger pattern of unequal social relations.

Several studies have suggested that race, class, sexuality, and gender are ever present as distinguishing characteristics in sport settings, especially in the building of masculinities and femininities (Birrell & Cole, 1994b; Foley, 1990; Grey, 1996; Messner, 1992). These studies contest the argument that sport is a natural site for the de-politicization of race, ethnicity, class, or sexuality, as well as a site for the creation and maintenance of community harmony. For example, Foley (1990) suggested that American high school football ritual, such as the homecoming ceremony, traveling to other communities, cheerleading, and pep rallies, reflected a hierarchy of privilege based on race, class, sexuality, and gender. Grey (1996) found that for many immigrant and minority students in U.S. educational institutions, sport becomes one of the most visible means to claim one's "American" allegiance. Thus, not unlike Lopez's story, these studies suggest that American sport provides students an opportunity to assimilate but not integrate, both on campus and in the larger community (Foley, 1990; Grey, 1996). More specifically, persons may be provided opportunities to adopt "American" dominant cultural practices, like Americanized sports and games, but

are not able to share their own cultural practices without being labeled "other." This naturalizes a particular "American" culture, while marginalizing all others.

More often than not, sport is a site where dominant cultural groups maintain their power and continue to shape sport and social interactions to reflect their own interests (Birrell, 1990; Dewar, 1993; Sage, 1990). This may be most apparent in elite women's athletics where it is largely white middle-class men who make significant decisions within sport organizations. For instance, in the case of transsexual, Rene Richards, it was men who had the power to decide if Richards was female enough to compete on the women's professional tennis tour (Birrell & Cole, 1994b). For the most part, female tennis professionals were left out of the debate about Richards' qualifications as a member of the women's professional tennis tour (Birrell & Cole, 1994b). In a similar way, the image of Nancy Lopez was co-opted to suit the needs of white, middle-class, heterosexual men and to a lesser extent, women. The images of Lopez as a wholesome, attractive, heterosexual, elite golfer distinguished her from stereotypical images of Mexican women and promoted her as a credentialed middle-class *American* woman. In this way, Lopez was able to appeal to a diverse audience and provide a much-needed boost in fan support for the LPGA. Clearly, the Richards case and the Lopez case hold material and symbolic significance as they reflect the power of white, heterosexual, middle-class men to construct notions of appropriate womanhood.

In spite of progress toward gender equity in sport, competing equities of race and class continue to impede opportunities for women and men of color in the world of sport (Abney & Richey, 1992; Corbett & Johnson, 1993). Eitzen and Furst (1993) found that racial preferences exist in the selection of athletes for particular positions in women's collegiate volleyball, while Corbett and Johnson (1993) revealed that stereotypical myths about sport-type preferences among African-American women persist, resulting in constricted opportunities for involvement in a wide range of activities. These studies strongly suggest that intergroup contact and increased visibility of minority athletes are not enough to challenge a gender order that is embedded in inequalities.

Moreover, the mere addition of race, ethnicity, or sexuality as variables to existing frameworks has not improved their analytical capacity, which suggests that additive models do not offer the comprehensive analysis necessary to understand the complexity of women's lives (Andersen, 1993; Birrell, 1990; Collins, 1990; Dewar, 1993; Smith, 1992). As Hall (1996) has suggested, "race does not merely make the experience of women's oppression greater; rather, it qualitatively changes the nature of that subordination" (p. 44). Consequently, African-American women, Latinas, Asian, and Native American women do not simply experience increased rates of oppression; their disadvantaged status in sport is qualitatively different from that of their white counterparts (Hall, 1996) as well as from that of each other. These analytic limitations have real consequences for women in sport and especially for understanding the cultural currency of particular women in sport. More importantly, they illustrate the need to examine gender as it is mediated by other systems of inequality.

Multiracial feminism offers the analytical rigor needed to comprehend Lopez's varied subordinated and dominant statuses and makes room for multiple standpoints and varied histories in making sense of the Lopez texts. Baca Zinn and Dill (1994) have suggested that:

> Multiracial feminism treats racial inequality as a vital shaper of women's and men's lives and advances a powerful and coherent premise—that racial ancestry, ethnic heritage, and economic status are as important as gender for analyzing the social construction of women and men. (p. 11)

Creative tensions in multiple feminist frameworks (e.g., Chicana feminisms, black feminisms, and white feminisms) have revealed what Collins (1990) has referred to as a "matrix of domination" operating in the lives of all women and men. For example, Lopez's multiple social statuses as a raced, classed, and sexualized woman intersect to locate her differently than white, heterosexual women or Latina lesbians. All women and men fit within this matrix, but they are situated at different intersections depending on their multiple statuses as raced, classed, and sexualized individuals. Moreover, these "intersecting forms of domination produce both oppression and opportunity" (Baca Zinn & Dill, 1996, p. 12). More explicitly, the intersecting forms of domination in Lopez's experience offer her privilege as a professional athlete, a financially secure woman, and a heterosexual woman, but oppression as a person of Mexican heritage and working-class heritage. These experiences directly point to the fluidity of privilege and oppression that come with varied locations within a web of inequalities (Baca Zinn & Dill, 1994, 1996; Collins, 1990, 1991).

The relational nature of domination and subordination is also a significant focus within multiracial feminism. That is, the significance of race is visible in "patterns of relations among minority women and White women" (Baca Zinn & Dill, 1996, p. 12) as well as among Latinas of different social classes or of varied sexual identities. For Lopez, the relational nature of gender was apparent as she came on the tour at a young age and as the only U.S. Latina on the tour. She was set apart by her brown skin, unique looks, age, and Mexican working-class heritage. Cultural ideology suggested that Lopez fell outside of the ideal woman status, and yet her golf skill gave her entrée to social and cultural locations that other 21-year-old Mexican women would not experience. Although Lopez earned entrée, her presence was constantly constructed in relation to an ideal type of woman and to an ideal type of athlete (e.g., male).

The comprehensive framework of multiracial feminism provides a lens through which Lopez may be seen as both oppressed and oppressor, especially in relation to other women on the tour. For Lopez, as it is for all women, gender is but one axis in a matrix of social structural domination. The intersection of these multiple axes (e.g., race, class, gender, ethnicity, sexuality) situates Lopez and other Latinas differently than it would white women, and yet Latinas take up diverse and dynamic locations within the matrix. That is, they are situated by more than racial or ethnic identities. Thus, the significance of the texts relied upon for this analysis lies in their ability to construct Lopez as a cultural marker of particular racialized, classed, and sexualized statuses in U.S. society and sport.

Constructing Race and Ethnicity

In the textual analysis that follows, I suggest that Lopez is constructed in various ways across axes of race, ethnicity, and class. An overarching purpose in these texts seems to be to differentiate Lopez from other Latinas. In reality, Lopez is different from other Latinas in many ways. For example, in contrast to nearly half of all U.S. Latinas, Lopez graduated from high school (U.S. Department of Commerce, 1996). Moreover, unlike many Latinos-Latinas who are compelled to leave college due to financial constraints, family needs, or feelings of isolation on campus (Nieves-Squires, 1993), Lopez left to join the tour—a career move that would further differentiate her from other Latinas. Perhaps most striking is the disparity between Lopez's earnings during her first full year on the tour (LPGA, 1997) and the median earnings of Hispanic women nearly 12 years later. In 1978, Lopez earned $189,817 on the LPGA tour, yet the median earnings of Hispanic women in 1990 were a mere $10,999, 21% less than that of non-Hispanic women (Mexican American Women's National Association, 1993). In spite of these visible differences in power and privilege, a variety of distinguishing characteristics were constructed or reconstructed in order to exploit Lopez in the particular project of each text. A large majority of these projects were connected to ideologies of race and ethnicity.

Culture As Villain[4]

Despite several advances in analytical and intellectual depiction of Mexican families (Baca Zinn, 1976; Ybarra, 1988), a *Sports Illustrated* (July 1978) article relied on a deficiency model to describe Lopez's father and family resources. Early in the article Lopez's father is described as "Domingo, who has a third-grade education and an auto-body shop in Roswell, New Mexico" (Deford, 1978, p. 24). The statement about his "third-grade education" suggests that Domingo Lopez stopped learning when his formal education came to an end. Intended or not, this may be read as code for a popular stereotype that most Mexicans do not value educational attainment and are content to operate at a lower educational level than others. Therefore, by choice, Domingo stopped his own education and, consequently, is no longer suitable to guide his daughter's social, professional, and educational development. In fact, Deford (1978) suggested that Lopez's father was:

> a natural athlete who could teach her golf, but however street-smart he may be, there is no way he can educate her in the school of marketing and six-figure affiliations that she has been ushered into. (p. 31)

The obvious message is that Lopez's family of origin has taken her as far as it can. Lopez must now leave her father's care in order to learn how to succeed in the more legitimized world of big contracts and big money deals. In a larger context, the coded message reinforces a belief in social mobility through sport. Clearly, Lopez's social ascent is symbolic of the American ideal of pulling oneself up by one's own bootstraps. The *suggested* separation of Lopez from her family of origin goes even further in solidifying a model for assimilation and social

mobility. As Sage (1990) has suggested, the well-publicized success of a few individuals aids in the maintenance of a belief in social mobility among the masses. Despite the limited extent of actual social mobility through sport, Lopez serves as a symbol to promote and sustain hegemonic ideology about widespread social climbing in the American social structure (Sage, 1990). Although Nancy Lopez was the 1980s "poster child" for Latino-Latina upward mobility, the careful distinctions made between her and her family of origin made this mobility one of individual assimilation rather than institutional transformation.

Culture As Rational Response

The Latino-Latina publications took a different perspective on Lopez's family of origin and their significance. The *Nuestro* publication suggested that "on a deeply personal level, [Lopez's] story is a tribute to the integrity of a Mexican American family" (*Nuestro*, 1978, p. 23). In contrast to the subordinated status attributed by the dominant media, the Latino-Latina media suggested that this is a family that maintained their Mexican pride, and yet made it in U.S. society. In the same publication, Nancy's father is described in the following manner, "Domingo was once a field hand who picked cotton under the broiling sun of west Texas. His education ended after the third grade" (*Nuestro*, 1978, p. 23). This information about Domingo symbolically solidifies Nancy Lopez's Mexican working-class heritage, and as we learn later in the article, illustrates her father's upward mobility from field hand to small business owner. This is a sharp contrast to the deficiency model used to construct the mainstream narrative about Lopez's family of origin.

In reality, the educational status of Domingo Lopez is but one example of the varied consequences of multiple inequalities facing immigrant and colonized Latinos-Latinas in the United States. Segregated schools, anti-Mexican sentiment, and the need to earn a wage forced many Latinos-Latinas of Domingo's era to curtail their formal education. During Domingo's school-age years, Latinos-Latinas in the Southwest fought segregation and demanded equality in the provision of educational resources (Meier & Ribera, 1993). In fact, in 1931, the Lemon Grove, California lawsuit marked the first successful legal challenge to school segregation (Meier & Ribera, 1993). Thus, low educational attainment is not an inherent Mexican deficiency, but rather a consequence of the social and political landscape during the early

1900s in the Southwestern United States (Meier & Ribera, 1993).

The longstanding estrangement from formal educational institutions, however, continues to have consequences in the lives of all Latinos-Latinas in the United States. For example, despite significant growth in numbers, U.S. Latinos-Latinas face lower college attendance and graduation rates, lower than average family annual income, and higher than average rates of poverty (Rumbaut, 1995). Inequalities such as these further restrict participation in various social institutions (e.g., education and sport) and predispose Latino-Latina youth to greater negative consequences during economic and political shifts in the social structure (Baca Zinn, 1992). The inequalities above are a striking contrast to the "successful" life of Nancy Lopez and are simultaneously representative of her family of origin. It is these contrasts that *Sports Illustrated* relies upon to construct Lopez herself as different from the unnamed white status group, but also different from other Mexicans. *Nuestro*, on the other hand, claims an understanding of Lopez's struggle as well as a vested interest in her achievements.

Resisting Ethnicity

After carefully constructing Lopez's father and family of origin in their respective manners, the *Sports Illustrated* text turned directly to Lopez for symbolic representations of racial, ethnic, and class statuses. For example, Deford (1978) noted that Lopez "put on" an accent when speaking to her sister on the phone and uttered the following words, "It's my seester" (p. 25), and "Hey beeg seester, I love you" (p. 25). The fact that Lopez "put on" the accent suggests that she may not actually speak Spanish, thus further removing her from her Latino-Latina heritage and solidifying her status as an appropriately assimilated Mexican. In yet another example of constructing Lopez as "other," her own public relations handler refers to her in a racially derogatory manner. During the course of a discussion regarding how and when to get Lopez to her next LPGA event, Lopez's public relations handler asked her caddie, "When are you going to get Taco Belle's car to Indianapolis?" (Deford, 1978, p. 25) In the very least, this is reflective of a lack of insight to white privilege and fails to acknowledge the potential for offending Latino-Latina readers. More specifically, this passage simultaneously constructs Lopez as the racial-ethnic other and trivializes the significance of her Mexican heritage (Birrell, 1990; Dewar, 1993).

A final touch to this construction of Lopez is obvious as her caddie refers to her as "Lopes" (rhymes with *ropes*) rather than calling her by her correct surname.

These particular examples of text suggest that Lopez's accent is make-believe and that her ethnicity is appropriately described by calling her "Taco Belle." Moreover, the failure to call Lopez by her name marks another form of resistance to her ethnicity. More than a casual nick-name, "Lopes" symbolizes the desire of a dominant culture to de-race Lopez and erase the political, historical, and cultural struggles of Latinos-Latinas in the U.S.: struggles that are deeply rooted in rights to culture, language, and naming of one's self. Together, these narratives construct Lopez as different from other Mexicans, especially those in her family of origin. This particular text also naturalizes the dominant status of Lopez's caddie and public relations man in relation to Lopez's subordinated status (e.g., as a woman, as a person of Mexican working-class heritage). The combined effect of these media representations is to render Lopez subordinate in the social construction of her own racial-ethnic identity and status, and to simultaneously uphold a white, male, middle-class status as the ideal.

Resisting Resistance

Nuestro made careful distinctions between Lopez's ethnic identity and social structural inequalities, rather than collapsing these two distinct categories of analysis into one culturally deterministic model. For example, Chavira (1977) suggested that Lopez "made it" despite the fact that "sex discrimination, lack of professional training, and money problems all stood in her way" (p. 34). Moreover, he acknowledged community financial support of the up and coming golfer when he suggested that "the chamber of commerce has raised money to help her enter tournaments" (Chavira, 1977, p. 35). Lopez reflected on economic difficulties and familial sacrifices, as she told Chavira, "My dad pays the expenses. He's not rich, so it's a real sacrifice. I've been very lucky my father has been willing to go all the way to help me make it" (Chavira, 1977, p. 35). This type of familial sacrifice and perseverance described in *Nuestro* reflects the reality of various forms of inequalities faced by Latinos-Latinas in the U.S. In fact, *Nuestro* magazine suggested that part of Lopez's appeal among Latinos-Latinas is the fact that Latinos-Latinas can relate to many of her challenges. *Nuestro* (1978) suggested that "perhaps we can identify more closely with this particular star's rise. Lopez has known the sting of discrimination too well to forget it" (p. 23).

Throughout the majority of Latino-Latina media accounts, Lopez is often named as Latina or Mexicana, her surname is spelled with an accent, and her family of origin is presented in a positive and significant light. The authors express a collective pride in Lopez's achievements, which they believe to be true for most of their readers. The *Nuestro* authors suggest that Lopez

> is a symbol for us. She symbolizes the increasing reality of crossing over into the American mainstream and making it. Hers, moreover, is a crossover accomplished without rage, without controversy, without (so far) selling out. (*Nuestro*, 1978, p. 23)

Reflective of Lopez's connection to multiple historical and political debates during the late 1970s, this text may be decoded in a number of ways. For example, the fact that Lopez has made her move into "mainstream" without "rage" or "controversy" may be read as discontent with radical and separatist tactics used by both the Chicano movement of the 1960s and 1970s and the predominantly white feminist movement of the 1970s (Meier & Ribera, 1993; Zavella, 1994). Many Chicanas were highly critical of white feminists' anti-male sentiment, particularly because they were aware that, like themselves, their own Latino brothers were facing varied and systemic subordinated statuses (Meier & Ribera, 1993; Zavella, 1994). Thus, rather than make a political scene about the patriarchal aspects of sport, Lopez moved quietly and yet noticeably into the "mainstream."

Yet, woven into this textual embrace of Lopez's ascent is an expectation that Lopez will achieve a balance between her Latino-Latina heritage and her status as a member a socially and financially elite class of U.S. society. *Nuestro* connects Lopez's struggles to the struggles of all Latinos-Latinas; therefore, her successes are also collectively owned and experienced. Despite Lopez's public closeness to her father and maintenance of her Spanish surname, the *Nuestro* text warns of the potential for Lopez to relinquish her ties to working-class Mexicanos-Mexicanas. Speaking about Lopez's financial advisors and their commercialization of Lopez, *Nuestro* (1978) writers stated the following, "Many people already call her 'Lopes' (to rhyme with dopes), thus making her less Latina, less foreign. And so far, Nancy seems to be accepting it all" (p. 26).

Although Lopez is revered for her quiet, sophisticated move into the mainstream, she is simultaneously admonished for not resisting attempts at making her "less Latina." In reality, Lopez's "bridge-building" is no different than that of other women of color who are consistently bridging cultural divides in the daily-ness of their lives (Anzaldua, 1987, 1990a, 1990b; Baca Zinn & Dill, 1994; Pesquera & de la Torre, 1995; Zavella, 1994). That is, Latinas are constantly involved in a dynamic process of maintaining ties to their working-class backgrounds, ethnic heritage, cultural heritage, and yet to prove their allegiance to social, economic, and educational progress in U.S. society (Anzaldua, 1987, 1990a, 1990b; Baca Zinn & Dill, 1994; Pesquera & de la Torre, 1995; Zavella, 1994). Lopez once again is co-opted, this time in the project of constructing and maintaining a particular Latino-Latina identity.

Constructing Sexualities

Additional examples of intersecting inequalities of race, ethnicity, class, gender, and sexuality lie in the stories of Lopez's marriage and pregnancies, especially as they became badges of middle-class and heterosexual status. In 1979, prior to returning to the tour for her second season, Lopez married Cincinnati sportscaster Tim Melton. The marriage did not last; moreover, the marriage the media has come to celebrate is that between Lopez and major league baseball player, Ray Knight. Lopez and Knight have been married since 1982 and have three daughters who were born in 1983, 1986, and 1991. As mentioned earlier in the paper, Lopez's marriages and parenting have been curiously absent or limited in coverage in the Latino-Latina popular print media, especially in the late-1980s. Consequently, this analysis focuses primarily on the *Sports Illustrated* texts.

Masculinities and Femininities

The stories about Lopez's marriages and motherhood provide examples of a modern-day apologetic (Felshin, 1981). The media countered Lopez's potentially emasculating skill with stories of her talents as wife and mother. The pregnancy comebacks were veiled forms of trivialization of Lopez's athleticism (Griffin, 1996), and her talent on the golf course was deemed "natural" (Newman, 1986, p. 38). For example, the *Sports Illustrated* author compared Lopez and Knight in the following manner: "Knight may have lacked her natural skills, but he was celebrated enough in his own right to have played in two All-Star Games" (Newman, 1986, p. 38). The naturalization of Lopez's talent not only disregards her hard work but also that of her only pre-professional coach, her father. In contrast, *Hispanic* (Alvarez, 1989) magazine acknowledged the discipline and hard work of Lopez and her family in the quest to build a career as a professional golfer.

Alvarez (1989) makes it clear that Lopez worked diligently to develop her skill in golf. In one passage, Lopez stated the following: "You're only going to be as successful as what you are willing to give. . . . I gave up a lot. I loved golf so much, and I just wanted to win. It wasn't given to me. I worked hard" (Lopez in Alvarez, 1989, p. 16). This acknowledgement of hard work and love for the sport contradicts the dominant attempts to trivialize Lopez's talent. Yet when flanked by the marriage and motherhood narratives, Lopez's hard work was annihilated.

The union between Lopez and Knight was constructed as the "very model of a modern marriage" (Newman, 1986, p. 34), despite the obvious hegemonic conceptions of masculinity and femininity that were operating. In fact, much of the text constructed Knight as a "new age," maybe even "pro-feminist" husband, who was not at all threatened by his wife's obvious ability to live independent of him. Lopez colluded in exalting Knight's willingness to support his professional, financially independent female partner as she stated: "After I married Ray, I felt that golf was second. He made me happier than golf did. But he never pressured me not to go anywhere to play golf, and I had often felt that pressure from Tim" (Lopez in Newman, 1986, p. 38). Thus, by comparison, Knight is less rigid in his gender role accomplishments. That is, Knight is able to be both husband and elite athlete without facing gender role conflict or questions of sexuality. In fact, he is so "modern" that he expresses support for Lopez's career goals in this way:

> I allow her to play golf because she has never put it ahead of me. I've never asked her to come home, and I never would. . . . It never entered my mind as a problem that she needed to play golf, as long as it doesn't affect my standing with her. But I married her as a woman; I didn't marry the LPGA tour. (Knight in Newman, 1986, p. 39)

Not only do these texts naturalize Lopez and Knight's roles as feminine and masculine subjects, they also serve to promote their heterosexual marriage as a bastion of equality, while inadvertently offering examples of embedded inequalities between women and men. Moreover, the last line in the above quote is especially interesting as it is a striking contrast to an earlier *Sports Illustrated* construction of Lopez as a "baseball wife" (Newman, 1986, p. 34). In concert with the role conflict theme, Alvarez (1989) pointed out that, "While at home . . . Nancy refuses to pick up a golf club. It is more important to devote herself to home and family in a traditional sort of way, cleaning, cooking, and playing with the kids" (p. 16). Yet, the *Sports Illustrated* article suggested that Knight built a batting cage in their backyard and that Lopez would feed the pitching machine while he took batting practice. So at home there was space for Knight's athletic pursuits, but Lopez supposedly left golf at the course to attend to Knight and the children.

This is a construction that is difficult to believe, especially in light of the *Hispanic* text that recognized Lopez's love for golf. Regardless, it works to perpetuate a model of family life, divisions of labor, and household power that benefits men and subordinates women. As Kane and Greendorfer (1994) have suggested, "Gender *difference* is translated into gender *hierarchy*, because in existing social arrangements women are defined not only as 'other than' but also as 'less than' their male counterparts" (p. 29). The underlying message is that even in this "modern" model of marriage, the socially constructed organizing principle of gender hierarchy reigns supreme.

Compulsory Heterosexuality

Not surprisingly, Lopez's marriages and pregnancies have also resulted in a social construction of her as a heterosexual woman. This was important, not only to the media, but also to the LPGA as it worked to market women's golf to a vast audience (Diaz, 1987). The representations of Lopez as a bona fide heterosexual woman maintain a sexist and heterosexist status quo and continue to co-opt sport in the service of compulsory heterosexuality. More significantly, they serve a larger project, which is to divide and silence women through fear tactics (Griffin, 1996; Lenskyj, 1987).

For example, Lopez's marriage and pregnancies were cleverly juxtaposed to the hidden social and sexual lives of other LPGA members, thus further silencing lesbians on the tour (Griffin, 1996). Much of the article in *Sports Illustrated* about the rivalry between Lopez and Pat Bradley was constructed around Lopez's pregnancy comeback and Bradley's psychological comeback. The subtext here is that Lopez's heterosexual married life is so good that the strength she gains from it enhances her game. In contrast, Bradley, presumably unmarried, needs professional help to keep her game up to par. The contrast was stated in this way:

> While Bradley was tearing up the tour [1986], Lopez had her second child . . . and played only four tournaments. . . . As she did in 1985 [after her first pregnancy], Lopez is drawing strength from her life away from competitive golf. (Diaz, 1987, p. 84)

Regardless of actual sexuality, this subtext suggests that heterosexual life is fulfilling and tantamount to a healthy lifestyle, while being unmarried (for whatever reason) is unfulfilling and has obvious consequences in one's personal and professional life, including the opportunity to choose motherhood.

Moreover, Lopez's pregnancies are symbolic of a type of reproductive control that white, heterosexual, middle-class women exercise at much higher rates than do women of color, especially lower-class Latinas (Mexican American Women's National Association [MANA], 1993). Thus, Lopez's pregnancies stand out as a dominant cultural symbol of reproductive freedom, a freedom that is not yet enjoyed by all U.S. women. Carefully woven into this text about Lopez's pregnancies is a class-based construction of motherhood. That is, Lopez's ability to "balance" family life and a career further legitimizes her as a "good mother." In actuality, because of her financial status, Lopez has been able to employ a nanny to help care for her children. Additionally, the fact that Lopez *does* motherhood within the credentialed status of heterosexual marriage puts her at less risk for losing her rights to reproduction and parenting as compared to most single, poor, lesbian, and non-white women (MANA, 1993).

Taken together, these texts use Lopez to project sexist, heterosexist, and homophobic images of women in sport. Griffin (1996) has argued that homophobia is manifested in women's sport in several distinct ways, two of which are silence and heterosexy images. The rhetoric underlying the Lopez-Bradley rivalry is that lesbians in sport are "nasty secrets that must be kept locked tightly in

the closet" (Griffin, 1996, p. 394). The power of the media to "out" Lopez as a heterosexual makes the silence surrounding the personal life of Bradley (and others on the LPGA tour) even more deafening. Constructing texts that uphold Lopez's heterosexuality and inclination toward motherhood as *natural* works to confer privilege and normalcy on particular social groups while holding others in contempt (Griffin, 1996). In this way dominant texts such as *Sports Illustrated* and *Hispanic* support and aid in the maintenance of existing social arrangements.

Conclusion

Perhaps what is most informative about decoding *Sports Illustrated*, *Nuestro*, and *Hispanic* media accounts of Lopez is the complexity of Lopez's multiple statuses—the very real experience of intersecting statuses of race, class, sexuality, and gender. More specifically, when the various Lopez texts are analyzed in the historical context in which they emerged, they offer insight to the pervasiveness of the project of white male superiority. When the histories of "others" are relied upon to decode mediated texts, a more complex, yet clarified, analysis of multiple inequalities is possible (Messner, 1993).

Nuestro and *Hispanic* in some ways offered what Gorelick (1991) called a "view from below," and what Collins (1991) termed the perspective of the "outsider within." These differentiated perspectives may offer a less partial view of the social world and perhaps a more accurate picture of what is really shaping social life (Collins, 1990, 1991; Gorelick, 1991). Anzaldua (1987) suggested that those persons who are most marginalized in any society have the potential to offer a more accurate view of the power structures and hierarchies that operate within the social system. Pronger (1996) echoed this perspective when he suggested that gay men are estranged in sport, and therefore offer a differently informed view of the social structure of sport. Taken together, these scholars make a strong argument for valuing multiple perspectives and standpoints in making sense of the social world. There is no one accurate perspective, but there are perspectives that are less partial than those that we have come to accept as the standard in sociological analyses of women's sport. The texts analyzed here offered varied perspectives on the significance of Nancy Lopez in the elite, primarily upper-class, and very white sport of golf.

In a complementary way, these textual constructions of Lopez provide insight into the fluid nature of gendered statuses and identities. They reveal the simple reality that gender is never the only appropriate category of analysis, nor can it be the most significant, because it is always mediated by other systems of inequality (Andersen, 1993; Birrell, 1990; Collins, 1990, 1991; Dewar, 1993; Smith, 1992). More than that, gendered identities fit within cultural and historical contexts that shape all women's lives but have different consequences for different groups of women (e.g., working-class women, heterosexual women, white women; Zavella, 1994). If one looks closely and simultaneously applies a broad framework, it is apparent that all women and men are in the process of traversing borders. It is our work as social scientists to develop the tools to make sense of these border crossings and to do so with regard to relevant historical, cultural, and political contexts.

References

Abney, R., & Richey, D.L. (1992). Opportunities for minority women in sport—The impact of Title IX. *Journal of Physical Education, Recreation & Dance*, **63**(3), 56-59.

Alvarez, A. (1989, June). Nancy Lopez: Balancing family and golf. *Hispanic*, **2**(5), 15-16.

Andersen, M.L. (1993). *Thinking about women: Sociological perspectives on sex and gender* (3rd ed.). New York: Macmillan.

Anzaldua, G. (1987). *Borderlands/la frontera: The new mestiza*. San Francisco: Spinsters–Aunt Lute.

Anzaldua, G. (1990a). Haciendo caras, una entrada. In G. Anzaldua (Ed.), *Making face, making soul: Haciendo caras: Creative and critical perspectives by feminists of color* (pp. xv-xxviii). San Francisco: Aunt Lute.

Anzaldua, G. (1990b). En rapport, in opposition: Cobrando cuentas a las nuestras. In G. Anzaldua (Ed.), *Making face, making soul: Haciendo caras: Creative and critical perspectives by feminists of color* (pp. 142-148). San Francisco: Aunt Lute.

Baca Zinn, M. (1976). Chicanas: Power and control in the domestic sphere. *De Colores*, **2**(3), 19-31.

Baca Zinn, M. (1992). Family, race and poverty in the eighties. In B. Thorne and M. Yalom (Eds.), *Rethinking the family: Some feminist questions* (pp. 71-90). Boston: Northeastern University Press.

Baca Zinn, M., & Dill, B.T. (1994). Difference and domination. In M. Baca Zinn & B.T. Dill (Eds.), *Women of Color in U.S. society* (pp. 3-12). Philadelphia: Temple University Press.

Baca Zinn, M., & Dill, B.T. (1996). Theorizing difference from multiracial feminism. *Feminist Studies*, **22**, 321-344.

Birrell, S. (1990). Women of color, critical autobiographies, and sport. In M.A. Messner & D.F. Sabo (Eds.), *Sport, men, and the gender order* (pp. 185-199). Champaign, IL: Human Kinetics.

Birrell, S., & Cole, C.L. (1994a). Media, sport and gender. In S. Birrell and C.L. Cole (Eds.), *Women, sport and culture* (pp. 245-248). Champaign, IL: Human Kinetics.

Birrell, S., & Cole, C.L. (1994b). Double fault: Renee Richards and the construction and naturalization of difference. In S. Birrell and C.L. Cole (Eds.), *Women, sport and culture* (pp. 373-397). Champaign, IL: Human Kinetics.

Chabran, R., & Chabran, R. (Eds.). (1996). *Lopez, Nancy. The Latino encyclopedia* (Vol. 3, pp. 915-916). New York: Marshall Cavendish.

Chavira, R. (1977, August). Three to cheer. *Nuestro*, **1**, 34-35.

Collins, P.H. (1990). *Black feminist thought: Knowledge, consciousness, and the politics of empowerment*. New York: Routledge.

Collins, P.H. (1991). Learning from the outsider within: The sociological significance of Black feminist thought. In J.E. Hartman and E. Messer-Davidow (Eds.), *(En)gendering knowledge* (pp. 41-65). Knoxville, TN: University of Tennessee Press.

Corbett, D., & Johnson, W. (1993). The African-American female in collegiate sport: Sexism and racism. In D.D. Brooks & R.C. Althouse (Eds.), *Racism in college athletics: The African-American athlete's experience* (pp. 179-204). Morgantown, WV: Fitness Information Technology.

Deford, F. (1978, July 10). Nancy with the laughing face. *Sports Illustrated*, **49**(2), 24-26, 31.

Dewar, A.M. (1993). Would all the generic women in sport please stand up? Challenges facing feminist sport sociology. *Quest*, **45**, 211-229.

Diaz, J. (1987, February 9). Time for the Pat and Nancy show. *Sports Illustrated*, **66**(16), 84, 87.

Duncan, M.C. (1994). The politics of women's body images and practices: Foucault, the panopticon and Shape magazine. *Journal of Sport and Social Issues*, **18**(1), 48-65.

Eitzen, D., & Furst, D. (1993). Racial bias in women's collegiate volleyball. In A. Yiannakis, T.D. McIntyre, & M.J. Melnick (Eds.), *Sport sociology: Contemporary themes* (4th ed., pp. 327-330). Dubuque, IA: Kendall-Hunt.

Felshin, J. (1981). The triple option . . . for women in sport. In M. Hart & S. Birrell (Eds.), *Sport in the sociocultural process* (pp. 487-492). Dubuque, IA: Brown.

Foley, D.E. (1990). The great American football ritual: Reproducing race, class, and gender inequality. *Sociology of Sport Journal*, **7**, 111-135.

Gorelick, S. (1991). Contradictions of feminist methodology. *Gender & Society*, **5**, 459-477.

Grey, M.A. (1996). Sport and immigrant, minority, and Anglo relations in Garden City (Kansas) High School. In D.S. Eitzen (Ed.), *Sport in contemporary society: An anthology* (5th ed., pp. 295-312). New York: St. Martin's.

Griffin, P. (1996). Changing the game: Homophobia, sexism, and lesbians in sport. In D.S. Eitzen (Ed.) *Sport in contemporary society: An anthology* (5th ed., pp. 392-409). New York: St. Martin's.

Hall, M.A. (1996). *Feminism and sporting bodies: Essays on theory and practice.* Champaign, IL: Human Kinetics.

Kane, M.J., & Greendorfer, S.L. (1994). The media's role in accommodating and resisting stereotyped images of women in sport. In P.J. Creedon (Ed.), *Women, media and sport: Challenging gender values* (pp. 28-44). Thousand Oaks, CA: Sage.

Lenskyj, H.J. (1987). Female sexuality and women's sport. *Women's Studies International Forum*, **10**, 381-386.

LPGA (1997, July). LPGA player biographies: Nancy Lopez (5 pages). LPGA [World Wide Web page]. Available: <**http://www.lpga.com/tour/bios/biohtml/lopez.html**>.

Meier, M.S., & Ribera, F. (1993). *Mexican Americans/ American Mexicans: From Conquistadors to Chicanos.* New York: Hill & Wang.

Messner, M.A. (1992). *Power at play: Sport and the problem of masculinity.* Boston: Beacon.

Messner, M.A. (1993). White men misbehaving: Feminism, Afrocentrism, and the promise of a critical standpoint. *Journal of Sport and Social Issues*, **16**, 136-144.

Mexican American Women's National Association (ca 1993). *In search of economic equity.* Washington, DC: Author.

Newman, B. (1986, August). The very model of a modern marriage. *Sports Illustrated*, **65**(5), 34-41.

Nieves-Squires, S. (1993). *Hispanic women in higher education: Making their presence on campus less tenuous.* Project on the status and education of women. Washington, DC: Association of American Colleges.

Nuestro (1978, September). Her drive to win. *Nuestro*, **2**, 22-23, 26.

Pesquera, B.M., & de la Torre, A. (1993). *Building with our hands: New directions in Chicana studies.* Berkeley, CA: University of California Press.

Pronger, B. (1996). Sport and masculinity: The estrangement of gay men. In D.S. Eitzen (Ed.), *Sport in contemporary society: An anthology* (5th ed., pp. 410-423). New York: St. Martin's.

Rumbaut, R. (1995, April). Immigrants from Latin America and the Caribbean: A socioeconomic profile. Statistical Brief No. 6. Michigan State University: Julian Samora Research Institute.

Sage, G.H. (1990). *Power and ideology in American sport.* Champaign, IL: Human Kinetics.

Smith, Y. (1992). Women of Color in society and sport. *Quest*, **44**, 228-250.

U.S. Department of Commerce, Economics and Statistical Administration, Bureau of the Census (1996). *Statistical abstract of the United States 1996: The national data book* (No. 241, p. 159). Washington, DC: Author.

Williams, L.D. (1994). Sportswomen in Black and White: Sports history from an Afro-American perspective. In P.J. Creedon (Ed.), *Women, media and sport: Challenging gender values* (pp. 45-66). Thousand Oaks, CA: Sage.

Ybarra, L. (1988). Separating myth from reality. In M. Melville (Ed.), *Mexicanas at work in the United States* [Mexican-American Studies Monograph, no. 5]. Houston, TX: University of Houston Press.

Zavella, P. (1994). Reflections on diversity among Chicanas. In S. Gregory and R. Sanjek (Eds.), *Race* (pp. 199-212). New Brunswick, NJ: Rutgers University Press.

Notes

1. LPGA tour players earn the Rolex Player of the Year by amassing points for "top 10" finishes.
2. LPGA tour players earn the Vare Trophy by posting the lowest scoring average per 18 holes for a minimum of 70 rounds.
3. A deficiency model locates the cause for social distress in the values and morals of individuals and groups. The culture of poverty thesis of the 1960s held the poor people had "distinctive values, aspirations, and psychological characteristics that inhibit their achievement and produce behavioral deficiencies likely to keep them poor not only within generations,

but also across generations through socialization of the young" (Baca Zinn, 1992, p. 72). This type of model was often misapplied to explain the structural challenges facing Mexican families.

4. I am indebted to Maxine Baca Zinn for her useful concept of "culture as villain," which she discussed in a 1989 article in *SIGNS: Journal of Women in Culture and Society.*

Acknowledgments

I am greatly appreciative of the comments by the reviewers of the *Sociology of Sport Journal* and Cynthia Hasbrook. Thanks also go to Diana Rivera, Lillian Castillo-Speed, Richard Chabran, and the journalism class at Goddard High School in Roswell, New Mexico, for their assistance in locating nondominant print media on Nancy Lopez.

Sport and Deviance: The Darker Side of Sportsworld

Objectives

The unit examines the underlying causes of deviance in sport and focuses on such activities as larceny, overconformity to the sport ethic, drug use, and aggression outside sport.

Sociologists define deviance as the violation of formal or informal norms. Whereas psychologists speak in definitive terms about behavior being either "normal" or "abnormal," sociologists avoid the pathological connotations associated with the latter term and take instead the position that "deviance is not inherent in specific behavior or attitudes but rather is a phenomenon of human interaction in a particular normative setting" (Theodorson & Theodorson, 1969, p. 111). Thus, behaviors that violate the normative structures of one community or society are labeled "deviant," whereas the same behaviors may be considered normal or acceptable in other social contexts.

Deviance within sport contexts may involve "violating the rules of a game or organization, going beyond the commonly accepted definitions of fair play and sportsmanship, and intentionally using illegal means to intimidate or injure an opponent" (McPherson, Curtis, & Loy, 1989, p. 263). Deviant acts committed by sport actors (e.g., players, coaches, booster-club members, team owners) can occur both on and off the field. Specific examples of deviance in baseball, for example, may include such on-the-field behaviors as doctoring the ball and corking a bat and off-the-field behaviors such as betting on one's own team or paying money to student-athletes under the table.

Deviance in sport often occurs in order to gain an edge or advantage, as in cases of cheating, taking performance-enhancing drugs, or using illegal aggressive acts to "take out" a particularly troublesome member of an opposing team. Off-the-field violence by athletes is more problematic for the social scientist because such behavior is not related to efforts to gain a competitive edge and is therefore more difficult to understand and explain. The subject of on-the-field (e.g., player violence) deviance as well as off-the-field (e.g., drugs, sexual assault) deviance is now receiving increasing attention by social scientists, probably because of its escalation and increased media attention.

The three selections that follow shed light on different aspects of this disturbing trend.

In the first selection, Hughes and Coakley argue that much of athlete deviance is grounded in the noncritical acceptance of the "sport ethic," that is, the norms and values of sport. Using performance-enhancing drugs as an example, the authors make the case that overconformity to the sport ethic (positive deviance) causes athletes to try anything to stay involved in sport or help their team even if it means engaging in illegal activity.

In the second selection, Snyder analyzes the case of a group of college athletes who were involved in a series of larcenies. Two important points about this case are that the athletes involved did not conform to the usual profile of individuals who commit such crimes and that material gain did not motivate their acts. The culprits came from upper-middle-class homes and had no prior history of criminal activity. So why did they commit these crimes and what relationship, if any, is there between their status as athletes and the commission of these acts?

The explanations of various authorities that emerged were focused on the collective influence of peer pressure in the athletic subculture, character flaws, alcohol consumption, and the quest for excitement. The author, however, employs an interpretive, case-study perspective that seeks explanations for the athletes' criminal activity by identifying and analyzing the "perceptions," "meanings," and "motives"associated with their deviant behavior.

Snyder suggests that their findings challenge the common assumption that sport "keeps kids out of trouble" and "builds character."

In the third selection, Nixon investigates how sports attitudes and athletic participation relate to physical aggression outside the sport context. He found that certain variables such as the value of toughness in sport, a belief held by both male and female athletes, was related to the commission of aggressive acts outside sport, particularly by male athletes. Further, the author notes that male athletes in team sports were more likely to have engaged in aggression outside sport than were male athletes in individual sports.

Both male and female participants in contact sports were also more likely to have aggressed outside sports contexts than were male and female athletes in noncontact sports. Twice as many males in contact sports, however, reported aggressing outside sport than did female athletes (in contact sports). Clearly, gender and the subcultural contexts associated with masculinity, sport, and the value attached to the toughness ethic are differentially interpreted, maintained, and promoted in men's and women's contact sports.

It is clear from this study that male athletes, and to some degree female athletes in contact sports, are more likely to aggress in nonsport contexts. Although self-selection factors may explain some of the behaviors, the author suggests that certain characteristics found in contact sports may also increase the athlete's tendency to aggress outside sport.

Although not a widespread phenomenon, aggression by athletes outside the sports context occurs frequently enough to be of concern to coaches, program administrators, and parents alike. It manifests itself in many forms, from assaults on women, gays, and

ethnically and racially different students on campuses nationwide to property damage, brawling, and the like. As the literature informs us, male athletes in heavy contact and collision sports such as football and basketball perpetrate much of the violence. One set of explanations suggests that athletes in these sports learn to get what they want by employing legal but rough physical means to attain their objectives (sometimes called instrumental aggression). When successful they are rewarded for such tactical uses of their bodies. Is it possible that the constant exposure to sanctioned sport violence eventually desensitizes them to the point where they can no longer empathize with the pain they cause to others, both within and outside sport? What role does the adulation and public attention they receive for their physicality play in legitimating their aggressive behavior outside sports contexts? Unfortunately, we do not know enough about the causes of aggression in sport to answer the question fully. And we know even less about the role sport plays as a trigger for violence by nonathletes away from the sport venue. For example, White, Katz, and Scarborough (1992) investigated the relationship between the timing and outcomes of the Washington Redskins' football games and violent assaults on women. What the authors found, which was somewhat unexpected, was that game outcome correlated with assaultive behavior against both men and women. When the team won, assaultive behavior against women increased. When it lost, assaults on women decreased, but assaults against men increased markedly. To explain their findings, the authors suggested that violent-prone men may be triggered into aggressive behavior against women (and people weaker than themselves) because they feel a sense of power by witnessing how violence on the field results in defeat and domination of the opposing team. That is, they learn that violence gets results. The authors are quick to point out that although football viewing is associated with assaultive behavior against women, not all men who watch football engage in such behavior.

Although many unanswered questions remain, we hope that raising probing questions, even of a speculative nature, will generate sufficient interest such that the reader will seek answers in class discussions and in research projects.

References

Hughes, R., & Coakley, J. (1991). Positive deviance among athletes. *Sociology of Sport Journal*, **8**, 307-325.

McPherson, B.D., Curtis, J.E., & Loy, J.W. (1989). *The social significance of sport*. Champaign, IL: Human Kinetics.

Nixon, H. (1997). Gender, sport, and aggressive behavior outside sport. *Journal of Sport & Social Issues*, **21**, 379-391.

Snyder, E. (1994). Interpretations and explanations of deviance among college athletes: A case study. *Sociology of Sport Journal*, **11**, 231-248.

Theodorson, G.A., & Theodorson, A.G. (1969). *A modern dictionary of sociology*. New York: Crowell.

White, G.F., Katz, J., & Scarborough, K.E. (1992). The impact of professional football games upon violent assaults on women. *Violence and Victims*, **7**(2), 157-171.

Discussion Questions

Robert Hughes and Jay Coakley

1. What is the sport ethic? Identify and discuss some of its major beliefs.
2. According to the authors, how does player deviance result from being "too committed to the goals and norms of sport"? Discuss and explain.
3. How does "positive deviance" among athletes differ from "negative deviance" among juvenile delinquents? Discuss and explain.
4. Identify two factors that help explain overconformity to the sport ethic.
5. Among which types of athletes is positive deviance most likely? Discuss and explain.
6. How do feelings of separateness, uniqueness, and camaraderie contribute to positive deviance among athletes? Discuss and explain.
7. Why does "deviance grounded in overconformity to the sport ethic present special control problems in sport"? Discuss and explain.
8. What is the danger of being overcommitted to "action in play"? Refer to the story of Daedalus and Icarus for the answer.
9. What can be done to discourage overconformity to the sport ethic? Discuss and debate in class.

Eldon Snyder

1. Provide a brief overview of the interpretive perspective.

2. According to the literature, what do we know about athletic involvement and delinquency? Discuss and explain.
3. Discuss the strengths and weaknesses of the author's methodology.
4. Discuss and comment on each of the four explanations offered in the paper to account for the athletes' criminal behavior.
5. If sport participation, as many argue, deters delinquency, how do *you* account for the behavior of these athletes? Discuss and explain.
6. How "good" an explanation is the interpretive model, including the concept of contingency, in helping us understand the deviant acts of these athletes? Discuss and speculate.

Howard Nixon II

1. Briefly summarize the research findings from the existing literature on athletes and aggression in and out of sport.
2. Briefly describe how the author conducted the study.
3. A "belief in toughness" scale is included at the end of the article. Respond to the scale and calculate your total score. Then compare your score with others in your peer group. How do you rate? Is there a relationship between your scale score and a proclivity toward aggression outside sport? Discuss and compare your scores with those of your peers.
4. The findings of the study suggest that men place a higher value on toughness than women. Discuss and explain this finding.
5. The findings suggest a relationship for male athletes between a belief in toughness and aggression outside sport. Discuss and explain.
6. The findings suggest that male athletes in team sports appear to be more aggressive outside sport than male athletes in individual sports. But this does not hold for female athletes. Why? Discuss and explain.
7. The findings suggest that male and female athletes in contact sports tend to be more aggressive outside sport than male and female athletes in noncontact sports. Why? Discuss and explain.
8. Briefly discuss how the author explains his findings. Do you agree or disagree with his interpretation and conclusions? Discuss and explain.
9. In your opinion, what is the connection, if any, between sport and aggression outside sport? Discuss and speculate.

Positive Deviance Among Athletes: The Implications of Overconformity to the Sport Ethic

Robert Hughes
Jay Coakley

The purpose of this paper is to develop a working definition of positive deviance and use the definition in an analysis of behavior among athletes. It is argued that much deviance among athletes involves excessive overconformity to the norms and values embodied in sport itself. When athletes use the "sport ethic"—which emphasizes sacrifice for The Game, seeking distinction, taking risks, and challenging limits—as an exclusive guide for their behavior, sport and sport participation become especially vulnerable to corruption. Although the sport ethic emphasizes positive norms, the ethic itself becomes the vehicle for transforming behaviors that conform to these positive norms into deviant behaviors that are prohibited and negatively sanctioned within society and within sport organizations themselves. Living in conformity to the sport ethic is likely to set one apart as a "real athlete," but it creates a clear-cut vulnerability to several kinds of deviant behavior. This presents unique problems of social control within sport. The use of performance enhancing drugs in sport is identified as a case in point, and an approach to controlling this form of positive deviance is discussed.

Since the mid-1970s the media have frequently reported cases of deviance among those connected with sports. Exposés on sport often infer that deviance is pervasive and that it is grounded in widespread disregard or rejection of norms by coaches and athletes, especially black athletes in highly visible or revenue producing sports, who underconform to commonly held rules of conduct. Since popular beliefs have traditionally emphasized the positive consequences of sport participation, the seemingly unending litany of publicized cases of deviance in sport has shocked and disappointed many people. In their disappointment, some have concluded that deviance in sport is simply proof that the moral basis of society is eroding. Many have called for new selection standards to keep "troublemakers" out of sport, tougher methods of rule enforcement, and stronger sanctions.

Often overlooked in these calls for more rigid external systems of social control is the fact that deviant behavior among athletes is a complex, diversified phenomenon, and that athletes' lives are already controlled through often repressive systems of social control. We argue that a significant portion of deviance among athletes does not involve disregarding or rejecting commonly accepted cultural goals or means to those goals, nor does it result from alienation from society. Instead, it is grounded in athletes' uncritical acceptance of and commitment to what they have been told by important people in their lives ever since they began participating in competitive programs; in a real sense, it is the result of being too committed to the goals and norms of sport.

Throughout their lives, athletes have heard again and again of the need to be dedicated, to set goals,

Reprinted from Hughes and Coakley, 1991.

to persevere until goals are achieved, to define adversity as a challenge, and to be willing to make sacrifices and subjugate other experiences generally associated with "growing up" all for the sake of their quest to become all they can be in sport. Coaches have emphasized the need to "pay the price," to "play with pain," and to "shoot for the top." These messages have been and continue to be repeated in the words of sport commentators who praise those who play with injuries as "courageous" and those who return to play after serious injuries as being "dedicated to the game" (Gifford & Mangel, 1977). Locker room slogans and sport publicity reinforce these norms (Snyder, 1972; Snyder & Spreitzer, 1989).

Most people in sport, including journalists, fans, owners, sponsors, commentators, coaches, trainers, *and athletes,* accept these norms. Indeed they often internalize them and use them as standards for evaluating themselves and others as "real athletes." In many cases, strict conformity to these norms becomes the basis for acceptance onto a team and a measure of status among athletes themselves. This encourages some athletes to overconform to these norms in ways seen as deviant within society as a whole and even within the governing bodies of sport itself.

This type of deviance is dangerous and certainly a case for concern. However, it is important to recognize that it is grounded in a different set of social dynamics than the deviance of young people who reject commonly accepted rules and expectations and engage in underconforming behavior. It is our contention that this difference between what might be called positive deviance and negative deviance must be taken into account when studying behavior in sport, and when recommending ways of controlling deviance in sport. This is *not* to say that all deviance in sport or all deviance among athletes is positive deviance; nor is it to say that overconformity to commonly accepted norms within sport is characteristic among the majority of athletes. But positive deviance does exist in sport, and that constitutes an especially serious challenge for those interested in reforming sport.

Positive Deviance and the Sport Ethic

This is intended as a working paper in which we outline a conceptual framework for explaining a special type of behavior within sport. Our inten-

tion is not to explain all behavior among athletes or all deviance in sport. Our hypothesis is simply that many forms of deviance in sport are not caused by a disregard or rejection of social values or norms; instead, they are caused by an unqualified acceptance of and an unquestioned commitment to a value system framed by what we refer to as the sport ethic.

The sport ethic refers to what many participants in sport have come to use as the criteria for defining what it means to be a real athlete. The criteria described below are not intended to be exhaustive, but informal reports from athletes and from coaches in coaching education programs, combined with information from autobiographies of numerous sport figures, strongly suggest that the following four beliefs are commonly accepted as factors defining what it means to identify oneself as an athlete and to be treated as an athlete by others in sport:

1. *Being an athlete involves making sacrifices for The Game.* The idea underlying this dimension of the sport ethic is that real athletes must love The Game above all else and prove it by subordinating other interests for the sake of an exclusive commitment to their sport. To prove they care about their sport, participants must have "the proper attitude" (a term commonly used by coaches), make a commitment, meet the demands of fellow athletes, and sacrifice to stay involved. In this sense, being an athlete means that a person will consistently do what is necessary to meet the demands of a team or the demands of competition. This is the spirit underlying the notion that athletes must make sacrifices, that they must be willing to pay the price to stay involved in sport. Pep talks and locker room slogans are full of references to this guideline (Snyder, 1972; Snyder & Spreitzer, 1989).

2. *Being an athlete involves striving for distinction.* The Olympic motto of *"Citius, Altius, Fortius"* (swifter, higher, stronger) captures the meaning of this normative dimension of the sport ethic. True athletes seek to improve, to get better, to come closer to perfection. Winning symbolizes improvement and establishes distinction; losing is tolerated only to the extent that it is part of the experience of learning how to win. Breaking records is the ultimate standard of achievement in sport. This is because real athletes are a special group dedicated to climbing the pyramid, reaching for the top, pushing limits, excelling, and exceeding or dominating others. Of course external rewards

may be associated with involvement, but the validation of one's identity as an athlete is primarily tied to one's immersion in the quest for distinction rather than gaining external rewards. It is worth noting here that sport scientists have intervened in sport in ways that certainly reinforce this guideline and promote overconformity to it; their development of and occasional unquestioned application of many new performance enhancing technologies has become an important part of this process of striving for distinction among athletes at elite levels.

3. *Being an athlete involves accepting risks and playing through pain.* According to the sport ethic, an athlete does not give in to pressure, pain, or fear. Many sport activities pose inherent risks of injury, but voluntarily accepting the possibility of injury is a sign of courage and dedication among athletes (Donnelly, 1980, 1981; Williams & Donnelly, 1985). In addition to courage in the face of physical challenges, moral courage is also implied in this normative guideline. This is reflected even in golf and tennis, for example, wherein athletes are expected to sustain high levels of physical performance under extreme psychological and social pressure. The idea is that athletes never back down from challenges in the form of either physical risk or pressure, and that standing up to challenges involves moral courage.

Furthermore, athletes are expected to display "coolness" (as conceptualized by Lyman & Scott, 1970, p. 145) and "composure" (as conceptualized by Goffman, 1967, pp. 222-223) as they willingly confront and overcome the fears and challenges associated with competition and accept the increasing risk of failure and injury that comes with higher levels of competition. As American athletes prepare for the 1992 Olympic Games in Barcelona, one of the most popular T-shirts at the U.S. Olympic Training Center carries the slogan, "No pain, no Spain." If the willingness to conform to this aspect of the sport ethic wanes, then sport physicians, sport psychologists, and other sport scientists will help athletes overcome and deal with risks, pain, and fears.

4. *Being an athlete involves refusing to accept limits in the pursuit of possibilities.* People in sport generally stress the possibilities for achievement and the imperative to wholeheartedly pursue them. An athlete does not accept a situation without trying to change it, overcome it, turn the scales. It is believed that sport is a sphere of life in which anything is possible, *if* a person lives by the sport ethic. An athlete is a person obligated to pursue dreams without reservation. External limits are not recognized as valid. True athletes are obligated to believe in *the attempt* to achieve success. And when the perception of limits threatens to impede achievement, there are many sport experts who will provide pep talks, therapy, or technology to alter those perceptions.

How is the sport ethic related to deviance in sport? Deviance is usually assumed to involve a rejection of norms (or at least allegiance to norms that conflict with other, more well-established norms), and it is also defined by most social scientists as negative in the sense that it is behavior that is morally condemned and punished. However, a portion of the deviance (i.e., behavior that is morally condemned and dangerous) among athletes does not involve a rejection of norms, or conformity to a set of norms not endorsed in the rest of society. Instead, many problem behaviors are created when athletes care too much for, accept too completely, and overconform to what has become the value system of sport itself, including both goals and means (cf. Merton's terminology from his 1957 discussion of anomie and deviance). This is especially true for high performance athletes, although it is certainly not limited to them; the phenomenon even occurs at youth league levels.

Although there is a need to empirically investigate this phenomenon, some studies have identified the existence of normative overconformity among athletes. Ewald and Jiobu (1985) found that serious athletes often zealously pursued and overconformed to the norms within their sport groups to such an extent that their sport participation was disruptive to everything from their family relationships and work responsibilities to their physical health and personal comfort. Other people saw these athletes as deviant, but the behavior of the athletes themselves actually reflected commonly held values and norms, although involving an unrestrained commitment and overconformity to these norms. Hilliard and Hilliard (1990) identified not only an awareness of and commitment to the guidelines of the sport ethic as it is explained in this paper, but also overconformity to the sport ethic among triathletes and weightlifters. Another study, developed along very different lines, found strong similarities between compulsive long-distance runners and anorectic patients in a treatment program (Nash, 1987). Both behaviors were classified as "addictive-like" overconforming responses to commonly accepted norms. In other words, the runners and anorectics went too far in conforming with the expectations that people should exercise and control their diets; they overconformed to the point that they engaged in positive deviance.

Similarly, 32% of the women athletes surveyed at a major university in the U.S. admitted to using various forms of pathogenic weight control behaviors in conjunction with their sport participation (Rosen, McKeag, Hough, & Curley, 1986). As with athletes in the other studies, the behavior of these women was deviant in the sense that they had gone too far in their efforts to live up to widely accepted expectations for physical appearance and for what it means to be an athlete.

We hypothesize that rates of positive deviance in sport are related to the special characteristics of sport experiences and systems of sponsorship in sport organizations. Overconformity to the sport ethic is prompted by the following factors:

1. Athletes find the action (Ball, 1972) and their experiences in sport so exhilarating and thrilling that they want to continue participating as long as possible.
2. The likelihood of being chosen or sponsored for continued participation is increased if athletes overconform to the sport ethic (i.e., coaches praise overconformers and often make them models for other athletes; furthermore, coaches often accuse athletes of lacking hustle, effort, and caring, and athletes can only prove hustle and effort through unquestioned conformity to the sport ethic).

Thus many athletes do not see their overconformity to the sport ethic as deviant; they see it as confirming and reconfirming their identity as athletes and as members of select sport groups. Following the guidelines of the sport ethic to an extreme is just what you do as an athlete, especially when continued participation and success in sport take on significant personal and social meaning.

Although developed here primarily in relation to sport, the concept of positive deviance has applications in many other contexts. However, our major point (to be developed below in the section on theoretical support) is that it identifies a type of behavior not easily explained by general theories of deviance. Through positive deviance people do harmful things to themselves and perhaps others

while motivated by a sense of duty and honor. Those who engage in such behavior do not claim or accept a deviant identity, nor do they see their deviant behavior as a basis for a master status (Wasielewski, 1991). They are not members of low status groups whose behavior threatens those with higher status; therefore, they are not generally labeled as deviant. *But* they clearly engage in extreme behaviors at a rate and in a manner that distinguishes them from others in society.

Despite its social implications, this kind of problematic behavior is often ignored by sociologists and left to be explained by psychologists, who refer to it in terms of individual differences. Yet we know that good people acting for good reasons have clearly done great harm to themselves and others. Milgram (1974), Zimbardo, Haney, Banks, & Jaffe (1982), and Arendt (1963) have shown that following the prescriptions for "being the best one can be" is an accurate albeit frightening explanation of the behaviors of Nazi prison guards. Furthermore, evidence to be summarized below shows that test pilots, mountain climbers, and scores of others consistently take unnecessary risks, exposing themselves and others to danger in order to prove they are good and worthy persons who have earned the right to claim a restricted (achieved) social identity.

Important to note is that attempting to change the behavior of such persons by helping them learn to conform to social rules and live up to social expectations would only increase their deviance. Although this paper deals with overconformity and positive deviance in the context of sport, the conceptual framework offered has implications for how sociology might define and explain a wide range of deviance outside the context of sport as well.

Conditions Leading to Overconformity

Not all athletes are equally likely to engage in overconformity to the sport ethic. We hypothesize that positive deviance is most common among the following:

1. Those athletes who have low self-esteem or who, for other reasons, are vulnerable to group demands and less able to withstand pressures to sacrifice themselves for the group;
2. Those athletes who see sport as an exclusive mobility route, and for whom mobility demands an extreme commitment to achievement and a willingness to make great personal sacrifices as they strive for achievement.

In other words, athletes whose identity or future chances for material success are exclusively tied to sport are most likely to engage in over-conforming behavior. This too needs to be explored through research, but it is expected that over-conformity to the sport ethic would be more characteristic among men than women (since men are more likely to use sport as an exclusive identity and/or mobility source), among low income minority athletes in revenue producing sports (for similar reasons), and among those whose relationships with significant others have been based exclusively on continued involvement and success in sport.

As self-identification becomes lodged within sport, a person is increasingly susceptible to control that is grounded in the demands of the sport and sport groups. Therefore, what we might refer to as the corruption of sport at least partially involves a process by which common restraints on behavior give way to encouragement to engage in potentially self-destructive behaviors in an effort to demonstrate worthiness for continued group membership and status within a specific sport group. It is the athlete's vulnerability to group demands, combined with the desire to gain or reaffirm group membership through overconforming to these demands, that is a critical factor in the incidence of positive deviance.

Along these lines, it has been suggested that one of the qualities of great coaches is their ability to create an environment that keeps athletes in a perpetual state of adolescence. This leads athletes to continually strive to confirm their identity and eliminate self-doubts by engaging in behaviors that please their coaches and teammates. When this dependency based commitment occurs, over-conformity to the sport ethic becomes increasingly common and many young people willingly sacrifice their body and play with reckless abandon in the pursuit of affirmation and approval as athletes. Coaches often encourage this, intentionally or naively. For example, Jerry Kramer, a former Green Bay Packer football player, alluded to this when he made the following observation about his coach, Vince Lombardi:

> I suppose I shouldn't have been, but I was amazed by how Vince Lombardi, the high school coach, paralleled Vince Lombardi, the professional coach, down to his insistence . . . that every player show up for every meeting and every practice not on schedule, but ahead of schedule. (Kramer, 1971, pp. 14-15)

Kempton (1971) also attributed Lombardi's success to his ability to keep groups of grown men at the maturity level of the average high school sophomore. A coach who can do this encourages, intentionally or naively, positive deviance in the form of overconformity to the sport ethic.

Overconformity and Bonds Between Athletes

Collective commitment to the sport ethic, especially under conditions of extreme stress, may also lead to the creation of special bonds between athletes in certain sport groups. To the extent that this occurs, these bonds not only reaffirm their unqualified acceptance of and commitment to the sport ethic on a day-to-day basis but also generate special feelings of fraternity, especially in groups of athletes in the same sports, and especially in sports wherein athletes are perceived to be unique because they endure extreme challenges and risks. These special feelings separate athletes from other people when it comes to what athletes see as a true understanding of the sport experience. Most athletes do not think outsiders know what it is really like to be an athlete; nonathletes just do not understand. This is illustrated by former professional football player Dave Meggyesy:

> Being a professional athlete was so strange. The real beauty of the experience is the actual play, the exhilaration of it, physically and emotionally. But because you have fans . . . who get so crazy about the game and feel so deeply about it, you have . . . people dissecting your every move and thought. [After the game] there are microphones all over the place, and everyone wants you to explain things: "Why did you screw up?" "Why did you hit that hole instead of the other one?" "How does it feel?" And you have to respond to all these people who never knew the first thing about what it feels like. . . . It's like making love and having to explain it to someone every time. (quoted in Remnick, 1987, p. 46).

When this sense of separateness and uniqueness is combined with the fact that athletes are often held in awe by outsiders and attract more media attention than heads of state, athletes may develop a feeling of superiority. Although there is a need to study the existence, origins, and correlates of these feelings of superiority, we suggest that they do exist among some athletes and that they are often accompanied by a sense of disdain for those "normal" members of the community who live their lives without sacrificing for sport, seeking distinction, taking risks, or pushing limits, and who therefore do not have an experiential basis for understanding the pure exhilaration of living life in this way.

Tom Wolfe (1979), in his analysis of test pilot/astronauts, identified very similar feelings of fraternity, superiority, and disdain for outsiders. These feelings were so evident that he captured them in the title of his book, *The Right Stuff.* Wolfe's description could easily be applied to athletes in many sport settings:

> in this fraternity, men were not rated by their outward rank . . . No, herein the world was divided into those who had it and those who did not.

> A career in flying was like climbing one of those ancient Babylonian pyramids made up of a dizzy progression of steps and ledges . . . and the idea was to prove at every foot of the way up that pyramid that you were one of the elected and anointed ones who had *the right stuff* and could move higher and higher and even . . . that you might be able to join that special few at the very top. (Wolfe, 1979, p. 24)

Wolfe further imagined how these feelings of separateness and uniqueness might affect a test pilot/astronaut's perception of "normal outsiders"; his words clearly infer the existence of disdain:

> From up here at dawn the pilot looked down upon the poor hopeless [city below] . . . and began to wonder: . . . how could they live like that . . . if they had the faintest idea of what it was like up here in this righteous zone? Danger, excitement, special standing, a way of life more significant than possible for all but a very few, a small slice indeed of mankind who can obtain it—facing danger, overcoming fear, shooting dice with death, a small price to pay for such extraordinary living, for the opportunity to be among the very best. (Wolfe, 1979, p. 39)

In the case of athletes in highly visible sports, this process of developing fraternity, superiority, and disdain for outsiders might also lead some of them to naively assume they are somehow beyond

the law, and that people outside the athletic fraternity do not deserve their respect. This could lead to serious cases of negative deviance including, for example, assault, sexual assault, and rape (including gang rape), the destruction of property, reckless driving, and alcohol abuse.

Another possibility is that this disdain can become such a part of an athlete's view of the nonsport world that it may even be turned inward and transformed into self-disdain or panic when athletes fail to overconform to the guidelines of the sport ethic in their own behavior, or when they must retire from active participation. This may be one of the reasons why athletes try so hard to extend their playing careers and why some even mourn its passing. Losing membership in the special and elite athletic fraternity presents difficulties in itself, but the threat of entering the disdained category of nonathlete or outsider is especially upsetting. Becoming separated from those few others who truly understand what it means to be an athlete can be a frightening experience, especially for those whose identity and feelings of significance and superiority are exclusively tied to sport. This is probably one reason why the retirement of highly competitive athletes has been conceptualized as a form of "social death" in some research (Brandmeyer & Alexander, 1982; Lerch, 1984; Rosenberg, 1984).

This may also be one reason why some athletes have knee surgery after knee surgery so they can play for "just one more year," and why others inject unbelievable amounts of hormones into their bodies on a regular basis without even thinking twice. The motivation is *not* just to win, or to make money, or to please a TV audience; more important, it is simply *to play, to be an athlete,* and *to maintain their membership in the special and elite athletic fraternity.* This is why a mediocre athlete on a second rate team may also engage in positive deviance such as taking performance enhancing substances, whether they be megadoses of vitamin B-12 or anabolic steroids: The athlete knows there are no championships to be won or money to be made, but there is an identity and moral worth to be established and reaffirmed, and a connection to a coach and a group of teammates to be honored. These are powerful motives.

This emphasis on the connection between positive deviance and identity and social relationships clearly grounds our model in a sociological framework. Our explanation of deviance cannot be reduced to a psychological model in which deviance is tied to an individual pursuit of self-interest in the form of external rewards.

Positive Deviance and Social Control Problems

Deviance grounded in overconformity to the sport ethic presents special control problems in sport. Owners, managers, sponsors, and coaches—all of whom exercise control within sport—often benefit when athletes overaccept and overconform to the sport ethic (Young, 1991). Having athletes who overzealously pursue the ideals framed by the ethic is seen by most of these people as a blessing. The fact that athletes have learned to use overconformity to the sport ethic as a gauge of personal commitment and courage for themselves and fellow athletes works to the advantage of those concerned with victories or entertainment. The issue of social control is even further complicated by the tendency to promote extreme overconformers into positions of power and influence in sport—after all, they have already proven they are willing to pay the price and live the sport ethic to the fullest.

This guarantees that athletes receive continued strong encouragement to overconform to the guidelines of the sport ethic. This also means that a powerful source of deviance and ethical problems among athletes lies in sport itself, in athletes' relationships with one another, and in their relationships with coaches and managers. Paradoxically, the sport ethic when taken to an extreme actually promotes the corruption of sport (see below).

Theoretical Support for the Concept of Positive Deviance

Sagarin (1985) and Goode (1990) have argued that positive deviance is an oxymoron—unless behavior is defined as different in kind and unless it is despised and punished, it does not qualify as deviant. However, even though a strong case can be made for the concept of positive deviance (e.g., Buffalo & Rodgers, 1971; Dodge, 1987; Ewald & Jiobu, 1985; Heckert, 1989), the debate is confusing because the sociology of deviance as a whole is characterized by theoretical chaos and by the tendency to ignore the relationship between deviance and social dynamics within total social structures (Ben-Yehuda, 1990).

Our purpose is not to enter this debate. In this working paper we follow the lead of Ewald and Jiobu (1985) and Dodge (1987), and suggest that many aspects of the problem behaviors engaged in by athletes cannot be explained simply as violations of sport norms or as conformity to a set of norms that are not endorsed within society at large. We argue that these problem behaviors, including such things as the use of performance enhancing substances (both legal and illegal) in excessive amounts, engaging in excessive on-the-field violence (both legal and illegal), and violating certain game or association rules (such as those restricting eligibility, limiting practice times, prohibiting participation in unsanctioned competitive events) are best explained as the result of overconformity to the norms of sport itself. In other words, they are the result of caring too much for or accepting too completely the goals and values of sport.

We are not arguing that athletes engage in what Merton (1957) has identified as "innovation" grounded in the acceptance of cultural goals and the concomitant rejection of accepted means to those goals. Merton's framework renders athletes as mere opportunists. This is inappropriate since athletes who engage in positive deviance accept goals as well as means to an extreme degree and without critical examination of either. Both goals and means are "overdetermined" and extended to an excessive degree. Instead of innovation, positive deviance in sport reflects more the notion of the hero's quest, or the extraordinary, rather than mere utilitarianism. Therefore if Merton's framework is applicable in any way, the behavior we are describing would best fit into an extension of the conformity category, but this misses the point.

Our approach is also slightly different from that proposed by Dodge (1987), and very different from that criticized by Sagarin since much of the publicized positive deviance athletes engage in is indeed negatively evaluated and sanctioned by those outside of sport, and often by administrators within the governing bodies of the sports themselves. However, these behaviors, even though defined as deviant, are different *only in degree, not in kind,* from behaviors valued positively in the rest of society. Again, it is emphasized that the norms of the sport ethic are positive norms; it is under the condition of uncritical acceptance and extreme overconformity that they are associated with dangerous and destructive behaviors. We are referring to deviance that would ultimately lead to fascism, not anarchy.

Our conceptualization of positive deviance is also somewhat different from "semi-deviance" as described by Etzioni-Halevy (1975). Semi-deviance refers to behaviors generally perceived as too extreme or bizarre to be normal, yet not negative enough to be defined as morally bad. In other words, Etzioni-Halevy infers that deviance can be conceptualized in terms of a continuum of behaviors varying from normal, to slightly deviant, to semi-deviant, to very deviant; semi-deviance "falls in to a no-one's land between behavior that is normatively fully condoned and that which is flatly condemned by a given group or society" (p. 356). However, describing deviance in this way infers that extremely conforming behavior is the ideal and that digressions from the ideal represent varying degrees of deviance. We would argue that this approach miscasts empirical reality.

Our intent is to abandon the traditional assumption that extreme conformity to an ideal pattern of good behavior should be considered the norm for evaluating human action across all social situations. When this assumption is made, there is the implication that the appropriate response to any deviant or problem behavior is to introduce additional programs of social control intended to increase conformity to the ideal. But if efforts to generate extreme conformity actually produced ideal moral behavior, there would be little or no deviance among the police, in the military, or among athletes for that matter. However, these groups are often the settings for serious problems of deviance.

Although abstinence from just about everything (the "just say no" approach) is the ideal proposed by numerous moral entrepreneurs and those in the clutches of moral panics of one form or another, we would argue that it is dangerous to accept such a definition of prosocial or desirable behavior. When conformity is conceptualized in terms of total abstinence, the analysis of deviance misrepresents what is normal, often necessary, and usually desirable in social life. After all, behaviors such as drinking, sexual expression, fighting, and questioning authority are not only socially acceptable and moral across a wide range of social situations but they are sometimes even necessary or morally prescribed.

Similar to our conceptualization of positive deviance, Wasielewski (1991) uses the notion of *defiance* to capture the idea that some kinds of deviance are created by groups who take good and acceptable behaviors, such as working for peace or physical fitness, to the extreme. She notes that the "deviance of the athlete and the [peace] activist resides not only in the acts in which they engage, but more precisely in the degree to which they carry these activities" (p. 85). For example, ultramarathon athletes thrive "on pushing the limits of physical and mental endurance" (p. 85). Wasielewski argues that although people who engage in extreme activities are deviant, their status as such is highly transi-

tory. She points out that deviance is not always or only a status created by others who label a person as deviant; sometimes deviance is grounded in self-initiated efforts to establish social uniqueness through a pursuit of specific goals. In this way, deviance is tied to "a process of self- and social discovery" (p. 89).

In addition to Wasielewski's discussion, there are several other discussions of deviance that are closely aligned with our conceptualization of positive deviance. For example, Cavan and Ferdinand (1981) and Dodge (1987) use the notion of a normal statistical distribution and conceptualize deviance as behaviors falling outside the middle range of the distribution. According to their conceptualization, most behaviors fall within a normally accepted range and the rest involve deviance in terms of either underconformity or overconformity to norms. Unfortunately, those using this model often infer that overconformity is associated with excessive virtue, or that it is the source of virtue, and that persons who deviate through overconformity tend to be rewarded positively for their extreme excellence.

This association between positive deviance and virtuosity has been seriously challenged by studies of alcohol use among adults (Valliant, 1983) and drug use among adolescents (Shedler & Block, 1990). For example, Valliant's study of drinking behaviors among adult males in the United States found that abstinence, as achieved by overconformers and the self-righteous, was *not* associated with psychological well-being or social adjustment. Adults who engaged in moderate social drinking exhibited the highest levels of overall mental health.

A similar pattern was found by Shedler and Block in their study of adolescent drug use: both substance abusers *and abstainers* seem to be psychologically impaired in serious ways and have social histories characterized by family relationships that created anxiety, inhibitions, and a lack of social responsiveness. Within the context of the 1980s peer subculture, it was the adolescents who had used alcohol and experimented with marijuana (without developing abuse patterns) who exhibited the highest level of psychological health, and whose social histories led them to score high on measures of social adjustment. In other words, in both these studies, overconformity was not found to always be a virtue or the source of virtue, and moderate amounts of social drinking or experimentation with drugs are not indicative of varying degrees of deviance (as some prohibitionists are now arguing).

The serious problems often associated with extreme conformity to cultural ideals have also been identified by Westkott (1986). She notes that many so-called personality disorders among women are the result of their tendency to overconform to traditional gender role expectations. According to Westkott's analysis, many distraught women are most accurately described as "supranormal" rather than abnormal. These women experience difficulties because their sense of self is not strong enough to overcome the demands for conformity to a set of expectations defined for them by others. As they conscientiously or desperately attempt to conform to these expectations, their selves are diminished and weakened and psychological problems arise.

The importance of distinguishing deviance (either positive or negative) that results from excessive compliance with norms from deviance originating in outright norm violations or conformity to alternative norms has been outlined in Tinto's (1987) discussion of Durkheim's original typology of the sources of deviance. Tinto views the relationship between the individual and the social order in terms of two dimensions: control and integration. A person may be overcontrolled (fatalistic) or undercontrolled (anomic), overintegrated (altruistic) or underintegrated (egoistic, i.e., alienated from an otherwise satisfactorily organized group). This typology indicates that inducements to deviance exist on the positive side of each dimension, that is, among those who are overcontrolled or overintegrated. Deviance in these cases results from external demands encouraging a person to act in the best interests of others rather than self (overcontrolled, fatalistic; e.g., gladiators or slaves, respectively), or to act out of a sense of membership in a group wherein one's status as a member calls for sacrificing self-interest and personal preferences (overintegrated, altruistic).

This conception of deviance differs from traditional conceptions in which negative deviance is seen as the result of (a) confusion about norms or rules, (b) being caught between conflicting norms or rules, and/or (c) feelings of alienation from established groups.

Finally, we suggest that excessive commitment to the sport ethic tends to be defined among many athletes as supranormal, in the sense of the Neitzschean "superman," and in the sense of the hubris that can emerge among those who feel or believe they are above the ordinary and live a life at the edge. This hubris, coming in the form of arrogance grounded in excessive pride, may include a disdain for those ordinary persons who only live by the rules to the extent that they never push limits. This disdain for others, as exhibited by many ath-

letes, may also be an important motivational source for their off-the-field deviance.

Positive Deviance and Identity Issues

Overconforming to the normative demands of sport involves a process in which the role of athlete (player, climber, skier, runner, etc.) becomes extremely salient to a person's identity. Since identity is social in nature, the acceptance and confirmation of one's status as an athlete is crucial (Donnelly & Young, 1988). The process of being defined and gaining acceptance in society as a real athlete is interactive, progressive, and voluntary.

By *interactive* we mean that the qualities used to define a person as able and acceptable as an athlete in a certain group must be demonstrated to others in a way that proves worthiness. As was pointed out in the discussion of the sport ethic, this usually takes the form of paying the price in one way or another.

By *progressive* we mean to call attention to the notion that continued participation in any sport generally demands increasing levels of commitment and the sacrificing of outside interests in order to keep moving up the hierarchy or the pyramid to the next competitive level. In baseball for example, this move would be from sandlot to Little League, to high school, to semi-pro or college, to minor league, to major league. If individuals drop out of this sequence at some point, they can continue participating in a recreational sense but will be denied status and identity as a real athlete. Since defining athlete as a status gives significance to obtaining social recognition of that which a person claims to be, this notion of the progressive demonstration of competence is as true for climbing and tennis as it is for football and volleyball.

By *voluntary* we mean to imply that a person can choose not to participate and suffer no general negative sanction (other than being called a quitter by some people), or the diminishment of life chances (as would be the case if the person dropped out of school or a job). Indeed, it is the voluntary nature of sport involvement that is key to its moral significance. When a person makes sacrifices for the sake of achievement and winning in sport, it is because a choice and personal commitment has been made. An excellent description of the process of taking on a voluntary and highly salient identity is provided by Dornbush (1955) in his analysis of the military academy.

Donnelly and Young (1988) also outline a similar process of establishing a sport identity in informal, self-controlled sport situations associated with climbing and North American rugby. The process they identify is characterized by a four-step sequence: presocialization, selection and recruitment, socialization, and acceptance/ostracism. They note that the process of identity construction and confirmation that occurs during socialization into a subcultural career "involves ceasing to consider outsiders [i.e., not athletes] as a valued audience" (1988, p. 224). Their findings certainly imply that rules created by persons external to the group are of limited importance. Similarly, Ewald and Jiobu outline a slightly different series of four steps leading to positive addiction for runners and bodybuilders. They point out that "What the outsider perceives as self-torture, the insider redefines as enjoyable and worthy of pursuing for its intrinsic rewards" (1985, p. 147).

Positive Deviance and the Commitment to Action

The process by which norms that encourage deviant and dangerous behavior actually emerge through the interaction of peers has been outlined by Sato (1989) in his "play theory of delinquency." Sato focuses on a more general, informal context than sport but uses concepts very similar to those describing the development of a sport identity. Sato argues that youth are naturally drawn to action, typically during their leisure time with peers outside the purview of adults. This action may involve some illegal activity but is most accurately characterized by comparing it to its opposite, which is sitting around the house doing nothing, being bored, or doing whatever parents want you to do all the time. Sato builds on this point and explains that this focus on action among young people is inherently volatile and subject to corruption. This process of corruption is conceptualized in the same way we are conceptualizing positive deviance as a form of overconformity. His words are informative:

> While the playlike definition of the situation can provide youngsters with a sense of meaning and purpose, *excessive commitment* to the definition sometimes leads to fatal and irrevocable consequences, because "action" has an inherent tendency towards "corruption" . . . There are at least three elements in "action" which lead to such consequences: collective encouragement, intense involvement, and a challenge to reach the limit. (1989, p. 203, emphasis added)

In other words, interaction among peers can lead to an excessive commitment to action. This action, used as proof of group membership or attachment to peers, often pushes limits and comes in extreme forms; the more extreme the behavior, the more one is able to demonstrate commitment to group norms. Initiation rites are institutionalized demands for excessive commitment to group norms.

This process is very similar to the process identified by Donnelly and Young (1988) and Ewald and Jiobu (1985) in their analyses of the behavioral implications of the development of sport identities. Seeking and participating in action is the norm; negative deviance occurs when a person avoids action altogether, and positive deviance occurs when a person becomes overcommitted to maintaining and extending action. Intensive involvement in a group in which there is collective encouragement to push limits and pay the price produces an excessive commitment to action that is destructive, not necessarily desired, and deviant. The "corruption of action" and the promotion of deviance, therefore, lie in the processes of group interaction among athletes themselves. This creates a situation in which what might be called the sport ethic is a crystallization of norms that tend to corrupt sport. It is *citius, altius, fortius* taken seriously, and to the extreme. This happens in the same way that norms among young peers in informal play situations tend to corrupt action.

The notion of being overcommitted to action in play, or to pushing the limits in sport, has been clearly explained in the account of Daedalus and Icarus:

> When Daedalus, who can be thought of as the master technician of most ancient Greece, put the wings he had made on his son Icarus, so that he might fly out of and escape the Cretan labyrinth which he himself had invented, he said to him: "Fly the middle way. Don't fly too high, or the sun will melt the wax on your wings, and you will fall. Don't fly too low, or the tides of the sea will catch you." Daedalus himself flew the middle way, but he watched his son become ecstatic and fly too high. The wax melted, and the boy fell into the sea . . . but Daedalus, who flew the middle way, succeeded in getting to the other shore. (Campbell, 1988, pp. 131-132)

Campbell follows this story with an interpretation of the tragic fates often endured by heroes and a word of advice to those who take the hero's journey:

> When you are doing something that is a brand new adventure, [such as living in a way] that is not what the community can help you with, there's always the danger of too much enthusiasm, of neglecting certain . . . details. Then you fall off. When you follow the path of your desire and enthusiasm and emotion, keep your mind in control, and don't let it pull you compulsively into disaster. (Campbell, 1988, p. 132)

Unfortunately, many athletes never bear these words of caution; they are not encouraged to seek excellence by "flying the middle way," by following the example of Daedalus. Instead they are encouraged to fly too high—into the sun. Not surprisingly, they get caught up in the adventure and, when they do, they frequently meet the same fate as Icarus. With this in mind, it is appropriate to use the positive deviance model to explain a specific form of deviance in sport.

Application of the Positive Deviance Model

The positive deviance model provides a useful explanation of athletes' use of performance enhancing substances, especially the potentially dangerous ones. For most athletes the use of these substances is not the result of defective socialization or lack of moral character. After all, users are often the most dedicated and committed athletes in sport! Nor are the users helpless victims of coaches and trainers who lack moral character, although when coaches and trainers get carried away in their endorsement of the sport ethic, they may directly or indirectly encourage the use of performance enhancing substances. But most substance use and abuse is clearly tied to an overcommitment to the sport ethic itself; it is grounded in overconformity—the same type of overconformity that leads injured distance runners to continue training even when training may cause serious physical problems, and American football players to risk their bodies through excessively violent physical contact week after painful week in the NFL.

Those sport critics who argue that an emphasis on winning or human greed is *the* cause of deviance in sport are creating a smokescreen, subverting efforts to deal with some serious problems. Ironically, these critics conclude that the only way to deal with problems in sport is to institute even more controls over athletes who are overcontrolled already! In this way, "humanistic" critics unwittingly offer recommendations that could have come from the pages of *Beyond Freedom and Dignity* (Skinner, 1971). At the same time, these critics ignore the fact that many athletes who clearly realize they will never win championships or make money from their athletic accomplishments still engage in deviance, including on-the-field violence and taking performance enhancing drugs. This is not to say that a desire to win or make money is irrelevant to athletes; both are important parts of the overall context in which many forms of deviance occur. But much deviance among athletes clearly rests in overconforming to the positive values promoted through the sport ethic itself.

The implications of this model become especially clear when programs to control the use of performance enhancing substances and other forms of deviance are considered. Making recommendations to try to control deviance grounded in overconformity to accepted values is a challenge, because one must realize that athletes themselves assume a good deal of complicity in perpetuating substance use. More rules and tougher rule enforcement are only of limited value when trying to control this type of deviance. For example, Terry Todd's own history of abuse of performance enhancing drugs as a power lifter (Todd, 1983) clearly shows how athletes continually seek to defeat rather than comply with drug testing programs.

As long as athletes are committed to the sport ethic without qualification, they will think it honorable to try anything to stay involved in sport. This is not only the spirit in which Ben Johnson took steroids but also the spirit in which a substitute football player on an American football team with a mediocre record takes steroids. Of course they want to win, but the main reason for their deviance is to live up to the ideal of being an athlete and to maintain membership in the athletic fraternity. Their goal is to show through their deeds that they belong in a special group, a group comprised of people willing to pay the price, strive for distinction, accept risks, and exceed limits.

This sense of membership and superiority is so important and powerful that it may be the reason why no other athletes blew the whistle on Ben Johnson's steroid use until he rejected his connection with them by naming so many others. Athletes know that the real measure of one's membership in the athletic fraternity is the response of fellow athletes; coaches and the rules of eligibility are only important in that they determine who competes in certain events.

Effectively controlling forms of overconforming deviance ultimately rests in getting athletes and others who are directly involved in sport to strike a balance between accepting and questioning the norms comprising the sport ethic, to fly the middle way. As in other settings, limits on commitment and conformity must be made more explicit so that athletes who engage in overconforming deviance will not be defined as heroes by those within sport or in the media. In appointing Arnold Schwarzenegger, a steroid user for 14 years, director of the President's Council of Physical Fitness, George Bush has certainly subverted efforts to discourage pushing limits in potentially self-destructive ways.

The questioning and qualification of the sport ethic also need to be combined with a process of creating new norms related to the use of medical science and technology in sports. This challenge of using new forms of technology in constructive ways is not unique; it is faced in many spheres of life apart from sport, although the pervasiveness of the sport ethic guarantees that it will create serious problems for athletes.

Specific changes suggested by the positive deviance model include the following:

- Lest we be hypocritical in our efforts to make changes, we need to eliminate the distinction between the so-called legal performance enhancing drugs or procedures that may harm the health of athletes and the illegal ones. Pain killers, massive injections of vitamin B-12, blood boosting, the use of erythropoietin to stimulate red blood cell production, playing with pins in broken bones or with high tech casts to hold broken bones in place during competition, and playing with special harnesses to restrict the movement of injured joints can be as harmful to health as taking anabolic steroids, and they must be regulated and controlled before the use of performance enhancing drugs can be effectively limited.
- Rules are needed to clearly indicate that risks to health are undesirable and unnecessary in sport.
- Athletes who are injured should not be allowed to play until certified as well, not simply "able to compete," by a physician outside

the athletic program; team physicians may be vulnerable to collective overconformity to the sport ethic within sport organizations.
- There is a need for new norms emphasizing an awareness of one's limits so that courage can be defined as being able to accept the discipline necessary to become well instead of disregarding the consequences of injuries.
- The goals of sport science must be reframed to emphasize the growth and development of athletes through the expansion of the sport experience at all levels of involvement. Concerns about the enhancement of performance must be informed by these goals, or sport scientists become high tech pimps. For example, sport psychologists should help athletes understand the consequences of their choice to participate in sport and to reduce the extent to which guilt or pathology influence their participation and training decisions. This is the alternative to the increasingly popular technique of "psycho-doping" which encourages positive deviance by making athletes more likely to give their all to sport without ever questioning why they are doing what they are doing.

The process of questioning and qualifying the sport ethic should be formalized and it should involve all sport participants. Unless this happens, deviance grounded in overconformity will continue to be commonplace and expected among athletes. Therefore athletes and coaches are the ones who need to develop new guidelines that discourage overconformity to the sport ethic, guidelines that emphasize health and development as well as performance. This is the major reason why dealing with most drug issues in sport requires the education of coaches, not just athletes.

At present we face a future without any clearly defined ideas about what achievement in sport means in light of the escalated rewards associated with participation, the increased importance assigned to sport participation in the lives of many young athletes, and the new technologies available to enhance performance. There is a need for new guidelines to replace the old ones. There is a need for new models of excellence shaped by a commitment to flying the middle way. Continuing to emphasize unquestioned acceptance of the sport ethic, and instituting increasingly invasive and repressive systems of social control, will not eliminate the self-destructive and dangerous behaviors characteristic in much of sport today.

References

Arendt, H. (1963). Eichmann in Jerusalem: A report on the banality of evil. New York: Viking Press.

Ball, D.W. (1972). What the action is: A cross cultural approach. *Journal for the Theory of Social Behavior, 2,* 121-143.

Ben-Yehuda, N. (1990). Positive and negative deviance: More fuel for a controversy. *Deviant Behavior, 11,* 221-244.

Brandmeyer, G.A., & Alexander, L.K. (1982). *A consideration of career disengagement as social death for professional baseball players.* Paper presented at the North American Society for the Sociology of Sport Conference, Toronto.

Buffalo, M.D., & Rodgers, J.W. (1971). Behavioral norms, moral norms, and attachments: Problems of deviance and conformity. *Social Problems, 19,* 101-113.

Campbell, J. (with B. Moyers) (1988). *The power of myth.* New York: Doubleday.

Cavan, R.S., & Ferdinand, T.N. (1981). *Juvenile delinquency* (4th ed.). New York: Harper & Row.

Dodge, D.L. (1987). The over-negativized conceptualization of deviance: A programmatic exploration. *Deviant Behavior, 6,* 17-37.

Donnelly, P. (1980). *The subculture and public image of climbers.* Unpublished doctoral dissertation, University of Massachusetts.

Donnelly, P. (1981). Four fallacies. *Mountain, 80,* 38-40.

Donnelly, P., & Young, K. (1988). The construction and confirmation of identity in sport subcultures. *Sociology of Sport Journal, 5,* 223-240.

Dornbush, S. (1955). The military academy as an assimilating institution. *Social Forces, 33,* 316-321.

Etzioni-Halevy, E. (1975). Some patterns of semi-deviance on the Israeli social scene. *Social Problems, 22,* 356-367.

Ewald, K., & Jiobu, R.M. (1985). Explaining positive deviance: Becker's model and the case of runners and bodybuilders. *Sociology of Sport Journal, 2,* 144-156.

Gifford, F., & Mangel, C. (1977). *Gifford on courage.* New York: Bantam Books.

Goffman, E. (1967). *Interaction ritual.* Garden City, NY: Doubleday.

Goode, E. (1990). *Deviant behaviors.* Inglewood Cliffs, NJ: Prentice Hall.

Heckert, D.M. (1989). The relativity of positive deviance: The case of the French Impressionists. *Deviant Behavior, 10,* 131-144.

Hilliard, D.C., & Hilliard, J.M. (1990). Positive deviance and participant sport. Paper presented at the annual meetings of The Association for the Study of Play, Las Vegas.

Kempton, M. (1971, Feb. 11). Jock sniffing. *New York Review of Books,* pp. 34-38.

Kramer, J. (Ed.) (1971). *Lombardi: Winning is the only thing.* New York: Pocket Books.

Lerch, S. (1984). Athletic retirement as social death: An overview. In N. Theberge & P. Donnelly (Eds.), *Sport and the sociological imagination* (pp. 259-272). Fort Worth, TX: Texas Christian University Press.

Lyman, S.M., & Scott, M.B. (1970). *A sociology of the absurd.* New York: Appleton-Century-Crofts.

Merton, R. (1957). *Social theory and social structure.* Glencoe, IL: Free Press.

Milgram, S. (1974). *Obedience to authority.* New York: Harper & Row.

Nash, H.L. (1987). Do compulsive runners and anorectic patients share common bonds? *The Physician and Sportsmedicine, 15*(12), 162-167.

Remnick, D. (1987, October 5). Still on the outside. *Sports Illustrated, 67*(15), pp. 44-54.

Rosen, L.W., McKeag, D.B., Hough, D.O., & Curley, V. (1986). Pathogenic weight control behavior in female athletes. *The Physician and Sportsmedicine, 14*(1), 79-84.

Rosenberg, E. (1984). Athletic retirement as social death: Concepts and perspectives. In N. Theberge & P. Donnelly (Eds.), *Sport and the sociological imagination* (pp. 245-258). Fort Worth, TX: Texas Christian University Press.

Sagarin, E. (1985). Positive deviance: An oxymoron. *Deviant Behavior, 6,* 169-185.

Sato, I. (1989). Play theory of delinquency: Toward a general theory of "action." *Symbolic Interaction, 11,* 191-212.

Shedler, J., & Block, J. (1990). Adolescent drug use and psychological health. *American Psychologist, 45,* 612-630.

Skinner, B. F. (1971) *Beyond freedom and dignity.* New York: Knopf.

Snyder, E.E. (1972). Athletic dressing room slogans as folklore: A means of socialization. *International Review of Sport Sociology, 7,* 89-102.

Snyder, E.E., & Spreitzer, E. (1980). *Social aspects of sport.* Englewood Cliffs, NJ: Prentice Hall.

Tinto, V. (1987). *Leaving college.* Chicago: University of Chicago Press.

Todd, T. (1983, August 1). The steroid predicament. *Sports Illustrated, 59*(5), pp. 62-78.

Valliant, G. (1983). *The natural history of alcoholism.* Cambridge, MA: Harvard University Press.

Wasielewski, P.L. (1991). Not quite normal, but not really deviant—Some notes on the comparison of elite athletes and women political activists. *Deviant Behavior, 12,* 81-96.

Westkott, M. (1986). *The feminist legacy of Karen Horney.* New Haven, CT: Yale University Press.

Williams, T., & Donnelly, P. (1985). Subcultural production, reproduction and transformation in climbing. *International Review for the Sociology of Sport,* **20**(1&2), 3-17.

Wolfe, T. (1979). *The right stuff.* New York: Farrar, Straus, Giroux.

Young, K. (1991). Violence in the workplace of professional sport from victimological and cultural studies perspectives. *International Review for the Sociology of Sport,* **26**(l), 3-14.

Zimbardo, P.G., Haney, G., Banks, W.C., & Jaffe, D. (1982). The psychology of imprisonment: Privation, power, and pathology. In J.C. Brigham & L.S. Wrightsman (Eds.), *Contemporary issues in psychology* (pp. 230-245). Monterey, CA: Brooks/ Cole.

Interpretations and Explanations of Deviance Among College Athletes: A Case Study

Eldon E. Snyder

This case study analyzes a group of college athletes who were involved in a series of larcenies. A focal point of the study is that these athletes did not fit the usual profile of deviants who would commit large-scale crimes. Furthermore, the athletes in question were apparently not committing the crimes for material gain. Differential interpretations that are given to explain the athletes' behaviors include defective character traits, the use of alcohol, peer pressure, and the quest for excitement. These interpretations and explanations are discussed within a broader interpretive model of behavior.

Folk knowledge as well as some formal studies support the position that sports serve to keep young people out of trouble. This assumption is incorporated into the broader belief that sport builds character, that through sport participation young people internalize the values and norms of conventionality and thus are taught to be good citizens. There is also the belief that coaches' training rules help reduce deviance among athletes relative to nonathletes. Accordingly, even if the athletes do not fully internalize the conventional social expectations, they will hesitate to violate the training rules for fear of being disciplined by the coach and losing their position on the team.

This topic has interested researchers in sports studies for years. Schafer (1969) conducted one of the earliest studies in the sociology of sport, focusing on the hypothesis that sport participation serves as a deterrence to delinquency. Schafer's findings among high school students demonstrated a negative relationship between sport participation and delinquency, as measured by the court records. Additional studies of high school students by Buhrmann (1977), Buhrmann and Bratton (1978), Landers and Landers (1978), Hastad, Segrave, Pangrazi, and Petersen (1984), and Segrave and Hastad (1984a, 1984b) likewise provide some empirical support for the deterrence thesis.

In another study, Segrave, Moreau, and Hastad (1985) investigated the relationship between participation in minor league Canadian ice hockey and delinquency and found no significant difference between participants and nonparticipants in the incidence of delinquent behavior. However, they did find that the hockey players were more involved in delinquency of a physically violent nature than nonplayers. Research by Thorlindsson (1989) on 12- to 15-year-olds in Iceland found a negative relationship between sport participation and drug related deviance.

The statistical facts and correlations of these studies, however, are not definitive evidence that sport participation serves as a deterrent to delinquency. For example, Hastad et al. (1984), Schafer (1969), Segrave and Hastad (1984a, 1984b), Sugden and Yiannakis (1982), and Yiannakis (1980) suggest that the causal inferences between athletic participation and delinquency should be qualified. More specifically, in the absence of longitudinal research

Reprinted from Snyder, 1994.

studies it is impossible to determine whether the findings are indeed attributable to sport participation; whether they are influenced by a selection process that tends to eliminate delinquents from the sport stream; or whether nonathletes are more likely to be labeled as delinquents. In general these quantitative studies only provide cross-tabulations and correlational analyses of athletic participation and some measure of delinquency. Although a number of theoretical explanations are suggested, the actual link between the athletic experience and deviant behavior is seldom manifest. These studies tell us little about how the deviance actually occurred and what meanings are attributed to the actions.

In his 1969 paper, Schafer considered several possible effects of sport participation on delinquent behavior. For example, if athletes interact primarily with other athletes and coaches, this "differential association" might reduce the likelihood of becoming involved in delinquent behavior (Sutherland, 1937). That is, athletes interacting primarily with like-minded friends theoretically are shielded from antiestablishment and deviant subcultural values, norms, and behaviors.

Schafer (1969, p. 37) also suggested that delinquency might stem from boredom or from an attempt to assert one's masculinity. Thus the delinquent behavior may be a way of getting kicks, thrills, and excitement through adventuresome or daring delinquent acts. These explanations are closely related to the notion that stimulus seeking and sensation seeking behavior may lead to delinquency. Consequently one might argue that athletic environments that can satisfy these desires through the sensations of vertigo, speed, and risk taking could reduce the probability of seeking these stimuli through deviance (Donnelly, 1981).

Other studies suggest there may actually be a positive relationship between athletic participation and deviance. Hughes and Coakley (1991) argue that the excessive commitment to the norms of sport can lead to extreme forms of behavior "in which there is collective encouragement to push the limits and pay the price [which] produces an excessive commitment to action that is destructive, not necessarily desired, and deviant" (1991, p. 320). Similarly, Donnelly and Young (1988) cite examples from sport subcultures wherein risk taking and camaraderie lead to postgame rowdiness, excessive drinking, souvenir-hunting escapades, and vandalism.

These studies provide some insight into the link between deviance and sport. The present study extends this research tradition through the use of qualitative research methods to gather data on and examine several explanations and interpretations of deviant acts committed by a group of college athletes. The primary thrust of this analysis concerns the way in which people construct and interpret explanations for deviance. In short, the interpretive approach does not focus on specific a priori theories and hypothesis testing; rather it is based on the emergent explanations within a naturalistic setting that includes the way family, friends, officials, and the athletes interpreted the deviant behavior.

The Interpretive Perspective

The multiple interpretations of motives and explanations for deviance outlined in this paper have a theoretical legacy in the writings of Weber (1947), Mills (1940), Scott and Lyman (1968), and Sykes and Matza (1957). Weber (1947, pp. 98-99) defined a motive as "a complex of subjective meaning which seems to the actor himself or the observer as an adequate ground for the conduct in question." This perspective was further developed by Mills (1940), who pointed out that motives are social in nature and vary with the situation. Thus, when behavior deviates from the norms within a social situation, motives are cited as reasons that justify the behavior in question. In short, motives are interpretations of behavior that serve to influence oneself and others about the rationale for the deviant behavior. Additionally, the motives people give to explain their behavior are described by Scott and Lyman (1968) as ways people account for behavior that may be discrediting in the eyes of others. In the study of deviance, accounts are similar to the "techniques of neutralization" described by Sykes and Matza (1957, p. 412). That is, delinquents often use accounts to neutralize the culpability of their deviant behavior by the denial of victimization or injury to anyone, denial of responsibility, condemning those who make the accusations, and because of their loyalties to others.

These interpretations are attempts to provide acceptable explanations for the deviant behavior, explanations that will deflect blame away from the person and protect his or her self-esteem—a goal many researchers have suggested is paramount in our social behavior. (See Becker, 1971, on maintenance of self-esteem; Heider, 1944, 1958, on causal attributions; and Goffman, 1967, on face-saving practices.) The interpretive perspective does not provide causal theories and methods of testing a priori theories. Rather, the presumed explanations and motives for deviance emerge within a social context to account for the untoward behavior.

In the present case, attempts to interpret and explain behavior are significant because they represent perceptions of reality used by the athletes, officials, and others to understand the deviance as well as to provide the rationale for the sentencing procedures. Whether the explanations provided by the people associated with this case are consistent with existing sociological theories or not, they are important because they were used in the court proceedings and sentencing of the athletes. To paraphrase Thomas and Thomas (1928, p. 572), we might say, The perceptions of causality were real in the sentencing consequences for the athletes. To illustrate this point, the court records indicate that the determination of the sentences was based on "the nature and circumstances of the offense, the history, character, and condition of the offender, and his need for correctional or rehabilitative treatment" (Clerk of Courts file).

Description of the Deviance

The deviant acts considered in this paper were committed by nine varsity athletes from a major university. Seven were on the men's swim team, one was on the men's track and cross-country team, and one was a former member of the women's swim team and a girlfriend of one of the male athletes. The athletes were described in the press as all-American white kids from middle- and upper middle-class homes in upscale Midwestern suburbs. Significantly, six of the athletes shared an off-campus apartment. In addition to practicing and competing together in their sport, the athletes spent much of their leisure time together and took many of the same business and computer courses. In general they would be described as good students majoring in prebusiness, business administration, accounting, and science.

They committed dozens of burglaries over a two-year period. The stolen property included approximately $50,000 worth of computers, telephones, answering machines, videocassette recorders, calculators, CB radios, lottery tickets, road signs, lawn furniture, and food. These items were stolen from university buildings, automobiles, and local businesses. Some of the stolen goods were stacked to the ceiling in a 5- × 10-foot rented storage locker. Two of the athletes were also convicted of arson when they broke into a rental office and, in an attempt to recover a rental lease, set fire to the file cabinets in the office. Those most involved in the crimes had become sophisticated in the use of burglary tools and a programmable scanner for monitoring the police. The investigating officer described them as "on the road to being career criminals with the burglary techniques that were equivalent to the skills of middle level career criminals" (investigating officer, interview).

Although the group was described in the news media as a "burglary ring," this is not entirely accurate since not all were equally involved in the crimes. One athlete had been convicted of burglary in high school and was apparently involved in all of the burglaries, but none of the others had a criminal record. Several of the athletes participated in many of the break-ins, others in some of the crimes, while still others were involved in few if any of the burglaries, yet were aware of the stolen property. Also, because some stolen items were viewed as common property and used by all the athletes, even those who were not involved in the actual thefts were implicated in the crimes. Additionally, some of the athletes were charged with and convicted of receiving stolen property when they helped dispose of some stolen goods prior to a police raid on their apartment.

In summary, two or three of the athletes were deeply involved in the criminal activities, three or four others were moderately involved, and the remainder were implicated either because they were aware of the stolen goods or helped dispose of the items. The lone woman among them worked at a local motel and gave a key to her boyfriend, who apparently used it to steal a television set from the motel.

There are several ways in which the deviant behavior of these athletes is linked to their athletic role. First, the connection is evident in the description of their crimes in the media. For example, initially five athletes were indicted and a major regional newspaper displayed the following headline: "Five Swimmers to be Arraigned in Burglaries." Other headlines included the following: "Arrest of Swimmers on Burglary Charges Surprises Coaches, Friends," "9th Ex-Athlete Gets Jail Term," "Swimmers Suspended From Team," and "Ex-Swim Captain Gets Prison Sentence." In short, over a period of several months a variety of headlines linked the athletes to their crimes and sentences.

One athlete suggested that if they had not been athletes the media would not have given so much publicity to their crimes. One might argue that their sentences, which in some cases were lenient, also reflect their athletic status. Further, the reaction of parents, friends, and athletic and university officials reflected the belief that because they were athletes the crimes were surprising and shocking; there are references in the records to their behavior as being "out of character," "they had everything going for them," "they were the best swimmers on the team."

Additionally, six of the athletes lived in the same house, which was known on campus as the Swim House, and the other three frequented the house. One news account indicates, "They [the athletes] spent countless hours together at practices and meets. Some took the same business and computer classes and they frequently threw parties at the house." In summary, their interaction as team members carried over into their living arrangements, academic and leisure time activities, and eventually their criminal behavior. The bonding that occurred within the sport related relationships, and perhaps the norms of sport, are important considerations in their deviant behavior (Hughes & Coakley, 1991). The significance of the team interaction in this case is similar to the fraternal bonding activities in sport discussed by other researchers in the context of sexist attitudes and violence (Curry, 1991; Kane & Disch, 1993; Loy, 1992).

Obviously, sport participation for these athletes was not a deterrent to their crimes, and their behavior calls the whole deterrence thesis into question. It is also evident that their deviance was inconsistent with their public image and a shock to the community. In short, this case study provides additional data and conceptual understanding of the link between sport participation and deviance.

Methodology

Several qualitative methods were used in gathering data for this study. Initially, background information was obtained from the newspaper accounts of the events. Later, notes were taken from the archival records on the individual cases filed as part of the public record at the office of the county Clerk of Courts. These case files included the criminal charge for each individual, statements from the prosecuting attorney, the disposition of the case, and often interviews and written statements from the accused, the judge, the legal counsel, prosecuting attorney, investigating officer, parents, and others. In some cases the files included letters and documents with requests for probation rather than a prison sentence, or a shock probation, and the rationale for lenient sentences. Analysis of these case files provided numerous references to motives and purported explanations for the athletes' crimes. A public record of the cases was also available at the campus security office, including data on the charges and a formal interview with each of the individuals detailing the extent of their involvement in the crimes.

These public records provided the primary accounts used to reconstruct the description and interpretations of the crimes. Additionally, interviews were conducted with the investigating officer, the university's director of standards and procedures, and two of the athletes involved in the crimes. In a follow-up interview, one athlete read a draft of this paper and generally concurred with the description of the deviance. (Having informants respond to observations or findings is a means of validating one's data [Shaffir & Stebbins, 1991, p. 161].) I also had informal conversations with the varsity coach whose team members were convicted of the crimes and other security and court officials who were familiar with the cases. The interviews and conversations provided little new information that was not already in the public record, but they did substantiate the accounts from the public documents. Combining these several sources of data achieved a form of triangulation that provides a greater degree of what Denzin (1989, p. 234) describes as "sophisticated rigor."

At least two athletes have graduated; one is attending medical school and the other is taking graduate courses. Definitive information on the other seven athletes is not available. Sketchy information provided by the athletes interviewed, their coach, and other university personnel indicates that all the athletes have completed their sentences and are continuing their education elsewhere or are working.

Explanations and Motives

As noted, one counterintuitive aspect of these crimes is that the perpetrators did not fit the stereotype of burglars. The investigating officer described the athletes as follows:

These kids came from upper middle-class homes. None of them had to use a public defender. They all had money for the attorneys' fees. If any needed a computer they could get one from their parents. But they didn't just steal one computer, they stole 6 or 7 systems. They didn't just need a computer. There is no way they could use all those computers. It is hard to understand. Yet they were all likable, handsome, articulate, and well mannered.

The university's director of standards and procedures described the case as "a real mystery, they were intelligent and every kid had money; relative to a lot of students I see, they were rich." Both officials indicated that the behavior of the student-athletes was "hard to understand" and "a real mystery." A news account noted, "But their futures as well as their team's, so bright a month ago, have taken a surprising turn. And university officials now are facing one of the worst scandals ever to hit an athletic team." In short, because of the perceived incongruence between the athletes' backgrounds and their criminal activities, their behavior was described as "hard to understand," "a real mystery," and "surprising."

One unusual aspect of these crimes is that, although stolen goods are usually kept for personal use or are sold, in this case much of it was stored in a locker, with rent paid on the storage space. All accounts of these criminal activities emphasize that, at the time they were caught, selling the stolen property was not their primary motive. In short, the ironic aspect of this study is that the deviants did not fit the profile of career criminals; yet the amount of property stolen was of the magnitude expected of professional burglars. The investigating officer reported on the case in this way:

> I don't know if I would say it [the stealing] was an addiction, but it was a group thing plus the excitement to see if they could get away with it. There is no way they could use all those computers. With property crimes the items are used or sold, but they didn't sell the things. They gave some away but they stashed most of it.

These athletes had the means to buy the goods they needed. Indeed the thefts went far beyond their needs, and their behavior seemed inconsistent with the conventional expectations of stealing for monetary reasons. This inconsistency is reflected in the accounts of their behavior as being "surprising" and "difficult to understand."

Furthermore, the data do not show that the athletes' attachment to the coach or their internalization of the conventional standards of behavior, values, and rules were sufficient to prevent their engaging in illegal activities. The control model of delinquency proposes that "middle-class youth traditionally have been 'insulated' from involvement in delinquent activities by conventional value commitments—such as hard work, delayed gratification, and so forth" (Cernkovich, 1978, p. 338). Ap-

parently this deterrence did not operate for most of the athletes. However, one athlete who was not directly involved in the burglaries said, "I was asked to go along, but I didn't want to because of the possible consequences." Question: "Were you thinking of the consequences from the coach if you were caught?" Athlete: "No, I was thinking of the consequences of breaking the law; suspension from the team and school were not primary in my thinking." For this athlete the possibility of punishment from breaking the law, rather than punishment from his coach, was sufficient to deter him from some of the illegal activities.

Another athlete refrained from some of the deviant activities because of the strong attachment to and time spent with his girlfriend: "The reason G. wasn't as involved is that his girlfriend took a lot of time, she controlled the relationship" (investigating officer's report). For at least one of these individuals, then, the limited involvement in the deviance might be explained by external attachments that served as social control mechanisms.

In general, the news reports and the accounts from officials and parents indicate that they felt the athletes had everything going for them—athletically, academically, socially—including their educational and occupational opportunities. They seemed to have little to gain, especially since profit was not the primary motive in the larcenies, and much to lose from their criminal activities. How did people make sense of the behavior? How did people interpret and explain the deviance that seemed inconsistent with the usual assumptions about criminal behavior? An analysis of the records and interviews uncovers four primary explanations: flawed character traits, use of alcohol, peer pressure, and thrill seeking.

Flawed Character Traits

The interviews and archival data indicate a number of references to some defect in the individual's personality or character traits as an explanation for the crimes. One attorney argued that his defendant's crimes can be explained by "flaws in his character, flaws which, as a young man, he was unable to recognize or control" (Clerk of Courts file). Interestingly, as this attorney pleaded for leniency for his client, he turned the argument around by suggesting that this "flaw" might be desirable for his rehabilitation. In his brief he wrote, "His youth and immaturity without a doubt contributed to his crimes, but at the same time they are evidence that he is amenable to rehabilitation and is not yet a hardened criminal" (Clerk of Courts file).

A letter in the court files from the mother of another defendant also suggests a character attribute—poor self-image—as a motivating factor in her son's crimes; she wrote, "I asked A. why he felt he had to follow these kids. I asked him if he didn't have a better self-image than that. As we talked it became evident to us that A. did not have a good self-image and hasn't for a long time—something that was a revelation to us."

Other references in the files point to some aspect of character or personality as an explanation for the deviant behavior. A coach testified for one of his athletes that "B. is mature, dedicated, and disciplined; the offenses were very much out of character for B." (Clerk of Courts file). By implication, however, his statement suggests that while the athlete had these desirable qualities, they were not strong enough to overcome other influences on his behavior. References in the files of other athletes likewise suggest an "inadequate character" and "the characteristic of being a follower" as reasons for their involvement in the crimes. In general this explanation of deviance rests on the assumption that behavior is primarily determined by dispositional personality traits rather than social situational factors. Further, it represents a type of explanation that excuses the deviancy because of an inadequate personality (Scott & Lyman, 1968).

Alcohol

Partying and drinking were typical activities at the house where six of the athletes lived. Several testimonies in the public records suggested that alcohol was a factor in the individuals' commission of the crimes because it lowered their inhibitions. One parent's testimony to the court illustrates this point: "A. was always a follower and looked up to older kids for whatever reason. He was also involved in alcohol and has admitted to this problem." This athlete was admitted to treatment for alcohol dependency the week after he was sentenced (Clerk of Courts file). Another example from the records also associates the use of alcohol with the commission of a crime; one athlete described the following incident:

C. said he and D. were walking through a parking lot. Both had been to a party and were very drunk. As they walked through the lot they were trying doors on cars for radar detectors. They found a car with the doors un-

locked and stole a musical instrument and a C.B. radio. (Clerk of Courts file)

The investigating officer pointed out that "to be part of the group they would often go out and drink, then steal." The implication of these statements is that drinking and stealing became mutually supporting activities of the friends, and the peer pressure to commit the crimes was magnified under the influence of alcohol. This interpretation was also suggested by an attorney for one of the defendants: "Profit was not D.'s motive. D.'s feelings and motivations at the time the crimes were committed were a mixture of alcohol, competitiveness, and peer pressure" (Clerk of Courts file). The following excerpts from interviews with the athletes provide additional examples of drinking in conjunction with criminal activities:

We came back from the bars, we picked up the bikes and D. said, "Let's go to the golf club house." We rode over there. D. was determined to get in. . . . He ended up pushing through the glass. We unlocked the window and went in there.

I started hating living in the house. I told D. I did not want to live there next year. At a party one night we were walking uptown to the bar. D. said we can get in the window [to the rental agency]. I looked through a lot of different files. I don't remember why we set the place on fire. . . . I was so drunk I dropped the matches.

We were walking out of X [bar] we were going to Y [bar] and we were walking by this van and I saw these videotapes in the van. The back window had been busted out, there was a piece of cardboard covering the window. . . . One of the guys boosted E. through the window and unlocked the side door. F. drove his car into the lot. We grabbed 3 or 4 boxes [of tapes]. (University Security Office files)

As these excerpts indicate, the use of alcohol and stealing became a group activity, and for some athletes these social activities were interconnected and further connected with peer group influence.

Peer Pressure

Because the crimes were primarily committed as a group activity, the element of peer influence was an important consideration in people's interpretations of the criminal behavior. One attorney's statement about his client demonstrates this point: "He attempted to gain the esteem of his friends by participating in these thefts, if not by out-striving them in committing the crimes" (Clerk of Courts file). This suggests that peer influence was important not only in terms of participating in the crimes but also in the element of prestige from the competition with others in the thefts. One participant who was marginally involved in a theft was implicated because of her relationship with her boyfriend. Obviously peer pressure was a factor in her involvement.

The investigating officer pointed out that one athlete had participated in thefts while in high school. According to one account, the high school thefts he engaged in took on a competitive game format, "He and his buddies would make a game out of going out to see who could get $1,000 in a single night" (interview, investigating officer). In the present case, the officer said, "D. was senior to the other guys; he would check things out and would say, 'we need this,' and get the others to go along. It was as if it was fun, exciting, and we can use it."

The university's director of standards and procedures described the peer pressure as follows:

One or two got started stealing, then others started. They got bolder. They didn't think there was anything they couldn't pull off. First they were getting things for their apartment, then they said, "I can get this"—so they were all getting things and the goods accumulated, things they didn't need. It started small, then it got out of hand, and when they got cold feet the leaders said they had to stay together or they would all go down together. There was a camaraderie and a feeling that "we can do anything."

Data from one of the athletes least involved in the crimes also supports the peer pressure interpretation; he gave the following statement in an interview:

I never went out and stole but I knew the TV and computer were stolen. You live, practice, eat, and go to class with them. People don't understand why I didn't leave [the house]. There is peer pressure. These are your friends, you hang out with them and you can't just leave that easily.

A letter from a mother illustrates her interpretation of both the peer influence and alcohol as factors in promoting the illegal activities:

A. said he felt more accepted because he could drink. . . . Peer acceptance was very important to him. . . . A. has always been extremely loyal to his friends and I know he was not aware of the guilt by association element. (Clerk of Courts file)

In summary, the peer influence emerges from the data as an underlying explanation for the athletes' participation in the crimes. These findings are consistent with the assumption that one learns criminal attitudes and behavior from the people he or she interacts with the most intensely and frequently (Sutherland, 1937). Obviously, sport participation in this case study did not serve as a deterrent to the criminal behavior.

As several of the quotations from parents, investigating officials, and the athletes themselves indicate, sport participation promoted the relationships and social pressure to participate in the criminal activities. In fact some of the athletes attempted to "neutralize" their deviant behavior by emphasizing their loyalty to their friends ("These are your friends, you hang out with them and you can't just leave that easily"). The data also suggest that some of the norms of sport were incorporated in their criminal behavior: they felt they could do anything, they could pull off anything, the stimulation of their camaraderie gave them courage and they were competitive. There remains an additional explanation that is evident in the records—the quest for excitement.

Quest for Excitement

The underlying paradox and perplexing question in this case was expressed by many of the observers who felt that the athletes' behavior "just didn't make sense." They stole too many items, the larcenies went far beyond their need for the goods, and if they were not stealing for profit, why did they do it? For example,

Police authorities recovered much of the stolen property in a storage locker. . . . D. generally did not profit from it. It is a strange circumstance. D. was rather like a magpie, or a packrat, observing shiny baubles, stealing them and stashing them. D.'s motivations may best be described as a combination of alcohol aided by peer pressure and thrill seeking. (Clerk of Courts file)

Here we find the control agents themselves offering accounts in an attempt to explain the athletes' deviant behavior. They offered the interpretations described above—character flaws, aided by alcohol, and peer pressure. Then, almost in despair they would say, "Maybe they were just seeking excitement or thrills." In the trials of several defendants the judge asked if their motivation for the crimes was the "thrill of stealing" or if their behavior was "just a lark" (Clerk of Courts file). One of the athletes interviewed provided a similar interpretation of their actions; he said that for some of his teammates, "There was more of a thrill than a need for the food and property." Another teammate said, "They didn't try to sell the things, a lot of it was still boxed, but they got excited by trying to out-fox the system and the thrill of stealing rather than the value of the items—there is no other rational explanation; the danger itself was thrilling."

The investigating officer suggested in an interview that they felt no one was being hurt by their actions (one form of neutralization)—the insurance would pay for the items, and there was "the excitement of seeing if they could get away with it. There was no way they could use all those computers. D. got to several of the 'in guys' on the team and he basically said, 'it is fun, exciting and we can use the stuff.'"

In short, as several athletes themselves suggested, there was a challenge in seeking out places that could be burglarized, the sophisticated use of tools to break in, and the logistics of carrying away the goods. These activities, including the mutual sharing of the experiences and the stolen property, can be interpreted as appealing, exciting, thrilling, and fun. Additionally, reports filed in the university security office indicate that on several occasions the burglars were almost caught. Escaping detection during these escapades would provide additional excitement. These activities became a source of competition and excitement that supplemented their athletic competition.

Interestingly, athletic competition is often advocated as a way to satisfy the need for sensation seeking and risk taking. Theoretically, the athlete might satisfy these desires through sports rather than through delinquent activities. Obviously this assumption regarding the deterrent effect of sport participation is not consistent with the facts of the present case study.

Discussion

The primary purpose of this paper is to analyze the way people in this interaction network interpreted and explained the criminal activities. The explanations that emerged were attributable to flawed character traits, the use of alcohol, peer pressure, and thrill seeking. A consideration of these explanations is significant for two reasons: (a) these accounts of the deviant behavior were important in the way people understood and dealt with the athletes, including the court proceedings and sentences that reflected these perceptions of causality; and (b) we can use these explanations to consider a more generic sociological explanation of the deviant behavior.

How might a sociological analysis go beyond the lay explanations discussed herein? The results challenge the common assumption that participation in sports is desirable because it "keeps kids out of trouble" and "builds character." While some of the earlier research does not support this hypothesis, the description and interpretations presented in this case study shed further light on this assumption. Certainly the athletes in question spent much of their childhood and adolescent years participating in sports. Yet they became involved in large-scale larcenies. When they were apprehended and their criminal activities exposed, their friends, families, coaches, and the public were shocked. Evidently the shock was based on the assumption that because they were athletes they were not expected to commit such acts. Schneider (1975) argues that irony often provides a framework for, or clues to, sociological analysis. The irony and counterintuitive elements of this case provide an opportunity to look beyond the recognized and manifest explanations to consider the latent and deeper accounts of the deviant behavior.

Certainly the ideas of Durkheim (1915) and the use of rituals to enhance group solidarity are helpful in the analysis of this case study. In fact the deviant acts and use of alcohol may be viewed as social rituals that contributed to group solidarity. Thus while sport participation may promote teamwork, group cohesion, and loyalty, it may have the unintended consequence of promoting an allegiance to a strong leader or an "in group" even when the group activities are deviant. Thus, ironically in this case, the "goodness" of sport—loyalty and group cohesion—promoted deviance (see Hughes & Coakley, 1991). Yet these integrative activities should not be considered as fixed entities that have the same effect on the behavior of all members. Indeed the data indicate there were variations in the degree of involvement in the deviant behavior by the athletes.

Furthermore, at present there is no assurance that sport participation will have a positive socializing effect. During the last decade we have become aware of too many examples of deviance in the sport world to believe wholeheartedly in the "sport builds character" dictum. We might speculate that the ethics of sport now approaches the precept of "the end justifies the means." Thus, contrary to conventional wisdom, the socializing process that takes place in sport may leave the individual open to social influences that lead to deviant behavior.

One tenet of the interpretive approach is that meaning emerges and is constructed in the process of interaction. Consequently, an explanation of the crimes based on flawed character traits depends too much on established personality dispositions of the individual athletes (i.e., psychological reductionism) rather than the interaction process among the athletes. On the other hand, while the notion of peer pressure helps provide a social situational context for explaining behavior, this structural explanation often does not recognize the reflective, evaluative, and decision-making capacities of human beings. If meanings are processual, emergent, and constructed through social interaction, the people one interacts with will be significant, but not deterministic. For example, not all of the athletes participated in the criminal activities to the same degree. Likewise, while the use of alcohol may reduce the athletes' inhibitions, not all athletes or other students who use alcohol become involved in large-scale larcenies or other forms of crime.

The motivation to commit some crimes for the thrill of it is an interesting model of deviance that has not been fully explored in the sociological literature. It is consistent with the interpretive and symbolic interactionist perspective because people create their own definitions of the situation, and behavior that appears to others as irrational is subjectively defined as fun, play, thrilling, and exciting. Further, what is defined as exciting and thrilling is socially constructed. In addition to the literature on sensation seeking cited earlier, several recent studies are consistent with this perspective. Katz (1988) argues that crime is often seductive and attractive, independent of the material gain. Especially in upper middle-class settings, "material needs are often clearly insufficient to account for the fleeting fascination with theft" (p. 52). The Katz thesis is persuasive when applied to the present study; as he points out, many nonviolent property crimes—vandalism, joyriding, shoplifting, burglaries—often by young people, provide "sneaky thrills" to their practitioners (pp. 52-53). This description seems to apply to the present study of deviance.

Another study provides a similar theoretical perspective of deviance. Sato's (1991) ethnographic account of motorcycle and automobile gangs describes young Japanese who "devote themselves to unlawful and often fatal racing" as a "pursuit of excitement and thrill rather than from considerations of gain and profit" (pp. 1-2). Sato, like Katz, explores the metaphor of crime as fun that provides action in the form of risk taking and thrills. In his work, Sato cites Csikszentmihalyi's research (1985) on ludic activities when the participants experience a feeling of "flow," an intrinsic pleasure and enjoyment, when there is an optimal challenge in relation to one's skill level.

Lyng (1991) argues that as our society has become increasingly safe and secure, many individuals seek experiences that are dangerous and risky (see also Elias & Dunning, 1970). Such voluntary activities that involve high-risk behavior—threats to one's physical or mental well-being—are termed "edgework." His high-risk activities include hang gliding, skydiving, scuba diving, and rock climbing. The skill, competence, and challenge that are displayed in the various forms of edgework produce, according to Lyng, feelings of self-actualization, exhilaration, and omnipotence.

In the present study several examples indicate that the thefts were a source of fun and excitement for the athletes. Their activities were described as follows: "They got bolder, they didn't think there was anything they couldn't pull off." They were motivated by "a combination of alcohol, aided by peer pressure, and thrill seeking." "There was the thrill of stealing." "The danger itself was thrilling." Apparently the burglaries escalated into edgework experiences that included a sense of hyperreality, excitement, and a feeling of self-determination in the face of the potential chaos of being caught.

This quest-for-excitement interpretation is consistent with several strands of research on risk taking behavior. A synthesis of these studies suggests that the risk taking behavior is a means of fulfilling some unmet needs by seeking exciting and thrilling activities that test one's abilities to cope with threatening situations. Certainly the daily grind of team practices, classes, examinations, and meeting the deadlines of assigned papers can be boring, constraining, unfulfilling, and alienating. Perhaps in this context the crimes had a creative appeal in that the perpetrators could display the norms of sport through the display of skill, competence, and control when "crowding the edge" of being apprehended.

Yet, I also feel uneasy relying too much on the quest for excitement as an a priori explanation (an independent variable) for the deviance of these athletes. Such a need for excitement was probably also true of other athletes and other students. Indeed, one of the athletes who lived in the house said, "I didn't want to get involved because of the fear of getting caught; the fear was greater than the desire for the goods or the excitement." A deeper analysis of this case suggests a more generic model of behavior that is grounded in the data and incorporates several of the previously discussed lay explanations.

In this regard the interpretive model argues for an understanding of behavior based on the concept of contingency. That is, while behavior does not occur at random, "Nothing *has* to happen. Nothing is fully determined. At every step of every unfolding event, something else *might* happen" (McCall & Becker, 1990, p. 6, italics in original). Furthermore, the concept of contingency includes the following:

> the balance of constraints and opportunities available to the actors, individual and collective, in a situation will lead many, perhaps most, of them to do the same thing. Contingency doesn't mean people behave randomly, but it does recognize that they can behave in surprising and unconventional ways. (McCall & Becker, 1990, p. 6)

Contingency asserts that there is a middle ground between the positions of the structural or cultural determinists and the psychological determinists. Behavior is a fluid process that reflects the back and forth nature of interaction between the actors within a social situation. In this case the meanings associated with deviance were socially constructed through social interaction. The lay explanations and several sociological theories are inadequate to fully explain the unexpected unfolding of the unconventional activities. The interpretive model of behavior appears to fit with the fluidity and processual nature of the deviance in this study.

This paper is not the place to detail the contingencies that promote involvement in deviance. Yet some implications of the contingency concept, framed within the interpretive model, are applicable to the present case study (several are modifications of analyses discussed in Prus & Sharper, 1991, pp. 159-168; see also Prus, 1984).

1. Through association with the other athletes who were in close contact with each other, especially those who lived together, the athletes form an orientation toward deviant behavior. These associations were reinforced and solidified by shared rituals of drinking and ultimately the deviant activities that were incorporated into their leisure. Again, the social bonding that emerged out of the team interaction was important in this process.

2. One or two of the athletes were leaders in recruiting and converting several other athletes to deviance. The leaders had accepted the "appropriateness" of deviant activities from earlier deviant experiences—they were "keynoters" in promoting the deviant acts. One leader was also a team captain and a three-year letter winner in his sport.

3. The orientation to deviance incorporated rationalizations and neutralizations that provided excuses for deviance: "No one is being hurt," "The insurance company will pay," "Because of my loyalty to my teammates, I'll go along with the activities" (see Scott & Lyman, 1968; Sykes & Matza, 1957). Again, the feeling of team loyalty was incorporated in these rationalizations.

4. Although the athletes probably had a general orientation toward conventionality, they entered the new situation wherein they could obtain computers, VCRs, food, and other items in a way that was inconsistent with their general orientation toward conventionality. In these situations the leaders became particularly powerful in nullifying the previous orientation toward conventionality. In short, most of the athletes were not predisposed toward deviance, as noted in the following point.

5. Orientations toward conventionality and deviance are not fixed entities. One's orientation is continually undergoing change as a result of interactions with others. Thus, friends influenced each other to participate in the deviance. For example, a girl became involved with a larceny because of her affiliation with her boyfriend, and another athlete did not become deeply involved because of his girlfriend. Another athlete who was implicated because he helped get rid of some stolen goods said, "I wanted to help my friends out of trouble. I knew the things were stolen, but I didn't think I had much to worry about. I was implicated because of the magnitude of the crimes." In short, the criminal behavior was emergent and processual.

6. People are also reflective and have the capacity to consider their options and to act in a way that is contrary to keynoters in the social situation. Indeed, some athletes did not become as deeply involved in the crimes as others did. In this respect, individual reflections are significant in maintaining personal orientations that may be contrary to the constructed norms.

7. Both personal and group orientations are a process that have emergent and unfolding characteristics. Information from this study indicates that the deviance started on a small scale with one or two individuals, then escalated beyond their original intent. One athlete suggested that in the beginning, "Someone had a computer, TV, or fuzz buster and another one of the guys would say, 'I could use one too.' Then one of the leaders would say, 'O.K. go with us and we'll get one for you.'"

8. Involvement in the deviant activities reflects the socially defined attractions of the activities to the individuals. While financial profit was not the primary attraction for stealing the items, all the athletes profited from using some of the stolen material. Additionally, the deviant activities were defined by some athletes as fun, thrilling, and in this respect enjoyable in contrast to the other dimensions of their lives. Further, the level of sophistication and success in the crimes apparently provided a sense of self-enhancement and a source of recognized prestige among the participants.

Conclusion

The significance of this study lies in its questioning the validity of the deterrence thesis and in its attempt to examine how the athletes "made sense" of deviance through their explanations and accounts. Such explanations and accounts took on particular importance since the crimes were perpetuated by middle-class athletes, individuals who did not fit the profile of deviants. Substituting the term "black high school dropout" for "middle-class athlete" may not have led to the same type of attempts to account for the behavior of the individuals involved. Also, the process by which one group's criminal behavior is another group's thrill seeking behavior is evident in the labeling and definitions attached to this case. It is even possible to argue that stealing for *need* is morally more defensible than stealing for kicks, but the legal authorities in this case were clearly more inclined to be perplexed than punitive.

This case study does not explain why these athletes turned to criminal behavior, but it does show how a particular set of meanings was constructed around that behavior. Not only did the athletes as well as their parents and lawyers engage in techniques of neutralization when accounting for their behavior, but similar accounts were offered by the various law enforcement authorities involved. Because all felt a need to account for the behavior, all of the involved parties shared in the construction of a particular set of meanings around these unexpected actions. They turned to a set of sociological and psychological explanations for deviance that have become common currency, and their acceptance of this set of explanations probably resulted in the relatively lenient sentences.

The lay explanations that are evident in the data—flawed character traits, use of alcohol, peer pressure, and thrill seeking—can be incorporated into the more generic interpretive model of behavior. The interpretive model, including the concept of contingency, fits as a model for understanding the deviant behavior that emerged within the interacting teammates. Furthermore, the interpretive approach provides a subjective and in-depth examination of people's perceptions, meanings, motives, and explanations of the criminal behavior rather than the numerical measures of sport and deviance used in the positivistic studies of the topic. We need additional studies that focus on the subjective interpretations of deviant behavior in the natural settings of sport to enhance our understanding of this topic.

References

Becker, E. (1971). *The birth and death of meaning*. New York: The Free Press.

Buhrmann, H. (1977). Athletics and deviance: An examination of the relationship between athletic participation and deviant behavior of high school girls. *Review of Sport and Leisure, 2,* 17-35.

Buhrmann, H., & Bratton, R. (1978). Athletic participation and deviant behavior of high school girls in Alberta. *Review of Sport and Leisure, 3,* 25-41.

Cernkovich, S. (1978). Evaluating two models of delinquency causation. *Criminology, 16,* 335-352.

Csikszentmihalyi, M. (1985). Emergent motivation and the evolution of the self. *Advances in Motivation and Achievement, 4,* 93-119.

Curry, T. (1991). Fraternal bonding in the locker room: A profeminist analysis of talk about competition and women. *Sociology of Sport Journal, 8,* 119-135.

Denzin, N. (1989). *The research act*. Englewood Cliffs, NJ: Prentice Hall.

Donnelly, P. (1981). Athletes and juvenile delinquents: A comparative analysis based on a review of literature. *Adolescence, 16,* 415-432.

Donnelly, P., & Young, K. (1988). The construction and confirmation of identity in sport subcultures. *Sociology of Sport Journal, 5,* 223-240.

Durkheim, E. (1915). *The elementary forms of the religious life.* New York: The Free Press.

Elias, N., & Dunning, E. (1970). Quest for excitement in unexciting societies. In G. Luschen (Ed.), The cross-cultural analysis of sport and games (pp. 31-51). Champaign, IL: Stipes.

Goffman, E. (1967). *Interaction ritual.* Garden City, NY: Doubleday.

Hastad, D., Segrave, J., Pangrazi, R., & Petersen, G. (1984). Youth sport participation and deviant behavior. *Sociology of Sport Journal, 1,* 366-373.

Heider, F. (1944). Social perception and phenomenal causality. *Psychological Review, 51,* 358-377.

Heider, F. (1958). The psychology of interpersonal relations. New York: Wiley.

Hughes, R., & Coakley, J. (1991). Positive deviance among athletes: The implications of overconformity to the sport ethic. *Sociology of Sport Journal, 8,* 307-325.

Kane, M., & Disch, L. (1993). Sexual violence and the reproduction of male power in the locker room: The "Lisa Olson incident." *Sociology of Sport Journal, 10,* 331-352.

Katz, J. (1988). *Seductions of crime.* New York: Basic Books.

Landers, D., & Landers, D. (1978). Socialization via interscholastic athletics: Its effects on delinquency. *Sociology of Education, 51,* 299-303.

Loy, J. (1992). *The dark side of agon: Man in tribal groups and the phenomenon of gang rape.* Paper presented at the North American Society for the Sociology of Sport Conference, Toledo, OH.

Lyng, S. (1990). Edgework: A social psychological analysis of voluntary risk taking. *American Journal of Sociology, 95,* 851-886.

McCall, M., & Becker, H. (1990). Introduction. In H. Becker & M. McCall (Eds.), *Symbolic interaction and cultural studies* (pp. 1-15). Chicago: University of Chicago Press.

Mills, C.W. (1940). Situated action and the vocabulary of motives. *American Sociological Review, 6,* 904-913.

Prus, R. (1984). Career contingencies: Examining patterns of involvement. In N. Theberge & P. Donnelly (Eds.), *5port and the sociological imagination* (pp. 297-317). Ft. Worth: Texas Christian University Press.

Prus, R., & Sharper, C. (1991). *Road hustler.* New York: Kaufman & Greenberg.

Sato, I. (1991). *Kamikaze biker.* Chicago: University of Chicago Press.

Schafer, W. (1969). Some sources and consequences of interscholastic athletics: The case of participation and delinquency. *International Review of Sport Sociology, 4,* 63-79.

Schneider, L. (1975). The sociological way of looking at the world. New York: McGraw-Hill.

Scott, M., & Lyman, S. (1968). Accounts. *American Sociological Review, 33,* 46-62.

Segrave, J., & Hastad, D. (1984a). Future directions in sport and juvenile delinquency research. *Quest, 36,* 37-47.

Segrave, J., & Hastad, D. (1984b). Interscholastic athletic participation and delinquent behavior: An empirical assessment of relevant variables. *Sociology of Sport Journal, 1,* 117-137.

Segrave, J., Moreau, C., & Hastad, D. (1985). An investigation into the relationship between ice hockey participation and delinquency. *Sociology of Sport Journal, 2,* 281-298.

Shaffir, W., & Stebbins, R. (1991). Introduction. In W. Shaffir & R. Stebbins (Eds.), *Experiencing fieldwork* (pp. 1-24). Newbury Park, CA: Sage.

Sugden, J., & Yiannakis, A. (1982). Sport and juvenile delinquency: A theoretical base. *Journal of Sport and Social Issues, 6,* 22-30.

Sutherland, E. (1937). *The professional thief.* Chicago: University of Chicago Press.

Sykes, G., & Matza, D. (1957). Techniques of neutralization. *American Sociological Review, 22,* 667-669.

Thorlindsson, T. (1989). Sport participation, smoking, and drug and alcohol use among Icelandic youth. *Sociology of Sport Journal, 6,* 136-143.

Thomas, W., & Thomas, D. (1928). *The child in America.* New York: Knopf.

Weber, M. (1947). *Theory of social and economic organization.* (T. Parsons & A.M. Henderson, Trans.) Glencoe, NY: The Free Press.

Yiannakis, A. (1980). Sport and deviancy: A review and appraisal. *Motor Skills, 4,* 59-64.

Acknowledgment

I appreciate the comments made by Stephen Cerkovich and Elmer Spreitzer on earlier drafts of this paper and would also like to thank the editor for his helpful comments and suggestions.

Gender, Sport, and Aggressive Behavior Outside Sport

Howard L. Nixon II

This study focuses on how sports attitudes and participation relate to physical aggression outside sport for college athletes. Data were derived from a survey of nearly 200 male and female athletes at a medium-size (11,500-student) comprehensive university. Physical aggression was measured by an item concerning whether the respondents ever physically harmed or injured other persons outside sport in fights or disagreements. Although exploratory, this study suggests potentially valuable insights about how gender, beliefs in the value of toughness in sport, accidentally or intentionally hurting other athletes in competition, and participation in a team or contact sport relate to physical aggression outside sport. Whereas attitudes, having hurt other athletes, and team and contact sport participation all were related to physical aggression outside sport for male athletes, only participation in a contact sport was related to physical aggression outside sport for female athletes.

Sexual assault on college campuses has received increasing public and scholarly attention in recent years. Among the factors thought to explain such assaultive behavior is membership on an athletic team (Boeringer, 1994; Crosset, Benedict, & McDonald, 1995; Ellin, 1995; Frintner & Rubinson, 1993; Jackson, 1991; Koss & Gaines, 1993; Koss, Gidycz, & Wisniewski, 1987; Malamuth, Sockloskie, Koss, & Tanaka, 1991; Melnick, 1992; Neimark, 1991). Several surveys have found that a disproportionate number of admitted acquaintance rapes on campus were committed by male athletes or fraternity members. Members of football, lacrosse, hockey, and basketball teams have been among those college men most likely to be accused of participating in gang rape. According to one authoritative source (Bohmer & Parrot, 1993), the most important characteristics of college men who engage in acquaintance rape are exaggerated masculine or "macho" attitudes, a pattern of antisocial behavior, and regular or binge alcohol abuse (p. 23). Criminal justice professor Michael Clay Smith of the University of Southern Mississippi argued that athletes are more involved in violent behavior than are their peers because they are physical people who are expected by others to be physically aggressive (cited in Lederman, 1990).

Mary Koss did pioneering work on sexual assault on campus in the 1980s. She and her colleagues explained the disproportionate representation of college athletes in cases of gang rape in terms of male bonding occurring on sports teams (Curry, 1991), which have subcultures of sexism, insensitivity, and aggression (Koss & Gaines, 1993; Koss et al., 1987; see also Messner, 1990). Curry (1991) found in his study of the locker room talk of two male intercollegiate sports teams that the competitive sports environment put male egos and self-esteem at risk. In this setting, peer group pressures and insecurities fostered antisocial talk and behavior as well as the affirmation of traditional masculinity. More specifically, talk often focused on sex and aggression and expressed sexist attitudes toward women, who were viewed in depersonalized and insensitive terms as objects to be used for a man's pleasure. Although it

Reprinted from Nixon, 1997.

is important not to make unfounded causal leaps, one could assume that where the main focus of male locker room talk is sex and aggression, male athletes may become more inclined to engage in sexual aggression against women.

Questions have been raised about whether such prevalence rates of sexual assault among male athletes have been exaggerated and whether higher rates of gang rape among members of male gender-segregated groups such as athletic teams necessarily imply that athletes are more likely to engage in sexual assault as individuals (Crosset et al., 1995). Studies of male college athletes and sexual assault raise broader questions about the relationship between athletic participation and violent or aggressive behavior of various types outside sport. Not long ago, Melnick (1992) proposed that "little is known about whether there is a correlation between on-the-field and off-the-field violence; yet one has to wonder about the interpersonal consequences of sports which teach participants to use their bodies as instruments of force and domination" (p. 33). The current research is an exploratory effort to begin addressing this issue.

A distinctive aspect of the research reported here is the focus on females as well as males. This article reports new evidence indicating how various aspects of college athletic participation are related to male and female physical aggression outside sport. It looks at sports variables given little direct attention in prior research, and it examines female aggressive behavior as well as male aggression. It also focuses on a more broadly defined concept of physical aggression than sexual assault.

Although physically aggressive behavior is generally associated with sport, the traditional exclusion of females from sport has resulted in little attention to the aggressiveness of female athletes. Although we talk about the macho male locker room and the aggressive and antisocial attitudes it might spawn, sport sociologists have had little to say about the possibility of comparable attitudes and subcultures in the female locker room. However, no evidence exists that shows whether female athletic participation is related to physical aggression outside sport. We may tend not to ask the question because we presume that aggression or violence and associated attitudes are unique products of the interaction, bonding, identity building, and beliefs that characterize male socialization and involvement in sport, especially when they are members of segregated all-male groups in sport. Evidence from a recent study of members of an elite women's ice hockey team in Canada (Theberge, 1993) indicates that there are female athletes who value physi-

cality and aggression. Even though the women in Theberge's research did not act in the antisocial or aggressive ways in which male athletes sometimes have been found to act, this research nevertheless gives a reason to look at the connection between sport and aggression for females as well as males.

The elements of aggression, pain, and injury in sport suggest the need for athletes to be "tough" to succeed or endure in athletic competition (Nixon, 1993). Those who are tough are not supposed to be afraid to face aggression or be aggressive toward others. Indeed, in sport and other environments where aggression is valued, being tough often involves being aggressive, which can be proof of one's manhood for male athletes. There is no clear stereotype of what female athletes learn about toughness and aggression when they are socialized into sport. But logically, if male or female athletes frequently engage in behavior that intentionally or unintentionally hurts their opponents, then we might expect a pattern to develop that carries over to roles outside sport. That is, we would expect athletes who learn to express tough attitudes and engage in aggressive or violent behavior as part of their sports role to be more physically aggressive or violent outside sport. These assumptions loosely follow findings in the sexual assault literature indicating that campus sexual assault is associated with macho attitudes and patterns of antisocial behavior.

The possibility that both males and females become generally more aggressive as a result of their sports involvement suggests that sport socialization reinforces stereotypical gender role learning for males and teaches females to act in nonstereotypical ways. Thus, the patterns of physical aggression may be stronger for males than for females, but a general socializing influence of sport is demonstrated if both learn aggression in sport and carry it over into interactions and relationships outside sport.

Among the aspects of sport thought to contribute to male aggressive behavior outside sport are involvement on a team and, especially, participation in a contact sport. Stereotypical male bonding and learning how to hit one's opponent are assumed to reinforce aggression as a normal or valued part of role-playing for males, which may be difficult to restrain in roles outside sport. In this article, I question the implicit notion that the culture and socialization of team and contact sports teach males alone to be more aggressive by considering whether females act more aggressively outside sport when they participate in these types of sports.

The arguments that have been presented suggest a number of hypotheses concerning gender, attitudes about toughness, aspects of sports involvement, and physical aggression outside sport. The purpose of the remainder of this article is to present evidence providing an initial test of hypothesized relationships among these factors. The results should point future research in this area in fruitful directions. For the ensuing hypotheses, the proposed relationship between variables is assumed to exist for both males and females, but these hypotheses also assume that the relationship will be stronger for males. This gender assumption follows stereotypical thinking about male and female aggressiveness. The hypotheses tested by this exploratory research are as follows:

Hypothesis 1: *Athletic participation and aggression outside sport.* Especially among males but also among females, athletes are more likely than non-athletes to engage in physically aggressive acts in everyday life outside sport.

Hypothesis 2: *Gender, attitudes about toughness in sport, and aggression outside sport.* Male athletes are more likely than female athletes (a) to express stronger beliefs in the value of toughness in sport and (b) to engage in physically aggressive acts in everyday life outside sport.

Hypothesis 3: *Attitudes about toughness in sport and aggression outside sport.* Especially among male athletes but also among female athletes, having stronger beliefs in the value of toughness in sport is associated with being more likely to engage in physically aggressive acts in everyday life outside sport.

Hypothesis 4: *Hurting people in sport and aggression outside sport.* Especially among male athletes but also among female athletes, hurting people in sport, either accidentally or intentionally, is associated with engaging in physically aggressive acts in everyday life outside sport.

Hypothesis 5: *Team and contact sport participation and aggression outside sport.* Especially among male athletes but also among female athletes, (a) team sport participants and (b) contact sport participants are more likely than their counterparts in individual sports and noncontact sports, respectively, to engage in physically aggressive acts in everyday life outside sport.

Methods, Measures, and Procedures

This research concentrated on college students and student-athletes. In the spring of 1992, students were surveyed at a medium-sized (11,500-student) southern comprehensive university that competes at the NCAA Division I level. Questionnaires were distributed by instructors to several introductory sociology classes, and students were asked to return their completed questionnaires by mail within two weeks. Questionnaires were distributed by student athletic trainers to the entire population of approximately 425 varsity athletes and cheerleaders, and these questionnaires were returned to a box in the athletic training room. Participation in this study was voluntary for both students and student-athletes. The convenience sample of introductory sociology students yielded 218 responses. A response rate of 45.9% yielded a sample size of 195 student-athletes, who represented the full range of 8 women's and 10 men's varsity sports teams and the coed competitive cheerleading squad.

The total sample size of 413[1] was a broad cross section of the student population. For the student-athlete population, females were overrepresented (37.9% of the sample versus an estimated 25.4% of the student-athlete population). However, females were underrepresented in the total sample (approximately 46% of the total sample versus 52% of the overall student population of this university). It was not possible to calculate the composition of the student-athlete population by race or class standing, but non-whites and freshmen were overrepresented in the overall student sample. The percentage of non-white respondents was nearly 14% (versus approximately 6% of the total student population), and the percentage of freshmen respondents was more than 41% (versus about 24% of the total student population). The overrepresentation of non-whites may be partially explained by the relatively high proportion of student-athlete respondents who were non-white (16.4%). The overrepresentation of freshmen is largely explained by the use of a convenience sample of lower level sociology classes to generate respondents from a cross section of students not involved in varsity athletics.

The main dependent variable of engaging in physically aggressive acts in everyday life outside sport was measured by one item that asked, "Have you ever physically harmed or injured another person *outside sport* in a fight or disagreement of some sort?" This item, admittedly, is a simple and gross measure of a potentially complex variable that could incorporate a variety of types of physical aggression in different contexts of everyday life. It is useful, however, in providing a first general indication of possible connections between sports participation and physical aggression outside sport for both males and females.

The toughness variable, concerning strength of belief in the value of toughness in sport, was measured by an attitudinal scale that was constructed for this research. The scale was derived from 11 items generally reflecting beliefs about toughness in dealing with pain and injury in sport that were highly loaded (from .46 to .66) on a factor analysis.[2] These items are in the appendix. The factor analysis included 31 statements about risk, pain, and injury in sport that were created on the basis of the results of a content analysis of approximately one decade of *Sports Illustrated* magazine articles (Nixon, 1993). Respondents indicated their agreement or disagreement with these statements on a 4-point scale ranging from *strongly agree* to *strongly disagree*. Three categories of belief in toughness—low, medium, and high—were created by reversing and combining the values of responses to the 11 component items. The response values of this scale were combined so that approximately one-third of the responses were in each of the three categories.[3] Other measures used in this data analysis were items indicating gender, whether or not the respondent had participated or was participating in college athletics, whether or not he or she had accidentally or intentionally hurt another athlete in competition, and whether he or she had participated in a team or individual sport or in a contact or noncontact sport.[4]

Results

Hypothesis 1: *Athletic participation and aggression outside sport.* Especially among males but also among females, athletes are more likely than nonathletes to engage in physically aggressive acts in everyday life outside sport.

Results. Among both males and females, there was no difference between college athletes and nonathletes in their likelihood of being aggressors outside sport ($p > .05$ for Pearson χ^2).

Hypothesis 2: *Gender, attitudes about toughness in sport, and aggression outside sport.* Male athletes are more likely than female athletes (a) to express stronger beliefs in the value of toughness in sport and (b) to engage in physically aggressive acts in everyday life outside sport.

Results. Table 28.1 reveals that a higher percentage of male than female athletes held the strongest belief (37.4% versus 21.1%) and a moderately strong belief (39.1% versus 33.8%) in the value of toughness in sport. Table 28.2 indicates that male athletes were more likely than female athletes (32.2% ver-

sus 10.8%) to have engaged in physically aggressive acts in everyday life outside sport. Both results agree with Hypothesis 2.

Hypothesis 3: *Attitudes about toughness in sport and aggression outside sport.* Especially among male athletes but also among female athletes, having stronger beliefs in the value of toughness in sport is associated with being more likely to engage in physically aggressive acts in everyday life outside sport.

Results. A statistically significant relationship between belief in toughness and being an aggressor was found for male athletes. Table 28.3 shows that 51.2% of male athletes with the strongest belief in toughness had been aggressors, 22.2% of male athletes with a moderately strong belief in toughness had been aggressors, and 22.2% of male athletes with the weakest belief in toughness had been aggressors. The distinction, therefore, is between those with the strongest belief in toughness and all others with weaker beliefs.

Hypothesis 4: *Hurting people in sport and aggression outside sport.* Especially among male athletes but also among female athletes, hurting people in sport, either accidentally or intentionally, is associated with engaging in physically aggressive acts in everyday life outside sport.

Table 28.1   Percentages of Female and Male Athletes Who Expressed Differing Beliefs in the Value of Toughness in Sport

Toughness	Female athletes	Male athletes
Low value of toughness	45.1 (32)	23.5 (27)
Medium value of toughness	33.8 (24)	39.1 (45)
High value of toughness	21.1 (15)	37.4 (43)

Note: ns are in parentheses. $\chi^2 = 10.51$, $df = 2$, $p < .01$; Pearson's $R = .23$, $p < .01$; $N = 186$.

Reprinted from Nixon, 1997.

Table 28.2   Percentages of Female and Male Athletes Who Reported Being Aggressors Outside Sport

Aggressor	Female athletes	Male athletes
Yes	10.8 (8)	32.2 (39)
No	89.2 (66)	67.8 (82)

Note: ns are in parentheses. $\chi^2 = 11.52$, $df = 1$, $p < .001$; Pearson's $R = .24$, $p < .001$; $N = 195$.

Reprinted from Nixon, 1997.

Results. The relationships of accidentally hurting someone in sport and trying to hurt someone in sport to aggression outside sport were statistically significant only for male athletes. Table 28.4 shows that male athletes who accidentally hurt other athletes were much more likely than those who did not (42.2% versus 3.2%) to have been aggressors outside sport, and table 28.5 indicates that male athletes who intentionally hurt other athletes were much more likely than those who did not (55.6% versus 25.5%) to have been aggressors outside sport.

Table 28.3   Percentages of Male Athletes With Differing Beliefs in the Value of Toughness in Sport Who Reported Being Aggressors Outside Sport

Aggressor	Low value of toughness	Medium value of toughness	High value of toughness
Yes	22.2 (6)	22.2 (10)	51.2 (22)
No	77.8 (21)	77.8 (35)	48.8 (21)

*Note: n*s are in parentheses. $\chi^2 = 10.19$, $df = 2$, $p < .01$; Pearson's $R = .26$, $p < .01$; $N = 115$.

Reprinted from Nixon, 1997.

Table 28.4   Percentages of Male Athletes Who Did Not and Did Accidentally Hurt Other Athletes in Competition and Who Reported Being Aggressors Outside Sport

Aggressor	Did not accidentally hurt another athlete	Accidentally hurt another athlete
Yes	3.2 (1)	42.2 (38)
No	96.8 (30)	57.8 (52)

*Note: n*s are in parentheses. $\chi^2 = 16.05$, $df = 1$, $p < .001$; Pearson's $R = .36$, $p < .001$; $N = 121$.

Reprinted from Nixon, 1997.

Table 28.5   Percentages of Male Athletes Who Did Not and Did Intentionally Hurt Other Athletes in Competition and Who Reported Being Aggressors Outside Sport

Aggressor	Did not intentionally hurt another athlete	Intentionally hurt another athlete
Yes	25.5 (24)	55.6 (15)
No	74.5 (70)	44.4 (12)

*Note: n*s are in parentheses. $\chi^2 = 8.66$, $df = 1$, $p < .01$; Pearson's $R = .27$, $p < .01$; $N = 121$.

Reprinted from Nixon, 1997.

Hypothesis 5: *Team and contact sport participation and aggression outside sport.* Especially among male athletes but also among female athletes, (a) team sport participants and (b) contact sport participants are more likely than their counterparts in individual sports and noncontact sports, respectively, to engage in physically aggressive acts in everyday life outside sport.

Results. A statistically significant relationship between team sport participation and aggression outside sport was found only for male athletes. Table 28.6 shows that male participants in team sports were substantially more likely than their counterparts in individual sports (43.4% versus 9.4%) to have engaged in physically aggressive acts in everyday life outside sport. Tables 28.7 and 28.8 reveal that a relationship between contact sport participation and aggression outside sport was found for both male and female athletes. Table 28.7 indicates that male contact sport athletes were much more likely than male participants in noncontact sports (49.0% versus 22.7%) to have engaged in physical aggression outside sport. A similar pattern was found among female athletes, as seen in table 28.8, with female contact sport participants significantly more likely than females in noncontact sports (22.7% versus 6.0%) to have engaged in physically aggressive acts in everyday life outside sport.

Table 28.6   Percentages of Male Individual and Team Sport Participants Who Reported Being Aggressors Outside Sport

Aggressor	Individual sport participation	Team sport participation
Yes	9.4 (3)	43.4 (36)
No	90.6 (29)	56.8 (47)

*Note: n*s are in parentheses. $\chi^2 = 11.91$, $df = 1$, $p < .001$; Pearson's $R = .32$, $p < .001$; $N = 115$.

Reprinted from Nixon, 1997.

Table 28.7   Percentages of Male Noncontact and Contact Sport Participants Who Reported Being Aggressors Outside Sport

Aggressor	Noncontact sport participation	Contact sport participation
Yes	22.7 (15)	49 (24)
No	77.3 (51)	51 (25)

*Note: n*s are in parentheses. $\chi^2 = 8.65$, $df = 1$, $p < .01$; Pearson's $R = .27$, $p < .01$; $N = 115$.

Reprinted from Nixon, 1997.

Table 28.8   Percentages of Female Noncontact and Contact Sport Participants Who Reported Being Aggressors Outside Sport

Aggressor	Noncontact sport participation	Contact sport participation
Yes	6 (3)	22.7 (5)
No	94 (47)	77.3 (17)

*Note: n*s are in parentheses. $\chi^2 = 4.33$, $df = 1$, $p < .05$; Pearson's $R = .25$, $p < .05$; $N = 72$.

Reprinted from Nixon, 1997.

Conclusion

Because the results are based on self-reporting by students at a single campus, and because the measure of the main dependent variable is a single item, caution must be exercised in generalizing. Yet, in breaking new ground in research on athletic participation and physical assault, these results bear serious consideration. In addressing a number of important hypotheses about sport and male and female physical aggression outside sport, this study points the way for future research with potentially important implications for college administrators and policymakers concerned about the occurrence of physical assault of various types on their campuses.

Several relationships among gender, sport, and physical aggression outside sport are suggested by this research. It appears that a belief in the value of toughness in sport is related to physically aggressive acts in everyday life for male athletes but not for female athletes. Similarly, accidentally or intentionally hurting other athletes in sport and participating in a team sport are related to physical aggression outside sport for male but not for female athletes. These results are consistent with the findings that male athletes were more likely than female athletes to have engaged in physical aggression outside sport and to hold highly or moderately strong beliefs in the value of toughness in sport. These finding also are consistent with stereotypical ideas in society about gender differences.

The chain of reasoning suggested by this research is that athletic participation by itself does not make people more likely to be physically aggressive in everyday life. The likelihood of such aggressive behavior seems to be increased for males by certain aspects or types of sports participation. A prominent factor increasing the likelihood of aggression outside sport for females as well as males is par-

ticipation in a contact sport, but a higher proportion of male athletes than female athletes tend to be affected by this factor. It may be that more aggressive females are attracted to contact sports or that recurrent contact in a sport leads to an internalization of aggressive patterns of behavior for females, which carries over to roles and relationships outside sport for a number of them. In view of the general pattern of findings in this study, we can reasonably speculate that contact sports have to reinforce or induce aggressive nonsports behaviors among females that attitudes about toughness, accidentally and intentionally hurting opponents in sports competition, and team sport participation do not possess. Among male athletes, all of these sports-related factors are related to a heightened tendency to engage in aggressive acts in everyday life outside sport.

It is important to move beyond speculation, correlations, and an undifferentiated conception of physical aggression outside sport to evidence from a variety of sports settings at different levels of sport showing the causal linkages between aspects of sports participation and different types and patterns of aggressive behavior outside sport. Although exploratory, this research clearly conveys the need to examine more extensively the factors that make female athletes more likely to engage in physical aggression outside sport. Even though a number of aspects of sports participation may increase or reinforce the tendency among males but not among females to engage in physical aggression outside sport, there are other aspects of sport, such as contact, that seem related to physical aggression outside sport for female athletes as well.

The competitiveness of women's intercollegiate athletics arguably has intensified over the past 15 years of governance by the NCAA. If female athletes seek to emulate male physical aggression and male macho values in team and contact sports as their sports become more competitive under male governance, we could see a closer approximation of male and female results concerning the relationship between aggression and related values in sport and physical aggression outside sport. This research has produced evidence that contact sport participation may induce, or at least reinforce, aggressive behaviors outside sport among females as well as males in intercollegiate athletics. By contrast, Theberge's (1993, 1995) recent study of an elite women's ice hockey team suggests that emphases on physicality and aggressiveness in highly competitive contact sports do not necessarily translate into the types of antisocial or aggressive behaviors in or out of sport that have been associated with male team and contact sports. Therefore, future research must address these apparent contradictions. More generally, what we must understand better are how particular types of norms, roles, identities, attitudes, relationships, and social influence processes associated with physicality and aggression in sport are linked to various types and contexts of aggressive acts in everyday life for both males and females. These understandings will enable us to address more effectively, through interventions ranging from education of coaches and athletes to a restructuring of sport, the risk factors in sport that make athletes more likely to engage in violence outside the sports arena.

Notes

1. The number of cases rarely added to 413 in the statistical analyses due to system and user missing values.
2. The items in the toughness scale (with letters from the appendix) and their factor loadings are as follows: g (must play), .66; y (show character and courage), .62; j (tough it out), .62; p (impress coach by playing hurt), .59; bb (must win), .54; l (expect injury), .51; k (coach wants healthy), .50; i (care about team), .50; b (no pain, no gain), .48; n (ignore pain), .48; and c (playing hurt deserves respect), .46. Items with negative loadings were recoded to facilitate interpretation of the results.
3. The frequency distribution ($N = 396$) for this scale is approximately 33% in the low category, 36% in the medium category, and 31% in the high category.
4. Contact sports are men's and women's basketball, women's field hockey, football, men's soccer, and wrestling. Noncontact sports are baseball, men's and women's cross country running, men's and women's indoor and outdoor track and field, men's and women's golf, men's and women's tennis, women's volleyball, and cheerleading. The team sports among these are baseball, basketball, cheerleading, field hockey, football, soccer, and volleyball.

References

Boeringer, S.B. (1994). Influences of fraternity membership, athletics, and male living arrangements on sexual aggression. Unpublished manuscript, Appalachian State University.

Bohmer, C., & Parrot, A. (1993). *Sexual assault on campus: The problem and the solution.* New York: Lexington.

Crosset, T.W., Benedict, J.R., & McDonald, M.A. (1995). Male student-athletes reported for sexual assault: A survey of campus police departments and judicial affairs offices. *Journal of Sport & Social Issues, 19,* 126-140.

Curry, T.J. (1991). Fraternal bonding in the locker room: A profeminist analysis of talk about competition and women. *Sociology of Sport Journal, 8,* 119-135.

Ellin, A. (1995, October-November). Out of bounds: Is student-athlete crime out of control? *Link: The College Magazine,* pp. 18-24.

Frintner, M.P., & Rubinson, L. (1993). Acquaintance rape: The influence of alcohol, fraternity membership, and sports team membership. *Journal of Sex Education and Therapy, 19,* 272-284.

Jackson, T.L. (1991). A university athletic department's rape and assault experiences. *Journal of College Student Development, 32,* 77-78.

Koss, M.P, & Gaines, J.A. (1993). The prediction of sexual aggression by alcohol use, athletic participation, and fraternity affiliation. *Journal of Interpersonal Violence, 8,* 94-108.

Koss, M.P., Gidycz, C.A., & Wisniewski, N. (1987). The scope of rape: Incidence and prevalence of sexual aggression and victimization in a national sample of higher education students. *Journal of Consulting and Clinical Psychology, 55,* 162-170.

Lederman, D. (1990, November 7). In glare of public spotlight, college officials struggle to deal with perceived lawlessness of their athletes. *Chronicle of Higher Education,* pp. A35-A36.

Malamuth, N.M., Sockloskie, R.J., Koss, M.P., & Tanaka, J.S. (1991). Characteristics of aggressors against women: Testing a model using a national sample of college students. *Journal of Consulting and Clinical Psychology, 59,* 670-681.

Melnick, M. (1992). Male athletes and sexual assault. *Journal of Physical Education, Recreation and Dance, 63*(5), 32-35.

Messner, M.A. (1990). When bodies are weapons: Masculinity and violence in sport. *International Review for the Sociology of Sport, 25,* 203-220.

Neimark, J. (1991, May). Out of bounds: The truth about athletes and rape. *Mademoiselle,* pp. 196-199, 244-246.

Nixon, H.L. II. (1993). Accepting the risks of pain and injury in sport: Mediated cultural influences on playing hurt. *Sociology of Sport Journal, 10,* 183-196.

Theberge, N. (1993, November). *Injury, pain and "playing rough" in women's hockey.* Paper presented at annual meeting of the North American Society for the Sociology of Sport, Ottawa, ON.

Theberge, N. (1995). Gender, sport, and the construction of community: A case study from women's ice hockey. *Sociology of Sport Journal, 12,* 389-402.

Appendix: Risk, Pain, and Injury Items

In the press and on television and radio, we read and hear a lot of different types of things about sports injuries and pain. Listed below are a number of statements about pain and injury. Please indicate how much you agree or disagree with each of these statements by circling one of the numbers following each one. Use the following key to interpret the numbers you can use for your answers:

$$1 = \text{strongly agree}$$

$$2 = \text{agree with reservations}$$

$$3 = \text{disagree with reservations}$$

$$4 = \text{strongly disagree}$$

b.	No pain, no gain	1 2 3 4
c.	Athletes who endure pain and play hurt deserve our respect	1 2 3 4
g.	Serious athletes have to play with injuries and pain	1 2 3 4
i.	Athletes who care about their team will try to play with injuries and pain	1 2 3 4
j.	Athletes should "tough it out" with an injury or pain today and not worry about the effects tomorrow	1 2 3 4
k.	Coaches only care about their players who are healthy and able to play	1 2 3 4
l.	Every athlete should expect to have to play with an injury or pain sometime	1 2 3 4
n.	Athletes should ignore pain	1 2 3 4
p.	Coaches are impressed with athletes who play with injuries and pain	1 2 3 4
y.	Playing with injuries and pain demonstrates character and courage	1 2 3 4
bb.	In sport, winning is everything and losing is nothing	1 2 3 4

Sport Subcultures: Alternate Sport Communities and Personal Identity

Objectives

The unit examines the role and structure of alternate sport communities, especially in creating and maintaining personal identity, in satisfying psychological needs, and in providing contexts for resistance to dominant sport ideologies.

Subcultures have been the subject of formal study for many years. Much is known about military, occupational, primitive, deviant, ethnic, high school, and adolescent subcultures. In recent years, an emerging group of social scientists with a special interest in sport has focused its attention on sport-specific subcultures. These scientists have generated a considerable body of knowledge about several sports, including boxing, skiing, karate, sky diving, and rugby.

Participation in sport subcultures can be a deeply meaningful experience for many. Orrin Klapp (1969) proposed that the need to join subcultures may stem from feelings of alienation, isolation, and the need for stability and order in a fast-changing world. Sociologist Louis Zurcher (1968) suggested that participating in sport subcultures enables individuals to enact "ephemeral roles" (roles of a tempo-

rary or short-lived nature) that often satisfy important psychological needs, needs that dominant role obligations (e.g., work roles) either thwart or fail to satisfy completely. For some, these ephemeral recreational roles become so significant that they eventually become essential aspects of the person's identity. Donnelly and Young describe the fascinating process of identity construction in the first selection of the unit.

Because most sport subcultures possess well-defined and sometimes even rigid social structures (e.g., the martial arts), the construction of identity and its role enactment demand a greater degree of psychic and physical commitment than found in most casual sporting activities. For example, sport subcultures such as rugby, karate, or hang gliding often require more than a casual encounter with the reference group. Role enactment in such contexts may be just as demanding as an individual's dominant role obligations (e.g., occupation).

To appreciate fully the dynamics of identity construction and its enactment in sport contexts, a brief description of the major characteristics of sport subcultures is useful. A sport subculture may be viewed as a subsystem of the larger society that is characterized by a distinguishing pattern of values, norms, shared symbols, beliefs, and material propeties (e.g., equipment and technology). Such groups also develop practices that serve to socialize new members; these practices help members deal with discord and dissent and help manage change in the group. Subcultures also develop ritual forms that help ensure the continuity of the system by reaffirming and celebrating its legitimacy for existing members and newcomers.

These and other elements provide a subculture with structural integrity and uniqueness. Thus we may speak of the subculture of boxers, skiers, joggers, hang gliders, and the like. What differentiates one sport subculture from another, however, is that each subculture develops its own value systems, meanings, and beliefs. Subcultures often attract participants from distinct socioeconomic backgrounds and use equipment, language, and symbols unique to their subculture. Sport subcultures may be analyzed as microsystems (e.g., a rugby team) or as macrosystems (e.g., rugby in the United States).

In studying subcultures we should heed the words of Donnelly and Young (1988), who caution that subcultures should not be investigated in isolation from their "structural, historical, and geographical" moorings. Without such contextualization, they say, "subcultural research will remain [only] an interesting appendage to more mainstream consideration of changing patterns of social development" (p. 238). Put another way, when we study subcultures we should also consider how the subculture fits in and interacts with the larger society, the historical forces that drive it (and society) at different periods in time, and, of course, the physical environment (geographically) in which it is located. Geographic location has implications for a subculture in terms of its accessibility, the availability of appropriate terrain, climatic influence, and population density.

In the first selection, Donnelly and Young provide the reader with an engaging account of the processes involved in the construction and confirmation of identity in two sport subcultures, rugby and rock climbing. Employing an interactionist perspective, the authors suggest that unlike previous thinking on the subject, identity formation is a more deliberate act involving a dialectic between the actor and the demands, opportunities, and expectations posed by the subculture. The authors identify several important concepts that are central to the socialization of the neophyte. These include

1. dealing with misconceptions about the subculture,
2. impression management,
3. composure under pressure,
4. paying homage to the subculture's focal concerns, and
5. dealing with the contradictions inherent in front stage versus back stage impression management.

Finally, the process of becoming a full-fledged member requires that the group recognize and affirm a neophyte's membership and status. Donnelly and Young call this identity confirmation. The authors point out, however, that "reputations are such that they must constantly be remade," suggesting that identity confirmation and reconfirmation are ongoing processes that members must constantly negotiate.

In the second selection, Klein takes us behind the scenes for a rare in-depth look at the world of competitive bodybuilding. On the basis of a four-year participant-observer study conducted in southern California, Klein describes how bodybuilders, in their effort to construct a viable identity, must resolve conflicts about the public's image of the sport, steroid abuse, homosexual hustling, and other contradictions. The author provides a detailed analysis of the dynamics of the weight room, discusses the feudal-like structure of its organization, and addresses the motives for joining such a subculture. Klein concludes that recruitment to the subculture "stems from real, felt, unmet needs and personality deficiencies. In short, poor self-image lurks in the background of most bodybuilders."

In the final selection, Wheaton and Tomlinson provide an in-depth look at the emerging sport of windsurfing. They discuss how the activity enables women to develop new and multiple identities. The authors explore a variety of themes and conflicts that beset women in this sport. Wheaton and Tomlinson suggest that the activity is a social terrain that provides women with opportunities to discover, test, and negotiate various identities, thus serving as a context for their potential empowerment. In particular, the authors note that women windsurfers are able to develop physical skills and abilities and "gain strength and masculary," features traditionally associated with men's empowerment. Further, the authors contrast the traditional female gender role with the role of the "windsurfing widows," while addressing issues surrounding commitment, physicality, multiple gender identities, competing femininities, and challenges to male hegemony.

What is most sociologically significant about this subculture is that the sport of windsurfing enables women to develop a sense of self, separate from other people or other people's standards of embodiment. It enables them to develop self-confidence and a sense of "subcultural solidarity," both of which are essential components of personal empowerment.

Finally, the authors point out that their findings illustrate how "both resistance and complicity to traditional notions of femininity" can coexist in the same cultural space, and how cultural change can be "contingent, gradual, partial, and a matter of negotiation." Although they see this as progressive, they also recognize the persisting power of patriarchy and its ability to thwart "uncompromising resistance" against the existing order of "gendered power."

References

Donnelly, P., & Young, K. (1988). The construction and confirmation of identity in sport subcultures. *Sociology of Sport Journal, 5*, 223-240.

Klapp, O. (1969). *Collective search for identity.* New York: Holt, Rinehart and Winston.

Klein, A. (1986). Pumping irony: Crisis and contradiction in body building. *Sociology of Sport Journal, 3*, 112-133.

Wheaton, B., & Tomlinson, A. (1998). The changing gender order in sport: The case of windsurfing subcultures. *Journal of Sport & Social Issues, 22*, 252-274.

Zurcher, L. (1968). Social-psychological functions of ephemeral roles. *Human Organization, 27*, 281-292.

Discussion Questions

Peter Donnelly and Kevin Young

1. Describe the processes involved in the construction of identity in the subcultures of rugby and rock climbing. Identify and discuss some of their similarities and differences.
2. What is meant by the term "identity confirmation"? Discuss the concept in relation to the subcultures of rugby and rock climbing.
3. Select a subculture and explain how the processes of identity construction and confirmation compare or differ from the processes found in rock climbing or rugby.
4. The authors indentify several essential concepts indigenous to the subcultures of rugby and rock climbing. These include dealing with misconceptions, impression management,

composure, paying homage, and dealing with contradictions. Discuss and explain each and provide examples to support your answer.
5. How does the rugby subculture demonstrate the values of generosity and fair play, and how do those values differ from the values found in mainstream North American team sports? Discuss and explain.

Alan Klein

1. Describe and explain how Klein conducted his study.
2. Describe and explain some of the contradictions that, according to the author, bodybuilders must resolve in constructing a viable identity. How do subculture members reconcile these contradictions?
3. The author describes the organization of bodybuilding as "feudal" in nature. What does he mean and in what ways does such a structure affect the behavior of bodybuilders? Discuss and explain.
4. Klein argues that because the sport needs acceptance, most, if not all, of its publicly expressed values are "ultimately betrayed." What does he mean? Discuss and explain.
5. The author argues that recruitment to the subculture "stems from . . . unmet psychological needs and personality deficiencies." Speculate and discuss what these needs may be and suggest how the subculture helps thwart or satisfy them.

Belinda Wheaton and Alan Tomlinson

1. According to the authors, involvement by women in the subculture of windsurfing is "heterogeneous and contradictory." What do they mean?
2. Describe the methodology used in this study.
3. What is meant by the term "windsurfing widow"? What are the characteristics of windsurfing widows?
4. How do female windsurfers gain acceptance and respect in a male-dominated activity? Does this differ from the process females use in other sports? Discuss and explain.
5. In what ways is windsurfing a source of empowerment and self-confidence for female windsurfers? Discuss and explain.
6. What is the "culture of commitment"? Discuss and explain.

7. In what ways do women surfers differ from surfer widows? Discuss such areas as identity, commitment, and attitude.

8. "The female athlete—and her body—have become a contested ideological terrain." Discuss and explain the meaning and implications of this statement.

9. In your opinion, does female participation in windsurfing represent a challenge to male hegemony in sport? Discuss.

The Construction and Confirmation of Identity in Sport Subcultures

Peter Donnelly
Kevin Young

It is usual in interactionist research to view the process of socialization into subcultures as, in part, a process of identity formation. However, we prefer to examine this process, at least in the case of sport subcultures, as a far more deliberate act of identity construction. That is, through a variety of means, the most significant of which is modeling, the neophyte member begins to deliberately adopt mannerisms, attitudes, and styles of dress, speech, and behavior that he or she perceives to be characteristic of established members of the subculture. Such perceptions among neophytes are usually far from being completely accurate and are frequently stereotypical. Thus, it is necessary to examine also the complementary process of identity confirmation in order to conduct a more complete examination of socialization into a subcultural career. These processes, and neophyte mistakes emerging in them, are examined with respect to ethnographies of climbers and rugby players conducted by the authors, together with supporting material from studies of other sports-related aspects of ethnographic research.

Since the earliest well-known ethnographies of sport/leisure subcultures (Polsky, 1967; Scott, 1968),

three principal themes have been apparent. The first and most prominent of these involves the description of characteristics of the subculture and behavior of the members—the presentation of "insider" information that is only accessible to the participant observer. While this theme is apparent in all subcultural ethnographies, the second and third themes—descriptions of typical subcultural careers and career contingencies, and descriptions of appropriate subcultural identity or demeanor—are presented less frequently, and even more rarely found in combination. For example, Faulkner (1975) and Pearson (1979) primarily emphasize the subcultural careers of hockey players and surfers, while Birrell and Turowetz (1979) and Klein (1986) are more concerned with the identities of gymnasts, wrestlers, and bodybuilders.

However, there are a few studies that implicitly or explicitly combine the concepts of career and identity with the implication that the act of becoming a member of a particular subculture is also the act of taking on an appropriate subcultural identity. For example, Rosenberg and Turowetz note that, "Ordinarily there is a sequence in role performance and its concomitant internalization of the role, its experience as part of one's identity. This sequence involves qualifying for the role performance, training, certification, and performance"

An earlier version of this paper was presented at a conference on "Qualitative Research: An Ethnographic/Interactionist Perspective," held at the University of Waterloo, Ontario, May 1985.

(1975, p. 567). This study also employs the concept of career to examine the processes of identity *construction* and *confirmation* in two specific sport subcultures.

More specifically, we propose that previous references to identity formation provide a far too passive characterization of this process, and even the notion of identity "work up" (Rosenberg & Turowetz, 1975) does not fully capture what is often a far more deliberate act of identity construction. That is, through a variety of means, the most significant of which is modeling, new members of subcultures begin to deliberately adopt mannerisms and attitudes, and styles of dress, speech, and behavior that they perceive to be characteristic of established members of the "achieved" subculture (Donnelly, 1981a).[1]

Such perceptions among neophytes are usually far from being completely accurate and are frequently stereotypical. Thus, it is necessary to examine also the complementary process of identity confirmation in order to conduct a more complete examination of socialization into a subcultural career. As if to symbolize the neophyte's position on the borderline between the larger culture and a specific subculture, identity construction is intended for two distinct audiences—members of the larger society and members of the subculture.

Because of stereotypes held by the neophyte, the initial attempts at identity construction are often inaccurate but are frequently confirmed by outsiders because they do conform to the stereotype. That is, the neophyte has achieved the first stage of distancing from nonmembers through their acceptance of his or her membership in the subculture. The second stage, having the identity confirmed by actual members of the subculture, is more difficult and, in the final analysis, involves ceasing to consider outsiders as a valued audience.

In addition, we propose a career model that is derived from several earlier models (e.g., Miller & Form, 1980; Prus, 1984; Rosenberg & Turowetz, 1975; Super, 1957) but that is more parsimonious and more appropriate to the particular subcultural careers under examination. A four-stage contingency model is suggested, with each stage playing a significant part in the development of actors' subcultural identities and in ensuring their (career) membership within the group: presocialization, selection and recruitment, socialization, and acceptance/ostracism.

Career Stages

Presocialization

Presocialization refers to all of the information an individual acquires about a specific subculture prior to initial participation in the subculture. Uninitiated knowledge and understanding of specific subcultures may be gained through a number of sources, including family and peer group awareness, direct or indirect contact with established members of the subculture and, most significantly, the media (Young, 1983). Media coverage may range from straight reportage and documentary accounts of the activities of a particular subculture to fictional and artistic accounts, and even joking references to the particular proclivities of a subcultural group (e.g., cartoons showing groups of roped mountaineers all falling together, or references to and samples of rugby songs). This knowledge may be absorbed to facilitate a process of anticipatory socialization whereby characteristics and roles of the subculture may be enacted before the actor's current audience. Presocialization represents the first phase of identity construction and, as noted previously, such tenuous knowledge of a specific subculture frequently results in a caricatured and stereotypical image of the group, and certain misconceptions regarding members' behaviors may be developed. Presocial-ization is an ephemeral stage that ends when an actor makes direct contact with the subculture and is recruited and/or received as a member.

Selection and Recruitment

Before more accurate identity construction can occur, an individual must actually become a member of a specific subculture. Donnelly (1980) has characterized the prerequisites for membership as opportunity, motivation, and interest. Thus, whether an individual selects and seeks out membership or is actually recruited by an established member, it is necessary to consider issues such as proximity, life circumstances, and even chance in the initiation of subcultural membership. Unlike presocialization, selection and recruitment is a flexible stage that may be renewed if the actor is geographically mobile and desires to maintain membership in a specific subculture.

Socialization

Socialization is an initially active but ongoing stage wherein members undergo training in the characteristics of the subculture. They soon discover whether early conceptions of the subculture developed during the presocialization stage are accurate or misplaced. Members learn to adopt the values and perspectives of the group, taking on new roles and modifying others, and thus establishing valuable new identifications with the politics and symbols of the group as a whole. In turn, these mechanisms function to cement in the actor a new concept of self, one that will continue to develop and guide the actor in his or her new subcultural career.

Acceptance/Ostracism

Acceptance in subcultures is directly related to demonstrations of appropriate job and/or skill requirements, appropriate roles and identities under specific circumstances, successful socialization procedures, and general value homophyly between the actor and the larger group. Acceptance may also necessitate the actor's flexibility toward activities he or she usually considers negatively but which are condoned in the larger context of the subculture. Whereas the first three stages in the model are concerned with identity construction, the crucial element of this final stage is the confirmation of that identity by established members of the subculture. As Stone suggested,

> When one has identity, he is *situated*—that is, cast in the shape of a social object by the acknowledgment of his participation or membership in social relations. One's identity is established when others *place* him as a social object by assigning to him the same words of identity that he appropriates for himself or *announces*. (Stone, 1970, p. 399)

However, when identities are not confirmed and role conflicts do arise, members of subcultures who are unable to meet role requirements (we say unable because it is unlikely that those unwilling to satisfy expectations would have been attracted to a subculture initially) may face ostracism and/or banishment from the group. While some subcultures will be less rigorous in their internal policing procedures and allow such role conflicts to persist, others will require unconditionally that they be resolved.[2]

This combination of identity construction and confirmation with the concept of subcultural career is examined with respect to previously conducted ethnographies of rock climbers and rugby players (Donnelly, 1980; Young, 1983), together with supporting material from studies of other sport subcultures.

The Construction of Identity

After the preconceptions, and frequent misconceptions, of presocialization, accurate identity construction begins during the socialization stage. Following selection/recruitment, early interactive exchanges and events such as initiation ceremonies represent the apprenticeships that novices in sport subcultures must serve before they may fully begin their subcultural career. This is a time when the construction of a subcultural identity already inaugurated during the presocialization stage comes to the fore for established members to view and perhaps confirm. However, we have also suggested that initial attempts at identity construction are often inaccurate, and thus it is common in subcultures for certain misidentifications, misrepresentations, and inappropriate comments to be made during early apprenticeship.

Of course, the number of gaffes made by rookies will depend on the accuracy of information received during presocialization. If an individual's preconceptions are accurate they will likely facilitate a good base from which a career in a subculture may commence. One rugby player, for example, gaining prior knowledge from an established player, was attracted to the sport's reputation for a boisterous social life, and found few surprises once he was on the inside:

> I had heard from a friend some of the things that had happened after games but had never really bothered to find out for myself. Then this guy told me a story about the players at his club playing a trick on a stripper that made her run off-stage. Apparently one guy made out that he was really interested in her while his friend knelt down behind her and bit her ass so bad that it bled. Now I've started hanging around with those guys I've never seen so much butt-biting in all my life![3]

On the other hand, one ex-football player, entirely misconstruing the essentially nonprofessional approach of rugby and fully expecting rugby behavior to be far less rowdy than tales predicted, found certain aspects of the sport rather alarming, and his preliminary attempts at identity construction grossly inaccurate:

> It was my first night and people had warned me that Rookie Night was a bit of an ordeal, but I'd just shrugged it off. Well we [the rookies] were forced to chug three full beers right at the start. After that things slowed down for a while and I thought it wasn't going to be so bad. Then they [veterans] lined us up and brought out the goldfish. Live goldfish! We had to bite each fish in half with our teeth, chew them, and pass them mouth to mouth amongst each other. I couldn't believe it. And it got worse!
>
> I didn't expect anything like it. We'd train real hard for two hours a day and then go down to the bar and get hammered; and [post-game] beer-ups . . . well, they're twice as bad. I was surprised because I thought the coach would be angry if we didn't try to keep in shape. In actual fact he condones it as much as the rest of us. If we were on the football or hockey team we'd have been benched by now.

Similarly, Thomson cites a far more serious example of rookie misconceptions:

> I was really mad at being cut from the football team because I was sure I had the ability to make the team. So when I first went out for rugby I started with the attitude that I was going to show them how tough I was. I was going to break people apart. Like in football, that's my attitude, that's the only way to win. All the guys have got helmets and pads on, and they think they are hot crap. Anyway I decided to go out at rugby and try to hurt as many people as I could. In one of the first practices I jumped on J's foot and broke two of his toes. In my first game I back off about ten yards and ran at this loose ruck. I hit one of the guys on our own team and broke two of his ribs. Then, in this game in Portland I dislocated a guy's shoulder, and I was really proud of myself for doing it. Then all of a sudden, you know, after all those games and going to parties afterwards and meeting all of the other players, I lost this attitude completely. I was starting to feel really ashamed of myself because this just isn't the rugby spirit. If you're

playing football that's something else. But in rugby as long as it's a good game you don't really mind if you win or not. I don't hold any animosity to anybody now. (Thomson, 1976, p. 113)

Because of such misconceptions, often made early in the presocialization stage, novices are frequently faced with some traumatic role-transitions that are vital to constructing an accurate subcultural identity. Implicit in the socialization of neophytes is a controlling function. That is, because individuals need to acquire new role definitions and behaviors that are appropriate to constructing a new career identity, they are in a sense being controlled extraneously. As Stryker (1980) has suggested, two mechanisms prevail here: first, actors will seek to validate their identity "by behaving in ways that elicit validating responses from others" (p. 64); second, because subcultural identity is important for all actors, they will play their roles in a manner that shows deference for the governing values of the group. Thus, in the interaction that occurs between actors in the subculture, impression management plays a significant role.

Whenever role conflict occurs, members may "role-take" or manage impressions to appear as though they identify with the values of the groups more than is actually the case. For example, novice climbers learn quite quickly about hiding obvious symptoms of fear and about never avoiding an opportunity to climb. While it is perfectly acceptable for an established climber to waste a day by being off-form, hungover, or just too lazy to do any climbing, a rookie can never appear unenthusiastic for fear of being thought of as a camp-follower/groupie type, or even a pseudo—an individual who seeks the glory without the risk:

> One of the wardens told me that there are people at the 'Gunks who go down to Rock and Snow [the climbing equipment store in New Paltz], outfit themselves completely with all the latest climbing gear, and then just parade up and down the Carriage Road [along the foot of the main cliff] and hang around at the Uberfall [a central meeting and gathering place at the foot of the main cliff] without ever doing any climbs. I never believed this until I saw two of them doing that very thing. It was quite obvious that they weren't climbers because they had a complete rack each and all of the nuts were threaded upside down! I watched them for a while and they just walked

up and down, stopped and had a drink, and every now and again they would put the rope down and chalk up [their hands] as if they were going to do a climb. Then they would pick up their gear and move on. Unbelievable!

Rookies must also take all opportunities to climb because to decline may lead to the offer not being repeated, the establishment of a negative reputation, and consequent difficulties with status advancement in the subculture.

It is also under these circumstances that novices may be tested by being taken on climbs that are well beyond their ability. While there is little actual danger to those not leading a climb, the experience can create a great deal of subjective terror. Novices, especially those who appear to be precocious or boastful, are sometimes given the "treatment" ("Let's take _____ on a route and scare the shit out of him!"). In order to pass this test, and in order for all novices to begin constructing an appropriate subcultural identity, it is necessary to manifest qualities of coolness and gameness to establish a reputation for reliability. A frequent sign of tension in novices is the shakes, or "sewing machine legs," the result of strain on the calf muscles from standing on small holds and the inability to relax on those holds. The ankles jump up and down spasmodically and uncontrollably, thereby increasing the novice's tension and fear that he or she will be shaken off the holds. The ability to control this phenomenon is a sure sign that one is beginning to relax in the stressful environment.

Overt displays of fear can destroy an individual's potential career (presuming that the individual would wish to continue) because it would be difficult to rely on such a person in genuinely dangerous circumstances. Donnelly (1980) describes an experience in which he had to effect the rescue of a novice partner who "froze" on a climb. The individual burst into tears upon reaching safety, but neither Donnelly nor the third member of the team could bring themselves to comfort him. By freezing, losing composure, he had jeopardized the safety of the party, and in the harsh and somewhat unfeeling social world of climbers he could not be forgiven. The incident was never discussed, the individual never climbed again, and the resulting awkward interaction led him to drop out of the circle of friends. A similar incident is described in Cherry's (1974, pp. 86-93) book on ironworkers and has similar consequences, indicating that in all avocations or occupations where risk and mutual dependence are involved, composure is perhaps the most important character trait.

Under less extreme circumstances, novices develop a variety of techniques to express composure when fear is actually felt. One method, often modeled for them by more experienced climbers, is to purposely overstate the degree of one's fear. An individual may state that he or she was "scared shitless," "gripped," or "sweating bullets," in each case employing the humor of exaggeration in order to diminish the degree of fear that is actually felt, or to indicate that no real fear existed in a situation where it should exist. In one sense it is a confessional act, but in another sense the message is, "If I really felt that scared would I be telling you?"

Similar forms of impression management may be apparent in rugby. As one player commented,

Sometimes I just don't feel like partying or singing and drinking my brains out at all but I feel I should. It's like, I don't want to be seen as not being one of the guys. So I go with the flow usually. . . . I do feel like there's an element of pressure to do all these things sometimes that, to be honest with you, really aren't my style. But when all the other guys are watching you, its really hard to avoid joining in, you know.

There is an important distinction to be drawn between roles played up front or on stage in a subculture and those played in the everyday course of events. The player in question, for example, was settled in a respectable professional career, participating in the rugby subculture on game days only. Thus, a peripheral member and a weekend deviant of sorts, he did not experience the same degree of role-identification as more central members, the latter being content to act out their disaffiliation (Goffman, 1963) on a more permanent basis, and deriving from it a significant sense of belonging.

As we have noted, in order to pay homage to the subculture's focal concerns (Miller, 1958), some novices will undergo anticipatory socialization procedures. That is, they will vicariously perform roles in various situations that they assume are expected of them. For example, a typical trait of novice climbers is to want to display to both climbers and nonclimbers that they are now climbers. This is part of the first stage of identity construction. Display involves wearing climbing clothes and boots in nonclimbing settings, carrying equipment, books, and magazines about climbing as conspicuously as possible, and turning the conversation to climbing as often as possible.[4] Novices have even been seen wearing the extremely uncomfortable boots designed specifically for rock climbing (removed immediately upon completion of a climb by veterans) in a number of nonclimbing situations such as attending class or in a bar. While they may claim to be breaking in the boots, such novices are invariably pleased that one has recognized their boots, thereby recognizing them as a fellow climber. In fact, the purpose of the display is to indicate to nonclimbers that one is now different, and to signal to other climbers that one is now a fellow member and may be approached as such.

Of course, what such display actually does is indicate to climbers that one is a novice. Experienced climbers have been known to take advantage of the novice's tendency to display by allowing them to carry all of the equipment, particularly if the approach to the cliff involves a long, uphill walk. While such an act may appear to be parasitic, it is actually symbiotic because the novice is allowed to indulge his or her tendency to display and may even fantasize (quite accurately, in fact) that nonclimbers who see the group may think that the novice is actually the leader because he or she is carrying the equipment. As novices become more experienced and more secure in their identity as climbers, their need for display will decrease, and they will gradually become conscious that such behavior is not "cool."

Overt display is a rookie error that highlights the subcultural values of coolness and understatement. While display is expected from novices, it may be ridiculed as the individual becomes more experienced. Normally, the more obvious signs of display are removed—ropes are removed from the outside to the inside of a backpack, climbing boots are removed and more comfortable shoes worn when not climbing, and conversations with other climbers turn to the subject more naturally. Recognition of other climbers becomes more subtle. Without quite realizing it, the individual begins to notice the rolled-up magazine, the guidebook in the hip pocket, and the cuts and scars on an individual's hands that could only have come from climbing rock. One climber, who worked in an equipment store, described a method of identifying the skill of climbers by their dress and demeanor:

> Those in beat-up looking clothes were either good or doing a lot. The ones in new clothes were usually beginners but they would talk as if they were good. The good climbers had an aura about them. They didn't talk about climbing all the time but they were very aware of equipment and knew their stuff. They did not come in the store during the day—only late at night and early morning.

As a novice becomes more confident in the construction of identity during the very active stages of socialization, he or she also becomes more certain and accurate in the reading of others' identities.

Anticipatory socialization may take other forms in rugby. Initiates in the rugby subculture frequently pick up on symbolic cues (Stryker, 1980) and act out anticipated roles. One neophyte in particular performed the requisite "Zulu" (or striptease) on rookie night without any of the usual coercion from veterans: "I knew I was going to have to strip but I didn't know when or how. I was feeling pretty hammered and I wanted to show the rest of the team that I could party as well as anyone, so away I went. I guess I was a little over-eager in retrospect!" Approximately three weeks in to the Canadian university rugby season, another neophyte, endowed with as much skill and talent as any of his teammates, found himself cut to the second team after a series of disappointing performances. The problem actually lay in the fact that he had, observing veteran members' behavior and modeling himself upon it, developed a habit of staying up all night drinking before games, rendering him tired and lethargic during games:

> I don't understand it. All those guys get away with it but I don't seem to be able to. Maybe it's because they've been doing it for so long they're used to it and I'm not. All I know is that when I stay up with those guys I play real lousy the next day.... I think I'm playing "seconds" rugby right now. So I'm going to have to make a choice here.

It seems that rugby players are aware from the presocialization and recruitment stages that certain forms of behavior are expected of them, and their subsequent behavior often shows something of a cyclical orientation. Conscious of bolstering their career identities by conforming to a set of subcultural role expectations, rookies and more established players make deliberate efforts to demonstrate modes of "typical" rugby behavior to other members of the group, and to undergo rituals, often before they are expected of them. Again, the construction of identity is an initially active, but essentially ongoing, process.

Perhaps the final and most important stage of identity construction involves the actor resolving, or at least learning to live with, the contradictions that characterize most sport and career subcultures. These contradictions are between the "front" and "back" regions of the subculture, or between the organizational and informal charters of the group (cf. Ingham, 1975; Vaz, 1972). Contradictions are readily apparent in both the rugby and climbing subcultures, and it is the novice's ability to deal with them that determines the final outcome of the process of identity construction. The true values of the subculture are acted out constantly for the novices by experienced members, and novices are expected to model the appropriate attitudes and behaviors. But the values are also continually emphasized in the gossip and in the repeated stories that become the myth and legend of a subculture.

The core values of rugby are truly mystifying for the average North American male who has grown up believing in success at all costs, ascetic training regimens, and high levels of fitness. The amateuristic aspects of rugby are demonstrated in a variety of ways, including the mandatory heavy drinking, but also in the stories of players who leave their cigarettes and matches next to the goalpost to be retrieved at halftime, in the legends of players who started the game in drunken stupors, and in gossip about who played with a massive hangover. In his ethnography of college and city rugby teams in North America, for example, Young (1983) discovered that a normative behavior, particularly of core members of rugby teams, was to pull all-nighters and to arrive at games hungover, unprepared, and generally devoid of energy following a night without sleep.

Other stories concern aspects of sportsmanship, in which players are lent to an opposing team in order to equalize the numbers, actions are taken to assist referees and officials, and players have great times fraternizing with opponents following hard-fought games. This is amply illustrated by one of Orloff's respondents in her study of the San Diego State rugby team:

> Rugby is the only sport I know of in the world where you can go out drinking with your opponents before the game, try to kill them during the game and then have a party afterwards. If you play any team anywhere, then the host team provides a party for the opposing team. This is a tradition. We also provide two kegs of beer for our opponents after every single game, and we would expect them to do the same. (1974, p. 45)

Such subcultural values of sportsmanship and generosity are also evident among British and Canadian ruggers. The general approach is epitomized in statements made, first, by a young college player in Canada: "Whether we win or lose it's important to us all that we enjoy the game and that both teams get together afterwards and party"; and second, by an English club veteran: "For me, the rugby club has always symbolized a type of second home and I think most of the lads feel that way. Over the years we've established some happy and lasting bonds with other clubs and we intend to keep it that way. Come to the clubhouse after any game . . . and you'll see what camaraderie really means."

As we can see from recent literature distributed by a provincial Rugby Union board in Canada, at the present time the administrators of North American rugby are clearly concerned with officially promoting the game as one that is rich in the ethos of sportsmanship: "Many . . . teams are providing athletes the facilities to enjoy the sense of loyalty and friendship . . . only the Rugby team spirit can provide." Noticeable here is an explicit attempt to elevate rugby above other North American sports because of this subcultural emphasis on sportsmanship and player fraternization.

A further set of rugby stories emphasizes playing with abandon, and mythologizes players who were found, upon completion of a game, to have suffered a broken leg, arm, or neck. But, the major set of stories concerns the rowdiness of postgame social behavior, and includes feats of drinking, damage to property and reputation, nights in prison, and who can outdo whom in terms of outrageous and obscene behavior. Young's (1983) cross-cultural ethnography of the rugby subculture is replete with cases of ruggers urinating in public and on tour buses, and bus drivers refusing to travel with them; conducting player stripteases and "mooning" in bars and other public places; being ejected from restaurants for having massive food fights; conducting souvenir-hunting escapades in bars, on road trips and in opponents' club houses; participating in public vandalism; objectifying and vilifying women and homosexuals in scatological songs and chants; staging "elephant walks"—a line of naked players marching one behind the other, to the tune "The Baby Elephant Walk," with one hand on the shoulder of the player in front and the other hand grasping the penis of the player behind—on campuses and through women's dormitories.

Examples are legion: After being requested to leave the premises of a popular restaurant following a mass food fight, a Canadian university rugby team drew away from the parking lot to a crescendo of breaking glass when players hurled empty beer bottles out of windows; one Canadian subject was arrested and jailed for attempting to steal an enormous mirror from behind a crowded bar while on tour in the U.S.; a Canadian university secretary revealed that on her way home from work during the rugby season she had never driven past the playing fields without team members dropping their shorts and "mooning" her and other passersby; one subject acquired legendary status at his English club for his pièce de résistance, which involved excreting down his pant leg while standing on top of the club piano and displaying the results to the audience at special events.

It becomes clear to rookies that these are the standards they will be expected to live up to, although some variation is clearly possible (see Note 2). The paradoxes lie in playing a vigorous game wherein victory is important but how one plays the game is even more important, in tackling opponents with abandon while knowing that one will be drinking with those same individuals after the game, and in practicing social habits that render one almost incapable of meeting the physical requirements of the game. (Donnelly & Young, 1985, have noted some additional paradoxes in rugby.) The construction of an identity as a rugby player proves to be an interesting balancing act for most individuals.

The contradictions in climbing are primarily between the public and private voices of climbers. The sport is subject to public criticism on occasion (as are most high-risk sports), particularly after accidents or expensive rescues. As a consequence, climbers and participants in other high-risk sports have tended to develop an entire mythology that is primarily for public consumption. This organizational charter emphasizes safety (it's not really dangerous if you know what you are doing), character-building, noncompetitiveness, and comradeship (the kinship of the rope) (Donnelly, 1981b, 1981c, 1981d, 1982a). Even novice climbers are presented with this view of the sport, but as Donnelly (above) and Vanreusel and Renson (1982) have shown, the reality presented to the novices both as models and in myth and legend is quite different.

It soon becomes apparent to many novices that real risks are frequently taken, character and friendship are by no means an automatic consequence of participation, and competition between climbers is rampant. Again, these values are modeled for the neophytes by established climbers and are represented in the gossip and lore of the subculture. For example, competition is evident in gossip concerning who may be working secretly on a new cliff in order to make first ascents before anyone else, who has cheated by not following the informal rule structure of the sport, and in legendary accounts of first ascents that were snatched from the grasp of unsuspecting opponents. The kinship of the rope is disputed in clique formations, in rivalries that are sometimes tense between adherents of different climbing areas, and in numerous stories of fistfights on the heights and tantrums during expeditions. And, the idea of character-building does not appear to be in complete accord with social behavior that is only rivaled, on occasion, by that of rugby players, by gossip about who was seen smoking what on a ledge several thousand feet up a cliff face, and by stories about how a whole valley full of climbers were able to achieve temporary wealth after a dope smuggler's plane crashed in a location that was inaccessible to police but not to climbers.

The major theme of climbing lore concerns risk and accidents, the significance of which may be determined from the number of terms used to describe these conditions. If climbing were actually safe for those who are knowledgeable, climbers would not be constantly talking about who was "gripped" on a particular climb, or about their latest epic. Recent accidents are analyzed, dissected, dwelled upon, joked about, and the victims mourned or vilified. Some accidents slip into the lore of climbing, and climbers will occasionally point out the site of accidents. Narrow escapes become even more famous because they indicate that there is always hope of survival, even in the most impossible circumstances. Individuals who fell the whole length of a cliff and then got up and walked away become folk heroes, even though the circumstances are often exaggerated with repeated telling.

Another class of story that provides additional reassurance regarding survival and a continued normal existence, and also carries with it the moral implication that it is all worth it, involves the remarkable or rapid recovery. In these stories, climbers dismiss themselves from hospitals, confound doctors' opinions by climbing again, and return to climbing while wearing their casts, or after losing fingers and toes, or even with artificial limbs. An example of this type of story concerns the climber who was badly hurt in an accident, and who was informed that he would be in the hospital for at least six months and that he would never climb again. The doctors also told him that alcohol would kill him during recovery, but his friends, feeling that his life was over anyway if he could not climb again, decided that he should part happily, and they continually smuggled beer and scotch into his hospital room. The climber dismissed himself from the hospital after two months and returned to climbing while still wearing a leg cast. The story clearly suffers from exaggeration and embellishment, but the point is that the exaggeration and constant retelling are precisely what make it revealing as a source of subcultural values. Similar stories are found in most high-risk sport subcultures and rarely become public knowledge, although Nicki Lauda's miraculously rapid return to Grand Prix auto racing after suffering nearly fatal burns in an accident has precisely the same point in its often exaggerated retelling.

Klein (1986) has recently shown how bodybuilders must learn to resolve, or at least cope with, yet another set of contradictions in order to develop an appropriate subcultural identity. In this case the contradictions are between the public image of rugged individualism and the reality of submitting to a feudal organizational structure, the public image of health and fitness and the reality of steroid abuse and extraordinary dietary practices, and the public image of heterosexual masculinity and the reality of homosexual hustling. The construction of normal identities as rugby players, climbers, or bodybuilders therefore frequently involves a complete turnaround from the preconceptions that may have been acquired during the presocialization stage—from courses, instructional books, television documentaries, and so on. While many subcultures are able to accommodate a wide range of internal differentiation, some individuals are unable to adjust during the active stage of socialization to a set of values that may be diametrically opposed to the public image of the sport.

The Confirmation of Identity

Under normal circumstances, identity confirmation is a relatively straightforward process. A novice begins to accept the actual values of the subculture and to leave behind any misconceptions. Confirmation may occur gradually, in rugby for example, in the process of making the team, undergoing the rigors of rookie night, and becoming more and more involved with established players both on and off the field. It is the process of establishing a reputation as a reliable individual whose values and behavior apparently conform to subcultural expectations. It is not necessary to do something crazy either on or off the field, but in the rugby subculture, crazy acts can certainly speed up and enhance the development of a reputation. In climbing, confirmation may be more immediate, for example, being asked to take the lead by an established member of the subculture.

In each case one's reputation is made, and one's membership has been confirmed. But reputations are such that they must constantly be remade, and it is this aspect of identity confirmation that is most interesting. The fragility of reputations has been an ongoing theme in interactionist sociology, and credentialing or verification procedures are a part of the norms of social conduct. New members of subcultures, geographically mobile members, and members who are attempting to have claimed achievements accepted each place their reputations, their constructed identities, at risk.

Based on Goffman's premise that all interactants desire smoothly flowing or euphoric exchanges, the rules of deference (particularly the rule of acceptance—"An individual's claims about himself must be accepted as valid unless proved otherwise" [Birrell, 1978, p. 267]) and demeanor (particularly the rule of sincerity—"The individual must be the person he has claimed to be" [Birrell, 1978, p. 265]) are most appropriate to the process of identity confirmation. If one or more parties to an interaction are suspected of not complying with the rules, then verification becomes an issue. A related concern here is the concept of trust. Garfinkel's (1963) definition, in which he refers to trust as taking for granted the constitutive expectancies or basic rules of the game, is clearly related to Birrell's derived rules of deference and demeanor. Henslin further suggests that, "Where the actor has offered a definition of himself and the audience is willing to interact with the actor on the basis of that definition, we are saying that trust exists" (1968, p. 140).

The actor's definition of self, or the front that is offered to an audience, may be seen as a coherence between the various parts of the front—the setting in which an actor appears, the appearance of the actor, and the manner of the actor (Goffman, 1959). If an actor is attempting to have a previous achievement accepted, we may add to these the appropriateness of the claim being made, and what is known by the audience of the actor's previous (verified) achievements. A coherence between these various parts of the actor's identity will usually result in trust, in the confirmation of the actor's claims.

Under normal circumstances, because record keeping is so much a part of sport and because of the requirements for third-party verification for claimed achievements, verification is not an issue in sport. Most individuals joining a team, for example, are either complete novices who need to establish a reputation or they arrive with a documented reputation. It is the exceptions to these conditions that are of interest. Donnelly (1978, 1982b) has examined verification procedures in climbing and birding, two activities that have no formal requirement for third-party verification,[5] and a recent study has examined verification as applied to geographical mobility in Canadian rugby clubs (Parnoja, 1985).

On the rare occasions in climbing when an individual is unknown to a particular group either personally or by reputation, or when an unobserved solo ascent is being claimed for which there is no photographic evidence, it is necessary for the safety of the members and the integrity of the subculture to determine the legitimacy of the individual. This is done by examining the coherence between the various parts of an actor's front, and possibly by engaging in the type of strategic interaction or information games outlined by Goffman (1969) and Scott (1968). For example, the pseudo-climbers mentioned previously were certainly making unspoken claims about their identity, but were easily revealed by experienced climbers because of an equipment error. However, it is apparent that poor climbers, or climbers who may have a tendency to panic, can be a very real hazard to climbers who accept exaggerated claims from them and who climb with them. Similarly, in cycling and particularly cycle racing, knowledge of and ability to use equipment (as in climbing) serves a gatekeeping function, because if one is unable to ride in a straight line at 60-70 kph one is a hazard to other riders (Albert, 1984).

In keeping with the old exploratory and geographical aspects of climbing, it is not customary to doubt the claims made by an individual, particularly if it is possible for the climber to have done what is being claimed (given such variables as the weather, ice and snow conditions, time available, and the climber's ability, equipment, and physical condition) and if the claimed achievement is in keeping with the individual's known ability, past experience, and previous reliability. If there are apparent reasons to dispute the claims, judgment is withheld, and an individual may suffer a loss of reputation (what might, in this context, be termed a disconfirmation of identity).

The problem of confirmation in rugby concerns players from other countries with a long tradition and reputation in the game (e.g., United Kingdom, New Zealand, South Africa) joining North American clubs. Such players arrive in North America with an aura of excellence that is sometimes undeserved. But because North American players, most of whom are new to the game, are primed to accept claims of excellence from these players, it is not unusual for the players from outside North America to take advantage of the situation by exaggerating their ability. As a result, sometimes a foreign player will make the team over some more deserving North American players. The Canadian players interviewed (Parnoja, 1985) were all aware of such a possibility and suggested that it would be

resolved in the long term purely on playing ability, particularly if there are no other ways to confirm the claimed identity.

In all of these cases, when there are genuine suspicions, or when an individual is being particularly tiresome by making obviously invalid claims, a number of sanctions are available to legitimate members of the subculture. Climbers have been known to take such a person on particularly terrifying routes, or to demonstrate his or her lack of ability in obvious and public ways. Cyclists have caused those who are unable to handle their bikes in an appropriately safe manner to crash. And rugby players note that tongues can be loosened and indiscretions revealed with the liberal application of beer (although, they also note, culprits can be punished in practice games).

Entrapment may be employed as a form of strategic interaction in order to reveal cheats (e.g., asking "How did you find the final overhang?" when it is known that there are no overhangs on the climb), the results of which are not necessarily shared with the culprit but certainly spread to all other members. Birders employ similar strategies against those members of the subculture who develop a reputation for being the only person in a region to see a particular species—often a sign of exaggeration or cheating. However, outright accusations are rare because of the tendency to avoid confrontation and the preference for euphoric exchanges; but when deliberate embarrassment does occur it is entirely appropriate in the manner outlined by Gross and Stone:

> embarrassment is deliberately perpetrated as a negative sanction as in "calling" one who is giving an undesirable (role) performance. Since embarrassment does incapacitate the person from performing his role, it can clearly be used to stop someone from playing a role that might discredit a collectivity. Empirical categories include public reprimands, exposure of false fronts, open gossip or cattiness, or embarrassment perpetrated as a retaliation for an earlier embarrassment. In some of these cases, a person is exposed as having no right to play the role he has laid claim to, because the identity in which his role is anchored is invalid. In others, the person is punished by terminating his role performance so that he can no longer enjoy its perquisites. (1964, pp. 14-15)

In the more formal sport subcultures, it is entirely possible to construct an identity that will convince nonmembers and even novice members that one has a reputation and a valid claim to membership. But the ongoing process of identity confirmation ensures that such individuals cannot do too much damage to the subculture itself, or to individual members.

Conclusions

The roles and identities of members of subcultures should not be thought of as static positions and entities. They are constantly undergoing revision and change due to a variety of processes both within and outside the subculture. We have argued that a career contingency model represents a useful means of characterizing subcultural membership, and that the active processes of cultural production in sport subcultures ensure that socialization is an ongoing stage, while acceptance/ostracism is likely to be a repeated stage. The key contingencies within this model, then, are the construction/reconstruction of an appropriate subcultural identity, and the confirmation/reconfirmation of that identity by other members of the subculture.

Although many subcultures are able to tolerate a great deal of diversity, there are frequently some critical aspects for which little tolerance is allowed. These typically concern circumstances wherein it is necessary to trust that a partner or opponent will play his or her part, that is, will have constructed and be prepared to display an appropriate aspect of subcultural identity. For example, professional wrestlers must be able to trust that their opponents will have learned and will play their parts appropriately, both for reasons of safety and to generate "heat" (Birrell & Turowetz, 1979); racing cyclists must trust that their opponents will have enough skill and composure to ride in a straight line at speed (Albert, 1984); hockey players need to trust that their teammates will come to their defense in the case of cheap shots or mismatched fights (Faulkner, 1974); birders must be able to rely on the integrity of the reports of fellow birders before embarking on long and expensive journeys to observe particularly rare species (Donnelly, 1982b); climbers must trust that partners will retain composure and not endanger anyone through panic or freezing (Donnelly, 1980); and rugby players need to maintain their sportsmanship in a particularly rough game, and not spoil the celebrations afterward by moderation or temperate behavior (Young, 1983).

In addition, resolving the contradictions of many subcultures exposes members to insider knowledge that must often be retained in order to maintain the integrity of the subculture. For example, much of the work as instructors, now available to many climbers, would disappear if insider conversations about risk reached a much wider audience; and bodybuilders need to retain insider knowledge about steroid abuse and homosexual hustling. Although some information inevitably leaks out through sociologists and ex-members, as long as the majority deny such information a level of plausible deniability is maintained.

The model developed here, concerning identity construction and confirmation in a subcultural career, is by no means limited to sport subcultures. Similar patterns of identity construction and confirmation, contingencies, and aspects of cultural production may be found in all achieved subcultures. Thus, whether reference is made to a greater range of avocational subcultures (leisure, hobbyist, and collector groups), to occupational and military subcultures, or to youth and deviant subcultures, the construction/reconstruction of an appropriate subculture identity and the confirmation/reconfirmation of that identity by other members are key processes.

This analysis of sport subcultures is grounded in interactionist approaches to the topic (cf. Fine & Kleinman, 1979). However, such focused views of specific processes within subcultures should not lead researchers to consider subcultures in isolation from their structural, historical, and geographical contexts, or to neglect the fact that "the dominant values of wider society are transmitted, resisted or negotiated" (Bishop & Hoggett, 1987, p. 32) through subcultures in general, but perhaps particularly through avocational subcultures. Without such contextualization, subcultural research will remain an interesting appendage to more mainstream consideration of changing patterns of social development.

References

Albert, E. (1984). Equipment as a feature of social control in the sport of bicycle racing. In N. Theberge & P. Donnelly (Eds.), *Sport and the sociological imagination* (pp. 318-338). Fort Worth, TX: Texas Christian University Press.

Birrell, S. (1978). Sporting encounters: An examination of the work of Erving Goffman and its application to sport. Unpublished doctoral dissertation, University of Massachusetts.

Birrell, S., & Turowetz, A. (1979). Character work-up and display: Collegiate gymnastics and professional wrestling. *Urban Life,* **8,** 219-246.

Bishop, J., & Hoggett, P. (1987, Summer). Clubbing together. *New Socialist,* pp. 32-33.

Cherry, M. (1974). *On high steel: The education of an ironworker.* New York: Quadrangle.

Donnelly, P. (1978, June). *On determining another's skill.* Paper presented at the Canadian Sociology and Anthropology Association Annual Meeting, London, ON.

Donnelly, P. (1980). *The subculture and public image of climbers.* Unpublished doctoral dissertation, University of Massachusetts.

Donnelly, P. (1981a). Toward a definition of sport subcultures. In M. Hart & S. Birrell (Eds.), *Sport in the sociocultural process* (3rd ed.) (pp. 565-588). Dubuque, IA: Wm. C. Brown.

Donnelly, P. (1981b). Four fallacies—I: Climbing is not really dangerous, *Mountain,* **80,** 38-40.

Donnelly, P. (1981c). Four fallacies—II: Climbing is non-competitive. *Mountain,* **81,** 8-31.

Donnelly, P. (1981d). Four fallacies—III: Climbing is character building. *Mountain,* **82,** 20-23.

Donnelly, P. (1982a). Four fallacies—IV: Climbing leads people to form close friendships. *Mountain,* **83,** 45-49.

Donnelly, P. (1982b). On verification: A comparison of climbers and birders. In A. Ingham & E. Broom (Eds.), *Career patterns and career contingencies in sport* (pp. 484-499). Vancouver, BC: University of British Columbia Press.

Donnelly, P., & Young, K. (1985). Reproduction and transformation of cultural forms in sport: A contextual analysis of rugby. *International Review for the Sociology of Sport,* **20,** 19-38.

Faulkner, R. (1974). Making violence by doing work: Selves, situations, and the world of professional hockey. *Sociology of Work and Occupations,* **1,** 288-312.

Faulkner, R. (1975). Coming of age in organizations: A comparative study of career contingencies of musicians and hockey players. In D.W. Ball & J.W. Loy (Eds.), *Sport and social order* (pp. 521-559). Reading, MA: Addison-Wesley.

Fine, G.A., & Kleinman, S. (1979). Rethinking subculture: An interactionist perspective, *American Journal of Sociology,* **85,** 1-20.

Garfinkel, H. (1963). A conception of and experiments with "trust" as a condition of stable concerted actions. In O.J. Harris (Ed.), *Motivation and social interaction: Cognitive determinants* (pp. 187-238). New York: Ronald Press.

Goffman, E. (1959). *The presentation of self in everyday life.* New York: Doubleday.

Goffman, E. (1963). *Stigma.* Englewood Cliffs, NJ: Prentice-Hall.

Goffman, E. (1969). *Strategic interaction.* New York: Ballantine.

Gross, E., & Stone, G. (1964). Embarrassment and the analysis of role requirements. *American Journal of Sociology,* **70,** 1-15.

Henslin, J.M. (1968). Trust and the cab driver. In M. Truzzi (Ed.), *Sociology and everyday life.* Englewood Cliffs, NJ: Prentice-Hall.

Ingham, A.G. (1975). Occupational subcultures in the work world of sport. In D.W. Ball & J.W. Loy (Eds.), *Sport and social order* (pp. 333-391). Reading, MA: Addison-Wesley.

Klein, A.M. (1986). Pumping irony: Crisis and contradiction in bodybuilding. *Sociology of Sport Journal,* **3,** 112-133.

Miller, D.C., & Form, W.H. (1980). *Industrial sociology* (3rd ed.). New York: Harper & Row.

Miller, W.B. (1958). Lower class culture as a generating milieu for gang delinquency. *Journal of Social Issues,* **14,** 5-19.

Orloff, K. (1974). Playgirl presents the San Diego State rugby team. *Playgirl,* **11**(1), 44-46.

Parnoja, J. (1985). A study of verification as it relates to foreign rugby players in Canada. Unpublished manuscript, McMaster University.

Pearson, K. (1979). *Surfing subcultures of Australia and New Zealand.* St. Lucia: University of Queensland Press.

Polsky, N. (1967). *Hustlers, beats, and others.* Chicago: Aldine.

Prus, R. (1984). Career contingencies: Examining patterns of involvement. In N. Theberge & P. Donnelly (Eds.), *Sport and the sociological imagination* (pp. 297-318). Fort Worth, TX: Texas Christian University Press.

Rosenberg, M.M., & Turowetz, A. (1975). The wrestler and the physician: Identity work-up and organizational arrangements. In D.W. Ball & J.W. Loy (Eds.), *Sport and social order* (pp. 559-574). Reading, MA: Addison-Wesley.

Scott, M. (1968). *The racing game.* Chicago: Aldine.

Stone, G.P. (1970). Appearance and the self. In G.P. Stone & H.H. Faberman (Eds.), *Social psychology through interaction* (pp. 187-202). Waltham, MA: Ginn-Blaisdell.

Stryker, S. (1980). *Symbolic interactionism: A social structural version.* Menlo Park, CA: Benjamin Cummings.

Super, D.E. (1957). *The psychology of careers.* New York: Harper & Row.

Thomson, R. (1976). *Sport and deviance: A subcultural analysis.* Unpublished doctoral dissertation, University of Alberta.

Vanreusel, B., & Renson, R. (1982). The social stigma of high risk sport subcultures. In A. Dunleavy, A. Miracle, & R. Rees (Eds.), *Studies in the sociology of sport* (pp. 183-202). Fort Worth, TX: Texas Christian University Press.

Vaz, E. (1972). The culture of young hockey players: Some initial observations. In E. Taylor (Ed.), *Training: A scientific basis* (pp. 222-234). Springfield, IL: Charles C. Thomas.

Young, K. (1983). The subculture of rugby players: A form of resistance and incorporation. Unpublished master's thesis, McMaster University.

Notes

1. *Achieved* subcultures are based on occupational, avocational, or deviant characteristics, in contrast to *ascribed* subcultures, which are based on age, race, social class, and so on. In addition, although the term *role* is employed here in its rather static and stereotypical sense, this is merely for convenience in order to simplify a rather complex process that involves both dynamic change and varying role expectations.

2. In the more informal subcultures the possibility of internal differentiation readily exists. For example, with reference to this paper, it is entirely possible to conceive of the creation of a fundamentalist Christian rugby team. And, in climbing, it is quite evident that many individuals who adhere to the public rather than the private image of the sport tend to move toward instructing or mountain rescue.

3. Unless otherwise attributed, all rugby quotations are from Young (1983) and all climbing quotations are from Donnelly (1980).

4. The use of language/argot in subcultures is also a distancing mechanism. Whether it is the windsurfer who claims never to rig until it's "blowing 15" or the swimmer constantly talking about "splits," language is a clear way of showing both insiders and outsiders that one belongs, and is also subject to error among novices.

5. Other sports may be included here, particularly caving. But verification is also important at an informal level in other sports. For example, fishermen and golfers are notorious for their exaggerations of lone achievements, but third-party verification is a prerequisite of formal competitions.

Pumping Irony: Crisis and Contradiction in Bodybuilding

Alan M. Klein

While the projection of ideal images is very important in American culture, it is in the subculture and sport of bodybuilding that it gets carried to the extreme. A 4-year study of bodybuilding's mecca—Southern California—revealed a fundamental set of discrepancies between what the subculture projects as ideal and what actually goes on. These discrepancies are examined to determine which ones result from changes that have taken place in bodybuilding and which are structural to it. It is shown that as the sport/subculture altered its image to achieve cultural respectability, it inadvertently created new problems. The shifts are examined within the context of studies of deviance and point to the need for long-term ethnography in sport sociology.

Sociologists and anthropologists have avoided disciplinary conflict in part because they have drawn territorial boundaries that complement each others' interests, a feat that has as much to do with avoidance as it does engagement. Subject matter and methodology were divided so as to avoid turf issues. According to this simplified scheme, anthropologists study exotic cultures (preferably non-white and non-European) while sociologists seek out Western societies. Anthropologists do qualitative analysis, while sociologists focus on quantitative. Enough is shared between them to constitute an intellectual demilitarized zone filled with anthropologists studying Western urban contexts and rural sociologists working in areas like Brazil and the Philippines.

The study of sport reflects both the separation and complementarity between sociology and anthropology. Sport sociology has been even more separate from anthropology than have other sociological fields, making the potential contributions from ethnography more promising. The following ethnographic study will speak to the fruitful relationship between the disciplines of sport sociology, urban anthropology, and studies of subculture. In particular, the relationship between cultural ideals and behavioral actuality will be examined. While both disciplines share an interest in this relationship, they have framed it somewhat differently (e.g., Durkheim, 1953; Becker, 1963; Diamond, 1972; Linton, 1945; Freilich, 1977). Using some of the more recent contributions from the field of subcultural studies, this paper focuses on the use of historical analysis and power relationships to look at discrepancies between ideal and real (Hebdige, 1983).

In sport analysis there is an immediate difference in the way the two fields define the appropriate subject of study. Sociologists study sport, while anthropologists deal with play. Play is certainly a broader category of behavior than sport, covering as it does, for instance, a child sitting alone making mud pies, as well as organized competition. By and large, however, anthropological studies of play view sport as less common in kin-based, nonstate societies, hence more properly the realm of other social scientists.

The association that each discipline forms also reflects these divisions. The North American Society for the Sociology of Sport (NASSS) studies Western sport or occasionally sport in Eastern industrial

Reprinted from Klein, 1986.

society (e.g., Cantelon & Gruneau, 1982; Eitzen, 1983). Exceptions are uncommon, such as Lever's study of soccer in Brazil (Lever, 1983). On the other hand, The Anthropological Association for the Study of Play (TAASP) tends to look at games and play in a Third World context (e.g., Stevens, 1977; Schwartzman, 1980; Blanchard & Cheska, 1983). The commitment to ethnography and fieldwork is noted in the work on sport carried out by anthropologists, while their sociologist colleagues lean heavily toward quantitative methods. It is the possibility of a *sport ethnography* within the sociological domain of contemporary industrial sport that represents a fruitful merger of anthropological orientation and sociological setting. This study attempts such a fusion.

Sport Sociology and the Ethnography of Sport

Sport sociologists occupy a position of low status within the hierarchy of sociological specializations. Studying almost any institution, be it law, family, corporations, even deviance itself, seems more legitimate than the study of sport. Among sport sociologists there is an unstated consensus about the negative views their colleagues outside the specialty have of them.[1] In partial response to this, sport sociologists have compensated with a hyperempirical methodology. Quantitative sport studies predominate, as evidenced by the citations of work in leading texts (Coakley, 1982; Eitzen & Sage, 1978; Leonard, 1980). Journals such as the *Journal of Sport and Social Issues* and *Sociology of Sport Journal* also point to a gap at least as large as the one that separates the disciplines of sociology and anthropology.

Anthropologists have increasingly carried out ethnographies and fieldwork on games (Blanchard & Cheska, 1985). With few exceptions, however, these studies have been on nonindustrial peoples (e.g., Geertz, 1972) or marginal groups within industrial societies (e.g., Tindall, 1975). While these are worthwhile anthropological contributions that deepen our understanding of culture, they do little to inform our understanding of American or Western society as it is affected by and through sport. This reinforces the oft-held view of anthropology as having little to say about the dominant society. Anthropologists have developed their analysis of small-scale societies, however, seeing them as a set of institutions and cultural variables which act to integrate and alter that society through consensus

and conflict. This is assessed through participant observation. More important, anthropologists stress the use of culture as a prism through which social life can be interpreted. While sociologists are aware of these techniques and perspectives, it is the anthropologists who have developed them more fully. As a result, they can be used to advantage where other perspectives have previously prevailed.

Sport ethnography is virtually nonexistent. Participant observation in the service of sport reporting is not in itself sufficient. On occasion, journalists with unusually keen insight and a sense of social analysis inadvertently cross over into the realm of ethnography (e.g., Lipsyte, 1975; Boswell, 1983). However, these efforts remain diletantish rather than being serious ethnography. The observations of Janet Lever in her thoughtful sociological work on Brazilian soccer (1983), or those of Brower (1975) or Devereux (1976) on Little Leaguers, are not the same as those of Colin Turnbull (1965) or Spradley (1970) or Lee (1979). Missing is the view of soccer or baseball as a self-contained, integrated whole, a cultural diorama. That totality and the insight and understanding that comes from the method and perspective of ethnography can be a critical element in the rise of sport sociology to a position of prominence.

Sport Ethnography and Subcultural Studies

The gap between sport sociology and ethnography can be bridged by looking at the analysis of subcultures. Although primarily the contribution of sociologists, anthropologists have not been altogether absent (e.g., Liebow, 1969; Spradley & Mann, 1975; Daner, 1976; Keiser, 1979). The theoretical debates have centered on the function, origins, and systematic workings of subcultures but have mistakenly placed such work within the area of deviance. Periodic reassessments (e.g., Matza, 1969; Brake, 1980; Hebdige, 1983) have done little to change this view. Anthropologists are uncomfortable with the way in which sociologists have lumped disparate subcultures under the heading of deviance. Despite cautioning us about the larger society's method of stigmatizing and labeling deviants, sociologists' continued use of the label sanctions it (see Hebdige, 1983). In anthropology the tradition of cultural relativism is sufficiently strong to promote a view of subculture that avoids deviance connotations, in part by focusing on the study of cultural entities via ethnography. Through relativism, and by partially sacrificing the subculture's ties to the larger society, the ethnography can intensively examine a subculture, giving it an integrity that ethnographic tradition often bestows upon its subject. Admittedly, unless one is careful the relations between the part and the whole (i.e., the subculture and the larger society) can be sacrificed; this hurts analysis but is more than made up for by affording a view of the subculture freed of the deviance label.

Some sociologists distinguish between subcultures on the basis of delinquency, thereby dichotomizing between delinquent and occupational subculture (Downes, 1966) or delinquent and subterranean subcultures (Matza, 1964). Sport subculture would seemingly fall into the category of the more acceptable work and countercultural groups. Many assume that sport as a whole is synonymous with socialization of norms (e.g., Phillips & Schafer, 1971). Others see this as the province of specific sport subcultures (Loy, McPherson, & Kenyon, 1978). Clearly there is a need for the establishment of a sport ethnography in looking at the machinations and function of sport subculture.

The neat division between delinquent and subterranean subculture that Matza (1969) points to, and the view of sport subculture as fitting neatly into the mainstream, is somewhat rattled by the case of competitive bodybuilding in Southern California.

Bodybuilding As Subculture

The respect by the larger society that has eluded bodybuilding for so long is finally within reach. This acceptance can be measured by the astounding growth in the past decade of competitive and noncompetitive bodybuilding. Trade publications estimate that as many as 85 million Americans engage in some form of weight training, and while only a tiny fraction will ever develop enough to compete, almost all of them are expecting to see bodily transformation. In that sense they are all bodybuilders, body shapers, or body designers. Over 100 countries now sanction and promote it as a sport, making bodybuilding the seventh largest sport federation in the world. Southern California, and Olympic Gym in particular, is the pulse of bodybuilding. It is the nexus between bodybuilding as sport and subculture, and as such it is the ideal place to study its cultural properties. As the self-styled core of bodybuilding, Olympic Gym has been home to almost every great bodybuilder of the past two decades.

Venice, California, is the perfect setting for a subculture as visually exotic as bodybuilding. Muscle Beach, Olympic, Gold's, and World's Gyms are all within a square mile of each other, making it easy for people to characterize the area as a haven for the practitioners of this sport. Venice, however, lends the entire complex a good deal of its own color. The ideologues of the sport—the Weider brothers who own the largest conglomerate of bodybuilding products in the world and who are headquartered nearby in Woodland Hills—view the free spirited and tolerant climate of Venice as somewhat excessive and potentially embarrassing. They strive to gain respect by projecting a persona of wholesomeness. By dovetailing with the fitness movement, the behemoths who determine bodybuilding's cultural images through their magazines are concerned with gaining cultural respectability rather than trendy popular cultural status. To come closer to mainstream culture, three values are heavily projected to the public via the leading publications: health, heterosexuality, and rugged individualism. As mainstream values, these three differ from values sought by other subcultures. Bodybuilding does not perceive the larger society as malfunctioning and in need of alternatives. If anything, the bodybuilding subculture is conservative, or as Matza might claim, an occupational subculture (1969).

A tension exists within bodybuilding's subculture, one between the ideal image as expressed in the three values listed above, and bodybuilding institutions that foster different and often contradictory behavior. In anthropology these discrepancies have been called "ideal versus real" culture patterns. First the status of bodybuilding in sports must be discussed.

Bodybuilding: Sport or Spectacle?

Bodybuilding rests precipitously between sport and spectacle. If professional wrestling or roller derby have become synonymous with spectacle, it is not because of their inability to meet basic definitions of sport. Structurally, they meet the outlines presented by Coakley (1982), who cites physical exertion, competition, and organization as three key traits all sports must have. Bodybuilding has some unique problems in meeting these criteria.

All three of Coakley's traits can be found in bodybuilding. The International Federation of Body Building (IFBB) is the dominant organization in the sport. Contests are highly competitive, but the physical exertion and demonstration of skills, which most people assume runs in tandem with organization and competition, is conspicuously absent. It takes place separately and is linked to the contest only as a visual reportage—a posing routine. This transforms the contest into a nonphysical event that outsiders often see as being like a beauty contest. Insiders defend against this by claiming that the sport is both sport and art: weight training is the sport, and posing and competitions are the art. Regardless of how they divide their field, the physical component is not contemporaneous with the organized competition, raising a claim that it is not a sport at all but a spectacle. Belly dancing is not a sport, yet many of its practitioners engage in weight training and enter competitions. Even within bodybuilding there has been a tendency of late to exaggerate the spectacle with the use of props and outrageous costuming and makeup (e.g., The Night of the Champions, a professional contest).

Definition of sport is mediated by other factors, however, most notably the media's willingness to accept an activity as such and the public's acceptance of that decision. Within the past decade just such a passive acquiescence seems to have occurred through the dramatic rise in popularity of "trash sports" (Sewart, 1983). Bodybuilding rode that crest, first through the attention received by the award-winning film *Pumping Iron,* and second with network telecasts of some of the better bodybuilding contests. This supported the view that virtually any sporting event would generate sufficient ratings, and contests along with prize money proliferated during the late 1970s. The advent of women's bodybuilding made the most dramatic impact, however, because it opened the sport/spectacle to a hitherto excluded group. And to the thousands of fans who willingly paid as much as $100 a seat to get into the Mr. Olympia contest, the temporal break meant nothing.

Closely related to bodybuilding is the internationally recognized sport of powerlifting. Here, one sees all three of Coakley's traits functioning at once. Both powerlifting and bodybuilding stemmed from the 19th-century strongman acts of Europe, with the former monopolizing the strength feature while bodybuilding focused on the physique. Between them exists an uneasy truce marked by the condescension of powerlifters toward their counterparts. The few powerlifters at Olympic (most prefer more utilitarian, austere gyms) were given a wide berth and respect granted only to the top people in the gym. Yet it is bodybuilding, not powerlifting, that has risen to cultural prominence, a rise that bears testimony to the media's ability to redefine cultural institutions and their definitions.

While the status of bodybuilding is not universally accepted, its position as a subculture is even more questioned. Many of the practices and beliefs held by bodybuilders have undergone a degree of change as a result of the new-found acceptance of the sport. Media attention exacerbates this, with the result being that discrepancies emerge between what is consciously being presented about the sport and what actually goes on. Three of the more glaring examples are (a) individualism as a self-definition versus socially determined self, (b) health versus illness, and (c) heterosexual projection versus homosexuality.

Individualism Versus Socially Determined Self

Bodybuilders prefer to be thought of as rugged individuals. Their very presence in such an individualized sport speaks to that preference. Those who came to the sport with a previous sport background invariably note their disdain for team sports and what it implies:

I began developing a strong sense of individuality quite early. I was always turned off by team sports. I just didn't like being part of a team and the backslapping and groupie sweating and all that. I would rather spend time in my basement pumping iron.

I liked football and all, but there was too much sharing. I just didn't wanna depend on anyone. I wanted to do something totally by myself. Bodybuilding is it.

A recent study of bodybuilders (Sprague, n.d.) used the Cattell 16PF psychology test on a random sample of people and found that bodybuilders were significantly more self-sufficient and less group-dependent than the mean population.

Of the numerous interviews conducted between 1979 and 1984, the expressed lack of ties among bodybuilders was typical, with characteristic comments like, "I'm a loner" or "I'm not easy to make friends with."

Question: Do you hang around with anyone in the gym?

Answer: No, no. You don't hang around with those guys. You're not gonna get it [acknowledgment] from them. The gym isn't really a social situation for me.

I don't think these guys make friends. You know what the problem is? Bodybuilders are selfish, and I been around for 10 years. They have to be. All they do is think about themselves. That's why _____ was so popular. Cuz in a sport where selfishness, size, and hustling count, he was the most selfish, the biggest hustler, and just the biggest.

Within the gym, however, there are distinct social[2] and psychological categories, the most significant being gender. Women are far more likely to be social, more likely to bond with others than men are. They are also more likely to lend mutual assistance (Klein, 1985b). However, because men make up the majority of the gym's population, and always have, the atmosphere still rings of indifference, and at times even surliness. The social solidarity of women is typified in the following:

Women are tighter. I've seen girls swap clothing, posing suits at contests. And they helped me with my hair and makeup when my hairdresser didn't show up on time.

Some of the girls really help each other. Like P. She had gas. She said to C, "I gotta get rid of this gas." So C. starts taking her through these stomach exercises that will help her move the gas around, and she massages her stomach for it. It was really neat the way she put her own considerations aside. . . . People help each other and that's what I like about the competitions.

The daily routine of bodybuilders and the relations they fashion and act in are all couched in atomistic behavior. Special dietary restrictions makes eating fairly dull and a more or less isolated act. The entire day is built around training, and much of the mental preparation is of the self-motivating form: no team sessions or mutual psyching (with one notable exception) as found in other sports. At the gym no one dares to break into someone else's routine or approach equipment until relatively certain that it is unused. Conversation, especially as a contest nears, is often kept to a minimum while working out.

While we're training, we don't wanna be bothered. It's much more social for non-serious bodybuilders. Those guys have time to bullshit in the gym.

I'm very sociable really. But I know when to cut it off. When I'm training I don't want to be bothered, like right now.

I can't talk now, man.

Thus while the gym may appear as if it is rocking in collective exertion, it is, with the exception of the training partnership, really a long sequence of individual efforts.

It is in competing, however, that one glimpses the extent of the individualism. All pretense at social bonding abandoned, each bodybuilder views others suspiciously. Competitors in bodybuilding (unlike most other sports) train together in the same place, and each day of contest preparation is dotted with confrontations and guarded acts lest one's physical condition be prematurely revealed. To assure this privacy the body is swaddled in sweat clothes, no information is given, and a hostile bravado supplants a tentative affability.

As the contest nears, conversation, which is already at a premium, virtually ceases. This is as much the result of the pernicious effects of dieting as it is the anxiety of competition. Men give and ask for nothing.[3] Backstage at the contest, sullen, scantily clad men stand alone in a crowd. The ruthlessness of actual competition is no more bruising than the isolated preparation that goes into it (Klein, n.d., chapter 4).

Economically, bodybuilders suffer as a result of their atomism. What each pro strives for are contest earnings as well as endorsements. Additionally, a world-class bodybuilder can parlay his or her winnings and titles into a lucrative mail order business. This is the economic ideal: individual competitive success followed by self-employment. The result is that every successful bodybuilder competes for a finite market against others, as well as the leading entrepreneurs. In the face of such fierce competition, more rational attempts to conduct business such as joining forces or not duplicating efforts would seem imminent. But the individualism that is so pervasive works to prevent this. Needless to say, the possibility of a bodybuilders' union, as was attempted in 1979, is doomed from the start.

Feudal Organization and Bodybuilding

Despite their individualism, bodybuilders do in fact form a community, rooted in their physical distinctiveness and what it symbolizes. Forced in upon themselves, bodybuilders have fashioned a subculture in Southern California's more tolerant climate. The gym, various contests, Muscle Beach, and media hype are additional factors making possible the expression of the subculture. In this context their individualism is actually fused into a social system that allows them their atomism while concealing social bonds. This social system has many traits in common with a feudal social system, yet exists within capitalism (Klein, 1981, 1985a).

To the outsider the gym appears as either a group-grope or a collection of individuals, yet there exists a clearly demarcated social hierarchy as well as different strata of political and economic entities. Beginning with the latter, and borrowing the feudal analogy, bodybuilding has a small class of powerful lords consisting of the largest entrepreneurs such as the Weider organization and to a lesser extent Olympic Gym. Beneath them and tied to individual lords through ties of dependence, one finds the various professional bodybuilders. These men and women vie with one another not only for prize money in contests but for closer political ties with the moguls. Amateurs competing for limited access to these same mentors, as well as the larger category of noncompetitive bodybuilders, are the serfs. They serve in the capacity of consumers for the products generated by the other strata.

The key to this feudal structure is the tie of personal dependence. Within each strata individuals compete for rank and economic opportunity, the result being the creation of vertical ties at the expense of horizontal ones. The primary relationship is one between a mentor and a subordinate, between a mogul and a bodybuilder. The paternalistic giants in turn vie with one another for the allegiance of the competitors. Group solidarity is virtually impossible in such a milieu, a condition that allows for an exaggerated view of individual autonomy.

One of the most sought after rewards for the aspiring bodybuilder is magazine space for one's ads.[4] Here is what several candid bodybuilders had to say about the control exercised over the access to ad space:

Of course it [success in the magazines] all depends on who you are. Tom P. and R. get a gratis thing [free ad space]. I know that Joe Weider doesn't like me, but then he doesn't like others also. I remember he said that R. would never appear in *Muscle and Fitness* but he did an article on him anyway. And somebody said that they heard Weider say that I didn't exist as far as he was concerned. But then I know that Joe is considering me for *Flex* ... oh he wants to sell me but he doesn't wanna work with me.

A. used to go to Joe [Weider]. He was one of the intermittent people. He wouldn't get a lot but he'd get something. He would never get a mail order ad, but he would get a couple hundred bucks when his face appeared in the magazine, whereas everybody else has to be perfect and kiss their ass to get in the mag. Then A. found out that if he asked Joe for help, "Joe, I need some help in my posing." Or "Joe, my diet. I can't get it quite right." You know, make him feel as if he's needed. Well it worked to get him in.

Responding to my question in 1979 regarding a failed attempt to put together a bodybuilders' union by some people at the gym, one top professional dismissed it, revealing the feudal-like political structure in the subculture:

I don't think bodybuilders need a union. The IFBB [the largest international federation in the sport, created and presided over by the Weiders] operates with the best interests of bodybuilders in mind. Whenever problems arise they're willing to listen and legislate or change the situation for the better. I think if things were so bad that there had to be a union, there would have been a union.

Social Organization of Olympic

Because of its influential position in the sport, a gym like Olympic has a unique social organization. Six distinct hierarchically organized groups exist. These are arranged in pyramid fashion, with the members constituting the largest group.

- Owners
- Professional bodybuilders
- Amateur bodybuilders
- Gym rats (noncompetitors)
- Members at large
- Onlookers and Pilgrims

The first three categories are self-explanatory and not particularly unusual except that at Olympic one tends to find whole clusters of professionals and amateurs, whereas at most gyms finding one is unusual. The category of gym rat is worth describing, however. All serious gyms have these men and women at their core. They come in religiously and train hard, but are distinguished from pros and amateurs because they do not compete. Hence, in gym hierarchies gym rats have less status. Members comprise that category of people who train less than the other categories. Of gym regulars, they have the least status, often not even looking like bodybuilders.

There's a pecking order with guys like Mike at the top. Maybe I'm put in there too. In terms of who gets to use a piece of equipment if three guys are waiting for it, and other things having to do with the gym.

Olympic, however, has another category of people who do not belong to the gym. Onlookers and pilgrims come there either to satisfy their curiosity or because they are bodybuilders who come to pay homage to the place. Since they are constant presences in the gym, they are given a place in the front of the gym. Commenting on the removal of one line of gym equipment that had brought in a flood of outsiders, one competitor summed up insider/outsider relations:

I'm kinda glad the water machines are out of the gym. I felt like I was training in a showroom. Those machines brought in a lotta sales people . . . and there was always those weirdos in business suits watching us all the time.

Get outta here. Go up there [pointing to the balcony] where all the weirdos gawk. I mean, where people train, you gotta prove yourself to be accepted. There's a lotta non-people in the gym, people who shouldn't be here.

This pyramidal organization is not a conscious one. Little in the way of formal organizational properties can be found in bodybuilding other than the organizing bodies that govern competition. Within the gym the only formal relationship is the training partnership. Usually made up of two (but sometimes three) people, training partners are responsible for pushing each other to their limits to enhance physical goals. This bond is formal and recognized as distinct from all other relationships. It is also a brittle bond, often lasting only as long as the preparatory period before a contest. Yet, through these partnerships a sequence of tentative bonds emerges, linking people in the gym together. The rarified nature of these bonds was succinctly stated by one female competitor: "It's easy to find a boyfriend, but a training partner is hard to find."

Health Versus Illness

In the past few years fitness and health have been the bodybuilder's ticket to cultural respectability. Weider changed the name of his magazine to reflect his going from *Muscle Power* to *Muscle and Fitness*. Bodybuilders now view themselves as nutritional and kinesiological experts, and for a fee will counsel others on matters of diet and training. Up on all the latest research in pop kinesiology, each has his or her idiosyncratic road to vigor and health and hypes it in comic books, exercise books, mail order ads, or most recently as guru-trainers to the stars. Certainly, in terms of fashioning their bodies into whatever form they desire, bodybuilders are advanced. Not only do they know what combinations of goods to consume, but also how to bulk up (increase mass) or cut up (reduce subcutaneous fat) on demand. This is fused with a mind-boggling array of weight training routines.

Self-mastery is the goal. Experiencing each repetition and calorie in terms of an overall plan for physical transformation is the means. One man had so mastered himself in terms of diet, training, and routine that he had no need of an alarm clock. At precisely 7:30 each morning he awoke with the urge to evacuate his bowels; at 11:30 A.M. his breakfast and food supplements were just kicking in and he could commence a 3-hour workout. Another had not missed a daily or twice-daily workout in 5 years. Illness is anathema, an admission of having failed to do things properly. Nutritional Calvinism is the philosophical tenet: bodybuilding success is partially predetermined (i.e., genetic), but good protein, complex carbohydrates, training, and so forth can help one realize his or her predetermined potential.

In direct contradiction to their public boasting of fitness and strength, we find bodybuilders' use of steroids and other drugs to be widespread. Despite the profoundly negative effects of steroids on health (e.g., the carcinogenic effects and negative impact on the liver), steroid use is virtually universal among male competitors and increasingly frequent among women and noncompetitors:

They all use drugs, even the Mr. Naturals. That year that S. won the Olympia [a professional contest], he told me that he used more drugs that year than he'd ever used in his whole life. They all use 'em, and when they say they don't, they're lying.

Drug peddling is so common among bodybuilders that conversations about drugs and drug deals are barely concealed. As well versed as these people are in matters of training and nutrition, they are equally unquestioning and naive on the subject of drugs. For instance, thyroid prescriptions from other countries are not even translated into English. In one instance this lead to an overdosing just before a contest:

> I had a reaction to thyroid medication. . . . I heard so much about a European product, I did something I hadn't been guilty of in the past—using it without knowing about it . . . I had all the symptoms of hyperthyroidism: nervousness, irritability, weakness, dizziness. You kinda feel subjected which is stupid, but you change so much during the last weeks before a contest. I mean bodybuilding is obviously not a healthy endeavor.

Drug related conversations are, ironically, quite lively, with a considerable sharing of information and misinformation. This is in marked contrast to other kinds of conversations.

The schizophrenic relationship of bodybuilding to steroid use involves outright denial and manifests itself in accusing others of drug abuse:

> I think we [referring to himself and friend] have the potential to be the best. All these guys [pointing around the gym] take steroids and we don't. Our structure is perfect. We don't take a lot. We been on steroids three times now [in the past 12 months].

In magazines bodybuilders espouse a competitive life free of steroids. Advice columns reject drugs as dangerous and not all that effective. Yet, among themselves they continue to consume dangerous quantities:

> Q. Did you use a lot of steroids over a long period?
>
> A. When I quit using steroids I had trouble finding a spot on my ass that I could inject.
>
> Q. Why?
>
> A. Cuz, calcium deposits build up when you inject certain steroids. And I'd been on a long cycle [using the drug for a protracted period].

One well-known pro read his own advice column aloud in the gym in mocking tones. As he read his quote on banning steroids, he and the others gathered around him rolled with laughter.

The top pros know best how to use as little of the "right" drugs and get the results needed. But lesser lights have little knowledge of drugs and experi-

ment freely on themselves. First-timers on oral steroids were, from time to time, seen doubled over in the corner of the gym. Another man handed me a box of hormones he was taking. The label cautioned, "Not to be used on horses that will be used for food."

The reason for drug use is that they help resolve a physical dilemma. The bodybuilder has to be as big as possible, yet achieve maximum muscular striation (getting "cut up"). This combination is usually incompatible. To facilitate striation a bodybuilder must diet down (perhaps as little as 1,000 calories a day) near contest time, but in doing so jeopardizes strength and the ability to retain size. Steroids are allegedly capable of enhancing strength and granting size, and in so doing permit one to continue to be large and achieve striation through dieting.

The extreme dieting preceding a contest also exacts a toll on the body as well as on the psyche. In conjunction with the anxiety surrounding the competition, many are not only weak but irritable as well. This is a time when bodybuilders lash out. Steroids only increase aggressiveness, and confrontations are kept to a minimum by judiciously limiting all social interaction. Immediately before the contest many even take diuretics to increase the striated look and overcome the bloating effect that many steroids create. As one pro said, "When we walk on stage we are closer to death than we are to life."

Courting dehydration and exhaustion, pumped with a variety of steroids and other drugs, many bodybuilders no longer represent the picture of health they so busily promote. Citing the prison he felt competition symbolized for him, one informant commented on his retirement that he was happy because, "I'll never have to take my shirt off again. From here on I train for me."

Following the contest there is an institutional gorging, accurately termed "pigging out." In groups and singly, bodybuilders go out to eat vast quantities of food. In a single evening some will gain 15 pounds. On one occasion an informant consumed 7 pies. Another downed 24 donuts. The way binging and dieting occur institutionalizes borderline bulimic and anorexic behavior. These we know are syndromes involving intrapsychic disorders, but in bodybuilding they become structured into an acceptable cultural product. Epidemiological research suggests, however, that rapid weight fluctuation is positively correlated with certain forms of cancer and cardiac irregularities.

As with so much of bodybuilding, the behavior is based on shortsightedness. Steroids foster short-term success at the risk of long-term illness. Underlying this preoccupation with the immediate is the demand for the new wealth coming to the sport. This collective grasping takes its sense of urgency from bodybuilding's past isolation and the fact it was held in disrepute. As late as the mid-1970s almost no practitioner could make a living from the sport. With the fitness movement in the United States came the opportunity for many who labored in obscurity to make money in the sport. Thus, the relative deprivation has had the effect of negating long-term, rational considerations. The apparent deleterious impact of drugs is explained away through a series of pseudoscientific facts that claim the contrary—that in moderation and in the right dosages one can use steroids without ill effects. Hence, the contradiction between health and illness is understood as an historico-economic problem, and one that will continue until the rewards are not so great.

Heterosexuality and Hustling

Heterosexuality is enshrined in the pages of *Muscle and Fitness*. Each issue abounds with full-color ads of men and women together, enjoying each other in some wholesome way. Forty years ago Charles Atlas' ads ran in comic books and also reinforced heterosexuality. In both Weider's and Atlas' ads the message is that if one looks like a man some woman will drape herself over him.

> Ya know in every age the women, they always go for the guy with muscles, the bodybuilder. [The women] never go for the studious guy. (Weider interview, March 1980)

The Atlas ad scenario underscores the same perspective. It begins with a young man out to impress his girl. They run into the physically imposing beach bully who insults the skinny man and kicks sand in his face, all of which is perceived as being emasculated. The girl is miraculously impressed with the bully's display, or so we are led to believe. An ad in his comic book leaps out at our unlikely hero, promising him a secure and permanent grip on his masculinity: a big body. Weeks later he avenges himself upon the bully by outsizing him and meting out physical punishment. In the course of this ludicrous scenario the woman is impressed and content to become the prize.

Size, masculinity, and physical appeal are equated with bodybuilding, and through magazines and ads that work by invidious comparison, they are hyped to an insecure public. Weider's latter-day versions of Atlas ads have not changed. The sexism is still present in his images of fit women seemingly delighted in being dwarfed by their he-men. The men all hold large impressive weights, while the women hold smaller, chrome plated versions of the same. It exaggerates their weakness to be cast in these scenes, but sales of these magazines have risen dramatically in the past 6 years.

For all this heterosexual posturing, bodybuilding has long existed under a cloud of suspicion. Be it the inordinate attention paid to oneself, the preoccupation with prancing about on stage wearing as little as possible, or an awareness that for all that form there is little function behind bodybuilding, many outsiders see bodybuilders as somehow associated with homosexuality.

Americans are perhaps the most homophobic people in the world. Crosscultural analysis on the subject indicates that most societies are not nearly as fearful of homosexuality (Karlen, 1971). In enculturating young men we seek to instill in them the notion that one's masculinity is determined in direct proportion to the repudiation of anything deemed homosexual. The latter is based in negative associations men have of women, and involves negating those traits. For many the ultimate man is the most macho-looking and sounding, the most aggressive-appearing and acting. "Real" men do not wince in the face of pain or trouble; they do not emote freely. Anything falling outside of this is considered weak and unfit, that is, womanly. The final link in this line of reasoning is that should one be biologically male, yet behave as a weakling or a woman, then he is an a priori candidate for homosexuality.

Building one's body becomes a necessary part of achieving the desired state of heterosexuality for many men. Hence, little boys are taught a modified version of the military male model: tough, disciplined, and stoic. Popular culture reinforces this as young boys are inundated with heroes such as Hulk Hogan, Rambo, or bodybuilder Arnold Schwarzenegger as Conan or the Terminator. Anthony Wallace (1970) has shown what the negative consequences of such one-dimensional expectations were for the 18th-century Iroquois Indian warriors. Buried under hypermasculine behavior, it was difficult for them to show need, dependency, or softness; and the greater the need the more it needed to be displaced. Caught in a similar quandary, many bodybuilders simultaneously search for requisite masculinity and a repudiation of homosexuality.

Ironically, the selling of sexual favors to gay men is widespread in Southern California bodybuilding. Estimates of the activity range from 40% to 75% depending on who is queried.[5] It is called "hustling" by people at the gym, but it only involves the male members of the community. Hustling is a range of transactions involving a bodybuilder and a gay male. Only on rare occasions is a woman the procurer of sexual favors. The act of hustling may entail selling one's time for "beefcake" photographs, or nude dancing at all-male events, but primarily it involves sexual acts. The latter might be passive or active, depending on one's conscience. Hustling is seen as distinct from being gay, a dichotomy made by both bodybuilders as well as myself. The two may merge, as when a gay bodybuilder engages in the act of hustling, but informants pointed out that very few of the bodybuilders they knew who hustled were also gay.

The process by which a bodybuilder moves from his conscious heterosexual upbringing to hustling is complex. Hustling is not found equally often among all strata in the gym. Pros, for instance, do not hustle that much, while amateurs do so relatively more frequently. The bulk of this behavior is found among males who compete but do not as yet earn any real income from bodybuilding. Elsewhere (Klein, n.d., chapter 8) I have interpreted male hustling as an "economic strategy," engaged in primarily by amateurs and noncompetitors. The reason for it is that amateurs have made the commitment to train full-time for competition but do not have enough economic security to do so. Proper training is an outgrowth of leisure time and money—time to mentally prepare oneself, to engage in lengthy training sessions. Given the educational background and work histories of most male bodybuilders, it is unlikely they would have the sorts of jobs that would allow them to train effectively. In Southern California, men train for the most prestigious contests (e.g., the Mr. California, or Gold's Classic, or the pro Mr. Universe or Mr. Olympia shows). This increases the caliber of training needed. The economic dilemma is answered through the gay community (or segments of it) that exist on the periphery of the subculture. Hustling is easy to initiate because of the proximity of men willing to pay for it. Once a hustler achieves any degree of security and can generate his own money, hustling is usually left behind.

There is a second and growing category of hustler—the bodybuilder who trains full-time without intending to compete. This man hustles purely to pay for his bodybuilding lifestyle. He has no intention of working his way up the ranks, and the presence of greater numbers of these men has been noted by many of the older informants who have been at Olympic for years (Klein fieldnotes, October, 1985).

Jennifer James' (1973) analysis of female prostitution holds valuable insights for this interpretation of hustling. She points out that for many of the young runaways who venture into the world of prostitution, the path is lined with people offering shelter and friendship but who, after a time, demand a payment (most often sexual). For young girls faced with the sudden pressure to reciprocate sexually for favors they thought were offered freely, the response is often based on guilt, shame, and capitulation. The sex they experience with their one-time protector or friend is often seen as the fall that makes all subsequent sex a moot point, and so they can move on to prostitution.

For many of the young men who go to Southern California and expect to be instantly successful at bodybuilding, the initial indifference they encounter can be jolting. Few come prepared emotionally, or with enough money to pay the dues demanded by the sport and lifestyle. These men are often the targets of advances made by other men. At first it might be just a token of friendship as when someone offers a badly needed job, or steroids, but later it is for services rendered. The quandary is quickly realized and while some bodybuilders reject these advances, many do not. It should also be noted that many hustlers as well as homophobic bodybuilders tend to see advances even where they don't exist. Hustling represents quick money, freeing them to train and meet expenses. To assuage guilt and facilitate acceptance of their impending status change, the men flirting with hustling will list all the great bodybuilders who have engaged in this behavior.

> People don't realize that in any given lineup of 20 competitors 10 are hustling.
>
> We have always had gays in the gym. . . . I learned from _____ who was hustling, that all the guys were doing it and that really opened my eyes. But now there is such a heavy gay concentration in the gym.

Hardly anyone is spared, allowing the novice to feel that hustling is a rite of passage rather than a deviant act.

Interviews taken also point to compartmentalization of experience, a psychological device that allows one to separate out kinds of behavior that might be contradictory or otherwise problematic. Hence, straight life is separated from the hustling life. As with any defensive strategy, however, it can at times break down. At that point the suppressed anxiety surrounding homophobia manifests itself in hostile encounters toward gays. The very people who hustle most often are the ones who talk endlessly about their women and sexual conquests around other bodybuilders, thereby denying anything that might implicate them. The following is typical of the line of reasoning given for *not* going out with women while hustling, that is, that they are too demanding.

> On any given time I can go out with a woman, but it's not very satisfying like a regular relationship. Women demand time. I don't have that right now. I lived with that girl [points to a photo] for a year and a half, but it's not that good. Several know what I'm doing. Some can handle it, some can't. I can't lie so that's why I'm not living with anyone until I get older.

The Jekyll-and-Hyde life they fashion enables them to juggle opposing moralities, but often the contradictions surface as hatred (often violent) of gays. Sometimes it takes the form of self-loathing and guilt, which on more than a few occasions has led to repudiation of the lifestyle and replacing it with Born Again Christianity. At other times it has led to suicide attempts. Reiss (1973) in his study of street hustlers documents the hatred that the hustlers had for gays. This expression of homophobia performs the function of separating the "peer" (hustler) from the "queer" (Reiss, 1973: 404-406). It is likewise found among bodybuilders I interviewed:

> I'll tell you being involved with the whole thing [hustling] reaffirmed my whole thing [being straight]. I remember in Venice I was involved in that, you know, community and saw so much that I began to wonder about their sanity and mine.

> Maybe 75% of the judges on any panel are gay. Well, they might understand this [the sane view of hustling] at the same time that they might hold it against you: the fact that you're working in that gay world, taking advantage of their people.

Here we see how hustling may fuel a hustler's homophobia as well as resentment on the part of gays. Viewing gays in a predatory way allows the hustler to continue the charade that lets him separate out his "straight self" identity from the hustling behavior he engages in. Gays who regularly seek sexual favors from bodybuilders often see the relation as predatory as well. Comments about getting the best of the deal are typical.

The positive role of gays in the world of bodybuilding, however, cannot be denied. As a group, bodybuilders tend to have (or have had) a poor sense of self. They generally require a strong dose of material and emotional support. It is in this context that various gay men have played a substantial role. When the society at large was indifferent or even hostile to bodybuilders, members of the gay community would lend support and admire them by acting in the capacity of fans and defenders. Gays essentially subsidized the sport in the difficult days of bodybuilding when the sport paid little.

The reasons for the attention paid by gays to bodybuilders stems from a psychological complex that merges heterosexual and homosexual issues. One is the notion that bodily form (and overall looks) is best understood and appreciated in a nonerotic way by members of the same sex. I refer here to the many studies pointing out that men dress for other men rather than for women, and the converse of that. This is based in part on self-love extended to encompass our gender, or appreciation of our gender as an extension of ourselves. I would call this *gender narcissism*, and it is universal, essential in the formation of bonds among members of the same sex. The excessive homophobia in our society, however, fosters a view of this otherwise healthy expression of gender narcissism as too close to homosexuality to allow expression. That gays have historically been supportive of bodybuilding therefore is seen in all cases to result from their erotic desires. The broader appreciation stemming from gender narcissism is fused with the erotic and suppressed. In doing so, however, we deny the capacity to appreciate any extension of our gender. Women, being less homophobic than men, are less likely to do this. It is, for instance, deemed suitable for women to state how attractive another woman may be, while one rarely hears something comparable from one man to/or about another.

The concern with presenting the sport in the best possible light has resulted in expunging any association with homosexuality and narcissism. The subculture of bodybuilding raises this possibility more than any other sport, but ultimately asks the question of sport itself.

Conclusion

In this study I have attempted to show how each publicly expressed value is created and then, because of the sport's need for acceptance, betrayed. New relations, within the subculture and between the subculture and society, stem from its increasing incorporation into contemporary capitalism. As a result a series of quasi-contradictions are brought to the fore. While the world of bodybuilding never envisioned itself as an alternative to status quo society, it nevertheless developed atypically and so fell within the domain of deviant subculture.

The sticking point that prevented greater cultural acceptance of the sport of bodybuilding has always been the vanity factor in addition to the sexual suspicions cast on its practitioners. Contrary to the Protestant Ethic, preoccupation with the body was seen as a frivolous, self-indulgent exercise in vanity. Recruitment to the subculture, however, stems from real, felt unmet needs and personality deficiencies. In short, poor self-image lurks in the background of most bodybuilders.

> I got caught up in the sport just cuz I was thin, and I wanted to put some body weight on, you know, get big.

> I was picked on when I was a kid. There was no support from my parents. I was always wrong in my parents' eyes.

> I was never dated, not even for the senior prom. . . . People used to laugh at me when I'd wear a bikini. They'd call me chicken legs. Now I can walk through a crowd and people go, "Check her out, what a bod."

Poor body image also results from emotional and other handicaps. Dyslexia, stuttering, eye problems, along with short stature and weight problems, were all documented as factors contributing to low self-worth among people at Olympic Gym. Considering their low self-esteem, mainstream views of bodybuilders as narcissistic and vain misses the point (Klein, n.d., chapter 9). This study sees the narcissism institutionalized in bodybuilding as therapeutic, a view also shared with bodybuilders who see it as a mark of how far they've personally come.

> Well, I would say that as a bodybuilder you have your mind so much into your body. You have to keep thinking positive. You may not be falling in love with your body, but you are positive that you're great in looking at yourself. I noticed that when I was more in love with my body and I'd look in the mirror; I dunno, it's something to do with muscle and

pain. Your mind has to be so positive. In the gym you have to be in love with your workout. You have to think about your pump [muscle worked to the point of failure]. So in a way I would have to say that bodybuilders are in love with themselves.

> These guys are drawn to bodybuilding for some reason, insecurities or whatever. That's why they flare their lats out like that.

Q. Do you think they're narcissistic?

A. Have you looked at the guys in this gym? Damn straight they're narcissistic. It's gotta be cuz of where these guys' heads are at, you know, insecurity.

It is at this point that deviant and occupational subcultures merge into a single category. The labeling of bodybuilders as deviant is then stood upon its head by the bodybuilders who turn the stigma into status-bearing criteria (cf., Hebdige, 1983). Thus narcissism becomes essential, leading to perfection, and hypermasculinity becomes the Mr. Olympia form.

More recently, the society at large seems to be altering its views on bodybuilding. Matza and Sykes (1961) point out that values associated with the dramatic rise of leisure since World War II foster a change in views of deviance. Values centering on excitement, disdain for work, hedonism, masculinity, and toughness are socially more highly regarded, and these are traits central to the bodybuilding subculture. Bodybuilding, then, stands to gain cultural acceptance by virtue of being what was previously most reprehensible, that is, self-indulgent, narcissistic, excessive, and sexually exotic.

Ironically the sport of bodybuilding has, according to its premier publication, chosen just this time to stress traditionally held cultural values such as hard work, wholesomeness of family, filial piety, God and country. Ideologues in this sport have missed the point that it is the oft-held view of bodybuilding as lurid, seamy, and excessive that is at the core of its newfound appeal. Instead, cover photos depict hulking men with their wives, girlfriends, or a model, but always lacking sexuality. Articles heralding the virtues of nutrition and drug-free lives abound, not to mention clichés about hard work and Horatio Alger snippets by the truckload. It is likewise ironic that many suspicions once held by outsiders turn out to have more than an element of truth. However, now those suspicions are fashionable—vanity and hedonism are in, as attested to by the popularity of the looks and messages of rock stars such as Madonna, Prince, and David Lee Roth.

In the course of this obstacle-strewn path to success, bodybuilding seeks to pay homage to tradition while appearing postmodern. This often creates more questions. As with the adult who earlier suffered humiliation, much of later life is spent responding to that hurt. So it is with bodybuilding, which can never completely enjoy its newfound success. The wound is historic and institutionalized as a set of behaviors. The recent rise in popularity of that subculture has generated a crisis in confidence because so much of the subculture was premised on social stigma that removing the barriers threatens many of the institutions within the subculture.

The work done on subcultures (e.g., Becker, 1963; Cohen, 1955; Brake, 1980), it seems, has understood the need to look at origins of subculture but has missed the value of looking at subsequent developments, such as removal of the stigmatization that can create new problems. These problems foster conflicts within the subculture precisely, as I have tried to show, because of the change in rules and structures. Sport ethnography goes a long way toward helping social scientists discern these crises.

References

Becker, Howard. 1963. Outsiders: Studies in the Sociology of Deviance. New York: Glencoe Press.

Blanchard, Kendall and Alyce Cheska. 1985. The Anthropology of Sport. South Hadley, MA: Bergin & Garvey.

Boswell, Thomas. 1983. How Life Imitates the World Series. New York: Penguin Books.

Brake, Mike. 1980. The Sociology of Youth Culture and Youth Subcultures. London: Routledge & Kegan Paul.

Brower, Jonathan. 1975. Little League Baseballism: Adult Dominance in a Child's Game. Paper presented at Pacific Sociological Association meetings, Victoria, B.C.

Cantelon, H. and Richard Gruneau. 1982. Sport, Culture, and the Modern State. Toronto: University of Toronto Press.

Coakley, Jay. 1982. Sport in Society. St. Louis: C.V. Mosby.

Cohen, Albert K. 1955. Delinquent Boys: The Culture of the Gang. New York: The Free Press.

Daner, Francine J. 1976. The American Children of Krsna: A Study of Hare Krsna Movement. New York: Holt, Rinehart & Winston.

Devereux, Edward C. 1976. Backyard Versus Little League Baseball: The Impoverishment of Children's Games. Pp. 179-192 in D. Landers (ed.), Social Problems in Athletics. Champaign, IL: University of Illinois Press.

Diamond, Stanley. 1972. "Review, man and culture: a philosophical anthropology" (A.W. Levy, ed., Dell Publ., NY). American Anthropologist, 74(3): 304-307.

Downes, D. 1966. The Delinquent Solution. London: Routledge & Kegan Paul.

Durkheim, Emile. 1953. "Value judgements and judgements of reality." Pp.37-55 in Society and Philosophy. New York: Free Press.

Eitzen, Stanley (ed.). 1983. Sport in Contemporary Society. New York: St. Martin's Press.

Eitzen, Stanley and George Sage. 1978. Sport in American Society. Dubuque, IA: W.C. Brown.

Freilich, Morris. 1977. "The meaning of sociocultural. " Pp. 20-33 in D. Bernardi (ed.), Concepts and Dynamics of Culture. The Hague: Mouton.

Geertz, Clifford. 1972. "Deep play: notes on the Balinese cockfight." Pp. 126-141 in The Interpretation of Culture. New York: Basic Books.

Hebdige, Dick. 1983. Subculture: The Meaning of Style. London: Methuen.

James, Jennifer. 1973. "The prostitute-pimp relationship." Medical Aspects of Human Sexuality, (Nov.), pp. 147-160.

Karlen, Arno. 1971. Sexuality and Homosexuality. New York: Norton.

Keixer, Lincoln. 1979. The Vice Lords: Warriors of the Streets (2nd Ed.). New York: Holt, Rinehart & Winston.

Klein, Alan M. 1981. "The master blaster: empire building and bodybuilding." Arena Review, 5(3): 12-15.

Klein, Alan M. 1985a. "Muscle manor: the use of sport metaphor and history in sport sociology." Journal of Sport and Social Issues, 9(1): 4-19.

Klein, Alan M. 1985b. "Pumping Iron." Society, 22(6): 68-75.

Klein, Alan M. n.d. No Pain, No Gain: The Subculture of Bodybuilding. In preparation.

Lee, Richard. 1979. The Kung San: Men, Women, and Work in a Foraging Society. Cambridge, UK: Cambridge University Press.

Leonard, W. 1980. A Sociological Perspective of Sport. Minneapolis: Burgess.

Lever, Janet. 1983. Soccer Madness. Chicago: University of Chicago Press.

Liebow, Elliot. 1969. Tally's Corner. Boston: Little, Brown & Co.

Linton, Ralph. 1945. The Cultural Background of Personality. New York: Appleton-Century-Crofts.

Lipsyte, Robert. 1975. Sportsworld: An American Dreamland. New York: New York Times Books.

Loy, J.W., B.D. McPherson and G.S. Kenyon (eds.). 1978. Sport and Social Systems. Reading, MA: Addison-Wesley.

Matza, David. 1964. Delinquency and Drift. New York: Wiley & Sons.

Matza, David. 1969 Becoming Deviant. Englewood Cliffs, NJ: Prentice-Hall.

Matza, D. and G. Sykes. 1961. "Techniques of neutralization." American Sociological Review, 27(4): 667-670.

Muscle and Fitness.1979-1984. Woodland Hills, CA: Weider Enterprises.

Phillips, J. and W. Shafer. 1971. "Athletics, aspirations, and attainments." Sociology of Education, 42(l): 102-113.

Reiss, A. 1973. "The social integration of peers and queers." In E. Rubington and M. Weinberg (eds.), Deviance: The Interactionist Perspective. New York: MacMillan.

Schwartzman, Helen B. (ed.). 1980. Play and Culture. West Point, NY: Leisure Press.

Sewart, John. 1983. Trash Sports. Paper delivered at 4th Annual Meeting of North American Society for Sociology of Sport , St. Louis.

Spradley, James. 1970. You Owe Yourself a Drunk. Boston: Little, Brown & Co.

Spradley, James and Patricia Mann. 1975. The Cocktail Waitress. New York: Wiley & Sons.

Sprague, Homer. n.d. Psychological profiles of bodybuilders. (unpublished manuscript).

Stevens, Phillips. 1977. Studies in the Anthropology of Play. West Point, NY: Leisure Press.

Tindall, B. Allen. 1975. "The cultural transmissive function of physical education." Council on Anthropology and Education Quarterly, 16(2): 10-20.

Turnbull, Colin. 1965. The Forest People. New York: Simon & Schuster.

Wallace, A.F.C. 1970. Death and Rebirth of the Seneca. New York: Alfred A. Knopf.

Notes

1. The feeling on the part of mainstream sociologists seems to be that if one teaches sport sociology, one suddenly has a joint appointment with the physical education department. Disparaging comments about those who study popular culture, media, and in this instance sports, are thinly veiled as jokes but show through as counterproductive elitism.

2. In 1983 the owners of Olympic Gym estimated their annual dues-paying members to be approximately 700, but as many as 2,000 come for shorter periods. The numbers of professional bodybuilders there range from 4 to 10 or more, amateurs from 10 to 30. Most gyms are fortunate to have a single pro or amateur in their ranks.

3. There is a term among Southern California bodybuilders for psyching out one's opponents: "the California treatment"; it is subtle, designed to destroy an adversary's confidence. Men are experts at this sort of behavior. Women have until recently been less likely to use it.

4. Ads in Weider's magazines are for the individual's mail order business. The space sells for about $2,500 per page per month. To defray the cost, a bodybuilder will seek to endorse Weider products. In return he or she will pay a reduced fee for the ad.

5. No informant I asked felt that hustling was insignificant. Most feel that it has increased in the past several years.

The Changing Gender Order in Sport?
The Case of Windsurfing Subcultures

Belinda Wheaton
Alan Tomlinson

New sports such as windsurfing have been perceived as the product of a postmodern society and culture in which sporting and physical activity offer a basis for the generation of new and multiple identities. Drawing on ethnographic work within England and across global subcultural networks, this article documents the persisting gendered basis of the subculture of windsurfing. It identifies the core principles of windsurfing's culture of commitment, the gender identities most prevalent within it, and the tension between dominant masculinity and the potentially empowering dimensions of the activity for women. The study also reiterates the importance of social class as a basis for the availability of life choices in sport and leisure, and of the centrality of ethnography and in-depth qualitative research in understanding how subcultures and their members live out gendered dynamics of power in the process of negotiating, renegotiating, and sometimes subverting the contemporary gender order.

The institutional organization of sport embeds definite social relations: competition and hierarchy among men, exclusion or domination of women. These social relations of gender are both realized and symbolized in the bodily performances. Thus

Reprinted from Wheaton and Tomlinson, 1998.

men's greater sporting prowess has become a theme of backlash against feminism. It serves as symbolic proof of men's superiority and right to rule. (Connell, 1995, p. 54)

Historically, sport has been so closely identified with men—and masculinity—that the two have become synonymous in many Western societies. Sport is among the most masculine of social institutions, created "by and for men" (Messner & Sabo, 1990, p. 9). These "cults of male physicality" encourage "men to identify with other men and provides for regular rehearsal of such identification" (Whitson, 1990, p. 21). A plethora of feminist-inspired critiques of sport institutions have demonstrated sport's role in the "structural and ideological domination of women by men" (Messner & Sabo, 1990, p. 2). Sport is a cultural space that has contributed to male empowerment and female disadvantage, and has thus played an important role in the reproduction of male hegemony (see Bryson, 1987; Hargreaves, 1994; Messner & Sabo, 1990).

It has been argued that a proving ground for masculinity, such as sport, can only be preserved by the exclusion of women from the activity (Whitson, 1990). Yet since the 1970s, women have penetrated many sporting spheres. With some erosion of male spatial domination, the role sport plays in the reproduction and/or transformation of contemporary relations between, and within, the sexes is a prime concern.

The Windsurfing Subculture

Windsurfing is a sport with a short history, having only been in existence since the late 1960s. In common with many other new or postmodern sports (see Wheaton & Tomlinson, 1995) that have emerged over the past 20 years—such as snowboarding, skateboarding, in-line skating, and mountain biking—windsurfing portrays a public image that emphasizes individuality, freedom, hedonism, and an anticompetition ethos. These characteristics differentiate windsurfing from more traditional, rule-bound, competitive, and "masculinized" sport cultures, themselves marked by combative competition, aggression, courage, and toughness. As Whannel highlights: "To be good at sport is to be strong, virile and macho" (Whannel, 1983, pp. 28-29; cited in Tomlinson, 1997, p. 138); sport is central to being a "real man." Thus, although traditional competitive institutionalized sport in Britain has been a central site for the creation and reaffirmation of masculine identities and the exclusion/control of women, are gender relations in alternative sports cultures like windsurfing renegotiated or even reconstructed? Does windsurfing afford women (and "other" men) opportunities to construct identities and control their own lives through the embodied experience of sport? As Hargreaves (1994) has highlighted, there is a need for empirical studies of sport that examine the lived realities of men's and women's sporting experience, particularly how changing values are linked to evolving masculinities and femininities in sport. In the spirit of Hargreaves' challenge, in this article we draw upon ethnographic work on leisure subcultures, conducted during 1994-1996, which focused on a windsurfing community on the south coast of England. The day-to-day experiences of the women within the windsurfing subculture are our primary focus.

The ethnography demonstrates that women's involvement in the subculture is heterogeneous and contradictory. The meaning of femininity and "being a woman" differs between groups of women in the subculture. For some of the women, windsurfing participation is an empowering experience and an important site for the creation and negotiation of a cultural identity that is detached from their roles as mothers and from their partners. For others, their lack of involvement and passivity conforms to traditional gender roles.

Gender Identities in Sport: Masculinities and Femininities

Over the past decade, the impact of the "difference" debates in feminism (and the social sciences more broadly) has contributed to a more fluid theory of gender within the sociology of sport. Carrigan, Connell, and Lee (1987), for example, describe the "gender order," in which gender is seen as a dynamic relational process, not a thing. Thus, as Messner and Sabo (1990) highlight, feminist theory that defines masculinity and femininity as separate and dichotomous entities ignores the processes through which power relations between men and women are constructed, negotiated, and contested (Messner & Sabo, 1990, p. 13). However, a feminist sensitivity to difference insists not only that gender is conceived as a continuum, but that the varied types of social oppression, such as diversity in race, ethnicity, class, sexuality, age, and religion, among women are considered (Hall, 1996). As Scraton (1994) argues,

> There is a need to research around difference in order to understand difference. We need to explore the leisure worlds of women. . . . It is only by starting from everyday experiences that we will be able to recognize the importance of difference and the significance of shared experiences. (p. 258)

The research reported in this article explores the similarities as well as the discords between the experiences of men and women windsurfers within the specific historical context and space of this leisure culture. Through the use of extensive interview vignettes, the multiplicity and complexity of the women's experiences are emphasized. In the wider research project (Wheaton, 1997a), some of the key issues about gendered identities and experiences within the windsurfing culture are explored, focusing in particular on the "discrepancies and contradictions" (Tomlinson, 1997, p. 137) of being male and female in the windsurfing culture. The demonstration of sporting prowess was identified as an important aspect of peer approval, which was achieved in relation to other men: men of other abilities (those who were less committed, less skilled, and less "go for it"); different ages, ethnicities; sexualities; socioeconomic categories; as well as in relation to women. Examining the relationships between men in the windsurfing culture has illustrated that although windsurfing is predominantly a site where middle-class white men construct masculine identities, a range of masculinities exists, each competing to become dominant, or hegemonic.

Methodology

The research from which the empirical data are drawn included three phases within an ethnographic approach.

- An 18-month participant observation phase focused on a windsurfing community centered on Silver Sands beach on the south coast of England. However, other beaches and communities were also observed along the south coast, the west country, and specific field trips abroad. As the field-worker was an active member of the subculture under study, and a journalist working for a British windsurfing magazine, the most appropriate approach for the participant observation phase was a complete participant role (Hammersley & Atkinson, 1983). So the field-worker adopted a covert role based on her established role within the group, and her familiarity with the main setting under observation (see Wheaton, 1995).
- In-depth, unstructured interviews were undertaken with 25 selected members of the British windsurfing community to develop the themes that evolved during the observation phase.
- A media research phase followed, linking analysis of media texts (windsurfing magazines and videos) with consideration of their consumption in the lived culture.[1]

In this article we draw upon all three sources of data for the overall interpretation, but participant observation and in-depth interviews supplied most of the reported data.

Women in the Windsurfing Subculture

The windsurfing sport and its culture were clearly dominated by men. Between 80% and 90% of the windsurfers who used Silver Sands, the main location in this ethnographic work, were male, with even higher proportions in the winter. The situation was similar at other coastal locations nearby, although according to traditional survey research, women constitute 30% of regular windsurfers around the United Kingdom (British Market Research Bureau, 1995).

Feminists investigating women's leisure have drawn attention to the gendered nature of leisure participation and demonstrated the nexus of structural, material, practical, and ideological constraints that severely limit the opportunities for women to indulge in active leisure, and particularly sport (see, e.g., Green, Hebron, & Woodward, 1989). Windsurfing, which places great demands on the participant's time, is a sport that is conducted in specific geographic locations and is often inaccessible by public transport. Furthermore, progress involves considerable capital expenditure (see Turner, 1983).[2] The recurring nature of such constraints and their effects on women's restricted participation in leisure and sport must be recognized as the backdrop to detailed studies of particular leisure and sport forms.

Privileged Women

At Silver Sands, almost all of the women who windsurfed were "privileged women": able-bodied, fairly well-off, and all but one were white. Most were professional women aged between 20 and 40 and not reliant on their partners for their income. Although Silver Sands is located in a particularly affluent part of Britain, survey data gathered nationally suggested that British women who windsurf regularly tended to be middle class, and in particular, professional women (Profile Sport Consultancy, 1994). Likewise, the 15 women interviewed in the study were all white, heterosexual women.[3] Their ages ranged from 22 to 66 and their commitment to windsurfing ranged from occasional participant to addict, including two who worked in the windsurfing industry (as competitors or teachers). They were predominantly middle-class women in professional employment such as teaching, advertising, promotions, journalism, and medicine. Two women were students, and one was retired.

Nevertheless, despite such shared characteristics, women's involvement in the subculture is contradictory and multiple. Women's association with the windsurfing subculture ranged from those who did not windsurf—in some cases, their partner's involvement in windsurfing was hated and resented—to women for whom windsurfing was a central part of their lives. Although in this article it is the experiences of the active sport women that are the primary focus, it is important to recognize the diversity of women's experience and the concomitant feminine identities in the windsurfing subculture. This is illustrated in the following brief description of the world of the "windsurfing widows," which can be usefully contrasted with the experiences and identities of the active women participants.

Traditional Gender Roles: Windsurfing Widows

Discussing the sexist nature of surfing subcultures in Australia, Fiske (1989) and Pearson (1982) comment on the gender order, where females are nonsurfers, passive, their role that of "passengers, spectators" (Fiske, 1989, p. 60). Many women's marginal role in the windsurfing subculture conformed to traditional inactive feminine roles. The windsurfers' own argot for the girlfriends or wives who spend days at the beach and are involved in the lifestyle but never or hardly ever sail, is windsurfing widows. As Scraton asserts: "Sport is seen primarily as a male pursuit bound up with masculine values. Young women spectate, support and admire: they do not expect to participate" (1987, p. 176). Many windsurfing widows of all ages did not participate in the sport, yet their leisure revolved around supporting their male partners: accompanying their partners to the beach, watching them, and supplying them with food and drink. For example,

> One smartly dressed woman in her 40s was carrying her husband's mast across the car park, which I remember thinking was an odd sight. She looked so out of place on the beach wearing "city" clothes with a windsurfing mast resting on her shoulder. I said to her "it looks like you drew the short straw—he goes windsurfing and you are carrying his kit." She replied, "as long as I don't have to get wet, I am happy." (Field notes, December 1994)

The category of windsurfing widows encompassed a variety of women, including marginal windsurfers, girlfriends, groupies,[4] and girlies. *Girlies* were predominantly younger windsurfing widows, including less committed female windsurfers, who negotiated an identity in the mixed sex environment by emphasizing their heterosexual femininity, particularly through their clothing and feminized appearance; Connell (1987) calls this "emphasised femininity" (see also Flintoff, 1997).

Women Windsurfers: "Real Women"

> Most women aren't that involved, because most women don't like the idea of getting cold. (Michael, male intermediate windsurfer)

Women windsurfers were expected to be, and mostly were, less proficient than the majority of the men. Contributing to this was the accepted convention that women were assessed by male standards of sporting prowess and commitment. Michael's statement (above) reflects a prevalent attitude, based on cultural stereotypes of femininity, that women dislike discomfort and are more interested in visual appearance than sport. Thus, women were less committed windsurfers than men (commitment was a key subcultural value). However, this stereotype of femininity, which predominates in explaining women windsurfers' behavior, does not acknowledge the diversity of experience and action, among both women and men, as highlighted by Stephanie, a core woman:

> I think you know there is that thing about "oh women won't windsurf because they don't like breaking their nails, or it's cold" and things like that. And a lot of women are like that. But I expect there's a good few men who only sail when it's warm as well. (Stephanie)

Despite the lack of expectation that women windsurfers would participate at the elite level, women could and did gain status in the subculture as active participants—albeit in distinctively gendered statuses. Yet paradoxically, as the observations of the female field-worker studying a male dominated subculture confirmed, the acceptance of women depended on their gaining status as windsurfers, not as women. One might assume that it would be hard for a female field-worker to gain full access to such a male-dominated sports culture. However, in many ways the field-worker's subcultural role was as "one of the lads." Due to her status in the subculture, based on windsurfing proficiency and commitment to the sport, she was able to participate in most sporting and social activities, including those of the core men. She had almost full access to the men's activities and conversations, including the time that their own partners were not welcome in the group.

Men's narratives also illustrate that women were respected as active sports women, and to a far greater extent than in other, more traditional sport cultures:

> Men's rugby despises women's rugby—it is seen as a joke. [But] yes, there is an awful lot of respect for the women who sail. . . . I have the greatest respect for Jane and Becky, as they are faster than I am. (Stephen, male racer)

Moreover, the women who were committed active sports participants and focused on their windsurfing gained more respect than the beach bunnies or girlies:

> The ones that are too feminine, or concentrate on being feminine have less rapport than those that get stuck in, and do the same things as men. So beach bunnies, nonsailors, definitely have less respect. (Scott)

Likewise, committed women windsurfers argued that the men differentiated them from the girlies and windsurfing widows.

> BW: Are we [windsurfing women] seen as a separate type of women by the men?
>
> Emma: Yes, . . . I definitely see that all the time. There are the women who windsurf who are actually thought of as a different breed by the men who windsurf, than the windsurfing widows, "the girlies." And the guys make comments about it . . . from more complimentary comments, like "you are the real women on the beach," to something more derogatory like "you are a man woman." We are thought of as different.

As Emma acknowledged, despite her status as a sport participant, her role as a woman windsurfer provoked a degree of ambiguity in the response of some men, highlighted by the term *man woman*. Feminists have argued that women who excel in sports that signify traditional male physicality are deemed masculine or at least not real women (Gilroy, 1989; Hargreaves, 1986).

Most men in the windsurfing culture, though, did not have that view, and real women themselves did not experience a sense of conflict between being a windsurfer and a woman.[5] Core women ardently denied that windsurfing was a masculine

sphere or that they as women were excluded. As Caroline, an elite French woman windsurfer, contended, windsurfing was an environment where women could engage in a demanding physical activity and express their femininity:

> I think if there is a sport that is made for women, then surfing and windsurfing is it, it is a sport that gives a chance to the femininity to give an expression, and because it is in a natural surrounding, you don't need to be strong . . . you only need to be strong if you do crazy loops, but not for planning, using the harness, gybing. If you have feeling you don't need to be strong, you just need to adapt your equipment. (Caroline)

Windsurfing As Empowerment: The Experiences of Real Women

> At the personal level, despite the fact that sport in Western society has been dominated by men and masculinity, the experience has been liberating for some women. (Theberge, 1987, p. 390)

Feminist theorists have explored the question of whether sports cultures are, or can potentially be, a source of women's empowerment, rather than their domination (e.g., see Birrell & Theberge, 1994; Gilroy, 1989; Hall, 1996; Hargreaves, 1994; Theberge, 1987, 1991). For many of these theorists, the empowering potential of sport is tied to its physicality: that power can be invested in the female body. As Theberge[6] argues,

> For some women, sport has become a means to realize their energy, creativity, and potential. . . . Through the bodily practice of sport some women have come to reclaim and reexperience their selves. (Theberge, 1991, p. 129)

Windsurfing is in two ways an empowering experience for some women windsurfers (see also Woodward, 1995).[7] First, the windsurfing culture is an important site of identity creation for committed women windsurfers, an environment in which female participants negotiate status and construct feminine identities as active sports participants. Second, windsurfing is a sphere in which, through corporeal activity, women windsurfers can experience and develop bodily skills and gain strength and muscularity—features that have traditionally been the source of men's empowerment (Hargreaves, 1994, p. 173).

In this article, we will focus on the former. However, although a full discussion of how women windsurfers negotiate meaning in physicality is beyond the scope of this article (see Wheaton, 1997b), we will highlight some aspects of this embodied dimension; that is, how women windsurfers who experienced their bodies as "strong and powerful, and free from male domination or control" (Theberge, 1987, p. 202) were acting as active agents, by investing power in their own bodies (Hargreaves, 1994).

Physicality and Power Invested in the Female Body

When learning to windsurf, and particularly acquiring more advanced skills, women developed stronger, more muscular bodies, especially around the upper body, arms, and shoulders. Despite skill being the main prerequisite for successful performance, there are times when brute force and determination can supplement (if not substitute for) skill and experience, such as when the wind strengthens, leaving the novice participant feeling vulnerable and unable to cope. Feeling in control in the windsurfing environment thus relates specifically to strength and confidence in the physical body. Although women, more than men, lacked confidence in their own ability, even those women whose lack of confidence severely limited their windsurfing participation argued that when they did achieve windsurfing goals it gave them a huge sense of self-achievement or confidence in themselves:

> Well I always feel better when I do start trying things out even if I fail to do them. The minute I get the courage up and spend half an hour attempting—I don't know—a duck jibe in the surf, or wherever and feel that I'm getting nearer to it I'm much happier. (Lucy)

This muscularity was associated with power and control over their bodies, which in Western cultures has historically been associated with masculinity (Bryson, 1987; Connell, 1985, 1987). Female interviewees took pleasure in their bodies during windsurfing, particularly such feelings associated with physical strength. As Lesley claimed,

> You feel stronger and more positive about yourself. If I am hooked in on a windy day, I feel strong and positive about what I am achieving. I come out and feel "yeah, like I am taking charge of the situation." . . . Windsurfing does challenge ideas about femininity—it is quite masculine, you are taking a masculine pose. (Lesley)

For many of the women interviewed, the power gained through physicality translated to a feeling of mental well-being. As elite American windsurfer Kelly Moore declared after learning to forward loop, "After that I was certain I could conquer the world" (as quoted in *Wahine*, 1996, p. 17). Women windsurfers' narratives stressed that they windsurfed for both the ephemeral bodily sensations and the more enduring feelings of mental or psychological well-being it gave them:

> Purely exhilaration. Keeping fit is an added benefit. (Claire)

Such physiological and psychological benefits of aerobic-type exercise such as windsurfing have been widely acknowledged (see Graydon, 1997; Haravon, 1995). Although, as Haravon (1995) notes, it is hard to articulate exactly how sport makes you feel better, in interviews women windsurfers expressed that they gained self-confidence not just in relation to their own windsurfing ability but also about themselves as women:

> [Windsurfing] definitely gives me confidence. If I have had a successful day's windsurfing it gives me a huge amount of confidence about myself. That is one of the reasons why I get so much out of windsurfing. . . . I feel better about myself as a person; it makes me a stronger woman. (Emma)

These experiences give support to Whitson's (1994) premise that learning and developing new skills leads to an increase in a person's confidence.[8] Moreover, as Gilroy (1997) suggests, the conversion of skill to confidence can usefully be thought of as what Bourdieu terms the conversion of physical capital to social capital, and in this windsurfing sphere, also to subcultural capital, or status. Thus, women windsurfers who experienced their bodies as "strong and powerful, and free from male domination or control" (Theberge, 1987) were acting as active agents by investing power in their own bodies (see Hargreaves, 1994).[9]

The Centrality of Leisure: Privileging Personal Pleasure

> For women who have historically been defined by their ability to nurture others, a commitment to nurture themselves, through windsurfing, or any other means, is a radical departure from what is expected of them. (Woodward, 1996, p. 6)

Studies that have demonstrated women's lack of involvement in active (and public) leisure have illustrated how ideologies of femininity contribute to women putting their domestic responsibilities and families before themselves (see, e.g., Deem, 1987). Although in this research, family commitments did curtail many women's involvement, the committed women in this research prioritized active leisure (as well as their professional careers) over traditional nurturing roles, without experience of guilt.

A Culture of Commitment

> I don't want babies because I want more time, more money. I think they are a bit of a luxury if you are a windsurfer. You know I don't want to give up windsurfing to have them. (Stephanie)

For the core members who formed the focus of this ethnographic study, windsurfing was a "culture of commitment" (Tomlinson, 1993; Wheaton & Tomlinson, 1995). Windsurfing was central in their lives: It organized their leisure time, their work time, their choice of career, and where they lived. Committed windsurfers, like surfers, defined windsurfing as a lifestyle and tended to identify with the values and culture of the defined role of windsurfer (see Farmer, 1992).

> It's a lifestyle thing. I'm willing to spend my whole year and set up my life so that when that day happens I'm ready and I can go. (Mike Waltz, professional windsurfer ("Southend on Sea," 1993, p. 70)

The core women windsurfers were dedicated, committed windsurfers, and in several cases more so than their male partners. As with dedicated men, their lifestyles were adapted to accommodate windsurfing. For example, Stephanie was an advanced windsurfer, more than 40 years old. She had been forced into part-time employment, but observed that despite her low income it gave her time and flexibility to windsurf. On several occasions, Stephanie confided in the researcher that her decision not to have children had been influenced by her desire to be able to keep windsurfing:

> I'm sailing whenever I can. . . . I never had kids because I thought it would interfere with my windsurfing too much. . . . In fact, I thought I was pregnant recently, which was one hell of a shock. . . . I don't think that it's possible to have kids and keep sailing seriously. Everyone I know that has had kids has ended up giving up the sailing, or at least it has made it very difficult. (Stephanie)

Many of the dedicated women windsurfers interviewed did not have children. They perceived that motherhood would severely limit their windsurfing. Due to the weather-dependent nature of windsurfing, it places great demands on the participants' time. Committed participants needed flexibility in their lives. Thus, it was the lack of flexibility that being a mother entailed that was deemed problematic. As Emma explained

> I'm sure it [windsurfing] has had a bearing on not wanting kids, well now—actually I can't see myself wanting kids . . . the flexibility, the need for flexibility in your life, that is a very strong need for me in my life. (Emma: core windsurfer, late 20s)

Multiple Gender Identities: Real Women's Identity in Leisure

The women whose experiences are the basis of the analysis provided in this article were advanced and expert recreational windsurfers, but they were not professionals: For them, windsurfing was no more than a "serious leisure activity" (Stebbins, 1992). Yet, their commitment to windsurfing was a disincentive to motherhood, a refusal—for the moment at least—of what has been perceived by some feminists as "the most ubiquitous element of the gender axis" (Bordo, 1990, p. 146). For many of these windsurfing women, their sense of gender identification was distinct from domesticity or their role of mother. As Bradley (1996) argues,

There are many ways of being a woman . . . awareness of gender may involve traditional ways of displaying femininity, through domestic or caring roles, motherhood, or assertion of sexuality. Given that gender experience is so differently felt by women of different ethnic groups, age, religions, nationalities or sexual orientations, it is evident that there are multiple versions of womanhood. . . . Gender identities, then are multiple. (Bradley, 1996, p. 106)

Moreover, contrary to the windsurfing widows who felt they were identified as appendages—their partner's nonsignificant other—the committed women, such as Stephanie, claimed that windsurfing offered a sense of identity, or self, that was detached from other people, particularly any identification as a girlfriend or wife:

Stephanie: It's having an identity as a person who is empowered to do their own thing, really or, you know, a professional identity is important, I think, too. I don't like the idea of being just someone's wife, or mother, or whatever. . . . It's given me a sense of identity, that is detached from other people.

BW: Do you think windsurfing is quite important for you within that identity, of being who you want to be?

Stephanie: It certainly has been—I am more relaxed about it now—I am not fussed in a way. I just like to do it—you know because it makes me feel good.

BW: You used the word empowering—do you think that it is empowering?

Stephanie: Yes—yes definitely, definitely—if I didn't windsurf I'd have to find some other thing that would do it for me. . . . So—yes it is empowering in a way. It's so kind of stamped into me as a person, that I don't even think of it as an identity thing, but it definitely is.

For real women, windsurfing gave them a sense of independence. As Sarah, a core woman, stated, "You should meet my friend Mary. She learnt to windsurf without a man. Actually, she is like me, she used it as a therapy to get away from men and relationships" (field notes, July 1995). Similarly, a recurring theme in the narratives of elite women windsurfers, interviewed in *Wahine* magazine,[10] is how windsurfing was empowering, articulated by the women as the freedom, confidence, independence, and sense of self procured through the activity:

It's a freedom thing. . . . you go out there and do what you want and express yourself in the way you want. . . . There is nobody to answer back to: it's just me and the water and the wind. (Jessica Crisp, *Wahine,* 1996, p. 14)

These women's dialogues emphasize that, as in the case of the women in this study, windsurfing was part of their feminine identity—their sense of self as a woman. Men, whether partners, husbands, or friends, did not play a part in their dialogues. The women stressed, above all, their independence:

I became more independent and proud of myself. . . being out there has helped me to open up and believe in myself. Windsurfing has been a sort of therapy. (Angela Cochran, *Wahine,* 1996, p. 15)

To summarize, for core women, windsurfing participation was an important site for the creation and negotiation of a cultural identity, one that was detached from their roles as mothers and from their male partners.

Subcultural Status: Competing Femininities?

Maybe one day I'll jump high off a wave and flip myself over the handle bars the way Kay Kucera does. Wishful thinking? Perhaps. But hey, at least I'm no wind widow. (Lisa Gosselin, 1994)

Real women, or core women's identities, were embedded foremost in being a windsurfer. These women saw themselves as different from the windsurfing widows, and in some cases, actively differentiated themselves from them, particularly girlies, who as previously discussed had a lower status in the subculture based on their low commitment to the windsurfing activity. Thus, although the social benefit of participating in the windsurfing community, especially attention from the men, was an important element for some windsurfing women, they differentiated themselves from the less committed women windsurfers who were more concerned about social and romantic relationships than doing the activity. As Stephanie explained,

I think you see that with people like Sarah who wasn't sailing this year. And, there's another girl who does the windsurfing, the racing, um, Julie. And I think she likes it because of the social things and all the men, and the attention and stuff—I may be really doing them a disservice, but I think that's as important to them as getting out there and sailing. And for me and Matthew doing the racing—the social side is very important—we love the social side of the racing—if that wasn't there we'd be less interested probably. But I think for some of the girls it's all the men around, definitely. (Stephanie)

Claire, a successful professional career woman declared that she considered the windsurfing widows to be "hopeless and pathetic." She described with contempt the "type of woman" who "fell by the way side" while she was learning to windsurf:

They were useless. They have all now got kids, are housewives, they are just appalling . . . but more they don't know what they are missing out on. (Claire)

For Claire, not to succeed in learning to windsurf was to fail, a fate comparable with merely "being a housewife." Claire sees the kind of women who easily gave up on windsurfing as lacking determination and commitment, values that she also associated with women who choose family or careers. Although Claire's view is an extreme one, it exemplifies some of the differences in attitudes and identities between some women who windsurf and those that do not.

Likewise, Lisa, a younger woman, explained that she had "nothing in common" with Jane, a windsurfing widow. Lisa declared that she hated when her partner's friend, James, brought his girlfriend Jane around their flat when he went windsurfing. As they were both women, he had assumed that they would get along. Lisa moaned that Jane would be there all day just sitting around, and Lisa was expected to entertain her. Jane did not windsurf, and Lisa thought she was "a complete bimbo," who had nothing to say. Lisa said she just wanted to go windsurfing herself (field notes, Hawaii, 1996).

One of the Lads?

Donna Haraway argues that:

Identities seem contradictory, partial and strategic. With the hard won recognition of their social and historical construction, gender, race and class cannot provide the basis for belief in "essential" unity. There is nothing about being "female" that naturally binds women. (Haraway, 1990, p. 197)

In the windsurfing subculture, the fact of womanhood itself was not a basis of any such unity or bonding. Being in a minority, core women windsurfers' subcultural role was as "one of the lads." Women claimed to share experiences depending on windsurfing proficiency and extent of commitment to the windsurfing culture and role, not gender. Stephanie's comments are revealing in understanding that although women windsurfers did have an affinity, particularly socially, when windsurfing and participating in any activities surrounding the sport, being a windsurfer, particularly a hard-core, advanced windsurfer, superseded her identity as a female windsurfer.

No, I don't give a stuff who it is really—actually it's never bothered me whether I've sailed with men or women. . . . I think some women can be as stupid or strange as men. You know it's people, you get some really strange women who come along on their own and they're probably feeling they're not confident, but I can think of a few that we all think "oh my god it's not her again." And there are men that are like that, and there are others that are great. So I'm really not particularly bothered about whether it's men or women. (Stephanie)

Likewise, other women discussed that it was important to windsurf with people of a similar performance level, irrespective of their sex. Thus, although core women's experiences of being a windsurfer differed from those of men, in the windsurfing environment their identities shared more with many windsurfing men than with nonwindsurfing women. The points of convergence between the experiences and leisure identification of committed men and women in the subculture were greater than between windsurfing widows and windsurfing women. Likewise, the experiences of some marginally involved men resonate with the experiences of the windsurfing widows: They were even called windsurfing widows.

In discussing the multitude of factors influencing the construction of a person's identity, Bradley (1996, p. 25) suggests that it is useful to differentiate between passive, active, and politicized levels of social or cultural identities. Adopting this differentiation, one could argue that for the active woman windsurfer, gender appears to be a passive identity. That is, while they windsurf, they think of themselves as a person, a windsurfer, not specifically as a woman. As Riley (1998) argues, our gender is not always at the "forefront of our awareness" (as cited in Bradley, 1996, p. 107). There are no doubt other times/spheres in these women's lives when they actively identify themselves primarily as a woman: "The burden of research certainly indicated that gender matters to women" (Bradley, 1996, p. 106). The windsurfing subculture has the capacity, though, to provide alternative and personally empowering identities.

Fluid Femininities

The fragmented, fluid, and culturally contingent character of identity has become a central concept in debates about changing contemporary Western societies. As Fraser and Nicholson discuss in relation to the destabilization of gender,

> Postmodern-feminist theory would dispense with the idea of a subject of history. It would replace unitary notions of women and "feminine identity" with plural and complexly constructed conceptions of social identity, treating gender as one relevant strand among others, attending also to class, race, ethnicity and sexual orientation. (Fraser & Nicholson, 1988, p. 391)

It is recognized too that people draw their sense of identity from an increasingly broad series of sources, including consumption patterns and leisure lifestyles (see Bocock, 1993). How do the ethnographic data reported in this article bear on such issues? Two main points emerge, concerning the capacity of women to forge their own self-identification in sport.

First, the analysis of the experiences of the women in the windsurfing culture has illustrated that a range of femininities was apparent within the middle-class, white, able-bodied, (heterosexual) women in this study. For the committed, core women, their leisure experiences and identities shared many aspects of unity with the windsurfing men. Second, these women windsurfers, who had overcome the ideological and structural barriers

constraining their participation, differentiated themselves from the nonactive and less committed women. Windsurfing women did not feel unity, or a bond of womanhood, with the nonactive windsurfing widows, who were identified in relation to their "emphasized femininity" (Connell, 1987). As Bradley (1996) argues, gender identities are themselves multiple. This research reiterates that women's relationships with men and other women are complex and variable (Hargreaves, 1994). "Gender might not be a global identity after all, even if it has profound breadth and depth" (Haraway, 1990, p. 222).

Power and Resistance: Challenging the Male Hegemony in Sport? Some Concluding Themes

Liberal feminists have argued that women's increased involvement and participation in physical activity is a form of resistance that challenges the naturalization of gender difference and inequality, and thus the male hegemony of sport. Michael Messner (1988) lucidly summarizes this debate:

> Increasing female athleticism in sport represents a genuine quest by women for equality, control of their bodies and self definition, and as such it also represents a challenge to the ideological basis of male domination. . . . In short, the female athlete—and her body—has become a contested ideological terrain. (p. 197)

There is no doubt that since the 1960s sport and physical exercise have become more widely available, popular, and significant in the lives of many (albeit predominantly young, able-bodied, professional, and white) women. Nevertheless, this liberal feminist agenda does not necessarily result in "freedom, equality, and social empowerment for women" (Messner & Sabo, 1990, p. 3). Sport continues to be defined and organized around the potential of the male body, particularly the latter's potential for physical strength and endurance. Thus, as Jennifer Hargreaves (1986, 1994) argues, women's influx into traditional male activities such as bodybuilding, boxing, and rugby is contradictory—there only appears to be a shift in the male hegemony:

> Women are being incorporated into models of male sport which are characterized by fierce

competition and aggression. . . . Instead of a redefinition of masculinity occurring, this trend highlights the complex ways male hegemony works in sport and ways in which women actively collude in its reproduction. (1986, p. 117)

Moreover, in "surveillance-dominated capitalism," "women's physical culture is embedded in and structured through a gendered panoptic—the exercise of power" (Cole, 1993, p. 87). Although men are increasingly affected by notions of the ideal body and body image, women's identity and sense of self tend to be linked to the outer shape of the body more than men's (Hartmann-Tews & Petry, 1997, p. 42). Feminist researchers have argued that despite the empowering potential of activities such as aerobics and bodybuilding, they do more to "maintain dominant ideologies of women's powerlessness than it does to liberate women through movement and action" (Haravon, 1995, p.23). Under what Hargreaves (1994) calls "the heterosexual gaze," women's attention is centered on their own bodies. Thus, the radical potential of strong and muscular women is subverted. Strong becomes sexy, or in the well-versed words of Judith Butler, "You only have permission to be this strong if you can also look this beautiful" (Butler, 1987, p. 122).

Emphasizing Physicality Not Appearance

Within the windsurfing culture, there were some similar contradictions between empowerment through the windsurfing activity and the "display of contrived femininity which symbolize manipulation" (Hargreaves, 1993, p. 65), most conspicuous in the representation of the female body in windsurfing magazines. Nevertheless, when asked about the reasons why they windsurfed, none of the women identified body sculpture, enhancing personal appearance, or health reasons. We are not suggesting that these women were not concerned about their appearance, or that windsurfing did not contribute to body sculpture, however it was not why they participated in windsurfing.

> I feel free. My hair is a mess; big purple bruises are blossoming on my legs. My throat feels raw from swallowing water, and my hands are blistered. I'm wearing no lipstick. I feel strong and happy. (Lisa Gosselin)[11]

These words, written by an American journalist after spending time windsurfing at Hood River (one of the epicenters of windsurfing in the United States), evoked exactly the physicality the female interviewees in this research discussed during and after going windsurfing. Alice, for example, divulged that she had a low body image and in the past had suffered from bulimia:

> The windsurfing, unusually, was more important to me than my sort of swimsuit potential really. . . . I don't know—I didn't care really. Mm if I did care, I just thought stuff it—and I know what I look like, which is the dog's dinner when I windsurf. . . . People usually respond to me being friendly and chatty and that sort of thing, more than what I look like anyway. (Alice)

Alice's use of the word *unusually* indicates that in other spheres she was concerned about her body being on display, in particular, whether her body was attractive, whereas when she was windsurfing, she did not have that concern. Windsurfing was one of the few activities and cultural spheres where she was not that concerned about her body appearance. Moreover, it gave her the confidence not to worry as much about her body appearance.

Core women's narratives suggested that they acknowledged that men judged them to some extent on how they looked, as well as their windsurfing ability. However, as we have outlined, being overly concerned about appearance, or displaying emphasized femininity by looking the beach babe was deemed the sphere of the girlies and the nonserious women windsurfers, who were only really involved with windsurfing for social reasons or to attract the attention of men. Despite the glamorous (media-induced) connotations, the reality of windsurfing participation in the United Kingdom is discomfort: blustery rain, cold weather, and often having to get changed in a car. This is not an environment that is conducive to bodily display:

> I mean most people look like shit when they windsurf. (Debby)

> It is very difficult to aspire to ideals of Western feminine beauty, if your hair is wet and you look like a drowned rat. (Maureen)[12]

Women's attention was centered on bodily experiences, specifically their strength and power, and the physically and mentally holistic embodied experience.

Scraton (1987) makes a similar argument for the value of initiatives such as self-defense, assertiveness training, and fitness programs that focus on physical well-being rather than appearance and physical attractiveness. She suggests that they

> indicate a qualitative shift in definitions of the "physical." Women in these programs are reclaiming the right to physical development and appearance on their own terms rather than the terms laid down in the traditions of "feminine culture" which are learned and reinforced at youth. (Scraton, 1987, p. 181)

Participation: Challenging the Macho Myth?

So are women windsurfers resisting the dominance of hegemonic masculinity and masculine hegemony in sport? Does windsurfing represent a challenge to the existing gender order in sport?

The mainstream and subcultural media focus on advanced windsurfing action and perpetuate imagery that denotes windsurfing as a male preserve, although women, particularly in advertising imagery, are displayed as passive compared to men. This ideology of gender difference conveyed in such imagery denotes the female windsurfer as the other. This emphasis on the hard-core element of the subculture and the symbolic exclusion of women is an enduring image, as Jason conceded:

> The media portrayal gives an impression you can't fail to hide, [that] you need to be fit and strong to enjoy sailing. . . . The sport is portrayed as being male dominated. (Jason)

Although such myths perpetuating the difficulty of windsurfing function to exclude all outsiders and wannabes, they particularly exclude women. The "ideology of biology" (Scraton, 1987) was one of the biggest deterrents to women's participation. Windsurfing widows and other newcomers stated that the sport was easier than they expected. Most men did not actively exclude women—the majority supported women's involvement, but the aura of this myth of the macho windsurfer, the naturalness of the association between masculinity and windsurfing, was extremely effective in marginalizing women's involvement.

Although recognizing the complexities of the male hegemony in sport (see Hargreaves, 1994),

particularly in conceiving of women's nonpassivity as empowering, in the context of windsurfing, women's entrance into this male-dominated and masculinist culture remains an important and imperative issue. As Birrell and Theberge (1994, p. 366) argue, "On both a symbolic and a real level, reclaiming physicality is a way for women to repossess themselves and intervene . . . to counter restrictive patriarchal practices." Women windsurfers by their actions and involvement, whether consciously or not, were challenging the norms of women's embodiment, and thus challenging enduring patriarchal ideologies that equate physical power and masculinity (see also Scraton, 1987). Their own bodies were the central site in their struggle over gender relations and identities, and as such, some would argue a "site for political territory" (Birrell & Theberge, 1994, p. 365). Whitson's (1994) argument about other new or lifestyle sports is pertinent in this context of windsurfing women:

> In living their bodies as skilled and forceful subjects rather than as objects of the male gaze, and especially in embodying power themselves, they challenge one of the fundamental sources of male power, the ideological equation of physical power itself with masculinity. (Whitson, 1994, p. 358)

New Sports, Old Battles

Participation in windsurfing gave women pleasure in physicality, self-confidence, and control over their bodies and their lives more broadly.[13] Active women windsurfers are judged less on appearance, the seen body, or traditional markers of femininity than in many other spheres of their lives. The windsurfing culture was an important arena for developing a sense of identification or self, separate from other people, and norms of female embodiment. Despite the individualistic nature of the activity, which as Scraton warns, denies women the opportunity to "develop group confidence and identity" (Scraton, 1987, p. 182), involvement in the subculture gave women a collective identity and a sense of community—"subcultural solidarity" (Whitson, 1994, p. 364). Clearly then, as Gilroy (1989) concludes, on the personal level sport can be empowering and a form of resistance "even if the women still seem to be functioning within a male sporting model" (Gilroy, 1989, p. 170).

Nevertheless, although in this article we have given centrality to the experiences of the core women windsurfers, it is important to emphasize the multiplicity of women's voices within the subculture—particularly those women on the margins who did not develop status based on sporting prowess or a sense of self that was detached from bodily image or appearance. The women were privileged women who had the opportunity to gain initial access to the culture. Many factors constrain women's involvement and consequent enjoyment of the windsurfing activity, particularly for those with low incomes and/or children due to the commitment in time and money required. Thus, it would be erroneous to suggest that windsurfing women, in any general sense, were contributing significantly to women's emancipation. Renegotiation of identity and the broadening of access to cultural and social space remain framed by the parameters of material and structural influences and constraints.

It is only ethnographic study that can provide a cultural analysis that does not just focus on public discourses or texts, but explores the "meaning and pleasure of these practices to those who participate in them" (Hall, 1996, p. 59). Thus, rather than conceiving of windsurfing women's experiences in terms of a dialectical struggle between empowerment and domination/constraint, it illustrates how both resistance and complicity to traditional notions of femininities coexist within the same cultural space and among middle-class, white women. Windsurfing women are both "active agents in the transformation of culture" and "determined by structures" (Hargreaves, 1994, p. 229). The ways in which they work within, rather than subvert, traditional patterns of gendered domination in sport illustrates how cultural change can be contingent, gradual, partial, and a matter of negotiation of and within existing social relations. That these possibilities of renegotiation in contemporary society exist is progressive. That such processes do not constitute a form of uncompromising resistance is testimony to the persisting power of patriarchy, and the realistic understanding of that power by those seeking to challenge, compromise with, or collude with the existing structures of gendered power.

Acknowledgments

The fieldwork was conducted for Belinda Wheaton's doctoral study (Wheaton, 1997a). We are grateful to the U.K.'s Economic and Social Research Council, which awarded the research studentship on which the doctoral study was based (ESRC Postgraduate Grant Number R00 429334379).

Notes

1. This phase of the research was developed to investigate the differences and interrelationships between the image of the subculture as it appears in the media and the lived dimensions of the subculture in everyday life.
2. Windsurfing is an expensive leisure activity, albeit less so than other water sports such as sailing.
3. Due to women's underrepresentation in the windsurfing subculture, interviews were conducted with a greater number of women windsurfers than with men.
4. Groupies are young women who had limited interest in the windsurfing activity but actively participated in the social activities that accompanied the lifestyle.
5. Interviewees highlighted that the image of the sport—in the media and other cultural products, an image signifying sexual difference and that windsurfing was a macho activity—affects outsiders' perception of the sport.
6. Theberge draws on Hartsock's feminist appropriation of Foucault—see also Hall (1996, p. 55).
7. Woodward (1995) makes a similar argument, claiming that "windsurfing like most sport, involves both entering a privileged masculine world and an active physicality which contravenes norms of feminine embodiment" (1995, p. 4).
8. See also McDermott's (1996) notion of self-possession.
9. Feminist researchers have argued that despite the empowering potential of activities such as aerobics—and bodybuilding—it does more to "maintain dominant ideologies of women's powerlessness than it does to liberate women's thought, movement and action" (Havron, 1995, p. 23). Central to this argument is empirical research that has demonstrated that women who participate in aerobics, or exercise classes, do so primarily to enhance and display their body appearance (see Hall, 1996; Hartmaan-Tews & Petry, 1997; Havron, 1995).
10. *Wahine* is a feminist women's sports magazine published in the United States that focuses on

all water sports, but surfing is the main emphasis.

11. In Women's Sport and Fitness (August 1994).

12. Interviewee in Woodward's study.

13. This connection between the physical and sociopsychological benefits has been reported in other studies of women's empowerment through physicality (see Guthrie & Castelnuovo, 1994).

References

Birkenfeld, K., & Moore, K. (1996). Windsurfing champions talk story. *Wahine, 2*, pp. 14-19.

Birrell, S., & Theberge, N. (1994). Feminist resistance and transformation in sport. In M. Costa & S. Guthrie (Eds.), *Women and sport: Interdisciplinary perspectives* (pp. 361-376). Champaign, IL: Human Kinetics.

Bocock, R. (1993). *Consumption.* London and New York: Routledge.

Bordo, S. (1990). Reading the slender body. In M. Jacobus, E. Keller, & S. Shuttleworth (Eds.), *Body/ Politics: Women and the discourses of science* (pp. 83-112). London: Routledge.

Bradley, H. (1996). *Fractured identities: Changing patterns of inequality.* Cambridge, MA: Polity.

British Market Research Bureau. (1995). *Target group index.* London: Author.

Bryson, L. (1987). Sport and the maintenance of masculine hegemony. *Women's Studies International Forum, 10*(3), 349-360.

Butler, J. (1987). Revising femininity? In R. Betterton (Ed.), *Looking on: Review of LADY, photographs of Lisa Lyon by Robert Mapplethorpe* (pp. 120-126). London: Pandora.

Carrigan, T., Connell, R., & Lee, J. (1987). Towards a new sociology of masculinity. *Theory and Society, 14*(5), 551-604.

Cole, C. (1993). Resisting the canon: Feminist cultural studies, sport, and technologies of the body. *Journal of Sport & Social Issues, 17*(2), 77-92.

Connell, R. (1987). *Gender and power.* Cambridge, UK: Polity.

Connell, R. (1995). *Masculinities.* Cambridge, UK: Polity.

Deem, R. (1987). The politics of women's leisure. In J. Horne, D. Jary, & A. Tomlinson (Eds.), *Sport, leisure and social relations* (Sociological Review Monograph 33, pp. 210-228). London: Routledge.

Farmer, R. (1992). Surfing: Motivations, values and culture. *Journal of Sports Behaviour, 15*(3), 241-257.

Fiske, J. (1989). *Reading the popular.* London: Unwin Hyman.

Flintoff, A. (1997). Learning and teaching in PE: A lesson in gender. In A. Tomlinson (Ed.), *Gender, sport and leisure: Continuities and challenges* (pp. 49-62). Aachen, Germany: Meyer & Meyer.

Fraser, N., & Nicholson, L. (1988). Social criticism without philosophy: An encounter between feminism and postmodernism. *Theory Culture & Society, 5*(2-3), 373-394.

Gilroy, S. (1989). The EmBody-ment of power: Gender and physical activity. *Leisure Studies, 8*(2), 163-171.

Gilroy, S. (1997). Working on the body: Links between physical activity and social power. In G. Clarke & B. Humberstone (Eds.), *Researching women and sport* (pp. 96-112). Basingstoke, UK: Macmillan.

Gosselin, L. (1994, July/August). Throwing caution to the wind. *Women's Sport and Fitness,* 56-61.

Graydon, J. (1997). Self-confidence and self-esteem in physical education and sport. In G. Clarke & B. Humberstone (Eds.), *Researching women and sport* (pp. 68-79). Basingstoke, UK: Macmillan.

Green, E., Hebron, S., & Woodward, D. (1989). *Women's leisure, what leisure?* Basingstoke, UK: Macmillan.

Guthrie, S., & Castelnuovo, S. (1994). The significance of body images in psychosocial development and in embodying feminist perspectives. In M. Costa & S. Guthrie (Eds.), *Women and sport: Interdisciplinary perspectives* (pp. 307-22). Champaign, IL: Human Kinetics.

Hall, A. (1996). *Feminism and sporting bodies: Essays on theory and practice.* Champaign, IL: Human Kinetics.

Hammersley, M., & Atkinson, P. (1983). *Ethnography: Principles in practice.* London and New York: Routledge.

Haravon, L. (1995). Exercises in empowerment: Towards a feminist aerobic pedagogy. *Women, Sport and Physical Activity Journal, 4*(2), 23-44.

Haraway, D. (1990). A manifesto for cyborgs: Science, technology, and socialist feminism in the 1980s. In L. Nicholson (Ed.), *Feminism/Postmodernism* (pp. 190-233). London: Routledge.

Hargreaves, J. (1986). Where's the virtue? Where's the grace? A discussion of the social production of gender relations through sport. *Theory, Culture & Society, 3*(1), 109-121.

Hargreaves, J. (1993). Bodies matter! Images of sport and female sexualisation. In C. Brackenridge (Ed.), *Body matters: Leisure images and lifestyles* (pp. 60-66). Eastbourne, UK: Leisure Studies Association.

Hargreaves, J. (1994). *Sporting females: Critical issues in the history and sociology of women's sports.* London: Routledge.

Hartmann-Tews, I., & Petry, K. (1997). Individualisation and changing modes of consuming in sport—some gender aspects. In A. Tomlinson (Ed.), *Gender, sport and leisure: Continuities and challenges* (pp. 35-45). Aachen, Germany: Meyer & Meyer.

McDermott, L. (1996). Towards a feminist understanding of physicality within the context of women's physically active and sporting lives. *Sociology of Sport Journal,* **13**(1), 12-30.

Messner, M. (1988). Sport and male domination: The female athlete as contested ideological terrain. *Sociology of Sport Journal,* **5**(3), 197-211.

Messner, M., & Sabo, D. (1990). Introduction: Towards a critical reappraisal of sport, men and the gender order. In M. Messner & D. Sabo (Eds.), *Sport, men and the gender order* (pp. 1-15). Champaign, IL: Human Kinetics.

Pearson, K. (1982). Conflict, stereotypes and masculinity in Australian and New Zealand surfing. *Australian and New Zealand Journal of Sociology,* **18**(2), 117-135.

Profile Sport Consultancy. (1994, March). *The United Kingdom windsurf report.* A joint publication between the Profile Sport Market Consultancy and the Royal Yachting Association.

Riley, D. (1988). *Am I that name?* London: MacMillan.

Scraton, S. (1987). "Boys muscle in where angels fear to tread": Girls' sub-cultures and physical activities. In J. Horne, D. Jary, & A. Tomlinson (Eds.), *Sport, leisure and social relations* (Sociological Review Monograph 33, pp. 160-187). London: Routledge.

Scraton, S. (1994). The changing world of women and leisure: Feminism, "post feminism" and leisure. *Leisure Studies,* **13**(4), 249-261.

Southend on Sea, Essex. (1993, December). *Boards,* **101**, 70.

Stebbins, R. (1992). *Amateurs, professionals and serious leisure.* Montreal, Canada: McGill/Queen's University Press.

The winds of Maui. (1996). *Wahine,* **2**, pp. 4-20.

Theberge, N. (1987). Sport and women's empowerment. *Women's Studies International Forum,* **10**(4), 387-393.

Theberge, N. (1991). Reflections on the body in the sociology of sport. *Quest,* **43**, 123-134.

Tomlinson, A. (1993). Culture of commitment in leisure: Notes towards the understanding of a serious legacy. *World Leisure and Recreation,* **35**(1), 6-9.

Tomlinson, A. (1997). Ideologies of physicality, masculinity and femininity: Comments on *Roy of the Rovers* and the women's fitness boom. In A. Tomlinson (Ed.), *Gender, sport and leisure: Continuities and challenges* (pp. 135-72). Aachen, Germany: Meyer & Meyer.

Turner, S. (1983). Development and organisation of windsurfing. *Institute of Leisure and Amenity Management,* **1**, 13-15.

Whannel, G. (1983). *Blowing the whistle: The politics of sport.* London: Pluto Press.

Wheaton, B. (1997a). *Consumption, lifestyle and gendered identities in post-modern sports: The case of windsurfing.* Unpublished Ph.D. thesis, Chelsea School Research Centre, University of Brighton.

Wheaton, B. (1997b). Covert ethnography and the ethics of research: Studying sport subcultures. In A. Tomlinson & S. Fleming (Eds.), *Ethics, sport and leisure: Crises and critiques* (pp. 163-171). Aachen, Germany: Meyer & Meyer.

Wheaton, B., & Tomlinson, A. (1995). *Consumer culture, gender identity and lifestyle in post-modern sports. Windsurfing subcultures.* Paper delivered at Shouts From the Street: Culture, Creativity and Change, the First Annual Conference for Popular Culture. Manchester, UK: Manchester Institute for Popular Culture, Manchester Metropolitan University.

Whitson, D. (1990). Sport in the social construction of masculinity. In M. Messner & D. Sabo (Eds.), *Sport, men and the gender order: Critical feminist perspectives* (pp. 19-30). Champaign, IL: Human Kinetics.

Whitson, D. (1994). The embodiment of gender: Discipline, domination, and empowerment. In S. Birrell & C. Cole (Eds.), *Women, sport and culture* (pp.353-71) Champaign, IL: Human Kinetics.

Woodward, V. (1995). *Windsurfing women, and empowerment.* Unpublished paper, November 1995.

Woodward, V. (1996). *Gybe round the buoys!—Femininity, feminism and windsurfing women.* Unpublished draft paper, March 1996.

UNIT XII

Sport and Globalization

Objectives

The unit examines the influences of globalization on local sport cultures and local sport practices.

Recently, one of the coeditors had the good fortune to take a sabbatical leave in Oslo, Norway. Despite its extreme northerly location (a considerable portion of Norway's land mass lies above the Arctic Circle), this country of just 4 million inhabitants has not escaped American cultural influences. Evidence of American style, taste, entertainment, and consumer products is found everywhere in the capital city. For example, at just about every major traffic intersection, a McDonalds, Burger King, or 7-Eleven beckons the hungry traveler. Food shoppers find supermarket shelves lined with popular American staples such as Jif peanut butter, Kellogg's Corn Flakes, Del Monte peas, and, of course, Coca-Cola. Evening television programming is dominated by popular American fare including *The Nanny, Ally McBeal, Friends,* and *Jerry Springer.* Movie theatres offer as many American-made films as they do European productions. Oslo newspapers share newsstand space with America's national daily newspaper, *USA TODAY.* On the radio, American country-and-western music commands its own station. What these examples demonstrate is that American popular culture, in all its many and diverse forms, is not confined to national borders but

is a global phenomenon reaching all corners of the world. The term Americanization is one of several used (e.g., others include CocaColonization, and Disneyfication) to capture the process by which "American cultural forms, products, and meanings are imposed on other cultures at the expense of the domestic culture" (Donnelly, 1996, p. 242). For some, the influence of American cultural products on other peoples and cultures of the world is seen as a form of cultural imperialism, an example of cultural hegemony because it occurs at the expense of the importing culture and local population.

In recent years, the discourse has broadened beyond a narrow focus on American cultural influence abroad to the recognition that the process is much more complex and global in nature. Rowe et al. (1994) define globalization as a set of forces that produce a complex and irresistible system of world economic, political, and cultural interdependence. These forces are seen as a threat not only to national integration and community structures but also to the collective identities associated with national spaces (Harvey & Houle, 1994). To be sure, U.S. capital and transnational corporations have enormous power to reshape the world in the image of American consumerism, freedom, and fun (Allen, 1999). But the concept of globalization also captures the interrelated phenomena of economic integration, ideological convergence, political consensus, and cultural homogenization (McShane, 1996).

Critical to Americanization and globalization processes and the creation of a shared, new "international information order" are the mass media. McLeod (1991) notes that "we have all become ensnared in this communication web whether we live in the first or in the tenth world. Our lives are molded and modeled by these media, our symbolic worlds are determined by them, even our clothes are fashioned by them" (p. 69).

The contribution of American-mediated popular culture to an ever expanding international mediascape and the creation of a homogenized, globally shared culture is hard to deny. But as Jackson and Andrews (1995) point out, an increased circulation of American commodity-signs does not necessarily lead to the creation of globally homogenized or "Americanized" patterns and experiences. Rather, they argue that global commodity-sign consumption is a complex process in which local environments are often the sites of negotiation and resistance. That is, the reach of the globalization process may be total or partial, and the local culture's response passive, participative, or conflictual (Houlihan, 1994).

It wasn't until the 1960s that sport sociologists first began to take a serious interest in the Americanization and globalization of sport. Recent interest in the subject has focused on the transnational migration patterns of sport labor, the relationship between global sport and new social movements, and the impacts of American sports on specific nation-states. Although research interests have clearly expanded since the early 1990s, researchers continue to examine and analyze the effect of American sport on the sporting culture of other nations. Wilcox (1993) notes that "as American sports television executives seek to counter domestic saturation through expansion into a larger European market, the preservation of traditional sporting values and practices becomes a major cultural concern" (p. 33). The extent to which this expansion constitutes a real threat to the sporting cultures of native peoples, as well as their national identity, is a much debated issue. The overseas marketing of the National Basketball Association (NBA) provides an interesting case. Today, NBA merchandise sales outside the United States are approximately 300 million dollars annually, televised games are seen in 199 countries, exhibitions and games that count in the league standings are played overseas, and six marketing offices have been created outside the United States. The aggressive efforts by the NBA and other professional leagues (e.g., National Football League, Major League Baseball) to develop international fan bases

raise important questions about the effect of American sporting culture worldwide. Bellamy (1993) frames the issue well when he asks, "To what degree is sport heritage susceptible to outside modification?" (p. 177).

The Americanization and globalization of sport and leisure is drawing increasing scholarly attention as we enter the new millennium. Some of the questions that will challenge sport researchers in the years ahead include the following:

1. How are the concepts of exile, migration, and diaspora relevant to the study of sport and leisure?
2. What effect does the globalization of sport have on nationalism?
3. How and in what ways does globalization alter the nature of amateur and professional sports?
4. Does globalized sport play a role in the production of "new ethnicities"?
5. How is the increased flow of sport information worldwide affecting local sport tastes and behaviors?

In the first selection, Harvey and Houle introduce several important concepts and issues that attend the sport and globalization debate. In particular, the authors discuss how globalization contributes to the emergence of new social movements and the role that communications technology plays in enhancing the globalizing process.

Ultimately, the authors would like to see the debate move away from a discussion of sport as a form of cultural imperialism. Instead, they encourage examination of the effects of sport as an emergent global culture on the development of a new world economy.

In the second selection, Klein examines the Americanization of baseball in the Caribbean and finds that the notions of cultural hegemony and cultural imperialism fail to capture the reality of the situation. In the case of Dominican baseball, we find several forms of resistance to American-style play. We learn about the existence of a palpable tension between the forces of hegemony and resistance in this very popular Caribbean sport. Clearly, sport can serve imperialistic agenda, but it can also serve as a site for struggle and opposition.

In the third selection, Jackson and Andrews contribute to our understanding of the current debate surrounding globalism and localism by locating the NBA, an American global-mediated institution, within the local New Zealand context. The authors make the case that globalization is not a uniform process that interacts with and influences all local cultures equally. To the contrary, we discover, perhaps to our surprise, that the NBA is helping to energize and reaffirm the local culture.

References

Allen, J.S. (1996, February 23). Capitalism globe trots with Jordan. *USA TODAY*, p. 6B.

Bellamy, R.V. Jr. (1993). Issues in the internationalization of the U.S. sports media: The emerging European marketplace. *Journal of Sport & Social Issues*, **17**, 168-180.

Donnelly, P. (1996). The local and the global: Globalization in the sociology of sport. *Journal of Sport & Social Issues*, **20**, 239-257.

Harvey, J., & Houle, F. (1994). Sport, world economy, global culture and new movements. *Sociology of Sport Journal*, **11**, 337-355.

Houlihan, B. (1994). Homogenization, Americanization, and creolization of sport: Varieties of globalization. *Sociology of Sport Journal*, **11**, 356-375.

Jackson, S.J., & Andrews, D.L. (1999). Between and beyond the global and the local: American popular sporting culture in New Zealand. *International Review for the Sociology of Sport*, **34**, 31-42.

Jackson, S.J., & Andrews, D.L. (1995). Michael Jordan and the popular imagery of post-colonial New Zealand: The necessary dialectic of global commodity-sign culture. A paper presented at the 16th annual conference of the North American Society for the Sociology of Sport, Sacramento, CA.

McLeod, J.R. (1991). The seamless web: Media and power in the post-modern global village. *Journal of Popular Culture*, **25**, 69-76.

McShane, D. (1996, February 23). Border skirmishes. *New Statesman & Society*, pp. 44-45.

Rowe, D., Lawrence, G., Miller, T., & McKay, J. (1994). Global sport? Core concern with peripheral vision. *Media, Culture & Society*, **16**, 661-675.

Wilcox, R. C. (1993). Imperialism or globalism? A conceptual framework for the study of American sport and culture in contemporary Europe. *Journal of Comparative Physical Education and Sport*, **15**, 30-40.

Discussion Questions

Jean Harvey and François Houle

1. What is meant by the terms "globalization" and "global culture?" Explain.
2. What has happened to nation-states in the face of powerful globalization processes? Discuss and explain.
3. How have globalization processes influenced and shaped sport today? Discuss and explain.
4. Discuss the concepts of imperialism (Americanization) and globalization. What do the terms mean and how do they differ?
5. How do transnational relationships and communications contribute to the emergence of a global culture and a global social reality? Discuss and provide examples.
6. What is the difference between analyzing sports as part of (a) Americanization processes or (b) globalization processes? Which paradigm do the authors favor? Discuss and explain.
7. To what extent has sport served as a focal point of new social movements? Discuss.
8. Does evidence suggest that new social movements create new sport forms and events? That is, do the spillover effects associated with general social movements affect sport? Refer to the sports of inter-crosse and the Tour de l'Ile of Montreal in answering the question.

Alan Klein

1. Where is Americanization most apparent in the Caribbean? Discuss.
2. What evidence indicates that Dominican baseball has subordinated itself to North American interests? Discuss and explain.
3. What role do North American baseball academies play in the Dominican Republic? Explain.
4. Have the Dominicans put up much resistance to the structural domination of their game? Discuss and explain.
5. Why is Caribbean winter baseball a source of contention? Discuss and explain.
6. What does the author's research study on "baseball hat preference" tell us about North American hegemony? Discuss and explain.
7. Why has baseball been chosen to confront American cultural imperialism? Discuss and explain.

8. Can you identify other examples of the tension between sport hegemony and sport resistance in other parts of the world? Discuss and explain.

Steven Jackson and David Andrews

1. What are discussions of globalization likely to focus on? Discuss and explain.
2. Identify the "local-global" debate. Contrast the positions of the "homogenizers" and the "heterogenizers."
3. To what extent has the National Basketball Association "gone global"? Explain.
4. Briefly describe the popular cultural context of New Zealand and, in particular, its mediascape.
5. Describe the NBA's effect on New Zealand popular culture.
6. Does any evidence show that New Zealand will resist global or American products if they conflict with local sensitivities? Discuss and explain.
7. Does the mere consumption of American products by local consumers equate with Americanization of that culture? Discuss and explain.
8. In what sense might the NBA play a role in energizing New Zealand's popular culture? Discuss and explain.
9. In your opinion, do the world's cultures have reason to fear transnational conglomerates like McDonalds, Kentucky Fried Chicken, Nike, Coca-Cola, and Pizza Hut? Discuss and explain.

Sport, World Economy, Global Culture, and New Social Movements

Jean Harvey
François Houle

This paper contributes to the ongoing debate on sport and globalization. In the first section of the paper major elements of the current debate are presented. The second section discusses the current literature on globalization and its related processes. Four elements are discussed in this section: the global economy, communications, new social movements, and the question of identity/culture. The third section comments on sport and key issues of the debate on globalization in light of the discussion in the previous section. An emphasis is put on the interrelationships between sport and new social movements.

Had we limited Sylvie Bernier to dive only in Ste-Foy swimming pools or Gilles Villeneuve to race on the San-Air race tracks in Trois-Rivières, these people never would have attained the levels of world excellence they reached. We have to give oxygen to our people, we have to give them the opportunity to go on the international level. We have to do it progressively and in a humane way. (René Lévesque quoted by Keable, 1993, p. 9; our translation)

When the late Prime Minister of Québec, René Lévesque, in his usual populist style, used a sport metaphor to explain to a handful of advisers and cabinet ministers what position he would like his government to adopt on the then proposed free-trade agreement between Canada and the U.S., he paved the way for the new nationalism of his government, which was open to the world economy. He also provided a vision of the role of Québec's high-performance athletes in a global sport system: to promote the Québecois (rather than Canadian) identity within the emerging world of interdependence. In other words, this quote can be interpreted as an example of a regionalist force recognizing the importance of the global culture and recognizing that globalization does not preclude the affirmation of a national identity.

Has contemporary sport entered into a process of Americanization or globalization? Is this process one of cultural imperialism, increased economic interdependency, or diffusion of modernity? Are these phenomena total and irreversible, or do we witness forms of cultural resistance? These questions summarize the state of the actual debate on globalization and sport. The purpose of this paper is to contribute to this debate through a discussion of globalization informed by the current literature in social theory. Moreover, the call for a debate reorientation includes an examination of forgotten dimensions, primarily the influence of new social movements.

In the first section of the paper, a summary of the major elements of the current debate is presented. The second section discusses the current literature in social theory about globalization and its related processes. This allows us to shed a different light on the relationships between globalization processes and sport. More specifically, four elements will be discussed: the global economy, mass

Reprinted from Harvey and Houle, 1994.

communications, new social movements, and the question of identity/culture. The purpose of this discussion is to specify which trends are present in globalization and what this concept means for our understanding of social, political, and economic dynamics. In the third section, we comment on some of the key issues in the ongoing debate on globalization and sport in light of our theoretical discussions. This concludes with focus on the new social movements and their interrelationships with sport within the context of sport globalization, so far a neglected topic in the sport studies literature.

Overview of the Debate

The status of the debate can be summarized around three lines of arguments, as noted in the introduction. First, is sport part of a process of Americanization or globalization? Second, is this a process of economic and cultural imperialism, or is it part of economic or cultural globalism? Third, are these processes irreversible and total, or is there room for resistance?

Maguire (1990) started the current debate in sociology of sport by examining the making of American football in England, situating this phenomenon in the context of the debates on the Americanization of British (English) culture. Maguire stipulates that the Americanization of English sport has to be understood in terms of the evolution of interdependencies between these two countries (1990, p. 216). He also underlines that cultural exchange is not one-way (the growing popularity of soccer in the U.S. would be an example). Moreover, Maguire argues, the struggle for hegemony is not confined to Britain, since the economic and cultural dominance of the U.S. has been challenged by Europe and Japan. Finally, Maguire suggests that a number of factors explain the development of American football in England, one factor being the process of commercialization of English sport itself. This process would have created a favorable environment for American commercialized sports to flourish in England.

In his contribution to the debate, Kidd (1991) suggests that, in the Canadian context, the term *Americanization* is a more appropriate term. More precisely, *American capitalist hegemony* describes the actual process into which Canadian sport is constantly overcome by American values and practices. From the perspective of the Caribbean countries, Klein's (1991) piece in this debate is also based on the concept of Americanization.

Wagner (1990) suggests that the effective process is "mundialization," not Americanization. He argues that (a) globalization of sport results as all major sports gain popularity around the world; (b) there is increasing motivation around the world to be part of international competition; (c) western mass media are influential in third-world countries and are able to generate increased interest in western sports; and (d) there is a growing awareness of the political importance of sport. In short, Americanization is, Wagner argues, just a part of a larger process, the homogenization of sports. Guttman's (1991) position is somewhat similar to Wagner's, although he suggests that globalization is part of the process of modernization.

Coming from a theoretically different perspective than Wagner and Guttman, McKay and Miller (1991) and McKay, Lawrence, Miller, and Rowe (1993) also argue against the term *Americanization*. They suggest that the most important fact is that we are witnessing a process of globalization of capital. In this argument based on the development of a world capitalist economy, the origin of capital is no longer an issue.

The second dimension to this debate concerns the type of process we are dealing with. Here the authors regroup differently. The first group consists of the adherents to the modernization thesis, Guttman and Wagner. They argue that as industrialization and modernization make ground, there is a process of cultural or ludic diffusion by which traditional sports are either gradually replaced by existing modern sports or transformed into modern sports.

The other group is formed by the political economists (Cantelon & Murray, 1993; Kidd, 1991; Klein, 1991; Maguire, 1993; McKay & Miller, 1991; McKay et al., 1993). Here, the analysis focuses not on a universalistic (despite the recognized backfires) process of modernization of the world (into which America, Europe, and Japan would only be among the more advanced) but on a process of development of capitalism and commodification of sport. For those in favor of the American imperialism thesis (Kidd, 1991; Maguire, 1990), the expansion of capital from dominant countries to the dominated countries engenders a process of cultural domination from the former over the latter, and results in a process of acculturation of dominated economies into the values and sport practices of the economies they are dominated by. Depending on which country is dominant, one would see Americanization or Japanization. Others, such as McKay and Miller (1991) and McKay et al. (1993), who base their arguments on a study of Australia, suggest that the political economy of sport can be best analyzed with "concepts like 'post-Fordism,' the globalization of consumerism, and the cultural logic of capitalism, all of which transcend the confines of the United States" (McKay & Miller, 1991, p. 86).

This leads us to the idea of a global culture, a notion that has been referred to by Cantelon and Murray (1993) and Whitson and Macintosh (1993). The latter, while focusing on the strategies of cities to promote themselves in a world tourist market by organizing major sport events, demonstrate the economic circumstances cities have to cope with in order to avoid marginalization. The goal is to be a "world-class" city, and in this race, sport complexes and major events become important tools. However, these cities have to develop world-class complexes and events. The so-called world-class complexes and events are designed according to highly homogenized concepts, and thus blur local distinctiveness. This is also true for other projects. "Many kinds of ex-urban leisure developments . . . that were once distinctive have become internationally ordinary" (Whitson & Macintosh, 1993, pp. 235-236). The end result would be the diffusion of a "highly capitalized consumer culture," in other words a "global culture" (Whitson & Macintosh, 1993, p. 236).

Finally, a third dimension to the debate is about the weight of domination. In other words, is Americanization or globalization a total and single-side process or is there resistance? On this issue, all the authors but Wagner (1990) seem to agree, more or less, that there is resistance. Klein's (1991) contribution, for example, using hegemony theory, illustrates the different forms of resistance from the people of the Caribbean. Kidd (1991) sees that process in a more complex way. He underlines the fact that Francophones in Canada, for example, "have taken up American practices in order to improve their chances to play and compete" (p. 180), which he sees as a way for them to overcome English Canadian domination. But we consider subsequently if there are forms of cultural struggles, other than local resistance, over dominant forms of sport practices and values.

Social Theory and Globalization

In this second section, we aim to show more clearly how the concept of globalization manifests itself in the real world and to examine what it implies for the paradigms that form the basis of our understanding of social, political, and economic forces. After all, the difficult economic transformation of recent years is often explained in terms of the demands and consequences of economic globalization. Since the mid-1980s, globalization has taken on an almost universal explanatory significance. Governments and corporations constantly cite globalization to justify a radical restructuring of social rights, the state's role in the economy, and the fordist wage compromise.

Through this analysis, we try to explain how the globalization process challenges our structures of national integration, identity, and community. We present the globalization process by examining its four dimensions: the global economy and the declining importance of the nation-state, communication, new social movements, and identity/culture. The first three are each considered separately. However, because these effects are not independent, it is impossible to consider any one of them without reference to the others. The fourth dimension, identity/culture, is so involved in the other three dimensions that it is incorporated throughout the discussion. Closer examination of identity/culture suggests the emergence of a global culture: a mass culture that penetrates every area of the world; a fragmented culture associated with the full development of modern individualism; the emergence of individuals with a fundamentally global ethos; and the creation of new forms of solidarity based on new links between individuals at the sub- and supra-national levels. Such examination also suggests that individual identity is partially defined by elements influenced by the globalization processes. We do not see the identity of the subject, its difference, as only defined by the self.

Economy and the Decline of the Nation-State

Recognizing the process of globalization that is in progress requires a radical change in the way we view our societies. Views which assume that the nation-state is the fundamental unit or which rely on the notion of imperialism may be outmoded. Because the nation-state can no longer negotiate its place in the world economy, its role has been reduced to adapting its national economy to the requirements of competitiveness established by global markets. States find themselves more or less restricted within a narrow and inflexible logic of making their policies and programs competitive with those of other states (Houle, 1987).

Contrary to Keohane (1984), we do not think that we should see international regimes as products of rational self-interest of national state under the leadership of the more powerful states. Nor should we see globalization as the domestication of international politics (Hanrieder, 1978). In a globalized system, national interest is not only modified, it becomes indistinguishable from the interests of the global system. Global dynamics and issues have become the basis of national interest. However, adapting to globalization does not simply require that we view state behavior in terms of international rather than domestic forces, that we substitute the international for the national; globalization is much more complex and multifaceted than such a simple substitution would suggest. We must develop analytical concepts that take into account the emergence of forces that are based not on the segmentation of the world into national political spaces but rather on integration within and across national political spaces.

Such a paradigm shift would alter our understanding of phenomena in the world of sports, for example. Sports are not evolving as a function of the intrusive forces of economic or cultural imperialism, or as part of a process of Americanization. Sports are being shaped by a myriad of globalization processes and at the same time are contributing to the development of those same processes. We return to this example in the third section.

An understanding of globalization that focuses exclusively on its economic aspects yields an oversimplified picture of this multifaceted phenomenon. In fact, even if globalization of capitalist markets is the most visible element of the globalization process, a narrow economic view of the process risks neglecting other important sub- and supra-national phenomena in the areas of communications, culture, and social movements. It would also neglect the issues which face our societies, and which are global, such as nuclear security and atmospheric pollution. In their own ways, and to varying degrees, all of these elements contribute to the globalization process.

According to Robertson (1990), the term *globalization* refers to the crystallization of the world into a single space. Giddens explains the same reality when he writes that globalization can be defined as the intensification of social relations at the world level, linking distant locations such that local events are structured by events occurring across the world (1990). Robertson identifies three factors that have contributed to world integration: capitalism, western imperialism, and the development of global

communications (1990). Giddens, on the other hand, describes globalization in terms of four dimensions: the global capitalist economy, the system of nation-states, the world military order, and the international division of labor. These four institutional dimensions of globalization fuel the process of cultural globalization occurring via communications technology and the media. Both Robertson and Giddens refuse to make the economic system the primary explanatory factor in the globalization process. In fact, even though they recognize the importance of the economy, they both place more emphasis on technology and communications.

Although both Robertson and Giddens place a strong emphasis on the role of the nation-state, we must not overlook the fact that the compression of space and the restructuring of social relations are occurring, in large part, independently of international relations. Falk (1990) has partially encapsulated this point with his notion of evasions of sovereignty (i.e., political action at the global level by nonstate actors). When we examine more closely what specific economic, social, and political activities are increasingly globally directed, and at what levels we are operating when we engage in these activities, we see that they decreasingly take place at what would be considered a national level.

Today's international economic interdependence contrasts sharply with historical forms of imperialism in the sense that the underlying forces of integration are different. A global economy does not integrate national spaces in the same way as an international economy. Imperialist theorists since J.A. Hobson have asserted that imperialism involves a particular type of relationship between nations. The domestic development of a peripheral nation occurs as a function of the interests of the imperial power. The economic resources of a peripheral nation are exploited according to the needs of a more advanced nation. The imperial relationship is therefore defined by a set of power relationships in which a periphery is dominated by a core state. Imperialism involves integration within a direct relationship that serves the national interests of a particular state, and that begins and ends with the national space.

By contrast, economic globalization involves the integration of national economic activities in a relationship where the dynamics and interests are globally directed. National economies are therefore involved in a relationship of interdependence at the global level (Michalet, 1976). In this relationship, large corporations dominate and determine the axes of economic development independently of national political economies, for their accumulation of profits is not dependent on national political spaces. However, the interdependence in this new reality may still be largely asymmetrical. The constraints imposed on national economies and states by the global economy are not the same for countries like Germany, the United States, or Japan, which exert a strong influence in defining the norms of global competitiveness, as for third-world countries with less competitive economies (see Gereffi, 1984).

Beyond this asymmetrical character it is also important to note that globalization does not imply the disappearance of the nation-state, for even if the nation-state is not the essence of the new international order, it may still be the most important component in most cases. As Thomson and Krasner (1989) have shown, the nation-state is the only actor capable of ensuring the stability of property rights, which are essential to the development and functioning of the global market. Similarly, Petrella (1989) has demonstrated how the state remains important, despite the fact that it is not the leading agent, and the fact that corporations increasingly bypass it by organizing on the basis of global industrial, financial, and service networks.

Finally, although the American economy is the most important economy at the global level, we must not let this obscure the actual dynamic at work. Speaking of globalization and a global economy suggests a very different understanding of the new reality we face than does speaking of Americanization and imperialism. What is important is that, although American corporations are playing an important role in the restructuring of the global economy, they are responding to a global logic rather than a domestic American logic.

Communications

The processes of globalization also depend on the creation of a vast network of transnational relationships and communications over which the individual state has only limited influence. Technological innovation and the growth of communications technology not only have reduced the costs of transportation and communication but also have strengthened relationships between corporations and between individuals, relationships that were previously, and almost unavoidably, organized on the basis of the nation-state. Although the increased availability of information also exists within national borders, its significance is much more important at the global level because it is leading to a re-

definition of our concepts of distance and space, as everything rapidly becomes more accessible. Not only are social relations becoming more global, but they are also being redefined on a spatial basis that is itself already in the process of becoming more global. According to Rosenau, this increase in the mass of available information is "the source of micro changes that may alter macro structures" (quoted in Thomson & Krasner, 1989, p. 204). Held also emphasizes its importance for the globalization of social activities: "What is new about the modern global system is the chronic intensification of patterns of interconnectedness, mediated by such phenomena as the modern communications industry and new information technology, and the spread of globalization in and through new dimensions of interconnectedness: technological, organizational, administrative and legal, among others, each with its own logic and dynamic of change" (1991, p. 206).

The development of multiple networks is one of the main factors that is making possible the creation of a global political culture, on the basis of which individuals are pursuing changes in national policies (Breton & Jenson, 1992, p. 41). These networks linking private individuals, groups, or corporations do not constitute a unified global entity but rather a global entity that is fragmented and segmented culturally, economically, and politically (Camilleri, 1990); these networks produce not a common perspective but a multitude of perspectives and diverse communities linking individuals independently of political boundaries.

Globalization does not simply involve the progressive development of a homogenized global metaculture, based on a global economy in which all individuals consume the same products. On the contrary, globalization at the cultural level involves, first, the emergence of certain elements of a common ethos, and of values shared by an increasing number of individuals with a sense of humanity's shared destiny. Here we see how globalization has as a corollary domestic fragmentation. Insecurity about environmental or military threats creates a sentiment of unity and solidarity transcending time and space. This common ethos develops at the transnational level through sub- and supra-national relationships and activities. Second, we also see the reaffirmation of many elements of regional and national identities within nation-states. These phenomena need not be seen simply as withdrawals, for they are also present in instances of transculturation. Third, the fact that the distant has become visible and immediate contributes to the emergence of global cultural phenomena and a global social reality. We need only think of the global character of an increasing number of events in the world of sports such as the Olympics or other large tournaments; in geopolitics, such as the Gulf War or the fall of the Berlin Wall; in economics, such as the global strategies of corporations and banks; and in other spheres, such as rock concerts like *Live Aid*. Technological innovations permit the media and other forms of communication to serve as a vehicle for the process of cultural globalization. These networks and flows of communication make possible the realization of this generalized networking, networking that challenges the collective identities associated with national spaces (Camilleri & Falk, 1992).

New Social Movements

It is not only individual actors who contribute to the development of international links and relationships. New social movements also make a significant contribution in this regard. As Hegedus (1989) has shown, these movements have important cultural and ethical dimensions that require the creation of networks that transcend national boundaries. They address issues in which the stakes and needs are transnational (Rosenau, 1993). If we consider the ecology movement, for instance, we notice that it is composed of a broad range of more or less interlinked groups, associations, and networks, some of which limit their activities to the local level, others to the provincial or national level, and others primarily to the international level. Individuals participating in these groups share values and a vision of the world, and they face common problems. They are conscious of their personal responsibility for the future of the planet and believe that national governments cannot meet this responsibility. The ecology movement therefore not only contributes to the integration of individuals through international networks (Friends of the Earth, Greenpeace, Sierra Club, etc.) but also ensures the development of a sense of belonging that approximates a kind of citizenship transcending national borders. In fact, several ecological groups attempt to pressure nation-states but very often do so via the international level. If they operate at the national level, it is because of an absence of effective institutions at the global level. Both the degradation of communal human goods, particularly water and the atmosphere, and the existence of strong globally based ecology movements contribute, separately and collectively, to the globalization process. First, by clearly showing that the stakes are global and

that the solutions cannot be viewed in strictly national terms, and second, by orienting their activities primarily to the global and local levels (both sub- and supra-national social movements, and the forces to which they are responding), new social movements put in question the principal paradigms that are the basis of the nation-state and the international order.

Breton and Jenson (1992) argue that new social movements involve a reconfiguration of political space in the sense that they contribute to the creation of communities that exist independently of national mediation. These communities emerge through networks of contacts that are not under the control, in terms of policy, of government. The emergence of such new political identities, transcending the self and the national space, is not only the product of globalization but also a contribution to the global reconfiguration of space, because it entails intensification of transnational relationships:

> The point about these antisystemic movements is that they often elude the traditional categories of nation, state, and class. They articulate new ways of experiencing life, a new attitude to time and space, a new sense of history and identity. Indeed, it may not be far-fetched to suggest that they are in the process of redefining the meaning and boundaries of civil society. (Camilleri, 1990, p. 35)

In so doing, they are contributing to the creation of a global ethos and networks of sub- and supra-national solidarity, and they thus contribute to the complexity of an increasingly unified world.

Globalization therefore means that the new global system will be much less state-centric. Because the state is no longer the only point of reference for explaining global integration, it is important, as Rosenau has suggested, to take into account the fact that nonsovereign sub- and supra-national actors also have an important role in the integration process; we should not substitute state actors by nonstate actors, and we have to recognize the influence of a plurality of actors (Rosenau, 1993). This means also that we must adapt our conceptions of the relationships between the nation-state and civil society, and between political authority and political community. The space in which social relations materialize and the community that contributes to the definition of our identity are less and less associated with our national space. As Breton (1993) notes, the space in which most individuals act every day does not correspond anymore with the borders of the society to which we belong.

In sum, we have attempted in this section to show how current trends in the global economy, in technological change, in communications, in social movements, and in identity/culture have each in their own way, and at their own pace, created interconnections within and across national spaces, and that this fact contributes to the globalization process. Recognizing that globalization is more than an interstate phenomenon has important implications for the paradigms we use to analyze the economic, political, and social phenomena of our time. We now consider more closely what this implies about our understanding of sport as an economic and cultural phenomenon.

Studying Sport in the Context of Globalization Processes

The topics of world economy and global culture have been widely discussed in the current literature on globalization and sport as noted. Our discussion also has pointed out different avenues for a better conceptualization of globalization processes, while emphasizing their impact on state/civil society relationships. In this section, we return to some of these points and discuss how they might be helpful in the current debate. Moreover, to date the topic of new social movements has been absent from the debates on globalization and sport, and we underline the importance of their study.

Analyzing sport as part of either Americanization or globalization processes implies different paradigms. Those who insist on an analysis in terms of imperialism start from the postulate of the primacy of internal logics to explain economical and cultural flows, as well as state action. Therefore, the Americanization or Japanization of sport would be a result of economic, cultural, and political dynamics predominantly specific to these countries. On the contrary, an analysis in globalization terms, while taking into account the existence of different nation-states, would underline how economic and cultural flows are the products of dynamics that are independent of these nation-states and that operate at the world level. Thus, linking sport to globalization leads to all analysis of sport as part of an emergent global culture, as contributing to the definition of new identities, and to the development of a world economy. Therefore, the debate between globalization and Americanization is more than a question of vocabulary. Indeed, it is a question of paradigmatic choice, which leads to completely different interpretations of a series of phenomena.

The sporting goods manufacturing industry, for example, is largely composed of multinational firms that not only aim at growing shares of a world market but also adopt global strategies of production, such as delocalization. Upscale (technology-intensive) products are manufactured in industrialized countries, while downscale (labor-intensive) products are manufactured in southeastern countries. Thus, according to Andreff (1988, p. 99), a new international division of labor is emerging. As a result, a growing portion of the population in developing countries is engaged in the production of goods for the reproduction of the lifestyles of those living in developed countries (Andreff, 1988). Take, for example, the ice skating and hockey equipment sector, which may be the only sector dominated by Canadian firms. Some of the production of the largest Canadian manufacturers like Canstar, SLM (Sport Maska/CCM), along with some production work of the smaller ones, is delocalized. While medium and high end of the market skates, as well as protective garments, are manufactured in Canada, gloves and some of the protective garments (i.e., shin and shoulder pads) are produced under license in Taiwan and other parts of Asia such as Korea and Pakistan (cf. Van Zant, 1993).

Moreover, corporations in the sport industry (manufacturers of sporting goods, professional sport franchises, etc.) are often only small divisions of industrial or financial conglomerates integrated into the global market, conglomerates that flourish regardless of national structures of accumulation. The fact that these firms are linked to American or Japanese capital is almost meaningless. The important point is that they participate in and respond to global, not regional, logics. Therefore, the association of sport with globalization has to be seen not only in the globalization of certain sports but also in the ownership structures of sport industries.

With regard to cultural flows, major sporting events (Olympic Games, tennis tournaments, the soccer World Cup, etc.) are ideal vehicles for multinational firms in their world market penetration strategies, thus contributing to the commodification and homogenization of cultures. Even if this homogenized culture is largely American, it is only the result of the relative importance of American culture and economy in globalization processes. As American firms act in the world market on the basis of their insertion into the world economy, rather than on the basis of specific American interests, American cultural forms are the ones dominating the emergence of a global culture because they are supported by American firms acting in the global market.

Besides, some sport forms contribute to globalization not by contributing to the development of a metaculture, but rather through a fragmented and segmented culture regrouping individuals independently from the national level. Such is the case, to a certain extent, for high-performance athletes whose identities are linked more to a network of training and competition than to any element of their national belonging, such as language or religion.

> Airline pilots, computer programmers, international bankers, journalists, show business stars, experts in ecology, demographers, accountants, professors, athletes, constitute a new breed of men and women for whom religion, culture and nationality only have a marginal importance in comparison to their professional life. (Barber quoted by Rosenau, 1993, p. 507; our translation)

Reducing the interpretation of these examples to cultural imperialism gives too much importance to the dominant character of a culture and neglects the fact that this culture is developing as an element of globalization processes. In the literature, there is a tendency to see any deviation from the global culture as a form of resistance to cultural imperialism. Rather, some of these deviations should be seen as contributors to globalization or, in other words, to the creation of a fragmented global culture. This is precisely the case with new social movements.

New Social Movements and the Globalization of Sport

"Social movements are phenomena that defy clear definition" (Thiele, 1993, p. 273). New social movements differ from older ones since they (a) are not linked to specific economic interests (such as the workers' movement), (b) work toward change in society's values, and (c) work for the collective good. They are fluid, their membership is diverse, they take different organizational forms, and they vary in size, composition, and forms of actions. They are often active at local, national, and transnational levels in the form of loose networks of groups and organizations. They are decentralized, open, and governed democratic structures. Some even lack any formal international structural organization. Thiele (1993) and others note that what is more important is their orientation to global citizenship. They deal with international problems: "The transnational nature of social movements has as much to do with their attitudinal and informal linkages

as their official organizational structure. The politics they practice are supposed to be global in intent, if not always in origin and effect" (Thiele, 1993, p. 281).

There is no example of sport-specific, organized, new social movements like feminism, pacifism, and ecologism. However, sport has been deeply influenced by and has contributed to these movements. The fact that there is no new social movement specific to sport does not diminish the relevance of this phenomenon. The following examples show the interrelationships between these movements and sport. Our examples range from strategies aiming at changes in sport at the global level, to local initiatives inspired by cultural changes promoted by the larger new social movements. Due to the limitations of this paper, our objective is not to provide a final account of this question but rather to call for more substantial analyses.

Feminism

The feminist movement has had the most significant impact on sport. Over the past century, this movement has been known by numerous names, and those involved in the movement have fought for many different causes and goals. One common cause, which is still a very prominent issue, has been the fight of women for equality in the Olympic games. Women joined forces behind Alice Millat and created the Fédération sportive féminine internationale, which was responsible for the organization of the Women's Olympics in 1922 and the Women's World Games in 1926, 1930, and 1934. The success of these games forced the male-dominated International Olympic Committee (IOC) to permit the participation of women in the Olympics, although the IOC maintained strict control by limiting women to a small number of disciplines. The members of the IOC justified their position because of the "ideal of the female frailty" (Theberge, 1991, p. 386), a belief that still seems to persist today among many IOC members.

During the 1960s, feminist movements in western industrialized countries expanded and eventually won more and more battles. The American feminist movement made significant inroads with Title IX (although this has since been seen to have produced only limited improvements). In Canada, a "second wave" (Keyes, 1991) of feminism in the 1960s also led to demands for more equity in the Canadian sport system. According to Keyes, in the 1980s, new developments marked the history of women in sport in Canada. The most significant event during this period was the establishment of the Canadian Association for the Advancement of Women and Sport (CAAWS) in 1981, an organization set up to press the Canadian government for greater equity in sport. Although CAAWS is funded by the same government it tries to lobby for changes, it can be seen as a sport branch of the Canadian women's movement. In fact, links are constantly kept between CAAWS and other organizations within the Canadian women's movement.

Women from all over the world have put pressure on the Olympic movement, as well as on sport organizations at the local level, in order to improve equity in sport and, as shown by Birrell and Richter (1987), are actively involved in creating feminist alternatives to male sport. Women from numerous countries are also involved in loose networks of information exchanges and lobbying efforts to achieve changes in sport. The action of feminists in sport is based on a set of shared values about equality (despite the existing debates within the movement about some elements of those values), which are not linked to any element of national culture but rather to a common view of citizenship. By acting at the infra- and supra-national levels, the feminist movement contributes to the development of global social relations, while these same global social relations are also a basis for their action.

Antiracism

The antiapartheid movement has been the most effective social movement in sport to date, while sport has been, at the same time, a key element in the spread of this movement. Indeed, with the recent demise of the apartheid regime in South Africa and corresponding changes in the sport structure, the objective of freeing South African sport from institutionalized race discrimination is in the process of being met. As noted by numerous authors (e.g., Ramsamy, 1991), racism in the Olympics has a long history. The anthropological games organized in conjunction with the St. Louis games in 1904 were one of the most blatant examples of overt racism, although these have to be put in the perspective of dominant Darwinian political ideas prevailing among the hegemonic nations of the time (cf. Hoberman, 1991). Even if South Africa has been plagued by racism since the beginning of colonial times, it was when the National Party came to power in 1948 that apartheid policy, the institutional segregation of races, was actually put in place. The first organization to try to gain recognition for nonwhite sport was the South African Sport Association (SASA). Eventually, it led to the creation of the South African Non-Racial Olympic Committee (SAN-ROC) in

1963. Finally, in 1979, the South African Council of Sport (SACOS) was created.

Meanwhile, protests and lobbying for the exclusion of South Africa from international competition were being organized. In 1964, after intense pressure, the IOC withdrew the invitation to South Africa to participate in the Olympics. Two years later, the Supreme Council for Sport in Africa (SCSA) was formed by the African countries. Threats as well as actual boycotts of the Olympics were soon issued to offset any possibility of South African participation in these events. Moreover, SCSA and SAN-ROC teamed to campaign for the exclusion of South Africa from the Olympic movement, and their objective was met in 1970. The next step was to cut South Africa off from any opportunity to participate in international sports competitions. Other boycotts were organized, such as the one to protest New Zealand's participation in the Olympics because a rugby team from New Zealand toured South Africa in 1976. As a result, 22 countries were not present in Montréal for the Olympic games. Several other measures were taken in order to isolate South Africa from international sport. In 1977, the Gleneagles Agreement was signed by the Commonwealth countries discouraging any contact between member countries in any sport exchange with South Africa, and to deny that country the opportunity to participate in the Commonwealth Games. In 1980, the United Nations issued a ban on any sport contact with South Africa. The most recent initiative of the Olympic community to monitor apartheid in South African sport was the creation of an Apartheid and Sport Commission by the IOC in 1988.

In the early 1990s apartheid started to vanish to the point that the first nonracial elections were held in 1994. In 1992, South Africa was allowed to participate in the Barcelona Olympics after recognition by the IOC of the newly appointed South African National Olympic Committee presided over by Sam Ramsamy, the former president of SAN-ROC.

Why has the antiapartheid movement in sport been so successful? Kidd believes the movement was led by "an extremely able group of men and women who shrewdly, sometimes audaciously, took advantage of the ideological claims of modern sport, the ambitions of sport federations and governments, and growing world concern about the crisis within South Africa to advance their cause" (1988, p. 648).

Also, in the late 1960s and the 1970s, the movement profited from the international affirmation trend of the postcolonial African countries and of the more general antiapartheid movement. Jarvie (1984, p. 83) pointed out that the struggles waged by the sporting proletariat in South Africa were as important as the international sport boycotts.

How can we understand the antiapartheid contribution to globalization processes? This movement leaned on a communication network at infra- and supra-national levels that was indeed independent of national structures. This movement aimed for a regrouping of individuals at a global level. The individuals in this movement shared an idea of the human condition based on race equality, in which one identified with "the other" independent of national differences. Finally, this movement was very active at the international level, lobbying the IOC and the UN. Moreover, the antiracist message promoted by the movement was addressed to each individual on the planet, making it more and more difficult for countries to maintain exchanges and economic relationships with South Africa.

Local Initiatives

New social movements also have inspired local initiatives to change sport, and we consider two examples of such initiatives: (a) "inter-crosse" and the Fédération internationale d'inter-crosse, and (b)"Vélo-Québec" and the Tour de l'Ile of Montréal. In these examples, we see how the values of new social movements have the ability to create new sport forms and events.

Inter-crosse was invented in 1980 by the Fédération québécoise de crosse (FQC—Québec Lacrosse Federation). A modified form of lacrosse (itself derived from a traditional game of native people), inter-crosse is played with an aluminum and plastic stick and a soft rubber ball. The sport was created by a group of leaders of the FQC in reaction to the violent nature of lacrosse, a contact sport in which the traditional hard wood stick can become a harmful device. The new sport was also designed to promote more equity among teams, including gender equity. The form of the game was inspired by pacifism and feminism. Inter-crosse promotes four values: "the value of *movement* and activity for everyone; the value of *autonomy* and freedom for everyone; the value of *respect* for opponents; the value of *communication* with partners and opponents" (Fédération internationale d'inter-crosse, 1991, p. 6). With its rules of play which, among other things, require the players to pass the ball often, force the team to use each player during a game, and avoid physical contact, inter-crosse rapidly gained appeal among physical educators in Québec as an excellent way to teach team sports. There are now approximately 35,000 young Quebecers playing inter-crosse in school leagues.

Due to the local popularity of the sport, its supporters decided to promote the sport internationally in 1984. The Fédération internationale d'inter-crosse was created and based in the same office as the Québec federation. At this time, original rules were adopted for international competition:

The basic formula is to establish, as a fundamental belief, a non political and non conflictual partnership amongst our members. We do not believe in opposing nations in competition and our annual Inter-Crosse World Games which have grown from 6 to 15 nations in 4 years is not only a refreshing idea in the actual politically dominated sport scheme but also a very efficient strategy to introduce new nations to a new world order. (Fédération internationale d'inter-crosse, 1991, p. 8)

In order to take into account the demographic and economic inequalities among nations, to create more fairness in international competition, and to increase opportunities for exchanges among players of the participating countries, the following procedures were adopted. First, national teams are required to be mixed teams, and second, at the competition site, all the names of the players are pooled and teams are drafted by a computerized random selection process. In that way, no nation can win the competition and, at the same time, athletes have many opportunities to fraternize. "Sport does not have to be a political enterprise. Sport does not have to be an economic enterprise. Sport does not have to be a mass media affair. Sport does not have to be a drug filled fallacy" (Fédération internationale d'inter-crosse, 1991, p. 8). Under these conditions, for obvious reasons, there is currently no government assistance or corporate sponsorship for inter-crosse national teams. Despite the lack of media exposure at international tournaments, inter-crosse continues to gain in popularity, as evidenced by the fact that there are now 22 national federations affiliated with the Fédération internationale d'inter-crosse. To some extent inter-crosse and korfball, which originated in Holland, share common characteristics (see Crum, 1988).

The Tour de l'Ile of Montréal provides the second example. An annual one-day event celebrating mass participation in sport, it was created by ecology groups who wanted to promote the bicycle as an ecological mode of transportation. In the 1970s ecology organizations such as Le monde à bicyclette ("the cycling people") in Montréal and Les roues libres ("the free wheels") in Québec City started to organize mass protests against the monopoly of cars in large cities and, in turn, promoted the development of cycling paths. The protests involved tactics such as blocking traffic during rush hours. The promotion involved organizing small group tours of Montréal for cyclists. In 1985, the Tour de l'Ile was organized for the first time by Vélo Québec, the Québec cyclotourist federation. The objective of the event was to give the city, for a day, back to the cyclists. Some 3,500 cyclists registered for the first tour. Since 1992, only the first 45,000 registered cyclists are allowed to participate in the event. In 1992, a special tour was organized for children, one day before the big tour.

Currently, there are similar tours in almost every major city in Québec on an annual basis. But Vélo Québec had bigger goals, and in 1992, the Groupe Vélo organized a world cyclist conference regrouping two former major cyclist conferences: the Pro-Bike of the Bicycle Federation of America and the Vélo City of the European Cyclists Federation. Moreover, the conference was sponsored by UNESCO and the United Nations Program for the Environment. The theme of the conference was "The Bicycle, Vehicle of the Year 2000." Soon after the conference, a world secretariat for cyclists, with the mandate of coordinating efforts to promote bicycling as an environmentally respectful mode of transportation, was set up in Montréal, under the supervision of Vélo Québec. Driven by an ecological ethos, local groups began their efforts by pressuring local governments for cycle paths and promoting cycling as a mass participation sport. They eventually created an international network and are presently involved with organizations of the UN.

Pacifism and ecologism did not only lead to local initiatives. One example is the Global Anti-Golf Movement (GAG'M), a network of ecologist organizations that, according to its statement, is fighting against golf as "a 'sport' which destroys environment, creates social disruptions and which is financially unsound" (see also An & Sage, 1992; Stoddart, 1990).

As noted, the preceding examples are not sport-specific examples of new social movements. However, they are examples of the spillover effects of more general social movements on sport. They show us how alternatives to dominant forms of sport are invented out of the values of the new social movements. They are also good examples of the loose networks of organizations influencing action at the local and global levels. New social movements may not lead to major reforms of sport, but their very existence and the international networks they have forged have already led to much more than local impacts. Indeed, as shown with the example

of inter-crosse, a new sport born in Québec based on the values of a new social movement has developed internationally. The initiatives of the Fédération internationale d'inter-crosse and of Vélo Québec have contributed through sport to the strengthening of identities associated with new social movements. Our examples show how new sport forms associated with globalization do not necessarily contribute to its elements of mass culture or commodification of sport, but rather to the development of a fragmented culture, yet another phenomenon associated with globalization.

Conclusion

The purpose of this paper was to propose a reorientation of the current debate on globalization and sport. So far this debate had focused on the problem of imperialism, which is a different set of issues than globalization. Imperialism refers to economic or cultural domination of one country over another. Globalization refers to processes that alter substantially the very notion of nation-state; it refers to forces at play that are not based on the division of the world into national political spaces but rather emerge from integration across national political spaces. Economic globalization involves the disintegration of national economic activities and the development of a global logic of a world economy that is not in the national interests of any particular state. National economies become interdependent and driven by a global process of accumulation, which is not to say that asymmetrical development has disappeared. Thus economic, technological, cultural, and social globalization processes are at work in the emergence of a world integrated into a single space. This theoretical approach to forces and processes at work at the world level sheds new light on different types of phenomena related to sport; we hope such analyses will prove to be more in touch with reality.

At the economic level, the sporting goods industry contributes to globalization processes. Firms are linked to multinational corporations for which the accumulation process is global. These corporations delocalize, restructure their labor process, and diversify their investments, not to allow economic growth within any national state borders but rather to cope with global competition. This is also the case with the major sport events industry. However, those major events also play an important role in the definition of elements of mass culture at the global level. But, at the cultural level there is not only a process of homogenization: Identity/culture develops in an important way on the basis of fragmented processes. This is linked to the presence of new social movements.

The relationship between new social movements and sport has not only had an impact upon the latter but has also meant that sport has become an important vehicle for the development of infra- and supra-national links, as well as for the development of a common ethos for individuals throughout the world. New social movements allow individuals to develop networks and a sense of community through sport independent of the presence of national political levels.

In this paper, we have demonstrated (a) that globalization as a concept to understand world reality has become more relevant than imperialism, (b) that globalization leads not only to homogenization but also to more fragmented civil societies and to the development of world-wide relationships, and (c) that the study of new social movements is important to the study of sport in the context of globalization because it allows us to understand both better. It is our hope that this paper demonstrates the utility of integrating research on new social movements, and the many processes of globalization, to the study of sport. More and more phenomena associated with sport are the product of, and at the same time contribute to, the various processes of globalization.

References

An, M., & Sage, G. (1992). The golf boom in South Korea: Serving hegemonic interests. *Sociology of Sport Journal,* **9,** 354-371.

Andreff, W. (1988). Les multinationales et le sport dans les pays en développement: Ou comment faire courir le tiers monde après les capitaux [Multinational firms and sport in developing countries: Or how to remake the third world run after capital]. *Revue Tiers Monde,* **29**(113), 73-100.

Birrell, S., & Richter, D. (1987). Is a diamond forever? Feminist transformations of sport. *Women's Studies International Forum,* **10**(4), 395-409.

Breton, G. (1993). Mondialisation et science politique: La fin d'un imaginaire théorique [Globalization and political science: The end of a theoretical imaginary]. *Études internationales,* **24**(3), 497-512.

Breton, G., & Jenson J. (1992). Globalisation et citoyenneté: Quelques enjeux actuels [Globaliza-

tion and citizenship: Some contemporary issues]. In C. Andrew, L. Cardinal, et al. (Eds.), *L'ethnicité à l'heure de la mondialisation* [Ethnicity in the age of Globalization] (pp. 537-546). Ottawa, ON: ACFAS-Outaouais.

Camilleri, J.A. (1990). Rethinking sovereignty in a shrinking, fragmented world. In R.B.J. Walker & S.H. Mendlovitz (Eds.), *Contending sovereignties—Redefining political community* (pp. 13-44). Boulder, CO: Lynne Rienner.

Camilleri, J.A., & Falk, J. (1992). *The end of sovereignty? The politics of a shrinking and fragmenting world.* Aldershot, UK: Edward Elgar.

Cantelon, H., & Murray, S. (1993). Globalization and sport: The debate continued. *Leisure and Society,* **16**(2), 275-292.

Crum, B. (1988). A critical analysis of Korfball as a "non-sexist" sport. *International Review for the Sociology of Sport,* **23**(3), 233-241.

Falk, R. (1990). Evasions of sovereignty. In R.B.J. Walker & S.H. Mendlovitz (Eds.), *Contending sovereignties—Redefining political community* (pp. 61-78). Boulder, CO: Lynne Rienner.

Fédération internationale d'inter-crosse. (1991). *Dobry den Polska.* Unpublished conference of the federation director in Legnica, Poland.

Gereffi, G. (1984). Power and dependency in an interdependent world: A guide to understanding the contemporary global crisis. *International Journal of Comparative Sociology,* **25**(1-2), 509-528.

Giddens, A. (1990). *The consequences of modernity.* Stanford, CA: Stanford University Press.

Gruneau, R. (1988). Modernization or hegemony: Two views on sport and social development. In J. Harvey & H. Cantelon (Eds.), *Not just a game* (pp. 9-32). Ottawa, ON: University of Ottawa Press.

Guttman, A. (1991). Sport diffusion: A response to Maguire and the Americanization commentaries. *Sociology of Sport Journal,* **8,** 185-190.

Hanrieder, W.F. (1978). Dissolving international politics: Reflections on the nation-state. *The American Political Science Review,* **72**(4), 1276-1287.

Hegedus, Z. (1989). Social movements and social change in self-creative society: New civil initiatives in the international arena. *International Sociology,* **4**(1), 19-36.

Held, D. (1991). Democracy, the nation-state and the global system. In D. Held (Ed.), *Political theory today* (pp. 197-235). Cambridge, UK: Polity Press.

Hoberman, J. (1991). Olympic universalism and the apartheid issue. In F. Landry et al. (Eds.), *Sport . . . The third millennium* (pp. 523-534). Québec, PQ: Presses de l'Université Laval.

Houle, F. (1987). Réfexions sur la restructuration de l'État au Canada [Reflections on state restructuration in Canada]. *Interventions économiques*, (18), 71-83.

Jarvie, G. (1984). Sports, hegemony and problems of popular struggle in South Africa. In *Sports and politics* (Proceedings of the 26th ICHPER World Congress, 1983, Vol. II, pp. 77-86). Jerusalem: Emmanuel Gill and Wingate Institute for Physical Education and Sport.

Keable, J. (1993). Pierre Fortin: Dans le courant de l'eau salée [Pierre Fortin: In the salty water school of thought]. *Interface*, **14**(6), 7-10.

Keohane, R.O. (1984). *After hegemony: Cooperation and discord in the world political economy*. Princeton, NJ: Princeton University Press.

Keyes, M. (1991). Feminist lobbying and decision-making power in fitness and amateur sport policies, programs and services: The case of Canada. In F. Landry et al. (Eds.), *Sport . . . The third millenium* (pp. 419-430). Québec, PQ: Presses de l'Université Laval.

Kidd, B. (1988). The campaign against sport in South Africa. *International Journal*, **43**(4), 643-664.

Kidd, B. (1991). How do we find our voice in the "new world order"? A commentary on Americanization. *Sociology of Sport Journal*, **8**, 178-184.

Klein, A. (1991). Sport and culture as contested terrain: Americanization in the Caribbean. *Sociology of Sport Journal*, **8**, 79-85.

McKay, J., Lawrence, G., Miller, T., & Rowe, D. (1993). Globalization and Australian sport. *Sport Science Review*, **2**(1), 10-28.

McKay, J., & Miller, T. (1991). From old boys to men and women of the corporation: The Americanization and commodification of Australian sport. *Sociology of Sport Journal*, **8**, 86-94.

Maguire, J. (1990). More than a sporting touchdown: The making of American football in England 1982-1990. *Sociology of Sport Journal*, **7**, 213-237.

Maguire, J. (1993). Globalization, sport, development, and the media/sport production complex. *Sport Science Review*, **2**(1), 29-47.

Michalet, C.A. (1976). *Le capitalisme mondial* [World capitalism]. Paris: Presses Universitaires de France.

Petrella, R. (1989). La mondialisation de la technologie et de l'économie—Une (hypo)thèse prospective [Globalization of technology and economy—A prospective hypothesis]. *Futuribles*, (135), 3-25.

Rail, G. (1992). Sport au féminin: Pour une réappropriation du corps [Women's sport: For a reappropriation of the body]. In M.-L. Garceau (Ed.), *Relevons le défi* [Let us take the challenge] (Proceedings of the conference on feminist intervention in North East Ontario, pp. 231-254). Ottawa, ON: University of Ottawa Press.

Ramsamy, S. (1991). Apartheid and olympism: On the abolishment of institutionalized discrimination in international sport. In F. Landry et al. (Eds.), *Sport . . . The third millenium* (pp. 537-546). Québec, PQ: Presses de l'Université Laval.

Robertson, R. (1990). Mapping the global condition: Globalization as the central concept. In M. Featherstone (Ed.), *Global culture: Nationalism, globalization and modernity* (A *Theory, Culture, & Society* special issue, pp. 15-30). London: Sage.

Rosenau, J.N. (1990). *Turbulences in world politics: A theory of change and continuity*. Princeton, NJ: Princeton University Press.

Rosenau, J.N. (1993). Les processus de la mondialisation: Retombées significatives, échanges impalpables et symbolique subtile [Globalization processes: Significant fall-outs, impalpable exchanges and subtle symbolics]. *Études internationales*, **24**(3), 497-512.

Stoddart, B. (1990). Wide world of golf: A research note on the interdependence of sport, culture, and economy. *Sociology of Sport Journal*, **7**, 378-388.

Theberge, N. (1991). Women and the Olympic Games: A consideration of gender, sport, and social change. In F. Landry et al. (Eds.), *Sport . . . The third millenium* (pp. 385-395). Québec, PQ: Presses de l'Université Laval.

Thiele, L.P. (1993). Making democracy safe for the world—Social movements and global politics. *Alternatives*, **18**(3), 273-305.

Thomson, J.E., & Krasner, S.D. (1989). Global transactions and the consolidation of sovereignty. In E.O. Czempiel & J.N. Rosenau (Eds.), *Global changes and theoretical challenges*. Lexington, UK: Lexington Books.

Van Zant, J.W. (1993). *The Canadian ice skating and hockey equipment sector*. Unpublished manuscript, Consumer Products Branch, Industry Science and Technology Canada, Ottawa, ON.

Wagner, E. (1990). Sport in Asia and Africa: Americanization or mundialization? *Sociology of Sport Journal*, **7**, 399-402.

Whitson, D., & Macintosh, D. (1993). Becoming a world-class city: Hallmark events and sport franchises in the growth strategies of western Canadian cities. *Sociology of Sport Journal*, **10**, 221-240.

Sport and Culture As Contested Terrain: Americanization in the Caribbean

Alan M. Klein

In looking at the "Americanization" of sport in other societies, we are essentially looking at a version of cultural colonialism. Sport, as a segment of popular culture, is certainly an effective form of promoting cultural hegemony. However, this essay argues for the use of cultural resistance as an opposing notion. Based on the author's study of Dominican baseball, the picture of a tension between hegemonic and resistant cultural forces is summarized and offered as a model to other sports researchers. The Dominican study examined the structural properties of major league baseball's domination of the sport in the Caribbean. Resistance to major league baseball was not structurally apparent and required looking at more subtle indices. Fans' preferences for symbols, content analysis of the sports pages in Santo Domingo, and examples of concrete behavior were looked at. Other researchers may find different indices more appropriate, but the use of sport related phenomena are felt to be valuable sources.

Studying the impact of one country's sport on another falls under the rubric of intercultural relations and, as such, calls for a cross-cultural perspective. The cultural relations discussed here are those between industrial and developing nations. These are, at their core, based on qualitative and quantitative power differentials. Rooted in the political-economy of colonialism, the gap in production, distribution, and consumption between industrialized nations and those still attempting to industrialize has in

virtually all cases remained unbridged. For sport sociologists, this means that the study of third-world sport may necessitate the use of slightly different, albeit compatible, tools and concepts from those we use to study Euro-North America or Europe. The issues of culture and political power are critical here.

At the level of political-economic relations, Euro-North American domination of developing countries reflects the latest expression of neo-colonialism. Collectively, the political economy of underdevelopment has been thoroughly analyzed by a host of scholars including Frank (1978), Wallerstein (1974), Wolf (1982), Mandel (1978), or de Jandry (1986). These experts may differ as to the causes and machinations of third-world exploitation, but none denies its occurrence.

However, the colonial domination that is manifested as exploitation is never complete. The tension between hegemony and counterhegemonic forces outlined by Williams (1977), and which has become a basic tenet of Gramcian cultural studies, is quite evident in colonial relations. Cultural resistance to colonial powers and to forces such as Americanization may take a variety of forms, and all aspects of culture may lend themselves to interpretation and reinterpretation as aspects of resistance. Thus, sport may easily be seen as contested cultural terrain (cf., Donnelly, 1988; Gruneau, 1983).

Americanization is apparent in all aspects of the Caribbean, but particularly in the Spanish-speaking islands and surrounding nations. In addition to colonialism, economic domination, and exploitation, the Monroe Doctrine has been used to repeatedly justify American intervention (e.g., Nicaragua)

Reprinted from Klein, 1991.

and invasion (e.g., Cuba, the Dominican Republic, Grenada, Panama). The prevalence of baseball as a major sport in the Spanish-speaking nations is one of the more obvious cultural manifestations of Americanization in the region. The case of baseball in the Dominican Republic provides an interesting example of these forces at work.

Baseball and Hegemony in the Dominican Republic

North American baseball interests in Latin America operate very much like other multinational corporations. They essentially locate cheap resources for manufacture and consumption elsewhere. While Latino players have been in the major leagues since the turn of the century, it is with the removal of the racial barriers in major league baseball in 1947 that large numbers of Latino players (most of them racially characterized as black) began to find their way into North America. This movement north was dominated first by the Cubans and then by the Dominicans.

Beginning with Ozzie Virgil in 1955 as the first Dominican major leaguer, their numbers grew to include the San Francisco Giants bonanza of the three Alou brothers and Juan Marichal, among others. Prior to 1980 there were 49 Dominican major leaguers, but the numbers have grown astronomically since then. In the 1990 winter meetings, 65 Dominicans were protected on major league rosters; 325 are playing in the minor leagues; and almost as many Dominicans are playing in the major leagues in this year as appeared in the 25 years prior to 1980.

The establishment of free agency in 1976 was a major watershed in Dominican baseball. Prior to that time, and dating back to the formal establishment of ties between professional Dominican teams and North American teams, the winter league was the backbone of Dominican baseball. From 1955, when major league teams formally established working relations with Dominican teams, the subordination of Dominican baseball to North American interests began in earnest. At first it included a shift in play from summer (which competed directly with North American play) to winter. In this format, major league teams would provide staff (managers, coaches, and even players) to the Dominican professional teams, while the Dominican teams would help scout talent and protect prospective players on their rosters. It seemed mutually beneficial, and it was.

Through the late 1960s and the 1970s, increasing numbers of Dominicans were found on major league rosters, and scouts and others focused more and more attention on the Dominican Republic as a baseball center. On a structural level, however, this boom facilitated increased dependency on major league baseball teams for the running of Dominican baseball. Prior to the second discovery of Hispaniola in 1955 (the first had been 450 years earlier), Dominican baseball (which dates back to 1890) exhibited an autonomy and self-determination. Dominicans developed their own style, their own heroes, their own traditions. With the coming of major league teams into the area, this cultural autonomy was eroded. No one seemed to mind that scouts regularly operated as brigands signing 13-year-olds, or failed to pay parents their due in signing bonuses, as the nation began to bask in the attention and glory being focused on its sport contribution.

By 1980 free agency, fueled by lucrative television contracts, had begun to affect all of the major league players' salaries. The meteoric rise in salaries had a particularly pernicious effect in Dominican professional baseball (Klein, 1989, 1991). When in 1970 the average salary for major leaguers was $29,300, the money earned ($2,100) in the course of a winter in the Dominican leagues was significant. By 1989 the average salary for major leaguers was approaching $600,000, making the $10,500 offered by Dominican owners meaningless. Multiyear contracts, often in excess of $1 million a year, had the effect of making potential players in the Dominican leagues think twice about risking their career to an injury.

The impact of this was to seriously impair the likelihood of Dominican stars (in the major leagues) from playing in their homeland. Professional baseball had reached a crisis point by 1989 when the fans began to stay away from stadia throughout the country.

The second major development that had a negative impact on the Dominican baseball scene was the establishment of major league baseball academies throughout the island. Prior to the academies, the best Dominican prospects were traditionally scouted as they played on the many amateur teams in the country. The refineries, the military and police, and the many company-sponsored teams made up a layered structure of amateur baseball. From here a prospect would try to attract the many visiting scouts from the United States and Canada or the attention of the powerful owners of professional Dominican teams.

By the late 1970s two clubs had established academies in which they would develop their own talent: the Toronto Blue Jays and the Los Angeles Dodgers. There are now 13 academies where the rookies are trained from the age of 17 (now the minimum age for signing a rookie), fed, clothed, and paid by the organization. To be signed, one needed to try out, and tryouts were regularly held at the academy. A prospect would come down on his own or at the invitation of one of the scouts associated with the club. Once signed, he was officially professional, receiving a signing bonus and monthly salary during the two seasons that he played. The rookie academies developed their own league, playing two seasons a year (summer and winter), and developed their own ties with professional Dominican teams to which they would send players. During his time at the academy, the rookie would be regularly evaluated and, if found to be improving, would be placed in one of the minor league rosters in the U.S.

The growth of the academies had the effect of weakening amateur baseball on the island. Rather than play on amateur teams for a number of years, young prospects would attempt to bypass the amateur leagues by trying out for the academies. If rejected, they would simply move to one of the other academies or even return a few months later. However it worked, the tendency to bypass the amateur leagues was pronounced enough by the late 1980s to warrant periodic editorials in the Santo Domingo dailies denouncing the academies as foreign intruders (Klein, 1991).

More recently, new evidence of the further erosion of Dominican baseball autonomy comes from the presence of Japanese academies. The Hiroshima Carp have begun building a new academy that is even more sumptuous than that of the Los Angeles Dodgers, with the goal of developing their own talent. This would at some point set off a bidding war between heavily invested North American teams and the heavily capitalized Japanese, one byproduct of which would be the further erosion of Dominican amateur baseball.

In a related development, the annual Caribbean World Series (newly renamed by the North Americans as "Winterball") played by the national champions of the Dominican Republic, Mexico, Venezuela, and Puerto Rico has also shown the effects of major league domination. Beginning in 1990 the annual round-robin tournament was shifted from its rotating base between the competing nations to Miami, Florida. The traditional source of national pride that resulted from hosting and/or winning the tournament has been shattered by being bought for the entertainment of American fans (no television coverage back to the represented countries). In return for allowing the series to be played in the U.S. from 1990 to 1992, the teams will be paid $60,000 (U.S.) each year. Last February only a few thousand Latino fans (those able to afford the trip) witnessed the series, while even fewer American fans paid to see it. All of the countries involved decried the conditions under which they played, and Mexico went so far as to claim they would not forego their turn to host the series. The symbolic loss of the series to North American interests only rankles those Latino nationalists who see so many of their cultural sources of pride being bought by rich foreigners, particularly North Americans.

Baseball As Resistance

Despite the increasing structural domination of Dominican baseball, Dominicans are not without their forms of resistance. Resistance may be active as in slave revolts or sabotage, or it may be more passive as in subtle forms of protest. Scott (1983) has presented these as "everyday forms of resistance," as have Genovese (1972) and Hebdige (1983) among others. Such forms of resistance work to keep alive alternative and/or forbidden traditions until such time as they may come to the fore. It is also important to understand that in developing nations the colonial heritage is strong enough to engender anger and resentment in the face of pronounced feelings of sociocultural inferiority. For them, nationalism is a manifestation of cultural resistance (Klein, 1988, 1991). The more they have to boast about, the better they feel, but the boasting never occurs in a vacuum; rather it becomes a symbolic slap at the class or foreign presence that may be in a position of superiority at the moment.

It was noteworthy that while the Dominican Republic has been undergoing a steady economic decline for some time, there has been little outrage on the streets or in the press directed against North Americans. Certainly, Dominicans have not been without their heroes in the fight against foreign occupation. The three founding fathers of the republic (Mello, Duarte, Rodriguez) were liberators from hated Haitian occupation; and many Dominicans are the descendents and survivors of the guerilla fighting against U.S. Marines during the first occupation in 1916-1924 and a second in 1965-1966. But now, in the midst of economic stagnation and ineptitude, there is little overt resistance, few who publicly point fingers.

This apparent absence of malice was betrayed in, of all places, the sports pages. A content analysis of the sports print media was my first index of resistance (Klein, 1991). There are two forms of baseball reporting in the Dominican daily newspapers: summer and winter. Both are revealing in that they fuel Dominican nationalism and act as a medium for rarely directed anger against the stifling North American presence.

During the summer, Dominican players are in North America among their various teams. The press works to highlight their accomplishments during that time. Lead stories and headlines boldly declare the achievements of Dominicans. While this may not appear unusual, what makes it so is that the outcomes of the games are secondary to the Dominican performance. During one 3-week stretch in 1988 , I counted only 3 out of 22 lead story headlines that had to do with non-Dominican events (Baltimore Orioles losing streak). The other 19 all had to do with Dominicans, not as representatives of their teams, but rather as stellar performers of the day. April 20th is typical of this. The main headline read, "Bell, Lee, and Pena All Strike Two Singles." In listing the accomplishments of three Dominicans, there was no concern for where they played: two played for the Toronto Blue Jays, the other for St. Louis. Clearly the emphasis is on how well Dominicans are doing in North America, not with whom. By grouping people along nationalistic lines there is an implicit comparison made against the "Norteamericanos."

Individual contests are subfeatures of all such reporting. Here too, the preoccupation was with Dominican presence and performance. In the absence of Dominicans, other Latino players would do, because the important point was that Latinos are up there in the major leagues, not only doing well but outperforming North Americans. The following entry is illustrative of the rampant nationalism of the sports press:

For Minnesota the *Panamanian* Juan Berenguer pitched one and two-thirds innings, permitted two hits, struck out four and walked one. For Toronto the *Dominican* Tony Fernandez was 1 for 5, his *countryman* George Bell was 2 for 4. The *Puerto Rican* Juan Beniquez added a run in two turns at bat. The other *Quisqueyena* [colloquialism for Dominican] Manny Lee hit a single in three trips and scored a run, while his *compatriot* Nelson Liriano went 1 for 4. (emphasis added to indicate nationalism)

Other forms of nationalism are found in the special types of stories one finds. Much is made of the salaries earned by Latinos or the honors bestowed upon them by their teams and leagues. However, there is also the establishment of a Latino notion of baseball excellence, which represents a universe of discourse free of North American influence but is judged as operating on a level every bit as high as major league baseball. Here I refer to the establishment of "All Latino" teams, or Latino All-Star teams regularly generated by Latino press, whether it be Dominican or other south-of-the-border nations.

During the winter the reporting is quite different. It deals with the playing of Dominican winter league baseball. Here the interference of North American teams in league play and structure has angered many. Whether it has to do with forcing Dominican or American players to leave the country before the end of the season or coercing local stars into forgoing play altogether, the meddling of major league teams has angered the fans, Dominican team owners, and the press. Many of these issues are met head on by owners and journalists who regularly call for the expulsion of major league teams from the country.

Yet another index of cultural resistance was found in a study of Dominican baseball fans and their symbol preferences (Klein, 1988). The consumption of North American culture by Dominicans is, given the Americanization of the Caribbean, predictably heavy. North American fashions, films, and music are often (although not always) uncritically consumed (Klein, 1991; Spitzer, 1972). Given this level of cultural colonialism, one would predict that in the context of baseball's dominance on the island, there would be further uncritical acceptance of major league teams.

I devised a questionnaire that asked fans to name their favorite North American team and the reasons for their choice, their favorite Dominican team, and why. Then I posed a hypothetical question to them. I made them choose between wearing a hat of their favorite North American team or their Dominican team, and I asked the reason for their choice. Based on larger cultural preferences for American products, I predicted that Dominicans would tend to choose American teams (especially those with many Dominican players) over local ones. The results of the survey ($n = 164$) were surprising: 78% chose the Dominican hat. When asked why, the answers were unambiguously nationalistic: for example, "I am Dominican." "This is my country, so I'll take Licey [local team]."

When analyzed by class position (from the demographic data obtained), we found that upper-class individuals (professionals/entrepreneurial) were twice as likely to choose a North American hat as were the poorer members of the sample. This is in keeping with notions of hegemony, since North American culture tends to be more slavishly followed by those with status. Still, of the upper class, 70% chose the Dominican hat. Clearly these symbol preferences were in a direction opposite to other forms of cultural consumption by Dominicans.

Finally, I looked at various forms of concrete behavior that might reflect cultural resistance. In a baseball context these ranged from foot dragging to confrontations between Dominicans and North Americans in which cultural issues were at the center. While such behavior is difficult to find, and motives are difficult to determine, the rumors and mythology that build up around these events or behaviors are as important as the event itself. What people falsely or accurately attribute to the event is as concrete and important as the event itself when it comes to cultural resistance because it enables one to build nationalism and express resentment.

Cultural resistance to the heavy presence of North American baseball interests is at odds with other cultural currents in the Dominican Republic. Whereas there is little expression of resistance elsewhere in the cultural interaction with North Americans, Dominicans have used baseball to express their resentment. The reason is not difficult to find: baseball is the only area of cultural interaction between the two countries in which the Dominicans exhibit an equality with or superiority over North Americans. Moreover, they do this in North America. Baseball enables Dominicans to see that their dominance in this arena is rewarded by North Americans materially as well as with a different view of Dominicans by those who in all other ways disregard them. Cultural resistance necessitates a break with the overvaluation of foreigners and the undervaluation of the social-self by engendering pride and nationalism (Klein , 1991).

Conclusion

The tension between hegemony and resistance in this study mirrors Donnelly's (1988) view of sport as contested terrain. Viewed in the context of the struggle between first- and third-world nations, the role of sport is enlarged and the contested terrain is more important than it would be in other cultural contexts. In discussing the penetration of the sport of football into England (Maguire, 1990), or comparable events in Canada, or the victory of any European country in World Cup competition, we are discussing a slightly different cultural phenome-

non. There is less at stake in winning or losing in the latter; the cultural symbols associated with these sport processes, while passionately felt, are less powerful. As I pointed out in my study, "Americans may love the game of baseball as much as Dominicans, but they don't need it as much as Dominicans do" (Klein, 1991, p. 4).

References

de Jandry, A. (1982). *The agrarian question and reformism in Latin America.* Baltimore: Johns Hopkins University Press.

Donnelly, P. (1988). Sport as a site for popular resistance. In R. Gruneau (Ed.), *Popular cultures and political practices.* Toronto: Garamond Press.

Frank, A.G. (1969). *Capitalism and underdevelopment in Latin America.* New York: Monthly Review Press.

Genovese, E. (1974). *Roll, Jordan, roll: The world the slaves made.* New York: Vintage.

Gruneau, R. (1983). *Class, sport, and social development.* Amherst: University of Massachusetts Press.

Hebdige, D. (1983). *Subculture: The meaning of style.* London: Methuen.

Klein, A. (1988). American hegemony, Dominican resistance, and baseball. *Dialectical Anthropology,* **13**, 301-313.

Klein, A. (1989). Baseball as underdevelopment: The political-economy of sport in the Dominican Republic. *Sociology of Sport Journal,* **6**, 95-112.

Klein, A. (1991). *Sugarball: The American game, the Dominican dream.* New Haven: Yale University Press.

Maguire, J. (1990). More than a sporting touchdown: The making of American football in England 1982-1990. *Sociology of Sport Journal,* **7**, 213-237.

Mandel, E. (1968). *Marxist economic theory* (2 Vols.) New York: Monthly Review Press.

Scott, J. (1983). *Weapons of the weak: Everyday forms of peasant resistance.* New Haven, CT: Yale University Press.

Spitzer, D. (1972). A contemporary political and socio-economic history of Haiti and the Dominican Republic. Doctoral dissertation, University of California, Berkeley.

Wallerstein, I. (1974). *Modern world system: Capitalist agriculture and the origins of the world economy.* New York: Academic Press.

Williams, R. (1977). *Marxism and literature.* New York: Oxford University Press.

Wolf, E. (1982). *Europe and the people without history.* Berkeley, CA: University of California Press.

Between and Beyond the Global and the Local: American Popular Sporting Culture in New Zealand

Steven J. Jackson
David L. Andrews

Abstract: This article examines how the National Basketball Association (NBA), an explicitly American, yet increasingly global media(ted) institution, can be located within the local context of New Zealand. Specifically, the article provides: (a) a brief overview of how and why the NBA transformed itself into a global sport commodity; (b) a contextualization of contemporary New Zealand along with a cursory examination of some empirical examples of the global/local nexus of the NBA; and (c) an analysis of how the NBA and American sporting culture serve as points of difference within what Robertson terms the "hegemonic global."

Key words: Americanization • globalization • Mass Media • New Zealand

Over the past decade globalization has emerged as one of the most debated phenomena within contemporary political, economic, cultural, technological and intellectual life (Albrow and King, 1990; Appadurai, 1996; Hall, 1991; Hirst and Thompson, 1996; King, 1990; Robertson, 1992a, 1992b). Though it undoubtedly oversimplifies the matter, contemporary discussions about globalization are concerned with the basis and consequences of postindustrial capitalism, economic flows, new media technologies, and the influence of largely, but not exclusively, American popular culture on contemporary social life throughout the world. In the sport-related literature scholars have adopted a variety of interpretive approaches: "globalization" (Bale and Maguire, 1994; Cantelon and Murray, 1993; Donnelly, 1996; Harvey et al., 1996, McKay et al., 1993; Maguire, 1994; Rowe, 1996a, 1996b; Rowe et al., 1994), "Americanization" (Jackson, 1994; Kidd, 1991; Klein, 1991; Maguire, 1993; McKay and Miller, 1991), "mundialization" (Wagner, 1990), and "creolization" (Houlihan, 1994). The most recent analyses, within both cultural studies generally, and the sociology of sport specifically, have focused on the complex debate about the relationships between global and local processes (Andrews, 1997; Andrews et al., 1996; Boyle and Haynes, 1996; Donnelly, 1996; Harvey et al., 1996; Jackson and Andrews, 1996; Maguire, 1993, 1994).

There are two key features of the global–local debate. First, how should we conceptualize the "local?" And, second, what is the nature and extent of global economic and cultural forces on local processes? With respect to the first point, Robins (1991: 35) conceptualizes the local as a "fluid and relational space, constituted only in and through its relation to the global." While this confirms the fact that the local should not be viewed as a self-contained, static, cultural site, the second question remains; that is, are global forces contributing to a process of *homogenization*, often characterized as "Americanization," or, alternatively, does an inherent uniqueness of local cultures enable them to transform, resist and

Reprinted from Jackson and Andrews, 1999.

indigenize global forces, thereby contributing to a process of accelerated *heterogenization*? According to Andrews et al. (1996), those who might be described as *homogenizers* pessimistically anticipate the emergence of a globally shared, universalized culture. Conversely, *heterogenizers* refute such a determinist view of globalization, arguing instead for a recognition and celebration of every particular localized culture. Thus, despite Robins's (1991) dialectic conceptualization of the local, there has been a theoretical dichotomization with respect to the effects of global process on local culture. In response, several theorists have called for a more dynamic, multidirectional approach to understanding the *global–local nexus,* one which returns us to the roots of cultural studies' focus on the relationship between culture and the economy (Appadurai, 1996; Featherstone and Lash, 1995; Grossberg, 1997; Robertson, 1995).

Grossberg (1997: 8) has argued that the "current thinking about globalisation is too often structured by an assumed opposition between the global and the local, where the local is offered as the intellectual and political corrective of the global." Such approaches tend to privilege "the local as a site of local knowledge/facts, of the real, of agency and resistance." In effect, the local becomes a celebrated "exemplar of the concrete" (1997: 9). In this way, Grossberg challenges the romanticization of the local espoused by those subscribing to the heterogenization perspective. Acknowledging Grossberg's reservations, we wish to make two observations in regard to current debates about globalization. First, like Robins, we emphasize that both the global and the local can only be understood in relation to each other. Second, we identify the need to recognize that globalization itself is constitutive of, and constituted by, multiple processes which are engaged to differing degrees, at differing intensities, and in differing spatial locations. In turn, such articulations result in the formation of what Appadurai (1990) refers to as *disjunctures*, based upon ethnoscapes, mediascapes, technoscapes, finanscapes, and ideoscapes. Here we use the term *disjuncture* to refer to the diverse set of consequences that result when global forces and local contexts meet. Thus, disjunctures can provoke conflict, incongruence, and resistance, but they can also refer to expressions of accommodation, acceptance, and even ambivalence. With respect to the asymmetrical effects of global processes, especially in terms of their political ramifications, we concur with Grossberg's (1997: 20) observation that:

> Too much attention to the global often leads
> critics to the unearned, pessimistic conclusion

that the victory—of capitalism, of American imperialism, etc.—is already sewn up. Too much attention to the local often leads critics to lose sight of the fact that someone is winning the struggle and, as we all know, it is rarely the periphery.

Hence, caution is required in both overstating and understating the effects of globalization. With this in mind we locate the presence of American sporting culture in New Zealand between and beyond the global and the local.

This study examines the global/local nexus of American popular culture, as represented by the National Basketball Association (NBA) and its attendant corporate and intertextual alliances in New Zealand. Thus, the aim here is to examine how the NBA, an explicitly American, yet increasingly global media(ted) institution, can be located within what Robertson (1995) has referred to as the *glocalized* context of New Zealand. Specifically, this article provides: (a) a brief overview of how and why the NBA transformed itself from a sport on the brink of failure to what many consider the world's most successful global sport entertainment organization; (b) a brief contextualization of contemporary New Zealand along with a cursory examination of some empirical examples of the global/local nexus of the NBA; and (c) an analysis of how the NBA and American sporting culture serve as points of *difference* which contribute to both the fetishization of the local and the fear and fascination of the "hegemonic global" (Robertson, 1992b: 29) in New Zealand.

Going Global: The (Trans) NBA

Considering its pre-eminent contemporary global presence, it is difficult to imagine a world without the NBA. Yet we should not forget the dramatic transformation that took the NBA from the verge of collapse in the late 1970s to its present success. In the years following its merger with the American Basketball Association in 1977, the NBA was at an all-time low in terms of image and economics (Voisin, 1991). Numerous factors have been identified to account for the league's troubles, including the fact that the league was widely viewed as being too regional, too black, and too drug-infested (Cole and Andrews, 1996). During the 1980s the NBA staged a remarkable comeback through the implementation of several innovations (e.g., anti-drug policies, collective bargaining, salary caps) as well as the timely emergence of a new generation of outstanding players (e.g., Magic Johnson and Larry Bird). However, on a semiotic level, the rising popularity of the NBA was engineered through the revolutionary way in which the league's administrators, guided by NBA Commissioner David Stern, creatively harnessed the expanding channels of the media in order to revive the game (Cole and Andrews, 1996). The astute Stern, who realized that American culture had become a "civilization of the image" (Kearney, 1989: 1), was responsible for transforming the NBA from an archaic professional sport industry into a multidimensional marketing and entertainment conglomerate, incorporating over 20 divisions, including NBA Properties, NBA Entertainment, NBA International, and NBA Ventures. By securing prime-time exposure on the major TV networks, regular billing on the expanding cable networks, and by developing in-house promotional programs, commercials, and prerecorded videos, Stern immersed the NBA within the "all engulfing dynamic of [televisual] promotion" which dominated post-industrial America (Wernick, 1991: 185). Thus, during the 1980s, the NBA experienced a remarkable transformation and had profound material effects on popular consumption practices. In quantitative terms the NBA's gross revenue has grown from $110 million at the start of the 1980s, to multi-billion dollar status today (Ryan and Cohen, 1996).

The NBA appeared to have found (or invented) the magic formula of corporate sporting success. Yet, in the American market the NBA had become a victim of its own prosperity (Andrews, 1997; Jackson and Andrews, 1996) and by the early 1990s was reaching a saturation point. As Don Sperling, director of NBA Entertainment, stated in 1991, "Domestically, we're tapped . . . Ratings have peaked. Attendance has peaked. The market here has peaked" (Voisin, 1991: F-1). Having outgrown its home market, the NBA realized that sustaining its anticipated growth would require the active cultivation of overseas markets. As Stern forewarned, "Global development is a certainty—with or without us" (Heisler, 1991: C1).

Consequently the NBA has become a *transnational* corporation. In order to attain its desired transnational presence the league formed an overseas division, NBA International (see Boeck, 1990) which became a key part of its organizational "commodity chain" (Korzeniewicz, 1994). In effect, this division cultivated the league's visibility overseas through TV and licensed merchandising deals negotiated in its regional offices in Geneva, Barcelona, Melbourne, Hong Kong, Mexico City, and Miami.

The TV coverage sold by NBA International has been touted as offering an avenue for integrated, cross-national promotional campaigns, "Global consumer-products companies are torn between a variety of ways to reach consumers . . . We're offering them one vehicle that does it all, that reaches a young and growing market base and that lends its own brand equity to theirs" (Grimm, 1992: 20). Consequently, a number of America's corporate icons have sought to enhance and refine their localized American identities within the global market, by joining forces with the NBA. Athletic footwear companies Nike, Reebok, and Converse have had particularly strong links with the NBA's global movement. Thus, the NBA is intertextually reinforced through the circulation of products such as caps, T-shirts, jackets, and a myriad of other items, all of which display one or more of the league's popular symbols, and hence act as effective promotional tools. The apparent omnipresence of these artifacts contributes to what Wilcox (1996: 123) describes as: "the 'worlding of America,' creating virtually seamless American representations of contemporary cultural issues and developments." However, while this position implies an imposition of an American flavored global culture, it is important to acknowledge that these products are often transformed and resisted as well as desired and demanded. The next section addresses this very issue by focusing on the presence of American sporting culture in New Zealand.

The "Trans" NBA and the Global/Local Nexus in New Zealand

Unlike many other multinational corporations who engage in an operational strategy known as "global localization," the NBA explicitly promotes itself as a signifier of cultural difference in an attempt to blend into the local culture and effectively become a part of the indigenous ethnoscape. It is through its exaggerated American identity that the league is able to appeal to local consumers. Consequently, the NBA's inverted rendition of global localization revolves around *not* becoming an accepted armature of the local culture by consciously developing the *authentic* NBA experience as an *authentic* American experience. However, we wish to assert that not only does "American" signify different things in different socio-cultural settings, but the precise signification and meaning of the explicitly "American NBA" is equally context-specific. At this point we return to the global/local nexus of American sporting culture in New Zealand. As a first step in understanding the global/local nexus of the NBA we briefly describe the contemporary context of New Zealand, particularly its media-scape.

Self-described as a "great little sporting nation" New Zealand is home to roughly 3.7 million people located in a relatively isolated position within the South Pacific (Jackson and Andrews, 1996). Historically a British colony, it is slowly shedding its colonial status in the post-World War II era and, like many nations, struggling to find its place and voice in the new world order. Once considered the *social laboratory of the world* because of its progressive social policies, New Zealand has undergone some dramatic social changes in the past 10 years. Indeed, it has become both the envy of and a model for other nations who are making dramatic shifts from social welfare systems to various forms of neo-liberal, economic rationalist, political frameworks (Haworth, 1994; Kelsey, 1996). Free-market analysts and political brokers alike have heralded the "success" of New Zealand's dramatic market deregulation, privatization, and the exodus of the state from many areas of social life (Duncan and Bollard, 1992). One area of deregulation that makes New Zealand unique particularly with respect to the influence of American popular culture is that associated with the media. According to Hutchison and Lealand (1996: 7) since deregulation in 1988-9, "New Zealand has witnessed a radical and revolutionary reshaping of its media-scape . . . that is unprecedented in the rest of the world." The significance of deregulation is that legally permitting 100 percent foreign ownership—an unparalleled situation within the OECD—enables those investors with enough resources to develop the infrastructure for satellite TV. In turn, due to the absence of sufficient local programming, it necessitates an increasing importation of foreign, largely American, media products (Spicer et al., 1996). For example, the emergence of the 24-hour SKY Sport network in New Zealand virtually demanded the securement of high-profile American sport programs. The NBA already had a small, but avid, following in New Zealand due in large part to weekly NBA highlight programs, weekly sports magazine shows, regular sport news coverage, and a domestic, national semi-professional league in which American imports competed. In sum, the shifting domestic mediascape, including the increasing demand for, and availability of, globally produced sports programs facilitated the NBA's emergence within New Zealand.

Globalization and Difference in New Zealand

Beyond televised sport there are a multitude of American cultural signs visible in New Zealand, including McDonald's, KFC, and Coca-Cola. There are also the less obvious, but equally influential, foreign economic investments including Telecom, TranzRail, SKY TV, TV3, and TV4. As in many other countries, some cultural nationalists have adopted reactionary stances condemning the influx of foreign, especially Asian and American, investment and commodities. Discourses dramatizing the threat of Americanization are rife, particularly when it comes to TV programming. However, sport is also being articulated to these discourses. For example, consider the following quote from Ian Robson, former Chief Executive Officer of the Auckland Warriors, a New Zealand-based professional rugby league team, which highlights one perspective on the supposed "threat" of the NBA and Americanization:

> . . . we're in a time now where . . . the most admired, recognised and acknowledged sporting hero is not a New Zealander, he's a black American by the name of Michael Jordan . . . if we . . . don't use the resources that men like Murdoch are now placing before us in a positive sense to re-establish and create heroes, create role models . . . I think that's the real challenge. Basketball in this country is the sleeping giant of all sports and if we sit back and don't meet and confront change we stand still at our own peril. (Robson, 1995)

The dialectic, or what Robertson (1995: 29) refers to as the "problematic of polarity" with respect to the homogenization versus heterogenization debates, emerges in Robson's warning. On the one hand, he expresses a nationalist concern that views American culture, as signified by basketball and its personification, Michael Jordan, as a threat to local culture. On the other hand, he also recognizes that the same global forces, whether they are satellite TV deals and/or major footwear company sponsorships that have made the NBA a threat are, in effect, a potential savior for local sporting commodities such as rugby union, rugby league, cricket, and netball. This point is confirmed by Rowe et al. (1994: 675) who note that: "Americanized marketing and presentational techniques may be 'imported' in order to protect localized forms of sport from external (including American) competition."

To date, there has been an absence of any complete, systematic analysis of the overall impact of American sporting culture in general, and the NBA in particular, on New Zealand. Here, we examine a few empirical examples of the global/local nexus of both America's and the NBA's presence in New Zealand. Three types of examples are presented: the relationship between local and global heroes; the meaning and market value of the NBA amongst a select group of "Kiwi" youth; and a point of disjuncture arising from a banned American-produced TV advertisement featuring a prominent NBA star.

First, two recent studies of sport heroes in New Zealand indicated that not only was Michael Jordan by far the number one choice among teenagers (Melnick and Jackson, 1996), he was also almost unanimously identified with respect to his corporate sponsors, confirming his commodity-sign status (Andrews et al., 1996). In addition, there are other insights provided by the global/local nexus of sport heroes in New Zealand. For example, Jeff Wilson, a superb New Zealand athlete whose talents allowed him the rare honor of playing for both the national rugby and cricket teams, recently revealed his own sport hero. When asked who he'd like to be for one hour of any day he answered: "Michael Jordan" (Johnstone, 1995: B2). Strikingly, Wilson and Jordan share a number of common features: both have competed at, or near, an elite level in two sports; both have contracts with Nike (and at one point Coca-Cola); and both are part of an ever-expanding worldwide web of self-reinforcing commodity signs. In a related point about the global/local nexus of sport heroes, it is interesting to note the media's representation of one of rugby's biggest international stars, All Black Jonah Lomu, who has been described as the "Michael Jordan of rugby" (South, 1995: B2). As Andrews et al. note (1996: 433):

> The comparison between Jordan and Lomu is particularly illuminating. First, it identifies two contemporary sporting icons, simultaneously celebrating Lomu's superb athletic talent while effectively subordinating him to Jordan. Second . . . it would appear the incongruence that may have existed for such a comparison only a decade ago has diminished to the extent that Michael Jordan and Jonah Lomu are not necessarily located in completely different worlds: cultural or corporate.

Like Jordan, Lomu has a sponsorship deal with McDonald's and has a burger named after him: the locally infamous "Jonah burger" (officially known as the MegaFeast). Though seemingly superficial, such examples highlight the complexity and dynamics of the global/local nexus. Transnational (American) corporations such as McDonald's not only reinforce the popular presence of American sporting icons such as Michael Jordan, they also construct and raise the profile of local heroes such as Lomu.

A second empirical example draws on informal interviews that were held with three New Zealand males aged 7, 8, and 11. While certainly not a random or representative sample, these individuals do provide some unique insights into the popular cultural presence of the NBA. Although their desire for NBA clothing was intriguing, the really fascinating aspect was the depth and intensity of their interest in NBA collectors' cards. These youths possessed both a genuine business savvy in relation to the exchange and market value of their collections and a broad knowledge base in relation to the players themselves: personal anecdotes, performance statistics, and much more. In many respects these youths were no different than those in many other countries. Perhaps that only serves to reinforce the "global" point. However, the most astounding fact was that none had ever seen an NBA game either live or on TV. This raises two important questions, the first of which relates to the issue of access, while the second question relates to why these kids were interested in the NBA at all. The question of how the children gained access to the NBA was alluded to previously. In all likelihood their involvement with the NBA was based on basketball highlight programs, sports news coverage, and perhaps most importantly, the vast array of TV commercials featuring NBA stars, their everyday interaction in trading cards, and, increasingly, their direct participation in basketball either informally or in PE classes. However, the question of what attracted these youths to the NBA, despite the fact that they live in a place where rugby union, rugby league, cricket, and netball reign supreme, remains largely unanswered. In their own words, trading NBA cards and wearing NBA caps and a pair of Nike shoes as they anticipate a trip to McDonald's or Pizza Hut is simply "cool." Arguably, one aspect of the "coolness" of American popular culture is that it is *different*.

The previous examples highlight the popular, if at times superficial, presence of American popular culture in New Zealand. Admittedly, the mere recognition and identification of American NBA stars by New Zealand youth fails to provide the type of in-depth insight desired. Nevertheless it provides a starting-point and a basis upon which to develop future investigations which will hopefully lead to a better understanding of how New Zealanders make sense of global cultural products. Likewise, it will be useful to explore how global or American products are transformed, indigenized, and/or resisted within local contexts. One example of resistance, which highlights disjuncture within the global/local nexus of American sporting culture in New Zealand, is briefly considered next.

It was previously noted that, despite an apparent fascination with American popular culture and an increasing dependence on it to fill air time, there is a small but active voice which clearly identifies the threat of Americanization in New Zealand. With respect to the media, one of the key threats is expressed through discourses about TV violence. New Zealand holds one of the most conservative, if not contradictory, positions with respect to its regulation of media violence (Weaver, 1996). Overwhelmingly, it is American programs that are targeted, though rarely empirically verified, as displaying the highest levels of gratuitous violence. While American sport, and the NBA in particular, have not been specifically identified within these attacks on violence, a recent debate about a Reebok shoe advertisement featuring an African-American NBA star has made the connection.

In brief, the advertisement features Shawn Kemp, then playing for the Seattle Super Sonics, but now with the Cleveland Cavaliers, who is shown competing in a game of one-on-one basketball against an animated Samurai warrior opponent. Kemp, nicknamed "Kamikaze" by his sponsors Reebok because of his fearless playing style, defeats his simulated opponent in a physical contest which ends in the loser exploding. In many respects this advertisement is similar to others currently featured on TV networks throughout the world. What is striking about this commercial is that it was banned by the TV Commercials Approvals Board, which acts in conjunction with the New Zealand Advertising Standards Complaints Board (ASCB), committees responsible for reviewing and censoring media content. A thorough interrogative analysis of the basis of the TVCAB's and ASCB's decision to prohibit the ad is currently in progress (Jackson, 1997) but what we do know is that it was banned because it featured *gratuitous violence* deemed irrelevant to the sale of athletic footwear (*Dominion,* 1995: 7). In part, the banning of the Reebok ad reflects New Zealand broadcasting's more stringent (and as previously noted often contradictory) codes of practice with respect to violence. However, it might also be interpreted as a form of resistance against threatening images of America, constructed through the intersection of sport, technology, and commodified images of violence and racial otherness. The apparent contradiction in public attitudes and censorship policy in the Reebok case highlights the complexity of the global/local nexus of American popular culture in New Zealand. Thus, while the NBA and its intertextual American popular cultural alliances are often desired because they express a notion of *difference,* they can also be challenged and resisted because they embody a difference which is deemed threatening and unacceptable.

Conclusion

Understanding the meaning and effects of the "global melange" (Nederveen Pieterse, 1995) exhibited by New Zealand youth wearing Nike shoes, collecting NBA cards, and idolizing African-American sport heroes, while simultaneously desiring a McDonald's Jonah Lomu burger may provide valuable insights into the debates surrounding globalism and localism. However, in order to comprehend the complexity of the global/local nexus, several issues, including relationships between culture and the economy need to be considered. As Rowe et al. (1994: 675) assert: "it is necessary to move beyond the simple logic of cultural domination and towards a more multi-directional concept of the flow of global traffic in people, goods and services." Thus, we must consider the global flow of local cultural products, and the local flow of global cultural products, as well as the forces that shape the contexts where they intersect. However, we cannot assume that globalization is a uniform process which interacts with, and influences, all local cultures equally, nor that resistance and agency are equal amongst all the global locals (Grossberg, 1997).

Second, any discussion of the opportunities and threats posed by globalization needs to recognize the politics and power relations associated with inventing a particular image of the local, that is, as an authentic "imagined community" (Anderson, 1983) through its juxtaposition to what Robertson (1995: 29) describes as the "hegemonically global." In short, there is a need to understand, and hopefully transcend, the politics of *fetishizing* the local and *fearing* the global.

Third, the mere consumption of American commodity-signs by these "peripherally located consumers" (Lash and Urry, 1994) cannot be equated with the Americanization of local cultures. Rather, it is the recognition of difference, in this case the NBA's signification as the American cultural Other, that establishes a form of opposition through which the local (national) cultural Self can be constructed. Relating this to the New Zealand context Lealand (1994: 34) asserts that:

American popular culture continues to be foreign because it is not New Zealand culture. Therein lies the source of its potency and attraction . . . youth dress themselves in the garb of American basketball stars not necessarily because they want to be little Americans. They seek a more vivid, fantastical world that is beyond the constraints of their age, family, neighborhood. They may be increasing the profits of global marketing interests, but their real loyalty is to a global tribal network.

If Lealand is correct, it could be argued that the accelerated circulation of *American* commodity-signs is not only contributing to the flow of global cultural products and practices, it is also leading to the rearticulation of national and local cultural identities, or what Robertson (1992b: 130) has described as "the global valorization of particular identities." Hence, rather than causing the dissolution of local identities through the establishment of a homogeneous global culture, the NBA may actually play a role in energizing multiple popular and local cultures.

In conclusion, it is recommended that future analyses consider the changing relations between different forms of capital, the changing nature and competing forms of production and formations of capitalism, the shifting terrain of labor and consumption, and the transforming nature of global relations with respect to both political and economic power. In other words we need to consider "how and where people, capital and commodities move in and out of the places and spaces of the global economy" (Grossberg, 1997: 10).

References

Albrow, M. and King, E. (1990) *Globalization, Knowledge and Society.* London: Sage.

Anderson, B. (1983) *Imagined Communities.* London: Verso.

Andrews, D. (1997) "The (Trans) National Basketball Association: American Commodity-sign Culture and Global-local Conjuncturalism," in A. Cvetovitch and D. Kellner (eds) *Articulating the Global and the Local.* Boulder, CO: Westview Press.

Andrews, D., Carrington, B., Mazur, Z. and Jackson, S. (1996) "Jordanscapes: A Preliminary Analysis of the Global Popular," *Sociology of Sport Journal* **13**: 428-57.

Appadurai, A. (1990) "Disjuncture and Difference in the Global Cultural Economy," *Theory, Culture and Society* **7**: 295-310.

Appadurai, A. (1996) *Modernity at Large: Cultural Dimensions of Globalization.* Minneapolis: University of Minnesota Press.

Bale, J. and Maguire, J., eds (1994) *The Global Sports Arena: Athletic Talent Migration in an Interdependent World.* London: Frank Cass.

Boeck, G. (1990) "NBA Expands its Horizons," *USA Today* (10 October): 2C.

Boyle, R. and Haynes, R. (1996) "The Grand Old Game: Football, Media and Identity in Scotland," *Media, Culture and Society* **18**: 549-64.

Cantelon, H. and Murray, S. (1993) "Globalization and Sport, Structure and Agency: The Need for Greater Clarity," *Loisir et Société/Leisure and Society* **16**: 275-91.

Cole, C. and Andrews, D. (1996) "Look—It's NBA Showtime!: Visions of Race in the Popular Imaginary," in N. Denzin (ed.) *Cultural Studies: A Research Volume*, vol. 1, pp. 141-81. Greenwich: JAI Press.

Donnelly, P. (1996) "The Local and the Global: Globalization in the Sociology of Sport," *Journal of Sport and Social Issues* **23**: 239-57.

Duncan, I. and Bollard, A., eds (1992) *Corporatization and privatization: Lessons from New Zealand.* Auckland: Oxford University Press.

Featherstone, M. and Lash, S. (1995) "Globalization, Modernity, and the Spatialization of Social Theory: An Introduction," in M. Featherstone, S. Lash and R. Robertson (eds) *Global Modernities.* London: Sage.

Grimm, M. (1992) "The Marketers of the Year: David Stern", *Brandweek* (16 November): 20.

Grossberg, L. (1997) "Cultural Studies, Modern Logics, and Theories of Globalisation," in A. McRobbie (ed.) *Back to Reality? Social Experience and Cultural Studies.* Manchester: Manchester University Press.

Hall, S. (1991) "The Local and the Global: Globalization and Ethnicity," in A. King (ed.) *Culture, Globalization and the World-System.* London: Macmillan.

Harvey, J., Rail, G. and Thibault, L. (1996) "Globalization and Sport: Sketching a Theoretical Model for Empirical Analyses," *Journal of Sport and Social Issues* **23**: 258-77.

Haworth, N. (1994) "Neo-liberalism, Economic Internationalisation and the Contemporary State in New Zealand," in A. Sharp (ed.) *Leap into the Dark: The Changing Role of the State in New Zealand since 1984.* Auckland: Auckland University Press.

Heisler, M. (1991) "Uncommon Marketing," *Los Angeles Times* (18 October): C1.

Hirst, P. and Thompson, G. (1996) *Globalization in Question.* Cambridge: Polity.

Houlihan, B. (1994) "Homogenization, Americanization and Creolization of Sport: Varieties of Globalization," *Sociology of Sport Journal* **11**: 356-75.

Hutchison, I. and Lealand, G. (1996) "Introduction: A New Mediascape," *Continuum: The Australian Journal of Media and Culture* 10: 1-11.

Jackson, S., (1994) "Gretzky, Crisis and Canadian Identity in 1988: Rearticulating the Americanization of Culture Debate," *Sociology of Sport Journal* 11: 428-46.

Jackson, S. and Andrews, D. (1996) "Excavating the (Trans) National Basketball Association: Locating the Global/Local Nexus of America's World and the World's America," *Australasian Journal of American Studies* 15: 57-64.

Jackson, S.J. (1997) "Sport, Violence and Advertising: A Case Study of Global/Local Disjuncture in New Zealand," Paper presented at the North American Society for the Sociology of Sport Conference, 5-8 November, Toronto, Canada.

Johnstone, D. (1995) "Wilson Ready to Prove White Men Can Jump," *Sunday Star Times* (11 June): B2.

Kearney, R. (1989) *The Wake of Imagination: Toward a Postmodern Culture*. Minneapolis: University of Minnesota Press.

Kelsey, J. (1996) *Economic Fundamentalism: The New Zealand Experiment—A World Model for Structural Adjustment?* Auckland: Pluto Press.

Kidd, B. (1991) "How Do We Find Our Own Voices in the 'New World Order'? A Commentary on Americanization," *Sociology of Sport Journal* 8: 178-84.

King, A. (1990) *Culture, Globalization and the World System*. Basingstoke: Macmillan.

Klein, A. (1991) "Sport and Culture as Contested Terrain: Americanization in the Caribbean," *Sociology of Sport Journal* 8: 79-85.

Korzeniewicz, M. (1994) "Commodity Chains and Marketing Strategies: Nike and the Global Athletic Footwear Industry," in G. Gereffi and M. Korzeniewicz (eds) *Commodity Chains and Global Capitalism*. Westport, CT: Greenwood Press.

Lash, S. and Urry, J. (1994) *Economies of Signs and Space*. London: Verso.

Lealand, G. (1994) "American Popular Culture and Emerging Nationalism in New Zealand," *National forum: The Phi Kappa Phi Journal* 74(4): 34-7.

McKay, J., Lawrence, G., Miller, T. and Rowe, D. (1993) "Globalization and Australian Sport," *Sport Science Review* 2: 10-28.

McKay, J. and Miller, T. (1991) "From Old Boys to Men and Women of the Corporation: The Americanization and Commodification of Australian Sport," *Sociology of Sport Journal* 8: 86-94.

Maguire, J. (1993) "Globalization, Sport Development, and the Media/Sport Production Complex," *Sport Science Review* 2: 29-47.

Maguire, J. (1994) "Sport, Identity Politics, and Globalization: Diminishing Contrasts and Increasing Varieties," *Sociology of Sport Journal* 11: 398-427.

Melnick, M. and Jackson, S. (1996) "Globalization, the Mass Media and Reference Idol Selection: The Case of New Zealand Adolescents," Paper presented at the annual meeting of the North American Society for the Sociology of Sport, Birmingham, Alabama, 13-16 November.

Nederveen Pieterse, J. (1995) "Globalization as Hybridization," in M. Featherstone, S. Lash and R. Robertson (eds) *Global Modernities*. London: Sage.

Robertson, R. (1992a) *Globalization: Social Theory and Global Culture*. New York: Russell Sage.

Robertson, R. (1992b) *Globalization*. London: Sage.

Robertson, R. (1995) "Glocalization: Time-Space and Homogeneity-Heterogeneity," in M. Featherstone, S. Lash and R. Robertson (eds) *Global Modernities*. London: Sage.

Robins, K. (1991) "Tradition and Translation: National Culture in its Global Context," In J. Corner and S. Harvey (eds) *Enterprise and Heritage: Cross-Currents of National Culture*. London: Routledge.

Robson, I. (1995) Quoted during special rugby edition of *Fraser*. Television One, Television New Zealand, Mark Champion producer, June 26.

Rowe, D. (1996a) "Editorial: Sport, Globalization and the Media," *Media, Culture & Society* 18: 523-6.

Rowe, D. (1996b) "The Global Love-Match: Sport and Television," *Media, Culture & Society* 18: 565-82.

Rowe, D., Lawrence, G., Miller, T. and McKay, J. (1994) "Global Sport? Core Concern and Peripheral Vision," *Media, Culture & Society* 16: 661-75.

Ryan, B. and Cohen, A. (1996) "Hoop Dreams," *Sales and Marketing Management* (December): 48-53.

South, B. (1995) "Jordan's Stardom Light Years Ahead," *Sunday Star Times* (17 September): B2.

Spicer, B., Powell, M. and Emanuel, D. (1996) *The Remaking of Television New Zealand 1984-1992*. Auckland: Auckland University Press.

The Dominion (1995) "Sport Shoe Ban Stuns Reebok" (20 June): 7.

Voisin, A. (1991) "NBA Takes Active Role in Dealing with AIDS Issue," *Atlanta Journal and Constitution* (3 December): F-1.

Wagner, E. (1990) "Sport in Asia and Africa: Globalization or Mundialization?" *Sociology of Sport Journal* 7: 399-402.

Weaver, K. (1996) "The Television and Violence Debate in New Zealand: Some Problems of Context," *Continuum: The Australian Journal of Media and Culture* 10: 64-75.

Wernick, A. (1991) *Promotional Culture*. London: Sage.

Wilcox, L. (1996) "Saatchi Rap: The 'Worlding of America' and Racist Ideology in New Zealand," *Continuum: The Australian Journal of Media and Culture* 10: 121-35.

Index

About the Editors

Andrew Yiannakis, PhD

Andrew Yiannakis, PhD, is currently the professor and director of the Laboratory for Leisure, Tourism and Sport at the University of Connecticut at Storrs.

Yiannakis was cofounder and the first president of the North American Society for the Sociology of Sport. He is also former president of the Sport Sociology Academy of the American Alliance for Health, Physical Education, Recreation and Dance (AAHPERD).

He has authored numerous articles on a variety of topics in the field and was the senior editor of four editions of the popular text *Sport Sociology: Contemporary Themes*. He is also senior editor of *Applied Sociology of Sport*, a book of readings explicating the relationship between theory and application. He currently resides in Coventry, Connecticut, with his wife, Linda. He enjoys horseback riding, reading historical novels, and teaching and participating in jujitsu.

Merrill J. Melnick, PhD

Merrill J. Melnick, PhD, is a professor of physical education and sport at the State University of New York College at Brockport. In 1998, he was awarded the university's prestigious chancellor's award for excellence in teaching.

Melnick is a founding member of the North American Society for the Sociology of Sport and a former president of the Sport Sociology Academy of the National Association for Sport and Physical Education. He has published more than 80 articles and presented both nationally and internationally in the area of sociology of sport. He coauthored the book *Sport Fans: The Psychology and Social Impact of Spectators* and also coresearched and coauthored three national studies for the Women's Sports Foundation.

Melnick lives with his wife, Shoshana, in Brockport, New York. He enjoys vegetable gardening, camping, canoeing, and playing tennis.

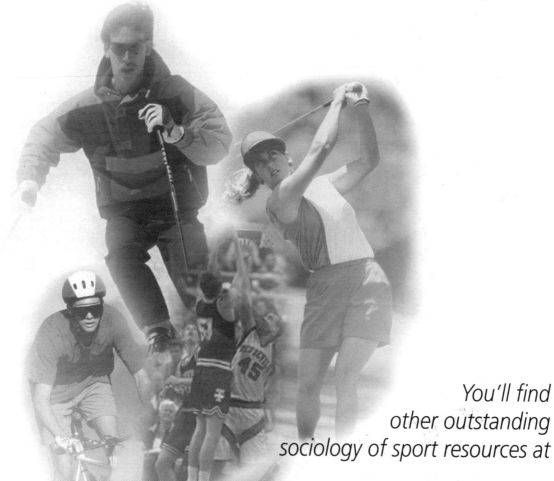